S0-ECM-390
Peace and World Structure

JX
1904,5
G34
V. 4

2/25/89 mm

Johan Galtung

Peace and World Structure

Essays in Peace Research

Volume Four

CALIFORNIA SCHOOL OF PROFESSIONAL PSYCHOLOGY LOS ANGELES

Christian Ejlers

Copenhagen 1980

Peace and World Structure
is set in Monotype Times New Roman

ISBN 87 7241 371 9
© Johan Galtung 1980
All rights reserved

 PRIO MONOGRAPHS from the
International Peace Research Institute, Oslo

1. Arne Martin Klausen: Kerala Fishermen and
the Indo-Norwegian Pilot Project, 1968

2. Johan Galtung: Members of Two Worlds.
A Development Study of Three Villages in
Western Sicily, 1971

3. Helge Hveem: International Relations and
World Images. A Study of Norwegian Foreign
Policy Elites, 1972

4. Johan Galtung: Peace: Research · Education · Action
Essays in Peace Research, I, 1975

5. Johan Galtung: Peace, War, and Defense
Essays in Peace Research, II, 1976

6. H. Hveem: The Political Economy of Third World
Producers' Associations, Universitetsforlaget, 1977.

7. Johan Galtung: Peace and Social Structure
Essays in Peace Research, III, 1978

8. Johan Galtung: Peace and World Structure
Essays in Peace Research, IV, 1980

9. Johan Galtung: Peace Problems: Some Case Studies
Essays in Peace Research, V, 1980

PEACE AND WORLD STRUCTURE

Contents of This Volume

ESSAYS IN PEACE RESEARCH, Volume IV

Peace and World Structure

Peace: Research · Education · Action

Peace in General

Peace
Entropy and the General Theory of Peace
Peace Thinking
Violence, Peace and Peace Research
Structural and Direct Violence:
   A Note on Operationalization
Is Peace Possible?

Peace Research

Peace Research
International Programs of Behavioral Science
   Research in Human Survival
Peace Research:
   Future Possibilities and Necessities
Peace Research:
   Science, or Politics in Disguise?
Peace Research:
   Past Experiences and Future Perspectives
Is Peaceful Research Possible?
   On the Methodology of Peace Research

Peace Education

Teaching and Infrastructural Problems:
   The Role of Universities and other Institutions
Towards a World Peace Academy: A Proposal
Education For and With Peace: Is It Possible?

Peace Action

Peace Theory, Peace Practice, and Peace Education
Social Structure, Religious Structure and the Fight for Peace
Peace as a Profession and New Peace Action Roles

ESSAYS IN PEACE RESEARCH, Volume II

Peace, War and Defense

On War and Arms Races

Belligerence among the Primitives
Balance of Power and the Problem of Perception
Two Approaches to Disarmament
The War System

Disarmament and Public Opinion

Atoms for Peace
Attitudes towards Different Forms of Disarmament
Public Opinion and the Economic Effects of Disarmament
Popular Inspection of Disarmament Processes

Peacekeeping, Peacemaking and Peacebuilding

Some Factors Affecting Local Acceptance of a UN Force
Participants in Peacekeeping Forces
Three Approaches to Peace:
    Peacekeeping, Peacemaking and Peacebuilding

Nonmilitary Defense

Pacifism from a Sociological Point of View
Two Concepts of Defense
On the Meaning of Nonviolence
On the Strategy of Nonmilitary Defense

ESSAYS IN PEACE RESEARCH, Volume III

Peace and Social Structure

Social Position Theory

Social Position and Social Behavior
Center—Periphery Concepts and Theories
Foreign Policy Opinion as a Function of Social Position
Social Position, Party Identification and Foreign Policy Orientation

Rank Disequilibrium Theory

A Structural Theory of Aggression
Rank and Social Integration:
  A Multidimensional Approach
The Dynamics of Rank Conflict

Social Structure Theory

Feudal Systems, Structural Violence and the
  Structural Theory of Revolution
A Structural Theory of Revolutions

Development Theory

Perspectives on Development:
  Past, Present, Future
The Structure of Traditionalism:
  A Case Study from Western Sicily
Social Structure, Education Structure and Lifelong Education:
  The Case of Japan

Ethnic and Racial Conflicts

Anti-Semitism in the Making
Towards a Theory of Race Relations

Conflict Theory

Institutionalized Conflict Resolution:
  A Theoretical Paradigm
Conflict as a Way of Life

ESSAYS IN PEACE RESEARCH, Volume V

Peace Problems: Some Case Studies

Peace Problems: The Area Approach

Europe Bipolar, Bicentric or Cooperative?

European Security and Cooperation: A Skeptical Contribution

The Middle East and the Theory of Conflict

On the Effects of International Economic Sanctions:
   The Case of Rhodesia

Divided Nations as a Process:
   One State, Two States and In-between: The Case of Korea

Japan and Future World Politics

Cuba: Anti-imperialism and Socialist Development

The United States in Indo-China:
   The Paradigm for a Generation

Peace Problems: The Issue Approach

The Cold War and the Artificial Satellites

Contact, Conflict and Summit Meetings

The "Limits to Growth" and Class Politics

Development from Above and the Blue Revolution:
   The Indo-Norwegian Project in Kerala

Human Needs, National Interests and World Politics

The Law of the Sea Conference

The Pugwash Movement as an International Actor

Towards a Theory of Freedom and Identity
   A New Frontier in Peace Research

Preface

The volume is part of a series of five volumes of edited essays on peace research, and two volumes on methodology. The essays, one hundred in total, were written over a period of fifteen years, between 1958 and 1973, half of them during the last five years, from 1969 onwards. Almost all of them were produced at the International Peace Research Institute. About one third have never before been published but have circulated in mimeographed form only. Some others have not been published in English before.

Why so many articles or essays, why not books? There is a simple reason for this. When peace research was initiated in Norway in 1959, an effort was made from the very beginning to avoid identifying peace research with one single theme of research, e.g. research on arms races, on conflict resolution, on problems of development. Peace research was conceived of as an approach rather than a discipline, as committed social science with no respect for any disciplinary or scholastic borderline in social analysis. The commitment was to a less violent world, violence being broadly conceived of. For that reason the research effort was spread over many fields and resulted in many articles rather than a few books with a more concentrated focus.

There was also a practical reason, not peculiar to peace research: the article form shortens the time period between research, publication, and feedback considerably. On the other hand, it also spreads the research product in all kinds of journals and books, so that in the end only the author sees any connection between them. Then, with the spread and growth of various forms of peace research around the world, the demand for more or less inaccessible articles also increases. It was felt that these reasons together help justify the publication of the essays.

The essays appear here as they appeared when first printed, although the unpublished ones have been updated somewhat. Each volume is more than a loose collection of essays, and not only in the obvious sense that the essays are edited and that there is an introduction, a sort of reader's guide.

Preface

From the very beginning there was a research program with a broad emphasis on three fields of research:

Peace, war, and defense
Peace and social structure
Peace and world structure.

But in the process of working within these three fields there were three "research fall-outs", so to speak:

Peace and peace research in general
Concrete case studies
Problems of methodology.

And these are, more or less, the titles of the six volumes. Since the work of editing them was started in 1969, efforts have been made to fill gaps both by directing research towards new fields, and by updating and carrying further some older research. Thus each volume is supposed to appear as a relatively integrated whole, where the articles complement each other.

The field of peace research has fortunately not yet developed consensus about basic definitions on paradigms and methods. An individual working in this field would have to be either sclerotic or isolated to avoid changes in his own scientific orientation throughout these last fifteen years. Some of these changes will be explicitly discussed in the introductions to the individual volumes, and they will indeed be evident to the reader. In earlier articles there are statements with which the author himself would not necessarily agree today, or agree only with so many ifs and buts that the statements become rather useless. So why publish them now? Because they are part of a more general process, here reflected or projected in the work of one author. Many social scientists either have been through that process, or are presently going through it, others are certainly going to have similar experiences. This process has the character of a change of identification. Dramatically stated we might say the changes in identification or orientation are from the ethnocentric to the global, and more importantly from oppressor to oppressed, from exploiter to exploited whether the reference is to nations, peoples or people. There is a parallel change in science ideology from seeing science as a reflection of the status quo towards conceiving of science as an instrument in the concrete, political fight for basic social change.

But for me this is an ongoing process more than a sudden conversion, and many fellow colleagues are in the same situation. In this process there are many phases and many paths. Human society and human beings themselves are infinitely complex. There are basic processes and basic analyses to be made but something significant will always escape, nay will even be created dialectically by the very analysis. Faced with this, no one is competent; and humility should be on the inside, not a tactical mask carried in self-defense in order not to stir the aggression of others. There is nothing final in any social analysis, for it is merely a part of the social process itself. Some readers may be in other phases of that process and find earlier articles more relevant. These articles are for them, not to exhibit the author's own intellectual odyssey — that is beside the point.

These volumes are published from the International Peace Research Institute in Oslo, of which I was a director for the first ten years and later a scientific co-worker. Some of the essays were written together with others at the Institute, but for most of them I alone should be held responsible for the views expressed. At the Institute there are many views and orientations, as there should be; and the Institute, or peace research, should certainly not be identified with the work of any one individual. The Institute is a setting that has made it possible for many, among them the present author, to do more work, and what to them appears as more meaningful work in social science than any other setting. Others may have other views, but to many of us this is a fact and an explanation more than any expression of gratitude.

However, there is one person whom I want to thank particularly: Erik Ivås, secretary, administrator, and friend through these years. Creative, conscientious, and devoted, he has exceeded every possible norm and expectation. His contribution, in one form or the other, is found almost verywhere in these pages.

And there are two others for whom words of gratitude also become pale, even misplaced: Ingrid Eide and Fumiko Nishimura. There is hardly an analytical point that has not been shared and discussed, and inspired — not to mention the emotive peaks and troughs experienced in any scientific process.

Finally, a vote of thanks to Susan Høivik, a marvellous editor, gently pushing my English closer to that of the natives and much more than that: cutting redundancies, urging precision, questioning and prodding and helping — a constant source of stimulation and inspiration.

Havana, August 1972
Dubrovnik, January 1974
Genève, January 1978 & 1979

Johan Galtung

15

Dedication

This volume is dedicated to UNESCO in general and to one person in particular, the late professor Julian Hochfeld, deputy director of the Division of Social Sciences in the early 1960s. In the whole UN system it was UNESCO that more than anyone else supported the peace research movement at the international level, thereby giving it a legitimacy that could be converted into financial and other forms of support from even relatively sluggish governments at the national level. Concretely this took three forms, and Julian Hochfeld played a positive role along all three dimensions of building transdisciplinary and transnational research.

First, there was the institutionalization in the form of an international organization supported financially by the UNESCO: the International Peace Research Association, founded in London, in Fall 1964 with Professor Bert Röling from the University of Groningen as its first secretary general, holding its first international conference in Groningen in 1965 (later conferences took place in Sweden 1967, Czechoslovakia 1969, Yugoslavia 1971, India 1974, Finland 1975, Mexico 1977, and Germany 1979). The UNESCO support was indispensable financially and morally: a good example of how an international organization with foresighted people in the secretariat can move much more quickly at the international level than ministries of education and science can at the national level. Professor Röling managed to give to this fledgling organization respectability, and not at the expense of relevance and audacity — as with UNESCO a fine example of tolerance combined with a sense of purpose.

Second, UNESCO established a directory of institutions engaged in peace research, the first edition published in 1967, the second in 1972, and the third in 1979. Through this work institutes not only increased their mutual visibility; they also developed more of a sense of having a common purpose. Thus, sometime during the 1960s a partial but very important transition took place in Europe: institutes used to seeing themselves as working in the service of the country or the political-military region where they were located started thinking and researching in terms of Europe as a whole.

17

Very important in this connection were the conferences of the directors of international relations and peace research institutes. The Council of Europe should also be mentioned in this connection: a study was carried out in 1967, interviewing policymakers in foreign offices in a score of countries, from the US to the USSR, from Norway to Greece (reported in Johan Galtung & Sverre Lodgaard, ed., *Co-operation in Europe*, Oslo, 1970). Cooperating, spelling out a common future rather than (or in addition to) pleading partisan views was a typical peace research perspective in a (relatively) horizontal conflict such as the East-West conflict.

Third, UNESCO started using peace researchers and peace research institutes for research, giving them tasks and contracts. UNESCO has often been criticized for the fragmentation of research money: on the contrary, by cutting the budget into relatively small pieces and stretching it around the world a high number of people can be involved and challenge each other. As one progresses from an OECD or Council of Europe via an all-European to a global, UNESCO-organized setting, problems become more and more complex and the styles of research, of disciplined inquiry, more and more disparate — which is another way of saying that the setting becomes increasingly realistic, to the great frustration of many attuned to the smaller worlds. UNESCO has played a great role as teacher and organizer of internationalism in this way, and also — although less so — of interdisciplinary research (the reason for the "less so" being that the UNESCO secretariat produces more transnationality than transdisciplinarity).

In saying all this it should not be concluded that there have not been different views within UNESCO of the role of peace research in general and any special orientation in particular — but whatever the changing orientations have been: UNESCO has been both an initiator and a supporter **and** continues to be so.

Alfaz, December 1978
Johan Galtung

Introduction

This volume focuses on *international relations*, peace and world structure — with some excursions into "technical assistance" and future perspectives. Thus, the focus is more on what to many would seem to be the immediate field of peace research, the structure of the world, including class, race, ethnic groups.

The general perspective is *structural*. We are not concentrating on the particular actors in the international arena, this and that state, that or this elite, party chairman, or president. The focus is on small states and big, poor states and rich, dependent and independent, exploited and exploiting — and on the structure of the interaction network in which they are found. The general idea is trivial: states are largely playing roles, as people do. The freedom of action of a "foreign policy elite", a "decisionmaker" or similar figures of speech is highly limited by the structure in which the state they supposedly head is embedded. This is the structure one has to understand, much more so than the detailed study of the idiosyncrasies of individual states, not to mention the individuals found at the pinnacle of the internal power pyramids. This is the iceberg once again: those elite figures are highly visible and capture the attention of the untrained eye — particularly when aided by the structure of foreign news, so trained on what elite people in elite nations do. Underneath the surface are the structures that remain more or less permanent from one day to the next, the constant molding, constraining and shaping whatever happens in the international arena — and sometimes given to volcanic eruptions accompanied by basic structural changes.

This is not to deny that there is also room for an actor-oriented perspective on international affairs. The analytical telescope or microscope may well be trained on the "decisionmakers", and not only in order to state the obvious: the decisionmakers in states on the top of the world pyramid will do their best to maintain status quo, the decisionmakers in states in the middle will try to get either themselves or the states they "represent" to the top: and the decisionmakers at the bottom will either try to bring themselves closer to the top through all kinds of linkages, particularly via international organizations of various kinds, or go in for destruction of the world pyramid. Depending on how one looks at it, this may be seen as expressions of a struggle for power (maintenance of the old, conquest of the new), defense of the national interest, in other words as expressions of *realism* — or expressions of *idealism*, the term often used for long-term realism, for actors who try to engage in rationality with a longer time perspective. There is space for more than this: for the study of irrationality, even of the suicidal, for the study of the colorful, the role of the idiosyncratic; or what even might appear random. But all this looks a bit like the study of snow falling on a gusty winter day: it moves up and down, back and forth, in all directions, but ultimately it falls *down*. The basic structure is defined by the law of gravity, but only a fool would deny that there are also other forces at work.

The purpose of these essays is more to elucidate fundamental, even crude to the point of the obvious, structures than what happens above and below that baseline. This is done by first focusing on international interaction as such, essentially elaborating one theme: the strong correlation that exists between the "rank" of the international actors, the states, and the amount of interaction — for good and for bad, constructive and destructive — that passes between them. Interaction is *rank dependent;* there is more interaction between two topdog states than between one topdog and one underdog, and, in turn, much more interaction than between two underdogs. Whatever happens, happens between those at the top.

The essays in the first section on international interaction are all related to this theme, but they focus on different types of interaction, and different parts of the world. In the first essay, originally presented at a conference on international relations theory at the University of Chicago in 1966, a general approach is indicated, based on what appeared as a goldmine in terms of structural insight relative to what international relations theory often produced: *small group theory*. The assumption is not that there is any automatic carry-over from one level to the other — only that findings and theory in small group research might serve as a heuristic device to produce hypotheses at the world level — and also vice versa.

The second essay, on summit meetings, was actually a byproduct of the first research project engaged in at the International Peace Research Institute in Oslo on "Contact, conflict and summit meetings" (stimulated by the Norwegian government's invitation to Khruschev to visit Norway in 1959, a highly emotional debate in the press and in the public, and the consequent refusal of Khruschev to come). The study gives some statistics on that particular form of diplomacy, popular at the time of the cold war since the logic of the cold war dictated that this should be, more or less, the only form of contact — and tries to explain some patterns in the distributions.

In the next two essays we move one step down, to ordinary diplomacy. No one will deny that the diplomatic network has its significance, more so previously than today when it is in competition with so many other networks (international organizations, governmental and nongovernmental; not to mention international news communication and multinational corporations). This, then, makes the international distribution of the diplomatic network rather important. That the pattern conforms to the basic underlying hypothesis goes without saying, but there are also exceptions of some interest. The first of these two essays tries to go into more depth by focusing on one particular foreign service, the Norwegian one, giving some data on career patterns and some elements of a theory about changing diplomatic styles.

At this point the distinction between person-oriented and structure-oriented comes in: the assumption being that the younger generation is more structure oriented in its outlook of the world than the older generation of diplomats (and that there is a middle generation of legalistically oriented diplomats). What is not known, of course, is to what extent there is something in the diplomatic service, itself highly personalized at the level of the *corps diplomatique*, that will not only facilitate but almost force a person-oriented perspective on the participants, regardless of their point of departure in orientation, as they grow old in the service.

The next essay does the same for international news communication: partly a study of the general pattern, partly a study, more in depth, of some particular news reporting in some Norwegian papers, concerning three "crises": Cuba 1960, Congo 1960, Cyprus 1964. Again, the difference between the person-oriented and the structure-oriented stands out as a key dimension of understanding: news is *personalized*, built around sentences where there are subjects doing something to objects — the latter human or nonhuman — and news is *discontinuous* in the sense that it reports what is today and was not yesterday. Otherwise this would not be news but "olds" — reports on that which is permanent, in other words, reports on the structured, the institutionalized. One conclusion from this is that news communication has a predominantly conservative function: it leads attention away from the permanent, good or bad, and focuses only on changes. Additionally. it was indicated quite strongly how news communication focuses on changes brought about by elite persons in elite countries. Like the essay on bilateral diplomacy this essay was written in cooperation with Mari Holmboe Ruge. An answer to some criticism of the theory is appended to the essay.

Air communication is a way of laying bare the international interaction structure, as argued in the introduction to this article, originally used in a presentation for the Peace Research Society (International) in Vienna, 1966, but unpublished. The bulk of the article is written by Nils Petter Gleditsch. In principle, all points in the world *can be* connected by air as long as an airstrip can be built, but not all points *are* connected. The difference between the potential and the empirical makes the structure. This structure is then examined in the Latin American case and the European case — the former a hegemonial pattern impossible to analyze without bringing in an outside party, the United States; the latter a bipolar pattern, particularly during the years that delivered the data for the analysis.

Finally this type of analysis is rounded off with an effort to study the case of one country: Norway. The essay is an exercise in two ways of coming to grips with a state "in the world community": in relative terms and in relational terms; in terms of differences and in terms of interaction. The study is mainly descriptive, with only some very few elements of a theory of Norway, focusing on Norway's use of shipping as a way of gaining position in the world community.

In the second section of the present volume, on *world structure*, there is an effort to go more deeply into the matter. The focus is no longer merely on the relation between rank and interaction for states, but on the relationship between different forms of rank, on how rank creates structure and structure creates rank (also dealt with in the opening essay in this book), on how new actors are brought into being through integration of various types — territorial, horizontal (associational), vertical (organizational) integration — and on actors that are not states, the non-territorial actors in the world structure. And finally, an effort is made to wrap up all of this in the essay "A structural theory of imperialism", where vertical interaction stands out as the major organizing principle in an effort to understand world structure, also bringing in themes from Volume III.

Why was this not introduced at an earlier stage? Because, as mentioned in the introduction to the preceding volume, of the difficulty in coming to grips with "vertical interaction", or "vertical division of labor"; less euphemistically and more accurately referred to as *exploitation*. All explanations in terms of exchange relations, voluntarily or involuntarily engaged in, were found unsatisfactory. There was a paradox that appeared and reappeared: given that the current relationship between the countries that export manufactured goods and the countries that export raw materials is exploitative, would the exploitation disappear if the terms of trade (simply conceived of as the number of units of raw materials needed to buy one unit of processed goods) were improved? If prices given for raw materials were doubled, trebled, increased ten-fold for that matter, would that be the end of exploitation?

This question is asked in the article "A structural theory of imperialism", originally presented as a paper at the International Political Science Association World Conference in Munich, September 1970, and the approach taken is that of giving a broader perspective on exploitation. Not only do the asymmetries in what goes on *between* the actors have to be taken into account, but also the differential spin-offs induced *within* the actors, the necessary and sufficient conditions. Only by doing this is it possible to understand the "gap" between "poor" and "rich" nations. This gap is the result of centuries of vertical division of labor, monopolizing the spin-off effects from manufacturing for the nations around the North Atlantic seaboard, creating periphery out of the rest, and then reproducing this vertical division of labor inside the nations of the world, inside their districts, and so on. It is difficult to see that this vertical division of labor is restricted to economic systems with private ownership of means of production alone; rather, it seems completely compatible with state ownership of means of production, moving production factors around so that they end up in a *center* where raw materials and raw labor are brought into contact with capital goods and taken away from a periphery reduced to the role of deliverer and consumer.

Still, vertical division of labor alone is not sufficient to constitute imperialism. There is also the building of bridges from the centers in the Center countries to the centers in the Periphery countries. This is conceived of as being done today precisely through that particular type of integration referred to as "international organization." Moreover, one Center country can attach to itself several Periphery countries just as a multinational corporation can have one head and many legs. But the condition for this to happen is a certain fragmentation at the bottom — and this is where the rank-dependent interaction structure enters the picture. And finally, the more the various rank dimensions, defined and created through vertical division of labor, are correlated, the more rank concordance there is, and the more solid is the structure of imperialism. When there is discordance of various kinds, states that are high on economic division of labor but low in the political or military fields; high culturally but low economically — not to mention groups within states in such positions — then aberrations of various types occur. That is the theme of the essay "International relations and international conflicts: a sociological approach", a plenary address to the Sixth World Congress of the International Sociological Association in Evian, September 1966. The theme is then carried further and made more specific in the article "Big powers and the world feudal structure", essentially a comparison between the United States and the Soviet Union

23

"interventions" in the Dominican Republic in March 1965 and in Czecho-slovakia in August 1968, witnessed by the present author. The article was presented in part at a peace research meeting in Budapest in early September 1968.

The essay on non-territorial actors is in two parts: a general theoretical essay and a report on a questionnaire study made in cooperation with Kjell Skjelsbæk and written up by him. The questionnaire was mailed to general secretaries in international organizations, to try to uncover some of the patterns of this particular "invisible continent". Needless to say, there are limits to this methodology, but the activities of the non-territorial actors are so much less visible than the highly publicized activities of the territorial actors, the states, that such methodologies will have to be considered. Besides, who is to say that a questionnaire investigation to the prime ministers of the world would not reveal interesting aspects of the territorial system?

In the short section on *technical assistance and world structure* the first essay represents an effort to link technical assistance in general, and "cultural assistance" in particular, to peace theory. The essay was originally commissioned by UNESCO but was never published by them. What the essay purports to do is to question the assumption that "cultural contact" will eventually lead to more "peaceful relations". Had it been written today, the notion of "cultural collective colonialism" of the weak by the strong might have been utilized. The essay also makes some conclusions about conditions under which cultural contact may function as an instrument of peace in a broad and positive sense.

In the next two essays the human factor in technical assistance is examined, in the form of "middle level manpower" (the case of the peace corps) and "high level manpower" (the case of the technical assistance expert, in this case in an Indo-Norwegian project). The paper on the peace corps is based on the author's observation of the US Peace Corps in its early phase of inception around the world, in 1961 and 1962, in a paper originally prepared for a conference organized by the US government on middle level manpower in Puerto Rico, September 1962 (but not published by them). And the essay on the Indo-Norwegian project in Kerala is based on field trips to Kerala in January 1961 and the summer of 1962 and is a report on the early stages of that project. (For a more complete report see *Essays* V, "The Blue Revolution"). The field reports on the US Peace Corps (in Ghana, Nigeria, India and Chile 1961—62), a content analysis of the US Congress debate on the Peace Corps, and a public opinion survey in Kerala were parts of the original projects, but have not been published. The reports are published as they were written, with only some minor stylistic changes.

Finally, there are three essays on *future perspectives:* one on the European situation, a plenary paper written for the Twelfth Annual Meeting of the Institute for Strategic Studies, Evian, September 1970, and two papers on international futures. The first, written in 1967, deals with growth of the international actors, with the transition from primitive via traditional and modern to what is called neo-modern (post-industrial) society, with how they gradually fill the territorial jackets provided for them by the concept of the territorial state, how they spill over, how the non-territorial actor is created in this squeeze, and so on. The second essay carries this theme further, exploitative relations are brought into the picture, a much more discontinuous, even convulsive image of the future world society is presented. Both of these papers were first presented at the International Future Research conferences, the first one in Oslo in September 1967 and the second in Kyoto in April 1970. This final essay also presents patterns of thinking that are at the core of the type of image of the future world developed much further in the author's *The True Worlds: A Transnational Perspective,* (New York: The Free Press/MacMillan, 1980).

In short: an image of a deeply maldeveloped world, profoundly vertical in the distribution of power and privilege, exploitation a major theme, much more important than even war as a form of violence. And with an uncertain future, except for one thing: there will be major transformations; the *status quo* being too unbearable.

Johan Galtung

IV.1. Small Group Theory and the Theory of International Relations *
A Study in Isomorphism

From M. Kaplan (ed.): *New Approaches in International Relations?*
(New York: St. Martin's Press, 1968). PRIO publication No. 1—5.

Notes on page *673*.

1. Introduction

No science of man seems to be as much torn between the ideographic and nomothetic traditions in science as the science of international relations. It has produced a wealth of descriptive information and interpretative accounts limited to one or a few nations in a limited time span, "the foreign politics of nation X between the wars," "relations between nations X and Y in the 'fifties'," etc. Typically the data of this science refer to proper names, and interpretations are often made using a maximum of information and connotations carried by these proper names. The scientific tradition, thus, resembles most that of the historian and only recently that of the sociologist or political scientist, as when students of international relations are talking about "actors" in general and "political systems" in general, and try to establish general invariances on the basis of sampling from well-defined universes.

In a sense this is strange, for international relations is so clearly a structural science. Unlike history it can never deal with the single unit. History may perhaps deal with one personality, but international relations will have to interpret one nation in the context of the nations with which it interacts. True enough, there exist studies on one nation. If a scholar from nation X writes about another nation Y this is sometimes referred to as "international relations," as if the distance between the author and his topic were the criterion. Merely to study and to write about what is far away may contribute to political science or political sociology; it is only when the international system or some subsystem thereof is considered *sui generis* that a study in international relations emerges. Thus one may say that the relationship between international relations and political science is the same as the relationship between sociology and psychology: it is the transition from the meticulous study of one unit at a time to the study of the interaction structure between the units that characterizes the relation between these pairs of sciences.

Just as much as sociology needs a theory of personality does international relations always need a theory of the national political system, but just as little as sociology is identical with a sum of studies of individual units is international relations equal to the accumulation of knowledge about political systems at the national level. Not even differential psychology or comparative politics will add up to sociology and international relations, because they do not consider the interaction structure. In Lazarsfeld's terms they remain at the level of *absolute* and *relative* variables, perhaps also *contextual* variables [1], but do not include *relational* variables. It may be objected that differences are not so sharp. However, this little exercise in classification of sciences has the advantage of indicating quite clearly which are the most relevant auxiliary disciplines for international relations: political science because of the information it provides about the participant units, and sociology, partly for the same reason as for political science, but more importantly because it is the only other social science that deals with the structure of interaction between social units *sui generis*. Considerably more peripheral is psychology, both because it deals with the wrong unit and because it does not deal mainly with interaction, by definition [2]. Structurally, sociology is the social science that stands closest to international relations by virtue of its heavy dependence on relational variables.

For easy reference, Table 1.1. presents this simplified classificatory scheme for social sciences.

TABLE 1.1 *A typology of social sciences*

| Type of variable | Type of actor | |
	Individual	*National*
Absolute	psychology	political science
Relative	differential psychology	comparative politics
Relational	sociology	international relations

Thus, the simple thesis of this paper is concerned with the utility of sociology, and some special parts of sociology in particular, as a reservoir of concepts and hypotheses for what has so far proved to be a relatively theory-poor social science. Typically, international relationists discuss how to construct theories more than they really try to do the work — as evidenced by some recent works in the field [3]. In that sense they are probably at the stage where sociology was one generation ago: the journals abounded with metatheory — theories about how to make theories — *and* with fascinating accounts of the human condition in particular cases, with a clearly ideographic orientation. However, nothing of what is said here should be interpreted to imply that such mental efforts are wastes of time or unimportant; they are of primordial importance, and it is only that they become dangerous if they dominate the intellectual field alone. Today both of them have almost disappeared from leading journals of sociology.

Obviously, if the theoretically more experienced discipline is to be of any relevance it will only be through interpretation and only through careful selection of what appears to be most suggestive. The key concept here is, of course, *isomorphism* [4]. It is easy to buy the general idea that the international system with about 135 actors called *nations* and perhaps 80 more units referred to as *territories* is an interaction system and for that reason should bear some similarity to intranational, social interaction systems. It is more difficult to establish this isomorphism in specific and scientifically productive terms.

2. Approaches to international relations

The point of departure is the (posited) correspondence between individuals at the social system level and nations at the international system level, and the (posited) correspondence between interindividual interaction and international interaction. "Interaction" is then defined as action where not only predictions as to the behavior of other units (actors) but also perceptions of the prescriptions held by these units towards oneself are taken into account [5]. Interaction is usually both ways: if A interacts with B, then there is a tendency for B to interact with A, i.e. to perceive that A expects (in the normative sense) something from him.

In what sense, then, do nations interact? On the answers to this will depend any judgment on the soundness of this approach, and there seem to be two distinct ways of answering. First of all, nations interact because the holders of collective, representative statuses (above all the head of state, the head of government, the foreign minister, and the persons to whom they delegate authority) are human beings who interact, and their interaction carries the burden of national interaction [6].

But is this all there is to it? Is international interaction "nothing but" the interaction between these individuals? If so, as some reductionists will claim, the problem of isomorphism is reduced to the simple problem of studying interaction systems in groups of top politicians concerned with international relations, and this would be a sub-branch of the sub-branch of general small group theory concerned with the interaction between

29

politicians in representative roles. But we shall defend the obvious position that there is more to international interaction than the interaction between top statusholders alone [7].

For if this were all there was to it, then international interaction would be predictable on the basis of solid knowledge and theory about the interaction between holders of top statuses. And quite a lot can no doubt be obtained on this basis. For a human group has so many layers, or subsystems, that a study of this particular type of interaction could be very rewarding if social scientists were permitted to get the data. Thus, from general sociological theory we can postulate the following phases in the development of a small group. First, members will explore each other and patterns of regularity will develop. Next, some of these patterns will be maintained by normative expectations, not only by predictions, and after some time any member will find himself surrounded by a set of expectations that define his roles in the group. At this point group *statuses* are born, for instance, by a process of division along the high — low and instrumental — expressive axes as suggested by Parsons and Bales [8], yielding four statuses. The group has now moved from a pattern of non-institutionalized interaction only, to institutionalized interaction, and from now on two processes usually take place. First, there is the process of *generalization* where the statuses become generalized so that they do not disappear when the members of the group change; but rather define holes that somehow have to be filled, such as the "best-liked man," the "best idea man," etc. [9]. The set of all these holes or statuses then forms the *structure* of the group. It is invariant under *substitution* (or nearly so), whereas the nongeneralized interaction that is tied to particular group members will change with them. And usually as a concomitant of this, there is the process of *formalization* whereby statuses become codified and are made explicit, and are identified by means of such tags as "president", "rapporteur", etc. Formalized statuses will usually also be generalized statuses, but the opposite need not be the case.

Thus, we have essentially three types of interaction. First comes the interaction that most easily meets the eye: the acting out of expectations that makes up *formal statuses*. Then comes the acting out of *informal statuses*. And then comes the rest, partly consisting of patterned interaction that is not generalized but linked to particular persons, and partly consisting of nonpatterned or noninstitutionalized interaction. Since both of these are connected with particular persons we can refer to them as *personal interaction* as opposed to substitutable status interaction. For this is crucial: one will have to know what is invariant under substitution of persons, and what depends on these particular persons. Once the group has arrived at a certain structure it will have a certain robustness when exposed to a high rate of turnover; when it is still in the first and formative stages it will be highly vulnerable to substitution.

Let us then return to the idea that the group is a group of foreign ministers or their representatives. In that case some of them by virtue of their personality will be able to dominate and influence the others, and if they meet sufficiently often generalized patterns will emerge with statuses that will be occupied by new foreign ministers when there is turnover (for instance, the status as "the one who knows what is formally correct," or "the one who knows how this was done when the organization was still young," or "the one who can serve as an in-between for the two camps," and so on).

It is now immediately seen how insufficient this will be as a model for the international system, and for that reason how fallacious this "nothing but" model is. For any foreign minister in addition to his personality and his status in the group of colleagues also carries with him the label of his nation. This means that in a small group of foreign ministers we can now postulate the existence of four interaction systems: 1. the *system of nations*, where each representative is allocated to his nation; 2. the *formal system*, with such statuses as president, chairman, rapporteur, etc.; 3. the *informal system*, with such statuses as "the experienced man," "the expressive leader," etc.; 4. the *personal system*, which is essentially a residual, idiosyncratic category. Thus, the *behavior* of any one representative is conceived of in terms of four components: the national component, the formal component, the informal component and the personal component, $B = N + F + I + P$.

Incidentally, this formula also points to the obvious methodology for the study of a system of foreign ministers (or their representatives) in interaction. Thus by keeping F, I, and P constant at various values one may study the impact of N (nationality) on verbal or nonverbal behavior; by keeping N, I, and P constant one may study the impact of F, and so on. By varying all of them one may also study interaction effects, for instance, the interaction between nationality and personality type (is a rigid person from a dictatorship more similar to a rigid person from a democracy or to a flexible person from a democracy, as both would be consonant with their systems?). Apart from our scant knowledge of the personality types of public persons, official records will give much material on the N and F components, and biographical material, memoirs, etc., on the I and P components. Thus, international relations as a field is very often far better off than sociology because better and more complete data are often readily available for the international system.

From general sociological theory quite a lot is known about social structures that consist of more than one system [10]. For instance, if there is a considerable amount of *rank disequilibrium* or *rank incongruence* present in the group instability will sooner or later result. This will be the case when the ranking of foreign ministers in terms of the power or prestige of their nations is not concordant with their ranking in the formal or the informal structure. Often the formal structure is used as a system of rank compensation: the foreign minister of a small nation is permitted to perform in a highly visible way when he is elected president, and then there is a rotational scheme that has the function of unfreezing any pattern of rank incongruence that may follow. More important is the case where the foreign minister of a small nation has *charisma* and the ability to influence people in the informal system, whereas the foreign minister of the big power is short on both. We would predict in this case a) that the former will often subdue his abilities in order not to challenge the latter [11], b) that they will avoid each other, c) (if b and a do not obtain) that they will start hating each other to a point that might have international consequences [12], and d) that the other small nation representatives will be on the side of the foreign minister from the big power until rank congruence has been established again — unless they can derive special benefits from the situation.

To take another aspect of the interaction structure that consists of more than one system: the case of *isomorphism between the systems*. In the system of nations, as is well known from general conflict theory, conflicts polarize interaction [13]. This means that positive interaction will tend to be within blocs and negative interaction between blocs, and foreign ministers are supposed to behave accordingly when they meet in the international system, and often also in the other two systems. But the other two systems may impose on them other interaction patterns because of the formal structure of the group or simply because of friendship and animosity patterns inconsistent with the pattern in the international system. The representatives may have been socialized to internalize this pattern so well that they feel dislike for the persons from the other bloc and attraction toward persons in their own — but then they also may not — and it is interesting to speculate on the function of various amounts of lack of isomorphism for the total structure to function. With complete isomorphism the system will function in a highly predictable manner but also exhibit extreme rigidity. With total lack of isomorphism social interaction will probably be impossible. And with some ingredients of lack of isomorphism a stimulus toward change and a drive toward consonance will be present in the structure; probably with N and F leading the way in a polarization process and I and P leading the way in a depolarization process — in general. In short, the problem of divided loyalties between the systems is found here as in all other human relations.

One can now imagine the science of international relations written from four vantage points, depending on which component in the behavioral equation one would emphasize most. The *personality* approach would emphasize the personal component of the interaction, the *informal* approach the informal component, the *formal* approach the formal component, and the *structural* approach the national component. The second approach is probably mainly of heuristic interest since relatively few properties of the international system would be invariant both of nationality of the representative, his formal status and of those of his personality characteristics that are not "soaked up" in the formal system. One is left, then, with the choice between the personality, formal, and structural approaches, where the last will present international relations in terms of everything that is invariant of substitution of individuals in the representative roles, and the first will present international relations in terms of what is invariant of the nationality of the representatives. Clearly, either of these two approaches will represent an exaggeration, together they may yield a rather satisfactory basis. For instance, typical examples that can only be derived from a simultaneous use of both personality and structural approaches are precisely the thesis about the importance of rank concordance in the systems, and isomorphism in case of conflict, dealt with above. The latter is facilitated by socialization and internalization of norms about conflict behavior, the former by the circumstance that bigger nations not only will tend to have more power but also have more trained people to choose from for such important jobs, so that chances are high that there will in general be a good correlation between the rank of the nation and the talent of the foreign minister. And should they not have sufficient talent available they can usually make up for it by the *number* of delegates they send to conferences.

There is no contradiction between the structural approach and the obvious dictum that nations as such do not act, just as little as there is any contradiction between the definition of sociology as the science of human inter-action and the definition of sociology as the science dealing with the invariants in social structure, under substitution of individuals. The structural approach studies how representatives of nations behave as a function of the position of that nation in the international system in order to arrive at propositions, for instance, about how a leader nation in a bloc will behave relative to the other members under varying degrees of conflicts with the other bloc. Persons will have to do what shall be done whether as soldiers, diplomats, commercial agents, technical assistance personnel or what not, but they are heavily constrained in their choice of appropriate actions by their national contexts. It is this common core that is the raw material of the structural approach.

This, then, gives meaning to two concepts of "international interaction": a *concrete* concept where representatives are interacting with each other in the three systems mentioned above, and an *abstract* concept where nations "as such" are interacting. The latter is very often reflected in the news when it is reported that "Nation X voted against, nation Y in favor," it hardly leads to any group-actor or group-soul fallacy and has the advantage of word economy. One does not have to refer to "substitution-invariant aspects of the foreign minister's behavior," but to international interaction as such.

This being said, it becomes obvious how sociology relates to international relations: as the *science* of the interaction between representatives from various nations when they meet, *and* as a *model* for the abstract concept of nations interacting. The former requires no concept of isomorphism, it is sociology plus the psychology needed to get insight into motivation patterns, etc., in each single individual case, plus the political science needed to understand the precise meaning of "representative status" in each single national case. But for the model approach isomorphism is needed. And the problem is: can we assume such an isomorphism between interpersonal and international interaction systems? The most obvious comment to make to this problem, as about any hypothesized isomorphism, is that the hypothesis a) constitutes no proof per se; and b) is not necessarily wrong just because it spans different levels of social organization, for instance from the individual actor to the national actor. A postulated isomorphism is a reservoir of hypotheses once a pattern of correspondence between elements/concepts at each level and between relations between these elements/concepts has been established.

It is rather obvious that "the proof of the pudding is in the eating," and that the isomorphism often will have to be established rather than discovered by suitable redefinition of old and introduction of new concepts. And to this task we now turn, concentrating completely on the contextual approach to international relations.

3. The sociology of small groups as a model

That the sociology of *small groups* is useful for the study of what we have called "concrete" international interaction above is obvious, but there also seem to be good reasons to say that this is the most rewarding branch of sociology for models of the "abstract" international system, at least at the present level of international organization. Some of the arguments are as follows:

1. Small groups and international systems can be regarded as isomorphic with the simple correspondences mentioned above (individuals to nations and interaction to interaction) because usually relatively few nations inter-

act together, which justifies the use of the word "small". Moreover, the international system has a relatively low level of organization which justifies the use of the word "group". To the extent more is needed, as in connection with international organizations, the theory of associations and perhaps also of simple organizations may be useful — but these branches may also be regarded as extensions of small group theory. Nothing as complicated as a full-fledged theory of social structure is needed, not to mention a theory of total societies, for there will be little or nothing at the international level that exhibits so complex interaction structures, at least at present.

2. Small group theory gives a theory of interaction in its most naked form, stripped of all extra connotations; it is to macro-sociology what chamber music is to the symphony orchestra.

3. Small group theory is empirically rather well established since it can draw on common sense insights, laboratory experiment, surveys, etc., as data. It has a degree of precision, but also a certain degree of artificiality. To the extent international interaction systems are to be studied directly, and not through simulation techniques for instance, it will not be through experiments but through observation, letting the system generate its own data. Thus, a better point of comparison would perhaps have been a vast amount of well-analyzed data about interaction processes in natural rather than contrived groups — but then one would perhaps not have obtained the insights currently at the disposal of social scientists. With this limitation small group theory nevertheless has the advantage of being based on a rich variety of relatively solid data.

4. Small group theory has not only well-established propositions but also a relatively high level of theoretical integration of them, at least as compared with other branches of sociology. This means that isomorphisms, once imputed and established, will be relatively rich in the sense of involving many relations between the elements.

We have now presented so many claims that the time has come to show there is some substance behind them. However, before that can be meaningfully done a dictionary will have to be written showing how terms in small group theory are supposed to be interpreted in the field of international relations. One suggestion is as follows (omitting such purely logical concepts as "weakly connected," "transitive relation," etc., that would be common to both).

TABLE 1.2 *Suggested dictionary for small group theory — international relations correspondence*

Small groups	International systems
individual	nation
group	alliance, group of nations
codified norms	international law
non-codified law	international practice
status, role	national status, role, patterned behavior
interaction	exchange, interaction
leader, power	leader nation, power
(absolute leader)	big power
slave	colony
slave owner	colonial power
democratic system	democratic system

The dictionary is not very rich, but serves to indicate some simple correspondences.

4. Examples of hypotheses

Several expositions of small group theory exist in print, but in our experience none of them quite equals the chapter on "Face-to-face relations, in small groups" in *Human Behavior* by Berelson and Steiner [14] when it comes to presenting the gist of the findings in a concentrated form. For that reason we shall explore that presentation systematically for its possible relevance as a reservoir of insights that can be brought to bear on international relations theory, using the dictionary above.

Since we do not claim that *any* small group is isomorphic to the set of *all* nations at any given point in time the method of isomorphism is meaningful only if a small group is conceived of as the model of a subsystem of roughly the same level of organization. Thus, a small group of nations would consist of anything from two nations to the maximum number of nations that *can be kept* cognitively present at the same time (20 is much too high, perhaps not more than 10 or 7) [15]; all nations *can interact with all other nations* (but not necessarily equally as much with all other nations); there is *consensus both within and outside the group as to which nations belong to it, and the pattern is extended through time*. There is no assumption to the effect that relations are positive or friendly. The interaction patterns may take on all values from extremely positive through indifference to extremely negative, but the net balance will usually have to be positive unless the group is forced to stay together as nations are when they crystallize into geographically contiguous and immobile states. Thus, a small group of nations is not the same as an alliance (which is a military organization of nations with a specific aim) nor the same as a trade area (which is an economic organization) nor the same as a federation (which is a political organization of nations) — it is a much more primitive unit with much less structure. Nevertheless, something can be said about it, and we shall follow Berelson and Steiner in their distinction between "formation," "influence" and "internal operation [16].

4.1. Formation

The basic finding from human groups is the idea that individuals that participate in a freely formed group under conditions of equality will tend to become like each other (share values and norms) [17] and tend to like each other. This relates interaction in general to friendship under two important conditions, and these conditions are not necessarily fulfilled in the dominance-oriented and highly stratified international society of nations.

International interaction will to some extent have to be based on one simple principle of organization, *geographical proximity*, if for no other reason than because our present concept of a nation is tied to the idea of a contiguous territory. Since most kinds of costs in connection with interaction will increase with increasing geographical distance, this means a forced overselection of geographical neighbors and underselection of distant nations. This, in turn, may have two possible consequences: the effects in terms of likeness or liking do in fact appear, which would mean that neighbor nations, on the average, should like each other most and be most like each other, *or* that they abstain from interaction or even engage in negative interaction since they are constrained (because of costs) to interraction with neighbors they do not like. Thus, one would hypothesize:

1. Over-representation of homologous nations among neighbors (likeness hypothesis);

2. Over-representation of friendly relations among neighbors (liking hypothesis);

3. Over-representation of aggressive relations among neighbors ("you are not the neighbor of my choice" hypothesis) [18].

Particularly the second hypothesis presupposes that the two conditions mentioned above are fulfilled. We know of no test of that hypothesis. Relative to the situation between nations, individuals have a number of advantages when they want to form groups — for instance, when they form the crucial group of 2 or dyad, known as a couple [19]. They have a *wider choice* since individuals are more numerous than nations, and in modern societies they can move so as to reduce the cost of interaction with the partner of their choice. Hence, they can rearrange the structure so as to align interaction patterns with liking and likeness patterns. Nations would be able to do so if they were not territorially but socially defined [20] and if the cost of interaction depended less on distance [21]. International society thus is very much like highly traditional societies based on the neighborhood principle.

It should be noted that this theory explains likeness between neighboring nations by deriving it as a consequence of ingroup interaction, not by cultural diffusion which obviously also depends on distance. The idea is that interaction forces homology because of the necessity for nation A to have in its status repertory the same statuses as nation B for interaction to proceed smoothly. This, in turn, will lead to homology, which is the same as similarities in systems and structure, and the result of this, in turn, is common if not shared culture.

In human groups much work has been done on the study of individuals who are members of two or more groups that may impose on the individuals conflicting standards of behavior so that the individual finds himself in cross-pressure, a situation which he resolves by cutting *one* of the ties or by decreasing *all* interaction [22]. In national groups geography again serves as a constraint: the nation in cross-pressure is not so free to choose because it is not free to move. Argentina, which by factor analysis can be shown to belong to southern Europe [23], nevertheless is located exactly where it is, bordering on nations like Bolivia and Brazil that in no way belong to southern Europe. For that reason one would expect nations to be less free to develop their potential of international interaction: caught in cross-pressures the only way out may be a decrease of interaction, and this in turn will reduce seriously the possibility of developing their internal potential. In a sense this may apply to Latin America as a whole: as developing nations they belong to the Afro-Asian group, as predominantly white nations they belong to the developed part of the world, and they are not quite accepted anywhere and caught in a conflict which cannot be completely resolved by severing ties. Data on airline connections give a good illustration of how much closer these countries are to the developed nations [24], data on opinion structure say something about how far away they are from them [25].

Then there are the traditional propositions in any theory of conflict about *polarization* (the more conflict between groups, the less positive interaction, and vice versa, until the breaking point is reached where interaction starts again, but this time of the negative variety); and about *consonance* (according to the well-known Arab sayings to the effect that "the friend of my friend is my friend, the friend of my enemy is my enemy, the enemy of my friend is my enemy, and the enemy of my enemy is my friend") [26]. Frank Harary, using graph theory, has proved that a system where all cycles are consonant is also a perfectly polarized system, with two camps and all positive interaction located within the camps and all negative interaction between the camps [27]. There is no reason why all this should not apply to nations as well [28], particularly since the mechanisms should be operative for the holders of representative statuses, *provided they identify with their nations*. And the concrete expression of polarization is of course the formation of alliances and blocs.

How does a group react to *new members?* Negatively, if many join at once; time is needed to adjust to new members and to prevent formation of subgroups by means of adequate integration so that there will be no polarization effect between oldboys and newcomers. But if a new member joins alone he will have to overconform and will feel inferior. This has important consequences for alliance-formation and for the formation of international organizations in general: never admit too many new members at the same time — it may have disruptive influence — rather admit them one at a time and make use of their initial period of overconformity to carry out tasks that older members would not care to do. On the other hand, if one does not want old members and leaders to dominate too much, but rather would like to preserve a certain pluralism, then new members should be admitted in blocs so as to arrive in the group with a common and shared definition of their status within the group. This probably also applies to groups of nations and could be tested systematically, for instance using data on the admission pattern to the United Nations.

4.2. Influence

Influence is but another word for power, although not of the kind usually referred to as "naked", which makes it a topic of immediate interest for any student of international relations. The main theme is the difficulty or almost impossibility of resisting majority values and attitudes — and the ease with which the individual deviant can be persuaded that he is wrong and be "influenced" so as to yield to the majority opinion, even in the face of evidence to the effect that he is right (Asch-Sherif effect). That individual and cultural differences are enormous here is obvious. There are also other conditions [29]: the more consensual the values, the more strongly they are held, the more ingroup interaction, the less secure other kinds of evidence, the more deviant or a newcomer the isolated individual and the more eager he is to stay in the group and receive a high ranking in the group — the more effective the efforts to bring him "in line".

That all of these factors mentioned above will be of some importance in a group of foreign ministers or other representatives seems reasonable, although they can also protect themselves from small group mechanisms by reference to mandates, ratification rules, etc., and by switching from the informal to the formal and even structural system. Much of the dilemma of conferences will consist in precisely this: trying to reconcile the informal, formal, and structural systems. The success will often depend on the degree of isomorphism, and particularly on the degree of rank concordance; they should be "neither too high, nor too low." But the theoretical problem is whether these factors can be held to be operative at the truly international level too, not only at its projection in the meeting halls.

This is less obvious than for the propositions discussed above. For one thing, all factors here must at some point or another pass via human minds; deviance must be perceived in order to trigger appropriate measures, even though it all seems to happen more or less automatically. But this does not mean it all has to take place in the meeting halls alluded to. Nations have other members that can perceive what is the norm (in the normative or in the statistical sense) and what is deviance, *provided other nations are visible to them*, and this depends on the channels of communication [30]. Thus, a pressure to bring another nation, a member of the group, in line may arise at the public opinion level and be proportionate to all factors mentioned at the human group level. This does not mean that pressure is effective; that will depend on the internal workings of the political systems, particularly on the degree of sensitivity of the decisionmakers to public opinion pressure. But the decisionmakers may themselves be the observers of the deviance and bring pressure on the deviant via sanctions in the interaction system, such as the cancellation of state visits, less favorable trade agreements, and so on. The meetinghall is not necessary; the international system is sufficiently isomorphic with the small group as it is since its elements can perceive, evaluate, and act and interact as long as channels of communication are open.

It may well be that the most important similarity would relate not so much to the operation of influence within one small group of nations as to an international system consisting of various groups. Findings from many studies suggest that "a major factor in influencing change in participatory groups is the power of the group itself over its members" [31]. Thus, he who wants workers to accept a salary freeze will have to argue with the trade union leaders, and they in turn with the leaders of the local unions, all on the assumption that these leaders are the "real" leaders of the "really important" groups. Similarly, acceptance of the goals of the UN probably presupposes their acceptance by regional organizations, which throws a certain perspective on the famous articles 51—54 of the UN Charter. They can be used as instruments of cooptation.

Another factor has been pointed out by William F. Whyte: "One of the most important functions [the leader] performs is that of relating his group to other groups in the district. Whether the relationship is one of conflict, competition, or cooperation, he is expected to represent the interests of his followers" [32]. Thus, a big power can remain the legitimate leader of its followers only as long as it handles external relations adequately, and since big powers, particularly in conflict, have a virtual monopoly on the major forms of external exchange, including communication, there is little opportunity for the lesser powers to control whether they in fact live up to their obligations.

4.3. Internal operations

The interesting thing about the pressure to conform, according to human group theory, is that it is strongest toward the leader of the group and toward the newcomer and the deviant; in other words, strongest at the very center of the group and at the periphery. Thus, one should expect the leader nation and the marginal nations in an alliance to be the nations that adhere most strongly to norms of polarization in a crisis [33]. This notion applies to the leader because he must conform to remain a leader (if he does not impose himself by sheer force, in which case he is not a leader but a despot), for the leader is the unit that best "represents or realizes the norms and values of the group" [34]. It also applies to the margina unit more than others because the marginal has to validate its claim to belong. For that reason the marginal unit will overconform and take all norms literally, where the more seasoned members know how to distinguish between norms that are only window-dressing and those to be followed to the letter. However, one interesting consequence is the kind of integration this factor should create between center and the extreme periphery, and this may serve as an explanation why the center often bypasses middle layers and finds its best support in some servile parts of the periphery, which then may be elevated to higher ranks (precisely what they have hoped for), with the consequence of alienating the middle layers but also of bringing some circulation and mobility into the system. Thus the big power, the leader of an alliance, may find its best support in the smallest powers not only because they are easily manipulated but because of this simple structural reason. This is exemplified by the relation the US has to a number of small Latin American nations and to the smaller NATO allies of the more marginal variety (Portugal, Greece, Turkey) compared with its relations to the "upper

41

class" of Latin America (Argentina, Brazil, Chile, and Mexico) and of Europe (Britain, France, Western Germany) [35].

If ranking depends on ability to realize values, its degree of consensus will depend on how consensual the values are. Since the system will function better in the sense of having less internal conflict the less rank disequilibrium and the less rank incongruence are found in the system, we get two conditions: 1. that values are consensual, and 2. that the group is organized around only one value or else that the ranking of the nations according to several values is concordant so that disequilibrium and incongruence are avoided [36]. This explains relatively well why military alliances have a tendency to break apart when the war is over. During the war there is one highly consensual value, the defeat of the enemy, and the nation that contributes most ranks highest. Since military contribution is relatively easy to measure, consensus about ranking will ensue, and the result will be a linear order according to prestige: superpower — big power — small power. After the war the "alliance for peace" is confronted with the difficulty in arriving at a consensual definition as to what constitutes peace, as to which are the new values to be maximized. If several values emerge it is probably an indication of different hierarchies of ranking, and hence of conflicts that will erupt sooner or later and disrupt the alliance because of rank disequilibrium and rank incongruence.

In human groups that problem can be solved by some rearrangements, by subgroups and new groups, by mobility — with nations this is not so easy, and changes of membership in groups of nations are highly visible and significant. Thus, if the alliance is kept it will probably be under one or both of these conditions: interaction is reduced to a minimum in order not to bring the conflict out in the open, meetings are rituals only and the alliance is kept in preparation to encounter new emergencies (which then may serve as a self-fulfilling prophecy) *or else* interaction is built around one new consensual and simple value. Two remarkable post-war examples are the *defeat of internal subversion* (anti-communism and red-baiting in the West, anti-capitalism and imperialism agent-baiting in the East) and the *devotion to national income per capita* as the supreme values of groups of nations. The criticism and dissatisfaction with the first of these dimensions has dominated political debate in the past; we bet that the dissatisfaction with the latter will dominate political debates in the near future. For there seems to be little in the international system that is quite as simple and consensual as military victory. As to income interest it seems now to be focused as much on dispersion as on averages and this may lead to rankings with relatively low rank-correlation. Moreover, there is no guarantee that a military superpower comes out on top — a fact both superpowers have been reminded of by their bloc members.

Who, then, are the leaders of a group? The list of characteristics for *human* groups include [37] *size* (height and weight), *physical appearance*, *self-confidence, sociability, energy*, and intelligence. Some of these characteristics are synonyms or correlates of power. Obviously, it would be futile to try to find national level counterparts to all these concepts, so the important point is really only one: leadership depends not only on achieved properties, but also very much on ascribed properties, probably also in an achievement-oriented system. Thus we assume this also to hold true for nations, where we define "ascribed" as a property handed over from one generation to the next, unchanged. Examples are [38]: size, population, location, past history (whereas present history is an achieved property, the achievement of the present generation). A nation that counts many square miles or tens of millions of inhabitants or is centrally located in the communication net or has a "glorious" history is difficult to bypass as a leader, for instance, when it comes to locating offices of important organizations [39]. Generalizing perception plays a role here: such a nation is believed to be great in general [40]. This then will produce precisely the same problems as it does in human groups: the small, peripheral, and "unglorious" nation may be a much higher achiever according to the values of the group of nations and yet not receive its share of the paraphernalia of rank, which may lead to alienation and to aggression because of the rank disequilibrium [41]. But then this may be less serious than the alienation of "old established forces," to speak in the Sukarno jargon, even if their claim to rank is based mainly on ascriptive criteria [42]. Thus, one key to de Gaulle's policy is his keen understanding of rank equilibration: it is not enough for France to indulge in ascriptive criteria, it must achieve to an extent that corresponds to its ascriptive rank, otherwise it will lag behind and its failure will be even more evident because it will be measured with past glories as the standard.

A measure has been devised to calculate the amount of disequilibrium in a rank profile, simply by adding all internal distances. Thus, if we give "1" to a topdog status and "0" to an underdog status, then the amount of disequilibrium in the profile TUTUT is 6, and the amount in the profile UTTTT is 4. However, this measure is purely mechanical and does not necessarily imply that the amount of, say, aggressiveness resulting from disequilibrium is proportionate to the measure. It may well be that a nation with the latter profile becomes much more aggressive, because it becomes possessed with the one missing topdog status. This dimension may refer to status as nuclear (T) vs. non-nuclear (U) power, rich vs. poor, growth vs. stagnation, and so on, and the despair resulting from non-nuclear status, relative poverty, or economic stagnation may become the primary concern of the nation and dispose it toward a choice of means it would otherwise abstain

43

from. Thus, aggressiveness may have a curvilinear relationship to rank disequilibrium.

In this connection it should be emphasized that a particular drive in the direction of aggressiveness may result from a disequilibrium between past rank and present rank. Both dimensions, past and present, would have to be included in the set to be analyzed. The theory would not distinguish between disequilibria resulting from downward or from upward mobility, but since there are many indications that either may result in aggressiveness this is not serious (the *nouveau riche* as well as the poor white).

Much and good small group theory is based on the distinction between instrumental and expressive roles, and particularly between instrumental and expressive leaders. The theory is so convincing, particularly because the well-verified proposition about the existence of incest taboos can be derived from it, that it would be nice if parallel concepts can be found. But it is difficult to see what would correspond to an expressive nation in the international system. Its people may be expressive, its foreign minister may be so in a meeting, but can the nation be so as such? Could there be a tradition for a nation to have foreign ministers that play expressive roles? Or could the nation be an exporter of cultural goods, of music, of religion? But this is not the important sense it has in small group theory, as the provider of integration of a noninstrumental kind, as the lubrication of the system providing it with phases of rest and tension release so that the system may go through new phases of instrumentality [43].

And then, this may be the point: the international system of nations functions so unsmoothly, among other reasons precisely because it lacks the expressive status. The system is forced to choose between instrumental achievement, with or without violence, on the one hand and inactivity on the other. And if it does not achieve, there is nothing corresponding to the consoling mother, there is only the bitterness of defeat and the withdrawal into inactivity till new energy, motivation and courage have accumulated. At the human level this would correspond to the efforts of the adolescent with no family support because he comes from a "broken home", and to the likelihood that his frustration, combined with rank disequilibrium, will result in delinquent activity. Similarly, we would postulate the parallel to this criminogenic factor at the international level: the bellicogenic factor. But much imagination should be brought to bear on the problem of finding, in spite of all this, the international system counterpart to the concept of the expressive status. It may well be that the answer lies in strong trans- and supranational organizations (INGOs and IGOs) and adequate expressive symbolism.

This is particularly important in a situation with many newly established nations. The experiments with small groups show that not only will the followers react against "bossy people", but when this dislike is openly expressed it may render the group virtually leaderless: no one wants to pay the price in terms of unpopularity. In cultures less sensitive to the reaction of the followers the leader may still lead, but the relationship may become authoritarian rather than democratic. Thus the choice often becomes one between autocratic leadership and a laissez-faire relationship combined with withdrawal, as is often found in relations between old colonial powers and their former colonies. Much of their nationalism is nourished by the antagonism against the bossy instrumental leader, and by negative actions during the first year of independence with consequent *imprinting* effect.

If we now turn to factors determining interaction frequencies, a number of interesting propositions should be valid also on the international level since interaction is a completely structural concept once the actors have been defined. Thus, that interaction increases with cohesiveness and decreases with dissensus (until the point of rupture is reached and negative interaction ensues) is rather obvious. It is less trivial (and certainly not necessarily true either) that interaction is primarily addressed more to deviants than to conformists. If interaction is generalized in the sense that one kind of interaction has a tendency to imply another, a member of a group of nations can attract interaction by defining itself as a deviant (referred to as "making itself interesting" in groups of individuals), provided it does not exaggerate so much that the other members no longer want to pay the interaction price necessary to keep the nation in the group [44].

More important are the main findings about the relationship between rank and interaction [45]:

1. The higher the rank, the more interaction received and emitted.

2. The more equal the rank between two, the higher the interaction.

3. There is more interaction from high to low than from low to high.

4. These rankings are highly correlated with [46]:
   a. the number of acts received by the units,
   b. the number of acts received by the units from a given unit,
   c. the number of acts sent by the units,
   d. the number of acts sent by the units to a given unit.

Of course, 4d implies 4c and 4b implies 4a, but not vice versa. Thus, if we symbolize the higher ranks by T (topdog) and the lower rank by U (underdog) we may hypothesize this ranking order of interaction [47]:

1. T to T
2. T to U
3. U to T
4. U to U

This strict ordering does not follow from the above, however. What follows from the above is only that T—T is higher than the other three combinations, and that T—U is higher than U—T. How U—U is located relative to T—U and U—T will have to be ascertained on some other basis. In the small group field we shall quote only one study to substantiate the hypothesis, a study of 18 three-man groups analyzed for patterns of support [48] (Table 1.3).

TABLE 1.3 *An example of positive interaction frequencies in small groups*

		As recipient		
		most active	medium active	least active
As *initiator*	most active	—	12.0	7.0
	medium active	11.1	—	3.8
	least active	4.0	2.5	—

From our point of view these data have two shortcomings: they concern only support or positive interaction, and there are only three members, whereas we would actually need four-man groups since we need two underdogs and two topdogs. However, the first difficulty is of minor importance since the focus is mainly on the intra-group interaction which will have to be predominantly positive anyhow (since we presuppose it is free-forming), and the latter is solved by using the "medium active" partly as topdog and partly as underdog. With these two assumptions the hypothesis is confirmed: the lowest levels of interactions are found between low and medium, the highest between medium and high, with the interaction between high and low located in-between as they should. Moreover, in all three cases we find higher levels of interaction from the higher to the lower than from the lower to the higher (12.0 as against 11.1, 7.0 as against 4.0, and 3.8 as against 2.5). And finally: this asymmetry is much more pronounced when the interaction is across two ranks than when it is across one only, as evidenced by the ratios (1.75 as against 1.08 and 1.06).

There is no reason at all why this should not also hold at the international level, except one: relations are often so formal that there is more of a norm of reciprocity, in the sense that if for instance nation A sends a head of state to nation B, then nation B is supposed to do the same with regard to nation A. This does not mean that we cannot hypothesize more diplomatic relations between topdog nations than between underdog nations, with topdog-underdog pairs in-between, only that we cannot hypothesize more topdog-underdog than underdog-topdog interaction for nations [49]. One important factor behind this crucial difference is the idea of sovereignty and formal equality, which can be preserved only by maintaining at least some kind of symmetry in relationship even across tremendous rank distances. But if instead of the crude differences of the "diplomatic relations present" vs. "diplomatic relations absent" variety, we operate for instance with the number of diplomats in each embassy [50], we shall probably be able to reconquer the lost distinction: the embassies of topdog nations in underdog nations are rather plentifully staffed, whereas the opposite is not necessarily the case.

With these comments the general hypothesis is eminently testable and a preliminary investigation seems to indicate that it is also tenable, at least for the Latin American system and the East-West system [51]. The implications of the hypothesis are so many that it should provide a relatively rich theoretical and empirical harvest for future investigations, but that will not be spelt out here [52].

The sociological findings dealing with conditions for successful performance of groups composed of individuals — that success depends on the harmony between group goals and individual goals, degree of co-operation, active discussion among members before decisions are taken — should be transferable to groups of nations; but they also have a touch of the trivial. When change is desired multilateral discussions seem to be more effective than bilateral discussions (usually the leader with the underdogs, but only one at the time) — whereas the latter probably is more efficient for control purposes and maintenance of traditions. "It is typically more effective to influence people as group members than to do so in an isolated individual-by-individual manner" write Berelson and Steiner [53] and this should hold a fortiori at the national level because of the importance attached to being consulted and being listened to, and to make visible to others at least parts of this procedure. One is reminded of the debate about secret vs. open diplomacy as an expression of the breakthrough of multilateralism, which again is an expression of formal equality between nations. Whether the "open covenants" are arrived at openly or not is a technical question — the meetings may well be secret as long as they are multilateral and not based on an accumulation of bilateral meetings of the T−T or T−U varieties only.

There is some small group theory support for the idea that the more open the communication, the more effective the group. Imagine a group with three members. There may be six lines of communication since there are three pairs, and communication can be in either or both directions. Imagine the network is complete and then gradually reduced by removing one line and then one more line. An ingenious experiment by Heise and Miller [54] shows that efficiency depends on the *number* of lines or arrows of communication as well as their *structure;* least efficient was a pattern of one-way communication in all pairs, then came a pattern with one central person in two-way communication in all pairs. The latter should not be confused with multilateral communication where there is not only two-way communication in all pairs, but also mutual visibility of all communication [55].

Another set of experiments by Bavelas [56] shows another effect of the communication network: the more central the position of a unit (as measured by the "associated number" in graph theory) [57], the higher the rank of the unit. Since we know from above that the reverse is also true — the higher the rank, the more central the position in the general interaction network — rank and centrality are related to each other by positive feedback [58]. On the other hand, the more centralized or asymmetric the interaction pattern, the less efficient the group. Hence maximum efficiency in the sense of utilizing the total potential of the units can be obtained only if something is done actively to counteract the tendency of the group to develop asymmetry [59]. This tendency seems to be a characteristic of all groups with a ranking structure, as developed above.

At the international level this can be easily interpreted in terms of the structure of the general interaction network: the more asymmetric it is, the greater the overutilization of the topdog nations and underutilization of the underdog nations. Hence research is once more directed toward the general interaction system (not only the pattern of economic interaction) as a cue to understanding how the international system functions.

In conclusion, let us see what small group theory has to say about the function of *size*, of the number of units in a group. In general the findings are contradictory in that something is lost and something is gained with higher numbers. Thus, with *increasing size* and other things being equal [60]:

1. *More formality* in the sense of clear leader roles (the critical point probably around five to seven);
2. *More tolerance of leader direction* (for otherwise chaos will easily ensue and the leader has only to demonstrate this to legitimate his claim);
3. *More inhibition at the underdog level*, which means more differentiation between high and low in the group;

4. *More tendency toward subgroup formation* (because there will be more to choose from, hence more likelihood of group formation according to the principles of likeness and liking);

5. *More disagreement* (because there will be more opinions to accommodate and less opportunity to express all of them, hence less opportunity to arrive at consensus);

6. *Less tension* (probably because of more centralization and clear authority definitions).

Berelson and Steiner conclude [61] with a recommendation of a group of *five* since it combines the virtues in the list above with the virtues of cohesion and the opportunity for every member for self-expression; moreover, there is no possibility of forming subgroups of equal size.

Again, there is no reason why all of this should not obtain at the international level too, and not only at the level of meetings of representatives. Thus implicit in this theory are conditions for lasting alliances, not necessarily in the literal sense that they should all have five-member nations, but in the sense that the principles are operative, and if too many of them are infracted a breakdown may be predicted. Thus it is probably wiser for a limited number of topdog nations with a high degree of consensus to stay together in a political and economic alliance than to try to increase the size by including a number of underdog nations. The latter may make good propaganda but bad social science — provided there is something to this general thesis at the international level as well. On the other hand, if a nation wants to dominate and satisfies the conditions as a leader (both of the achieved and ascribed varieties), it is wise to increase the size of the group to legitimize the need for one upper hand, and then present its credentials as that upper hand. A group of three is probably too limited for this purpose, whereas a group of ten may too easily be a victim of disruption and subgroup formation; hence it may be that groups of five or seven are ideal for this purpose. But we shall of course not infer that this is the only reason why EEC and EFTA and the Warsaw Pact seem to have less internal dissensus than NATO and the OEA, and it may also be disputed whether this assertion is true.

Concluding this list of examples of hypotheses one might perhaps try to relate this approach to the distinction made in section 2 above between the components in the behavior of any representative of a nation state in an international system. There were four such components: the national, formal, informal and personal; the idea being that in groups of such representatives national belongingness is only one component among several. But how does this "national component" help steer the behavior of individuals? Perhaps some insights can be gained simply by dissolving it, using the same approach once again. In a group of nations, there will also be a formal system and an informal system with relatively well-defined statuses, such as "big power" vs. "small power", "colonial power" vs. "colony" (whether they are defined in terms of traditional colonialism or neo-colonialism). Thus, big powers probably expect small powers to expect them to solve their problems, and many such expectations are codified in international law. Regardless of where one draws the borderline between the formal and informal systems there will always remain an idiosyncratic, non-structural component of interaction that is not substitutable. Bilateralism is actually an expression of this: it is a codification of the interaction nation X has with nation Y, and not necessarily invariant under any substitution of X and Y. Characteristic of multilateralization is precisely the idea of substitutability: the relations X has with Y are the same as the relations X, by a multilateral convention, pledges itself to have with Z. A typical case is the extension of the MFN (most favored nation) treatment. The distinction between formal and informal, then, is the distinction between what is explicit, codified and what is not.

This means that it is meaningful to distinguish between six components: formal, informal and nonsubstitutable, at both the national and the personal levels. And this makes the general problems of consonance and congruence even more complex. In their relations representatives will partly try to mirror what they perceive as the patterns between the nations they represent, partly try to anticipate trends in these patterns. Much of the art in diplomacy will probably consist in the ability *not* to mirror too accurately corresponding relations between the nations but rather to work into the interpersonal relation an element of audacity, almost to the point of being frivolous. For the moment interpersonal relations at the formal, informal and idiosyncratic levels reflect accurately the corresponding interstate relations the latter tend to be frozen. Thus, representatives can consciously create rank incongruences, break down isomorphisms, make interpersonal relations less rank dependent, etc.; in short try to avoid the pitfalls of perfect equilibrium and consonance that may lead to strong identification and feeling of behaving correctly, but also to strong rigidity.

5. Conclusion

Thus, small group theory constitutes a reservoir of hypotheses for the student of international relations, some of them far from trivial, most of them readily testable, some of them even partly confirmed. The present article certainly does not exhaust the theme, since mostly we have used as a basis what one recent text has skimmed from the wealth of insights and findings in the field. But to the extent the isomorphism holds we are actually developing a general (social) systems theory, just as analogies between domestic and international law point to a general legal theory. However, one cannot conclude without some words of caution, by specifying in concrete terms some of the implications of the truism that "nations are, after all, not human beings." For we have, in fact, used small group theory not only to explore similarities but also to pinpoint better where the isomorphism does not hold, where the dissimilarities are located.

Nations are aggregates and so are the decisionmaking bodies. All nations are ruled by oligarchies most of the time and by autarchs some of the time, where the autarchic regime may be seen as a limiting case of the oligarchy. Imagine that the size of the oligarchy is N and that the course of action suggested by a member in a situation is A_2. The course of action pursued by the nation is, then, $A = f(A_1, A_2, \ldots A_n)$. For the sake of simplicity, let us assume that the function is a weighted average, $A = w_1 A_1 + w_2 A_2 + +\ldots+w_n A_n$. In a completely autarchic system all but one of the weights would be equal to 0; in the simplest system based on arithmetic means all weights would be equal and hence equal to $1/N$. If the dispersion of the distribution of suggested courses of action for the A_2 is σ, then the dispersion for the arithmetic mean is $\sigma / \sqrt{N}$, and similarly for the case of unequal weights. Thus, the range of action for nations that are not autarchies is smaller than the range of action for individuals because of the compromise effect, in comparable cases. And as a consequence of this there is a lag in reaction time for nations relative to individuals, because of the time required for collective decisionmaking [62]. Thus, things are happening less quickly and fewer things are happening than in the world of individuals, but what happens may be much more consequential. Only a system of autarchies will resemble a system of individuals very closely.

Other dissimilarities have been pointed out above. Nations do not have geographical mobility as long as the concept of a nation is tied to that of the state, defined as a political system based on a contiguous territory. If "nation" is defined as an aggregate of individuals tied together by affinity rather than by vicinity, we might arrive at something approximated by what today is known as an international organization. One could imagine a process of "pakistanization" whereby a contiguous territory is subdivided into a set of noncontiguous parts till one reaches the social atom, the indivisible individual — in other words, the case of the nation "without a country" of Jews before the State of Israel (but with a stronger political system than Zionism). Such nations would possess a degree of geographical mobility that would make for much closer isomorphism with the structures studied at the level of the formation of small groups. As it now stands the international system is not isomorphic to any small group, but bears many resemblances to a system of villages, or heads of family within one village, in a country so traditional that mobility is minimal. The system is frozen. Problems remain in the system for a long time because the system cannot be defrozen by mobility — every issue has to be solved or to be a part of the existence — one cannot simply move away from it by permuting all the elements a little.

Another major difference hinted at above lies in the structure of international interaction relative to human interaction in modern nations. Broadly speaking, it looks as if the international system is much more "feudal" in the sense specified below, which, of course, would tie in with its lack of geographical mobility and also with its slow reaction time. By and large, the international system seems to be much more dominated by big powers than national systems, and the interaction between nations seems to be extremely dependent on rank [63]. Big powers interact with each other for good and for bad, small powers with big powers but less so, and between the small powers there is very little interaction. This makes the system particularly vulnerable to the whims of the big powers, even if their influence is harnessed somewhat by the network of international organizations that at least give to lesser powers a say and a vote, if not much power.

But, as indicated above, this "feudal" characteristic of the international system is already found at the level of interaction between strangers in small groups; it is only epitomized in international systems. Other characteristics of the contemporary international system do not have their counterparts in small group theory. After all, the international system does have institutions; there is a supranational stratum, however imperfect relative to some models of supraindividual strata found in some national societies. This points to richer structures than small groups as reservoirs for hypothesis-formation: organizations, for instance, even total institutions and societies. In the latter case it may well be that organizations and associations, not individuals, should be seen as the homologues of nations in the international system.

This approach, by no means novel, is probably of the type that may influence the science of international relations in some periods, after which people become disenchanted and look for properties of the international system *sui generis*, whereupon new insights can be utilized from the lower-level social sciences because of new advances in the field, or new isomorphisms that had passed unnoticed before. And this exchange is a two-way process, the lower-level social sciences can learn from international relations much in the same manner. The condition for this exchange, viz. interdisciplinary milieus with sufficient exchange of theory and methods, is not easily satisfied, however.

In conclusion let us also point out how fruitful this perspective is for the discipline of *peace research*. Peace research is an applied science concerned with conditions that further or impede peaceful relations between major groupings of human beings. As such its field is at the same time wider and more narrow than international relations: it is concerned with group conflicts (between races, ethnical groups, classes) as well as with international conflicts; but it focuses on what is directly relevant for the peaceful settlement of disputes and the emergence of cooperative patterns of interaction. What is then more natural for peace research than to say the following: just as lower-level social systems in general form reservoirs of hypotheses for the study of international systems in general, let us use lower-level peaceful, cooperative and egalitarian systems as reservoirs of hypotheses in peace research. And with all the pitfalls inherent in this approach it seems to be one of the major avenues of progress in the field [64].

IV.2. Summit Meetings and International Relations*

From *Journal of Peace Research* I/1 (1964). PRIO publication No. 4—1. Notes on page *681*.

1. Introduction

The world is a system of elements called nations that are, at least potentially, highly consequential for each other. But nations are collectivities and do not act; only individuals act. Hence, one focus for the study of international systems is on crossnational interaction between individuals. But not all such interaction is of equal interest. Particular theoretical and practical emphasis is rightly put on the study of individuals in representative statuses, whose function it is to interact with similar individuals from other nations. These representative statuses are so strongly embedded in the national systems that they have become a profession, called diplomacy [1]. However, interaction takes place both below and above this professional international activity. The present study is devoted to some aspects of the international interaction above the level of the diplomats, where 'above' is taken in the sense of social rank [2].

This is not necessarily the same as 'summitry' or summit meetings. Any definition of 'summit meeting' will have to give a precise answer to two questions: *between which statuses?* and *from which nations?* To both questions increasingly tolerant answers may be given: 'only heads of state and heads of government, foreign ministers included, all ministers included' to the first question; and 'only the two superpowers, the big powers, all nations' to the second. This gives a set of nine possible definitions, ranging from the most narrow one that would rate as a summit meeting only meetings between the US president and the Soviet president and/or premier, to the broadest definition that would give any meeting between two ministers from different nations the status of a summit meeting. We shall strike a compromise between these two extremes, defining as a 'summit meeting' *any* ad hoc *meeting of heads of state, heads of government and/or foreign ministers where at least two of the big powers are represented.* 'Big power' is then defined as 'China, France, UK, USA, and USSR', changing from Nationalist China to the People's Republic after the revolution in 1949. Narrower or broader definitions might also point to phenomena worth studying systematically, but this definition directs our attention to the politically most meaningful forms of summit diplomacy for reasons that will be given in the following. It should be noticed that this definition does not include institutionalized meetings, e.g. in the United Nations or in one of the alliances (but it includes the meetings to found these institutions).

Thus, the summit meeting is a phenomenon that can be registered, counted and characterized. We have chosen the recent twenty years' period from when East and West found a common enemy in Nazi Germany on June 22, 1941, until the summit meeting twenty years later between Kennedy and Khrushchev in Vienna on June 3—5, 1961. During this period East-West relations underwent sweeping changes, from a period of alliance through a period of conflict and bloc-formation to a period of coexistence (if not always equally peaceful). In this period 147 meetings satisfying the definition were held, out of which 40 were held between East and West, according to information given by *Keesing's Contemporary Archives* and other reference works. What this study now proposes to do is to analyze this meeting aspect of summitry [3] as a function of the various phases of East-West relations.

We shall start by formulating two hypotheses about summit meetings between East and West that will be made more precise and operational later on. Both hypotheses relate the same two variables to each other: the nature of East-West relations and the level of summitry. Where the latter is concerned we shall only make a distinction between more or less *restricted* or *limited*, using these vague and generic terms for a set of quantitative and qualitative indicators that will be made clear later. As to the nature of East-West relations in the period 1941—1961 we think they can be characterized for our purposes by two main variables. On the one hand there are various degrees of *polarization* in the East-West system throughout the period, on the other hand there are various degrees of *predictability* in the system. By 'polarization' or bi-polarization, then, we mean the extent to which the international system is divided into two blocs with all positive relations within the blocs and all negative relations between the blocs. And by 'predictability' we mean the extent to which there is complementarity in the role-expectations in the international system, so that each nation knows, for good or bad, more or less how any other nation inside or outside the blocs will react to a given stimulus.

The two hypotheses can now be presented:

H_1 (the polarization hypothesis): *The higher the polarization, the more restricted or limited the summitry.*

H_2 (the predictability hypothesis): *The higher the predictability, the less restricted or limited the summitry.*

The first hypothesis is close to a tautology, since polarization is defined as a concentration on intra-bloc interaction — except for bellicose interaction, of course (for which the summit meeting would hardly serve). The second hypothesis derives from considerations such as the following: no nations will engage in activities that can endanger the prestige of their top leaders and hence a nation will only engage in high level summitry if the effects on one's own bloc, the other bloc, and third parties can be predicted with a reasonable margin of error. This does not mean that summit meetings will only be used in times of amity; enmity may serve as an equally good or better basis for prediction about the outcome.

We can now combine the two hypotheses by combining the two variables used to characterize East-West relations:

TABLE 2.1   *Phases in East-West relations 1941–61*

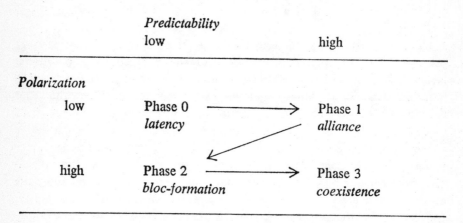

Predictability

	low	high
Polarization		
low	Phase 0 *latency*	Phase 1 *alliance*
high	Phase 2 *bloc-formation*	Phase 3 *coexistence*

The arrows indicate one way of conceiving of East-West relations in the period. The common enemy made for low polarization in 1941 but there was a carryover of low predictability (i.e. uncertainty about each other) that made for a short phase of latency before an efficient alliance pattern was activated. This alliance pattern between East and West against the Axis was low on polarization and high on predictability as in any efficient partnership. But with the common enemy conquered, latent conflicts became manifest again and led quickly to a complete and drastic change to the opposite pattern, characterized by high polarization and low predictability. Then predictability increased again through years of training in cold war, a predominantly peaceful coexistence and completed bloc-formation, maintaining a high level of polarization.

Since phase 0 probably was of very short duration we shall only work with the three phases called 'alliance', 'bloc-formation' and 'coexistence, and can now use the hypotheses and Table 2.1 to deduce one master hypothesis:

H_3 (the polarization-predictability hypothesis): *Summitry was more restricted or limited in the phase of bloc-formation than in the phases of alliance and coexistence.*

It should be noticed that this hypothesis has a high level of falsifiability [4]. The independent variable is the phase-movement of the East-West relation, given as a trichotomy, divided into three phases. We are going to present a set of indicators of how limited or restricted a summit meeting is, and the level will then be calculated for each phase. From each phase to the next there are three possibilities: the level remains the same, it increases, or it decreases. Since there are two such transitions from one phase to the next we get nine possible distributions. Out of these only one will be predicted by the hypothesis, and this one distribution will be either V-shaped or A-shaped, never always increasing or always decreasing or with plateaus of constancy. Thus, the degree of *a priori* falsifiability, assuming all distributions equally probable *a priori*, is 8/9, or 0.89. Hence, confirmation of the hypothesis is far from trivial.

Let us then have a closer look at the variables we shall use to test this hypothesis.

The basic variable is *time*, or rather *phase*. To test the theory we have to divide the twenty years' interval from 1941 to 1961 into three parts. Consequently, we have to choose two cutting points so that the three phases correspond more or less to the definition given in Table 1. Also, the phases should preferably be of relatively equal length, so that the same amount of summit activity could have taken place in the intervals.

We have chosen not to use any particular event to define the point where the alliance phase ends and the phase of bloc-formation and open conflict starts. One might have used the 'Truman doctrine' of March 1947 or the events in Czechoslovakia in February 1948. Or one might have used some earlier or later episode. We have chosen January 1, 1948, as a point in time where it was reasonably obvious, regardless of interpretation and distribution of guilt, that the wartime alliance pattern was no longer operative. This does not mean that we see this cutting point as the 'beginning of the cold war', but as a point where a more continuous pattern of enmity between East and West became fully apparent again [5].

In the period that followed both East and West engaged very quickly in a polarization process with mutual disengagement and separate alliance formation. April 4, 1949, and May 14, 1955, are the points in time where the Western and Eastern alliance-formations were formalized, and we could have used these two dates as the two extremes of the second phase. However, this would have been unrealistic, since it is obvious that it took some time, at least one year, to build up to the formation of the NATO alliance. It may also be that the Eastern alliance was completed much before the signing of the Warsaw Pact, but we find the formal signing of the treaty significant enough to use it as a point indicating the end of the second phase. The blocs had now been formed, the world was divided and the borderlines clear: everything was ready for a war or for coexistence, but not for a really positive peace according to any reasonable definition.

Obviously, such sharp borderlines in time are never appropriate when processes are analyzed. They conceal the continuity in the process, and are also more or less arbitrary within an interval of a year or two. For that reason all findings presented here have been checked to see whether they are invariant of some variations in the cutting points, and have been found to stand the test, although in some cases at the expense of a reduction in percentage differences.

Finally, it should be noticed that our analysis includes the meetings within the blocs, what we call the intra-meetings, to serve as an analytical contrast for the study of the inter-meetings.

2. Testing the hypothesis

We shall now conceive of H_3 as a basis for deducing hypotheses by interpreting the term 'restricted', and start by the simplest possible meaning, the purely quantitative meaning:

$H_{3,1}$: *There were fewer summit inter-meetings in phase 2 than in phases 1 and 3.*

To test the hypothesis we present:

TABLE 2.2 *Type and phase of the summit meetings 1941—61*

Type	Phase 1	Phase 2	Phase 3	Sum
Intra-West	22	33	44	99
Intra-East	0*	3	5	8
Inter-East-West	21	5	14	40
Sum	43	41	63	147

* By definition.

We have not percentaged the Table since it is interesting in both directions [6]. Both kinds of intra-meetings show a steady increase, the Western meetings also when seen relative to the total summit activity. But the meetings between East and West show the predicted dip in phase 2. In spite of the approximately equal length of the three phases there were three times as many meetings between East and West in phase 3, and four times as many in phase 1 as in phase 2. And the inter-meetings make only 12% of the total activity in phase 2, as against 49% in phase 1 and 22% in phase 3. So the hypothesis is clearly substantiated, and the finding is not an artefact due to short duration of the phase or general decrease in summit activity (e.g. due to the personalities of the top executives), for this would also have shown up in the intra-meetings.

The low level of intra-East activity deserves some comments. First of all, only from 1949 are there two big powers in the 'Socialist camp' for a meeting to have any meaning. Secondly, there are probably meetings satisfying the definition that are less known in the West, and some of the meetings may take place in ways that are less prominent in the West, e.g. as meetings in the international communist movement because of the dyarchic structure with parallel state and party bureaucracies. Finally, the relations between the Soviet Union and China recently have been relatively conflict-loaded. This should be contrasted with the steady growth in intra-West summitry, partly an expression of the growth of the Western apparatus, partly an expression of a general process of internationalization.

We then turn to qualitative aspects of summitry, and the first question is simply: *Who* meet? Which statuses, and which nations? We shall start with the statuses.

There are three of them according to the definition, and the rank order is clearly 1. head of state, 2. head of government, 3. foreign minister. But this rank order is formal and depends, for instance, on how the nation balances the power between the head of state and the head of government. Also, we see no clear hypothesis that relates phase of conflict to rank. One may argue that intense conflict should favor a concentration on the rank summit, that only interaction at the highest rank possible would be permitted to ensure that the action is really on behalf of the nation. But one may also argue that crises do not lead to willingness to let the other party enjoy the presence of one's own top leader. But instead of using rank or power we tried to use the instrumental-expressive dimension. On the one hand we assume that summit activities as part of international interaction have an instrumental component, a clearly goal-directed activity where the goal is an agreement; and an expressive component which is more emotional and symbolic of common values (such as common enemy, victory, welfare, peace). On the other hand we assume a concentration of the expressive component on the top, with a division of labor assigning expressive activities to the higher rank. Thus, we hypothesize that the prime minister will play an instrumental role if accompanied by the president or king, but an expressive role if accompanied by his foreign secretary. And the latter will need some subsecretary or the company of another minister to be free to engage in expressive activity [7].

The link with conflict theory is the hypothesis that symbols of *Gemeinschaft* will be eliminated earlier than instrumental activity, for the latter also serve one's own nation directly or indirectly in times of crisis. Thus, we predict:

$H_{3,2}$: *There were more summit meetings with only foreign ministers and fewer with heads of government in phase 2 than in phases 1 and 3.*

To test this hypothesis we used:

TABLE 2.3 *Participants to summit inter-meetings 1941−61, %*

Participants	Phase 1	Phase 2	Phase 3
Only foreign ministers	48	100	22
Heads of government			
present	52	0	77
(N)	(21)	(5)	(14)

The hypothesis is clearly confirmed, and the percentage differences are substantial.

The data in Table 2.3 give information in a gross way geared to $H_{3,2}$. But it is tempting to go one step further and ask how the nations adjusted the levels so as to obtain rank equivalence, i.e. participation of leaders of some or equivalent rank from the various nations. Rank equivalence is important both from the instrumental and expressive points of view: it implies equivalence in symbolic exchange, and equivalence in instrumental impact, at least if the nations are relatively homologous. Rank equivalence is like any form of value equivalence: it is a question of seeing to it that the other party does not get more out of the exchange than one gets oneself. It is a kind of institutionalized stinginess, and should be most prevalent in times of crisis. Thus, we predict:

$H_{3,2}$: *There are fewer summit inter-meetings where the persons participating are not rank-equivalent in phase 2 than in phases 1 and 3.*

We cannot say that this hypothesis is really confirmed by the data even though the data are consistent with it, because there are so few meetings where rank-equivalence is not present [8]. Thus, the Western powers have never had meetings with China that were not rank-equivalent, but they have had four such meetings with the Soviet: three in phase 1, none in phase 2 and one in phase 3. Rank-equivalence is the general rule in international affairs, as it probably is in most places where organizations interact. Thus, of the 147 meetings, including the intra-meetings, only 16, or 11%, were not rank-equivalent, and seven of them according to a common pattern: the foreign minister of the USA meeting the prime minister of Britain or France. This can probably be explained by means of two simple properties of the USA. It lacks one of the three top statuses, so that even if the foreign minister is too little to meet a prime minister, the president is too great — and statuses are probably to some extent weighted with the power of the nation so that the USA can do with less in a meeting than Britain or France — not to mention smaller powers.

Let us then look at participation in terms of *nations*. We are dealing with nations in conflict, at times in bitter, dangerous conflict — nevertheless they meet. What are the minimum precautions they could take in the most critical phase, in terms of national participation? The two blocs are clearly structured with the USA and the USSR as the leading nations during the conflict period of the study. Hence there are two simple problems: rank-equivalence between nations, not only between statuses of the individual participants; and number of countries participating. As to rank-equivalence our hypothesis is simply:

$H_{3,4}$: *There are fewer summit inter-meetings where the nations participating are not rank-equivalent in phase 2 than in phases 1 and 3.*

The closing of ranks in times of conflict, the preoccupation with a show of strength, and the fear not so much of letting inferior powers on one's own side deal directly with the top power of the other side as of one's own top nation coming to feel let down and the other top nation interpreting the move as an advance — all this contributes to $H_{3,4}$: few meetings where only one of the superpowers is present.

The hypothesis is confirmed by:

TABLE 2.4 *Superpower participation in summit inter-meetings 1941–61, %*

No. of superpowers	Phase 1	Phase 2	Phase 3
0	0*	0	0
1	38	20	29
2	62	80	71
Sum	100	100	100

* By definition.

But the percentage differences are small. It is worth noting as an extra result that direct summit meetings between France and Britain on the one hand and China on the other did not take place in the period, which is a good indication of this effect of conflict: rank-and-file direct inter-action is ruled out. It is also a good illustration for the consternation that the current relations between France and China bring about. Table 2.4 demon-strates clearly how the general rule is participation by both superpowers, and the tendency is slightly more pronounced in the critical phase 2.

But who else are present? Do they bring their allies? They do and they do not. There are several reasons why we would predict a tendency to bring allies (i.e. to have fewer bilateral meetings) between the blocs than within the blocs: it is a show of strength and unanimity, it is a sign of super-power confidence in their allies, it is a method of control and of having witnesses present of what happened and it is a way of making maximum use of an inter-bloc meeting, which is not so easily arranged. Thus, we would predict:

$H_{3,5}$: *The proportion of bilateral summit meetings is lower for meetings between the blocs than for meetings within the blocs, and lower in phase 2 than in phases 1 and 3.*

The prediction is borne out by:

TABLE 2.5 *Proportion of bilateral summit meetings 1941—61, %*

	Phase 1	Phase 2	Phase 3
Within West	82	67	87
Between East and West	38	20	72

We then turn our attention from *who* to *where*, with two dimensions of the location: political alignment of the host country, and ecological setting. That meetings within the Western bloc are usually held in the West does not merit comment, and it is also fairly obvious that:

$H_{3,6}$: *There are more summit inter-meetings in neutral countries in phase 2 than in phases 1 and 3.*

The hypothesis is confirmed in Table 2.6.

The tendency to use neutral countries like Switzerland in situations of crisis is clear. It is also clear that the willingness to use summitry as a method in diplomacy has been most pronounced in the East, if willingness to con-

TABLE 2.6 *Location of summit inter-meetings 1941—61,* %

	Phase 1	Phase 2	Phase 3
In the West	48	40	50
In the East	43	0	21
In neutral countries	9	60	29
Sum	100	100	100
(N)	(21)	(5)	(14)

cede to using the other party as a host is a measure. This has given the East an opportunity to demonstrate its willingness to participate, although it may also be partly explained on such bases as relative ease in traveling (there are more participants from the West, and they probably have to stay closer to the political bodies they are responsible to, especially the US President). If one believes in the importance of maintaining top contact in a period of conflict the importance of geographically centrally located neutral countries is well borne out by Table 2.6.

But the ecological aspect of where they met is probably just as important. The distinction is between using big towns and small, relatively isolated places as the location of a summit meeting. Obviously, if the participants want an agreement, an agreement can be reached whether the room of negotiation is located in one of the capitals, in Geneva or in Camp David. One is dealing with the world's most expert politicians, and although they are in all probability influenced by small group mechanisms inside the meeting room (we do not have data to demonstrate this), they can hardly be much influenced by the location of the room itself. But the choice of meeting place is significant because it has some *symbolic* value. It is hardly farfetched to say that the big town symbolizes work, efficiency, easy visibility and control by others, and contractual relationships; and the isolated, small place intimacy, friendship, privacy, primary relationships. In short: the choice of a town as meeting place indicates instrumentality, the choice of the isolated place expressiveness. These two dimensions are, of course, not exclusive: the expressiveness in the town meeting can be symbolized by well-publicized garden parties and parades, and the instrumentality in the Camp David type of summitry is well symbolized by the concept of 'withdrawing to the working room' — whether the top people actually negotiate, play a game of cards, or just do nothing.

In line with the general hypothesis that the expressive component will suffer the most severe cut in a conflict we get:

$H_{3,7}$; *The proportion of summit meetings held in small and isolated places is lower for meetings between the blocs than for meetings within the blocs and lower in phase 2 than in phases 1 and 3.*

The prediction is confirmed by:

TABLE 2.7 *Proportion of summit meetings held in small and isolated places*, %

	Phase 1	Phase 2	Phase 3
Within West	36	9	22
Between East and West	14	0	21

Of course, Table 2.7 also demonstrates another function of the 'small and isolated place', viz. secrecy, which was important in the war part of phase I. But this is not the only factor operating, as shown by the clearly V-shaped pattern of the distributions.

After how many, who and where, the natural next question is *when*. By this we do not think in terms of the distribution on phase — that has already been treated in Table 2.2 — but distribution on month of the year, and, in connection with that, the duration of the meetings. One may object that these are extremely external aspects of summitry, but they form a part of the general image of the summit meeting and may shed some additional light on the structure and function of these meetings.

The annual cycle in political life has a certain structure, and the nations of the world are to a considerable extent attuned to each other, both as a cause and as an effect of the interaction in the international system. There is a distinction between the in-season and the out-season, although one may dispute the location of the cutting points. We have used the regular sessions of the major national assemblies and the United Nations and one additional principle of a purely methodological nature: we wanted to cut the year in equal parts, preferably both in terms of number of months and in terms of total summit activity, counting both intra- and inter-meetings. Using these principles we arrived at these definitions: *in-season* from January to April, and October-November, and *out-season* from May to September, and December. We coded each summit meeting according to the month in which it took place (permitting double coding if it was located on two months, and even triple coding since 7 meetings lasted more than one month) and got the 147 meetings distributed over a total of 169 meeting months. April was highest with 17 meetings, and November lowest with 8 — the average was 14. And our statistical goal was obtained insofar as 82 meeting months were in the season and 87 outside it.

How should one reason, then, concerning the choice of month for the inter-meetings? An inter-meeting is a big event, and it may be argued that there is not sufficient time for it in the heat of the political season — just as much as it has to be preceded by a political season for the sake of preparation. On the other hand, if these important top meetings are taken out of the season and put in the summer months they are less strongly coupled to the political machinery so that any positive impact will be less quickly followed up. But on the other hand again, a weak coupling serves as a protection against a failure. A summit meeting in the summer is like a love affair in vacation time: it may be defined as a parenthesis that can be closed. This, of course, is only a pro-argument if failure is more or less expected and summitry is engaged in for fear of repercussions if one refuses, not with the hope of achieving anything positive. And then there is the expressive-instrumental axis: the out-season has a higher symbolic loading; it symbolizes the extraordinary, the willingness to use one's time reservoir for the sake of world peace, etc. In short: there are bases for predictions in either direction.

Nevertheless we feel there is a basis for predicting a tendency to place the inter-meetings out of the season. One grants the other party vacation time with its implications as indicated above. But, more importantly, one also implies that the other party is not admitted to one's own office during office-hours, so to speak. It is much like meeting a disagreeable relative or business acquaintance at a restaurant instead of inviting him to one's home, or having a summit meeting in a neutral country instead of at home, to use the findings from Table 2.6. In short, we predict:

$H_{3,8}$: *The proportion of summit meetings held outside the season is higher for meetings between the blocs than for meetings within the blocs and more pronounced in phase 2 than in phases 1 and 3.*

This is a precise hypothesis that predicts a correlation between the two variables 'intra-inter' and 'in-season-out-season' for the unit 'summit--months', in general; and a higher correlation for phase 2 than for phases 1 and 3 in particular. The hypothesis is amply confirmed by Table 2.8.

TABLE 2.8 *The time distribution of summit meetings, 1941—61*

Phase:	Phase 1		Phase 2		Phase 3		Total	
Season:	in	out	in	out	in	out	in	out
Intra-meetings	10	12	21	17	30	22	61	51
Inter-meeting	9	20	2	7	10	9	21	36
Correlation, Yule's Q	0.30		0.62		0.10		0.34	
Correlation, % difference	14%		33%		6%		17%	

The correlation patterns are as predicted for two different correlation measures. Of course, one could also have calculated the proportion of summit-months out of season for the inter-meetings, and for each phase (the pattern would be 69%—79%—47%), but this A-shaped pattern could also have applied to the intra-meetings. In the way we have done it the intra-meetings are used as basis of comparison, and the differences between intra-meetings and inter-meetings are as predicted.

One can now wonder whether all the reasons we have given as arguments for or against having summit meetings in the summer enter as causes or as functions. That is, are they consciously perceived motives or are they possible consequences; are they manifest or latent functions in contemporary sociological jargon? We do not know, nor are we particularly interested. International relations are governed by many principles which politicians would not be conscious of, not to mention formulate. And international relations are not governed by some of the principles they do formulate. These are two good reasons why we prefer this kind of methodology to the traditional kind of quotation methodology. But it is interesting to speculate a little bit more on the function of the time of year as a variable in politics.

Almost for the fun of it, we found out the national days of 106 nations [9] — that day in the tumultuous history of any nation that has been chosen to symbolize its birth — and broke these down by month of the year. The three summer months June-July-August were clearly overrepresented (38% as against a chance probability of 25%) and the three winter months December-January-February underrepresented (16% as against 25%). But if one splits by geographical location, the tendency is much more pronounced: of the countries to the North of the tropical zone [10] only 3, or 6%, had their national holiday in the winter, and of the 8 countries to the South of the tropical zone only one had its national day in June-July-August — which is winter in the Southern hemisphere. Thus, there is a clear tendency to locate the national holidays in the summer or spring: if we control for the geographical location, more than 70% of the holidays are found in this period (depending somewhat on how the time-cuts are made, but with a clear overrepresentation for all reasonable cuts).

There are at least two interpretations. It may be that certain types of stirring, important events take place in spring and summer rather than in other periods. But it may also be that among the various possible dates that could be used to symbolize the 'birth of the nation', a date in spring or summer is preferred to enhance festivity. We do not have data to decide from, but doubt that the second interpretation can account for more than a small fraction of the difference. Spring and summer seem to be periods overselected for the extraordinary, the audacious, the extreme, the periods where 'love comes to young people and heroism to the generals', as they say in Latin America. This is also well known from another form of extreme activity: suicide. According to Durkheim [11], for the periods and countries he studied, the rate of suicide is highest in summer (June-July-August), with spring next. These are the periods where despair and *dysphoria* in general are most strongly noticed, for these are the periods where others reach highest in *euphoria*, so that the relative deprivation is greater.

To summarize: it may be that summit meetings are found more in these months than in others, not so much because they are outside the political season, as because of a general tendency towards risk-taking and extraordinary behavior. This is well in line with our findings, because the consequence would be that the cautiousness during intense conflict would be too strong for the low risk-potential in the political season, and require the higher potential of the summer period for a summit meeting to emerge. Thus we have a kind of beak-like image of Political Man: he spends the better part of the year in hibernation, maintaining the system, and then has a period of extraordinary and other-oriented activity for good or for bad before he goes into hibernation again.

We then turn to the question of the duration of these meetings. The following hypothesis hardly needs comment:

$H_{3,9}$: *The proportion of lasting summit meetings is higher for meetings between the blocs than for meetings within the blocs and more pronounced in phase 2 than in phases 1 and 3.*

Intra-bloc meetings can be short and businesslike; there may be a well-defined agenda and a lot of preparation made beforehand. Between the blocs one has to calculate with the incalculable. If there were a well-defined agenda and routine matters to be discussed, ordinary diplomatic channels would probably be used. On the other hand, if the climate is such that the parties would prefer being responsible for breaking negotiations to being responsible for keeping them going, then there would probably not have

TABLE 2.9 *The duration of summit meetings, 1941—61*, %*

	Phase 1 1 week or less	More	Phase 2 1—2 days	More	Phase 3 1—2 days	More	Sum	(N)
Intra-meetings	77	23	64	36	59	41	100	(17)
Inter-meetings	43	57	20	80	21	79	100	(40)
% difference		34		44		38		

* The time cut is different in phase 1 because of the much longer average duration of the summit meeting and right after the war.

been any agreement about a meeting either. Hence, it will probably be in the interest of both parties to keep the meeting going, at least for some time, and more so the more conflict-loaded the situation (Table 2.9).

The first part of the hypothesis is well confirmed, the second part is also confirmed, but the tendency is not so strong. The intra-meetings are quite short — 87% of them lasted one week or less — but the inter-meetings had a considerable duration, only 15% more than one month but over half of them more than one week. From a communication point of view one might say that this shows the common interest in visibility of a peace initiative: a meeting of two days is over before the maximum build-up of interest can be reached, whereas a meeting that lasts more than a month becomes an institution.

Finally, in this long discussion of external aspects of summit meetings we come to what we shall call *extra-meetings:* they are meetings within the West immediately before, during, or immediately after a summit meeting between East and West [12]. That such meetings were held during the war, is obvious: the difficulties with travel and telecommunications that could be intercepted are convincing reasons. But these reasons do not obtain after the war, or are at least considerably less important. Such meetings are important manifestations of intra-bloc cohesion and not merely an expression of the need to rationalize and cut down on travel expenses. This is indeed perceived by politicians, as witnessed, for instance, by the following quotations. To start with a typical phase 1 meeting: Churchill wanted a meeting between Britain and the USA before the summit meeting with the Soviet Union that was under preparation in November 1942, but Roosevelt wrote Churchill, saying:

I do not want to give Stalin the impression that we are settling everything between ourselves before we meet him [13].

According to Plischke, the same thing happened before the Tehran conference.

Compare this with what Eden said in connection with the summit meeting in Geneva in 1955:

I would have been happier if it had been possible to arrange a preliminary meeting of the three Western Heads of Government before we went to Geneva. I thought this would be helpful to ourselves and educative for the Russians. It would be good for them to see how close was our accord in advance of the meeting. I tried to fix this in London. M. Faure was willing, but the President could not get away [14].

This was, apparently, an old idea with Eden according to what Cordell Hull writes in connection with the Moscow conference in phase 1 (October 1943):

> British Foreign Secretary Eden had cabled me suggesting he and I meet for a preliminary conference at Cairo before going on to Moscow. I replied that our Russian friends were rather suspicious generally, and that it might look as if Britain and the United States were forming a common policy in advance of discussing it with Russia [15].

One can almost hear both kinds of arguments prior to each summit meeting in any phase. But there is probably also an argument here that is not made explicit: the words by Roosevelt, 'The President' (meaning Eisenhower), and Cordell Hull may express that 'the Soviet Union is what interests us, not Britain'. However that may be, it seems reasonable to suppose that:

$H_{3,10}$: *The tendency to have extra-meetings within one bloc before or during a meeting between the blocs, will be highest in phase 2 and lowest in phase 1.*

In this hypothesis we go one step further than in all the others by predicting phase 1 relative to phase 3, since it seems obvious that the type of consideration expressed by Roosevelt and Hull above will be much more listened to in phase 1. Even here we get a confirmation, but the frequencies are so low that the confirmation is not strong (Table 2.10).

TABLE 2.10 *Proportion of intra-meetings within West relative to inter-meetings, 1941—61, %*

	Phase 1	Phase 2	Phase 3
Before and during the meeting	50	100	73
After the meeting	50	0	27
Sum	100	100	100
(N)	(6)	(2)	(11)

That Western powers meet after the inter-bloc summit meetings to 'compare notes', so to speak, is not strange — but, as one sees, the symbol of courtesy alluded to by the Americans has not been utilized much, even in the co-existence phase. A preconference meeting is a kind of protection of oneself, a way of arriving at and symbolizing a united front — and as such a conflict phenomenon.

That concludes our testing of the main hypothesis.

3. Discussion

From our hypothesis H_3 a total of ten consequences were derived, leading to predictions that all had an *a priori* degree of falsifiability equal to 8/9 — or at least equal to 3/4 if we do not count the possibility of two relative frequencies being equal. All predictions (or rather postdictions, since they refer to material in the past) were confirmed, or at least not disconfirmed. Thus, there is little doubt that there is some pattern in the data, and that our hypothesis predicts it: the pattern is too consistent to be the result of randomly operating factors.

This, of course, does not confirm the hypothesis and the reasoning about the interplay between polarization and predictability. Other hypotheses, i.e. alternative interpretations, may lead to the same or similar predictions, and our data are not of the kind that enable us to rule them out. We shall discuss, very briefly, two such alternative interpretations.

First of all: there is the classic interpretation in personality terms. It is well known that Roosevelt bypassed his foreign service also for reasons extraneous to East-West relations, that Mendès-France was his own foreign minister, that Eisenhower had a very 'strong' foreign minister, that the Stalin period had to be followed by more openness, etc. History does not permit us to run over the period from 1941—61 again with different personalities in the top positions. But we have a hunch that it would not change much. Our intuition is certainly no proof, but it can be argued that the different phases of East-West relations: 1. favored the selection of different personality types, 2. made it possible for these personalities to act out that aspect of their personality that corresponded, in the way predicted by the theory, to the international situation in which they found themselves. In other words, we do not think these statesmen were at liberty to act in any way they wanted, nor were they psychologically limited to only one pattern. The external situation interplayed with their personality so as to produce the result we know. But we know of no way of proving this, particularly since we would not claim that personality is irrelevant, only that it is more an intervening than an independent factor.

Secondly, the idea of 'polarization' has to be examined more closely. As we have defined it there are four dimensions of polarization [16]:

1. the extent to which the *whole* international system is aligned in the bipolar system [17];
2. the extent to which there are *no positive links between* blocs;
3. the extent to which there are *no negative links within* blocs, and
4. the extent to which there is *alignment of attitudes* and emotions with the bipolar bloc system.

70

Although we have probably been right in assuming both a high level of polarization and a high level of predictability at the beginning of phase 3, both are in a process of erosion, and, it seems, at an accelerating rate. Thus, as of January 1, 1956, the United Nations had 75 members. Fourteen of them were members of NATO, and 9 were members of the Warsaw alliance (counting White Russia and the Ukraine since they are members of the UN, not counting the two Germanies since they are not members). Thus, 31% of the UN membership were directly engaged in the main power blocs. If we add the SEATO and CENTO countries that are not in NATO we get 7 more countries, or 40% of the membership. But it would not be farfetched to add to this 20 Latin-American countries (this was after the Bolivian revolution of 1952, but before the first Cuban revolution of 1959), Nationalist China, Spain, and perhaps some others, which brings us up to 70%.

Eight years later the UN had 113 members, but of the 38 members admitted in the meantime 36 are formally nonaligned (not counting Japan which was admitted December 18, 1956, and Mongolia, admitted October 27, 1961). This means that the two main alliances are surrounded in the UN by 80% that are not alliance members. They are not for that reason necessarily non-aligned but become increasingly so, at least in the formal sense, building on the nucleus of nations that stayed non-aligned all the time.

The cold war lines are blurred, as witnessed by the establishment of a France-China diplomatic axis, or by the crisscrossing effect on Latin America of Cuba as a Western outpost of the Eastern system. Or to use the SEATO countries as an example: the pact was signed in Manila on September 8, 1954, presumably as a protection against the People's Republic of China. Today Pakistan sees the conflict with India over Kashmir as salient enough to permit an *approchement* with China, whereas Britain, Australia and New Zealand are concerned with the protection of Malaysia against Indonesia, with the Philippines, Thailand and the United States intervening. At the same time negative links are appearing *within* the systems, centered on France and China, and the attitudinal *approchement* between the US and Soviet is expressed rather often by top leaders.

But if there is this decrease in polarization accompanied by a decrease in predictability, what would be the impact both on our interpretations and on our predictions for the period following 1961? We have a number of comments on this.

First of all, we think it is fair to assume that there is a certain lag between international situation and type of summitry — and this has actually been an assumption underlying the choice of time-cuts and the analysis all the time. Thus, we are fully aware that the alliance-phase broke down before January 1, 1948 [18], and that the two blocs were actually completed before May 14, 1955, for instance by the time joint military commands had been established in both East and West. But we think there is a general tendency to inertia: one tries to go on with the pattern from the days of the alliance even if it is not attuned to the events, and one continues with the pattern from the coldest days of the cold war even though important parameters have changed values. Similarly, one will continue a pattern of interaction tuned to high polarization and high predictability for some time before one discovers that both polarization and predictability are decreasing. Thus, granting the decrease in polarization and predictability, we stick to the prediction from Table 2.1 and hypothesis 3 with a definition of phase 3 lasting up to June 1961, because of the lag.

Secondly, this process of depolarization started possibly with the death of Stalin but hardly gained momentum till the events mentioned above. Thus, the real increase in the number of non-aligned national actors, the 'difficulties' with France and China, the *approchement* between the Soviet Union and the USA are phenomena of the sixties and not of the fifties that dominate phase 3 in our analysis. We mention this as well as the point above for one particular reason. If these points are not granted some validity, the interesting V- and A-patterns in all distributions studied so far could perhaps be better explained on the basis of an hypothesis of a V--shaped pattern of polarization: the higher level of summitry in phase 3 could also be due to less polarization. It is impossible to deny some validity to this, but we tend to stick to our original interpretation. That is: *after the completion of the bloc-formation there was a kind of predictability because of the high level of structural polarization that permitted inter-bloc activity.* Before that the concentration on intra-bloc work as well as a lower degree of predictability made for very restricted summit meetings of the kind we have discussed.

It is difficult to choose between these two interpretations, but we have two sets of indicators that seem to favor our position.

If the higher level of summitry in phase 3 was really due to a lower level of polarization and a less conflict-loaded situation in general we would expect the summit meetings in phase 3 to bring some results as they did in phase 1. On the other hand, if the higher level is due to predictability because of the rigid position and the relatively tight bipolar system, they should produce fewer results — they should be, in fact, a kind of ritual, a gesture to public opinion and the non-aligned — and to each other. To test this we studied for each meeting what had been the outcome. Of the 147 meetings there was no communiqué at all from 26 of them; 9 (all of them intra-meetings) were without any result according to the communiqué; 32 were dedicated to the 'exchange of points of view', which is certainly not a very positive characteristic; 25 were reported as having been 'positive' in some general sense and 55 of them led to concrete agreements. This is 37 % of the total, so one cannot possibly claim that summitry only leads to empty talking. We did not study in detail what happened to these agreements — even to reach an agreement is positive, and at least a symbol of some kind of togetherness. And we would even go so far as to include the meetings that were characterized as 'positive' — but to omit them from Table 2.11 changes nothing in the shape of the distributions [19].

TABLE 2.11 *Proportion of summit meetings with agreements or charac-*
terized as 'positive', 1941—61, %

	Phase 1	Phase 2	Phase 3
Intra-meetings	50	67	53
Inter-meetings	67	60	14

For the first time we see a quite different pattern: the J-shaped pattern with a steady decrease in the positive outcome of East-West summitry. This is clearly not a general trend due to impotence of the politicians participating, for there is no similar pattern for the intra-meetings; they have a relatively constant level of achievement (it is higher in phase 2 probably because they would not publish any failure in that critical period). *Rather, the summit meetings are dying as they grow:* they are at the highest level possible according to the data, but they achieve less than ever, even much less than in the phase of bloc-formation.

It may be objected that two years after the end of our phase 3 came the test ban treaty, and that Table 2.11 also may be interpreted as an indication that the agreements were reached at a lower level so that only the impossible was left for the summit meetings. But the period up to and including the Vienna meeting in June 1961, or including the Cuba crisis of October--November 1962 for that matter, was certainly not characterized by agreements reached between East and West. Rather, we feel there is a clear extrapolation from the bottom line of Table 2.11 to the Cuba crisis, and from the Cuba crisis to the test ban treaty.

The second set of indications that phase 3 is different from the phase we are now in, characterized above as less polarized and at least somewhat less predictable and hence conducive to a more circumscribed kind of summitry according to Table 2.1 and hypotheses 1—3, is more impressionistic. It is based on the simple fact that from June 1961 to June 1964 there have been no meetings at the very summit, but some foreign minister activity and the Moscow meeting in connection with the treaty. It is too early to say, but it looks so far as if this phase 4 in which we find ourselves is going to be more like phases 0 or 2, where summitry is concerned, than phases 1 and 3 — which is according to the theory. But this remains to be studied — for instance in 1968.

At this point we feel we have more than exhausted our data and turn to the general conclusion. It can be formulated as follows: a model of social conflict in terms of polarization assuming that interaction will decrease both quantitatively and qualitatively with time once the polarization has started, is much too simple. It neglects the possibility of arriving at a point where the bipolar system is reached with a sufficient level of predictability to resume interaction, maybe from what is referred to as a 'position of strength' (read 'predictability'). But this resumption of interaction is not necessarily productive of anything even if it is made in phase 3 according to the model of phase 1 (Eisenhower's many references to his wartime cooperation with Zhukov). It is formally similar to interaction without polarization, but not substantially similar. And this, again, does not mean that it is useless — only that it serves other functions than in a truly de-polarized system. This distinction between formal and substantial inter-action and the applicability of the polarization hypothesis to the latter but only partly to the former (till the conflict groupings have become orga-nized) is the theoretical implication of our findings [20].

4. Some policy implications

We then turn to the problem of whether there are any practical implications, which immediately leads us away from our data to some kind of (hope-fully guided) speculations.

For the sake of these speculations, let us assume the validity of the three preceding sections of this article. What they purport to show, essentially, is how the form of summitry depends on the international situation. Specu-lations about policy implications would have to turn this around and ask: how could the international situation be brought to depend on the form of summitry? In other words: can the form of summitry be used as an inde-pendent variable with a positive, however weak, coupling to the inter-national situation? We shall discuss this, but only within the limits set by our relatively external variables.

What we have done has essentially been to present two models of sum-mitry (Table 2.12).

Summitry as a system is oscillating between the two according to a certain pattern, described by the modified polarization hypothesis. There are now two clearly distinguishable conclusions one may draw. First there is the *conservative* conclusion: 'Align your policy with this tendency, use the conflict model when there is conflict'. And there is the *radical* conclusion.

TABLE 2.12 *Two models of summit contact*

	Cooperation model	Conflict model
1. No. of meetings	many	few
2. Participants	above foreign minister	only foreign minister
3. Rank-equivalence, persons	not always observed	observed
4. Rank-equivalence, nations	not always observed	observed
5. No. of nations	also bilateral	rarely bilateral
6. Location, country	any country	neutral countries
7. Location, ecology	less in big cities	more in big cities
8. Time of the year	in-season	out-season
9. Duration	short	long
10. Intra-meetings	after inter-meetings	before inter-meetings

'Choose the opposite policy of this tendency, use the cooperation model *a fortiori* when there is conflict.' To choose between the two is probably a very general type of problem in peace research. For theoretical and/or empirical reasons a certain tendency is found to be 'normal'. Shall one align oneself with the 'normal', assuming that the system has somehow found the best course — or shall one oppose it?

On the one hand it is obvious that there are conditions under which the cooperation model can bring the system a number of turns down the conflict spiral — that it can hook the system on to a pattern of cooperation, so to speak. This means many meetings, at the very summit, with little or no rank-equivalence, permitting bilateral meetings between the top nation of one bloc and a rank and file nation of the other — not to mention permitting meetings between two rank and file nations — held in the lion's den, out of easy visibility, in the middle of the season, even short and businesslike, and with all kinds of pre- and post-conferences added to it. It is clear from our data that this would indeed be extraordinary and be the opposite of alignment with system processes as they seem to be now.

On the other hand, it is also obvious that there is a limit to how much the system can stand in any given situation. The different types of polarization are probably protected by some very fundamental aspects of the structure of human psychology as it is found in our culture (we do not believe it is immutable), and are certainly protected by a set of expectations about how foreign policy should be carried out. The extraordinary would be too extraordinary, and the ordinary would be too indicative of conflict and not sufficiently conducive to conflict control. The obvious answer to the dilemma would lie in making the extraordinary ordinary.

Concretely, this might take the form of *institutionalizing* summit meetings according to a cooperation model so that one is not forced to choose between *ad hoc* arrangements over a wall of protests urging for a conflict model meeting, or no meeting at all. Institutionalization might cover the question of which nations should meet, which statuses, where, when and for how long — with the possibility of pre- and post- conferences according to any bilateral or multilateral pattern. One form would be a yearly meeting at the UN of the heads of government of the big powers, with the UN Secretary General present. There are heavy arguments for and against tying it to the opening of the UN General Assembly, but that is of less importance than the general idea of reducing the component of the extraordinary by making all aspects of the meeting predictable — except the content. The meetings should be defined as discussion and contact meetings more than as working meetings — so that any additional output is a positive surprise.

Such meetings would constitute a minimum base with a built-in motive to participate, for withdrawal would probably be defined by third parties as negative for the total system. Over and above this base one might superimpose an oscillating pattern of *ad hoc* meetings, *among other reasons to give the big powers a means of sanctioning the other bloc* — positively by using the cooperation model and negatively by using the conflict model, or by having no meeting at all.

To conclude: the world is a system and some needs have to be satisfied for the system to function with at least some degree of adequacy. Two needs are: 1. a certain level of contact to increase predictability, exchange views and at times even reach agreements towards negative and positive peace, and 2. a range of sanctions short of war yet serious enough to be meaningful in a conflict. One such sanction is reduction of the level of summitry along the dimensions we have used in this article; a more serious sanction is the complete cancellation of summitry. Superficially viewed these two functions contradict each other: like lower levels of diplomacy it may look as if one cannot both break relations and maintain relations. But that is not true: one can maintain relations via third parties (e.g. the US--China contact via the ambassadors to Poland) not to mention in the setting of the United Nations. Our suggestion is to do the same for summit meetings: use institutionalized meetings within the neutral framework provided by the UN to satisfy the permanent need for contact and agreement, and superimpose on this the *ad hoc* meetings that can be used for sanctions and the sudden, drastic efforts to make these brave steps forward that any summit participant, after all, would like to be remembered for.

IV.3. Patterns of Diplomacy

A Study of Recruitment and Career Patterns in Norwegian Diplomacy*

From II/2 *Journal of Peace Research* (1965). PRIO publication No. 13—1. Notes on page *683*.

1. Introduction

To study the structure of the institution of diplomacy certainly requires no defending among students of international relations in general, and peace research in particular, but it is an institution that has been seriously understudied by sociologists [1]. In a sense this is strange, because the field has much to offer for almost any type of sociological imagination.

Thus, the structurally minded sociologist might like to study the character of the *world network of diplomacy* as a web of bilateral and multilateral links between nations. The sociologist out to study institutions and organizations might be attracted by a study of the *foreign service of a nation:* its social structure, its stratification system, its division into such branches as 'ministry', 'consular service', 'bilateral diplomacy', and 'multilateral diplomacy' — and the social exchange this institution has with other social institutions, national and international. The sociologist concerned with social interaction in general, and particularly with its similarity to economic markets, might be interested in a study of the *corps diplomatique* of any capital to analyze its mores and structure. The small group sociologist would find most *diplomatic missions* a fine field of inquiry, richly stratified and complicated in their task-solving process. And the sociologist with a more social psychological bent would be attracted by the *status of the diplomat*, how he reconciles his many roles and the norms impinging on him, how personality and status may conflict with each other, how they both undergo changes throughout the life-time career of the diplomat [2].

There is enough to choose from — but the unfortunate compartmentalization of the social sciences has impeded a growth of knowledge that might be both interesting and useful. In addition there is the general difficulty in applying standard techniques of sociological analysis, such as interviews and questionnaires, to persons belonging to one of the national or international elites [3].

Our purpose in the present article is closest to the second of these five fields of research on diplomacy, but will occasionally touch on the other four. We are not arguing any really systematic and 'streamlined' theory of diplomacy, but are rather trying to develop perspectives on the institution and illustrate our ideas with some data from Norwegian diplomacy. Thus, this article should be conceived of as the first of a series of studies where the institution of diplomacy is related systematically to the general problem of peace and war.

2. Some perspectives on diplomacy

2.1. Some phases in the history of diplomacy

The point of departure is, of course, that the international system is composed of territorial units most of which are referred to as (independent, autonomous) *nations*. In addition there are some other territories, some of them with colonial status and others with a semi-colonial status, running to a total of about 160 units. The number of such units has indeed varied through the history of mankind, and presently we are witnessing both a tendency towards the emergence of very many new and small units and the amalgamation of older units into super-units of various compositions.

From the fact of territorial division of the world alone nothing can be derived about diplomacy. Thus, one could imagine two extreme kinds of worlds where no institution of diplomacy would exist: the fully disintegrated and the fully integrated world. In the disintegrated world nations are not interdependent; they stand in the same relationship as is approximated today by the relationship between, say, Norway and Nepal. Neither of them needs to take the other into account. This state of the world was approximated to when the world consisted of roving tribes with virtually no points of contact [4], but is today a fiction of analytical value rather than anything that can be used as an empirical model.

In the fully integrated world a superstructure would exist that would take care of most if not all of the interaction between the units, so that no separate institution would be needed to carry out the interest of nation *A* versus nation *B* and vice versa. The relationship would be much as between the counties or other territorial subdivisions in a contemporary modern nation-state; organizations and private citizens in these units may enter into some pattern of exchange, but counties as such usually do not have anything corresponding to embassies and diplomatic relations. Their relationships are regulated at a higher level.

Thus, diplomatic relations correspond to an intermediate stage in the general growth of mankind into a world state. The major implication of this is that diplomacy must have come into existence at a point where inter-dependence between nations or city-states got beyond a certain threshold so that some institution was needed to stabilize the relationship and make it more predictable. A second implication is that this very institution of diplomacy will disappear or will gradually merge into a world government in due time.

Moreover, it is obvious that the institution of diplomacy itself will have reflected this kind of growth of the world society into a world-state, and this growth has probably been along two dimensions. First of all, there has been a change from what one might call *ad hoc* diplomacy where the parties meet when circumstances so demand and permit, to *institutionalized* diplomacy. The latter can actually be subdivided into two categories: *permanent* diplomacy and diplomacy at *regular* intervals [5]. On the other hand there is the crucial distinction between *bilateral* diplomacy that involves two nations only, and the *multilateral* diplomacy that involves more than two nations. This last category can also be subdivided into two: multilateral in the sense of 'some' nations, and multilateral in the sense of (practically) all nations (Table 3.1).

TABLE 3.1 *Phases in the history of diplomacy*

	ad hoc	*institutionalized* 'regular' and 'permanent'
bilateral (two nations)	I diplomacy by envoys→	II residential diplomacy
multilateral ('some' or 'all' nations)	III conference diplomacy→	IV organizational diplomacy

There is a considerable difference between the diplomatic pattern found in the upper left-hand corner and in the lower right-hand corner; this is the difference between the occasional exchange of envoys found between 'primitive' tribes or between Greek city-states [6] on the one hand and the United Nations on the other. Nevertheless, the first form was quite important as late as five centuries ago and the second form is of major importance today, which means that the history of diplomacy in a sense telescopes an important aspect of the history of world development into a couple of centuries. This, in turn, points to the possibility of using the institution of diplomacy as a case for the study of the emergence of the world-state. The transition from the bilateral to the multilateral and from the *ad hoc* to the institutionalized forms of diplomacy are both major steps in this development, and by studying the diplomacy of today and the conflicts between the requirements imposed by bilateral diplomacy and by multilateral diplomacy, one is studying an important aspect of the world integration process.

We have indicated the phase numbers and some arrows in Table 3.1, not because of any exact chronological order from one phase into the next, but because of a certain logical relationship, and also a rough chronology. The four phases represent four steps from the disintegrated to the integrated world, both of them different from the two extreme phases described above as the fully 'integrated' and the fully 'disintegrated'. Historically, the overlap between the phases is considerable. Thus, we may still be said to live in a period where phase II is dominant, with the major part of the diplomatic services of most countries devoted to residential diplomacy (see Table 3.4). Residential diplomacy involves the idea of a *sender--nation* and a *host*-nation with the diplomatic mission permanently located in the host-nation, or else there is a system of accreditation with regular visits. This is a far step from *ad hoc* arrangements, particularly because the institutionalization makes it possible for the diplomats to work without any necessary suspicion that something extraordinary is going on. The *ad hoc* is by definition extraordinary.

The diplomatic mission acts as an intermediary between public or private interests in the sender-nation and public or private interests in the host-nation, whether these interests are located in the sender-nation or in the host-nation. The task may take the form of representation, negotiation and/or information feedback [7], and it is customary to make a distinction between the diplomatic and the consular branches of diplomacy. Exactly where this borderline is located need not worry us here, as long as it is relatively clear that relations between public interests in the sender-nation and public interests in the host-nation belong more to the diplomatic sphere and relations between private interests in the sender-nation and private interests in the host-nation belong more to the consular sphere. The intermediate combinations are perhaps less easily located, just as the distinction between 'public' and 'private' is by no means a clear one. There should be some implications in terms of growth-rates here. With increasing internationalization we would expect multilateral diplomacy to increase, if necessary at the expense of bilateral diplomacy. But we would also expect the consular branch to increase since more and more private persons, firms, etc., have such foreign interests as tourists, participants in conferences. Thus, residential diplomacy may survive as consulates.

2.1. Styles of diplomacy

The task of diplomacy is of course not only to serve as an intermediary, but to see to it that the interests of the sender-nation are taken care of as well as possible. It will be very wrong to add to this kind of definition the clause 'if necessary at the expense of other nations, even of host-nation'. First of all, the pattern of residential diplomacy makes it difficult for the diplomat to act very much and very openly against the interests of the host-nation, since he is after all supposed to go on living there and the *ad hoc*-pattern would, for that reason, generally be better suited for that kind of diplomatic activity (or no diplomatic relation at all). And secondly there is no need to assume that foreign ministries, diplomats or people in general feel loyalty towards and identify with their own nation alone. If they did so, then the zero-sum game model of diplomatic activity might be useful — and it would certainly obtain in some places at some periods. In general, much more complicated cooperative models would be necessary and this should be reflected in any attempt to define 'diplomacy' normatively or descriptively. We feel this is rather uninteresting, however, and content ourselves with the definitions given in this and the preceding section.

The problem that remains, however, is the problem of distinguishing between different styles of diplomacy. Since the ultimate task of diplomacy is to obtain something by influencing people, styles should be classified according to the technique of influence. Efforts have been made in this direction, for instance by Morgenthau, Sorokin and Etzioni, and they come out with a very similar trichotomy (Table 3.2).

TABLE 3.2 *Techniques of influence in diplomacy*

Author	System reference personal	social	physical
Morgenthau [8]	persuasion	bargaining	force
Sorokin [9]	familistic	contractual	compulsory
Etzioni [10]	normative	remunerative	coercive

This scheme is too general to be very useful for an analysis of diplomacy, but we shall borrow the idea of using patterns of influence as a basis. One can influence another person by letting him anticipate negative or positive consequences of what [11] he is doing, depending on what course of action he chooses. These negative and positive consequences may be located in three different spheres of human reality, here referred to as the 'personal', 'social' and 'physical'. Thus, what Morgenthau has called 'persuasion' is an effort to show the other person that a certain course of action would be in agreement with that person's values so as to give him what could be referred to as a 'good conscience'. Usually this should be accompanied by an effort to show that any other course of action would give him a 'bad conscience'. If this does not help, Morgenthau's 'bargain' comes into the picture: an administration of negative or positive social sanction depending on the course of action the other party chooses. And if this does not help either, Morgenthau's third category may become useful: the *threat* of force, for the actual *use* of force is the prerogative of another institution, the military. This would then be aimed at the physical system of the other party itself, but would certainly also have its connotation of (strong) negative social sanction. These comments also apply to Sorokin's and Etzioni's schemes. There is also a correspondence between this scheme and Nicolson's famous schools of diplomacy [12].

As they have been presented here there is probably a simple hierarchy involved in the sense that persuasion is preferred to bargaining and bargaining is preferred to force. But which means to choose as a major technique of influence will obviously depend on the position of the nation in the international social system and its traditions in general: many nations may not make use of threats of force, not because they want to abstain from it, but because their force is not impressive enough. The same applies to bargaining, for simple economic reasons, and this means that many nations in practice are left with persuasion alone as their diplomatic technique [13].

However, we shall now try to present a slightly different scheme that seems to have a more direct bearing on the problems of diplomacy. It is a truism that the task of the diplomat is policy-making and not analysis alone, but it is also a truism that his policy-making will have to be based on some kind of analysis. Now an analysis can be done in many ways, and a basic distinction seems to be between person-oriented and structure--oriented analysis. To someone who is person-oriented the world presents itself essentially as a stage with human actors. They are influencing each other according to their free will and along the lines of a giant plot, but this plot can be understood and even manipulated if one knows as much as possible about the persons participating. This image of the world is individualistic and usually also elite-centered since not all people would count equally much: persons in the elite should be studied perhaps even to the complete exclusion of others. Their desires and whims, their strong and weak points should be meticulously mapped, and particular emphasis put on their relations with each other. The analysis of the world becomes a dramatic endeavor in sociometry: every elite person's relation to every other elite person is to be explored, and the diplomat equipped with this knowledge should know how to maneuver. He should have the tools of persuasion in his hands since this tremendous sociometric analysis will give him insight into the right path of influence for him to take.

To the structure-oriented analyst the particular characteristics of persons, and even elite persons, play a minor role. Societies have structures of different kinds, and these structures develop according to laws or at least principles of development. These also apply to the international social system, and the good analyst is the person who is maximally well acquainted with knowledge and insights of this kind. The persons, and even the elite people, are seen more as playing certain roles, as being harnessed by their positions in the social structure, than as persons who can act in any way they choose and aim for anything they want. This point of view, then, is deindividualized, much less elite-centered (although it may be interested in the *structure* of the elite of a nation; not, however, in the personalities of the people occupying this position and in knowing them personally in order to deal with them), and is often referred to as 'materialistic'. Just as the person--oriented point of view may be found in its extreme version in some philosophical orientations associated with conservatism, the structure-oriented point of view may be found in its extreme versions in philosophies associated with Marxism. One may also recognize in this distinction the extreme vantage points for analysis often claimed by psychologists on the one hand and sociologists on the other hand, and the obvious synthesis of these points of view in the efforts made by social psychologists to find a focus for understanding the human condition by analyzing it at the point where the constraints of the social structure impinge on the variety of human personality.

In spite of its crudeness this trichotomy seems to point to a very real difference between styles of diplomacy. There is a difference between knowing people and understanding structures. The first is consistent with a style of diplomacy that is built around conferences, meetings, parties and social gatherings among elite people, with the idea of filling in the sociomatrix of the place as quickly and as well as possible. And the second is consonant with the idea of a more academic approach, with the reading of a maximum of articles and books about the social, economic and political structure of the host-nation, with a maximum of observation of all strata and sectors of the society in order to arrive at a maximum of insight into the laws governing this society. One immediate implication of this distinction again is that the first style of diplomacy is very consistent with the traditional upper-class style of life based on forms of intercourse that are courteous enough to permit association with many people, yet informal enough to permit thorough friendship with some selected few, whereas the second style is more consonant with patterns found in the academic community, in faculties of social science. And this also points to implications in terms of recruitment: the first style would need people who are maximally fit for the type of life that gives them access to elite people, in other words upper--class people well versed in the mores and folkways of upper-class life — in other words the offspring of upper-class people themselves, or their satellites. And the second style would ask less for talent in associating with people and more for talent in understanding social structures, in other words for people with a social science degree or some similar kind of training.

The latter will be less interested in what they could persuade the ruler of a country into doing than in knowing what he can possibly offer, given the social structure of his nation and its position in the international social structure. The person-oriented diplomat will have achieved his goal when an agreement is reached and be less equipped to understand whether it is at all consistent with the possibilities of the nation. This is where he has his shortcomings, just as the structure-oriented diplomat will run up against the difficulty that he is better equipped to understand how and why people act, than to get on good terms with them and change their patterns of action. The structure-oriented will try to align himself with patterns of development more or less according to the Spinozistic line of thought that 'freedom is insight into necessity'.

Needless to say, the two types we have depicted here are extremes that may be approximated to but perhaps never really found in social reality. Most diplomats will harbor both elements in different ratios, and most diplomatic services will probably try to cultivate both types and mix them in an appropriate way. But what can generally be said is that probably the trend in this generation has been, as perhaps it will also be in the generation to come, from the person-oriented towards the structure-oriented. One simple reason for this is the growth of social science, which has made the second perspective more meaningful. But a less trivial reason is the notion, apparently quite generally accepted, that person-oriented analysis was much more warranted before than it is today. In earlier centuries Europe has been depicted [14] as ruled by a thin layer of inter-marrying princes with a tightly knit social relationship that would have to be understood thoroughly by anyone who wanted to do diplomatic work. Today, 'social forces' are held by many to play a more fundamental role. One indicator of this is the growth of parliamentary democracy as an institution, giving the 'people' access to power, and the idea that the people are somehow more representative of social forces than the elite. To focus on the elite alone becomes ideologically incompatible with democratic thought. However, we find it extremely difficult to arrive at a meaningful and precise version of the problem of who is more right, the person-oriented or the structure-oriented. But diplomacy has come in for severe criticism in the last decades and much of the basis for this criticism can be seen in terms of proponents of the second style arguing against the proponents of the first style [15].

There is, however, a second distinction that also seems to play a major role. If the idea of diplomacy is to influence the other party, the problem nevertheless remains of whether the result should be made explicit or not. A treaty is an agreement in formal and explicit form, but is certainly not necessarily typical of diplomatic procedure. Characteristic of the treaty is 1. that it is visible to others (we disregard secret treaties), 2. that there is a high degree of consensus among the partners to the treaty as to what the consensus leading to the treaty was about, 3. that other people in the host-nation and in the sender-nation may be called upon to ratify the agreement, and 4. that nations that are not parties to the agreement nevertheless exercise some kind of influence as witnesses and because they are defined as non-signatories to the treaty. This is the 'open covenant' in President Woodrow Wilson's parlance, and whether it is openly agreed upon or not need not concern us here.

More important is the question of what one would find at the other end, as the opposite of the treaty described above. The opposite seems to be some kind of insight into the other party that can be used to manipulate him, even without his knowledge. This is where insight into propositions about intranational and international structure enters: if the insight is good, one should be able to use it as a lever to influence the behavior of the nation concerned. Thus, we get essentially three types of diplomatic styles (Table 3.3).

TABLE 3.3 *A typology of diplomatic styles*

	implicit, informal	*explicit, formal*
elite-oriented	personal manipulation	treaties
structure-oriented	structural manipulation	treaties

We have not distinguished between elite-oriented and structure-oriented styles when they result in explicit agreement, since the treaties will probably look very much the same. Hence, one ends up with what we shall call *the elite-oriented, the treaty-oriented*, and *the structure-oriented* diplomatists. Put in these terms it is rather obvious what kind of training one would expect these people to have: the first type should preferably have a background of solid upper-class training in general, the second type should be a legal expert in order to negotiate and draft ratifiable treaties that are consistent with other legal norms and be trained to discover implications that might be harmful, and the third type should be a social scientist of any discipline or persuasion. It does not seem unreasonable to assume that the treaty-oriented type represents a kind of interlude between the purely elite-oriented and the purely structure-oriented diplomatist, making himself felt at a point in time when the idea of the ratifiable treaty was very important and the social sciences still in their relative infancy — the between-war period. The treaty was, perhaps, a way to recreate the belief in stability and predictability in a society where one could no longer predict on the basis of knowledge of princes. And mid-century events destroyed much of the belief in treaties, and this, perhaps, paved the way for structure-oriented diplomacy.

2.3. The high status of the diplomat

An investigation made by Svalastoga in Denmark some years ago shows that out of 75 occupations, 'ambassador' was ranked highest by a sample of 3,000 Danes [16]. Thus, it was given a rank superior even to that of prime minister, and was probably given royal connotations. This means not only that it gets a high average rank in the population, but also that 'ambassador' is the kind of status the high rank of which seems to be very consensual. It is not difficult to find the functional explanation of this: the diplomat is supposed to associate with the power elite of the host-nation, and since contact in general is supposed to be best and least circumscribed when it is based on at least near-equality of rank the ambassador should be given a rank that corresponds to the level at which he is supposed to interact. How this is expressed in terms of the paraphernalia of the highest diplomatic status, that of the ambassador, is well known: it means above all that all the symbols of high status shall be easily available to the diplomat, he shall be second to none when it comes to meeting the highest-rank people on equal terms. This is also supposed to be reflected in his style, his command of languages, his general manners, etc. But there are some other less trivial implications.

First of all, the kind of rank the diplomat obtains is only partly *achieved*, it is mainly *ascribed*. There is little the diplomat has to do himself to obtain it: he will probably have to pass some examination to get into the foreign service, but from that point on he will, in most foreign services, be granted access almost automatically to at least the lower echelons of the highest rank levels, if he is only willing to wait long enough for it. In highly achievement-oriented societies, like most Western societies, this is likely to lead to difficulties for the diplomat. He may feel that he is accorded more than is actually his due, that he is not entitled to that high rank he enjoys. This probably led to very few problems for people of the old, elite-oriented diplomatic style, with a solid upper-class background, for they only changed from one basis (family) to another (diplomacy) for enjoying the privileges of upper class life. But the legally trained treaty-oriented diplomat and the structure-oriented diplomat versed in social science will probably have some difficulties. They may compare themselves with other professionals with the same training and find little reason why they themselves should fare so much better. Jackson [17] has a very interesting hypothesis to the effect that a person who ranks high on an ascribed dimension but low on an achieved dimension (for instance the poor white in the Southern part of the United States) will develop stress symptoms and in general be intra-punitive since he has not achieved the equivalent of what society gives to him in terms of rank. This does not quite correspond to the kind of problem we indicate here: in the case of the diplomat it is more a question of a person who may feel that he is not up to what is expected from him, not on two different dimensions, but on the same dimension. In short: he may feel that he enjoys the privileges of the wrong status and feel his status as a source of alienation: 'this is not really me.'

But the diplomat will probably answer himself by pointing out that the rank he receives when he occupies the status of diplomat is not to remune-rate him personally, but is, rather, a compensation for staying abroad, and above all to make it possible for him to perform the task he has; it should be compared with the skilled worker who does not have to pay for the instruments and tools he uses in the factory. Foreign services that use a rotational system whereby the foreign service man is supposed to return home and work in the ministry for some time several times during his career may use these periods to put the diplomats on an equal footing with other professionals with the corresponding level of training, and thus remind him that his high rank is artificial. The diplomat may also ridicule his own status among friends to show that he has not been spoilt. Never-theless, it would be strange if some of these high-rank effects were not some-how to rub off and our hypothesis is that they might lead to some stress symptoms and certainly to a number of practical problems with the sudden drops and jumps in prestige and income.

Our second point about the high status of the diplomat is very much related to this. The ambassador is entitled to be called 'His Excellency', and is subject to a kind of deferential behavior usually accorded only to members of royal families and members of governments. One aspect of this deferential behavior is that people will take care not to let him feel inferior and perhaps also take care to see to it that he always feels superior. People interacting with him will feel subject to certain norms of servility, and even though the ambassador may be perfectly aware of this, it would also in this case be strange if something did not rub off. In other words, one would expect that after some time the ambassador begins to believe that the deference he is met with is due to him personally and not to his status. In some cases this may of course also be true, but to the extent that it is not, the danger of overestimation of one's capability and a certain amount of conceit will be there. One very concrete implication of this is a difficulty in asking questions to extract information from inferiors, since excellencies presumably already know. They may receive unsolicited information but not betray that the information was not known to them [18].

Another point in the same connection has to do with rank as something with relative rather than absolute value. The status of the diplomat is high, but if he associates almost only with people of the same profession and rank he will be one *inter pares*, and for that reason not enjoy the fruits of high rank relative to social surroundings of lesser privilege. And even if he leaves the cocktail-circuit and enters the host society in general, high rank will in general not be as enjoyable to him as to a person who enjoys it at home. To the extent that people are interested in high rank as a criterion of achievement or as something to show off, the value of high rank will probably to a considerable extent depend on what people are there to join the circle of admirers. If we buy the assumption that much of what ambitious people do is done in order to impress 'significant others' — peers from childhood and adolescence, parents and other relatives, friends from college and university — then the diplomat had chosen the wrong profession. He eats cherries with the 'big' people, but there is nobody there to watch him doing so — the people who are present eat the same cherries (and they may also all be painfully aware of the circumstance that the cherries have been imported duty-free and with special privileges from the international firms specializing in merchandise for diplomats, which makes consumption conspicuous, but less costly) [19]. The diplomat can make up for some of this difficulty by going home in his vacations, but he cannot possibly bring with him all of his status symbols, and moreover, although he may have spare money, he is not an ambassador in his home country, only in his host-country, because only there is the relevant role-set accessible and visible. Besides, he is rarely at home long enough to build up a public image sufficient to give him high rank there. Thus, the major possibility for him if he wants to demonstrate his status to significant others lies in having them come over as friends and visitors and giving them the red carpet treatment.

A fifth and final point in this connection has to do with retirement. A person who retires will always suffer a certain drop in status, and the higher up he has been located the more may he fall. A retired ambassador probably still has considerable rank, but this is in more abstract terms. A retired professor may be surrounded by grateful students who know him from his days of active work; a retired physician may enjoy the gratitude of cured patients. A retired ambassador does not have his role partners around him, and he may also have spent so much time outside his own country that he is virtually a stranger there. This he may indeed anticipate, and view with horror during the last years of his active service. At the same time he may counteract some of the status-drop by settling abroad, and preferably in a country where there is a sufficiently high probability that he can meet people with whom he has interacted in his days of maximum rank and power (this need not necessarily be one of his former host-countries). A pattern sometimes found is the retired ambassador who continues to move around much as he did before retirement.

2.4. The problem of contact

This is a much discussed problem, and an ever-recurring item in the criticism raised against diplomats and even against the whole institution of diplomacy [20]. The argument is probably that negotiation and representation can best be taken care of at a very high level of interaction, but for the purposes of information feedback, contact with other parts of the society is indispensable. This is particularly true for a structure-oriented style of diplomacy. To discuss this we make use of the simple model of a society in Fig. 3.1.

The differences between the two societies are: 1. a secondary sector of economic activities has been developed (industrialization) and 2. a middle class has emerged; this is usually referred to as 'development'.

The diplomat will associate mostly with people very high up in the tertiary sector, since this is where the administration is located. But in addition he is more likely than not to be acquainted with top people on the primary sector ('the landed gentry'), and in modern societies with people high up in the secondary sector ('capitalists'). When it comes to meeting people in the middle and lower classes the hypothesis is that these people are likely to be located almost exclusively in the tertiary sector. First of all, these are the people with whom he will have to interact for service purposes (people working in shops, restaurants, transportation, administration, trade, etc.). With these people he would stand in a clear relationship of exchange: he gives something, usually money, and receives a service; or he may interact with them by virtue of his profession as a diplomat. But secondly, the sections crossed out in Fig. 3.1 represent very low foci of interaction for the diplomat because there is so little meaningful interaction he can have with them. In the lower echelons of the primary and secondary sectors are

FIGURE 3.1 *The social structure of traditional and modern societies*
(Marked field indicates low contact with diplomat)

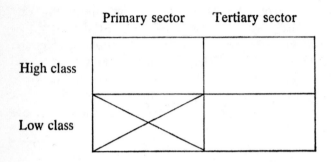

people (peasants, workers) who in most societies, except the most developed ones, interact mainly with people higher up in their own sector: with the foremen, or the owners of the means of production. Interaction with the tertiary sector where the diplomat is typically located is more often than not indirect, via high class people in their own sector. Of course, modern organization and the money economy facilitate direct interaction with lower and middle classes in the tertiary sector (commerce and transportation particularly, and the lower echelons of the administrative sector), but at no point do they come into meaningful interaction with the foreign diplomatist.

The consequence of this is that the diplomat will get a highly biased picture of the society in which he lives. His impressions of 'the people, will easily be based on some few contacts he will have in the lower strata of the tertiary sector, which would make disproportionately much of the content of his reports about the 'mood' of the people contingent on what his driver, his servants and the different kinds of artisans working in the embassies, mixed with the proverbial taxi-drivers and waiters, have told him [21]. His patterns of contact are adjusted to elite-oriented diplomacy but are incompatible with the needs of structure-oriented diplomacy.

Another effect of this is an easily developed negative bias towards the society of the host-nation. People in the tertiary sector will see the diplomat as an object of easy exploitation, not because of any particular greediness, but because this is built into their roles. Their task is to offer service for money, and unlike people lower down in the primary and the secondary sectors there is usually no upper limit on this exchange. A peasant or a worker offers his labor and receives a stipulated salary and that is it; a peddler, a shopkeeper or an agent of a travel agency has no fixed salary, what he can gain is dependent on how much he can sell. The implication of this is only that the diplomat will have to be almost superhuman to correct for the image he will get of the native population as mainly interested in offering and selling objects and services at a maximum profit and uninterested in the kind of regularly performed work found more typically in the primary and secondary sectors. The diplomat will meet with a combination of greediness and servility and less typically with the more autonomous and dignified behavior found among well-organized peasants, workers and students.

2.5. The theme of loyalty

The instructions given to the diplomat of any country will underline themes of loyalty to the sender-nation. These norms can be internalized by means of formal pledges [22], but the extent to which they are really followed will also depend on the structure of the diplomatic institution in which the diplomat works. We shall only emphasize some points in this connection.

Loyalty depends on identification, and identification is to a large extent a function of the volume of meaningful and egalitarian interaction with other people. All interaction abroad that fulfills these conditions when the diplomat is stationed in his host-country, and all sources of irritation and rejection relative to his home-country should, thus, contribute towards a change in the focus of identification away from the home-country and towards the host-country. The host-country is where the diplomat is treated well: here he is an excellency, he enjoys the highest status available outside the very summit of the host-nation, and he may enjoy gracious living with people who, though they may cause him difficulties, also flatter him [23].

At the same time his relations towards his ministry at home may be strained. Relative to the ministry he is one among many ambassadors. This is also true relative to the host-country: he is one of many members of the *corps diplomatique*. There is a difference, however: although he might like some special favors from his superiors at home in his ministry he will probably generally accept the idea that the ministry should treat everybody according to 'universalistic' criteria, for instance seniority mixed with achievement. Relative to the government of the host-country, however, he will probably have no objections to the idea that he is treated better than others. On the contrary, he will probably willingly accept a status as 'most favored ambassador' and also accept that other ambassadors have that status. He may compete for it, but that will be a part of the game. If he is promoted too quickly at home he will probably feel uneasy in front of his colleagues; if he is given special treatment by the government in the host-country he will, on the contrary, probably feel extremely well and proud in front of his colleagues, the other ambassadors.

The consequence of this important asymmetry in his relationship to home- and host-countries is that he is likely to have his triumphs abroad and his defeats at home, or so at least he may perceive it. The antagonistic relationship between the home office and the field offices of any organization is probably universal; at least it seems to be ubiquitous in the foreign service. To the diplomat abroad the foreign ministry is an organization that never reads his dispatches, that never answers his letters (and if it does so, on the basis of very general criteria that do not apply correctly in his particular situation), that treats him rudely or not at all when he is home on vacation and that does not take sufficient notice of his important advice [24]. To the ministry the diplomat in the field may appear as a person who has become provincial, who does not follow world events sufficiently closely to evaluate what he has picked up of gossip and solid information in the host-country, who is difficult and unreasonable in his claims and unable to see his own situation relative to his colleagues in other countries and makes unjust demands on an already overworked ministry. Above all he is a person who overrates the importance of his own mission [25].

With the host-country as a source of gratification and the home-country as a source of deprivation a change in the focus of identification seems likely, and the traditional answer to this is the rotation pattern of diplomats whereby their stay in any host-country is limited to a maximum of three or five years [26]. It is probably also a rather effective answer, since we would imagine that the psychological reaction of the diplomat would be to protect himself against the reality of the famous proverb *partire è un po' morire* by not developing too close friendships in the host-country. This should also lead to a certain artificiality in his general pattern of behavior: he may fake more friendship than he is willing to risk; he wants it for the sake of easy transfer of information and persuasion, but he avoids it because of emotional risks.

However, loyalty should not necessarily be conceived of as some kind of material that can be given either to the home-country or to the host-country, in the sense that if one of them receives it, then the other does not [27]. First of all, loyalty, like love, is probably divisible in the sense that a person may be capable of giving a good share to more than one person so long as this does not bring him into impossible conflicts. Thus, if the host-country needs settlers from his country and his own country asks him not to encourage emigration he may get into difficulties if he has multiple loyalties, unless he is inventive enough to make use of the many compromises that can be found. In a sense this may be one of the major problems of the diplomat and requiring the utmost diplomatic skill: how to distribute what he has to offer of loyalty in a reasonable way between home- and host-country.

In this game his home-country has one major advantage: he is dependent on it for his career. His skills as a diplomat, unlike the skills of a qualified worker, a farmer, a mathematician, a physician, a natural scientist (but not a lawyer, nor a specialist in national history, geography, etc.) are not easily transferable. If he has other skills, for instance as businessman, he may pass the borderline literally speaking. But if he depends on a position as a diplomat for a living his general skills will be in low demand (because they may be easily acquired) and his special skills are linked to his country of origin — a transfer of them is tantamount to treason. He may be willing to commit treason, but that is the rather high price set on the complete change of loyalty in this case. For that reason we would imagine that he has to defend himself against the problem, and here his biased pattern of contact mentioned above may come in handy: he may use his negative impressions of the host-country to shift the balance of loyalty in favor of his country of origin. But at this point it should be noted that these advantages of the home-country do not hold up against a temptation to enter an *international* organization, because this could not be defined as treason to any specific nation and his special skills would still have some value.

But there is a second objection to the simplified either-or model of loyalty according to which a person who is not loyal to his own nation must be loyal to another and hence a potential traitor: the idea that the diplomat can identify with some kind of super-national structure. If he is a member of a delegation to one of the international organizations this may be built into his role. He is supposed not only to represent his own nation's interests relative to that organization, but (probably) also to identify with the organization and find a solution that is optimal from the organization's point of view. But the diplomat engaged in bilateral diplomacy may also find a focus of super-national identification in the local *corps diplomatique*. To what extent this really takes place, that is, to what extent the *corps diplomatique* conceives of itself as a little local United Nations, a projection from the international community on the local scene, we do not know. More often than not the *corps diplomatique* will probably conceive of itself as a trade union for negotiating the common interests of the diplomats *vis-à-vis* the host-government — and these interests may be of a very material nature such as problems of customs duties, protocol matters and housing conditions. Nevertheless, we list it as a fascinating problem for future research because here the contemporary resident diplomatic structure may be provided with an avenue of transition from bilateral to multilateral diplomacy.

3. The growth of Norwegian diplomacy

We shall now present some data about structural aspects of the Norwegian foreign service, mainly based on data available from *Utenrikskalenderen*, a directory published at uneven intervals with information about the personnel of the Norwegian foreign service [28]. Obviously, there are changes in this structure over time and it seems that these can be relatively well accounted for by means of five factors:

1. *Special factors in Norwegian history.* Norway has become independent three times during the last 150 years, in 1814 (from Danish domination), in 1905 (from Swedish domination) and in 1945 (from German domination). Since the foreign service of a nation is particularly vulnerable to foreign domination this has had obvious impacts. The foreign service in general and the ministry in particular had to go through phases of reconstruction.

2. *Changes in Norwegian social structure.* During the last 150 years Norway has undergone a socio-economic change roughly corresponding to the transition from Rostow stage I to Rostow stage V. This has obvious implications for the occupational distribution of the Norwegian population etc.

3. *Changes in Norwegian central administration.* During this period the central administration of Norway has been subject to a number of changes that will also have been reflected in the structure of the foreign ministry.

4. *Professionalization of the Norwegian diplomat.* One general characteristic of our time is the professionalization of almost any activity, and this

will have implications in terms of homogenization, as well as in other terms.

5. *Changes in styles of diplomacy.* We have hypothesized a general change from the elite-oriented via the treaty-oriented to the structure-oriented styles, and a parallel trend from bilateral to multilateral diplomacy. There should be some structural counterparts to these trends.

However, in our analysis of the structure of the Norwegian foreign service we shall not give equal emphasis to these five factors. The first three are mainly of interest to Norwegians, and their relation to the growth of the Norwegian foreign service will be elaborated in another article. The minimum of knowledge that is useful in this connection is presented in the Appendix. Thus, we shall mainly concentrate on the last two factors and see how and in what sense they are consistent with our data.

As a point of departure let us present the composition of the Norwegian foreign service at the turn of each decade of this century (Table 3.4).

TABLE 3.4 *The composition of the Norwegian foreign service,* %

	1910	1920	1930	1939	1951	1960
Ministry	23	28	32	32	30	35
Diplomatic service	41	41	38	40	43	41
Consular service	36	31	30	28	22	19
Delegation	0	0	0	0	5	6
Sum	100	100	100	100	100	101
(N)	(55)	(91)	(84)	(100)	(164)	(201)

The first and rather obvious comment is in terms of the growth of the institution, which amounts to almost 400 over a period of fifty years. If, in addition, one should count the diplomats associated with the service in 1960 but not at that time in a regular position, the growth would be about 500 %. This is probably as good a reflection as any of the growth of a nation into the international society and the increasing importance of international interdependence [29].

As to the composition of the service the conclusion is easily drawn. Bilateral diplomacy is kept constant during the period with small ups and downs, the ministry is increasing, the consular service is decreasing regularly, and the last decades have seen a growth of a newcomer on the diplomatic scene: the delegation (to international organizations). The latter is an expression of multilateralization, the growth of the ministry is an expression of the extent to which diplomatic work becomes political work that cannot be resolved in the field but has to be referred to the ministry, requiring more and more expertise, and the decrease of the consular service should probably be seen in the light of a corresponding enormous growth of the field organizations and field offices of commercial agencies, shipping lines, airlines, organizations, etc. [30]. Nevertheless, we predict a growth for the consular services later in this century.

As can be seen from Table 3.5 more than 50 % of the total force at any point in time is located outside Norway. Where are they? We calculated this for the diplomatic, consular and delegation services (Table 3.5).

TABLE 3.5 *The location of personnel in diplomatic and consular services,* %

	1910	1920	1930	1939	1951	1960
Scandinavia	10	8	12	12	9	9
European Big Powers	40	31	28	23	20	18
Other European States	12	17	12	15	17	20
USA	12	17	16	19	20	19
USSR	12	5	9	6	3	3
Asia and Australia	10	6	12	12	10	13
Africa	0	3	2	4	3	2
Latin America	5	14	9	9	10	7
Delegation embassies	0	0	0	0	8	9
Sum	101	101	100	100	100	100
(N)	(42)	(65)	(57)	(68)	(115)	(132)

The four most remarkable features that emerge from Table 3.5 are rather easily explained. In 1910 the USA and Russia exercised the same pull on the Norwegian foreign service, that is 11 %; in 1960 the USA had increased to 18 % and the USSR was down to 3%. The importance of both nations has increased considerably, so this is a clear expression of cold war polarization, among other factors.

In 1910 European big powers accounted for almost half of the foreign service personnel of Norway; in 1960 this was down to one fifth. The decrease is not compensated for numerically by the increase in delegations, but there is probably a functional equivalence. In 1910, when the Norwegian foreign service was very young, Norway gained her membership in international society by tying herself to the big European capitals. In 1960 international society exists in its own right and membership is obtained through direct participation in the international organizations. Moreover, 'society' at the international level is no longer Europe alone. Thus, the tendency is towards growing dispersion with growing internalization.

But Asia and Africa are nevertheless remarkably constant during that time span of 50 years, whereas Latin America is down from 14% in 1920 to 7% in 1960. This is probably one more expression of the drop in status which that continent has suffered during the period.

The last problem in this connection has to do with the rank-composition of the foreign service. The data are given in Table 3.6.

TABLE 3.6 *The rank distribution of the Norwegian foreign service,* %

	1910	1920	1930	1939	1951	1960
Ambassador I [31] Secretary General	0	0	14	11	5	15
Ambassador II, Consul General, Director General	29	29	20	22	24	12
Deputy Director	0	0	0	0	0	1
Ambassador III, Counsellor, Consul, Chief of section	22	22	22	21	22	22
1. secretary embassy, 1. Vice consul, First secretary	31	36	27	13	14	21
2. secretary embassy, 2. Vice consul, Secretary	13	10	17	26	26	15
Attaché	5	3	0	7	6	10
Special service at the disposal of the ministry	0	0	0	0	3	4
Sum	100	100	100	100	100	100
(N)	(55)	(91)	(84)	(100)	(164)	(201)

There is a magic line in the Norwegian foreign service, as in most other organizations, between the 'high' and the 'low' in the organization, and this line is as drawn in Table 3.6. Below are the 'tjenestemenn' and above are the 'embetsmenn' — the former are appointed by the ministry, the latter are appointed by the Government. As can be seen from the Table there is a remarkably constant division of the personnel with 50% above and 50% below the line all through the period. As a matter of fact, there is so little change in the Table that it looks as if each year in the foreign ministry has been a true copy of the preceding year regardless of external circumstances.

Our data show that apart from the two last phases, which contain persons who have been in the service for too short a time, between 80 and 90% of the officers in the first four phases have crossed the magic line at step 4. And if one considers this together with the fact that 'practically all who have become "embetsmenn" sooner or later are appointed to a top position in the foreign service' [32], it becomes easy to see the importance of this division. Up till now the major question has not been *whether* a young member of the foreign service will in due time be an ambassador or a consul general, but rather *when* he will have a chance to reach the top. The trend has been one of increasing homogeneity: in phase II there was a bimodal curve as 20% reached the counsellor level in less than 10 years and as many as 29% had to wait more than 15 years for this important promotion. In phases III and IV, however, the mode is 10—14 years after entering the service. Those who are promoted sooner are probably regarded as fairly successful. The study group wants even more emphasis to be put on the differences between step 5 and step 4: '(It seems) natural to promote into the "embetsmenn"-group only those who are considered qualified to serve as chief of mission. This would also be a clear reminder to those who are lagging behind that their chances for a further career are limited' [33]. The scarcity of top-level positions is the kind of structural condition that can create tensions that in turn can be expressed in terms of generational conflict. More particularly, conflicts of interest may be translated into conflicts of ideology — and it is our hunch that this will take place along the lines of bilateral versus multilateral, national versus international, elite- and treaty-oriented versus structure-oriented, etc., alluded to above.

4. The social background of the Norwegian foreign service

In order to study the social background of the Norwegian foreign service, data have been collected for all people who have served or are currently serving [34]. This gave us a total of N = 398, out of which 228, or 57%, are currently serving. To study the trends in the data the material was divided into six *phases*, determined by crucial developments in the institution of the Norwegian foreign ministry (see Appendix) [35]. Thus, phase I is the phase prior to 1905, phase II covers the period from 1905 to the reform in 1922, phase III covers the period from 1922 to the end of the war, phase IV covers the period from 1945 to 1949 when a more profession-oriented basis for recruitment was reintroduced, phase V is the period from 1949 to the end of the 1950s, and phase VI is from 1960 up to the end of 1964. Some of the analysis is carried out with phases V and VI combined, some of it with phases V and VI separately in order to study the most recent development. There are also Tables where we have to use a phase V* from 1950 to the end of 1962 because of difficulties with the data for 1963 and 1964.

A diplomat is allocated to a phase according to the year in which he entered the service. Thus, to the extent that we make a diachronic analysis by following the diplomats through time, analysis of one phase will essentially be a kind of cohort-analysis. This will also be the case later in connection with the analysis of career patterns.

The first focus of interest for any analyst of a social institution is the social background, for instance as expressed by father's position. Data are given in Table 3.7.

TABLE 3.7 *Father's position for Norwegian foreign service,* %

	Diplomat	Superiors public admin.	Intellec. academ.	Profes sionals	Officers	Business	Func- tionaries	Teachers	Workers Crafts Sailors Farmers	No info.	Sum	(N)
I	5	8	13	15	23	26	5	0	8	0	103	(39)
II	5	12	13	13	6	26	9	3	5	8	100	(97)
III	5	12	4	24	8	27	11	3	1	5	100	(74)
IV	3	11	16	14	2	20	11	6	9	8	100	(64)
V+VI	3	4	8	18	2	19	18	7	12	9	100	(124)

As can be seen at a glance, the changes through the five phases are not very startling, especially when compared with other trends to be presented below. The distributions for phase I and for phase V are dissimilar, but not very much so. The most important characteristics are the following: officers are out (for phase VI alone it is down to zero), business is down, as are intellectuals and academic people, and functionaries are up as well as teachers [36, 37]. Self-recruitment, the case where the son follows in the footsteps of his diplomat father, is negligible — which is partly due to the circumstance that Norway as a young nation always had few people who were or had been diplomats and to the circumstance that they did not produce many children in the first phases (see Table 3.11).

In particular, it is evident that the basis of recruitment in the last phases cannot be said to be much more 'democratic' (a euphemism for 'proportionate') than in the first phases. There is a slight dislocation of the point of gravity downwards in the social structure, but it is still solidly in the tertiary sector and solidly upper middle-class, in spite of a certain increase in the lowest recruitment category [38].

Also remarkable is the similarity in the dispersion of social background. Four or five categories accounted for more than 10% each in all phases. In phase I the foreign ministry drew its personnel above all from two categories in the Norwegian population: business people and officers. After the First World War the basis looks somewhat broader, although, as noted, still located within a particular social class. This does not take into account the meaning of the category 'officer' in phase I, however. At that time to be an officer probably signified something different from what it does today: it was a part of a gentleman's education and less than a fully-fledged profession [39]. Thus, 'officer' may be a synonym for upper-class to an extent which is not the case for later phases and particularly not for the phases after the Second World War [40].

Whilst we are discussing this it might be interesting to look at the second interpretation of 'democratic recruitment'. In addition to proportionate representation of social categories there is the idea of an easy transition from the lower echelons of an institution to the higher echelons. Applied to the foreign ministry this would involve the mobility of cipher clerks, secretaries, office assistants, etc., into the ranks of the diplomats, so that they could finally end up as ambassadors. We looked into this and found that 92% of the recruitment had been from outside the organization, 1% from the ministry itself, 4% from the diplomatic branch and 3% from the consular branch [41]. And the trend was here away from this kind of 'democratization': before 1905, 82% of the personnel were recruited from outside the organization as against 97% in the post-war period. Thus, the organization osmosis from below to above is negligible, and this is also reflected in a pronounced sex difference: in 1960, one out of 201 'flyttepliktige' was a woman, whereas 123 out of 215 of the 'ikke-flyttepliktige' were women [42].

To complete this survey of the social background of the diplomats it might be worth while looking at the father-in-law. The difficulty is only that the data are very scant indeed, but to the extent that we have been able to get them (we have no information for as many as 42% of the cases) they seem to indicate 1. a more narrow concentration of the fathers-in-law in the same strata as the fathers themselves and 2. a slight tendency for the diplomats or diplomats *in spe* to marry up. The latter is a relatively logical consequence of the circumstance that problems of equivalence in marriage may be solved for the young diplomat by adding the rank of his own father to his own rank, as at least a coming diplomat, so as to arrive at a sum equal to a father-in-law higher up than his own father. How this works in practice we do not know [43], but the impression one gets from the data is that the diplomats are solidly embedded in a narrow segment of the population, and that this is reinforced through marriage [44]. But we would also like to add at this point that we know of no convincing theory to the effect that a broader dispersion in social background would in any sense add to the value, efficiency or general usefulness of the institution [45].

When it comes to geographical background there are few interesting trends in the data. The recruitment to the foreign ministry, probably like other ministries and other Norwegian organizations for that matter, shows a slight trend away from Oslo as the basis of recruitment. But the trends are slight and the impression is more or less the same as for father's position: throughout this period of two generations the basis of recruitment has changed very little.

Let us then turn from the basis of recruitment to the family founded by the diplomat. First of all, there is a remarkable tendency to be seen in their marital status. That there are still people in phases V and VI who are not married is certainly not strange when age is taken into consideration. Much more interesting is the circumstance that as many as 23% were not married in phase I. There may have been particular reasons for this but it is consistent with a different orientation towards diplomacy as a whole. In that early period diplomacy must have been conceived of much more as *a calling*. It must have had a connotation of the monastery, a male society devoted to diplomacy 24 hours a day, 365 days a year. By forsaking marriage diplomats could symbolize even more effectively and visibly their devotion to the national cause. Through growing professionalization this becomes less and less necessary, and the end result would be the diplomat who, just like any other Norwegian, marries, and begets children [46] (Table 3.8).

If there is anything in this theory, then, one would predict, for those who are married, a strain in the period between more fully-fledged professionalization of the diplomat and the culture of the calling. And this seems to be precisely what we find from the data about divorce (Table 3.8): in phase II diplomats married much more than in phase I, but they also achieved an exceptionally high divorce rate and a corresponding rate of remarriage. Both these rates are going down with time and even though diplomats in phases IV and V, not to mention phase VI, still have much time ahead of them to produce divorces and remarriages, our prediction is nevertheless that they will under no circumstances catch up with the phase II level.

TABLE 3.8 *Marital status of the diplomats,* %

	Not married	Married once or more	No information	Sum	Widower	Divorce	Remarried
I	23	72	5	100	18	3	5
II	5	91	4	100	16	22	24
III	5	92	3	100	8	12	16
IV	0	97	3	100	0	13	11
V	2	96	2	100	0	9	8
VI	26	66	8	100	0	0	0

Another consequence of this hypothesis would be that diplomats in phase I married much later (not only somewhat later as would be normal relative to changes in the population at large) [47] — and that diplomats in the first phases had a higher tendency to marry after they joined the service. Both predictions are amply borne out by Table 3.9.

First of all one may note the strongly growing tendency to marry before one joins the service. To some extent this is due, as we shall see later, to a different age distribution at the time when they enter the service, but that accounts for only a minor fraction of the difference. Rather, as is

TABLE 3.9 *When did the diplomats marry?* %

	20—24	25—29	30—34	35—39	40—45	45+	marriage first
I	5	15	5	15	15	10	5
II	3	19	23	11	14	8	19
III	2	28	34	16	7	4	12
IV	6	39	33	6	3	0	31
V*	19	55	16	3	1	0	53

seen from Table 3.9, there have been two trends: towards much younger age at marriage, and towards much less dispersion in the age of marriage. This is a typical expression of what will also turn up many times later, that is, the diplomats start becoming typical Norwegians, with the same patterns in terms of when to marry and when to enter on a life career.

This is, of course, reflected in the nationality of the spouse (Table 3.10).

TABLE 3.10 *Nationality of spouse of Norwegian diplomats,* %

	Un-married	Nor-wegian	Scandi-navian	Euro-pean	Other	No infor-mation	Sum	(N)
I	23	39	0	21	5	13	101	(39)
II	5	56	7	11	6	14	99	(97)
III	5	68	5	5	12	4	99	(74)
IV	0	76	5	9	2	8	100	(64)
V	2	73	9	7	5	4	100	(86)
VI	26	53	5	5	5	5	99	(38)

We shall not put so much emphasis on the last line since they have not yet had time to marry. The general tendency is clear: Norwegian diplomats tend to marry Norwegian girls, so they become 'normal' also in that respect. There may perhaps be some ups and downs on the curve, but the trend is there and is a typical consequence of the normalization mentioned. Thus, in phase I as many as 21 % of the diplomats married Europeans: this is consistent with their late age of marriage and also with where they were placed (see Table 3.5). But more significant than the cause of this tendency is its possible consequence: diplomats in that period probably had more occasion to identify themselves as *Europeans* than diplomats of today. They belonged to the upper stratum of the European society, whereas the diplomat today is more of a Norwegian paying a short-term visit to international society.

The diplomat in the first phases was probably also a much more mobile person, not only because of his late marriage-age, if he married at all, but also (consequently) because of the low number of children he produced. This is reflected in Table 3.11. Again, phase VI should be disregarded,

TABLE 3.11 *Number of children of Norwegian diplomats,* %

	One child	Two children	Three children	More
I	13	15	8	3
II	21	29	8	7
III	16	38	20	11
IV	13	41	25	8
V	16	45	19	6
VI	16	13	8	0

but in spite of the youth of phase V they have nevertheless already produced many more children than were produced in phases I, II and III, on the average. All this points towards a tendency to gravitate towards Norway, which is again consistent with the slight growth in the foreign ministry itself, as was seen in Table 3.4.

5. The training of the diplomat

The story of the change in the training of the Norwegian diplomat is the story of normalization, professionalization and homogenization. Table 3.12 will surprise nobody.

TABLE 3.12 *High school graduation ('artium') — field,* %

	No 'artium'	Human-ities	Science	Classics	Other	Abroad	Field not known	Sum	(N)
I	13	0	15	21	8	3	41	101	(39)
II	9	21	14	10	11	2	32	99	(97)
III	8	10	28	31	7	4	12	100	(74)
IV	5	25	34	13	9	3	11	100	(64)
V*	2	35	29	8	6	2	17	99	(96)

The percentage not having 'artium' was already low and is now, in most recent years, for all practical purposes equal to zero [48]. At the same time there is a trend away from the study of classics in high school to a concentration on the more modern disciplines — recently above all in the direction of 'humanities', which means a specialization in the English language. This trend away from classics is, however, to a large extent a reflection of a general trend in Norwegian education. As can also be seen from Table 3.12, making some guesses about the 'not knowns', there is less dispersion in the educational background of the diplomat in phase V than in the first phases. Hence, one more indicator of homogenization.

And this is much more pronounced if we look at the marks they obtained at high school graduation (Table 3.13).

TABLE 3.13 *High school graduation ('artium') — marks, %*

	No 'artium'	S	M	T	Ng	Not known	Sum	(N)
I	13	7	13	18	3	46	100	(36)
II	9	6	24	22	3	35	100	(97)
III	8	4	28	15	5	39	99	(74)
IV	5	3	39	22	0	31	100	(64)
V*	2	7	49	14	0	27	99	(96)

The four symbols in Table 3.13 are very meaningful to any Norwegian: S is the very best, which may be obtained by about 3% of the graduates [49]. As can be seen from the Table there is a trend towards better grades (the modus was 'T' in phase I, but with a very clear lead for 'M' in phase V*). And the relatively even distribution has disappeared: in phase I no mark accounted for as much as 20% of the data; in phase V one mark alone accounts for half of the data.

We then turn to the university degree (Table 3.14).

TABLE 3.14 *University degree — field, %*

	No degree	Huma- nities	Law	Science	Econo- mics	Social Sciences	Other	Abroad	Incom- plete	Sum	(N)
I	18	0	77	0	0	0	0	3	3	101	(39)
II	31	4	52	0	7	0	1	2	3	100	(97)
III	22	0	53	0	11	0	4	4	7	101	(74)
IV	19	5	44	2	17	0	6	3	5	101	(64)
V	4	9	44	0	9	16	5	13	0	100	(86)
VI	8	8	38	0	16	8	5	18	0	101	(38)

We get a corresponding decrease for people with no degree, so pronounced that it looks as if the university degree is becoming *sine qua non* for a foreign service man. At least there will be a stabilization with a very low in-flow of people without university degrees.

But the most interesting finding emerging from Table 3.14 is the strong degree of complementarity between law and social science, where we include economics. During the entire period law is down from 77% to 38% and social sciences and economics are up from 0% to 24%. Both changes are almost monotone and very consistent with the theory about the decrease in the treaty-oriented style and a corresponding increase in structure-oriented diplomacy.

There are, however, a number of comments that should be made. First of all, this change is a reflection of a general trend in the universities. Law was formerly probably considered the proper training of the 'generalist', the training of the person who wanted to prepare himself for a very wide variety of positions both in the public and in the private sectors; being the only Social Science field of its time. It is quite possible that law is now becoming a more specialized field training for more particular positions, and that a person with a law degree is now considered less fit for the wide variety of positions he entered earlier, including politics. It may also be that economics and the social sciences, particularly political science, are gradually taking over as adequate preparation for the Norwegian generalist — but this is difficult to confirm or disconfirm for the time being. At any rate, the university turnout of lawyers proportionately speaking is decreasing and the turnout of social scientists is increasing, the latter certainly in part due to the circumstance that political science and sociology were ntroduced as subjects at the University of Oslo in 1947 and 1948 [50].

Whatever the precise combination of factors that have contributed to this trend, the importance from our point of view is its compatibility with a certain change in style of diplomacy. It should be noted that the legally trained diplomat of phase I probably was eminently fit as an elite-oriented diplomat, and the social scientist of phases V and VI should excel in structure-orientation. It goes without saying that at any period in the history of diplomacy the diplomat had to know *something* in order to carry out his work, and this something was and is more often than not of a very trivial nature and usually includes a detailed knowledge of rules, legal or not. Thus, it is in a sense surprising that the system is experiencing such a decrease in legally trained people, and one would expect the service to call for more persons with that background. Nevertheless, in spite of the need for legally trained diplomats the trends are unmistakable. In a sense it looks as if the social scientists are knocking at the door of the lawyers telling them 'look, now it is our turn'. Since the phases are also generations this will easily be translated into conflicts between generations in the service [51].

What remains to be seen is, of course, who will knock at the door of the social scientists and tell them that their time is up. This will not happen, we assume, before the percentage of social scientists has increased considerably and reached its apogee — and that will probably take a good fraction of what remains of this century. In the meantime it might be wise to notice that the change where field of study is concerned does not reflect itself in lower scholarship — on the contrary (Table 3.15):

TABLE 3.15 *University degree — marks* [52], %

	No degree	'laud'	'haud'	No marks	No infor- mation	Sum .	(N)
I	18	23	26	0	33	100	(39)
II	31	26	21	1	22	101	(97)
III	22	42	8	1	27	100	(74)
IV	19	45	12	5	19	100	(64)
V*	3	50	6	13	27	99	(96)
Total	19	38	14	5	25	101	(370)

We get precisely the same tendency as for the matriculation degree: much less dispersion, and higher quality as measured by marks. This indicates more achievement-orientation and less use of social background as the basis of recruitment. Still, a closer scrutiny shows that the people entering diplomacy are not necessarily the very best in terms of high school or university examinations — but, rather, good second bests.

In addition to this formal training most of them had one form or another of additional training before they entered the service. This is presented in Table 3.16. To the left is the entrance-test of the foreign service, 'aspirant-

TABLE 3.16 *Additional training before service,* %

	'aspirant pröven'	mercantile	military	practice – own field	practice – not own field
I	0	10	10	46	14
II	1	16	23	63	29
III	50	28	15	57	19
IV	3	25	14	69	33
V	76	16	13	29	22
VI	100	0	24	35	15

pröven'. The test was introduced in 1922 and marks the transition from phase II to phase III. The emergency situation during the war made it impossible to use such tests. It was reintroduced in 1949 at the beginning of phase V, but did not become 100% effective before phase VI, as can be seen from the data [53]. In a sense this column is a good illustration of what it means to become an independent nation: in phases II and IV Norway had to fill her foreign service with people regardless of entrance tests, very often by virtue of the fact that they had done some service in the ministry or for the nation before. But after such a period comes the period when the ministry takes shape and becomes formalized adequately; and that includes the entrance test and the subsequent year of training with its control, learning and 'socialization'.

As can be seen from the fourth and fifth columns, phases II and IV are also the phases where people with practice in their own field (for instance, of university training) or some other field were admitted more than in the other phases: both distributions have their peaks in these phases. As the service becomes more regular the tendency to bring in people with outside practice decreases — and the tendency towards homogenization increases.

Some information we have about publications produced by the diplomats may serve as a little illustration of all this. This is a decreasing activity: 'no publication' was registered for 74% in phase I, and then follow 73, 89, 95, and 98% in phase V*. In phase I 10% wrote their memoirs and in phase II 20% produced professional or political publications. It may be said that the young people in phase V* would still have to wait some time before they write up their memoirs — nevertheless it is our prediction that they are not going to do so. For the diplomat in phase I the memoir is the logical outcome: he is elite-oriented and the elite had scarcity value since journalists had less access to them in those days. Correspondingly, political publications are the logical outcome of the career of the diplomat in phase II: he is legally trained, he is treaty-oriented according to the hypothesis and may concentrate his experiences in such publications. The same might apply to phase III, but for phases IV and V we would predict no publication at all (most people in most jobs after all do not publish even in Norway), or else *analyses* as the typical outcome. The skillful analytical article in a professional journal about the problems of some country or international organization, not necessarily with any normative, political conclusion, should be the archetype of publication in these phases, since the phases should be characterized by a predominance of structural orientation.

6. Some trends in the career patterns

Data were obtained for every diplomat who had served in the Norwegian foreign service, about where he was placed, what was his position, in which branch he served and for how long — all these four for every step in his career. For this analysis we have only made use of the data up the end of 1962, since it is obvious that the personnel joining the service in 1963 and 1964 have not yet had sufficient time to leave any career patterns behind them.

Many times in the foregoing we have had occasion to hypothesize that diplomats in the earlier phases had a much wider dispersion when it came to the age at which they joined the service: they were both younger than diplomats of today and older. This is borne out by the data in Table 3.17.

TABLE 3.17 *Age when entering the service,* %

	20—24	25—29	30—34	35—39	40+	Sum	(N)
I	21	46	21	8	4	100	(39)
II	23	38	12	11	14	100	(97)
III	24	57	12	2	5	100	(74)
IV	5	54	30	2	9	100	(64)
V*	4	74	16	4	0	100	(96)

As is seen at a glance there is a very heavy concentration in one category in phase V* and a corresponding dispersion in phases I and II. The two periods of independence, phases II and IV, make themselves noticed with a higher proportion of older people entering the service, but apart from this the tendency is clear: fewer very young people and fewer relatively old people joining the service.

They were then fed into the service at different levels according to the phase, as can be seen from Table 3.18.

TABLE 3.18 *First step in career — position,* %

	attaché	secretary	middle levels	top levels	Sum	(N)
I	31	49	5	15	100	(39)
II	50	40	4	6	100	(97)
III	58	38	4	0	100	(74)
IV	69	25	2	5	100	(64)
V*	81	16	1	2	100	(96)

What this Table says is actually nothing but the truism that it takes some time to build up a national foreign service. The projection from these data is that in some time close to 100% will start as attachés, which again is an expression of the normalization of the profession. It should also be noted that the fraction of personnel entering at the middle or top level has decreased from 20% to 3%, which can be interpreted both as democratization and professionalization.

Another expression of this is found in Table 3.19.

In the old days the newcomer started in the consular branch and, as will be mentioned below, abroad; nowadays he starts in Norway and in the ministry. He has been broken in, so to speak, under the full supervision of his superior and is socialized, we assume, more successfully into a more standardized pattern. Again the two phases of independence make themselves noticed: in phases II and IV there is a particularly large input to the ministry because of the necessity of building up the service, if not from scratch at least from a new point of departure.

TABLE 3.19 *First step in career — branch,* %

	Ministry	Diplomatic branch	Consular branch	Delegation	Sum	(N)
I	18	18	64	0	100	(39)
II	42	17	41	0	100	(97)
III	32	41	26	1	100	(74)
IV	75	14	11	0	100	(64)
V*	66	25	6	3	100	(96)

When it comes to *where* they started their careers the patterns are relatively obvious consequences of what has already been said. The percentage starting in Norway increases from 10% [54] to 66%, and the concomitant decreases are found in Scandinavia (10—3%) and Europe (59—20%). But more interesting is the duration of the first step and that is given in Table 3.20. The conclusion is rather simple: in the old days one stayed for a short or for a very long period; nowadays the diplomats stay for a regular period of one or two years [55]. Again the dispersion is less and the homogenization higher, with a trend towards a shorter period of service at each single place. This may be seen as an expression both of a desire for a pattern of rotation, a desire for more control over the diplomat by

TABLE 3.20 *First step in career-duration,* %

	6 months	6—12 months	1—2 years	3—4 years	4 years	Sum	(N)
I	26	26	15	13	20	100	(39)
II	13	27	34	12	13	99	(97)
III	20	26	27	12	15	100	(74)
IV	14	27	42	14	4	101	(64)
V*	11	21	59	7	1	99	(96)

bringing him home at regular intervals, and of a desire on the part of the diplomat for being at home — the latter would be consistent with our general finding that he is now a more typical Norwegian.

However this may be, the obvious consequence would be a lower number of steps in the career for the first phases than for subsequent phases, and this is also what we find in Table 3.21.

Of course, the diplomats in phases IV and V* have still not had sufficient time to take any steps in their career; nevertheless the pattern seems to be in the predicted direction. In practice this means that even though the old diplomat perhaps was more of a genuine European, he was a European

TABLE 3.21 *Number of steps in the career,* %

	0—6	7—10	11+	Sum	(N)
I	28	26	46	100	(39)
II	29	26	45	100	(97)
III	20	26	54	100	(74)
IV	14	53	33	100	(64)
V*	68	27	5	100	(96)

at fewer places; and even if the young diplomat is more of a Norwegian residing abroad, he is residing at very many different places. In this there is no contradiction: whereas the former grew roots abroad, this is less true of the latter.

And thus we could continue: a scrutiny of the second step in career, for instance, brings out exactly the same pattern as for the first step. The effects of the two periods of independence make themselves felt through a number of steps, and shape the distribution of people in the ministry at step n for high value of n.

Finally, let us look at the conditions under which the diplomat leaves the service. The simplest facts are summarized in Table 3.22. What this Table shows is actually only how young the Norwegian diplomatic service is, since the majority are still serving, and the decrease of the consular branch as the last stage, at the expense of the ministry and the diplomatic branch. Thus, in phase I as many as 41% of the total left the service as consuls general, as against only 36% as ministers. But already in phase II the pattern had changed: 18% left as consuls general as against 20% as ministers. The consul general was the typical final reward of the Norwegian

TABLE 3.22 *Leaving the service,* %

	Ministry	Diplomatic branch	Consular branch	Still in service	Sum	(N)
I	8	40	52	0	100	(39)
II	17	44	36	4	100	(97)
III	3	15	3	78	100	(74)
IV, V*	3	1	1	95	100	(160)

foreign service in those days, and this fits in well with everything which has been said so far: the elite-orientation, the generality in training and background, the tendency to settle in one country and rotate much less than is usually the case nowadays, bilateral rather than multilateral diplomacy, and so on.

Phase I was, everything considered, a rather happy phase which is clearly seen by the circumstance that more people left the service because they reached the age of retirement in that phase than in the subsequent phase II. In that phase 30% left the service earlier at their own request (as against 23% in phase I) and many of them as early as between the ages of 30 and 49 (28% as against 10% in phase I). Again this is what a new nation had to reckon with: it calls on personnel from other fields and will to some extent have to give them back again. This tendency will certainly decrease with increasing professionalization.

7. Discussion and implications

We are now at our journey's end and can try to summarize and discuss more fully some of the most important patterns that have emerged. Much of this will be rather tentative, but we have been struck by the consistency in the data, by some striking similarities with corresponding data about English and American diplomats, and so we feel justified in making some projections.

It is easy to envisage some possible future states of the world where the structure and function of diplomacy are concerned. An invariant feature of these models would be professionalization. But it is difficult to see how this could be consistent with continued generalized rather than specialized training, and a continued use of the pattern of rotation between the three or four branches of the service. For this pattern to continue when professionalization and specialization are among the gods of our time one would have to create people who are specialists in general diplomacy. This is probably as good a formulation as any of what one has tried meaningfully and successfully to do in the past, but that will hardly be possible in the future.

Today the diplomat generalist will have to be a universal genius to compete meaningfully with international organizations, experts, peace corps and the news media when it comes to information feedback. In the past he did not have to share his access to the power elite of the host-nation with so many. Moreover, to the extent that person-oriented diplomacy is yielding to structure-oriented diplomacy he will also have to compete with social scientists, area specialists, etc., and is then severely hampered by the bias of his contacts in the host-society. And something of the same probably applies to negotiation. In the past he could concentrate on some (European) powers, today the diplomat at large will have to face a much larger span of heterogeneity in the personalities and social backgrounds of his counterparts. With increasing homogenization of world culture we may again enter a period where the world elite has a shared culture, talks the same language, knows one another well, etc., but ours is rather a period of both heterogeneity and much interaction.

There is still the function of representation which can be carried out more according to standard patterns. However, referring to the element of strain due to the artificiality of the rank of the diplomat the task of representation alone will hardly attract the best members of the service. Actually, it all amounts to this: the structure of diplomacy, with its high rank and upper-class style of interaction, is lagging behind, even though diplomacy (we assume) is changing from elite-oriented to structure-oriented, bilateral to multilateral, and *ad hoc* to institutionalized patterns. To insist on generalization and not specialization, rotation and not concentration is to invite the successful competition of research organizations and others that offer these two virtues of our time. From attracting second bests diplomacy may run the risk of attracting third bests only.

Thus, later on in this century, if the trends revealed by our data 1. continue and 2. are fairly typical, we would not be surprised to find the following:

1. Bilateral, government-to-government diplomacy will be considerably reduced, and mainly be used between antagonists (there may come a period when entering bilateral diplomacy may be a sign of hostility, not of friendship). In its place will come:

a. Multilateral diplomacy, regional and universal, in rapid growth. First there will be a tendency for nations to negotiate via their ambassadors to the international organization — which is bilateral diplomacy within a multilateral framework. Later these negotiations will gradually be built into a truly multilateral structure, the secretariat will make preparations, criteria applying to more than the two nations at stake will be developed, etc.

b. Consular services to take care of private citizens and firms, etc., abroad, and for representation. However, there are three alternatives to this development, and they are perhaps just as likely:

1. Host-nations will consider this to be their task by extending services given to foreigners — on a basis of reciprocity.

2. International organizations, governmental and non-governmental, will take care of their members. Thus, professional associations, Rotary Clubs, etc., probably already handle a much higher volume of such transactions than consulates.

3. Non-governmental organizations in the home country may have branches for this particular purpose. The best examples are the commercial networks created by firms, shipping companies, travel associations and bureaux, etc.

c. Internationalization of news communication to provide for consensual reporting about world events. This will probably be increasingly professionalized, and combine person-oriented news with structure-oriented analysis.

2. The personnel of the new diplomacy, essentially multilateral, will be professionals trained according to the same pattern but with the opportunity to specialize in particular international organizations and functions. There will be considerable crises of identity in the relationship between one's own country and the international organization to which one is accredited, and these crises will be more difficult to resolve since one's own nation is a member of the international organization. To begin with they will probably rotate between the office of their own nation in the international secretariat and the office of the international organization in their own foreign ministry; later they may settle at either end of the channel, and they may become members of the international staff. Internationalization will probably proceed precisely by integrating more and more foreign service officers into the staffs of international organizations, thus counteracting inbreeding in international organizations.

Thus, we are rapidly growing into a period where the diplomat will be an International Man, or at least a regional man, a specialist on some functions of his organization much like any national ministry officer. His hobbies will no longer be Portuguese art, Turkish coins and stamps or vases from the Ming dynasty, but rather something less bound to areas and nations and more practicable anywhere his missions may bring him. His publications will be less tied to nations and persons and more to problems and structures and functions. He will possibly be a less colorful person, less of a reservoir of style, charm, wit, general knowledge and talented gracious living, and more of a secretariat member, like anyone else, only more skillful. Above all, one International Man will pretty much resemble another International Man — there will be less variety in training, prior experience and life-career patterns. They may pass through different countries, but their tie to the international organization will be so strong that they will experience more or less the same things. In short: they will be normal people living in the growing international layer encapsulating the world.

But even if this is about as far as we can see for the moment, with the addition that it will probably be realized before we think — this is not the situation of today. Today's problems for most foreign services probably center around the difficulties of balancing homogeneity with heterogeneity, specialization with generalization, and so on, and with the difficulties arising from the lag between structure and function in modern diplomacy. All we can say where this is concerned is the truism that any inadequacy in the machinery of diplomacy, so crucial for us all, is potentially threatening, and should be counteracted by speeding up the process towards what one can reasonably assume to be future forms of diplomacy. Thus, insights in trends may strengthen these trends, but may also make one disregard other possibilities. But for more insights into these problems more data and other kinds of data are needed, so we shall postpone further discussion for future articles.

Appendix

A short chronology of major events in the Norwegian foreign service

1814 May: Norway independent from Denmark after more than 400 years of union. November: Personal union between Norway and Sweden. Common foreign service and consular administration.

1905 June: Norway independent from Sweden. Provisional diplomatic envoys appointed. November: Independence officially accepted by the Swedish Government. The first ordinary diplomatic envoys appointed.

1906 First Norwegian law for the Foreign Service enacted. First instructions for diplomats and consuls.

1912—13 First Foreign Service Commission at work, partly as a result of complaints from business circles that the service was not capable of taking care of Norwegian commercial interests. No formal reorganizations came out of this partly because of World War I.

1919—20 Second Foreign Commission at work. Proposed to merge the different branches of the service.

1922 New law for the foreign service enacted. The diplomatic and consular branches merged. Formal training course *(aspirant-kurset)* started. Efforts to economize and cut back on the number of positions.

1923 Second instruction for the foreign service.

1940—45 The Foreign Office in exile with the rest of the Norwegian Government in London.

1946—47 Third Foreign Commission *(Reformutvalget)* at work, with the special mandate to suggest changes in the foreign service intended to meet the demands of the changed world situation after the Second World War.

1948 New law for the foreign service according to the principles of *Reformutvalget*. The law supposed a new instruction to be worked out. The work with the new instruction entailed the need for some changes in the law of 1948, which led to

1958 New law for the foreign service. This law is rather similar to the principles for the administration and organization of the foreign service as laid down in the Law of 1948.

1960 New instruction for the foreign service.

1961 A committee appointed *(Brinchutvalget)* with the mandate to suggest changes in the Norwegian diplomatic representation abroad, with special reference to recently independent nations etc.

Bibliography

[1] *Almindelig instruks for Utenrikstjenesten* av 10. august 1923, med kommentar. (Kristiania: Nationaltrykkeriet, 1924) pp. 5—309.

[2] *Almindelig Norsk Konsulatinstruksjon* av 24. juli 1906.

[3] ANDVORD, ROLF. *Med hånden på hjertet.* (Oslo: 1964) 374 pp.

[4] CARDOZO, MICHAEL H. *Diplomats in International Cooperation: Stepchildren of the Foreign Service.* (Ithaca, New York: Cornell University Press, 1962) 142 pp.

[5] COLBAN, ERIK. *Femti år.* (Oslo: 1952) 264 pp.

[6] FAY, HANS. *På post i fem verdensdeler.* (Oslo: 1959)

[7] HAYTER, WILLIAM. *Diplomacy of the Great Powers.* Norw. ed.: *Stormaktenes diplomati.* (Oslo: J. W. Cappelen, 1962).

[8] *Innstilling fra Reformutvalget for utenrikstjenesten.* (Oslo: Utenriksdepartementet, 7. januar 1947)

[9] *Innstilling fra Studiegruppen vedrörende utenrikstjenesten.* (Oslo: 10. juni 1964) 75 pp. mimeo.

[10] *Innstilling fra Utenrikskommisjonen av 1919.* (Kristiania: 1, 28. juni 1920. 2, 14. mars 1921)

[11] *Innstilling fra Utvalget til gjennomgåelse og vurdering av Norges utenriksrepresentasjon.* (Oslo: 20. desember 1962, St. meld. nr. 37, 1962—63) 65 pp.

[12] *Instruks for utenrikstjenesten*, fastsatt ved Kgl. resolusjon av 11. mars 1960, med kommentarer, vedlegg og formularer.

[13] *Instruksjon for Gesandtskapene* av 25. august 1906.

[14] IRGENS, FRANCIS. *En norsk diplomats liv. Minister Johannes Irgens, (1869—1939).* (Oslo: 1952) 160 pp.

[15] KELLER, SUZANNE, 'Diplomacy and Communication', *The Public Opinion Quarterly*, Vol. XX, No. 1, Spring 1956, pp. 176—82.

[16] KERTESZ, D. STEPHEN and FITZSIMONS, M. A. (Eds.) *Diplomacy in a Changing World.* (Notre Dame: University of Notre Dame Press, 1959).

[17] LANGE, HALVARD. *Administrative problemer i norsk utenrikstjeneste.* (Oslo: 1954)

[18] LEDERER, WILLIAM J. and BURDICK, EUGENE. *The Ugly American.* (New York: W. W. Norton & Co. Inc., 1958) 284 pp.

[19] LIE, MICHAEL. *Fra mitt liv som diplomat.* (Oslo: 1929)

[20] *Lov om Diplomat- og Konsulatvaesenet* av 12. juni 1906.

[21] *Lov om utenrikstjenesten* av 13. desember 1948.

[22] *Lov om utenrikstjenesten* av 18. juli 1958, med motiver. (Oslo: Utenriksdepartel mentet, 1962) 12 pp.

[23] *Lov om Utenriksvesenet* av 7. juli 1922 (Kristiania: Nationaltrykkeriet, 1924) pp. 1—4.

[24] NICOLSON, HAROLD. *The Evolution of Diplomatic Method.* (1954).

[25] NICOLSON, HAROLD. *Diplomacy.* (London: Oxford University Press 1960, 2nd edition) 248 pp.

[26] NUMELIN, RAGNAR. *The Beginnings of Diplomacy.* A sociological study of intertriba and international relations. (London: Oxford University Press, 1950; Copenhagen: Ejnar Munksgaard, 1950)

[27] NUMELIN, RAGNAR. *Diplomati.* (Stockholm: 1954)

[28] OMANG, REIDAR. *Norsk utenrikstjeneste, Vol. I Grunnleggende år.* (Oslo: Gyldendal Norsk Forlag, 1955) 329 pp.

[29] OMANG, REIDAR. *Norsk utenrikstjeneste. Vol. II Stormfulle tider, 1913—1928.* (Oslo: Gyldendal Norsk Forlag, 1959) 588 pp.

[30] *Reglement om rekruttering og utdannelse i utenrikstjenesten,* fastsatt ved Kgl. res. av 14. mai 1948, 17. sept. 1948, 14, nov. 1952, kr. pr. reg. s res. av 9. mars 1956 pg Kgl. res. av 5. sept. 1963.

[31] RAEDER, JOHAN GEORG J. *Glimt fra et langt diplomatliv.* (Oslo: 1950)

[32] SATOW, ERNEST. *A Guide to Diplomatic Practice.* (London: 1932, 3rd edition)

[33] SPAULDING, E. WILDER. *Ambassadors Ordinary and Extraordinary.* (Washington, D. C.: Public Affairs Press, 1961) 302 pp.

[34] STEINER, ZARA S. *Present Problems of the Foreign Service.* (Princeton, N. J.: Center of International Studies, Woodrow Wilson School of Public and International Affairs, Princeton University, March 20, 1961, Policy Memorandum No. 23) 57 pp.

[35] THAYER, CHARLES W. *Diplomat* (London: 1960) 288 pp.

[36] The Committee on Foreign Affairs Personnel. *Personnel for the New Diplomacy.* (Report, December 1962, 2nd printing January 1963) 161 pp.

[37] VOGT, BENJAMIN. *Indtil 1910 og Efter 1910.* (Oslo: 1941)

[38] WEDEL-JARLSBERG, F. H. H. *Reisen gjennom livet.* (Oslo: 1932)

IV.4. The Structure of Foreign News

The Presentation of the Congo, Cuba and Cyprus Crises in Four Norwegian Newspapers *

From *Journal of Peace Research* II/1 (1965). PRIO publication No. 14—2. Notes on page *690*.

1. Introduction

In this article the general problem of factors influencing the flow of news from abroad will be discussed, following the kind of reasoning given by Östgaard in his article [1], but in a somewhat different way. A systematic presentation of factors that seem to be particularly important will be followed by a simple theory and the deduction of some hypotheses from them. No claim is made for completeness in the list of factors or 'deductions'. Some of these hypotheses will then be tested on data relating to the presentation in four Norwegian newspapers of three particular and recent crises abroad. Gaps in our present knowledge will be indicated and some possible policy implications drawn.

The point of departure is our world as a geographic structure divided roughly into 160 territories, most of which are called nations and are 'autonomous'. The international community of nations is structured by a number of variables and highly stratified into 'topdog' and 'underdog' nations so that the world is geography on which are superimposed two relatively similar levels of human organization: the interindividual and the international. The two levels are not independent of each other and the more they are linked (the more population and leadership in any nation are interdependent), and the more nations are interdependent because of increasing efficiency of communication and military action [2], the more valid is the old sociological slogan about 'everything's relevant for everything else'.

Thus, the world consists of individual and national actors, and since it is axiomatic that action is based on the actor's image of reality, international action will be based on the image of international reality. This image is not shaped by the news media (press, radio, TV, newsreels) alone; personal

118

impressions and contacts, professional relations abroad, diplomatic dispatches, etc., count too — whether less, equally much or more, we do not know. But the regularity, ubiquity and perseverence of news media will in any case make them first-rate competitors for the number-one position as international image-former. Since the adequacy of an action is often, but by no means always, positively related to the adequacy of the image on which it is based [3], research into the adequacy of the image the news media give of the world is of primary importance.

At the interpersonal level the relationship between the *events*, the *perception* with all the selective and distorting factors that are operative under different circumstances, and the final *image* is relatively well explored. At the level of collective perception, where perception is made on behalf of others to be relayed to these others later, the situation is much more complicated. From world events to personal image we have the chain of communication presented in Figure 4.1.

FIGURE 4.1 *The chain of news communication*

```
world  events → media   → media → personal   → personal
              perception ↑ image      perception ↑ image
                 selection                selection
                 distortion               distortion
```

We are concerned with the first half of this chain, from world events to news image, or, to be more specific, to the printed page in the newspaper since our data refer to that. In other words: *how do 'events' become 'news'?* This does not mean that the second half is unimportant — on the contrary, it is the personal image, not the newspaper that counts, but this will be discussed in a later article. In analyzing the first half we shall treat the news media as non-personal indivisible entities and not distinguish between the journalist in the field in the news sending country, the local press agency bureau, the district bureau, the central bureau of the press agency, the district bureau on the receiving end, the local bureau in the newsreceiving country, the news editor in the receiving newspaper, the layout man, and what not — to indicate a chain with some seven or eight steps in it [4]. The chain may of course be much shorter if the newspaper has a correspondent; it may then be reduced to event correspondent editor, which involves two steps only. Östgaard has indicated many of the problems along this chain [5] and detailed analysis here is certainly important for future research, but our analysis will treat news media *in abstracto* and limit itself to some reasoning from first principles.

2. The theory

To do this a metaphor with sufficient heuristic power to offer insights (but certainly not proofs) is useful. One such metaphor is as follows. Imagine that the world can be likened to an enormous set of broadcasting stations, each one emitting its signal or its program at its proper wavelength (another metaphor might be of a set of atoms of different kinds emitting waves corresponding to their condition). The emission is continuous, corresponding to the truism that something is always happening to any person in the world. Even if he sleeps quietly, sleep is 'happening' [6] — what we choose to consider an 'event' is culturally determined. The set of world events, then, is like the cacophony of sound one gets by scanning the dial of one's radio receiver, and particularly confusing if this is done quickly on the medium-wave or short-wave dials. Obviously this cacophony does not make sense, it may become meaningful only if one station is tuned in and listened to for some time before one switches on to the next one.

Since we cannot register everything, we have to select, and the question is what will strike our attention. This is a problem in the psychology of perception and the following is a short list of some obvious implications of this metaphor:

F_1: *If the frequency of the signal is outside the dial it will not be recorded.*

F_2: *The stronger the signal, the greater the amplitude, the more probable that it will be recorded as worth listening to.*

F_3: *The more clear and unambiguous the signal (the less noise there is), the more probable that it will be recorded as worth listening to.*

F_4: *The more meaningful the signal, the more probable that it will be recorded as worth listening to.*

F_5: *The more consonant the signal is with the mental image of what one expects to find, the more probable that it will be recorded as worth listening to.*

F_6: *The more unexpected the signal, the more probable that it will be recorded as worth listening to.*

F_7: *If one signal has been tuned in to the more likely it will continue to be tuned in to as worth listening to.*

F_8: *The more a signal has been tuned in to, the more probable that a very different kind of signal will be recorded as worth listening to next time.*

Some comments on these factors are in order. They are nothing but common-sense perception psychology translated into radio-scanning and event-scanning activities. The proper thing to do in order to test their validity would be to observe journalists at work or radio listeners operating with the dial — and we have no such data. For want of this the factors should be anchored in general reasoning and social science findings (but references to the latter will be given in the notes only since they are not essential to our reasoning).

The first factor is trivial when applied to radio sets, less so when applied to events in general. Since this is a metaphor and not a model we shall be liberal in our interpretation of 'frequency' and proceed as follows. By the 'frequency' of an event we refer to the time span needed for the event to unfold itself and acquire meaning. For a soldier to die during a battle this time-span is very short; for a development process in a country to take place the time span may be very long. Just as the radio dial has its limitation with regard to electro-magnetic waves, so will the newspaper have its limitations, and the thesis is that *the more similar the frequency of the events is to the frequency of the news medium, the more probable that it will be recorded as news by that news medium.* A murder takes little time and the event takes place between the publication of two successive issues of a daily, which means that a meaningful story can be told from one day to the next. But to single out one murder during a battle where there is one person killed every minute would make little sense — one will typically only record the battle as such (if newspapers were published every minute the perspective could possibly be changed to the individual soldier). Correspondingly, the event that takes place over a longer time-span will go unrecorded unless it reaches some kind of dramatic climax (the building of a dam goes unnoticed but not its inauguration). Needless to say, this under-reporting of trends is to some extent corrected by publications with a lower frequency. A newspaper may have a habit of producing weekly 'reviews', there are weeklies and monthlies and quarterlies and yearbooks — and there are *ad hoc* publications. If we concentrate on dailies, however, the thesis is probably valid and probably of some heuristic value when other aspects of news communication are to be unraveled.

The second thesis is simply that there is something corresponding to the idea of 'amplitude' for radio waves. What this says is only that the bigger the dam, the more will its inauguration be reported *ceteris paribus;* the more violent the murder the bigger the headlines it will make. It says nothing about what has greater amplitude, the dam or the murder. It can also be put in a more dichotomous form: there is a threshold the event will have to pass before it will be recorded at all [7]. This is a truism, but an important one.

The third hypothesis is also trivial at the radio level but not at the news level. What is 'signal' and what is 'noise' is not inherent; it is a question of convention [8], as seen clearly when two radio stations are sending on the same frequency. Clarity in this connection must refer to some kind of one-dimensionality, that there is only one or a limited number of meanings in what is received. Thus interpreted the hypothesis says simply the following: the less ambiguity, the more the event will be noticed. This is not quite the same as preferring the simple to the complex, but one precization of it rather; an event with a clear interpretation, free from ambiguities in its meaning, is preferred to the highly ambiguous event from which many and inconsistent implications can and will be made [9].

The fourth hypothesis also deals with meaning but not with its ambiguity. 'Meaningful' has some major intepretations. One of them is 'interpretable within the cultural framework of the listener or reader' and all the thesis says is that actually some measure of *ethnocentrism* will be operative: there has to be *cultural proximity*. That is, the event scanner will pay particular attention to the familiar, to the culturally similar, and the culturally distant will be passed by more easily and not be noticed. It is somewhat like the North European radio listener in, say, Morocco: he will probably pass by the Arab music and speech he can get on his dial as quaint and meaningless and find relief in European music and French talk.

The other dimension of 'meaningful' is in terms of *relevance:* an event may happen in a culturally distant place but still be loaded with meaning in terms of what it may imply for the reader or listener. Thus the culturally remote country may be brought in via a pattern of conflict with one's own group [10].

The fifth hypothesis links what is selected to the mental pre-image, where the word 'expects' can and should be given both its cognitive interpretation as 'predicts' and its normative interpretation as 'wants'. A person *predicts* that something will happen and this creates a mental matrix for easy reception and registration of the event if it does finally take place. Or he *wants* it to happen and the matrix is even more prepared, so much so that he may distort perceptions he receives and provide himself with images consonant with what he has wanted. In the sense mentioned here 'news' are actually 'olds', because they correspond to what one expects to happen — and if they are too far away from the expectation they will not be registered, according to this hypothesis of consonance [11].

The sixth hypothesis serves as a corrective to the fourth and fifth. The idea is simply that it is not enough for an event to be culturally meaningful and consonant with what is expected — this defines only a vast set of possible news candidates. Within this set, according to the hypothesis, the more unexpected have the highest chances of being included as news. It is the unexpected *within the meaningful and the consonant* that is brought to one's attention, and by 'unexpected' we simply mean essentially two things: *unexpected* or *rare*. Thus, what is regular and institutionalized, continuing and repetitive at regular and short intervals does not attract nearly so much attention, *ceteris paribus*, as the unexpected and *ad hoc* — a circumstance that is probably well known to the planners of summit meetings [12]. Events have to be unexpected or rare, or preferably both, to become good news.

The seventh hypothesis is the idea that once something has hit the headlines and been defined as 'news', then it will *continue* to be defined as news for some time even if the amplitude is drastically reduced [13]. The channel has been opened and stays open partly to justify its being opened in the first place, partly because of inertia in the system and partly because what was unexpected has now also become familiar. Thus F_7 is, in a sense, deducible from F_3 and F_6.

The eighth and final hypothesis refers to the *composition* of such units as evening entertainment for the family around the radio set, the front page of a newspaper, the newscast on radio, the newsreel on TV or in the cinema, and so on. The idea is this: imagine the news editor of a broadcasting station has received only news from abroad and only of a certain type. Some minutes before he is on the air he gets some insignificant domestic news and some foreign news of a different kind. The hypothesis is that the threshold value for these news items will be much lower than would otherwise have been the case, because of a desire to present a 'balanced' whole. Correspondingly, if there are already many foreign news items the threshold value for a new item will be increased.

As mentioned, these eight factors are based on fairly simple reasoning about what facilitates and what impedes perception. They are held to be culture-free in the sense that we do not expect them to vary significantly with variations in human culture — they should not depend much on cultural parameters. More particularly, we would not expect them to vary much along the east-west, north-south or center-periphery axes which we often make use of to structure the world. In particular, these factors should be relatively independent of some other major determinants of the press. A newspaper may vary in the degree to which it caters to mass circulation and a free market economy. If it wants a mass circulation, all steps in the news chain will probably anticipate the reaction of the next step in the chain and accentuate the selection and distortion effects in order to make the material more compatible with their image of what the readers want. Moreover, a newspaper may vary in the degree to which it tries to present many aspects of the situation, or, rather, like the partners in a court case, try to present only the material that is easily compatible with its own political point of view. In the latter case selection and distortion will probably be accentuated and certainly not decrease.

But there is little doubt that there are also culture-bound factors influencing the transition from events to news, and we shall mention four such factors that we deem to be important at least in the northwestern corner of the world. They are:

F_9 : *The more the event concerns elite nations, the more probable that it will become a news item.*

F_{10}: *The more the event concerns elite people, the more probable that it will become a news item.*

F_{11}: *The more the event can be seen in personal terms, as due to the action of specific individuals, the more probable that it will become a news item.*

F_{12}: *The more negative the event in its consequences the more probable that it will become a news item.*

Again, some comments are in order. That news is *elite-centered*, in terms of nations or in terms of people, is hardly strange. The actions of the elite are, at least usually and in short-term perspective, more consequential than the activities of others: this applies to elite nations as well as to elite people. Moreover, as amply demonstrated by the popular magazines found in most countries, the elite can be used in a sense to tell about everybody. A story about how the king celebrates his birthday will contain many elements that could just as well have been told about anybody, but who in particular among ordinary men and women should be picked for the telling of the story? Elite people are available to serve as objects of general identification, not only because of their intrinsic importance. Thus in an elite--centered news communication system ordinary people are not even given the chance of representing themselves. *Mutatis mutandis*, the same should apply to nations.

More problematic is the idea of *personification*. The thesis is that news has a tendency to present events as sentences where there is a subject, a named person or collectivity consisting of a few persons, and the event is then seen as a consequence of the actions of this person or these persons. The alternative would be to present events as the outcome of 'social forces', as structural more than idiosyncratic outcomes of the society which produced them. In a structural presentation the names of the actors would disappear much as they do in sociological analysis and much for the same reason — the thesis is that the presentation actually found is more similar to what one finds in traditional personified historical analysis. To the extent that this is the case the problem is *why*, and we have five different explanations to offer:

1. Personification is an outcome of *cultural idealism* according to which man is the master of his own destiny and events can be seen as the out-

come of an act of free will. In a culture with a more materialistic outlook this should not be the case. Structural factors should be emphasized, there will be more events happening to people or with people as instruments than events caused by people.

2. Personification is a consequence of the need for meaning and consequently for *identification:* persons can serve more easily as objects of positive and negative identification through a combination of projection and empathy.

3. Personification is an outcome of the *frequency-factor:* persons can act during a time-span that fits the frequency of the news media, 'structures' are more difficult to pin down in time and space.

4. Personification can be seen as a direct consequence of the *elite-concentration* but as distinct from it.

5. Personification is more in agreement with modern techniques of news gathering and news presentation. Thus, it is easier to take a photo of a person than of a 'structure' (the latter is better for movies perhaps), and whereas one interview yields a necessary and sufficient basis for one person-centered news story, a structure-centered news story will require many interviews, observation techniques, data gathering, etc. Obviously there is an egg-chicken argument implied here since it may also be argued that personification came first and that techniques, the whole structure of news communication, were developed accordingly.

We only offer those explanations without choosing between them; first of all because there is no reason to choose as long as they do not contradict each other, and secondly because we have neither data nor theory that can provide us with a rational basis for a choice. It is our hunch that future research will emphasize that these factors reinforce each other in producing personification.

When we claim that *negative* news will be preferred to positive news we are saying nothing more sophisticated than what most people seem to refer to when they say that 'there is so little to be happy about in the news', etc. But we can offer a number of reasons why this state of affairs appears likely, just as we did for the factor of personification. We shall do so using the other factors relatively systematically:

1. Negative news enters the news channel more easily because it satisfies the *frequency* criterion better. There is a *basic asymmetry* in life between the positive, which is difficult and takes time, and the negative, which is much easier and takes less time — compare the amount of time needed to bring up and socialize an adult person and the amount of time needed to kill him in an accident: the amount of time needed to build a house

and to destroy it in a fire, to make an airplane and to crash it, and so on. The positive cannot be too easy, for then it would have low scarcity value. Thus, a negative event can more easily unfold itself completely between two issues of a newspaper and two newscast transmissions — for a positive event this is more difficult and specific. Inaugurating or culminating events are needed. A. p.r.-minded operator will, of course, see to that — but he is not always present.

2. Negative news will more easily be *consensual and unambiguous* in the sense that there will be agreement about the interpretation of the event as negative. A 'positive' event may be positive to some people and not to others and hence not satisfy the criterion of unambiguity. Its meaning will be blurred by other overtones and undertones.

3. Negative news is said to be more *consonant* with at least some dominant pre-images of our time. The idea must be that negative news fulfils some latent or manifest needs and that many people have such needs. Of the many theories in this field we prefer the cognitive dissonance version because it is falsifiable. The theory, however, presupposes a relatively high level of general anxiety to provide a sufficient matrix in which negative news can be embedded with much consonance. This should be the case during crises [14], so a test of this theory would be that during crises news that is not related to the crisis tends to be more negative and not more positive (as a theory of compensation rather than of dissonance/reduction would predict).

4. Negative news is more *unexpected* than positive news, both in the sense that the events referred to are more rare, and in the sense that they are less predictable. This presupposes a culture where changes to the positive, in other words 'progress', are somehow regarded as the normal and trivial thing that can pass under-reported because they represent nothing new. The negative curls and eddies rather than the steady positive flow will be reported. The test of this theory would be a culture with *regress* as the normal, and in that case one would predict overreporting of positive news. This is exemplified by news about the illness of an important person: the slightest improvement is over-reported relative to a steady decline.

Again we do not have sufficient theory to make a choice between these possible explanations — nor do we have to do so since they do not exclude each other.

As to these last four factors it was mentioned that they seem to be of particular importance in the northwestern corner of the world. This does not mean that they are not operating in other areas, but one could also imagine other patterns of relationship between the set of events and the set of news. Table 4.1 shows some examples.

TABLE 4.1 *Some patterns of news structure*

Pattern	F_9 nation	F_{10} people	F_{11} personification	F_{12} negativization
I	elite-centered	elite-centered	person centered	negative centered
II	elite-centered	elite-centered	structure centered	positive centered
III	elite-centered	elite-centered	both	negative centered
IV	non-elite-centered	elite-centered	person centered	positive centered

Pattern I is the pattern we have described above. Pattern II would, where the last two aspects are concerned, be more in agreement with socialist thinking, and where the first two are concerned, with big-power thinking. It might fit the news structure of the Soviet Union, but with the important proviso that one would probably use pattern III to describe Western powers. Similarly, a newly independent developing nation might use pattern IV for itself, but also reserve pattern III for former colonial powers. But all this is very speculative [15].

Let us then list systematically the twelve factors we have concentrated on in this analysis with subfactors.

Events become news to the extent that they satisfy the conditions of:

F_1: *frequency*
F_2: *threshold*
$F_{2.1}$: *absolute intensity*
$F_{2.2}$: *intensity increase*
F_3: *unambiguity*
F_4: *meaningfulness*
$F_{4.1}$: *cultural proximity*
$F_{4.2}$: *relevance*
F_5: *consonance*
$F_{5.1}$: *predictability*
$F_{5.2}$: *demand*
F_6: *unexpectedness*
$F_{6.1}$: *unpredictability*
$F_{6.2}$: *scarcity*
F_7: *continuity*

F_8: *composition*
F_9: *reference to elite nations*
F_{10}: *reference to elite people*
F_{11}: *reference to persons*
F_{12}: *reference to something negative*

As mentioned, these twelve factors are not independent of each other: there are interesting inter-relations between them. However, we shall not attempt to 'axiomatize' on this meager basis.

Let us now imagine that all these factors are operating. This means, we hypothesize, three things:

1. *The more events satisfy the criteria mentioned, the more likely that they will be registered as news* (selection).
2. *Once a news item has been selected what makes it newsworthy according to the factors will be accentuated* (distortion).
3. *Both the process of selection and the process of distortion will take place at all steps in the chain from event to reader* (replication).

Thus the longer the chain, the more selection and distortion will take place according to this — but the more material will there also be to select from and to distort if one thinks of the press agencies relative to special correspondents. In other words, we hypothesize that every link in the chain reacts to what it receives fairly much according to the same principles. The journalist scans the phenomena (in practice to a large extent by scanning other newspapers) and selects and distorts, and so does the reader when he gets the finished product, the news pages, and so do all the middle-men. And so do, we assume, people in general when they report something, and, for instance, diplomats when they gather material for a dispatch to their ministry — partly because they are conditioned by their psychology and their culture, partly because this is reinforced by the newspapers.

In general this means that the cumulative effects of the factors should be considerable and produce an image of the world different from 'what really happened' — for instance in the ways indicated by Östgaard [16]. However, since we have no baseline in direct reports on 'what really happened' on which this can be tested we shall proceed in a different direction. Our problem is how the factors relate to each other in producing a final outcome.

Imagine that all factors, for the sake of simplicity, are dichotomized so that an event either possesses them or does not possess them. A given event can receive a score from $0-12$ according to this system, and we claim that this is as good a score of that elusive concept of 'newsworthiness' as any, in a culture where F_8-F_{12} are valid. This has two theoretical implications that will be spelt out. The first one is almost too simple to mention:

Additivity hypothesis: The higher the total score of an event, the higher the probability that it will become news, and even make headlines.

This may be seen as a hypothesis about how journalists work, about how the night editor reacts to incoming newsscript or about how the reader reacts when he scans his newspaper for something worth reading. It may be more valid in the first two than in the last case — we do not know. But it is interesting to put down some pairs that should be considered particularly newsworthy:

(9, 10): *news about elite people in elite nations* [17].

(9, 12): *news of a negative nature relating to elite nations — in other words, big power conflict*

(10, 12): *news of a negative nature relating to elite people — in other words, struggle for power etc., at the top of society*

(11, 12): *news of a negative nature relating to persons — in other words, scandals.*

It is hardly necessary to make a content analysis to substantiate the claim that these four categories account for a sizeable fraction of the news presented by newspapers in most parts of the world.

But there is another hypothesis that is less trivial. An event obviously does not have to score 12 to hit the headlines. Imagine the floor level for acceptance is at score 6, which can be obtained in $\binom{12}{6} = 924$ different ways. (This high number, by the way, explains why factors may be operating and still not be noticed by the public: the variety is too great). The implication of this is only that if the event is low on one dimension or factor *it may compensate for that by being high on another*, and still make the news. For instance, the less an event refers to persons as actors the more negative will it have to be (earthquakes, accidents that are presented in terms of technical errors, not in terms of 'the human factor'). The more culturally close and hence meaningful the event, the less does it have to refer to elite people — and vice versa: the more culturally distant the event, the more should it refer to elite people, *ceteris paribus* (which corresponds to the impression that rank-and-file people are highly under-reported when they live in far away countries). And so on, and so forth: this will be spelt out in section 5 below.

Since we have 12 factors this principle gives rise to $\binom{12}{2} = 66$ hypotheses, all of the following form:

Complementarity hypothesis:

$\mathrm{F_i} \overset{\longrightarrow}{\underset{\longleftarrow}{}} \mathrm{F_j}, \; i \neq j; \; i, \, j = 1, \, 2 \ldots \ldots \ldots \ldots 12$

The reasoning is always the same; if an event is low on F_i, then it will have to be high on some F_j to make news at all. For a low F_i the probability that any F_i is high is greater than for a high F_i — since a high F_j has already contributed towards the total score. According to the additivity hypothesis there will also be news where both are high, and much prominence will be given to them. But events where both are low will not be admitted as news.

Thus, for the simple case of two factors only, F_i and F_j, we have the three kinds of events indicated in Table 4.2.

TABLE 4.2 *A trichotomy of events according to newsworthiness*

	F_i	F_j	Score of news-worthiness
Type 1. *Prominent news*	high	high	2
Type 2. *Ordinary*	high	low	1
	low	high	
Type. 3. *Events, not news*	low	low	0

The additivity hypothesis focuses on type 1 and the complementarity hypothesis on type 2 — one might then add the obvious *exclusion hypothesis* that would focus on type 3.

We then turn to the presentation of our data and to a systematic testing and discussion of a selection of the hypotheses mentioned.

3. The data

We have selected four Norwegian newspapers, three international crises, and for each crisis a number of variables to use in the content analysis of what the newspapers wrote about the crises. The rationales behind our selections are as follows.

3.1. The newspapers

Newspapers play an important role in Norway [18] and appear in a relatively decentralized pattern. However, when it comes to foreign news only newspapers in the bigger cities would give sufficient coverage to merit a content analysis, and particularly the newspapers in the capital, Oslo. They are 10 in number, and we have selected 4 according to Table 4.3.

No. I is the government paper, no. II the afternoon paper of the widest circulation, no. III a conservative paper and no. IV a conservative afternoon paper, of tabloid format. Apart from the conservative morning paper

TABLE 4.3 *The newspapers in the sample, and their average circulation*

		Morning				Afternoon		
Radical		I				II		
	1960	67,494	1964	67,000	1960	98,352	1964	95,000
Conservative		III				IV		
	1960	21,204	1964	16,800	1960	37,040	1964	38,000

circulation figures have been constant during the period. As usual the morning papers are considered more 'serious', and indeed are, at least in terms of lay-out, use of headlines and vocabulary — this holds true for the radical as well as for the conservative press. But these political terms are generic terms and do not imply that the papers in the same category follow the same party line [19].

The reason for this particular choice lies in the experimental design we obtain: by means of the two axes in the Table we get a sufficient dispersion to provide a setting for replication. A finding that holds true for all four papers will receive a higher degree of confirmation when the papers are different than when they are similar [20].

3.2. The crises

We have selected three crises, and according to a very simple experimental design. We wanted both synchronic and diachronic comparisons to check for consistency in the way news was presented in the four Norwegian papers. For that reason two crises were selected that occurred simultaneously and otherwise were roughly comparable: the Congo and Cuba crises in the summer of 1960. In 1964 a third crisis occurred that had some of the same characteristics, viz. the Cyprus crisis, and we decided to give it the same kind of analytical treatment. Obviously none of the three crises have very definite points of initiation and termination, so we had to select more or less arbitrary cutting points. For the Congo and Cuba these cuts were made so as to coincide almost with the month of July 1960, which will be remembered as a rather conflict-laden one. For Cyprus the month of March and the first half of April 1964 were included. In three appendices we have given chronological surveys of what happened in the three areas during the periods mentioned, according to *Keesing's Contemporary Archives*. We do not claim that they represent well-defined chapters in the books about these crises —nor is that in any sense essential for our purpose.

It may be objected that these three crises are much too special to give a basis for assessing the structure of foreign news, and we would agree with that assertion. On the other hand, the three crises contain elements of particular interest and relevance in the current world situation. The conflicts are acted out in theaters remote from the elite northwestern corners of the world — but with traditional powers in that corner deeply involved — Belgium, France, USA, Britain. In all three cases world conflicts, both of the East-West and the North-South variety, are superimposed on local conflicts or vice versa: local conflicts develop from world conflicts. The UN intervened in the Congo and Cyprus conflicts and not in the Cuba conflict. In short, many elements of the contemporary international situation are present. In addition the conflicts are so similar that roughly the same analytical scheme can be used so as to obtain comparability.

3.3. The variables

The 'unit of analysis' is the press cutting as defined by the newspaper itself when it typographically sets a unit apart from its surroundings, such as a news story, an editorial, an article (reportage, interview) or a letter to the editor — to quote the categories we have used. The contextual unit is the newspaper itself, which means that for all units we have two kinds of variables: contextual variables referring to the newspaper (its name, party color, date, etc.), and proper variables that refer to the unit itself. These variables may again be subdivided into variables that apply to the cutting as a whole (its presentation in the newspaper, its length, its 'type' as above, the source in terms of press agency, person quoted, etc.) and variables that apply to what is written. As to the latter we have worked with a list of items and coded a unit according to the presence or absence of these items.

More specifically we have been interested in:

1. *Nation*	underdog (colony)		topdog (motherland)			
2. *People*	top leader	elite	rank-and-file			no people
3. *Perspective*	East-West	East-colony	West-colony	motherland-colony	UN-colony	intra-colony
4. *Mode*	negative	positive			neutral	(both or neither)
5. *Focus*	economic	political			social	cultural

We have used the generic terms 'underdog-colony' and 'topdog-motherland' for, respectively, Congo-Cuba-Cyprus (Greek or Turkish) on the one hand and Belgium/France-US-Britain/Greece/Turkey on the other. The terms denote a difference in rank and a dependence relationship that is basic to the crises — and nothing else. As can be seen at a glance the list covers some but certainly not all of the factors we are interested in, according to the theory — nevertheless they can be brought to bear on a number of the hypotheses.

Let us then give in Table 4.4 a brief survey of the nature of our data.

TABLE 4.4 *Survey of the press cuttings coded,* %

Paper	Congo News	Other	(N)	Cuba News	Other	(N)	Cyprus News	Other	(N)
I	89	11	(112)	98	2	(37)	96	4	(171)
II	96	4	(100)	89	11	(43)	88	12	(178)
III	90	10	(103)	88	12	(65)	91	9	(241)
IV	87	13	(108)	93	7	(29)	92	9	(75)
Total	91	9	(423)	91	9	(174)	91	9	(665)

Although it makes little sense to pool the data from the four newspapers — the sample is made for replication and not for estimation — unless they can be shown to be sufficiently homogeneous, it is interesting to see that 91 % of the cuttings are news messages in all three cases. Thirty-six units were editorials (divided 23—4—9 on the three crises) and there were 58 articles etc. (divided 25—8—25). But out of a total of 1,262 pieces this means 3 % and 5 % respectively — and the number of letters to the editor was less than 1 % of the total. Although we shall certainly not neglect this 9 % in the total picture we nevertheless feel justified in focusing the analysis of what was written in these four papers on the news items.

And this brings us to our main justification in presenting these data at all, the answer to the obvious 'Who cares about four Norwegian papers in the world? — at most half a million Norwegians'. We are concerned with who has transmitted the news and for each unit we have put down the press agency or agencies quoted as a sources (Table 4.5).

The Table substantiates what we are after: the sources of the news in these Norwegian newspapers — among the most important politically — are international. 'Own correspondent' is quite insignificant as a category, which is not strange, taking into consideration the economy of Norwegian newspapers and the distance to these particular theaters.

This means, briefly, that foreign press agencies account for about 95 % of the news items about these three crises, and the news items account for 91 % of the total number of units appearing in these papers about these crises. That, in turn, means that four foreign press agencies take care of 95 % of 91 %, or about 87 %, of the total — which again means that Norwegians, *in casu*, are rather dependent for their images of how the international system functions on the quality and quantity of news delivered through these agencies [22].

133

TABLE 4.5 *The distribution of the news messages on the press agencies*, %*

	Congo	Cuba	Cyprus
Associated Press (AP)	12	20	9
United Press International (UPI)	20	17	17
Reuters	31	22	52
Agence France-Presse (AFP)	19	15	24
Norsk Telegrambyrå (NTB) [21]	28	20	54
Tass	1	2	0
Others	4	1	4
(N)	(382)	(158)	(612)
Own correspondent	2	1	7**

* Percentages do not add up to 100% since items from different agencies are often pooled together in one unit, and sometimes there is no reference to agency.
** 43 cuttings out of which 37, or 86%, are due to paper II — it had a correspondent in Cyprus and this accounts for 23% of its coverage.

Consequently our study is a study of a part of the foreign news system, using how it impinges on four Norwegian newspapers in three crises as twelve case studies.

4. Testing the hypotheses

We then proceed to tests of the theory of the structure of foreign news with the data we have. All we can do is to exhaust the possibilities our data give for tests of the theory, and we start with:

H_1: *The more distant the nation, the higher the tendency to report elite action.*

If a nation is 'distant', here of course taken in the cultural and not in the geographical sense, identification with rank-and-file people will be correspondingly low. At the same time, to become news, events will have to fulfill some other requirements. We shall first test this hypothesis on the Congo and Cuba crises since here what is close and what is distant is so obvious (Table 4.6).

Reading downwards one would expect decreasing percentage differences according to the hypothesis; each percentage difference should be lower than the preceding ones. This holds in five out of the six cases and gives us a degree of confirmation of 0.84 using that as a criterion. Rank-and-file Americans went underreported in Cuba — and this is certainly understandable if one compares this with the Congo case. There is a difference between

TABLE 4.6. *Distance of nation and rank of people reported,* %

Crisis	Congo			Cuba		
Nation	Congo	Belgium	%diff.	Cuba	USA	% diff.
Top leader	47	15	+32	53	23	+30
Elite	50	40	+10	47	39	+ 8
Common people	30	35	— 5	24	6	+18
(N)		(158)			(382)	

nationalizing industrial enterprises and open conflict: the former is more abstract and does not give rise to the same amount of stories about women and children, for instance.

Let us then turn to the data from Cyprus. They are complicated by two factors. First of all, we do not at all have a clear pattern with two parties to the conflict, as between the Congo and Belgium and between Cuba and USA in July 1960. At least five parties are involved at three levels of dominance. At the bottom there is the conflict between Greek Cypriots and Turkish Cypriots. Related to either and at an intermediate level is the conflict between Greece and Turkey, partly over Cyprus, partly over anything else that can be added. Above that level again looms Britain and other big powers, but we have concentrated on Britain because of her past as a colonial power in Cyprus and her present as the holder of major airforce bases on the island. Thus, there is no clear bipolar pattern here as in the other two cases, with clear foci of identification [23].

Secondly, the ethnical dimension is harder to apply. Greeks and Greek Cypriots, Turks and Turkish Cypriots are hardly very different relative to, say, Norwegians, although the Greeks are probably somewhat more familiar. But Britain can be set apart relative to the other four.

The data in Table 4.7 are quite interesting and confirm more or less everything we have said, with one important proviso: The British are the only case where there is a clear increase in the percentage of reporting as we move down the social ladder.

TABLE 4.7. *Distance of group and rank of people reported, Cyprus,* %

	Greek Cypriots	Turkish Cypriots	Greeks	Turks	British
Top leader	30	7	11	13	5
Elite	4	4	6	5	12
Common people	40	34	6	9	15
(N)		(612)			

This is in agreement with the hypothesis of closest identification with the UK since none of the other four percentage-sets have a correspondingly clear and monotone pattern. But if we look at the rest an interesting suspicion emerges: that there has been more identification with the Turks than with the Greeks. Although the differences are small they are there: the common people/top leader ratio is 1.3 for the Greek Cypriots and 4.9 for the Turkish Cypriots, 0.6 for the Greeks and 0.8 for the Turks. Of course, the over-reporting of Makarios may be explained on such bases as the fact that he was well known from the fight against the British and that he, not the Turkish minority leader Dr. Kutchuk is the President of Cyprus. Nevertheless, there is the suspicion of differential identification built into the structure of the news. This is not a part of the hypothesis, however, since cultural distance can hardly be said to be a factor here. But it is nevertheless consistent with what was reported by one Norwegian with special insight into the area, as to British and Turkish views and perspectives being favored in general in the Norwegian press [24].

A particular way of looking at this hypothesis is by counting the number of times people are *quoted* in the news. To many readers it will be obvious that common people are quoted in only 2 of the 612 cuttings from the Cyprus crisis, to take one example (more frequently in the Congo news where relative identification with the Belgians was stronger). The elite and the top leaders are very frequently quoted and in general the ratio between cuttings where people are mentioned with quotes and mentioned without quotes decreases rapidly with decreasing rank. This, then, is one more factor of identification that favors the elite.

These general findings were checked for newspapers and stood up against the test — the finding is replicated.

After the relationship between distance of nation and rank of the person reported we turn to the relationship between what we have called 'mode' of reporting and rank of persons reported. We have coded for each cutting whether it reports something 'negative' (something is destroyed, disrupted, torn down) or something 'positive' (something is built up, constructed, put together) and we are interested in knowing, for each of our three rank levels where people are concerned, whether they are seen in a context that is negative or positive (we omit the cuttings where the event-context is coded as 'neutral', 'both' or 'neither'). The obvious hypothesis to be deduced from the complementarity principle is

H_2: *The lower the rank of the person, the more negative the event.*

We tested this hypothesis not only within each crisis but also for each country or nationality, which gives a total of nine cases (Cuba, the US, the Congo,

Belgium, Greek Cypriot, Turkish Cypriot, Greece, Turkey, Britain). For each case we had three ranks (top leader, elite, rank-and-file) and for each rank the event could be either negative or positive since we discarded all cuttings that were not clear. To arrive at a composite measure − 1 was given to a negative cutting and + 1 to a positive one, and the average 'mode' was computed. Thus, with 80 negative cuttings and 35 positive we would get:

$$\frac{-80 + 35}{80 + 35} = \frac{-45}{115} = -0.39.$$

In general the index ranges from − 1 to + 1, but the limits were hardly attained; the news was almost never completely one-colored.

The data are given in Table 4.8.

TABLE 4.8 *Rank of the person and mode of the event*

	Top leader	Elite people	Common people
1. Cuba	—0.66	—0.51	—0.59
2. USA	—0.91	—0.72	—1.0
3. Congo	—0.39	—0.45	—0.47
4. Belgium	—0.08	—0.33	—0.45
5. Greek Cypriots	+0.16	—0.20	—0.38
6. Turkish Cypriots	+0.13	—0.43	—0.47
7. Greece	+0.21	—0.10	0.20
8. Turkey	—0.26	—0.18	—0.38
9. Britain	+0.39	—0.20	—0.33

Out of the nine cases the hypothesis is clearly confirmed in cases nos. 3, 4, 5, 6, 7 and 9; which means in 6 of the 9 cases. In the other three the trend from 'elite' to 'common people' is as it should be, but the three top leaders are seen in a more negative context than one would predict from the theory. Two of these cases, nos. 1 and 2, concern Cuba-US relations, which were then in a very critical phase with both top leaders declaring negative actions against one another in an escalating sequence. The third case has to do with the Turkish top leader who in that period used a language characterized by threats and invasion menaces (see Appendix III). However, any exception from the rule can always be 'explained' away by invoking some special circumstances, so we shall be satisfied by noticing that out of a total of 27 numerical relationships (three for each case) 23, or 85%, are in the expected direction, i.e. increasingly negative with decreasing rank. This is high even though the 27 relationships are not independent.

The general finding was checked for newspaper and for press agency and stood up well against that additional source of variation.

Thus, we have been brought a step forward towards the idea that common people have to appear or be presented in a negative context to make news, much more than is the case for people higher up — relatively speaking. It may well be that the total volume of negative events reported in connection with elite people — whether happening to them or having them as causes — is higher, due to the elite concentration reported above. But the proportion of negative events relative to the total number of contexts is higher the lower down in society the news comes from. Or, in other words, where positive events are reported they will be more likely to occur as contexts for an elite person than as something surrounding the common man.

However, one thing is context, another thing is who is seen as the cause of the event. According to our hypothesis one would expect the same pattern if the news stories are analyzed for their tendency to attribute causes to somebody, and this is what we actually get, as Table 4.9 shows.

TABLE 4.9 *Rank of causal agent of an event and the mode of the event**

	Yule correlation Q	Percentage difference	% negative in the news from the group
1. Cuba	1.0	21	79
2. USA	1.0	4	96
3. Congo	0.47	15	91
4. Belgium	0.46	18	76
5. Greek Cypriots	0.80	44	65
6. Turkish Cypriots	1.0	25	94
7. Cypriots, not specified	0.93	51	87
8. Greece	0.76	40	86
9. Turkey	0.57	18	90
10. Britain	0.57	27	67

* Top leader and elite have been pooled.

Thus, the hypothesis is confirmed in 10 out of 10 cases: the lower the rank of the causal agent, the lower also the chance that he is seen in a context of something positive happening.

From here we may turn to the next hypothesis, thus completing the triangle we have made of variables:

H_3: *The more distant the nation, the more negative the event.*

The data in Table 4.9 are relevant for the hypothesis and do not appear to give any clear pattern of confirmation. We have used the data about causal agents only, not the data where a nation may also appear as the victim of a negative act. As can be seen the British, as a total, with the three rank categories pooled, appear as the causes of negative events less frequently than do the others, with the exception of the Greek Cypriots. Correspondingly, the Belgians are causes of negative events less than the Congolese. But the US are producers of negative acts more than the Cubans. One reason may be that negative acts were not actually seen as negative by the agencies reporting them, often AP and UPI — but as adequate reactions in a situation of intense conflict.

It should be kept in mind that although the material includes all news from the Congo, Cuba and Cyprus in the periods of analysis, this is not the case with the 'mother countries': Belgium, the USA, the UK, Greece, and Turkey. News from those places which has no relevance to the areas of crisis has appeared in the papers in addition to the coded items. (Just to mention one example: the death and funeral of King Paul of Greece took place in the middle of March, causing Greece to appear quite heavily in the news stories for a week.) In the case of culturally close countries like the UK, the USA and Belgium, a great variety of news stories reaches the papers every day, regardless of major events. This would serve to balance off the negative impression these countries give as partners in the colonial crises analyzed. Nevertheless we do not feel that H_2 has been confirmed, although it has not been disconfirmed either.

Another way of looking at these data now is to ask the question: Cuba, the Congo and Cyprus are far away places, they are 'culturally distant' (factor $F_{4.1}$). How do the events come to be represented at all as news? Because they are made 'relevant' (factor $F_{4.2}$). Thus we get the hypothesis

H_4: *The more culturally distant the theater, the more relevant must the event appear to be.*

Unfortunately, we do not have data from theaters with a wide range in cultural distance, but we can get some idea about the validity of this hypothesis in Table 4.10 from the distribution of the news stories on what might be called the 'perspective'.

A purely cold-war perspective involving East and West alone has not been made much use of, but East and West reappear in their relations with the 'colony', thus increasing relevance by linking the conflict to the East-West system. Most important, of course, is the 'motherland-colony' perspective, appearing in more than half of all the news stories. It may be said that this was what the conflicts were about, but that is not so obvious. There are many ways of presenting an event, and particularly many ways of presenting what to many appeared as fights for independence.

TABLE 4.10 *Location of the theater and perspective of the news story,* %

| Crisis | Relations between | | | | | | (N) |
	East-West	East-'colony'	West-'colony'	Motherland-'colony'	UN 'colony'	Intra-'colony'	
Cuba	9	35	22	59	9	20	(158)
Congo	9	20	20	52	41	36	(382)
Cyprus	0	4	8	54	59	29	(612)

Thus, nationalization of industries, independence of a new nation and the fight between a majority and a minority might all have been presented as fairly internal events with local actors only and the 'motherland' appearing more as a constant condition that could be mentioned in, perhaps, 10% of the stories. But this would have presupposed a much higher degree of identification, up to the level one probably had in the newspapers from the Congo, Cuba and Cyprus during those periods. Instead, events are seen as unfolding themselves in the periphery of the 'motherland' with no real local autonomy. The 'colonies' are not causally self-sufficient. News stories that have an 'intra-colony' perspective exist, but there are two simple explanations for that. The first one is in terms of F_{12} — the idea that events will have to be negative — and simply refers to the fact that in both the Congo and Cyprus local conflict is at the root of the 'crisis'. Even under this condition, however, the local conflict is not enough: some familiar groupings, such as the East, the West, the motherland, the UN, have to be added to it to make it really newsworthy. And the other explanation is in terms of F_7: since the theater is already in the news it will probably remain in the news because an apparatus has been established that requires a certain quantity of news stories to be maintained.

That there are explanations of the *mechanism* underlying this in terms of such factors as the nationality of the press agencies and the training of some of the journalists, whether they are foreign or local by nationality, is obvious. Thus, one would expect the news from Cyprus to be much concerned with events seen as relevant to Britain, since the British agency Reuters appears in connection with 52% of the news stories. One consequence of this is found in the circumstance that Cyprus is seen in its relationship to Britain in 31% of the stories, which is a high percentage if one conceives of the conflict as essentially limited to the Greece-Turkey-Cyprus triangle.

There is another way of testing the hypothesis, taking as in Table 4.11 the focus of the news story as point of departure.

The figures are quite clear and tell the kind of story one would predict: the three countries in the world periphery enter by way of variables that

TABLE 4.11 *Location of the theater and focus of the news story,* %

Crisis	Focus Economic	Political	Social	Cultural	(N)
Cuba	63	56	0	1	(158)
Congo	13	86	11	2	(382)
Cyprus	10	95	1	0	(612)

link them to the center part of the world. 'Social' and 'cultural' are more internal and do not have the same immediate ramifications to the topdog nations. The only variation in the focus is from economic to political as one moves from Cuba via the Congo situation to Cyprus, and that corresponds well to most images of 'what really happened'.

Again, the findings hold up against the variation in newspaper and press agency. We let this suffice as an indication of how hypotheses derived from the complementarity theory can be tested.

It may be objected that what we have said is an artefact of the three crises we have picked for our sample. There is no other way of exploring this objection than by means of a new project.

5. Discussion

On the basis of what we have presented we feel that it would be unreasonable not to have some confidence in the general hypothesis. There is probably such a phenomenon as *complementarity of news factors* although much remains to be done in terms of refinement of the hypothesis. Under what conditions will the effect be more pronounced or less pronounced; which pairs of factors tend to produce the strongest (or the weakest) effect of complementarity; how do the factors combine in patterns of three and four, etc.? We leave this for future research, and turn to a discussion of what this implies — under the assumption of the general validity of our thesis.

A discussion of this kind can best be done by selecting out of the 66 possible pairs some crucial pairs that are particularly important in terms of their consequences for the kind of image of the world that they will promote. The numbers refer to the list of twelve factors. These hypotheses are bivariate only, and coming research in this field will have to carry the thinking and the analysis up to, at least, the level of three variables or factors at the same time.

(1,4): *The more distant a nation is, the more will an event have to satisfy the frequency criterion.*

In other words: the distant nation will have to produce events that capture attention particularly easily in order to be recorded. The consequence of this is an abruptness and unconnectedness that the news from such countries will display. Natural disasters and accidents will play an important role, and changes of government. The build-up of events, based on small quantitative changes, will go underreported — it is only when they lead to the big qualitative changes that they make news. This again may provide readers with an image of these countries as places where things happen all of a sudden and in an unpredictable way — in other words inherently dangerous and inherently different places.

(4,3): *The more distant an event, the less ambiguous will it have to be.*
The remote and the strange will at least have to be simple if they are to make news — complexities can be taken care of if they are found within one's own culture, but not if they are found at a considerable distance. The implication of that is obvious! The culturally distant acquires a presentation in terms of 'ideal types'; whole nations and continents are described in sweeping terms and this may leave the impression of a uniformity and homogeneity that is not present in the reality of that nation. One's own nation is described in complex terms which will correspond more to the idea most people have of a 'civilized existence'. On the other hand, the phenomenon indicated here will tend to foster the idea of a simple, primitive and more 'human' kind of existence in remote countries.

(4,5): *The more distant the nation, the more consonant will the news have to be.*
For a far away nation to make news it will be particularly necessary that the news should fit a pattern of expectation. Thus the *golpe militar* in Latin America, according to this hypothesis, will make news exactly because that is what is expected — it is a case of news being 'olds'. The opposite development will not so easily fit the expectation pattern and for that reason less easily be reported, because probably it will, consciously or unconsciously, be registered as a quasi-event that will not last. Any story of sexual extremism from Sweden will receive an *a priori* credibility that will make it pass many filters of news communication, whereas stories or statistics to the opposite effect may be seen as atypical or even fake and propaganda, and not be reported. The consequence of this will be that distant nations appear as essentially unchangeable whereas one's own cultural sphere undergoes real, basic change.

(7,2): *The higher the continuity effect, the lower can the threshold be.*
We only list this hypothesis for the sake of completeness, for it is actually

the definition of the continuity effect. Once an event has 'made it' the news channel will be more readily open for the follow-up events, at a lower threshold value. The effect of this will be the creation of 'news strings' that may create artificial continuities just because the channel is open.

(8,2): *The higher the composition effect, the lower can the threshold be.* This is also listed for the sake of completeness, since it is already included in the definition of the composition effect. The idea is simply that news can enter because of underrepresentation of categories that should be represented according to some overall judgment — not because they are important by themselves. This, in turn, means that in periods where little else happens abroad the limit defining newsworthiness may be drastically lowered so as to include news items that score relatively low, and this in turn may produce images of discontinuity that do not correspond to the real world.

(1,12): *The less negative the news, the more important the frequency con-*
dition.
This is already referred to in connection with the theory for the negativism of the news. But here it is put in a stronger form: positive events will have to be particularly short of duration to appear as news. This means, essentially, that a premium will be put on the ability to make ceremonies where developments can be telescoped into an event that is reportable. Obviously the more elite people can be added to it the better for the newsworthiness, and this has a double effect. First of all it may contribute to a false image of how positive developments come about, since the amount of planning and painstaking work, mostly and in most cases by non-elite people, goes underreported. Secondly it forces many people into a kind of activity usually referred to as P.R. — public relations — that is often accepted as a part of their work, where one might question the wisdom of the structure of the news communication instead.

(9,4): *The lower the rank of the nation, the lower must the cultural dis-*
tance be.
This only means that if a nation is low in terms of rank it must compensate for that in terms of proximity. Or, in other words: the topdog nations of the world will each have their own set of underlings that they overreport from, relative to what they report from other low rank nations. For the US it will be Latin America; for France, Communauté Française; for Britain, the Commonwealth countries; for the Soviet Union, the socialist bloc; for China, (probably) selected countries in South and Far East Asia. This pattern, in turn, will tend to reinforce existing divisions of the world since reporting will probably make for some kind of identification.

(9,5): *The lower the rank of the nation, the more consonant will the news have to be.*

This is very similar to the hypothesis of the relationship between distance and consonance — but whereas that hypothesis emphasized consonance with what one would expect from more or less stereotyped conceptions of a foreign culture, we are here concerned with stereotypes about low rank. The typical example would be news that emphasizes the difficulties low rank nations have: signs of 'immaturity' in terms of payment crises, political instability, murder at the top of society, etc. The consequences are the same as for hypothesis (4,5) above.

(10,6): *The lower the rank of the person, the more unexpected will the news have to be.*

This has actually been touched upon in different contexts already and the idea is simply that whereas elite people can have their day-to-day routine reported, rank-and-file people will only make news when something happens that stands in a very marked contrast to their ordinary existence. The good examples are sudden acquisitions of wealth and negative actions.

(9,10): *The lower the rank of the nation, the higher will a person have to be placed in that nation to make news.*

This may lead to an image of the world underdog nations as extremely elite-dominated with a non-existing mass of rank-and-file people. In political terms this image will probably tend to reinforce the conditions that make such images warranted. This will also make for poor identification particularly if elite action in low rank nations is also negative.

(9,12): *The lower the rank of the nation, the more negative will the news from that nation have to be.*

In other words, when something positive and good is happening it will have to be located in a high ranking nation — from the underdog nations of the world, typically, news reports will be overwhelmingly negative. The Latin American proverbial case of the *golpe militar* is one example; all the disaster news from such nations is another. The thesis is that positive things that happen in the underdog countries will go under-reported and this will promote an image of those countries as being unable to govern themselves, and as inherently inferior to the topdog countries.

(10,12): *The lower the rank of a person, the more negative will his actions have to be.*

In other words, the thesis is that common people must do something negative to make news, and the lower down the person is, the more negative should it be. At the bottom of society one enters the news pages more easily as a cri minal — but sport should of course be mentioned as the big compensating m echanism. It may also be regarded as so important, together with the arts and entertainment, that it actually invalidates the hypothesis. Nevertheless, the kind of positive action the rank-and-file person has it in his power to perform is, perhaps, more likely to be of a kind that will never make the news — not only for the reason mentioned in the hypothesis but because it does not satisfy the criteria of frequency, threshold, unexpectedness and continuity either. If the ordinary man is to enter positively, it will probably have to be in an article, reportage, etc. It may be objected that he enters when he wins in the lottery — but this is not an act of his — it happens to him, like a catastrophe. The implication of all this may easily be a kind of reinforcement of class society in the sense that the top is overrepresented with the good and the positive that occurs, and the lower layers of society are portrayed as producers of less fortunate events·

(11,12): *The less personal the news, the more negative will it have to be.* In other words, when something positive happens it is more likely to be attributed to people, whereas something attributed to non-people will have to be negative to hit the news. In a sense this may also be seen as a reflection of the dominant idea of man as the maker of his own progress against the forces of nature that tend to inundate him with floods, shake him to pieces with earthquakes, etc.

It may be worth while to collect together what has been said about nations that are culturally distant and nations that are low in international rank [25]. We can combine it because what we have said should *a fortiori* be valid when these two criteria — negative for newsworthiness — are superimposed on each other. In short, from such countries news will have to refer to people, preferably top elite, and be preferably negative and unexpected but nevertheless according to a pattern that is consonant with the 'mental pre-image'. It will have to be simple and it should, if possible, provide the reader with some kind of identification — it should refer to him or his nation or group of nations. This will, in turn, facilitate an image of these countries as dangerous, ruled by capricious elites, as unchanging in their basic characteristics, as existing for the benefit of the topdog nations, and in terms of their links to those nations. Events occur, they are sudden, like flashes of lightning, with no build-up and with no let-down after their occurrence — they just occur and more often than not as a part of the machinations of the ruling or opposition elites.

The consequence of all this is an image of the world that gives little autonomy to the periphery but sees it as mainly existing for the sake of the

145

center — for good or for bad — as a real periphery to the center of the world. This may also tend to amplify more than at times might seem justified the image of the world's relatedness. Everything's relevance for everything else, particularly for us, is overplayed. Its relevance to itself disappears:

> Mr. Mboya complained of the Press (foreign-owned) in Africa behaving and writing as though it were operating in London, Paris or New York 'where the problems and anxieties are entirely different from those current in Africa'. He said these and many other questions kept coming up in the minds of many Africans as they try to figure out what freedom of the press meant in the African context. He was of the view, therefore, that it was important that the Press should concern itself with finding out what goes on in the African mind. The world's verdict on Africa, however, was often reduced from subjective dispatches of foreign journalists paying short visits to the various parts of Africa. The result was that news coming out of Africa was often related to the already biased and prejudiced mind that keeps asking such questions as: 'is this pro-East or pro-West?' but nobody asked: 'is this pro-African?' [26].

This is particularly dramatic in connection with new countries. Their newness, which is probably the major fact for the majority of their inhabitants, is not stressed except as reports from the independence ceremony if there is any (because it satisfied F_1). Instead the news is interpreted in a context of the old, and since all three countries were centers of major events in the periods we have analyzed, they have probably for many people come to be defined for some time through these crises. This, in turn, may influence people's behavior towards the nations in question, and if they are very young nations serve as a kind of imprinting experience [27], with the consequences that implies for later relationships. It would be interesting to know something more precise about how far behind political independence what one might call causal independence (or auto-causation, causal autonomy) is lagging.

As to the developed countries the general implication of the above has already been mentioned: conflict will be emphasized, conciliation not [28].

6. Some policy implications

The policy implications of this article are rather obvious: try and counteract all twelve factors. More specifically, this means:

1. More emphasis on build-up and background material in the total media output. Journalists should be better trained to capture and report on long-term development, and concentrate less on 'events'.

146

2. Occasional reports on the trivial even if it does not make 'news', to counterbalance the image of the world as composed of strings of dramatic events.

3. More emphasis on complex and ambiguous events, not necessarily with any effort to interpret them.

4. More reports from culturally distant zones even if the content has no immediate relevance for oneself. Experiments with newspapers in different countries exchanging local columns might prove even more interesting than reprinting what was said in the newspaper fifty or a hundred years ago.

5. More emphasis on the dissonant, on that which does not fit stereotypes. Training of journalists to increase their insights into their own stereotypes so as to facilitate their awareness of the consonance factor.

6. More emphasis given to the predictable and frequent, for the same reason as under 2 above.

7. More awareness of the continuity factor — and at the same time more emphasis on follow-ups even if the chain of events has been interrupted for some time. Often one has the impression that one hears about something negative that has happened but not about how it has been counteracted, if the time-span is so long that the continuity has been broken.

8. More awareness of the composition factor in order not to create news artefacts.

9. More coverage of non-elite nations.

10. More coverage of non-elite people.

11. More reference to non-personal causes of events. Special training is probably needed here.

12. More reference to positive events.

These implications work on one factor at a time and would, if implemented, reduce the effects of the factors. However, the combined effects of the factors might still persist even if the effect of any one factor is reduced.

One might say that all or much of this is what the elite paper tries to do, and that is probably true. However, elite papers are probably mainly read by elite people and this may increase the distance between center and periphery where international perspective is concerned.

Hence one additional need is for a more widely dispersed style of news communication in agreement with these principles. It should be emphasized, however, that the present article hypothesizes rather than demonstrates the presence of these factors, and that these factors, if present, will have certain effects among the audience.

Appendix I

A short chronological survey of events in Cuba, July 1960. (From *Keesing's Contemporary Archives*)

29/6 The Cuban Government confiscates Texaco's oil refineries.

1/7   The Cuban Government confiscates Esso's and Shell's oil refineries because all the refineries had refused to refine Soviet crude oil.

5/7   British protest against the confiscation of the Shell refinery. United States reduces its import of Cuban sugar by 700,000 tons.

6/7   American protest against the confiscation of the Texaco and Esso refineries.

8/7   The Cuban Government refuses to accept the protests, referring to the obligation of the refineries to refine any crude oil. Dr. Miro Cardona requests political asylum in the USA.

10/7 The Government of the USSR announces that it will buy 700,000 tons of Cuban sugar in addition to its usual quota.

11/7 The Cuban foreign minister accuses the USA of 'economic aggression', in the UN Security Council.

18—19/7 Debate in the Security Council concerning US-Cuban relations. Decided to hand the matter over to the OAS before any UN steps are taken.

17—21/7 Raoul Castro visits the Soviet Union.

23/7 The Cuban Government confiscates four US sugar refineries. Trade agreement between Cuban and China concerning a yearly sale of 500,000 tons of Cuban sugar for five years.

Appendix II

A short chronological survey of events in the Congo, July 1960. (From *Keesing's Contemporary Archives*)

30/6—1/7 The Congo independent at midnight. Speeches by King Baudouin, Prime Minister Lumumba and President Kasavubu. Lumumba attacks the Belgian colonial administration.

2/7   Lumumba demands the immediate withdrawal of all Belgian troops from the Congo.

5/7   Mutiny among private Congolese soldiers in Thysville and Leopoldville against their Belgian officers. Lumumba and Kasavubu intervene in order to restore order, but with no great success. The anti-European feelings spread to other provinces.

7/7   Europeans in the Leopoldville province flee to Congo—Brazzaville.

8/7   The Belgian Government announces that troop reinforcements will be sent to the Congo.

10/7 Belgian forces attack Congolese in various places.

11/7 The Congolese Government appeals to UN for assistance. Tshombe declares Katanga an independent state.

14/7 The Security Council adopts a resolution concerning the immediate sending of UN forces to the Congo, and asks Belgium to withdraw its troops. The Congo breaks off diplomatic relations with Belgium.

15/7 The first UN troops arrive in Leopoldville.

17/7 The Congolese Government informs the UN that it will ask for Soviet troops if the UN does not succeed in getting the Belgian troops out of the country within 72 hours.

17/7 Vice-Secretary-General Ralph Bunche reports that an agreement has been reached with the Belgian authorities to withdraw the Belgian troops from Leopoldville.

20/7 Tshombe warns the UN against entering Katanga, states that any support of the central government against Katanga will lead to war between Katanga and the rest of the Congo.

21/7 The Security Council adopts a resolution requesting Belgium to withdraw its troops from the Congo as soon as possible, and which authorizes the Secretary-General to take the necessary steps to execute the resolution. The Belgian Government declares that its troops will stay in the Congo until law and order have been restored.

23/7 Belgian troops entirely withdrawn from Leopoldville.

24/7 Lumumba arrives in New York to confer with Secretary-General Hammarskiöld.

26/7 Hammarskiöld goes to Bruxelles and Leopoldville.

27/7 Hammarskiöld meets Prime Minister Eyskens and King Baudouin in Bruxelles. The Congolese Government issues its political program, stating the wish for cooperation with Belgium and that the foreign policy of the Congolese Government will be characterized by 'positive neutralism'.

28/7 Hammarskiöld arrives in Leopoldville for talks with Kasavubu. The Belgian Government issues a detailed report on atrocities in the Congo. The report estimates the number of raped white women to be 291. Number of killed not given. The number of UN soldiers in the Congo is given as 10,000. The number of refugees from the Congo is officially given in Bruxelles as 35,000.

29/7 The Belgian Government announces that the withdrawal of some of the troops in the Congo will start at once. No information on when all the troops will be withdrawn.

30/7 Announcement after Hammarskiöld's meeting with the Congolese Government that agreement had been reached concerning the task of the UN in the Congo

Appendix III

A short chronological survey of events in Cyprus, December-April 1964. (From *Keesing's Contemporary Archives*)

6/12 President Makarios reportedly sends a memorandum to Vice-President Kutchuk concerning his desire to amend certain provisions of the Constitution, such as the separate majority vote on taxation laws, separate courts of justice, separate municipalities and certain other 'unreasonable rights'.

21—26/12 Communal violence in Cyprus, in which 200 Greek and Turkish Cypriots were believed to have been killed.

25—28/12 Turkish military movements, in and outside Cyprus.

26/12 A joint Greek, Turkish and British force, under British command should restore order. This was accepted by all the governments.

27/12 Cypriot representative in the UN protests to the Security Council.

28/12 The British Colonial Secretary, Mr. Duncan Sandys, arrives in Nicosia for talks with the local leaders.

30/12 Vice-President Kutchuk denounces the protest of the Cypriot UN representative, Mr. Rossides. Since the fighting the Turkish Cypriot ministers had refused to attend meetings of the Cabinet, which in consequence had become representative only of the Greek Cypriot community.

1/1 The Cypriot Government accepts a proposal that a UN representative should be stationed in Cyprus.

16/1 General Gyani appointed UN representative in Cyprus.

15/1 A conference in London to decide the future government of Cyprus, attended by the Greek and Turkish Foreign Ministers, Greek Cypriot and Turkish Cypriot delegations, and chaired by Mr. Duncan Sandys, UK. The conference ended in deadlock towards the end of the month.

31/1 An Anglo-American plan for a NATO emergency force to be placed in Cyprus, including the Greek and Turkish forces already on the island.

1/2 The Greek and Turkish Governments accept the proposals.

2/2 Vice-President Kutchuk accepts the plan in principle.

4/2 President Makarios's Government rejects the plan, while stating that it would accept an international force under the Security Council.

7/2 Premier Khrushchev protests against the planned NATO force.

11—13/2 Heavy fighting in Limassol.

15/2 Requests from the British and Cypriot Governments to the Security Council to consider the situation in Cyprus.

Latter part of February. Greek and Turkish military preparations, threats of intervention.

2/3 Common Turkish-American and Greek navy maneuvers started.

4/3 UN Security Council unanimously approves the formation of an international force and the appointment of a mediator.

4—5/3 Shooting in both Greek-Cypriot and Turkish-Cypriot villages.

6/3 General Gyani appointed leader of the UN forces.

7/3 Secretary-General U Thant asks member governments for voluntary financial contributions to the force.
Hard fighting in the village of Ktima.
Forty-nine Turkish hostages released on Makarios's orders.

8/3 Cease-fire in Ktima after negotiations led by Gyani. 228 Greek hostages released.

9/3 Cease-fire broken.

10/3 Vice-President Kutchuk accuses the Greek-Cypriots of intending to eliminate the Turkish—Cypriot society before the arrival of the UN force.

13/3 About 13,000 Turkish troops embarked at Iskenderun.

14/3 The first part of the Canadian force arrives in Nicosia; the rest to be flown in during the next two weeks.

16/3 A secret meeting of the Turkish Parliament agrees to give the Government permission to start a military intervention in Cyprus if necessary.

25/3 Ambassador Tuomijoja appointed UN mediator in Cyprus.

27/3 The UN force formally established.

31/3 President Makarios informs the Greek and the Turkish Prime Ministers that the formation of a UN force had ended the agreement under which Greek and Turkish military units had served under British command, and requested that these units be withdrawn to their camps.

1/4 Prime Minister Inonu replies that the Turkish troops would not be withdrawn. About $ 5.3 million of contributions promised.

2/4 Tuomijoja arrives in Nicosia.

4/4 President Makarios informs Prime Minister Inonu that Cyprus has ended the alliance treaty with Turkey.

6/4   The Turkish Prime Minister warns Makarios that the Turkish Government regards the treaty as still valid, and will take all necessary steps in case of aggressive actions intended to prevent the Turkish—Cypriot minority exercising its rights.

7/4   The British force in Cyprus reduced to 4,500 soldiers.

8/4   U Thant asks Sweden, Ireland and Finland to increase their forces by 300 soldiers each. Sweden and Finland agree to do so.

11/4   President Makarios arrives in Athens for talks with the Greek Government and with General Grivas.

14/4   Makarios returns to Cyprus.

IV.5 International Air Communication*

PRIO publication No. 5—3/79 and No. 21—11.

Notes on page *694*.

1. Introduction

Why study international air communication? The study of *interaction* need hardly be justified in sociology or international relations. While units or actors are the building-blocks of social structures, the study of interaction is the study of how the blocks fit together into a whole greater than the sum of its parts. International air communications is a good indicator of international interaction patterns. It is *global*, it is *new* (and thus modern and prestigious) but not so new as to be a mere rarity, and it is *unhampered by geographical pecularities* of different regions of the world. Studies of surface communication are handicapped by the lack of comparability between different areas. Rail and road are based on a land connection, ships on a sea connection (even if ferries and canals make such distinctions less absolute) and their integrative value is not simple to compare. Land and sea transport can be combined, but the combination is highly dependent on the development of ports and to trace the links is a formidable task. Not all pieces of land are equally connectable, there are deserts and mountain ranges. The polar caps are largely impenetrable both to land and sea communication. The geography of the earth is so rich in asymmetries and inpediments of various kinds that a single "natural" interaction link on the surface is hard to imagine.

By contrast, air communications should be conditioned mainly by the *motivation* and the *capability* of the actors. This is not to ignore geographical factors, only to rule out the geographical whims of particular areas. No doubt most if not all countries have a limited capacity to overcome the cost involved in interaction at a distance. But a strong motivation to reach out can be a great equalizer relative to distance and thus an indicator of the importance of the link. In fact, this is so important that air communication tends to be a government monopoly or under strong government control, and not only for military reasons. Costs being high and the potential interaction partners many, the choices are so visible and so much an expression of "national interest" that governments cannot stand aside and leave such decisions to the market alone.

In short, our basic assumption is that a study of air communication will give us a purer expression of the international inclinations of all countries, largely unfettered by the hazards of nature and the idiosyncracies of private citizens. Probably much of this could be learnt by studying telecommunication. However, unified data are much less simple to come by and, at least until recently, the difference between telecommunication by land and by sea has made comparison difficult. Possibly the best approach would be to study a long cocktail party for UN ambassadors, each of them free to choose their conversation partners. Apart from the low probability or our being able to organize and observe such an event, the cocktail party would perhaps be *too* unfettered by geographical factors. The topology of the party differs from the globe as we know it. In international air communication the distance factor is present, but manageable — which is basically why we want to explore it.

2. The theory

2.1. The indicator

This paper concentrates on how the airlines link different nations and territories. No consideration will be given to domestic flights, whatever their frequency and importance. Nations will be considered as points on a social map. Busy international airports, such as Los Angeles and New York in the US, or Kano and Lagos in Nigeria, will be considered as one point, whether or not they serve different countries. We shall use only one indicator: the frequency of weekly scheduled passenger flights between all pairs of countries. For the most part we shall use this indicator in a dichotomized form, *whether or not there is at least one weekly scheduled flight*. This indicator, then, tells us whether two countries are *connected*, or not. In characterizing countries in terms of this indicator, we shall speak of the total number of *connections* (i.e. the number of countries to which the country is linked) and *flights* (the total number of flights to these countries). Operational definitions are discussed more carefully in section 3.1 and in several footnotes, as are various problems encountered in the data collection process.

We shall theorize about the possible linkages between nations (in terms of air connections) from the following perspectives: 1) air connections as an intrinsic value; 2) the dependence of interaction in a pair on the total

153

rank of the pair; 3) clique formation on the basis of similarity of traits and of past history; and 4) trends over time. Many predictions will be generated on this basis, and several of them will be tested. The major focus of this paper, however, is on the trends over time.

2.2. Air connections as an intrinsic value

Clearly, we would expect large countries to have more connections than smaller ones. Large populations generate more travel, they create larger markets; this leads to more trade, which in turn leads to more traffic, both of goods and human beings. More wealth means more tourists and leisure travellers. A larger economy can support a national airline geared to the needs of its home country [1]. In turn, the availability of good air (and other transport) networks also stimulates trade and development.

All this is closely related to the expected relationship between interaction and *rank*, to which we shall return in the next section. Here, however, we are more concerned with the 'magic' associated with having a national airline and the availability of good communications. It has been pointed out that national airlines are important status symbols to newly independent states [2]. The establishment of such national airlines, as well as other pressures to maximize communication with the outside world (such as the fact that decisionmaking groups also tend to be frequent guests of the airlines, cf. Gleditsch, 1975), must be expected to stimulate a process of steady growth of airline connections, independently of the other factors to be discussed subsequently.

2.3. Interaction in stratified systems

Sociologists and social psychologists assert that stratification in social systems has effects on the patterns of communication and on interaction in general. Thus, Berelson and Steiner (1964), summing up the literature on social stratification, state the following general propositions [3]:

1. The higher the rank, the more the contact with people of various ranks, and the greater the geographical range of contacts.
2. Organizational memberships are more frequent among the higher classes.

Galtung (1966a) in reviewing the implications of small group studies for international relations, reformulates Berelson and Steiner's propositions concerning face to face interaction in small groups [4]:

3. The higher the rank, the more interaction received and emitted.
4. The more equal the rank between the two, the higher the interaction.
5. There is more interaction from high to low than from low to high.

Elsewhere, Galtung (1966) has called this a *feudal* interaction pattern [5]. He points out the similarity (p. 149) between polarization and 'between-block feudality' (notably in the case of hostile blocks), but also asserts that there will be 'within-block feudality'. If for a moment we disregard the conflict dimension and further take account of the fact that an air connection is a symmetric indicator (eliminating the possibility of distinguishing between topdog to underdog interaction and underdog to topdog interaction) the scheme is simplified somewhat, and we can adopt Galtung's more detailed specification of the hypothesized rank order of interaction frequencies in pairwise terms. For a system with only two ranks (topdog and underdog) this is as follows: TT > TU > UU. By summing up the ranks for the pairs and ordering the pairs according to total rank, we can, of course, generate the same kind of prediction for a system with any number of ranks. In the following we deal with a system of topdogs, middledogs, and underdogs. With three ranks, there are six combinations of ranks, and the prediction of the rank order of interaction frequencies is as shown in Table 5.1.

TABLE 5.1 *Predicted interaction frequencies for all pairs in a system with three ranks. The feudal hypothesis*

1.		TT
2.		TM
3.	MM	TU
4.		MU
5.		UU

We are not making a prediction as to the rank order of MM and TU interaction, since the total rank of these two pairs is the same. However, proposition 4 above (concerning equal rank) would lead to the prediction that MM interaction would outrank TU interaction.

As evidence for the feudal hypothesis in small groups, Galtung cites only one example from work in the Bales tradition [6]. However, as noted by Galtung, a weakness of this example is that there is only one topdog member, and hence no intra-topdog interaction was measurable. A greater weakness is that the ranking is in terms of activity, which makes the outcome somewhat tautologous. In general, research in the Bales tradition is not too applicable to testing the feudal hypothesis, since the groups are small and have only one leader of each type (commonly a task leader and a social/emotional leader) [7].

However, there is also small-group evidence bearing more directly on the feudal hypothesis. Hurwitz, Zander, and Hymovitch (1960) investigated, among other things, interaction patterns in groups where the members had been assigned positions of high and low power (or, in our terms, high and low rank), Controlling for a 'response effect' — i.e. how frequently a recipient communicated to communicator — they obtained the following average interaction frequencies [8]:

High response		Low response	
TT	4.89	TT	1.87
TU	3.66	TU	1.63
UT	3.61	UT	1.14
UU	2.76	UU	0.92

The data fully support the hypothesis of rank dependence. We also note that since this is an asymmetric indicator of interaction we can — and do — confirm hypothesis 3 above, that there is more interaction from high to low than from low to high.

Newcomb, Turner, and Converse (1965) in reviewing these findings and similar results in Newcomb (1961) caution against generalizing to larger communities: 'The ... finding ... that low-status men do not associate with one another ... obviously does not apply to the larger scene of total communities'. They cite Warner et al. (1949) as evidence that association between underdogs is as frequent as association between topdogs. In view of later work in social stratification, as summed up above by Berelson and Steiner, this conclusion appears doubtful, however.

In the international system, considerable support has been found for the feudal hypothesis, notably for the Latin American 20 republics (see Galtung, Schwartzman, and Araujo, 1964; and Schwartzman, 1966); for East-West interaction (Galtung, 1966); and for international organizations (Smoker, 1966, p. 46 ff.).

While there is considerable empirical support, then, for the hypothesis of rank dependent interaction, there is less clarity regarding its theoretical rationale. Hurwitz, Zander, and Hymovitch discuss two theoretical interpretations. *One* is that the underdogs will behave in an ego-defensive manner, and will attempt to reduce uneasiness by tending to like topdogs and to overrate the extent to which topdogs like them. Further, they will communicate infrequently, and when they do, talk mainly to topdogs. The *second* interpretation is that of 'restraint against' the participation of underdogs in groups involving members of unequal status, and an outright expectation that underdogs should not participate too much (a well known phenomenon in the case of children [9]). In the case of nations, it is equally well known that representatives of topdog nations are increasingly irri-

tated that underdog nations at the UN General Assembly and other international parleys 'talk too much' and pass too many resolutions — although
without effective influence. (They are 'over-active deviants' in Bales' terminology [10].)

Newcomb, Turner, and Converse (op. cit.), on the other hand, reason
that in Newcomb's study of a student boarding house, interaction between
unpopular men would be low inside the house, because it would be preferable for these men to interact elsewhere. In total communities there is
no outside social system to interact with. However, as mentioned, we question
the assumption that the total interaction rates of topdogs and underdogs
are in fact the same, although this explanation may account for some of
the difference. — Galtung (1966b, p. 149) briefly refers to 'the common-
sense experience that topdogs ...control their systems and, hence, prefer
interaction patterns consonant with this'. Since the topdog powers exercise
a large influence over interaction generally (through their control over
international shipping and trade, market prices, major airline companies [11],
international news agencies and radio stations, etc.) it is not too far-fetched
to assume that this kind of 'control' could be asserted over the underdogs,
against their will. If, in addition, we assume that the underdogs, to avoid
dissonance, tend to conform to the same pattern, the picture becomes
even more complete.

Finally, let us note that while the Berelson and Steiner propositions
relate rank of an actor to his total interaction, the feudal hypothesis relates
total rank of a pair to amount of interaction in the pair. At first glance
the latter theory may appear more specific. However, if topdogs have more
total interaction than underdogs, it is also reasonable to expect more interaction, the higher the total rank of the pair. Using a probablistic model,
Deutsch and Savage (1960) have developed a formula for 'correcting for' the
size of total interaction by calculating an expected amount of interaction
for each pair and the deviation of the actual from the expected in per
cent of the expected (relative acceptance). Using this indicator, Karl Deutsch
has frequently concluded that between topdog interaction is lower than
'expected', and that e.g. European integration has been stagnating since
ca. 1957—58 [12]. We shall not discuss here the various pros and cons of
this model, except to note that it points out the possibility that the feudal
hypothesis asserts merely that the high-ranking actors have higher total
interactions, plus a chance distribution of the marginals over the pairs
in the interaction matrix [13].

However, even if this is the case it may still be important to look for a
feudal structure as a means of describing the international system, e.g.because
of the *consequences* such a pattern may have. Furthermore, by analyzing
interaction in pairs rather than interaction summed by country, we can

test the influence of other characteristics of the pair, such as geographical proximity and colonial ties [14].

2.4. *Clique formation on the basis of similarity of traits and past history*

It is a well-known proposition that similarity and interaction tend to be positively associated (cf. Homans 1951). One important example of this general rule is the tendency to homogamy in marriage, for which there are at least two theoretical explanations: that liking is an intervening variable, and that persons who are similar are more accessible to each other [15].

There is no reason not to expect the same to hold for nations. Hence, we would expect similarities of a wide range to be relevant for interaction patterns. Similarity of rank has already been mentioned in the preceding section; cultural traits, religion, political systems, etc., are other possibilities. None of these will be discussed systematically in relation to our data. Instead, we shall concentrate on two other types of 'similarity' which seem particularly important: geography, East-West affiliation, and colonial affiliation.

The *relevance of East-West affiliation* to interaction patterns was demonstrated by Galtung (1966 b). The hypothesis of clique formation on the basis of similarity positively favors intra-system interaction. In addition, Galtung points out that polarization and a history of conflict tends to limit intersystem interaction [19].

The same applies to *colonial affiliation*, although here the positive effect of similarity and historical ties is probably more important than polarization between colonial systems, at least in the post-colonial period. It should be noted that by 'colonial affiliation' we mean colonial systems in the broadest sense.

2.5. *The geographical factor*

The relevance of geography to interaction has already been touched on in the introduction. We have argued that air communication, unlike surface communication, is relatively independent of the distinction between land and water and other geographical peculiarities of different regions. For the earliest part of our study, this is not strictly true. In 1930 commercial planes could not cross the Atlantic in scheduled flights, and much less the Pacific. However, these gaps were bridged before the war and other absolute geographical barriers, such as mountain ranges, have also been overcome. The last barrier of this kind, the polar region, was broken with the first truly trans-polar flight in 1957. (There are still no flights across the South Pole, but this is because of the long distances and the weak traffic generating potential of the adjoining countries, not because it represents any great technical challenge).

This is not to say that geographical distance in itself is irrelevant. On the contrary, studies at all levels of human behavior indicate that the distance factor permeates all interaction [16]. Even the global and unified aviation network of today cannot be expected to be independent of distance. Although the most modern planes can fly very long stretches, it is frequently uneconomical to do so.

Flights between contiguous points are cheaper. And even where there is a traffic potential between distant points, it is frequently more economical (or necessary for technical reasons) to stop over at intermediate points. This generates extra flights at shorter distances.

Several specific models for the relationship of distance to interaction have been developed by geographers and economists. Particularly well-known is the so-called gravitation formula [17]. In this article, however, we shall limit ourselves to studying the negative relationship between distance and interaction with any precise explicit model [18].

2.6. Inter-relationships between the hypotheses

We would expect the association between rank and interaction to be almost universal, for reasons given in section 2.3. That is, we would expect to fiind this relationship both for the total system, and for various subgroups. The propositions that interaction depends on rank, and that similar nations tend to interact more, need to be qualified. Within a subsystem (defined on the basis of the other trait) we would expect the hypothesized ranking: TT interaction greater than TU, etc. On the other hand, low-rank interaction *in* the subsystem should be higher than low-level interaction *between* subsystems, and similarly for pairs of higher rank. We shall not attempt here to 'weight' the relative influence of the two factors, or to compare e.g. intra-system UU interaction with inter-system TU interaction.

2.7. Trends over time

A first and obvious trend to be predicted is a steady increase in number of air connections. These are accumulated as a value in themselves, as noted earlier; and although there is an upper limit to *connections* (the number of nations minus one), there is no limit to the number of *flights*. Furthermore as the data will indicate, the system is far from 'saturated' in terms of connections, and we would therefore expect fairly rapid growth, such as represented by an exponential curve or the first part of a logistic curve, rather than the last part of a logistic curve. However, it seems unlikely that there will ever be connections between small and very distant countries like Luxembourg and Western Samoa; we must therefore expect the upper limit to be located well below 100%.

The effect of colonial affiliation we should expect to be declining. The colonial empires are shrinking, and some former colonies are breaking out entirely of the old patterns of allegiance. There are also other major nations than the former colonial powers competing for influence in the new nations. Most important, we would expect the United States — and to some extent the Soviet Union — to increase rapidly interaction with ex-colonial territories.

Similarly, the effect of geography should be on the decline. Faster, more long-ranging planes will be used on the longer routes, linking countries directly over great distances. This will not necessarily in itself lead to an increase in flights, since the utility of intermediate stops will decrease. These would now have to be justified in terms of local traffic. This would indicate a steady increase in number of air connections for the larger countries, and countries with their own airlines, but possibly a decline in the number of connections for the smaller and non-airline countries. In other words, flights will be more dependent on rank, and particularly on wealth.

However, since air connections are a value that nations strive to maximize, national airlines may tend to grow, if outside airlines cease to perform their present function. The operation of domestic airlines may offset the loss of connections due to fewer transit flights; still, we would expect a momentary dip or at least declining growth rates for the more peripheral countries.

The effects of the Cold War we would also assume to be on the decrease, although there may be new conflict lines forming, particularly around China. However, the countries in her orbit are few. So this will probably take the form of an isolation of one or a few countries.

Similarity, in terms of race, culture, religions, etc., we would assume to have a more or less constant effect on air connections, for lack of other hypotheses. The same applies to the dependence of rank on interaction.

All these trends are *ceteris paribus*. The joint effect — provided that no major new bipolar splits occur — should be to strengthen the process assumed more or less universal: the positive association between interaction and rank. This then should be discernible in our over-time data. However, in terms of connections, at some point there must necessarily be a ceiling effect. When the topdog countries come closer to 100%, the underdog countries should start catching up. However, to believe that 'full equality' of interacting will then be attained is naive. Rather, this means that our indicator is no longer able to discern the differences in the interaction opportunities of different countries. At this point, therefore, we would have to introduce more discriminating indicators, like the number of *flights*, and whether or not flights are *direct*. But meanwhile we shall see what can be done with our first, rather simple indicator.

3. The data

3.1. Sources and procedures

This study is longitudinal, using four time-points: 1930, 1951, 1958, and 1965. These were chosen to have at least three post-war time-points, with seven-year intervals (the first interval, however, is three times seven) for convenience, and, finally, according to what data were available. (The 1930 European guidebook seems to be the first source of its kind).

All the data were collected from flight schedules. These were found to be quite reliable, and, considering the amounts of data collected, relatively few coding decisions had to be made. These are detailed in Appendix 3, along with other comments on the methodology of the study.

For practical reasons, also explained in the Appendix, the 1965 data are for 220 nations (all nations and territories) while the other three time-points are limited to 125 nations, only independent nations. Since the airline schedules give the routes city by city, even such a large number of countries as 220 did not present any problem with regard to obtaining complete information [20]. In this article, the 125 nation world will be used most of the time.

3.2. Some operational definitions

An (air) *connection* between two countries exists if there is at least one regularly scheduled passenger flight between them. By a *flight* we mean that the same plane flies all the way, without change in 'flight number' [21]. This is less restrictive than the *direct flight* without intermediate stops at all; however, it is more restrictive than the *connected flight*. We felt that the former would be too dependent on physical geography; the latter impossible to code reliably. Pure mail and cargo services have been disregarded, as have unscheduled and chartered flights. If included, none of these would probably add any new *connections*, although obviously they would increase the number of *flights*. Finally, connections, and flights are assumed to be *symmetric*: if there is a flight from A to B there must also be one from B to A [22].

3.3. Air connections as a measure of integration: validating the indicator

One might object that air connections alone are not a good indicator of integration or even of interaction. We will not attempt a formal definition of integration here, but will assume that integration and interaction are closely related, and that interaction patterns may be the most practical means of measuring integration, and particularly convenient for the pur-

pose of deriving relatively formal measures. The relationship between structural variables and interaction patterns, on the one hand, and attitudinal
variables, on the other, will not be dealt with here. However, even if we
bypass this problem, the question remains whether air connections capture
a *central* aspect of a general interaction pattern, or whether, as some skep-
tics have commented, 'it's just traffic'.

Patrick McGowan, in an interesting unpublished paper (1967), included
aviation agreements when he analyzed ten indicators of interaction between 32 African states and the Warsaw Pact countries. Starting with a
matrix of product-moment-correlations, he obtained by factor analysis three
common factors and one specific factor of interaction. Rotating the solution
to a pattern closely approaching simple structure, he reports the following
factors with the corresponding variables with factor loadings greater than
.50 (the factors are ranked according to the amount of common variance
explained, and the variables according to their loading on the factor)
(Table 5.2).

TABLE 5.2 *Factors and their corresponding variables for interaction between
32 African countries and the Warsaw Pact countries. Patrick
McGowan's data*

Factor	'Name'	Variables
1	'Bloc aid'	Military personnel
		Military aid
		Economic aid
		Diplomatic missions
2	'Civil exchange'	Student exchange
		Foreign trade
		Civil aviation
3	'Political economic interaction'	Bloc technicians UN voting
4	(Specific)	Press services

The names of the factors are debatable, and the theoretical significance of
the distinction between these types of interaction is unclear. The interesting
thing, however, as McGowan notes, is that all the ten indicators tend to
vary in the same direction. For the whole correlation matrix (45 correlations) the maximum is .88, the minimum .05, and the median correlation
.55. Thus, at a higher level, everything merges into one general, higher-
-order factor of 'interaction'. And in this cluster of interaction indicators,
'civil aviation', has a central location. The correlations with *all* the other
variables are .50 and up, and particularly close are 'foreign trade' and
'student exchange', themselves frequently-used measures of inter-nation
interaction [23]. However, McGowan's aviation measure is 'a composite

score for each training program, equipment assistance program, and regularly scheduled passenger service agreement'. Thus McGowan's measure partly overlaps ours, but takes more into account. Mali, for example, which had no scheduled flights to any of the Warsaw Pact countries in 1965, received the highest score on McGowan's indicator (in a four-way tie). We therefore added our own data for the same 32 countries, and produced the extended correlation matrix. Since only Egypt had more than one scheduled weekly flight to any Warsaw Pact country, it seemed unnecessary to distinguish between *connections* and *flights* to the Warsaw Pact countries. However, we added the *percentage* which connections to Warsaw Pact countries constituted of all connections for the African countries included. These two variables correlated quite well with McGowan's 10 variables, as the summary comparison in Table 5. 3 indicates.

TABLE 5.3 *Correlations of three air interaction variables with other interaction variables. Data on African interaction with Warsaw Pact countries*

Air interaction variable	Correlation with other interaction indicators		
	Maximum	*Median*	*Minimum*
Aviation (McGowan)	.83	.62	.50
Connections to Warsaw Pact countries	.87	.67	.37
% Connections to Warsaw Pact countries	.76	.52	.21

Our variable fares well in comparison, so we may conclude that it would have served satisfactorily as a measure of interaction in a study of Africa and the Warsaw Pact countries. However, can we generalize from this to interaction generally?

Suspecting that interaction with the Warsaw Pact countries for African states would be as much a reflection of a general tendency to interact with the outside world as a tendency to an 'Eastern orientation', we included several variables of airline interaction with the world in general and with the West. By a simple clustering procedure [24] on the resulting 28×28 correlation matrix, we found evidence to confirm this suspicion. *Diplomatic missions to Warsaw Pact countries* loaded primarily on a 'general interaction' factor and correlated highly (.77 and .71 respectively) with variables like *no. of flights to all countries*, and *connections to Warsaw Pact countries*. Other variables, such as *trade with Warsaw Pact countries, % of connections to Warsaw Pact countries*, etc., were primarily located in one of two groupings of 'Eastern interaction', while still highly correlated with the vari-

ables measuring general interaction with the rest of the world, or interaction with the West.

In conclusion, there seems to be enough evidence in this limited study
to warrant the use of airline connections as a general measure of interaction, although strictly speaking we have only shown that it is a valid indicator for the interaction of 32 African countries [25].

If our aim were to produce a general index of interaction, the 'dimensions
of interaction', as uncovered by a factor or cluster analysis, would be of
more concern to us. We are instead primarily interested in testing a theory
of interaction patterns, and a good fit for the airline variable will give us
considerable confidence that other interaction variables conform to the
same pattern.

4. Findings

4.1. Introduction

The collected data appear as four 125 × 125 matrices with 0 or 1 in the
cells. For 1965 the complete matrix is 220 × 220 with frequencies in the cells
ranging from 531 (UK-Ireland) to 1 (India-Nigeria and 371 other pairs).
Appendix 1 presents the information for the four time-points, summed
by country. There is a general increase in number of connections, to be
commented on in section 4.2, but the rank order of the countries in terms
of number of connections is quite similar, as shown by Table 4. The
correlations between 1930 and the others are the lowest, as one would
expect.

TABLE 5.4 *Rank order correlations (gammas) for the number of connections*
of the 125 countries

	1930	1951	1958	1965
1930	—			
1951	.37	—		
1958	.45	.71	—	
1965	.38	.61	.76	—

The number of countries with no connections at all is shown in Table 5.5.
For the three post-war time-points at least, the number of zeros is so small
that we can meaningfully use airlines as a measure of integration for the
whole world. Furthermore, for all post-war points, the subgraph of non-
isolated nations is *strongly connected* (or 'strong' [26]), i.e. all points which

have any connections at all are reachable from each other by air, directly or through one or more intermediary nations. The 1930 airline graph, howver, is *disconnected*, split in several parts, with no connections between e.g. the Western and the Eastern Hemisphere.

TABLE 5.5 *No. of countries with no connections at all*

Year	1930	1951	1958	1965
n	55	9	3	1
%	44%	7%	2%	1%
		(n = 125)		

The three standard measures of central tendency, as well as the standard deviation, Pearson's coefficient of skewness and a Gini-index for the 'inequality' of the distribution of connections over the set of nations [27] — are given in Table 5.6.

TABLE 5.6 *Measures of central tendency, dispersion, skewness, and inequality for the number of connections for each nation. All four time points, 125 nations*

	Central tendency			Dispersion	Skewness	Inequality
Year	*Mean*	*Modal deciles*	*Median*	*Standard deviation*	*Pearson's coefficient*	*Gini index*
1930	4	1	1	5	1.8	0.64
1951	13	1	9	12	0.9	0.48
1958	19	2	13	15	1.1	0.44
1965	21	1.3	18	17	0.5	0.43

Table 5.7 sums up the information by region for all four time points.

Table 5.8 gives the number of pairs of countries (i.e. the number of possible connections) within and between each region. Since the indicator is symmetric and domestic connections are not counted, the number of pairs is found as follows: with n_a nations in region a and n_b in region b, there are $1/2 \, n_a \, (n_a - 1)$ pairs within region a and $n_a n_b$ pairs between them. The connection matrices in Table 5.7 are obviously also symmetric.

TABLE 5.7 *Connections within and between regions*

Year	Region	Region Africa	America	Asia	Europe	Australia/ Oceania	Grand total
1930	Africa	14	0	4	13	0	
	America	0	92	0	0	0	
	Asia	4	0	14	18	0	
	Europe	13	0	18	88	0	
	Australia	0	0	0	0	0	
	Total	31	92	36	119	0	243
1951	Africa	120	15	26	79	1	
	America	15	114	14	80	4	
	Asia	26	14	86	99	7	
	Europe	79	80	99	132	2	
	Australia	1	4	7	2	2	
	Total	241	227	232	392	16	781
1958	Africa	142	12	28	133	1	
	America	12	148	23	98	4	
	Asia	28	23	152	201	14	
	Europe	133	98	201	190	10	
	Australia	1	4	14	10	1	
	Total	316	285	418	632	30	1,157
1965	Africa	170	21	40	184	9	
	America	23	125	22	117	5	
	Asia	40	22	166	203	20	
	Europe	184	117	203	227	13	
	Australia	9	5	20	13	1	
	Total	426	292	451	744	48	1,325

TABLE 5.8 *Number of pairs of countries within and between each region*

Region	Region Africa	America	Asia	Europe	Australia/ Oceania	Grand total
Africa	703					
America	912	276				
Asia	1,216	768	496			
Europe	1,064	672	896	378		
Australia	114	72	96	84	3	
Total	4,009	2,700	3,472	3,094	369	7,750
						$(=^1/_2 \cdot 125 \cdot 124)$

Table 5.9 gives the fraction of connections in terms of the possible connections. In the following, for convenience, we shall refer to this fraction as the *density* of the airline network.

TABLE 5.9 *Density of the region-to-region airline network (connections over pairs). 125 nations. Data for all four time points (1930 top, 1965 bottom)*

	Africa	America	Asia	Europe	Australia/ Oceania	Total
Africa	.02					
	.17					
	.20					
	.24					
America	.0	.33				
	.02	.41				
	.01	.54				
	.03	.45				
Asia	.00	.0	.03			
	.02	.02	.17			
	.02	.03	.31			
	.03	.03	.34			
Europe	.01	.0	.02	.23		
	.07	.12	.11	.35		
	.13	.15	.22	.50		
	.17	.17	.23	.60		
Australia/	.0	.0	.0	.0	(.0)*	
Oceania	.01	.06	.07	.02	(.67)	
	.01	.06	.15	.12	(.33)	
	.08	.07	.21	.16	(.33)	
	.01	.03	.01	.04	.0	.03
	.06	.08	.07	.13	.04	.10
	.08	.11	.12	.20	.08	.15
Total	.11	.11	.13	.24	.13	.17
No. of pairs	4,009	2,700	3,472	3,094	369	7,750
No. of countries	38	24	32	28	3	125

* In parentheses since the number of pairs is only three.

4.2. The saturation of the system

The first thing to note about these matrices is the very clear expected trend in the direction of higher densities. Table 5.7 gives the trends over time in number of connections for the world as a whole, as well as for the five regions. In every case, there is overall growth over the whole period. For the complete region-by-region matrix, the information is summed up by Table 5.10.

TABLE 5.10 *Testing the hypothesis of monotonic growth from 1930 to 1965. Confirmation ratios * for all combinations of regions and for all totals*

Region	Region				
	Africa	America	Asia	Europe	Australia/ Oceania
Africa	100%				
America	83%	83%			
Asia	100%	83%	100%		
Europe	100%	100%	100%	100%	
Australia	92%	92%	100%	100%	(58%)***
Total**	94%(30)	88%(30)	97%(30)	100%(30)	100%(30)
	100% (6)	100% (6)	100% (6)	100% (6)	100% (6)
Grand total**	94%(90)				
	100% (6)				

* The confirmation ratio is somewhat similar to a tau or gamma correlation coefficient. According to the hypothesis of monotonic growth the densities should be ranked 1965, 1958, 1951, 1930. The percentage of pairwise comparisons that actually conform to this pattern is the confirmation ratio. A tie is counted as half an agreement.
** Two totals (and two grand totals) are given. The first row is the sum of the corresponding columns of the matrix (only half the matrix is included because of the symmetry); the second is based on the totals in Table 5.9 directly. In parentheses is the number of comparisons on which the percentage is based.
*** In parentheses since the number of pairs here is only three.

The agreement is quite convincing. The only partial exception, America, has two plausible explanations, one general and one particular. The particular explanation is that Cuba, in the years following the revolution, lost all its air connections in the Western hemisphere (as well as most other peaceful interaction with its neighbors) while not gaining elsewhere. (Two connections gained with Czechoslovakia and the USSR are cancelled out by the two lost to the Netherlands and Britain). If Cuba had retained its 1958 level (24 connections) in 1965, intra-American connections would have had a higher total. The more general explanation is that intra-American air interaction was highly developed at an early stage; hence the saturation effect may have occurred in America before elsewhere.

At the nation level the picture is similar. Appendix 1, in addition to the total number of connections by country, gives the confirmation ratios for these four totals. Again, in all regions, most countries get a near-perfect score although America again is somewhat lower than the others. 11 countries (8.8% of all) score 50% or worse. The information is summed up by region in Table 5.11.

TABLE 5.11 *Confirmation rates by country, summed up by region. As a fraction of all countries in the region.*

Confirmation level	Africa	America	Asia	Europe	Australia	Total
0	0	0	0	0	0	0
8.3	0	0	0	0	0	0
16.7	0	.04	0	0	0	.01
25.0	0	.04	0	0	0	.01
33.3	0	0	0	0	0	0
41.7	0	.13	.06	0	.33	.05
50.0	0	.08	0	.04	0	.02
58.3	.03	.04	.03	0	0	.02
66.7	.08	.08	.03	.07	0	.06
75.0	.10	0	.09	.11	0	.08
83.3	.29	.29	.34	.18	0	.27
91.7	.13	.08	.13	.07	0	.10
100.0	.37	.21	.31	.54	.67	.37
Total	1.00	1.00	1.00	1.00	1.00	1.00
(n)	(38)	(24)	(32)	(28)	(3)	(125)

We predicted above that some peripheral countries might have less than perfect confirmation ratios. The 11 countries with 50% or below are Costa Rica, Cuba, Dominican Republic, El Salvador, Haiti, Honduras, Malta, Nicaragua, North Korea, South Korea, and Western Samoa. With the partial exception of Cuba and the Koreas — for which special circumstances can account — these are all small countries, many of which have lost their significance as transfer stops for connections between larger countries (Central America losing out to the Caribbean, Western Samoa to the Fiji Islands).

Finally, we shall look at this at the dyadic level. Since at this level we only know whether there is a connection or not, confirmation of the hypothesis is calculated in terms of whether a connection, once established, has been retained. With 4 time-points, 16 patterns are possible; the percentages of pairs in each pattern are set out in Table 5.12.

TABLE 5.12 *Testing the hypothesis of monotonic growth. Pairs of countries with different patterns of connection over time. (For each time-point 'I' signifies a connection.)*

Pattern	Connection in —				Intra-region %	All pairs %
	1930	1951	1958	1965		
1	0	0	0	0	55	79
2	0	0	0	1	6	4
3	0	0	1	0	3	2
4	0	0	1	1	8	4
5	0	1	0	0	2	0.7
6	0	1	0	1	1	0.6
7	0	1	1	0	1	0.7
8	0	1	1	1	13	6
9	1	0	0	0	1	0.2
10	1	0	0	1	1	0.3
11	1	0	1	0	0.4	0.1
12	1	0	1	1	2	0.5
13	1	1	0	0	0.1	0.0
14	1	1	0	1	0.1	0.0
15	1	1	1	0	1	0.2
16	1	1	1	1	7	2
Sum					100.0%	100.0%
(n)					(1,856)	(7,750)

TABLE 5.13 *Testing the hypothesis of monotonic growth: % of pairs consistent with hypothesis*

Pattern in Table 12		Intra-region %	All pairs %
4, 8, 16	Consistent	27	12
6, 7, 10, 11, 12, 13, 14, 15	Weakly inconsistent	6	2
3, 5, 9	Strongly inconsistent	6	3
1, 2	Irrelevant	61	83
	Sum	100	100
	(n)	(1,856)	(7,750)

To interpret Table 5.12 we collapse all those pairs where a connection, once established, is not broken *(consistent* with hypothesis); those where a connection once established, is broken immediately and not re-established *(strongly inconsistent);* those where an established connection is broken, but not immediately re-established *(weakly inconsistent);* and those where no connection has ever been established or only in the last period *(irrelevant)* (Table 5.13).

Again, the hypothesis is confirmed. The overwhelming number of pairs have, of course, never had a connection. Among those who have, a large majority follow the predicted pattern.

If we view the connections over time as a Guttman scale (with four two-valued items) we notice that the five scale-types (1, 2, 4, 8, and 16) account for 95% of all pairs and 88% of the intra-region pairs. Since this percentage corresponds to the *coefficient of reproducibility* for a Guttman scale, we may conclude that four 'items' form such a scale for the total of all pairs, according to the (rather arbitrary) figure of 90% often set as a criterion for 'scalability' (Stouffer *et al.*, 1966, p. 77).

A slightly different way of looking at this is to calculate the relative probability of having a connection broken once established (Table 5.14).

TABLE 5.14 *Conditional probability of breaking a connection established in or before 1930, 1951, 1958*

	The connection was established in or before		
	1930	1951	1958
p =	.41	.22	.18

All three probabilities are lower than .5. Hence, the probability (when randomly selecting a connection) is better than even that the connection will not be broken later, although not very much better for a connection established in 1930.

The three preceding tables indicate that not only has the number of air connections been increasing steadily, but also reveal something about the process itself: *an air connection is 'sticky': once established, it tends to last.* It is tempting to draw an analogy with the *positive lock-in* on cooperative behavior found in gaming experiments (e.g. Rapoport, 1967). A weakness of the analogy is, of course, that while gaming experiments have uncovered a corresponding tendency to 'lock in' on non-cooperative behavior, this cannot be found here since we only have a dichotomy of positive or no interaction, and no negative interaction. The absence of an air connection cannot reasonably be interpreted as non-operative behavior: two countries may just be disinterested, too small, or too far away [28].

Granting that the growth in connection has been monotonic in the past, is this likely to continue? We have remarked that there is an upper limit, that a ceiling effect must necessarily occur at some point. Fig. 5.1 gives the densities plotted over time. Insofar as we can say anything at all on the

FIGURE 5.1 *Densities for all regions and world total, plotted over time*

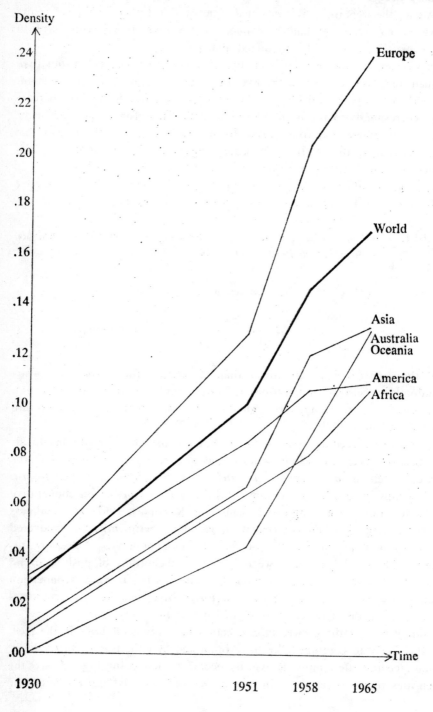

basis of four points, the pattern seems to be logistic rather than exponential. In other words, we would expect some growth, but less rapid than before, and eventually stagnation. The exception is of course Africa, the 'youngest continent', and the least developed one in terms of connections.

With the corresponding growth rates for countries, however, the picture is less clear. While some major countries (France, West Germany) have ollowed the same (logistic) pattern, others (such as the US) have not. It is also interesting to note that if a linear trend is projected onwards from these four timepoints, the three leading countries (US, UK, France) will not achieve 'saturation' (i.e. be connected to all countries) until the early nineties, and no other country until after the turn of the century.

4.3. Two divisions of the world

We shall now discuss the findings with regard to some of the other hypothesized relationships. In so doing, we shall proceed in a different way, following and elaborating upon a certain tradition in several studies of the influence of rank on interaction in international society (e.g. Galtung 1966b). We shall divide the world up in parts, characterize the parts and their interrelation in terms of the relevant variables (rank, distance, colonial affiliation), and then analyse the interaction patterns between and within these subgroups of the total international system [29].

Two such partitions of the world will be used in the following. The first, very crude model, is the 'regional model' with the five regions used below. This is basically a geographical division, so we shall simply assume that geographical distance within region is low, between regions high. Furthermore, we shall assign a generalized rank to each of the regions, as shown in Table 5.15.

TABLE 5.15. *The regional model: rank of five regions*

T Topdog	Europe
M Middledogs	America, Australia/Oceania
U Underdogs	Africa, Asia

This division is based on an impression of total impact of variables of size, power, status, and economic development of the countries in these regions. Note that only the 125 countries are included in the following; for the universe of 220 countries, Australia/Oceania would clearly be an underdog continent, and it might also be unreasonable to lump Africa and Asia in the same category.

In addition to this admittedly crude division, we shall use another somewhat more complex one, which we shall call the 'colonial model'. The 'systems' to be used in this model [26] are 'colonial' systems in the broadest sense of the word. A nation was classified as belonging to a system if and only if it had belonged to it as late as after World War II and had not joined another system since then, nor clearly established itself as an independent center of world affairs. Thus, of the four parts of former French Indo-China, North Vietnam was put in a group called 'Asian Communists' in the 'Communist' system, South Vietnam and Laos in a group called 'Western Asians' in the US orbit, while Cambodia for lack of other affiliation remained in the group 'former French colonies' in the French system. The Arabs and Latin Americans were regarded as independent systems although French North Africa (under some doubt) was maintained in the French group. For analytic purposes, however, Latin America will be incorporated into the US orbit. Cuba forms a separate group of 'American Communists', while Israel is the only single nation to form its own system.

A remainder category was necessary for Asia (3 countries) and Africa (5 countries). The groups have been assigned 4 ranks: topdog (T), middledog (M), higher underdog (HV), and lower underdog (LV). In a way this corresponds to a classification in terms of upper class, middle class, working class, and *Lumpenproletariat*, but we would not make too much of this, as we are not investigating enough behavioral characteristics and attributes to make such a sweeping analogy. However, it is interesting to note that the stratification pyramid *in terms of nations* (but not in terms of population), is quite similar to the intra-societal pyramid with a pyramidal shape from the higher underdogs up, but a narrowing below the HUs.

The complete pattern, with systems, groups, and nations is given in Appendix 2. Only the 125 nations for which we have over-time data are included. The nametags for the various groups should not be taken too literally; they are given for easy reference, with no claim to an accurate or complete description.

As before, we will assume *intra-group* geographical dstance to be *low*, and intergroup distance to be high (including intrasystem distance). The ranking of the nations into four groups was also done on the same intuitive basis as for the previous model. What this model gives us in addition, then, is the *colonial affiliation* variable, plus a greater number of combinations of groups.

A number of predictions will be tested. A brief survey of these follows (Table 5.16). All the predictions follow from the theoretical statement in sections 2.2.–2.7. The new element here is that the testing procedures are spelled out in detail.

TABLE 5.16 *Predictions using the colonial model and the feudal hypothesis and other hypotheses above*

1. *Intra-system predictions*
   a. Short distances: the predicted relationship between rank and interaction (TT interaction greater than TM greater than MM etc.).
   b. Large distances: same.
   c. Total rank of pair constant: short distance pairs have more interaction than large distance pairs.
   d. The higher the rank of a pair, the lower the negative influence of geographical distance.
2. *Inter-system predictions*
   a. Rank constant: intra-systems pairs have more interaction than inter-system pairs.
   b. Inter-system pairs only: the predicted relationship between rank and interaction.
3. *Inter-system interaction with conflict*
   a. Total rank constant: inter-system interactions are smaller when the systems are in conflict than when they are not.
4. *Predictions over time*
   a. The differences found in 2a decrease over time, i.e. there is a decreasing influence of colonial affiliation.
   b. The differences found in 1a, 1b, 1d, and 2b are relatively constant; i.e. the impact of rank, other factors constant, is stable.
   c. The difference in 3a is decreasing (as far as the East-West conflict is concerned, not with regard to the Israeli-Arab conflict or the isolation of China and her allies).
   d. The difference found in 1c is decreasing. Furthermore, the percentage of intragroup interaction decreases.
   e. The bivariate relationship between rank and interaction is strengthened (i.e. when other factors are not kept constant).

4.4. Influence of geographical distance

To test the predictions with regard to influence of geographical distance, we could give data on the percentage of connections that are intra-region, for each rank level and over time. While these would be comparable over time, the figures for different rank levels, would not be comparable, however, because 'intra-region' or 'intra-group' would mean a different proportion of the total number of pairs in each case. Thus, both the numerator and the denominator need to be normed by the number of pairs of nations. Furthermore, it is not clear whether dividing by or subtracting total density from intra-group density gives the most meaningful comparison. Both are given in Tables 5.17 (the regional model) and Tables 5.18 (the colonial model). The first thing to note about these Tables is that there are very few negative numbers (in the second half) or numbers lower than one (in the first half). Furthermore, whenever a difference is negative in the second half of Table 5.18, the number in the first half is zero, indicating that there is no intra-group interaction at all (Rest Asia, Rest Africa in 1930, and Asian Communists).

175

TABLE 5.17 *Intra-region densities divided by density for the region as a whole, and the difference between intra-region and total density. Over time, 125 nations*

	Intra-region density divided by total density				Prediction 4d. confirmation
	1930	1951	1958	1965	
Africa	2.6	2.8	2.6	2.3	83% (6)
America	9.8	4.9	5.1	4.2	83% (6)
Asia	2.7	2.6	2.5	2.6	83% (6)
Europe	6.1	2.8	2.5	2.5	83% (6)
Australia	—	(15.4)	(4.1)	(2.6)	(100% (3))
	Total density subtracted from intra-region density				Prediction 4d. confirmation
Africa	0.01	0.11	0.12	0.14	0% (6)
America	0.30	0.33	0.43	0.35	17% (6)
Asia	0.02	0.11	0.19	0.21	0% (6)
Europe	0.20	0.22	0.28	0.36	0% (6)
Australia	(0.000)	(0.62)	(0.25)	(0.20)	(50% (6))

In Table 5.17 intra-region densities are always greater than the total. Clearly, geographical distance has persisted as a limiting factor on airline interaction.

Comparing the figures over time we notice a clear difference between the first and the second halves of the two Tables. When the baseline is subtracted, the importance of geography seems to be on the increase; when it is used as the denominator in a fraction, the picture is reversed, although not so clearly. We may conclude that the growth rates for inter-region and inter-group densities are larger than intra-region and intra-group densities. Yet, the difference in growth rates is not large enough to allow the inter-region and inter-group densities to catch up [30]. Whether one prefers to say that the influence of geography is increasing or not is partly a matter of taste. For our part we prefer to formulate it as follows; *the influence of geographical distance as a restraint on interaction has decreased, yet the impact of geography has increased and — if present trends can be extrapolated — will continue to do so for some time, until the system becomes more saturated in the parts which are geographically close and the intra-region and intra-group growth rates decrease even further* [31].

In the following differences rather than ratios will be used in most of the analyses. We caution the reader to remember that taking the ratios might give different results in many places. We have chosen *differences*, however, because we are more interested at present in the *impact* of different factors, and are working from the hypothesis that the difference

TABLE 5.18 *The colonial model. Intra-group densities divided by total density for the group, and the difference between intra-group and total density. Over time, 125 nations. (Only groups with more than one nation included)*

System	Group	Intra-region density divided by total density				Prediction 4d. confirmation
		1930	1951	1958	1965	
British	White empire	0.0	3.5	3.5	2.8	50% (6)
	Colonies	1.7	1.7	1.3	1.4	67% (6)
French	Colonies	2.7	4.0	3.9	2.9	50% (6)
American	Latin America	8.1	4.9	5.4	5.1	67% (6)
	West Asia	3.1	2.3	4.2	4.2	33% (6)
Western Europe		4.2	2.9	2.3	2.2	100% (6)
Rest Africa		0.0	3.8	3.6	3.8	33% (6)
Rest Asia		—	—	0.0	0.0	50% (1)
Belgian	Colonies	—	19.4	14.8	14.2	100% (3)
Arabs		2.5	4.1	2.9	2.9	50% (6)
Sino-Soviet	Eurocomm.	9.5	10.5	8.3	5.6	83% (6)
	Ascomm.	0.0	0.0	0.0	0.0	50% (6)

System	Group	Total density subtracted from intra-region density				Prediction 4d. confirmation
		1930	1951	1958	1965	
British	White Empire	—0.002	0.29	0.36	0.32	16% (6)
	Colonies	0.01	0.06	0.04	0.05	33% (6)
French	Colonies	0.01	0.17	0.18	0.18	0% (6)
American	Latin	0.29	0.27	0.43	0.39	33% (6)
	West Asia	0.03	0.10	0.46	0.46	17% (6)
Western Europe		0.14	0.30	0.33	0.33	17% (6)
Rest Africa		—0.01	0.25	0.24	0.37	17% (6)
Rest Asia		0.00	0.00	—0.03	—0.05	92% (6)
Belgian	Colonies	0.00	0.95	0.93	0.93	50% (6)
Arabs		0.03	0.29	0.31	0.33	0% (6)
Sino-Soviet	Eurocomm.	0.45	0.36	0.69	0.73	17% (6)
	Ascomm.	—0.01	—0.01	—0.01	—0.01	58% (6)

is perceived more clearly than the ratio and hence is politically more significant. If the system were very much closer to saturation, differences might be less significant [32]. Furthermore, since most of our theory is on the synchronic level (i.e. for one time-point only) we shall for the most part be interested in the degree to which our 'static' model fits the data at the different time-points. Therefore, if the confirmation rate of a synchronic prediction is 100% for all four time-points, minor changes in percentages or ratios are not very important relative to the fact that the model fits the data 'perfectly'. And if the confirmation rate is increasing monotonically (as in

Table 5.23, below) this again indicates a better fit of the data to the model over time.

We mentioned that by dividing and subtracting densities rather than number of connections, comparisons are meaningful not only horizontally, but also vertically, thus giving an impression of the relative degree of 'introversion' or 'extroversion' of different regions and groups. However, we must remember that a low ratio or difference intra-region to inter-region density may signify not just high extroversion, but also low development of internal communications. Africa, for example, has a low density ratio in Table 5.17, but this is due mainly to a low numerator, while Asia's low ratio to a larger extent is caused by a high denominator. Also, of course, ranks enter the picture — we would expect Africa to have more inter-regional interaction because this includes interaction with topdogs and middledogs. The next tables shed light on these issues. The first relevant comparison is horizontally, between the high distance and low distance columns (Tables 19, 20). All the differences are positive (low distance interaction is higher than high distance interaction), at both rank levels and all time-points. Hence, prediction 1c is confirmed. However, the differences are generally growing rather than decreasing, so that 4d is disconfirmed again. (Confirmation is 16% for MM pairs, 0% for UU pairs.)

TABLE 5.19 *Interaction in pairs with high vs. pairs with low geographical distance. Total rank of the pair held constant. The regional model. Over time, 125 nations*

| Time | Pair | Rank | Interaction (density) | | |
			High distance	Low distance	Difference
1930	MM	4	0.00	0.33	0.33
	UU	2	0.003	0.02	0.02
1951	MM	4	0.06	0.42	0.36
	UU	2	0.02	0.17	0.15
1958	MM	4	0.06	0.53	0.47
	UU	2	0.02	0.25	0.22
1965	MM	4	0.07	0.45	0.38
	UU	2	0.03	0.28	0.25

Prediction 1d is also disconfirmed on these data, since geographical distance appears to have a larger impact on MM interaction than on UU interaction. However, we would not make too much of this, since distance is much larger in the case of MM interaction than UU interaction, so the comparison is highly biased. Furthermore, the differences due to geographical distance for MM pairs are increasing much more slowly (and have a reverse for the last period) than that for UU pairs.

The corresponding data for the colonial model are found in Table 5.20. Only intra-system interactions are compared in this Table, and only two systems have intra-system intergroup interaction at rank levels MM and UU (the Soviet and American systems). Hence, the basis for comparison is weak. The pattern, however, is strikingly similar to that in Table 5.19. All differences are positive (confirmation of 1c) and increasing (disconfirmation of 4d) and larger for MM than UU pairs (disconfirmation of 1d). The same reservation must be taken with regard to the last comparisons, too, since the only intra-system inter-group MM interaction is that of China to Eastern Europe. The absence of any connections here is certainly a striking illustration of the weak position in international interaction of the Middledogs in the Sino-Soviet system, but may also partly be accounted for by the particularly large distance.

TABLE 5.20 *Interaction in pairs with high vs. pairs with low geographical distance. Total rank of the pair held constant. Intra-system interactions only. The colonial model. Over time, 125 nations*

Time	Pair	Rank	Interaction (density) High distance	Low distance	Difference
1930	MM	4	0.0	0.24	0.24
	UU	2	0.0	0.11	0.11
1951	MM	4	0.0	0.44	0.44
	UU	2	0.0	0.24	0.24
1958	MM	4	0.0	0.62	0.62
	UU	2	0.03	0.34	0.31
1965	MM	4	0.0	0.64	0.64
	UU	2	0.03	0.35	0.32

Karl Deutsch has argued (1956) that nations may be becoming more introvert, in the sense that they are directing a larger share of their transactions towards their own nations. We have no way of testing this on our data, since we have no information on domestic flights. However, insofar as directedness toward the immediate geographic surroundings is concerned, Deutsch would appear to be correct, although the differences in results obtained when using ratios and when using differences must be kept in mind. Furthermore, it is doubtful whether this is really a sign of introversion, since all transactions — domestic, regional, and international — are increasing very rapidly and all that these findings really indicate is that the international interactions cannot quite keep pace with domestic and regional ones.

4.5. Influence of rank and colonial affiliation

Using the regional model first, we shall now look into the relationship between rank and interaction (Table 5.21).

TABLE 5.21 *Rank and interaction. The regional model, over time*

a. *high distances only*

Pair	Total rank of pair*	Densities 1930	1951	1958	1965
TM	5	0	0.11	0.14	0.18
MM	4	0	0.06	0.06	0.07
TU	4	0.02	0.09	0.17	0.20
MU	3	0	0.02	0.03	0.04
UU	2	0.003	0.02	0.02	0.03
Confirmation rate		3%	89%	89%	89%
No. of pairwise comparisons		(9)	(9)	(9)	(9)

* Note that MM and TU have the same total rank, hence the densities for these two pairs are not compared.

b. *low distances only*

Pair	Total rank of pair	Densities 1930	1951	1958	1965
TT	6	0.23	0.35	0.50	0.60
MM	4	0.33	0.42	0.53	0.45
UU	2	0.02	0.17	0.25	0.28
Confirmation rate		67%	67%	67%	100%
No. of pairwise comparisons		(3)	(3)	(3)	(3)

Overall confirmation (high and low distances)

	1930	1951	1958	1965
Confirmation rate:	42%	83%	83%	92%
No. of pairwise comparisons:	(12)	(12)	(12)	(12)

Confirmation rate for the whole table: 75% (n = 48)

The overall confirmation is quite convincing, although for 1930 and high distances the expected pattern is not found. However, in 1930 there were relatively few connections, and, most important, no transoceanic flights to connect the topdog group with either of the middledog groups, or the latter with each other. Furthermore, we notice in the bottom row of Table 5.21 a tendency to better confirmation with time. This we may see more clearly if we calculate all the relevant differences in densities (Table 5.22).

TABLE 5.22 *Differences in densities for all relevant comparisons*

Pairs high distance	Total rank difference	1930	1951	1958	1965	Confirmation
TM VS MM	1	0	0.05	0.09	0.11	100% (6)
TM VS TU	1	—0.02	0.02	—0.02	—0.02	33% (6)
TM VS MU	2	0	0.09	0.12	0.15	100% (6)
TM VS UU	3	—0.00	0.09	0.12	0.15	100% (6)
MM VS MU	1	0	0.04	0.03	0.03	100% (6)
MM VS UU	2	—0.00	0.04	0.03	0.04	100% (6)
TU VS MU	1	0.02	0.07	0.16	0.16	100% (6)
TU VS UU	2	0.01	0.07	0.14	0.16	100% (6)
MU VS UU	1	—0.00	—0.00	0.00	0.01	100% (6)

Total confirmation rate: 86% (n = 54)

low distance						
TT VS MM	2	—0.10	—0.07	—0.03	0.15	100% (6)
TT VS UU	4	0.21	0.18	0.26	0.32	83% (6)
MM VS UU	2	0.31	0.24	0.29	0.17	16% (6)

Total confirmation rate: 67% (n = 18)

Grand total confirmation rate: 84% (n = 721)

In the whole Table 5.22 there are only two exceptions to a monotically increasing difference over time, and in each case a pair with the smallest rank difference is involved. In the comparison of MM and UU interactions the difference in geographical distance must also be considered, as noted before.

Obviously, the regional model is a very crude one, and the results may be partly spurious. However, let us look at the corresponding tables for the colonial model. Ideally, the test should proceed in three phases: we should first look at the correspondence between the act and the hypothesis *within* each of the systems, then at the interactions of the systems with the outside, and finally at the pairwise interactions of all systems. This would yield a large number of tables, necessitating a correspondingly large number of calculations. Hence, we will limit ourselves somewhat with regard to the latter two steps. First, however, we shall look at *all* the predictions with regard to intra-system interactions (Table 5.23).

TABLE 5.23 *Intra-system densities, high distance only. Over time, 125 nations**

Pair	Total rank	1930 System			1951 System			1958 System			1965 System		
		Brit.	Am.	Sino-Soviet	Brit.	Am.	Sino-Soviet	Brit.	Am.	Sino-Soviet	Brit.	Am.	Sino-Soviet
TM	5	0.00	—	0.11	0.60	—	0.67	1.00	—	0.89	1.00	—	0.89
MM	4	—	—	0.00	—	—	0.00	—	—	0.00	—	—	0.00
TU	4	0.00	0.52	0.00	0.35	0.85	0.00	0.80	0.89	0.25	0.90	0.96	0.75
MU	3	0.00	—	0.03	0.16	—	0.00	0.17	—	0.03	0.26	—	0.08
UU	2	—	0.00	0.00	—	0.00	0.00	—	0.03	0.00	—	0.03	0.00
Confirmation		50%	100%	67%	100%	100%	72%	100%	100%	.83%	100%	100%	83%
No. of pairwise comparisons		(3)	(1)	(9)	(3)	(1)	(9)	(3)	(1)	(9)	(3)	(1)	(9)
Total confirmation		65% (13)			81% (13)			88% (13)			88% (13)		

Table 5.23 indicates that the hypothesis of increasing interaction with increasing rank of the pair is confirmed for all systems at all four time-points, with the exception of the British system in 1930. We might now go on to calculate the differences in densities for all comparisons of pairs (as we did for the regional model in Table 22), but this is not really necessary. The main dividing line running through the whole Table is that between pairs which involve topdogs and those which do not. Clearly, *the gap between the pairs involving topdogs and the others is widening drastically over this period*, while the difference between TM and TU interaction in the two systems where this comparison can be made, is decreasing in the later periods.

The corresponding comparisons for low geographical distance are not given system by system, since only two systems have relevant groups to compare. However, for both systems together the differences can be seen from Table 5.20 to be in the wrong direction. Again this is due to the peculiarly weak interaction of the two Middledog groups in the Sino-Soviet system.

We are not giving data here for the relationship of rank to interaction for all systems at a time (but controlling for geographical distance). Clearly, what is found to hold for the three major systems must also hold for the world as a whole. However, Table 5.24 presents the corresponding data for inter-system inter-actions (prediction 2b). Here and in most of the following Tables we present all inter-system interactions together, rather than looking at all pairwise combinations of systems or data for each system against all others.

TABLE 5.24 *Inter-system interactions (densities). The relationship of rank to interaction. Over time, 125 nations*

		Year			
Pair	Rank	1930	1951	1958	1965
TT	6	0.17	0.50	0.67	0.83
TM	5	0.25	0.49	0.61	0.73
MM	4	0.10	0.21	0.32	0.39
TU	4	0.02	0.16	0.23	0.34
MU	3	0.01	0.07	0.12	0.14
UU	2	0.01	0.05	0.06	0.07
Confirmation:		86%	100%	100%	100%
No. of comparisons:		14	14	14	14

Again, we shall not go on to calculate the difference for all relevant comparisons of pairs. The picture is fairly similar to that in Table 5.23 with the exception that for inter-system interactions the MM pair has a high density (consistently higher than TU). Clearly, the differences between pairs of high and pairs of low on total rank are increasing. Tables 5.23 and 24 together seem to warrant the conclusion, therefore, that *rank has increased in impact on interaction patterns over this 35-year period.*

The influence of colonial affiliation can be investigated by comparing the densities for intra-system and inter-system pairs. The difference (intra-system minus inter-system) are presented in Table 5.25.

Table 5.25 indicates that colonial affiliation does have a positive influence on interaction, although the confirmation rates are not very high. The MM and UU groups are giving us trouble again, since there are few of these that are intra-system and not intra-group. The comparison of intra-group, intra-system and inter-system interactions at these three rank levels in Table 5.26 makes this clear. Interaction is overwhelmingly concentrated within the system, both for MM and UU pairs. However, this can be accounted for both by the difference in geographical distance and by colonial affiliation, or the joint effect of the two. When we try to separate the effects, as in Table 5.25, a distortion occurs because of the low number of comparisons. However, for the other three pairs the effect of colonial affiliation is clear.

TABLE 5.25 *Differences in densities for intra-system and inter-system pairs, and confirmation rates at each time-point of the prediction that these differences be positive*

Pair	Rank	Difference in density			
		1930	1951	1958	1965
TU	5	—0.18	0.15	0.32	0.20
MM	4	—0.10	—0.21	—0.32	—0.39
TU	4	0.24	0.41	0.62	0.59
MU	3	0.001	0.05	0.02	0.09
UU	2	—0.01	—0.05	—0.04	—0.05
Confirmation		40%	60%	60%	60%
No. of comparisons		5	5	5	5

TABLE 5.26 *Intra-group, intra-system, and inter-system interactions at rank levels MM and UU. Densities. Over time, 125 nations*

Year	Pair	Intra-system		Inter-system
		Intra-group	Inter-group	
1930	MM	0.24	0.00	0.10
	UU	0.11	0.00	0.01
1951	MM	0.44	0.00	0.21
	UU	0.24	0.00	0.05
1958	MM	0.62	0.00	0.32
	UU	0.34	0.03	0.06
1965	MM	0.64	0.00	0.39
	UU	0.35	0.03	0.07

The pattern over time is also clear. While the effect of colonial affiliation increased up to 1958 for two of the three pairs where comparison is meaningful, the differences decline for every pair except MU for the last seven-year period. The effect is seen most clearly in Fig. 5.2, which presents the same data in graphical form. It would appear then, that *colonial affiliation has been increasing in importance over most of the period under investigation, but that the reverse trend has now set in.* The reverse coincides, of course, with the period in which political decolonialization received its strongest impetus. Interestingly the decline is smallest where the rank difference is greatest, i.e. in the TU pair. Here, following Reinton's terminology (1967), interaction is on the least equal terms; it is characterized by *dominance*.

This concludes our discussion of data relevant to the predictions on rank colonial affiliation, and interaction. In general these predictions have been

FIGURE 5.2 *The effect of colonial affiliation.*
The data from Table 5.25 plotted over time

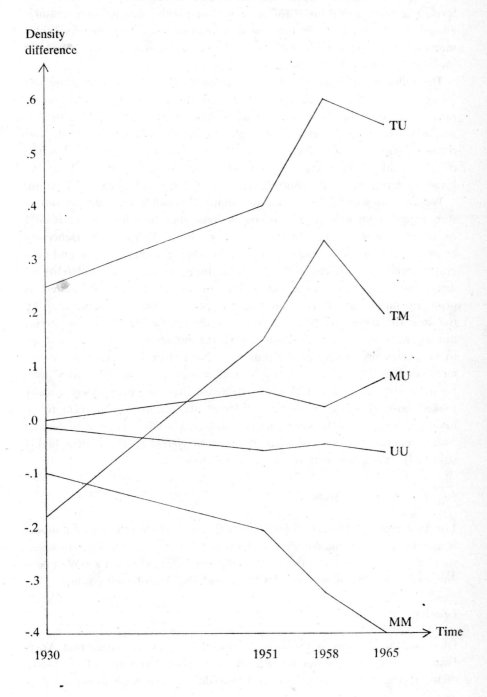

confirmed: interaction is positively associated with rank, both at the intra-group or intra-region level, at the intra-system level, and at the inter-system level. The relationship holds for all four time-points, although not unambiguously for 1930 (no doubt because air transport was a new means of communication at the time and because the 'colonial model' does not fit the world equally well before the war).

The influence of rank was only predicted to be constant over time, although on the bivariate level we predicted an increase in the impact of rank since other factors were assumed to have a declining effect. However, we have found the effect of geography to be increasing somewhat, and colonial affiliation only decreasing in the last period. In spite of this, the effect of rank on interaction was found to be increasing, not only at the bivariate level, but even controlling for geography and colonial affiliation.

We have mentioned before the possibility that while underdog countries start catching up with regard to connections, they may lag further behind on other indicators (the number of flights, direct flights, etc.). Hence, by choosing new indicators we may find increasing influence of rank and geography, and even of colonial affiliation. In particular, the availability of direct flights is highly dependent today on geography and this effect is probably increasing. It is interesting to speculate that the same may be the case for colonial affiliation. Without data to guide us at this point, our guess is in the negative: we believe the influence of colonial systems to be decreasing, whatever the indicator. Nevertheless, another possibility mentioned in the theoretical discussion, that 'new colonial affiliations' may be increasing while old affiliations decrease, has not been systematically looked into. However, such 'new colonial affiliations' would seem to be mainly a function of the joint effect of rank and conflict, i.e. one is dealing with a general Western and a general Eastern system (both of them highly stratified) and a few nations squeezed in between.

4.6. The impact of conflict

For analyzing the impact of conflict on the present data the regional model is useless, and even the colonial model is not entirely satisfactory. However, we shall comment on the three following conflicts: the 'old' East-West conflict, the 'new cold war' around China, and the Arab-Israeli conflict.

Israel vs. the Arabs

Of these, the last one is the most clear-cut, so clear-cut indeed that Arab-Israeli interaction densities for all four time-points are zero! (This in spite of the fact that Israel is located in the middle of the Arab world, so geographical distance between them is low.) Furthermore, since both internal Arab and external Arab and Israeli interaction has been increasing (Table 5.27) the relative impact of this conflict is all the greater.

TABLE 5.27 *Arab and Israeli interaction patterns (densities). For all four time-points, 125 nations*

Interaction	Densities			
	1930*	1951	1958	1965
Arab. intra-group	0.04	0.38	0.47	0.51
Arabs to all others	0.02	0.09	0.16	0.18
Israel to all	0.00	0.20	0.11	0.19
Arab-Israeli	0.00	0.00	0.00	0.00

* 'Israel' in 1930 = Palestine.

One interesting aspect of the Arab-Israeli conflict is that although there is a total lack of interaction between them, there is no effective 'secondary boycott', i.e. countries are not prevented from having connections to both Israel and the Arabs, and even the same airline can include Israel and Arab countries as intermediate stops on alternate days on their long distance routes. And contrary to what one might expect, Israel and the Arabs are *not* largely connected to different countries [33]. Both serve as important stop-over points for routes from Europe to Asia [34] and no less than 22 countries (or 17.6%) had connections to *both* Israel and the Arabs in 1951 and 1965 (Table 5.29). Naturally, the Arabs have a larger total, reflecting in part intra-Arab interaction, but also more interaction with Africa, as well as with the Soviet Union and Eastern Europe. The lack of Israeli connections to Eastern Europe obviously signifies a polarization, and a .growing one, since Arab interaction with Eastern Europe is increasing

TABLE 5.28. *To what extent are the Arabs and Israel connected to the same countries?*

	1930	1951	1958	1965
Countries connected *both* to one or more Arab countries and to Israel	0%	18%	11%	18%
Countries connected to Arabs but not to Israel	12%	17%	39%	36%
Countries connected to Israel but not to Arabs	0%	2%	0%	0%
Countries connected to neither	88%	63%	50%	46%
Sum	100%	100%	100%	100%
(n)	(125)	(125)	(125)	(125)

187

The dip in common interaction with third parties in 1958 (Table 5.29) and the corresponding drastic increase in the percentage of connections to Arabs only might indicate that a secondary boycott was in effect until 1958, possibly as a result of the 1956 Suez crisis. However, since the interaction rate of Israel with countries *not* interacting with any Arabs also went down, the whole phenomenon would seem better understood as a general decrease in Israel's connections in this period (cf. the total densities in Table 5.27).

The 'old' East-West conflict

The impact of the East-West conflict is less clear, since in comparing inter-action between East and West we must take into account not only conflict but also the fact that the East lags far behind in developing its air interactions. This can be seen clearly from the comparison of total densities for some Eastern and Western groups in Table 5.29.

TABLE 5.29 *Total interaction densities for East and West. Over-time data, 125 nations**

	1930	1951	1958	1965
topdogs				
West	0.14	0.40	0.54	0.62
East	0.02	0.07	0.12	0.31
Difference	0.11	0.33	0.42	0.31
underdogs				
West	0.05	0.17	0.27	0.28
East	0.05	0.04	0.09	0.16
Difference	—0.00	0.14	0.17	0.12

* Only Europeans plus the US are included in this table, to get at the 'old' East—West conflict exclusively, and to lessen the impact of geographical distance. The only country removed from the rest, the US, is the country for which geographical distance is least of a restraint. The Eastern topdog is the Soviet Union, the Eastern underdogs the remaining 8 European Communist countries (including Albania and Yugoslavia). Western topdogs are the US, Britain and France, everything else in Europe (including neutrals) is included in the Western underdog group. (Note that the Eastern underdogs were of course not 'Eastern' in 1930.)

Table 5.29 alone would lead us to suggest that the East-West conflict has had a major impact, but that it is of decreasing importance. For a topdog, the Soviet Union is extremely low (in total density in 1965 it is far below a European middledog like Netherlands and only slightly above Belgium). Eastern European underdogs, on the other hand, reversing a trend found almost everywhere else, decreased total interaction in the period 1931—51.

This can hardly be explained except as a result of East-West polarization and resulting isolation of the East.

We must emphasize that in the polarized situation of the fifties, there was by no means a split between two equals. The West was overwhelmingly superior, particularly in its interaction with countries outside Europe. The question of exactly *how* superior is answered in Table 5.30 which shows how deeply the four topdogs 'penetrate' into each other's systems.

TABLE 5.30 *Interaction within and between systems. High distance interactions only**

1. 1951	Topdogs			
Underdogs	British	French	American	Soviet
British	0.350	0.200	0.200	0.000
French	0.056	0.500	0.167	0.000
American	0.296	0.223	0.852	0.000
Soviet	0.125	0.250	0.000	0.750
2. 1958				
Underdogs	British	French	American	Soviet
British	0.800	0.400	0.400	0.000
French	0.056	0.944	0.167	0.000
American	0.222	0.408	0.889	0.000
Soviet	0.250	0.375*	0.000	0.875
3. 1965				
Underdogs	British	French	American	Soviet
British	0.900	0.400	0.400	0.300
French	0.056	0.944	0.444	0.222
American	0.481	0.519	0.963	0.037
Soviet	0.750	0.875	0.250	0.875

* The nations included represent a reduced version of the colonial model with only two ranks. Only 'British colonies' are included in British underdogs, and 'European communists' in the Soviet underdogs. The American underdogs include both Latin America and 'West Asia'.

Table 5.31 gives the differences in densities for intra-system and inter-system topdog interaction, and compares these differences for systems with and without conflict. All the comparisons indicate that the differences are smaller for systems without conflict, at all three post-war time-points. However, it looks as if the Soviet Union is becoming somewhat more closely integrated with the underdogs of the French and British system, while the interaction with the American system (compared with the interaction of the French and British systems to the American underdogs) is extremely low. Indeed, it is between the American and Soviet systems that we see the polarized and feudal interaction pattern most clearly (and, since the conflict there is the greatest, this is where we would most expect it). However when the US and the Soviet Union decided formally to establish an air connection between their two capitals in the mid-nineteen sixties they opened up interaction at the top of the system — and we should then expect that the great

TABLE 5.31 *Interaction with the underdogs of other systems. Differences in density between intra-system and inter-system interactions. With and without conflict*

		Difference in density between intra-system topdog- -underdog interaction and inter-system		
Year	Underdogs	(1) Between systems with conflict*	(2) Between systems without conflict	(2) — (1)
1951	British	0.35	0.15	0.20
1958		0.85	0.45	0.40
1965		0.60	0.50	0.10
1951	French	0.50	0.39	0.11
1958		0.94	0.83	0.11
1965		0.72	0.69	0.03
1951	American	0.85	0.59	0.30
1958		0.89	0.57	0.32
1965		0.93	0.46	0.46
1951	Soviet	0.63	—	—
1958		0.67	—	—
1965		0.25	—	—

* Systems without conflict: American, British, and French. Systems with conflict: those three vs. the Soviet system.

potential for interaction between the lower levels of the systems should now be exploited.

The situation is not quite symmetrical, since while the US interacts with Soviet underdogs, the Soviet Union hardly interacts with US underdogs. However, if Western Europe had been included in the group of Western underdogs, the situation would have looked different. Several European NATO members, such as Denmark, have connections both to the Soviet Union and her European allies (particularly Czechoslovakia).

There are two interpretations of this. One possibility was mentioned above, namely, the prediction (contrary to the feudal hypothesis) that big nations in conflict might be using their underdogs as a testing-ground for interaction. Hence, the US-Soviet air agreement should be seen as a successful conclusion of a period of successful testing. A different interpretation, and a more likely one, in our opinion, (and not contrary to the feudal hypothesis), is that European interaction, by air and otherwise, was so well established before the Second World War and in the immediate period afterwards, that no amount of Cold War could disrupt it completely (although the data indicate that interaction between Eastern and Western Europe decreased during the first period of Cold War [35]. The geographical proximity of these parts of two opposing blocs also made for interaction between them. Outside Europe, however, the situation is a radically different one. Just as the Soviet Union has no interaction to American underdogs, other than Iran, the US has no connections to the three Asian and one American communist underdog states. Here, in a sense, the East-West conflict is more salient. But with regard to the Asian underdogs of the Sino-Soviet system it fuses with the 'other Cold War' which we shall examine next.

Finally, we shall comment on the other Cold War: the conflict between China and the West. In terms of airline interaction this split is very clear. Table 5.32 gives the total number of countries to which China had connections at the various time-points.

TABLE 5.32 *China's connections over time*

Countries	Year			
	1930*	1951	1958	1965
	Japan N. Korea S. Korea	—	Burma Mongolia USSR	Burma Cambodia Indonesia N. Korea N. Vietnam Pakistan USSR
Total	3	0	2	7
%of all countries	2%	0%	2%	5%
(n)	(125)	(125)	(125)	(125)

* The three connections in 1930 were all Japanese connections to occupied territory. Unfortunately, the data give no indication of the extent of China's involvement in the international air network immediately before the revolution. However, airline maps in the 1951 guidebook still retain connections to several Chinese cities — although these connections had not been operating for some time. — The difference between 1958 and 1965 may be due to an error in the 1958 guidebook.

The China vs. the West situation is similar to that of the Arabs vs. Israel, in that the split is a total one. However, there is the very marked difference that while the Arab-Israeli conflict has not resulted in the isolation of either of the two parties (or at most, a little in the case of Israel), China is completely isolated, although a little less so in 1965. Against the baselines of the growing density of the world airline network generally, of China's population, its growing military power and involvement in world afffairs — against almost any baseline — the isolation of China is dramatic [36]. The same applies to the two socialist countries in its orbits. North Vietnam and North Korea — but these are small countries, and their low interaction is therefore (partly) explainable in other terms. However, the comparison in Table 5.33 indicates that this does not explain everything, since there is also a clear difference between the two halves of Vietnam and Korea. This difference is clearer in the case of Vietnam than of Korea. However, if all the 220 nations are taken into account, South Korea's connections increase to 4, while North Korea's do not increase. More importantly, however, South Korea is connected with countries with a high number of connections, so as to give it a more central location in the network as a whole.

TABLE 5.33 *Some smaller Asian countries: a comparison*

Country	Population (1961)	Air interaction (connections)		
		1951	1958	1965
North Vietnam	16.7 mill	3	0	2
South Vietnam	14.5 mill.	9	20	20
North Korea	8.6 mill.	0	0	2
South Korea	25.4 mill.	3	2	3

TABLE 5.34 *Cuba's connections over time*

Year	Total no. of connections	World rank (percentile)*	Connections in America	Rank in America (percentile)**
1930	15	3.2	15	8.3
1951	21	19.6	17	12.5
1958	24	26.4	20	8.3
1965	4	90.4	4	100.0

* World rank (in terms of total no. of connections) divided by the number of countries (125) times 100. Tied ranks are averaged.
** Rank among the countries in America in terms of intra-American connections.

The only parallel elsewhere in the world [37] is the case of Cuba [38]. From a central location in the inter-American airline net of the fifties, Cuba has become totally isolated, with connections only to four European countries. Table 5.34 illustrates the change.

5. Conclusions and policy recommendations

Having surveyed at some length the trends in air interaction between nations we have identified a number of factors with substantial influence on inter-action patterns. The impact of geographical distance we found to be large and, if anything, increasing. Affiliation to a 'colonial' system also was increasing until the late fifties, but has recently been decreasing. We have found the Cold War to be diminishing in impact, while a new Cold War has developed around China and around Cuba. The Arab-Israeli conflict continues to prevent air interaction between the two parties. Above all, the rank of a nation was found to influence its interaction patterns. As a means of integration, then, the airline network has served mainly to link the nations of high rank. Underdog nations have also increased their inter-action, but with a bias towards their geographical neighbors, nations in their own 'system', and nations with which they (or their corresponding topdogs) are not in conflict. It seems likely that, even if present trends continue, at some point the underdog nations must start catching up. As we have repeatedly pointed out, however, this does not mean that equality will come nearer, only that we need other indicators than a simple 'con-nection' variable to measure the inequality (such as 'flights', 'direct flights').

If a policy of international development includes the following two aims — the wisdom of which we have not shed any light on in this article — *integration across conflict lines* and *the creation of a welfare world*, then it would appear that the current trends cannot just be allowed to drift: rather, attention must be turned to the development of more 'democratic' interaction patterns as an integral part of an international development policy.

Just as national governments have been responsible in developed countries for ensuring that all parts of the country are accessible to each other (by railroads, aviation, interstate highways), the central coordinating organ of the world community should see it as its responsibility to facilitate inter-action between underdog countries, between geographically distant coun-tries, and between countries in conflict. This organ is, of course, the UN family, and in particular the relevant special agency of the UN, the Inter-national Civil Aviation Organization.

It remains entirely outside the scope of this article to undertake a critical discussion of the policies and organization of ICAO, in relation to the aims mentioned above [39]. However, the following few suggestions may be worth considering:

1. The 'division of labor' between ICAO and IATA (International Transport Association) should be critically reviewed. The IATA is a private organization with the national airlines as members. Naturally, with their powerful position in international air traffic, the major Western companies are a dominant force in IATA. Some of the powers of the IATA, such as the determination of prices on international traffic, might be transferred to ICAO on the grounds that fixing price levels is a matter for government and not for private cartels.

2. Efforts should be made to expand ICAO and IATA into truly universal organizations. In particular, the absence of the Soviet Union, China, and the East European countries must be deplored.

3. As a first step towards the universalization of ICAO, the secretariat should be instructed to compile their statistics on a universal basis, wherever the information is available, and not just for member nations.

4. The practicability of a system of subsidizing certain international routes by taxation on the more profitable ones should be looked into. While such a scheme may not be politically realistic today, such plans will have an important function whenever the time is ready to move towards some form of international taxation. Such proposals might involve an internationalization of all air-space (outside certain defined limits) and heavy use of this space would be subject to taxation.

5. The possibility of an international airline operated by ICAO or another international agency should also be explored.

Appendix 1

Connections by country for all four time-points and confirmation ratio for the hypothesis of monotonic growth in the number connections.

Number [40]	Name	Year 1930	1951	1958	1965	Confirmation ratio, %
101	Algeria	2	14	14	14	75
105	Burundi	0	2	5	7	100
106	Cameroons	0	11	8	15	83
108	CAR	0	3	6	5	83
109	Chad	0	2	6	6	92
111	Congo (Brazzaville)	0	10	13	15	100
112	Congo (Kinshasa)	0	18	21	19	83
113	Dahomey	0	5	8	10	100
114	Ethiopia	0	9	5	14	83
115	Gabon	0	9	4	5	67
116	Gambia	0	3	9	10	100
117	Ghana	0	17	17	34	92
118	Guinea	0	5	7	19	100
122	Ivory Coast	0	11	16	22	100
123	Kenya	5	24	22	27	83
124	Liberia	0	12	13	30	100
125	Libya	1	7	21	21	92
126	Malagasy Rep.	0	5	6	5	75
127	Malawi	0	4	5	5	92
128	Mali	0	5	7	12	100
129	Mauritania	3	0	2	4	67
131	Morocco	4	11	9	19	83
133	Niger	0	7	9	6	67
134	Nigeria	0	13	23	31	100
136	Rhodesia	0	12	14	16	100
137	Rwanda	0	2	2	3	92
140	Senegal	3	27	31	30	83
142	Sierra Leone	0	6	9	11	100
143	Somalia	0	4	3	4	75
145	South Africa	0	16	26	27	100
149	Sudan	5	20	26	20	75
151	Tanzania	5	4	10	17	83
152	Togo	0	9	5	5	58
153	Tunisia	3	11	9	20	83
154	Uganda	5	1	11	17	83
155	UAR	9	36	39	55	100
156	Upper Volta	0	2	5	7	100
157	Zambia	0	4	12	9	83
202	Argentina	12	22	29	27	83
207	Bolivia	1	0	9	10	92
208	Brazil	7	22	27	26	83

Number	Name	Year 1930	1951	1958	1965	Confirmation ratio, %
209	Canada	1	29	22	22	58
212	Chile	5	7	21	26	100
213	Colombia	14	11	18	21	83
214	Costa Rica	9	9	10	7	42
215	Cuba	15	21	24	4	50
217	Dominican Rep.	7	7	9	5	42
218	Ecuador	5	9	15	16	100
219	El Salvador	10	7	9	7	25
224	Guatemala	3	8	13	9	83
227	Haiti	7	5	6	3	17
228	Honduras	9	7	11	8	50
229	Jamaica	0	13	8	11	67
231	Mexico	10	9	16	25	83
234	Nicaragua	9	7	12	7	42
235	Panama	9	21	23	23	92
236	Paraguay	1	8	14	11	83
237	Peru	6	13	20	22	100
244	Trinidad and Tobago	7	11	8	9	67
246	US	17	58	66	76	100
247	Uruguay	11	14	22	20	83
248	Venezuela	9	14	21	22	100
302	Afghanistan	0	0	6	9	92
307	Burma	0	5	30	21	83
308	Cambodia	0	2	3	21	100
309	Ceylon	0	7	23	18	83
310	China	3	0	3	7	75
311	Cyprus	0	10	10	12	92
313	India	5	32	38	43	100
314	Indonesia	1	3	24	27	100
315	Iran	6	15	29	35	100
316	Iraq	6	19	32	26	83
317	Israel	0	25	14	23	67
319	Japan	3	12	31	37	100
320	Jordan	0	2	6	13	100
322	North Korea	3	0	0	2	42
323	South Korea	3	3	2	3	42
324	Kuwait	0	6	11	21	100
325	Laos	0	0	3	2	75
326	Lebanon	3	20	46	43	83
328	Malaysia	0	7	13	16	100
330	Mongolia	0	0	2	1	75
332	Nepal	0	0	1	2	92
333	Pakistan	5	30	35	39	100
335	Philippines	0	13	29	24	83
339	Saudi Arabia	0	17	23	22	83
341	Singapore	1	13	23	30	100
342	Syria	1	20	31	30	83

Number	Name	Year 1930	1951	1958	1965	Confirmation ratio, %
343	Taiwan	0	4	6	5	83
344	Thailand	0	23	37	32	83
346	Turkey	10	18	38	30	83
347	North Vietnam	0	3	0	2	58
348	South Vietnam	0	9	20	20	92
349	Yemen	0	0	1	1	83
401	Albania	1	1	3	5	92
403	Austria	13	12	28	38	83
404	Belgium	6	25	36	37	100
405	Bulgaria	7	4	13	21	83
406	Czechoslovakia	12	17	24	42	100
407	Denmark	7	29	44	45	100
409	Finland	2	11	13	19	100
410	France	23	44	72	79	100
411	East Germany	13	2	10	18	67
412	West Germany	18	32	59	69	100
414	Greece	14	28	46	55	100
415	Hungary	10	6	23	23	75
416	Iceland	0	4	8	9	100
417	Ireland	0	11	21	12	83
418	Italy	10	53	62	69	100
420	Luxembourg	0	0	6	9	92
421	Malta	0	6	5	3	50
423	Netherlands	9	39	56	65	100
424	Norway	4	8	9	8	75
425	Poland	4	10	13	19	100
426	Portugal	0	34	42	34	75
427	Romania	8	4	11	15	83
429	USSR	3	8	15	38	100
430	Spain	5	26	34	46	100
432	Sweden	9	29	42	18	67
433	Switzerland	8	33	51	64	100
434	UK	11	45	60	75	100
436	Yugoslavia	10	3	16	36	83
501	Australia	0	13	23	34	100
515	New Zealand	0	4	8	15	100
523	Western Samoa	0	1	0	0	42

Appendix 2

Systems, groups, and countries for the 125-nation world

System	Group rank	Group	Country
British (n = 26)	T	Britain	Britain
	M	White Empire (n = 5)	Australia
			Canada
			New Zealand
			Rhodesia
			South Africa
	U	Former British colonies (n = 20)	Burma
			Ceylon
			Cyprus
			Gambia
			Ghana
			India
			Jamaica
			Kenya
			Malaysia
			Malawi
			Malta
			Nigeria
			Pakistan
			Sierra Leone
			Singapore
			Tanzania
			Trinidad and Tobago
			Uganda
			Zambia
			Western Samoa
French (n = 19)	T	France	France
		Former French colonies (n = 18)	Algeria
			Cambodia
			Cameroon
			Central African Rep.
			Chad
			Congo (Brazz.)
			Dahomey
			Gabon
			Guinea
			Ivory Coast
			Malagasy Rep.
			Mali
			Morocco
			Niger
			Senegal
			Togo
			Tunisia
			Upper Volta
American (n = 28)	T	US	US
	U	West Asia (n = 8)	Iran
			Japan
			Laos
			Philippines
			Taiwan (Formosa)
			Thailand
			S. Korea
			S. Vietnam
	U	Latin America (n = 19)	Argentina
			Bolivia
			Brazil
			Chile
			Colombia
			Costa Rica
			Dominican rep.
			Ecuador
			El Salvador
			Guatemala
			Haiti
			Honduras
			Mexico
			Nicaragua
			Panama
			Paraguay
			Peru
			Uruguay
			Venezuela

System	Group rank	Group	Country
Belgian (n = 4)	M	Belgium	Belgium
	U	Former Belgian colonies (n = 3)	Burundi Congo (Kinshasa) Rwanda
Dutch (n = 2)	M	Netherlands	Netherlands
	U	Former Dutch colonies	Indonesia
Western Europe (n = 15)	M	Western Europe (n = 15)	Austria Denmark Finland Greece Iceland Ireland Italy Luxembourg Norway Portugal Spain Sweden Switzerland Turkey West Germany
Israel (n = 1)	M	Israel	Israel
Rest of Africa (n = 4)	U	Rest of Africa (n = 4)	Ethiopia Liberia Somalia Sudan

System	Group rank	Group	Country
Rest of Asia (n = 2)	U	Rest of Asia (n = 2)	Afghanistan Nepal
Arabs (n = 10)	U	Arabs (n = 10)	Iraq Jordan Kuwait Lebanon Libya Mauritania Saudi Arabia Syria United Arab Rep. Yemen
Sino-Soviet (n = 14)	T	Soviet Union	Soviet Union
	M	China	China
	M	European comm. (n = 8)	Albania Bulgaria Czecho-slovakia East Germany Hungary Poland Romania Yugoslavia
	U	American communists	Cuba
	U	Asian comm. (n = 3)	Mongolia North Korea North Vietnam

Appendix 3

The data collection

The data used in this study have all been collected from flight schedules. The first set of data is on all international *flights* for 220 nations and territories in August 1965. The 220 nations and territories are from the PRIO *list of nations* (available in mimeo from the International Peace Research Institute, Oslo). This list aims at including *all* nations and territories, provided they fulfill all of the following criteria: 1. have an indigenous population (thus Greenland was included but not Spitsbergen); 2. are administered separately (thus the islands of Barbuda and Barbados each constitute a unit, while the several islands of Netherlands Antilles also count as just one unit); 3. must be territorially non-contiguous to the 'mother country' (thus, Puerto Rico and the Faeroe Islands are separate units, while Wales and Scotland are not); 4. must be either considered a separate unit by a significant segment of the population or must be in clearly subservient relationship to the mother territory (hence Alaska and Hawaii, which have gained statehood and apparently have no significant independence movements, as well as East Pakistan, which is an integral part of a divided country, do *not* qualify, unlike Puerto Rico, which is an 'associated free state' with an independence movement).

The reliability of the guide-books we have assumed to be near-perfect for our purposes. Officials of international (International Civil Aviation Organization, International Air Transport Association) and national agencies (Civil Aeronautics Board of Washington, D. C., Scandinavian Airlines System in Oslo, Norway) have all expressed their belief that virtually all international connections are listed, although many domestic flights may be missing, particularly in countries like China (for which information is too scarce) and the US (where flights are too numerous). However, we are not concerned here with domestic flights at all. If there is any systematic error at all, it would most probably be in the direction of underreporting flights not originating in the North Atlantic area.

Two problems arose in the 1951 guidebook. First, the book states that 'SABENA provides scheduled services throughout Belgian Congo'. The guide-book map indicated that this included flights to the (now independent) territories of Burundi and Rwanda, as well as between the two. All three connections were therefore coded. A more serious problem was announced as follows in the section on Air France: 'Also scheduled service within French West Africa, French Equatorial Africa, and to many points throughout the continent of Africa, including the islands of Madagascar, Mauritius and Reunion'. Again, the missing information could partly be found in the map section. Also, an Air France map in the schedules section was of some help. We were satisfied that all connections to Europe had been coded. As for the African routes there was disagreement between the three sources, and the maps did not indicate the endpoints of the flights. As a minimum assumption all *direct* flights on the map were added, except for one which seemed to have been replaced by a different route. (In general, the maps in the flight schedules have been found to be out of date. Thus the maps in 1951 still included flights to the Chinese mainland). Compared with a reasonable guess as to how the routes in fact did , in, we have missed a total of 11 connections between French African countries. However, 4 of these did not have a connection in 1958 either, so the loss might in fact be as low as 7.

The second set of data are on *connections* (but not *flights)* between 125 countries in 1930, 1951, and 1958. The basis for selecting these countries was that they were all independent as of August 1959. An explicit exception, however, was made in the case of (Southern) Rhodesia, which proclaimed independence in November 1965 and had considerable autonomy in advance. Among the small countries excluded from the short list are several semiautonomous small states and sheikdoms (such as Bhutan, Sikkim, Andorra, Liechtenstein, San Marino, Monaco, Qatar, Trucial Oman). Unlike some authors in international relations, we make no claim that this is a representative sample of nations, or that it includes all 'significant' nations; the limitation was dictated exclusively by practical considerations. The effect of restriction of the number of countries is, of course, that the 'density' of the world airline network is exaggerated. The choice of the time-points was dictated by the availability of information (the 1930 flight schedule was the earliest one we could find) as well as a desire to evaluate the over-time trends on the basis of at least three post-war time points.

The following sources were used: For 1930: *International Air Guide*, 1931, and (for inter-American flights) the *Official Aviation Guide of the Airways*, August 1930. For

1951 and 1958: *Official Airlines Guide*. For 1965: *ABC World Airways Guide*. The latter two guide-books are the two main contemporary guide-books, published in the United States and in Britain respectively. The *International Air Guide*, published in Paris in 1931, appears to be a unique publication. Although titled 'no. 1, 1931' we have found no record of a second edition. It is a heavy-bound, expensive-looking work, prefaced by Prince Bibesco, president of the *Fédération Aéronautique International*. Both Prince Bibesco and the publishers hail the book as a historical publication, a landmark in the history of aviation. The sponsorship of the *Fédération* and various remarks in the introductions indicate that the publishers have had ample access to all records of scheduled airlines at that tine. Hence, with the exception of the intra-American lines, the guide should be quite reliable. However, it was decided to code the book as 1930 instead of 1931, for several reasons. First, the production-time for this large volume must have been considerable, all the more so since the editors started from nothing. Furthermore, for several scheduled operations it is indicated that 'this route should be in operation by 1931' (these have not been coded and could not have been since no information is given on intermediate stops). The (American) *Oficial Aviation Guide*, which was used to supplement the information for the Western Hemisphere, is probably more up to date. This is a monthly publication, a slim paperbound volume which no doubt relied on short publication time and high accuracy to sell regularly. Also it had been published for several years. We have therefore assumed that the August 1930 edition of this work corresponds in time to the other book.

It should be noted that for all four time-points we are using the same number of countries. However, during these 35 years important changes in the number and location of countries have occurred. Former colonial territories have been split up, and some united and the Second World War created a number of new boundaries in Europe. Instead of trying to 'define the world' at each of the four points we projected today's world backwards. Hence, future trends can be projected only on the basis of our world. We believe that the general propositions will not be affected vitally, but more descriptive characterizations of particular areas may change as the 'composition of the world' changes. In any case, we would not expect great territorial changes in the near future.

Various problems arose with regard to how cities and regions which have changed 'ownership' should be coded. The most important coding decisions are recorded in the Table below.

City/region	Coded as	Affects connection with	Year
Estonia	USSR	Finland	1930
Königsberg et al.	East Germany	several	1930
Berlin	East Germany	—	1930
West Berlin	West Germany	—	1951
Rijeka (Fiume)	Italy	Italy (i.e. not coded)	1930
Lwow	Poland	several	1930
Manchuria	China	Japan	1930
Biak	Netherlands New Guinea	i.e. ignored	1958

A few times 'Berlin' is listed with no indication of whether it is East or West. We have assumed that routes continuing to the West land in West Berlin, those originating in the East and ending in Berlin land in East Berlin. Again, there are other routes overlapping some of these, so even if we have made a few mistakes here, the number of connections will probably not be affected.

Bibliography

ADLER-KARLSSON, G.: *Western Economic Warfare 1947—67.* (Stockholm: Almqvist & Wiksell, 1968)

ALKER, H. R.: *Mathematics and Politics.* New York: Macmillan, 1965.

ALKER, H. R. and RUSSETT, B. M.: 'On Measuring Inequality', *Behavioral Science*, vol. 9, no. 3, July 1964.

BALES, R. F. and SLATER, PH. E.: 'Role Differentiation in Small Decision-Making Groups', In Parsons, T. and Bales, R. F.; *Family, Socialization, and Interaction Process.* Glencoe: Free Press, 1955.

BERELSON, B. and STEINER, G. A.: *Human Behavior: An Inventory of Scientific Findings.* New York: Harcourt, Brace and World, Inc., 1964.

COLEMAN, J.: *Introduction to Mathematical Sociology.* New York: The Free Press, 1964.

DEUTSCH, KARL W.: 'Shifts in the Balance of Communication Flows: A Problem of Measurement in International Relations', *Public Opinion Quarterly*, vol. 20, 1956.
— 'The Halting of European Structural Integration: The Evidence of Transactions'. In Deutsch, K. W. et al.: *France, Germany, and the Western Alliance: A Study of Elite Attitudes on European and World Politics.* New York: Scribner, 1967.

DEUTSCH, KARL, W. and SAVAGE, I. R.: A Statistical Model of the Gross Analysis of Transaction Flows'. *Econometrica*, vol. XXVIII, no. 3, 1960.

GALTUNG, JOHAN. 'Small Group Theory of International Relations: A Study in Isomorphism', mimeo, International Peace Research Institute, Oslo, 1966. (1966 a) In this Volume of *Essays in Peace Research.*
— 'East-West Interaction Patterns', *Journal of Peace Research*, vol. 3, no. 2, 1966. (1966b).

GALTUNG, JOHAN; MORA Y ARAUJO, MANUEL; and SCHWARTZMAN, SIMON: 'El Sistema Latino-americano de Naciones: un Analisis Estructural', *America Latina*, ano 9, no. 1, 1966.

GLEDITSCH, N. P.: "Trends in World Airline Patterns", *Journal of Peace Research*, vol. 4, no. 4, 1967, pp. 366—408.

GLEDITSCH, N. P.: *The Structure of the International Airline Network*, Mimeographed thesis, Oslo, PRIO 1968, 190 p.

GLEDITSCH, N. P.: "The International Airline Network: A Test of the Zipf and Stouffer Hypotheses", *Papers, Peace Research Society (International)*, vol. 11, 1969, pp. 123—153.

GLEDITSCH, N. P.: "Rank Theory, Field Theory and Attribute Theory: Three Approaches to Interaction in the International System", *Research Report* no. 47, Dimensionality of Nations Project, Department of Political Science, University of Hawaii, 1970, 58 p. (1970 a).

GLEDITSCH, N. P.: "Rank and Interaction: A General Theory with Some Applications to the International System", *Proceedings of the IPRA Third Conference*, Assen, van Gorcum, 1970, vol. 1, pp. 1—21 (1970 b).

GLEDITSCH, N. P.: "Interaction Patterns in the Middle East", *Cooperation and Conflict*, vol 6, no. 1, 1971, pp. 15—30.

GLEDITSCH, N. P.: "Time Differences and International Interaction", *Cooperation and Conflict*, vol. 9, no. 2, 1971, pp. 190—192. (1971 a).

GLEDITSCH, N. P.: "Slow is Beautiful. The Stratification of Personal Mobility. With Special Reference to International Aviation", *Acta Sociologica*, vol. 18, no. 1, 1975, pp. 76—94. (1971 b).

GLEDITSCH, N. P.: "Towards a Multilateral Aviation Treaty", *Journal of Peace Research*, vol. 14, no. 3, 1977, pp. 239—61.

HARARY, F.; NORMAN, R. Z.; and CARTWRIGHT, D.: *Structural Models: An Introduction to the Theory of Directed Graphs*. New York: Wiley, 1965.

HOMANS, G. C.: *The Human Group*. London: Routledge, 1951.

HURWITZ, J. I.; ZANDER, A. F.; and HYMOVITCH, B.: 'Some Effects of Power on the Relations among Group Members', in Cartwright, D. and Zander, A. F.: *Group Dynamics: Research and Theory*. 2nd ed. New York: Harper and Row, 1960.

HØIVIK, TORD & GLEDITSCH, N. P.: "Structural Parameters of Graphs: A Theoretical Investigation", *Quality and Quantity*, vol. 4, no. 1, 1970, pp. 193—209.

HØIVIK, TORD & GLEDITSCH, N. P.: "Best Interaction Models", *Quality and Quantity*, vol. 12, 1978.

JAMES, P. K, and JONES, C. F. (eds.): *American Geography: Inventory and Prospects*. Syracuse, NY: Syracuse University Press, 1960.

LINDBEKK, T.: 'Utdannelsen i Norge'. In: Ramsøy, N. R. (ed.): *Det Norske Samfunnet: En Sosiologisk Beskrivelse*. Oslo: Gyldendal, 1968.

LINNEMANN, H.: *An Econometric Study of International Trade Flows*. In *Contribution to Economic Analysis*. Amsterdam: North-Holland, 1966.

McGOWAN, PATRICK: Unpublished paper, Department of Political Science, Northwestern University 1967.

MILLS, TH. M.: 'Power Relations in Three-Person Groups', *American Sociological Review*, vol. 18, pp. 351—357, 1953. Reprinted in Cartwright, D. and Zander, A. F., op. cit. (see above under Hurwitz et al.).

NEWCOMB, T. M.: *The Acquaintance Process.* New York: Holt, Rinehart and Winston, 1961.

NEWCOMB, T. M.; TURNER, R.; and CONVERSE, PH.: *Social Psychology: The Study of Human Interaction.* New York: Holt, Rinehart and Winston, 1965.

RAPOPORT, A.: *Games That Simulate Escalation and Deterrence (Peace Research Reviews.)* Canadian Peace Research Institute, 1967.

REINTON, P. O.: 'International Structure and International Integration'. *Journal of Peace Research* vol. 4, no. 4, 1967, pp. 334—365.

RUMMEL, R. J.: 'Some Dimensions in the Foreign Behavior of Nations'. *Journal of Peace Research*, vol. 3, no. 3, 1966.

SCHWARTZMAN, S.: 'International Development and International Feudalism: The Latin American Case'. For full reference, see Smoker (1966).

SEALY, K.: *The Geography of Air Transport.* London: Hutchinson, 1957.

SIMON, H.: *Models of Man: Social and Rational.* New York: Wiley, 1960.

SMOKER, PAUL: 'A Preliminary Empirical Study of an International Integrative Subsystem'. In *IPRA Studies in Peace Research: Proceedings of the International Peace Research Association Inaugural Conference.* Assen: Van Gorcum, 1966.

STOUFFER, S. L., et al.: *Measurement and Prediction.* Princeton: Princeton University Press, 1950.

WARNER, W. L.; MEEKER, M.: and EELES, K.: *Social Class in America.* Chicago: Social Science Research Associates, 1949.

WEEKS, GEORGE: "Wings of Change. A Report on the Progress of Civil Aviation in Africa." *Africa Report*, vol. 10, no. 2, February 1965.

ZIPF, G. K.: *Human Behavior and the Principle of Least Effort.* Cambridge, Mass.: Addison-Wesley, 1949.

IV.6. The Latin American System of Nations: A Structural Analysis*

From B. Höglund & J. W. Ulrich (eds.): *Conflict Control and Conflict Research* (Copenhagen: Munksgaard, 1972). PRIO publication No. 21−1.

Notes on page *698*.

1. Introduction

In this article the Latin American system will be described and studied as a system of twenty actors in interaction, just as if it were a small group. This means than an important aspect of the analytical tradition in sociology will be utilized at the level of international interaction: the analysis of behavior as conditioned by structural factors. In sociology this has a relatively precise meaning. When a sociologist describes and analyzes human interaction, this is usually done with reference to such "background variables" as age, sex, occupation, educational level, social rank, social status, belongingness to groups. The names of the individuals are not mentioned. And the reason for this is not any kind of aversion against names, but simply the idea of trying to find the explanation of human phenomena in terms of general, explicit and observable characteristics of human beings, and not in terms of all the special and idiosyncratic information that one can obtain about a particular Pedro Sanchez. This means that the sociologist disregards more diffuse information about the persons he studies, even if this information might perhaps give him a more profound insight in order to gain, on the other hand, in economy, generality and precision. He may say something like this: "These are the variables I am going to make use of. I shall measure them in such and such a way, and I want to investigate how they combine in the empirical reality and how much I can explain of the behavior of the individuals in terms of these variables. If nothing comes out of this, then I have to search for other variables, for example personality characteristics. But if I can explain a considerable fraction of the variance in behavior by means of these variables, so much the better."

Applied to the study of international systems this means that one programmatically declines from using a lot of lexicographic insight about anything related to the Latin American nations, collected by the numerous scholars studying Latin America who have much to say about this international subsystem in particular, much of it unverifiable and some of it even verified. But this procedure is in general far from the principle pronounced by Occam several centuries ago: *entia non sunt multiplicandem præter necessitatem.* The tendency is to explain any new phenomena in terms of a new "entity" or variable, and not to stick to a limited set of selected variables to see how much can be explained in terms of them. Besides, the basis for description and explication are usually not very explicit. A scholar says something about "Bolivia", and makes use of a considerable amount of intuition and common sense knowledge, but he does not thereby contribute to generalized findings. In order to provide the basis for general propositions the theory about Bolivia has to be made in terms of variables on which Bolivia is given a precise value, with indication of how other countries can be measured and placed on the same variables. And this is the approach of this article, the names of the countries will only be used as tags of identification, not in order to draw upon some surplus of their meanings of a less explicit nature.

2. Theory

Our point of departure is the simple idea that an international system, just as national system, can be regarded as stratified and that the interaction patterns between the actors will depend, both in intensity and in other characteristics, on the position the actors occupy in the stratification system [1]. In order to speak properly about a system of stratification two conditions are necessary:

1. The existence of *rank dimensions* that order the countries from "high" positions to "low" positions.
2. The existence of *a certain consensus* with regard to how to classify the countries that belong to this system.

These two conditions are *interdependent*. A rank dimension is a variable, and like all other variables its values, called "ranks", are mutually exclusive and exhaustive, in the system of units (individuals, nations, etc.) for which the dimension is defined. But contrary to other types of variables, a rank dimension is always ordered (it has the properties of the ordinal scales) and a clear meaning is given to "high ranks" at one extreme and "low rank" at the other. But even under these conditions it is only meaningful to talk about rank dimensions to the extent that one can find a consensus in the system according to which the high ranks are really pursued and the low ranks are really avoided, or at least that the high ranks are not avoided and the low ranks not pursued.

Or in other words: the rank dimensions are defined for a specific system, and it is the very existence of this system, with its particular consensual value system, that gives to these variables their character of being rank dimensions. And here we more or less take it for granted that our twenty nations can be regarded as a system. The very fact that the general term "Latin American nations" is used about them, the existence of international organizations of a regional character, their geographical proximity, the fact that they are characterized as "developing" (implying that the consensual value "development" is not fulfilled) — all this justified the idea that the Latin American system exists, and the study of its characteristics.

The problem is now how to define the variables of stratification, the rank dimensions. There are many possibilities for analysis once this perspective is chosen, depending on whether one wants to consider one or more rank dimensions at a time, and whether one wants to consider one or more units (nations) at a time. Table 6.1 gives a general and systematic idea of the analytical possibilities.

TABLE 6.1 *The dimensions of rank analysis*

| | | number of dimensions | | |
		one	two	many
number of units	one	rank	total rank of the unit rank equilibrium and disequilibrium	(generalization)
	two	total rank of the pair rank equality and rank difference	rank equivalence or inequivalence rank congruence or incongruence	(generalization)
	many	(generalization)	(generalization: rank agreement, criss-cross)	(generalization: rank concordance, etc.)

Detailed comment on this table follows later. What interests us here is a special type of social structure which we shall call the *feudal system*, an over-used term to which we shall try to give a more precise meaning [2]. By a feudal system we mean a system of units with two characteristic properties:

1. *Rank concordance, i.e. the rank dimensions are strongly correlated with each other.*

207

2. *Interaction in pairs of nations is strongly dependent on the total rank of the pair.*

By "rank concordance" we mean the extent to which all the *m* units in the system are ordered in the same way by the *n* dimensions that are defined in the system. Thus, if rank concordance is present, then some units will tend to be high on all dimensions and other units will tend to be low on all dimensions. The theoretical hypothesis that develops from this is the idea that *the higher the rank concordance, the higher the probability that generalized rank-roles* will emerge. In other words, the more rank concordance, the more will there be a tendency for units that are high on all dimensions to behave in such a way that they will continue to be high on these dimensions, and similarly for the units, that rank low. This is tantamount to indicating that rank concordance is self-reinforcing.

Rank concordance means not only that the same pair of units will always find itself in the same relative rank regardless of which dimensions are used to measure the rank, but that each individual unit will find itself in the same position on each dimension. Both of these factors contribute to the structural condition under which units will be trained in generalized rank-roles, as "high", "middle" or "low". An implication of this is that in a rank-concordant system switching from one focus of interaction to another, which usually means switching from one rank-dimension to another, is easy because the same high-class units will always encounter the same low-class units in the same social relation. This means that a constant pattern of interaction can be maintained, that deference always flows in the same direction, for instance.

But this is not the only thing we mean by a feudal system, although rank-concordance is a highly important element. The other element is the idea that the interaction should depend strongly on the rank of the pair of units. The perfect and extreme case of a feudal system would be a system divided in two classes, a high class and a low class (and also a middle class if that status exists in the system), in such a way that the interaction is heavily concentrated in the high rank units and there is some interaction between high and low, but no interaction between the units with low rank. At the other extreme is the completely a-feudal system, where there is no concordance of rank. Instead there is rank-discordance, and interaction does not in any sense depend on the total rank of the pair. The feudal system is by definition *both* high on rank-concordance *and* high on the extent to which interaction depends on the rank of the pair.

The main consequence of the existence of a system of a feudal type as we have defined it is that this is a self-sustained system, *both* in the sense that both of its characteristics is self-reinforcing *and* in that the two characteristics are mutually reinforcing.

We have already mentioned the concept of generalized rank-role. For a unit with, say, three high statuses, the social position it has been given signifies a resource which can be utilized to conquer other statuses with high rank, whereas for a unit with only low statuses a type of inhibition and dependence will be built into the unit. This will generate a generalized behavioral pattern which not only will prevent the unit with low status from conquering a high status, but will also add to the probability that the unit will accept more statuses of low rank.

With reference to the second characteristic of a feudal system, it has been relatively well established with small groups under experimental conditions that they tend to stratify, and that the interaction is more intense between members of the high statuses. There is successively decreasing intensity in the interaction between one unit that is high and one unit that is low, and between units from the low strata. This pattern is self-reinforcing, because once it has been established interaction will be so much more gratifying where it has already taken place. But all units will try to interact upwards, because that is where the reward is. In general, any unit will succeed in getting another unit on the "interaction-hook" to the extent that the other unit finds that the first unit is interesting enough — and this will again depend on how high a rank it has. The result is a high degree of interdependence between rank and volume of interaction. The reason why the two characteristics of a feudal system reinforce each other is very simple. Rank is a "good" thing and rank-concordance means that there is a heavy concentration of this type of value on persons who have much on all dimensions, and a similar deprivation in resources among those are low on all dimensions. Since interaction has to do with the exchange of goods, this means that the rich will enrich themselves by a heavy pattern of interaction and the poor deprive themselves even more the lower their level of interaction is.

Our working hypothesis now is that *the Latin American system of nations satisfies the two characteristics of a feudal system.* If this is the case this will imply that the existing differences between countries will tend to increase, not to decrease. The difficulties of integration and cooperation between countries will be more pronounced the more inferior the position of the countries in the system, which is tantamount to saying that the more the countries are in need of integration and cooperation, the less they will be able to get it. The consequence of this again is that the feudal system, *when left to itself,* will tend to perpetuate or aggravate its own situation, unless some external factor, intentionally or not, can correct this kind of development.

3. The stratification in the Latin American system of nations

Latin America is an international system that is strongly stratified. Regardless of which rank dimension one takes, one will find nations participating in the system and representing extreme positions where rank is concerned, even if one takes as a point or reference the world international system. *The World Handbook of Political and Social Indicators* (Russet, 1964) gives the countries in the world ordered according to 75 variables and rank dimensions that are then each of them divided into ten deciles of rank. Table 6.2, taken more or less by chance from the book, demonstrates how different Latin American nations are located in the different deciles for some variables.

TABLE 6.2 *Location of different Latin American countries in the international system*

rank deciles	per capita income	literacy	area	radios per inhabitants
1	(USA)	(Austria)	(USSR)	(USA)
2	— — —	Argentina	— — —	— — —
3	— — —	Chile	— — —	— — —
4	— — —	Panama	— — —	— — —
5	— — —	Colombia	— — —	— — —
6	— — —	Brazil	— — —	— — —
7	— — —	Bolivia	Brazil	Uruguay
8	Venezuela	— — —	— — —	— — —
9	Uruguay	Haiti	Argentina	Venezuela
10	Mexico	— — —	Haiti	Honduras

The total rank of a country in a stratified system is a resultant of the rank that this country occupies on any one of a series of rank dimensions. However, in a system of strong rank concordance the total rank is not only an additive index based on a series of isolated ranks, but has a direct and important sociological reality about it because of the phenomenon referred to above as generalized rank-roles. This means that one could try to determine the rank of a given country not only by means of an *objective* technique, leading to the position that a country occupies on a series of rank dimensions that are considered relevant, but also by means of a *subjective* technique, where the problem is to get hold of some kind of general rank concept that is present in the minds of the individuals living in these countries in the system. We shall make use of both these approaches.

The objective technique would essentially consist in constructing an additive index of international position, which one would get by adding together the position that the nation occupy in a series of rank dimensions. The selection of these dimensions, the weight one wants to give to any one of them as well as the positions that shall be attributed to the countries on the dimensions all lead to methodological problems that are difficult to tackle and that will demand investigations to determine the relevance of any one dimension in terms of consensus and explicative power. But there is of course also the possibility of taking the index at face value, using it as it is in order to see whether the result gives something of theoretical interest. Thus, we construct an additive index taking into consideration four factors: the *size* of the country measured by means of global variables that characterize a dimension of power; the *distribution of goods*, measured by means of analytical variables and leading to a dimension measuring relative wealth; some characteristics of *social structure* and finally the dimension of *race* which probably is a sociologically relevant dimension in this connection. For the first three of these four we have three indicators for each one, and this gives us a total of ten rank dimensions.

TABLE 6.3 *Index of international position: rank dimensions*

dimension	item	source
a. *Size*	1. Area	UN, *Statistical Yearbook* (1963).
	2. Population	UN, ibid.
	3. Gross National Product	B. M. Russet et al.: *World Handbook of Political and Social Indicators* (Yale, 1964).
b. *Distribution of goods*	4. GNP per capita	id., ibid.
	5. Illiteracy	DESAL, "Tipologia Socio-Economica Latinoamericana", *Mensaje*, Oct. 1963, Santiago, Chile.
	6. Communications (newspapers per population)	id., ibid.
c. *Social Structure*	7. % of population in middle and high strata	id., ibid.
	8. Urbanization (pop. in cities of more than 20,000 inh.)	id., ibid.
	9. % of active pop. in industry	id., ibid.
d. *Race*	10. % of population white	Angel Rozemblat, *La Poblacien Indigena en America;* UN *Demographic Yearbook* (1956).

TABLE 6.4 *Index of international position: rank of the nations*

country	score	rank position
Argentina	20	1
Chile	18	2.5
Cuba	18	2.5
Venezuela	17	4
Brazil	16	5.5
Uruguay	16	5.5
Colombia	15	7
Mexico	14	8
Costa Rica	11	9.5
Peru	11	9.5
Panama	9	11
Ecuador	8	12
Bolivia	6	13.5
Paraguay	6	13.5
Dominican Republic	5	15
El Salvador	4	16
Guatemala	2	17.5
Nicaragua	2	17.5
Haiti	1	19.5
Honduras	1	19.5

TABLE 6.5 *Index of international position: intereorrelations*

	2	3	4	5	6	7	8	9	10	index total
1. Area	.94	.93	.10	—.04	.06	.17	.12	.15	.20	.41
2. Population		.96	.10	—.08	.07	.20	.14	.12	.17	.46
3. GNP			.30	—.21	.24	.36	.41	.22	.30	.58
4. GNP per capita				—.41	.58	.57	.60	.20	.23	.67
5. Illiteracy					—.83	—.88	—.80	—.66	—.71	—.78
6. Communications (newspapers/population)						.87	.90	.62	.66	.79
7. % of population in middle and high strata							.90	.70	.80	.85
8. Urbanization								.72	.64	.85
9. % of active population in industry									.56	.61
10. % of population white										.60

The countries were ordered from 1 to 20 according to each dimension, and then divided into three groups of about equal size [3], giving to the nations of *high, middle* and *low* rank the values 2, 1 and 0 respectively. Thus the total index ranged from 0 to 20, and the 20 countries were then divided into three groups according to their position on this scale of total rank. Table 6.3 gives the details of the index, and Table 6.4 the results we arrived at.

To what extent can we now say that the stratified system of nations that emerges from this index satisfies the condition of rank concordance and the idea of generalized rank roles depending on total rank? Where the first point is concerned it is necessary to examine the internal consistency of the index by means of the intercorrelations between its components.

What emerges from Table 6.5 is the existence of two relatively well characterized factors, one that corresponds to a dimension of *development* and the other that corresponds to a dimension of *size*, with high internal correlations and low correlations between the two dimensions [4].

This indicates that the condition of rank concordance is not completely satisfied, although it seems to obtain for either one of these two dimensions. If there had been complete rank concordance then the big nations would also have been the most developed nations — but the existence of such nations as Brazil on the one hand and Costa Rica on the other lower the total rank concordance considerably.

To see to what extent our index corresponds to a socially existing image of a stratified system, to a generalized concept of rank, a questionnaire was applied to a number of students of social sciences in different Latin American countries (mainly Brazil, Argentina and Chile). One of the purposes of this questionnaire was to get hold of the *subjective image of stratification of the Latin American system,* and to do this students were asked to distribute the twenty Latin American nations in three classes, "high", "middle" and "low", according to the prestige or importance they thought these nations had in the Latin American system. Table 6.6 gives the final rank, as well as a measure of dispersion of "votes". For the computation the values 3, 2 and 1 were given to the classes high, middle and low respectively, and the arithmetic mean was then calculated with the range of 1 to 3. We excluded the student's ranking of their own countries, and this explains the variations in the N, which may also be partially explained by the "no answers". It is noticeable that the frequencies of "no answers" are not random, but strongly correlated (rank coefficient .75) with the rank order [5].

The comparison between Tables 6.4 and 6.6 indicates that our objective index renders relatively well the image that one gets from the subjective estimates emerging from the interviews. Thus, *the correlation coefficient between the two measures is as high as .93.* The major deviant cases — Mexico, Cuba, Brazil — show the importance of the factor of size, or power. Thus, it seems that the most important determinant of the prestige of a nation is not so much the means of distribution of goods — according to which both Brazil and Mexico would rank fairly low — but the existence of very modern sectors in the country — which is also an important characteristic

TABLE 6.6 *Subjective stratification of the Latin American countries*

Country	score	rank position	modal category	frequency of modal category	N	total of "no answers"
Argentina	2.84	1	3	85%	204	8
Mexico	2.78	2	3	81%	313	13
Brazil	2.69	3	3	75%	198	9
Chile	2.34	4	3	45%	261	14
Uruguay	2.34	5	2	46%	312	15
Venezuela	2.21	6	2	51%	300	21
Cuba	2.13	7	2	44%	307	22
Peru	1.79	8	2	55%	292	36
Colombia	1.70	9	2	60%	300	28
Panama	1.39	10	1	66%	285	42
Costa Rica	1.37	11	1	66%	293	36
Ecuador	1.33	12	1	68%	297	31
Bolivia	1.24	13	1	78%	304	25
Paraguay	1.21	14	1	79%	306	23
Guatemala	1.19	15	1	82%	280	48
Dominican Republic	1.19	16	1	84%	297	32
Nicaragua	1.18	17	1	84%	284	45
El Salvador	1.13	18	1	88%	282	41
Honduras	1.11	19	1	89%	285	41
Haiti	1.08	20	1	92%	298	30

of development. Thus Mexico probably ranks high because of what Mexico City stands for, and Brazil ranks high because of what southern Brazil (São Paulo, for instance) stands for. It is also possible that some political factors enter when the image of the country is formed. We tried to correlate the two measures of international rank with an index of political instability [6], and found that the subjective index correlated better with political stability than the objective one (the correlations were .52 and .46 respectively, not a very large difference). This could be interpreted to mean that political stability is also in itself a factor contributing to prestige.

If we examine the measure of dispersion given in Table 6.6 (fourth column) we find that there is high consensus as to the existence of a "high class" of countries that are big and well developed (Argentina, Brazil, Mexico), and also that there is high consensus with regard to a "low class" of nations that are small and underdeveloped. Colombia is the typical case of a "middle class" nation, with both size and level of development in the medium category. The consensus with regard to other nations in the middle class is much lower, especially for countries that are small but relatively well developed such as Chile and Uruguay, not to mention Cuba with is particular political situation. Cuba has the lowest consensus measure of them all.

The conclusion that we arrive at is that in spite of some deficiencies in the objective index there seems to be little doubt that there exists a Latin American stratification system with elements of strong rank concordance. We now have to see to what extent the second condition of a feudal system is also present, that is to what extent the interaction between the countries depends on the position that the countries occupy in the stratification system.

4. Interaction patterns between the Latin American countries: relational variables

The study of interaction between the Latin American nations necessitates a unit of analysis that no longer considers each nation individually, but pairs of nations (and in principle also triples, quadruples, etc., of nations). If we have 20 nations, this gives us a total of

$$\frac{20!}{2!\,(20\text{-}2)!} = 190$$

pairs, which from now on are our new units of analysis [7]. For these pairs the following analysis will give us occasion to explore how their rank properties are related to some measures of interaction, as required by the definition of a feudal system. But in addition to this we shall also use a measure of geographical distance, which, however trivial, no doubt is important in determining the interactions between nations. Our list of relational variables, hence, is as follows:

a) total rank of the pair of nations
b) differences between the rank of the nations in the pair
c) geographical proximity
d) surface communications
e) air communications
f) trade.

a) Let us imagine that a system has three ranks, *high, middle* and *low*. If we now give, as we have done on page *212* the scores 2, 1 and 0 respectively to the three ranks, the total rank will be given by (Table 6.7).

To obtain this all we had to do was to trichotomize the *subjective index* in three classes of relatively homogeneous countries, the high ranging from Argentina to Venezuela, the middle from Cuba to Paraguay, and the low including the rest. But in addition to this we could also have proceeded as follows: order all countries from 1 to 20, that is from Haiti to

TABLE 6.7 *Rank of the pairs*

	high (2)	middle (1)	low (0)
high (2)	4	3	2
middle (1)	3	2	1
low (0)	2	1	0

Argentina (the range is now from 3 to 39) and then trichotomizing the set of pairs according to whether they have a total rank which is high, middle or low. The result is approximately the same as what we would get with the method indicated above, with the difference that the trichotomization makes it possible for us to work with a smaller and more homogeneous number of categories.

b) The rank differences were determined in the same way as the rank totals, with the only difference that instead of adding we subtracted. The significance of this simple measure is, of course, in its indication of the amount of lack of equivalence in the pair.

c) The factor "geographical proximity" may certainly play a powerful and decisive role in the international communication and general interaction structure, and this factor is the basis for the theories of the geopolitical type in the field of international relations. As to this factor two types of reasoning were considered.

First of all, imagine that we find a pattern of interaction which is partly explicable in terms of geographical proximity. Even though this is the case, this by no means invalidates the *functional* importance of the relation, for instance a relation of a feudal type. One thing is to ask "why" a phenomenon exists, another and not less important is to ask what are the consequences of this phenomenon. Thus, a phenomenon is not "explained away" even though it can be shown that geographical proximity accounts for much of it. Thus it might well be that an ascribed characteristic such as geographical position could have the effect of reinforcing a feudal interaction structure, which then, in turn, could reinforce the importance of these "purely" geographical factors. This would be particularly true for the more classical means of communications, that are linked to the surface of the earth, and less true for the new means of communications that make use of the air, not to mention space, and that will gradually decrease the importance of the geographical factor. In this modern world distances are more appropriately measured in social terms than in terms of kilometers. Thus, Caracas or Rio de Janeiro are much closer to New York or

Paris than to La Paz, where air transportation is concerned, as well as for almost any other kind of contact, and it makes very good sense to say that the road between two South American capitals very often goes via Europe or United States [8].

In order to control for this factor it is necessary to make use of a measure that takes into consideration the distance as well as the existence of natural obstacles, etc. It is not so much the distance between the frontiers that is of interest, as the distances between capitals, or the most important urban centers, since interaction mostly takes place between these centers. Thus, an index of geographical distance could be constructed taking all these elements into consideration: 1. the distance between the most important urban centers in the nations of each pair, 2. the existence of natural obstacles (oceans, mountains, etc.) and 3. the existence or absence of a common frontier.

However, we shall simplify and only make use of the third criterion, which means that the 190 pairs of countries are ordered as follows in three groups:

— nations that have frontiers in common,
— nations that do not have frontiers in common, but have frontiers in common with at least one third country. For simplicity, we shall refer to these pairs as "proximity by one step".
— nations that do not satisfy conditions a or b.

In all its simplicity, this index has considerable explicative power, as we shall see later on.

d) As to surface communication, what we did was to inspect good maps of Latin America to find out which countries are connected by railway communications or roads. In the same way as for geographical proximity the pairs of nations were classified as follows:

— nations with at least one road or railway in common
— nations that have at least one other nation in common with which they have land communication. We shall refer to this group of pairs as "communications by one step".
— nations that do not satisfy conditions a or b.

e) The interaction patterns by air between the nations were determined by means of the *ABC World Airways Guide*, edition of November 1964. We classified as a flight between two nations each flight between them where at least one of the two capitals was involved, whether as final destination or not. If there was a change of planes in between it was nevertheless considered as one flight, provided the Guide book regarded it as such. The following cities were considered equivalents to the capitals: São Paulo and Rio de Janeiro in Brazil, Medellín and Barranquilla in Colombia, Guayaquil in Ecuador and La Paz in Bolivia. These cities were included because of their importance or because they function as alternatives to the respective capitals for the airlines. When a flight between two cities could not transport passengers because of particular regulations then it was not counted as a flight.

In Table 6.8 the general data about the international air transportation between the Latin American nations can be seen.

f) Trade is, of course, one of the most important interaction variables and has been so considered in the literature [9]. The volume of trade between two countries will depend, among other things, on the size of the country (in terms of its GNP), on its economic structure, especially its position in the international division of labor, on geographical proximity and, we assume, on the position that the countries occupy in the international stratification system.

TABLE 6.8 *Latin America, international flights (number of weekly flights)*

Country	flights with						
	USA	*Europe*	*Africa*	*Asia*	*subtotal*	*Lat. America*	*Total*
Argentina	26	18	12	2	58	251	309
Brazil	31	22	12	0	65	88	153
Mexico	27	11	0	2	40	92	132
Chile	13	14	7	2	36	81	117
Venezuela	15	15	0	0	30	40	70
Uruguay	12	8	5	0	25	157	182
Cuba	—	6	0	0	6	4	10
Colombia	18	6	0	0	24	56	80
Peru	38	11	0	2	51	119	170
Costa Rica	7	0	0	0	7	63	70
Bolivia	6	0	0	0	6	22	28
Ecuador	13	4	0	0	17	54	71
Panama	39	1	0	0	40	161	201
Paraguay	4	2	1	0	7	39	46
Nicaragua	6	0	0	0	6	51	57
Guatemala	8	0	0	0	8	80	88
El Salvador	7	0	0	0	7	86	93
Dominican Republic	13	1	0	0	14	15	29
Honduras	7	0	0	0	7	48	55
Haiti	7	0	0	0	7	7	14
Total	299	119	37	8	463	1514	1977

TABLE 6.9 *Foreign trade in Latin America (1961)*[1]

a) Grand total (exports plus imports)
b) Total of external trade with Latin American countries
c) Total trade with USA
d) b/a(%)
e) c/a(%)

| Country | (millions of dollars) | | | | |
	a	b	c	d	e
Argentina	2,587.0	245.7	511.3	9.6	19.6
Brazil	2,865.2	240.2	1,077.6	8.4	37.0
Mexico	1,846.2	38.6	1,299.9	2.1	70.4
Chile	1,092.4	85.5	410.8	8.0	36.7
Venezuela	3,363.4	254.9	1,481.2	7.7	44.0
Uruguay [2]	—	—	—	—	—
Cuba [2]	—	—	—	—	—
Colombia	974.1	34.3	538.8	3.5	55.3
Peru	965.4	69.3	385.3	7.2	40.0
Costa Rica	81.1	14.4	47.3	17.7	58.0
Bolivia	153.8	23.1	57.4	15.0	37.3
Ecuador	197.3	20.9	107.2	12.0	54.0
Panama	144.8	49.5	84.2	34.1	61.0
Paraguay [3]	61.2	21.1	12.5	34.4	20.4
Nicaragua	142.9	11.8	68.7	8.2	48.0
Guatemala	377.6	27.3	152.7	7.2	40.5
El Salvador	227.6	33.3	82.8	14.6	36.3
Dominican Republic	226.8	2.1	128.1	2.0	56.7
Honduras	140.1	20.8	80.6	14.8	57.5
Haiti [2]	—	—	—	—	—

[1] About the reliability of these data, see [10].
[2] The Direction of International Trade does not give data for these countries.
[3] About 20% of the total trade of Paraguay is given as "unclassified" which makè the percentage figures highly doubtful.

The construction of a measure of commercial interaction was based on the data published by the *Direction of International Trade*, United Nations (1962) [10]. In order to investigate the specific effect that international stratification had on this type of interaction we made use of the "directional trade ratio F_{mn}", an index of commercial relations developed by Paul Smoker (1965), because this index gives the measure of the relative trade between two countries according to the formula

$$F_{mn} = \frac{1}{2}\left(\frac{t_{mn}}{t_m} + \frac{t_{nm}}{t_n}\right)$$

where $t_{mn} = t_{nm}$ corresponds to the trade volume (imports and exports) between two countries m and n, t_m and t_n to the total trade volume of m and n in the Latin American system. Table 6.9 gives us some general data about the external trade of the Latin American nations.

What emerges from these tables, especially from Table 6.9, is the rather limited volume of inter-Latin American trade. There are many reasons that can be given for these circumstances. Not the least important is certainly that the Latin American countries in general have a tendency to produce the same type of products for export. Whatever the reason, it is important to study the possible effect of this limited trade on the relations between the countries, regardless of underlying causes.

5. The feudal system

Since we have now established the existence of international stratification in Latin America and selected the relational variables with which we are

TABLE 6.10 *Rank of pairs and interactions* (%) — I

Surface communications	Total rank of pair [1]				
	4	3	2	1	0
direct	27	12	9	2	33
1 step	13	21	11	4	0
none	60	67	80	94	67
Sum	100	100	100	100	100
(N)	(15)	(48)	(64)	(48)	(15)
Flights					
more than 6 a week	33	23	16	11	46
1—6	53	46	22	6	0
none	12	31	62	83	54
Sum	100	100	100	100	100
(N)	(15)	(48)	(64)	(48)	(15)
Relative trade [2]					
more than 20	50	15	4	0	27
10—20	0	3	11	11	18
1—0	50	51	37	23	9
none	0	31	48	66	46
Sum	100	100	100	100	100
(N)	(10)	(35)	(46)	(35)	(11)

[1] According to Table 6.6.
[2] According to Table 6.5-A (see [4]).

going to work, we are now ready to investigate to what extent the second characteristic of the feudal system — that the interaction patterns in pairs of countries depend strongly on the total rank of the pair — is satisfied. Tables 6.10 and 6.11 show us the relations between rank and interaction, with regard to our three relational variables, and for the two types of cutting points that we used in order to classify the 190 pairs according to total rank.

TABLE 6.11 *Rank of pairs and interactions* (%) — II

| | Total rank of pair | | |
	high	middle	low
Surface communications			
direct	16	8	11
1 step	9	16	8
none	75	76	82
Sum	100	100	100
(N)	(57)	(67)	(66)
Flights			
more than 6 a week	25	15	21
1—6	40	23	12
none	35	60	67
Sum	100	100	100
(N)	(57)	(67)	(66)
Relative trade			
more than 20	23	5	5
10—20	2	13	11
1—10	40	54	20
none	35	28	64
Sum	100	100	100
(N)	(43)	(39)	(55)

The consistency of the tables is remarkable. The higher the rank of the pair, the more the nations communicate by land or by air, and the more trade they have. An important exception to this generalization, however, is found among the pairs of total rank 0, that is the pairs formed by Nicaragua, El Salvador, Dominican Republic, Honduras, Haiti and Guatemala. All of them are Central American and Caribbean nations, small and close together. The immediate explanation for this finding is that the geographical position of the countries is an important factor shaping the interaction patterns. To what extent this is true we should be able to discover in Table 6.12.

221

TABLE 6.12 *Geographical proximity and interactions* (%)

	Geographical proximity		
	boundaries	1 step	none
Surface communications			
direct	64	0	0
1 step	18	53	0
none	14	47	100
(N)	(27)	(30)	(130)
Flights			
more than 6 a week	66	23	10
1—6	30	64	15
none	4	13	75
(N)	(27)	(30)	(130)
Relative trade			
more than 20	38	8	5
10—20	25	8	5
1—10	29	44	34
0—1	8	40	56
(N)	(24)	(25)	(88)

The influence of the geographical factor is also remarkable. The countries that are close together have much more land communication, more air communication, and more trade — as one certainly would have expected. As to the land communication this is so evident that no further comments are necessary. As to the air communication the emerging pattern seems to be a type of local air traffic.

Where trade is concerned it seems necessary to consider a little more closely the meaning of the "directional trade ratio" which we are using here. The meaning of this index is clear when its value is high or low, but is less clear when its value is in the middle. When it is high, it indicates that almost all of the external trade of the pair in the system considered is concentrated in this relation, and the contrary for the low values. But a middle value can mean two different things; on the one hand that the importance of the trade in the pair is in the middle range for both countries if the volume of their commerce in the area is about the same; on the other, that the relationship is strongly asymmetric, very important for one and almost without significance for the other. At the least we can say that the index gives an idea of the relative significance of trade for the pair within the area, even without considering the effect of the asymmetry factor. But we can also see that the interactions tend to concentrate in the pairs with smaller rank difference. This is explained by the general idea that equal rank favors interaction, and even more so when we have a feudal system in which the stratification has a definite socio-logical meaning. Table 6.13 shows the relationship between rank equality (or rank difference) and interactions; the data confirm our ideas.

TABLE 6.13 *Rank difference and interaction (%)*

	Rank difference		
	0	*1*	*2*
Surface communications			
direct	24	6	2
1 step	12	13	5
none	64	81	93
(N)	(58)	(96)	(36)
Flights			
more than 6 a week	35	17	5
1—6	27	26	17
none	38	57	78
(N)	(58)	(96)	(36)
Relative trade			
more than 20	21	7	4
10—20	12	7	8
1—10	29	37	44
none	38	49	44
(N)	(42)	(70)	(25)

When we calculate the percentages in Table 6.11 horizontally, we see that 67% of the cases where relative trade exceeds 20 occur among the countries of high rank, while pairs of countries of low rank make up 57% of the relationships in the bottom group. At the other extreme the same analysis in Table 6.10 shows that 25% of the high relationships (more than 20) belong to the group of total rank 0. The commercial relationships actually seem to be a function of rank or of a geographical dependence that does not allow the small countries to get free of local ties.

We now want to take a look at the relationship between rank and geo-graphical position. It is possible to make an index of geographical position in the continent. The rank correlation between this index and the rank order is almost zero (.07), showing that we have two independent factors. But if rank does not depend on geographical position, it is possible, nevertheless, that the influence of the geographical factor will be determined by rank, in other words that there is interaction between the two. The influence of rank on the importance of the geographical dimension can be seen in Table 6.14.

TABLE 6.14 *Rank of the pair, geographical proximity, interactions (%)*

Geographical proximity	Rank of the pair high			middle			low		
	bound	1 step	none	bound	1 step	none	bound	1 step	none
Surface communications									
direct	62	0	0	62	0	0	86	0	0
1 step	15	33	0	25	60	0	14	67	0
none	23	67	100	13	40	100	0	33	100
(N)	(13)	(9)	(35)	(8)	(15)	(44)	(7)	(6)	(53)
Flights									
more than 6 a week	54	22	15	76	20	2	86	34	11
1—6	46	67	31	12	67	11	14	50	8
none	0	11	54	12	13	87	0	16	81
(N)	(13)	(9)	(35)	(8)	(15)	(44)	(7)	(6)	(53)
Relative trade									
more than 10	64	33	6	63	0	12	66	33	7
1—10	36	17	47	37	62	55	0	33	21
none	0	50	47	0	38	33	33	33	72
(N)	(11)	(6)	(26)	(8)	(13)	(18)	(6)	(6)	(43)

It is clear enough that the geographical factor works on each level of rank. If we ordered Table 6.14 differently, to study how the rank factor behaves at each level of geographical proximity, the conclusion would also be that the influence of this factor is constant. *How* important the geographical factor is on each level for rank can be measured by the range of variation (i.e. the difference between the extreme percentages) for each level (Table 6.15).

TABLE 6.15 *% of the variation explained by the geographical factor*

	Rank of the pair high	middle	low
Surface communications			
direct	62	62	85
none	77	87	100
flights			
more than 6	39	74	75
none	54	75	81
Relative Trade			
more than 20	58	51	59
none	47	33	39

The interpretation of Table 6.15 for variables of communication is that the countries of lower rank are much more dependent on geography than those of high rank: the network of air traffic, for instance, is twice (75/39) as dependent on geographical contiguity for the former as for the latter. The data about trade, however, are not conclusive about this, but show how the influence of the geographical factor is constant and significant. We are led naturally to try a combination of these two determinants of feudal interaction, and assume that this combination will explain more than each of its elements by itself. We combine them according to Table 6.16 and the results are indicated in Table 6.17.

TABLE 6.16 *Index of feudal position (pairs)*

| | Geographical proximity | | |
	boundaries (2)	*one step (1)*	*none (0)*
Total rank			
High (2)	4	3	2
Middle (1)	3	2	1
Low (0)	2	1	0

TABLE 6.17 *Feudal position and interactions (%)*

| | Feudal position | | | | |
	4	*3*	*2*	*1*	*0*
direct surface communications	62	35	10	0	0
more than 6 flights a week	55	21	8	2	2
more than 20 in relative trade	54	47	25	2	11

It is remarkable that, for the two variables of communication, the effect of this combined index grows progressively as the total score diminishes, which will give a J-shaped curve.

We have now demonstrated that the second condition of a feudal system is present; i.e. the interactions in this system are dependent on rank position, in such a way that the interactions will be more intense the higher the total rank and the less the rank inequality. Another fact demonstrated by our data is that the interactions are dependent on the relative geographical position of the countries. The combination of these two factors led us to a new proposition which is partly confirmed by our data: *in an international system of a feudal type the more the interactions will be determined more by geography, the lower the position of the units in the system of stratification.*

6. Latin America and the international system

So far we have been dealing with Latin America as a system in itself. We did so when we ordered the rank dimensions according to rank position in Latin America, when we used the total amount of trade in the system to construct our measure of relative trade, and so on. This is because the twenty republics are a set of countries very well characterized as a specific subsystem, for geographical, historical and cultural reasons, and must be studied as such. But it is evident that this system is related to other countries and systems. Tables 6.8 and 6.9 presented some data about air interactions and trade with countries outside the Latin American system, which we shall now examine more closely.

Regarding flights, it is striking that all the Latin American countries have direct flights with USA, only 13 with Europe, 5 with Africa and 4 with Asia. Moreover, all the "high class" countries are included among the 13 which have flights with Europe, and they have 74% of these flights. When we calculate the ratio between flights with USA and other continents, the correlation between the countries ordered according to this ratio and the international stratification is .81, showing that the lower the position in the stratification system, the higher the concentration of flights with USA. It is not surprising, then, that this concentration of flights to the USA is also correlated with the indicators of development, as can be seen in Table 6.18.

TABLE 6.18 *Flights with the* USA *and indicators of development-correlations*

Indicators	Correlations
illiteracy	.62
per capita income	—.52
newspapers by inhabitants	—.57
population in industries by active population	—.62

In short: the less literate, the poorer, the less industrialized, the less equipped with media of internal communications a country is, the more it will tend to concentrate its external interaction with the USA.

Regarding trade, Table 6.9 shows the general fact that 45% of all the Latin American external trade is concentrated in the USA, and only 12.1% with all the other Latin American countries. In contrast, USA trade with all the 20 Latin American republics is less than 19% of all the external trade of that country. This concentration of the external trade with the USA apparently does not depend on the position in the system of stratification, the correlation coefficient between these two dimensions being approximately 0. But perhaps this dependence would appear if we had controlled factors like the characteristics of the export products, the relative importance of the externla trade for the economy of the country, etc. However, this would demand a special study.

The Latin American system is an open system, then, to the United States, and relatively closed to other continents. If the trend of regarding flights is more general, we can say that this exclusive openness to the United States is a major characteristic of the countries of low rank. If we consider the United States as a member of the system, the resultant image will be that of a relatively closed system only open to the external world through the countries of higher rank. A simplifiied and exaggerated scheme of this is shown in Fig. 6.1,

FIGURE 6.1 *Latin America and the international system: interaction pattern*

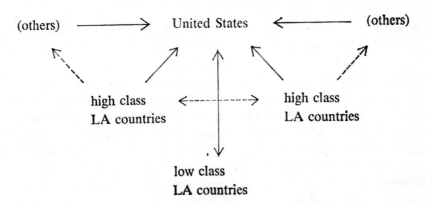

But this is not all. The international system of nations seems to follow, also, the feudal pattern. Regarding flights, a simple fourfold division of the world, as follows,

	Western hemisphere	Eastern hemisphere
North (high class)	North America	Europe
South (low class)	Latin America	Asia and Africa

reveals that there were 440 weekly flights connecting the two Northern continents, and only 45 between Latin American and Asia and/or Africa. An analysis of the items in the *Keesing's Contemporary Archives* (1963), or the news indexed on the headings of "relations with" (which includes

227

positive as well as negative interactions among countries, mainly on an official level) showed that, from a total of 600-odd references, referring to 100 countries, 25% included at least one of the five Big Powers (USA Soviet Union, France, Peoples Republic of China, Britain). The study of the trade figures among the NATO and Warsaw countries also shows a heavy concentration of trade among the top countries of both systems, which fits our image of feudal interaction.

All this seems to suggest the image of a system of "Chinese Boxes" where many feudal systems are superimposed. Our data indicate at least four levels:

1. The world level, having the Big Powers as the high class.
2. The Inter-American level, having USA as the high class.
3. The Latin American level, with Argentina, Mexico, Brazil and Chile occupying the top positions.
4. The Central American level, with Costa Rica, Panama and Cuba in a special category, having the high positions.

The main question is now to what extent this structure determines the behavior of the countries in international affairs, and the consequences, if any, that this behavior has for the internal development of the countries. It is possible, for instance, that the top countries in a system or subsystem will try to increase the value of their position giving the maximum of relevance to this subsystem, while the low-class countries will try to emphasize the dependent relationship that is considered more profitable to them. This could explain, for instance, why it is exactly among the top Latin American countries that the opposition to the Inter-American system is stronger, and the same reasoning could explain why the internal oppositions in the Western system are stronger in the high countries of the European subsystem, the same holding again for the relationship between the Eastern system and the top countries of the Asian subsystem. (We are thinking, of course, of Mexico and Chile in the first case, France in the second and the Peoples Republic of China in the last).

Another possible inference would be that the countries of low rank which are the less able to solve the problems of development by themselves, will tend to transform the internal conflicts into replications of international conflicts, with strong possibilities of escalation. This would be not only because these countries are in general in a bad situation where development is concerned, but also because of their situation of isolation regarding other low countries and of dependence regarding the high-class countries. This will tend to impede the establishment of regional cooper ation and the search for social and political paths different from the dependence on blocks and the violent and conflict-ridden movement from one block to another.

7. Conclusions

The Latin American countries were studied as a system of actors, using structural variables which define the positions the countries have in the system of stratification and interaction. In spite of the simplicity of our measurements, it was possible to construct an image of Latin America as a clearly stratified system, with interaction patterns dependent on this stratification. At the same time one could see how the geographical factor enters into this picture, and some insights emerged about the relationship between this particular subsystem and the international system.

Although very general and by no means surprising, our conclusions correspond to a necessary first step in the understanding of the international system. This kind of analysis will allow us to make predictions with some assurance about the long-term development of the foreign policy of the Latin American countries, and about the fate of the attempts to change these policies.

The fact that we arrived at outcomes more or less well known only indicates that we are on the right path. The difference between our point of departure and our terminal point is that our image of Latin America is no longer something intuitive and diffuse, but an explicit and verifiable scheme from which the characteristics of the system can be deduced and tested empirically. It is important, initially, that the results reconstruct the diffuse image already existing. Subsequently many things will follow less from the idiosyncratic characteristics of each country and more from the structural characteristics of the system. We hope that the expansion of this line of analysis by the use of more extensive and reliable indicators, as well as through the examination of the more refined hypotheses that follow from a structural approach (regarding rank congruency, rank equilibria, criss-cross, etc.) may give rise to a less intuitive image of this and other international systems, and at the same time to more possibilities for explanation and prediction.

Bibliography on page 230

Bibliography

ELLISON, FRED P. 1964 The Writer In J. J. JOHNSON (ed.) *Continuity and Change in Latin America*. Stanford: Stanford Univ. Press.

GALTUNG, JOHAN 1965 Rank and Social Integration. A Multidimensional Approach. In BERGER ZELDITCH and ANDERSON (eds.) *Sociological Theories in Progress*. Boston: Houghton Mifflin.

GALTUNG, JOHAN 1966 International Relations and International Conflicts: A Sociological Approach. *Transactions of the Sixth World Congress of Sociology*, *1*, 121—161. International Sociological Association.

LAGOS, GUSTAVO 1963 *International Stratification and Underdeveloped Countries*. Chapel Hill, North Carolina: Univ. of Carolina Press

MORA Y ARAUJO, M.; and SCHWARTZMAN, S. 1966. The Images of International Stratification in Latin America. *Journal of Peace Research* 3: 225—244.

RICHARDSON, LEWIS F. 1960. *Arms and Insecurity*. Pittsburgh: The Boxwood Press.

RUMMEL, R. J. 1966. The Dimensionality of Nations Project. In R. MERRITT; and S. ROKKAN (eds.) *Comparing Nations*. New Haven: Yale Univ. Press.

RUMMEL, R. J.; SAWYER, JACK; GUEZKOW, HAROLD; and TANTER, RAYMOND *Dimensions of Nations*.

RUSSET, BRUCE M.. ALKER, HAYWARD R.; DEUTSCH, KARL W.; and LASSWELL, HAROLD D. 1964. *The World Handbook of Political and Social Indicators*. New Haven: Yale Univ. Press.

SMOKER, PAUL, 1965. Trade, Defence and the Richardson Theory of Arms Races: A Seven Nation Study. *Journal of Peace Research* 2: 161—177.

IV.7. East-West Interaction Patterns

From *Journal of Peace Research* III/2 (1966). PRIO publication No. 21—4.

Notes on pages *700*.

1. The theory

The purpose of this paper is twofold: to explore the pattern of interaction of different kinds between the nations that are members of the NATO and the Warsaw treaty systems, and to explore the implications of some suggested changes in these interaction patterns.

Since we, in order to do this, need a perspective on international systems in general and the East—West system in particular, we shall make use of a recently-developed theoretical perspective [1]. According to this perspective, the world is conceived of as consisting of nations ranked according to a number of dimensions, such as size, wealth, military power, degree of development, etc., in various degrees of interaction, negative and positive. However, in this complexity, two simple ordering principles appear:

1. the *rankings* have a tendency to be *concordant*, in the sense that a nation that ranks high on one dimension has a tendency also to rank high on other dimensions; and a nation that ranks low on one has a tendency to rank low on other dimensions as well. We shall refer to the former as topdog nations and to the latter as underdog nations.

2. the *interaction* has a tendency to be *rank-dependent*, in the sense that there is much interaction between nations high in the ranking system, less between one nation that is high and another nation that is low, and much less between two nations low in the system. Thus, the degree of interaction is strongly dependent on the *total rank* of the pair.

An international system satisfying these two properties will be referred to as a *feudal system*, because the interaction patterns tie together the elements that are high up in the system — sew together the system at the top, so to speak — and split the system at the bottom, because the underdogs direct their interaction potential towards the top more than towards each other [2].

But this system bears in it the seeds of its own destruction, because it permits more exploitation of the underdogs than the underdogs will, in the long run, tolerate; because of the subutilization of human and national resources; and for other reasons. Thus, it can be destroyed if the underdogs unite and change the interaction pattern so that there is less rank dependence — and we get a *class system*. Or, it can be changed by breaking down the rank congruence, permitting all kinds of mixed rank patterns, and we get what can be referred to as a *mixed system*. Also, both processes may take place, in which case we arrive at an *egalitarian system*. However, according to our theory, the egalitarian system is not stable either, but will tend to relapse to the old dimensions defining the old feudal system, or some new dimensions will emerge defining a new feudal system. In this pendulum process between the feudal and egalitarian extremes there may be a dampening factor, so that the extremes are not really attained. Moreover, since the feudal end of this spectrum is more stable, we actually assume that the system will usually stay at the end.

In this chapter we shall discuss the case not of one system, but of two systems in various degrees of conflict with each other. In general, the units may be individuals or nations, and it helps theorizing in this field to draw on common-sense thinking and research from both levels of human organization. We shall call the two systems S_1 and S_2, where the first is split into a set of topdog nations T_1 and underdog nations U_1; and the latter, similarly into T_2 and U_2. Then, *within* each system we assume that there is more interaction between the T's, than between the T's and U's, and finally the lowest level of interaction between the U's. It may also be that the systems are less feudal, that they approach more the egalitarian model — but we assume that the topdogs can nevertheless be singled out (for instance the big powers in the NATO and Warsaw treaty systems). Table 7.1 gives this general picture.

TABLE 7.1 *The general scheme*

System	S_1	S_2
Topdog	T_1	T_2
Underdog	U_1	U_2

As seen from Table 7.1, our total system has four types of actors: T_1, T_2, U_1 and U_2. It is fruitful to speculate what would happen if one strengthened the degree of interaction between the units, nations in our case, in all possible ways, and made it more positive. Thus, there may be more *within-*

interaction in the sense that the T_1's start interacting more with each other, the T_2's more with each other, and so on — four cases altogether. And there may be more *between*-interaction, with T_1's interacting more with the U_1, or more with T_2 — or more with the U_2, and similarly for T_2 — six cases altogether. However, since there is complete symmetry between the two blocs we can reduce this to six cases; three within-bloc and three between-bloc:

1. *More T_1-T_1 interaction and more T_2-T_2 interaction.* This would make the blocs more feudal because of tighter integration between the topdog nations. In the NATO case, France has been pressing for a system of this kind, where decisions are virtually made by the three big powers in the bloc [3]. In the world of individual relations, this would correspond to more upper class, capitalist, employer cohesion.

2. *More T_1-U_1 interaction and more T_2-U_2 interaction.* This would lead to a reinforcement of the blocs, which are then often referred to as *regions*. They would tend to become more self-sufficient; the smaller powers would look to the bigger powers for the solution to their internal and external problems. In the world of individual relations, this would correspond to employers carrying out welfare policies towards their employees, employer-employee associations and cooperation, etc.

3. *More U_1-U_1 interaction and more U_2-U_2 interaction.* This would lead the blocs into the class system phase, where the smaller powers would tend to coordinate their behavior towards the bigger powers, and start pressing for what they regard as more equitable prices for their exchange with the bigger powers. In the world of individual relations, this would correspond to local trade unions, and increased underdog cohesion would probably lead to increased topdog cohesion — i.e. to process 1 above.

4. *More T_1-T_2 interaction.* This would lead to a tendency for the big powers to regulate their conflicts over and above the heads of the smaller powers for instance by means of summit meetings. In the world of individual relations, this would correspond to covert and overt agreements between capitalists to coordinate economic activities.

5. *More T_1-U_2 interaction and more T_2-U_1 interaction.* This would lead to big power jealousy — T_2 would feel excluded in the first case and T_1 in the latter. In the world of individual relations, this would correspond to workers in one firm negotiating contracts with the employers of another enterprise.

233

6. *More U_1-U_2 interaction.* This would lead to some kind of class system for both systems. The process would be resented by both types of topdogs and may force some type of cooperation between them, which means that it may induce a type 4 process. In the world of individual relations, this would correspond to the idea of horizontal, national trade unions whereby employers from different enterprises also are united.

Thus, these six processes are easily identifiable in the world of political and social behavior, at both levels of human organization. Can we now assume that they are completely unrelated, in the sense that a system consisting of two subsystems in conflict is free to do what it wants — or are there principles that regulate the processes relative to each other? Our answer lies, of course, in the latter direction. Although the tendencies towards a coupling of the processes may not be strong, it would be contrary to theory and data in the social sciences to postulate relative independence.

More concretely, we may offer three propositions with subpropositions which bring considerable theoretical order in this system of concepts and processes. We shall refer to these as the *homology* propositions, the *feudality* propositions and the *polarization* propositions respectively. The system of propositions is as follows:

1. *Homology propositions*: Systems that are comparable and in interaction will tend towards structural similarity (isomorphism, homology)
1.1. *Vertical homology propositions*
    1.1.1. Process 1 will lead to process 3, within each bloc, and v.v.
    1.1.2. Process 4 will lead to process 6, between blocs and v.v.
1.2. *Horizontal homology propositions*
    1.2.1. T_1-T_1 interaction will lead to T_2-T_2 interaction and v.v.
    1.2.2. U_1-U_1 interaction will lead to U_2-U_2 interaction and v.v.
    1.2.3. T_1-U_1 interaction will lead to T_2-U_2 interaction and v.v.
1.3. *Diagonal homology propositions*
    1.3.1. T_1-U_2 interaction will lead to T_2-U_1 interaction
    1.3.2. T_2-U_1 interaction will lead to T_1-U_2 interaction.

2. *Feudality propositions*: The higher the total rank of the pair, the easier the interaction process.
2.1. *Within-bloc feudality propositions*
    Process 1 is easier than process 2, which is easier than process 3, within each bloc.
2.2. *Between-blocs feudality propositions*
    Process 4 is easier than process 5, which is easier than process 6, between blocs.

3. *Polarization propositions*: The lower the total rank of the pair, the higher the tendency to break off interaction in case of conflict.

3.1. *Horizontal polarization propositions, between blocs*

    3.1.1. Process 6 will first be broken, then process 5 and then process 4.

    3.1.2. Processes 1, 2 and/or 3 will be strengthened.

3.2. *Vertical polarization propositions, within blocs*

    3.2.1. Process 2 will be broken in case of class conflict.

    3.2.2. Processes 1 and 3 will be strengthened.

We shall make some brief comments on these propositions.

The homology propositions are all based on ideas of communication which leads to imitation, and the need for structural similarity, whether the relation between the two parties is positive or negative. Each party has to find its "opposite number" in the other party; each party will easily believe that a reorganization on the other side will strengthen that side relative to itself, and that the best counter-tactic is to do the same. NATO was followed by a military supreme command in the East, and by the Warsaw treaty; EEC by Comecon, and so on [4]. Employers' unions and employees' unions are closely geared to each other [5].

The feudality propositions have already been commented upon many times. Let it suffice to say that these are nothing but efforts to put in proposition form the common-sense experience that topdogs draw more attention than underdogs, and that they control their systems and, hence, prefer interaction patterns consonant with this.

The polarization propositions can be seen as descriptions of conditions that precede destructive conflict behavior and/or result from them. The essence of the proposition is that the topdogs trust only themselves and consequently want to dominate interaction, and more so the more conflictive they deem the situation to be. They do not rely on the underdogs for direct contact, but prefer the contact to go via the topdogs. Nor do they rely on their own underdogs for contacts with the topdogs of the other party — for fear that they will start negotiating special deals for themselves [6]. To avoid this, the topdogs have to pay for the decrease in interaction with the other party with increased interaction within the bloc, simply to provide for the needs of the underdogs. In general, the topdogs are forced all the time to convince their underdogs that they have more to gain by staying in the bloc than by attaching themselves to the other party — and if this cannot be done on the basis of bargaining, it has to be done by means of persuasion and/or force.

Thus, in a sense the topdogs will be most interested in breaking contacts of the type described in process 5, since contact with the topdog on the other side potentially is more rewarding to one's own underdogs. Nevertheless, in proposition 3.1.1. we have assumed that process 6 will be broken first, then process 5 and then process 4. This is because there may be cross-conflict topdog cooperation in preventing interactions of the type described in process 6 — but not for the types described in process 5, where either side will enjoy underdog renegades from the other side.

It should be noticed that the polarization propositions are similar in form to the incest propositions [7], if we compare Table 7.1 with Fig. 7.1.

FIGURE 7.1 *Types of incestuous relations (broken lines)*

	Male	*Female*
Topdog	Father	Mother
Underdog	Son	Daughter

The incest taboos are against relations structurally similar to relations outlawed by norms of polarization. This can be generalized to other types of small groups as well [8], and probably contributes to learning generalized patterns of polarized behavior [9].

However, the most remarkable feature of our set of propositions is the similarity between the feudality propositions and the polarization propositions: the former say that interaction at the top is favored in feudal systems; the latter, that interaction at the bottom is the first victim of polarization tendencies in a conflict. Concretely, this means that, *with a feudal relationship between two blocs or systems, polarization is already built into the system.* In other words, to the extent two systems have a relationship obeying the feudality propositions, to that extent are they already "stripped for conflict action", to use Coleman's excellent expression [10].

At this point let us go straight to some conjectures for which we do not have sufficient data, although they are certainly testable:

1. Inter-nation relations tend to be more rank-dependent than inter-group relations within a nation [11] and

2. The more rank-dependent a relation between two systems (nations, groups), the more violent the conflicts between them [12].

These propositions, are no doubt, valid under some conditions, but since we know little or nothing about the conditions under which they are valid we shall not use them as more than heuristic devices. For the obvious implications are 1. that international systems are more dangerous, which we generally hold to be true [13], and 2. that they can probably be made less dangerous by counteracting rank-dependence in them.

Hence, our tasks in the following sections are these:

1. To explore with as good data as possible the exact nature of the inter-action patterns between the two power blocs in order to see to what extent the degree of interaction, both positive and negative, is really rank-dependent; and how this varies with changing phases in the between-bloc conflict.

2. To explore in detail what the possibilities of decreased rank-dependence would be, to see whether the thesis above seems reasonable.

2. The data

To get data about East-West interaction patterns we sent a questionnaire to all Oslo embassies and the foreign ministries of GDR, Albania and Norway, of the 15—8 nations that were members of the two systems in spring 1964, and asked for information about interaction with the other 22 nations. Only one embassy (the embassy of the German Federal Republic), refused to cooperate, whereas others were fairly late in their response and much direct correspondence with embassies and government offices had to be carried out. The responses were then checked and additional data were obtained through international yearbooks, particularly those of the United Nations, and *Keesing's Contemporary Archives*. The interaction variables we wanted information on were the following fifteen:

1. *Diplomatic relations*
   1.1. Establishment of diplomatic relations
   1.2. Diplomat restrictions imposed and cancelled
   1.3. Expulsion of diplomats

2. *Political relations*
   2.1. State visits
   2.2. Notes exchanged
   2.3. UN interaction

3. *Economic relations*
   3.1. Trade agreements
   3.2. Trade restrictions imposed and cancelled
   3.3. Trade volume

4. *Cultural relations*
   4.1. Cultural agreements
   4.2. Cultural institutions closed

5. *Travel*
   5.1. Visa requirements
   5.2. Tourist restrictions imposed and cancelled
   5.3. Tourist volume
   5.4. Flight connections

Other types of interaction can certainly be imagined, but we felt that this was sufficient to test our hypothesis about the general pattern of interaction. Moreover, there are six negative types of interaction: 1.2, 1.3, 2.2, 3.2, 4.2, and 5.2. But in the period under discussion no directly belligerent activities took place between the present regimes in the nations belonging to the two systems — we do not count the Axis powers.

As *time variable* we shall use the phase variable for describing cold war relationships developed in an earlier article [14]. Thus, phase 1 is from June 22, 1941 to December 31, 1947, phase 2 from January 1, 1948 to May 14, 1955, phase 3 from May 15, 1955 to June 5, 1961, and phase 4 from then on to the end of 1965.

As *rank variable* we shall use the simple distinction between big powers and small powers mentioned above — where the big powers are the Security Council veto powers [15]. But whether that distinction functions is an empirical question to be tested in the next section.

3. Testing the hypothesis about rank concordance

We shall now explore to what extent our model of the world as a feudal system is valid, and turn first to the problem of concordance for the ranks in the blocs. Table 7.2 summarizes some of the most important data about the big and small powers in the two alliances, and we have also added some information about (the People's Republic of) China. To add perspective to the comments on the Table we shall use the propositions about rank disequilibrium [16] and rank incongruence [17] as sources of change and (possible) conflict.

First of all, it should be noticed how remarkably concordant the eight dimensions dealing with *size* and *power* are, at least as long as we only deal with 'big' versus 'small' nations. For the Warsaw Pact nations the concordance is perfect, insofar as the Soviet Union ranks highest by a factor around 10 on the first four dimensions and is the only nation with nuclear arms, veto power, a world language and a sphere of interest. By and large this also applies to the NATO alliance, which means that the hypothesis is confirmed. *But there are some highly important exceptions in the* NATO *case:*

1. Germany ranks above two of the big powers in population, Italy ranks above one.
2. Canada ranks above all three in area, Italy and Germany above one each.
3. Germany ranks above France in GNP.
4. Germany comes very close to United Kingdom in armed forces.
5. Canada also speaks the world languages English and French.

6. Belgium speaks French (and Flemish).
7. Germany also has a "sphere of interest".

Thus, one would predict less rivalry and a higher degree of cohesion in general in the Warsaw Pact system than in the NATO system, because of the extreme rank dominance of the big power in the former, making for complete rank equilibrium and rank congruence. Of course, there may be important cases of rank disequilibrium or rank incongruence 'in the small', among the small powers. Thus, the German Democratic Republic ranks lower on area and on armed forces than it should according to population and GNP, relative to Poland and Czechoslovakia.

In the NATO system each disequilibrium, and particularly the cases of incongruence with big powers, may lead to internal conflicts, potentially weakening the alliance (in times of peace; one should of course not infer that these conflicts will not lose salience and even be forgotten in times of war or threats of war). Germany, Canada and Italy have been singled out for attention in this connection. Some years ago, the disequilibrium due to the 'no' for France as to nuclear power was a major source of conflict — and some of the conflicts centering around France may still be attributed to the wounds created by that disequilibrium. Today the incongruence caused by Italy's population is of minor significance, particularly because of the low GNP per capita of that nation. But Germany and Canada and Italy are, nevertheless, the nations that rank highest among the small powers as to nuclear power potential, with Belgium (the only other country to be mentioned in the disequilibrium list above) as a poor No. 4 (with 56 possible bombs per year). Thus, the list serves as a very good predictor of nuclear power potential, partly because size and economic potential permit this type of development — and partly, we presume, because of the motivation provided by the disequilibrium and/or incongruence itself. And this particular type of development, under international supervision or not, is probably a key to present and future power distributions.

Secondly, it should be noticed that it costs to be a big power, not only in absolute terms, but also relatively speaking. Big powers have to spend a much higher fraction of their GNP than smaller powers on defense — even though Germany comes very close to France. Grossly speaking, they also allocate a higher proportion of their total central government expenditure on the military sector, although these figures are difficult to interpret because of the differences in political structure in the countries involved.

Thirdly, when we add one of the per capita variables, the GNP per capita, the whole picture changes. The big are still big, but less so. In fact, whereas the five nuclear powers in the world also are the five nations with the largest armies, with veto power except for the anomaly where China's seat in the

Security Council is concerned, with world languages, etc., and are among the top 6 in GNP (West Germany is no. 4), and among the top 12 in population (United Kingdom is no. 10, France is no. 12) — we find that they are only among the top 101 as to GNP per capita. Thus, United States is no. 2 (after Kuwait!), United Kingdom no. 10, France no. 13, Soviet Union no. 21 and China 101 [18]. This means that in a world where the emphasis changes from absolute to per capita indicators — a world more concerned with the status of the individual than with the status of the nation — the small powers would mix very well with the big powers. But in a world where military power is salient, this will not be the case for some time to come, for in a war absolute power counts more than power per capita. If military personnel as a percentage of population (aged 15—64) counted most, then the six leading nations would be Taiwan, North Korea, Israel, South Korea, Jordan and Albania — with France as no. 7, Soviet Union as no. 11, United States as no. 17, United Kingdom as no. 23 and China as no. 59 [19].

Finally, there is China. She has suffered more from rank disequilibrium and rank incongruence than any other nation, having ranked low on nuclear power, veto power and GNP per capita. The first of these three sources of strain has been overcome [20]; the US policy of refusing the People's Republic of China membership in the UN and a seat with veto power in the Security Council [21] has blocked equilibration at this point so far and probably contributed to withdrawal and extreme aggressiveness [22] and the lag in GNP per capita has led to extreme efforts to improve productivity [23]. At the same time a sphere of interest exists, the limitation of which is not well known; and, as long as the motivation produced by rank disequilibrium lasts, one will probably also have efforts to have the sphere of interest recognised.

It is interesting to compare the profiles for Soviet and China. The Soviet Union is above China in area, GNP and GNP per capita, and China is above the Soviet Union in population — as to armed forces they are more equal. Thus, the rank incongruence theory is good basis for predicting that the two would not join forces in an Eastern alliance; according to the theory they would live in isolation, in conflict or in both, and they would seem to have chosen 'both'. Contributing to this rank incongruence is probably the Soviet self-definition as a young nation, at least compared with China. If the Soviet Union prefers to define itself as being in continuity with old Russia, she may claim up to 1000 years of existence, as compared with China's three millenia or more [24]. From the Chinese point of view both the Soviet Union and the United States may both appear as *parvenus*.

That, of course, does not mean that China and the Soviet Union would necessarily have been friends, had they been of the same age. Thus both of the two superpowers today are newcomers on the international scene, filling the gaps of such powers as the United Kingdom, France, Germany, Italy and Austria (some of which earlier filled gaps left by Spain and Portugal). They are essentially struggling for the same goal, ascendancy over other nations, and, since the goal is scarce, the basis for conflict exists. And in this process they obtain rank incongruent positions relative to older nations and cultures — an incongruence the French seem to have felt particularly heavily.

China has now joined this struggle, and it is easy to see that she will have to build her own sphere of interest, since she is rank-incongruent with the other two superpowers. Moreover, she will probably only look for nations still lower in GNP per capita to avoid rank incongruence. That gives North Korea and North Vietnam, Burma, Laos, Mongolia, and Nepal among her neighbors (and India, Pakistan and Afghanistan among the more remote neighbors) — but not Thailand, Cambodia, Ceylon and Indonesia [25]. Thus, the theory predicts instability in China — Indonesia relationships until China's GNP has surpassed Indonesia's, and predicts which nations would more easily attach themselves closely to China.

Thus, in general the essentially very simple theory put forward is both well confirmed and found to be fruitful. On the one hand, the predominant feature of the two blocs is rank concordance; on the other hand, where rank concordance does not occur the theory predicts conflicts and these conflicts seem to be easily identifiable empirically. More particularly, the difference in degree of overt external conflict in the NATO and Warsaw blocs is predicted by the theory. For instance, if one selects as rank dimensions the first four in Table 7.2, population, area, GNP and armed forces, the average degree of rank disequilibrium is 0.6 for the Warsaw powers as against 2.6, or more than four times as much, for the NATO powers [26]. In both blocs the highest (USA and Soviet Union powers) and the lowest (Luxembourg and Albania) powers are best equilibrated (perfectly so for the two Warsaw treaty powers), but then the differences in degree of internal disequilibrium emerge. However, it should of course be noticed that all this depends very much on which dimensions one selects for the calculation of degree of disequilibrium. On the other hand, the general finding is invariant of which set of the rank dimensions one uses.

And it should also be noticed that perfect rank concordance with one power on top is not necessarily stable in the long run: the smaller powers may unite against the big power. But this is unlikely to happen unless there is some measure of rank disequilibrium present in one or more of the smaller powers — preferably in one of the highest ranking of them — producing the kind of aggressiveness that can be easily converted into drive for change [27].

TABLE 7.2 A comparison between big and small powers, West and East, and China

			population (mill.)	area, km, (thous.)	GNP US $, 1957, (bill.)	armed forces, (thous.)	nuclear power	veto power	world language	sphere of interest	nuclear power potent., possible bombs/year	Defense expenditure: % of GNP	% of central gov't expenditure	per capita GNP US $, 1957
			Size				Power				Additional info.			
North Atlantic Treaty Organization	Big powers	US	194	9363	443	2660	yes	yes	yes	yes	—	8.9	53	2577
		UK	54	244	61	440	yes	yes	yes	yes	—	6.7	26	1189
		France	49	551	42	557	yes	yes	yes	yes	—	5.1	22	943
	Small powers	Average all 12	17	101	12	168	zero	zero	low	low	52	3.4	18	863
		G.F.R.	56	248	50	438	no	no	no	yes	187	5.0	34	927
		Italy	51	301	25	390	no	no	no	no	134	3.3	16	516
		Canada	19	9974	32	120	no	no	yes	no	240	3.7	23	1947
Warsaw Pact Nations	Big power	USSR	228	22403	122	3150	yes	yes	yes	yes	—	5.7	16	600
	Small powers	Average. all 7	15	145	7	160	zero	zero	zero	zero	4	3.0 a	8.0 b	492
		Poland	32	312	13	277	no	no	no	no	0	3.5	8.5	475
		Czech.	14	128	9	235	no	no	no	no	30	3.9	9	680
		G.D.R.	17	107	10	112	no	no	no	no	0	2.5	—	600
	Big power	China	650	9761	46	2486	yes	no	yes	yes	—	—	—	73

a Albania not included
b GDR and Albania not included.

4. Testing the hypothesis of interaction dependence on rank

We shall now investigate in detail how interaction between pairs of nations, one in the West and one in the East, depends on the total rank of the pair. By "total rank of the pair", then, we mean what we arrive at when we give 0 to an underdog nation and 1 to a topdog nation, and then calculate the sum for the two nations in the pair. Thus, two big powers get a score of 2, one big and one small get a score of 1 and two small powers, make 0 — yielding three types of pairs. According to the hypothesis there should be more interaction the higher the total rank of the pair, and the differences should even be quite pronounced.

At this point one may object that this is trivial: that there is, for instance, more diplomatic activity between the big than between the small is a simple consequence of the circumstance that they are big. For that reason we are not simply trying to prove that there is more interaction, the higher the total rank of the pair, but also that there is more interaction relative to what one might expect, given the interaction potential. The precise meaning of this will be made clear for each case below, when types of interaction will be treated in the same order as they appear in the list in section 2 above. Since the NATO bloc is divided into three big and twelve small, and the Warsaw Pact bloc into one big and seven small, we get 3 pairs with total rank 2, 33 pairs with total rank 1, and 84 pairs with total rank 0 — in all, 120 pairs. Imagine now that we have an interaction phenomenon that is not measured in degrees, it either takes place or not, like the existence (or not) of diplomatic relations, state visits, flights, etc. To explore the degree of interaction dependence we calculate the percentage of pairs where the interaction is found, for each of the three groups, and compare these percentages. Examples of possible distributions are shown in Table 7.3.

TABLE 7.3 *Some examples of types of interaction dependence (hypothetical)* %

Type of pair	big East big West	big East/West small West/East	small East small West	% diff.
Total rank of pair	2	3	0	
Complete rank dependence	100	50	0	100
Partial rank dependence	80	50	20	60
Low rank dependence	60	50	40	20
No rank dependence	50	50	50	0
Inverse rank dependence	20	50	80	—60

In the first case, the case of complete rank dependence, the situation is very feudal indeed: the small do not interact directly, interaction goes via one or two of the big. Evidently this is an extreme case, but well approximated in the rules of interaction in some bureaucratic organizations. It should be noticed that there are actually two dimensions at work here: not only degree of rank dependence but also average level of interaction. Thus, systems may be low on both (10—10—10), high on one but not on the other (50—30—0 or 80—80—80) and high on both (100—70—40). We expect most distributions to be of the "partial rank dependence" variety. Cases of no-rank dependence, not to mention the unlikely case of inverse rank dependence, would be clear cases of disconfirmation, but even cases of low rank dependence do not confirm the hypothesis.

We then turn to the detailed examination of the relation between rank and interaction, using the fifteen types of interaction outlined in section 2 above.

4.1.1. Diplomatic relations

As the exigence of diplomatic relations has long been regarded as an important indicator of the nature of the relations between two countries, we shall start with that kind of data. There are three values of the variable: embassy or legation exists, embassy or legation is not established, and the intermediate value of *accreditation*. In the last case, diplomatic relations have been established, but for economic and/or political reasons the ambassador or minister resides in another capital, usually in a neighboring country.

The data are presented in Table 7.4 [28].

TABLE 7.4 *East-West diplomatic relations, 1966,* %

	big East— big West	big East/West- small West/East	small East— small West	total
Embassy or legation both ways	100	82	39	53
Accreditation one way	0	0	7	5
Accreditation both ways	0	0	12	8
No diplomatic relation	0	18	42	34
Sum	100	100	100	100
(N)	(3)	(33)	(84)	(120)

The trend is as predicted. If we collapse the three types of diplomatic relation we get the following percentages for diplomatic relations: 100% — 82% — 58%, and a percentage difference of 42%, which is quite high. Thus, 41 pairs of the 120 pairs of nations did not have diplomatic relations.

However, it should be noticed that the two Germanies accounted for a total of 21, or 51%, of these gaps (the German Federal Republic has diplomatic relations with the Soviet Union) and if we add Portugal, which did not have diplomatic relation with any nation in the East, we account for a total of 28 of the pairs, or 68%. But this is no falsification of the hypothesis, only more detailed information about the mechanisms. The point is that the gaps in the diplomatic network matrix are not located at random, but are concentrated in the lower levels — the tops of the system are completely sewn up in terms of diplomatic relations. Thus, accreditation is also found at the bottom: of the 26 cases of accreditation 21, or 81%, stem from the three smallest NATO powers (Luxembourg, Iceland, Norway).

4.1.2. Diplomatic restrictions imposed and cancelled

Restrictions on the freedom to move for diplomats were typical of the activities in phase 2, although some of them (mainly involving the US and the Soviet Union) are still in force. The distribution is shown in Table 7.5 [29].

TABLE 7.5 *Restrictions imposed on diplomats, phase 2*

	big-big	big-small	small-small
No. of ordered pairs with diplomatic relations	6	58	64
No. of restrictions	6	29	16
% restrictions of total	100%	50%	25%
% difference		75%	

The hypothesis receives a very clear confirmation. And the interesting thing about this Table is that we are concerned with negative interaction, yet nevertheless find the same type of relationship. Thus, one might have imagined that diplomat restrictions would come more easily in relations between small nations, since relations are already so meager — but the fact is as predicted by the theory, that *all* kinds of interaction are, if not monopolized, at least overrepresented by the big powers. Interaction is between them, and between them and the smaller powers; the others are spectators and reflections.

4.1.3. Expulsion of diplomats

We perused *Keesing's* for material on the expulsion of diplomats. This relation is clearly not symmetric by definition, since country A can expel a diplomat from country B, without country B expelling a diplomat from country A. However, by and large the relation tends to be symmetric; B will have a tendency to find a pretext to reciprocate, and such pretexts are probably easily found. Nevertheless, we shall treat the data asymmetrically and calculate the percentages of cases of expulsion on the basis of diplomatic relations both ways. Moreover, as in Table 7.4 we shall use as a basis for the calculation not the total number of (ordered) pairs of nations (240 in phase 4), but the total number of ordered pairs with diplomatic relations — since expulsion cannot take place where there are no diplomatic relations.

As shown in Table 7.6, the hypothesis is confirmed for all three phases, especially phases 2 and 4. It may be objected that these percentages should

FIGURE 7.2 *Expulsion of diplomats in the East-West system and nuclear test series*

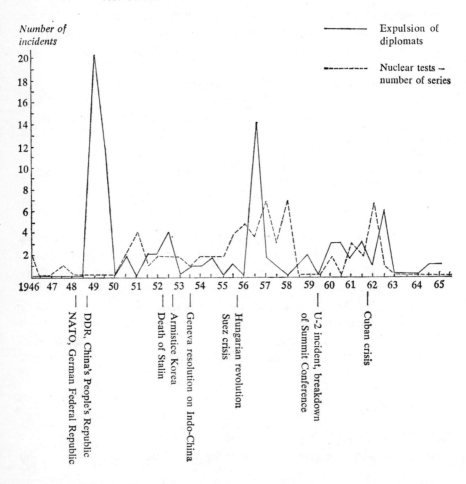

have been calculated on the basis of the total number of diplomats, not on the basis of the total number of diplomatic relations. If this were done, the percentage differences would be reduced, but the trend would still be there (except, possibly, for phase 3).

Let us then look at the total number of expulsions as a function of time, but in a more detailed manner. In phase 1 we had the crises leading up to and including the formation of NATO, in phase 2 no particular crisis but continuously bad relations, in phase 3 the Hungarian—Suez crises, and in phase 4 the Cuba crisis. How are they reflected in the curve for expulsion of diplomats ?

If one should speculate on this meager basis, then one might read three hypotheses into this curve.

First of all, expulsions are concentrated, peaked and connected with important events. Thus, the three crises mentioned seem to account for about 50 percent of the total number of expulsions found in the period.

Secondly, there seems to be a dampening in the system; the peaks become lower with time. To establish this, one would need an objective indicator of the relative severity of the three crises, and we do not have that. However, it does not seem reasonable to assume that the Cuba crisis was that much less severe that the Hungary—Suez crises, and that they in turn were that much less severe than what happened in 1948—49. Thus, the system has probably become more trained, more able to absorb shocks over a period of time.

Thirdly, the two intervals are equal, both to seven years. It would be foolhardy to see any kind of regularity in this and predict that the next East-West crisis occur in 1970 (and extrapolate from the peaks to the number of diplomats that will be expelled prior to, during and after that crisis). Nevertheless, it does seem reasonable that crises will either increase in number and decrease in interval, eventually leading to war; or else decrease in number and increase in interval, eventually leading to

TABLE 7.6 *Expulsion of diplomats East-West, phases 2, 3 and 4*

	Phase 2			Phase 3			Phase 4		
	Big: big-big	Big: big-small	Small: small-small	Big: big-big	Big: big small	Small: small-small	Big: big-big	Big: big-small	Small: small-small
No. of ordered pairs	6	58	64	6	54	70	6	54	72
No. of expulsions	4	12	4	2	11	0	4	7	2
% expulsions of total	67%	25%	6%	33%	20%	0%	67%	13%	3%
% difference		61%			33%			64%	

247

positive peace — or else stabilize at a level that might well be every seventh year. It takes time to repair relations after a crisis, to enjoy the honeymoon feeling of resumed relations, and it takes time to build up a new crisis — so why not seven years altogether, provided the basic inter-bloc relations are the same?

4.2.1. State visits

We counted as a "state visit" all cases reported in the questionnaires and/or in *Keesing's* where a head of state, a head of government or a foreign minister had been on an official visit in a country belonging to the other bloc. Thus, summit meetings or private conversations are not counted, unless they fall under the definition given above. The data distribute as shown in Table 7.7.

TABLE 7.7 *Ordered pairs with state visits,* %

	Phase 1	Phase 2	Phase 3	Phase 4
big-big	0	0	67	33
big-small	1.7	0	7.5	16.7
small-small	0.8	0	0.6	0
% difference	—0.8	0	66	33

Thus, there is a clear confirmation in phases 3 and 4. In phase 2 the state visit activity was at its lowest, just as we found for summit meeting activity in another study. It should be remembered that phase 4 only covers a period of 4 years, whereas the other phases are 6—8 years long.

4.2.2. Notes exchanged

Keesing's was perused for material about notes between governments. Since the number of notes very often exceeded the number of pairs of countries, we preferred to compare the distribution of the total activity of note exchange with the distribution of the number of pairs, and obtained the results presented in Table 7.8.

Here the confirmation is extreme, since we get percentage differences in the neighborhood of 70. Of the 407 notes we were able to locate, for the total period, 3% of the pairs of countries accounted for 51% of the note activity, while the small-small pairs, representing 70% of the total, accounted for only 7%. One or more big powers were involved in 93% of the activity, and even if *Keesing's* is biased towards big power reporting, this

TABLE 7.8 *Distribution of notes, and pairs of countries,* %

	Phase 1			Phase 2			Phase 3			Phase 4		
	Notes	Pairs	Diff.	Notes	Pairs	Diff	Notes	Pairs	Diff	Notes	Pairs	Diff.
big-big	40	3	37	52	3	49	50	3	47	48	3	45
big-small	60	30	30	40	27	13	46	27	19	52	27	25
small-small	0	67	—67	8	70	—62	4	70	—66	0	70	—70
Sum	100	100	0	100	100	0	100	100	100	100	100	0
(N)	(5)	(98)		(266)	(120)		(113)	(120)		(23)	(120)	

almost identifies notes with big powers. It is also part of the picture that more notes went from big powers to small powers than vice versa; 98 against 74 to be precise. Topdogs are trained in taking the initiative, and notes from the small to the big are most likely to be responses triggered by the stimulus of a note from the top [30].

Table 7.8. also gives a nice confirmation of the finding from an earlier article about summitry: phase 2, the bloc-formation phase, was also the phase highest on negative activity — and the content of the notes is almost always negative one way or the other. Thus, of the total period of close to 25 years, that particular 6-year period (less than one quarter of the time) accounted for two-thirds of the note output.

4.2.3. UN *interaction*

What is the contact network in the United Nations among the member nations of the two systems? Is the pattern the same or is it very different? To get an impression of this we examined data from Chadwick Alger's study of interaction in a committee (the fifth), of the United Nations General Assembly [31]. The methodology is simple: an observer located in the room where the meeting is held takes notes whenever informal communication takes place. These data are from the 17th session in 1962, where the committee held 70 meetings. Eighteen of these meetings were used to get to know the identity of the delegates, so the data are from the remaining 52 meetings. Since 94% of the interaction situations were bilateral, between two delegates, we can restrict ourselves to bilateral interaction. If we use the same division of countries as in Table 7.2, with the exception that the two Germanies do not appear since they are not members of the UN, and with Byelo-Russia and Ukraina joined with the Soviet Union, we get the interaction shown in Table 7.9.

The Table can be read in many ways. One way is to focus on the very low frequencies. Thus, the NATO countries almost do not deal informally

TABLE 7.9 *Informal, bilateral interaction in the* UN *Fifth Committee, 17th session 1962*

To:	USA, UK. France	Canada. Italy	The rest, NATO(9)	USSR etc.	Poland, Czecho-slovakia	The rest Warsaw (4)
From:						
USA, UK, France	17	46	53	7	18	1
Canada, Italy	40	1	21	0	0	1
The other NATO countries (9)	48	36	38	2	4	1
USSR etc.	11	0	2	12	21	11
Poland, Czechoslovakia	6	3	7	17	13	20
The other Warsaw countries (4)	3	0	0	13	9	1

with the small Warsaw Countries at all, the idea probably being that "they don't count". On the Warsaw side this is reciprocated only for the small Warsaw countries — the result being that from the very small in one bloc to the very small in the other there is no informal interaction at all. This comes as no surprise bearing the general hypothesis in mind but is nevertheless interesting since the informal forces might be less strong. In fact, they are: the Table indicates a lot of interaction that does not correspond to the pattern for note exchange, for instance. But to study this we have to compare the interaction that takes place with the number of pairs in each category, and make use of the cruder distinction between big and small only.

First of all, Table 7.10 shows that there is more interaction within bloc than between blocs, relative to what one might have expected. Secondly, the NATO system conforms better to the hypothesis than the Warsaw powers — there is more activity at the bottom. And the relation between blocs is interesting. Thus, the big powers in the West seem to avoid the Soviet Union, Ukraine and Byelo-Russia, and to prefer the smaller powers — then, perhaps, to communicate the results to the small NATO-powers. The Warsaw powers seem to have different tactics: direct communication from big to big, and much discussion in the group. A more detailed inspection seems to indicate that the West uses Netherlands in addition to the big powers as a medium of communication with the East, and the East makes use of the Soviet Union and Poland. Obviously, personality characteristics play a considerable role here.

The picture is more refined than the predominantly feudal image we have obtained so far: the UN is an agency that gives more possibility for the smaller powers, because the feudal structure of the international society

TABLE 7.10 *Ratio between number of interactions and number of pairs, for each category of countries*

From:	big NATO (3)	small NATO (11)	big Warsaw (3)	small Warsaw (6)
To:				
big NATO (3)	1.9	3.0	0.8	1.1
small NATO (11)	1.2	0.2	0.1	0.1
big Warsaw (3)	1.2	0.1	1.3	1.8
small Warsaw (6)	0.5	0.5	1.7	1.2

is not mirrored completely in the world of delegates; it gives more leeway. However, the interaction is still directed towards the big on the other side.

4.3.1. Trade agreements

We perused *Keesing's* and other sources for material on trade agreements, starting with some data on the number of trade agreements in existence at different levels of total rank of the pair, and for different phases in East-West relations. We also included phase 1 for comparisons, and got the results presented in Table 7.11.

TABLE 7.11 *Existence of trade agreements East-West, phases 1—4*

	Phase 1			*Phase 2*			*Phase 3*			*Phase 4*		
	big-big	big-small	small-small	big-big	big-small	small-small	big-big	big small	small-small	big-big	big-small	small-small
No. of pairs	3	29	66	3	33	84	3	33	84	3	33	84
No. of agreements	3	13	6	2	1	2	1	9	4	2	13	7
% agreements of total	100%	45%	9%	67%	3%	2%	33%	27%	5%	67%	39%	8%
% difference		91%			65%			28%			59%	

The hypothesis is confirmed in all cases. In phase 1 the two Germanies were not included in the system. All percentages are higher than for all other phases, reflecting some of the effects of the East-West polarization that took place later on. But the strong dependence of interaction on total rank was as pronounced as ever. On the other hand, one should not draw too many conclusions on the basis of the relative sizes of the percentage differences, since they are extremely vulnerable: one more big power trade agreement and the percentages as well as the differences jump 33%.

We also investigated the average length of the trade agreements, but although there was a tendency for agreements on the top to be concluded for a longer period at the time, the correlations were unclear and unimpressive.

One reason why the rank-dependence is so pronounced for the first phase is probably the influence of the war. World trade had to be reopened, and it was natural, in a sense, that the big powers took a lead in this. It was their task, their responsibility in a world where the big powers play the role of the family fathers to provide for the small and the weak (not to mention for themselves) through a system of agreements. Later on the rank-dependence decreased, but the low rate of trade agreements among the small was maintained. We shall see later, in section 4.3.3. below, that this is clearly reflected in the data on trade volume.

Again one should be warned against taking these data too seriously. Much trade may go on without a trade agreement, and there may be trade agreements without much trade. Nevertheless, in the cold war system the trade agreement is tantamount to some kind of positive interaction and as such of interest in our context of analysis.

4.3.2. Trade restrictions imposed and cancelled

Some of the crucial characteristics of the history of cold war trade restrictions emerge from this survey:

Trade restrictions imposed:

1951, 1 September: USA cancels agreements with Albania (trade and monetary agreement)
Bulgaria (agreement of 1932 cancelled within 3 months)
German Democratic Republic
Hungary ('most favored nation' in its treaties of friendship, commerce and consular rights, treaty of 1924)
Poland (do.)
Rumania (agreement of 1930 cancelled within 30 days)
Soviet Union (agreement of 1937 cancelled within 6 months)

1951, 2 October: USA cancels agreement with Czechoslovakia ('most favored nation' from its treaties with regard to commerce)

1952, 24 February: USA enters into agreement with 10 other NATO nations to increase export control to countries in East. The countries:
Belgium, Denmark, France, German Federal Republic, Italy, Luxembourg, Netherlands, Norway, Portugal, United Kingdom

1952, 20 October: The agreement mentioned above is extended to
Canada, Greece

1955, 3 November: USA relaxation of non-strategic goods to countries
in East, according to promise given at summit conference

Trade restrictions cancelled:

1954, 15 August: All NATO-countries except Iceland relax trade restrictions as follows:

1. Items on the complete strategic embargo list reduced from 250 to 170
2. Items on quantitative export control list cut from 90 to 20
3. A further 60 items put on a "watch list"

1958, 14 August: All NATO-countries except Iceland passed that

1. the strategic items on the embargo list to be reduced to 118
2. the quantitative restrictions for 25 items be abolished

1958, 6 November: USA agrees to this.

Thus, the story begins with a superpower and ends with a superpower,
and no such moves of the kind mentioned here are made without superpower and, indeed, big power, participation.

4.3.3. Trade volume

Trade data are problematic, but, since we are mainly concerned with gross
characteristics of the trade in the East-West system, we have relied on
the data given in the Europa Yearbook, and some United Nations statistics.
For any pair of nations (excluding Luxembourg and Iceland) data have
been obtained on the volume of 1. A exports to B, 2. B imports from
A, 3. B exports to A, and 4. A imports from B. The difference between
1 and 4 is A's trade balance relative to B; the difference between 3 and 2,
B's trade balance relative to A; there is no necessary reason why they should
be 0. But 1 should be equal to 2, and 3 should be equal to 4, and where
this is not the case we have used the arithmetic mean as the best estimate.
Usually the discrepancies are of a small magnitude relative to the amount
involved.

As trade is not exactly the same as power politics, we have chosen a
different division where rank is concerned this time. The total export matrix
for the East-West system was inspected and nations were ranked within
each bloc according to the magnitude of their exports and their imports
in this system. The rank order correlation for import and export was almost
perfect (0.91 for NATO, 0.98 for Warsaw), so we used this rank order to
divide the NATO powers into "high", "middle" and "low" as to trade volume, and the Warsaw powers into "high" and "low", as shown in Table
7.12.

TABLE 7.12 *Divisions of* NATO *and Warsaw Pact nations as to trade*

	NATO *nations*	Warsaw Pact nations
High	1. United States	1. Soviet Union
	2. German Fed. Rep.	2. German Dem. Rep.
	3. United Kingdom	3. Czechoslovakia
	4. Canada	4. Poland
	5. France	
Middle	6. Netherlands	
	7. Belgium	
	8. Italy	*Category not used*
	9. Denmark	
Low	10. Norway	5. Hungary
	11. Turkey	6. Romania
	12. Greece	7. Bulgaria
	13. Portugal	8. Albania

Thus, in the "high" classes are included not only the big powers but also the highest-ranking smaller powers according to the analysis made in 3 above. We have thereby reduced the complexity of the system from 21 nations to five categories of nations, four of them consisting of four nations each, and one consisting of five nations. In other words, the total trade in the system is divided into $5 \times 5 = 25$ categories of trade, and we are interested in the relative size of these trade volumes, measured in millions of US dollars.

One way of doing this is to set the total trade equal to 100, and calculate the 25 percentages. This gives the figures in Table 7.13 [32].

TABLE 7.13 *The relative magnitude of trade within and between East and West. Based on Europa Yearbook, 1964,* %

		to NATO countries			to WARSAW countries		
		high	middle	low	high	low	Sum
from NATO countries	high	35.0	16.8	3.2	1.9	0.5	57.4
	middle	13.2	4.9	0.8	0.6	0.2	19.7
	low	1.7	0.5	0.0	0.1	0.0	2.3
from Warsaw	high	1.6	0.6	0.2	10.8	3.4	16.6
countries	low	0.5	0.2	0.0	3.1	0.2	4.0
	Sum	52.0	23.0	4.2	16.5	4.3	100.0

One should be careful with interpretations of Table 7.13. Within each of the four blocs the Table is divided into there is a monotonic decrease in all percentages, from the upper left to the lower right hand corners of the subtables — as predicted by the theory. Trade is highly rank-dependent — but trade has also been used to determine the ranks. However, it is obvious that the results would be fairly much the same if we adhered to the criterion for dividing the nations into big and small used in Table 7.2.

Thus, we are not saying that it is in any sense strange that the data distribute as they do above: this it easily explained in terms of total capacity for import and export. The remarkable fact about the Table is rather how much of the total trade is in the hands of relatively few nations. Thus, if one looks at the exports one finds that the nine countries classified as "high," or 43% of the total number of countries (39% if we include Luxembourg and Iceland), account for 74% of the export, whereas the countries classified as "low," 38% of the total number, account for as little as 6.3% of the export. If we look at the data from the point of view of imports, then the "high" group accounts for 68.5% and the "low" group for 8.5%. Thus, it is also part of the picture that the "high" group has a positive and the "low" group a negative balance in the system. The consequence of all this is once more that the world interaction machinery is dominated by the big, far more than their number should warrant.

But most remarkable, in a sense, are the four cells indicating low-low trade relations: three of them are empty (very low trade levels). So, except for intra-East trade, where the distribution is less feudal, the tendency is to direct trade from "low" NATO countries away from other "low" countries, whether these countries are in the NATO or the Warsaw Pact systems. Thus, with the exception mentioned, there is underselection of the low by the low relative to what one would predict from import and export potentials.

4.4.1. Cultural agreements

The data on cultural and scientific agreements signed, according to the questionnaires and to *Keesing's* distribute as shown in Table 7.14.

TABLE 7.14 *Percentage of ordered pairs with cultural agreements*

	Phase 1	Phase 2	Phase 3	Phase 4
big-big	0	0	100	100
big-small	6.9	6.1	15.2	30.3
small-small	1.5	0	0	1.2
% difference	—1.5	0	100	100

The pattern is parallel to the pattern we find in Table 7.7 for state visits, which is not strange since cultural agreements usually are on the agenda for such visits. And even if they were not, the two would be correlated since they are both aspects of the polarization-depolarization game between the big powers. Again, the general hypothesis is confirmed for two phases, but it should be noticed that phase 4 still is rather short, so the percentages have some more years to grow.

4.4.2. Cultural institutions closed

Seventeen cases of limitation of cultural freedom were found for the years 1950 (June) to 1953 (December); starting with the United Kingdom and Czechoslovakia closing each other's information offices, and ending with USA and Rumania stopping publication activities. Big powers were involved in 16 of the 17 cases — but this must of course be evaluated relative to the distribution of information offices etc., which already show a very heavy overselection of big powers. Nevertheless, the pattern is as predicted.

4.5.1. Visa requirements

"Is there a visa requirement for tourists?" was one of the questions we asked. At this point there is no simple hypothesis, since a visa is not a form of interaction, but only a factor facilitating or impeding interaction. Actually, an hypothesis in this field of visa requirement might run the other way, predicting that big powers would impose more visa requirements than small powers, since it is compatible with their bigness — and still expect a disproportionately high quota of tourists and other visitors.

Actually, what we find is that the factor does not permit any test of any hypothesis of patterns between East and West, since all nations in East require tourist visas of all nations in West, and vice versa. Thus, the factor does not discriminate. But it does discriminate within the blocs. In the NATO alliance the United States is the only country consistently requiring visas of everybody (except its neighbor Canada) and unilaterally — the visa requirement is not reciprocated. Greece and Turkey also require visas of each other, since the Cyprus conflict, and Iceland requires visas of Portuguese tourists. With these exceptions tourist traffic is free, i.e. for 93% of the 210 possible (ordered) combinations. The corresponding figure for the countries belonging to the Warsaw Pact is 59% — to the best of our knowledge. Most of this is due to the visa policies of Albania and the German Democratic Republic.

4.5.2. Tourist restrictions imposed and cancelled

The major source of restriction in tourist volume is, of course, found in the visa regulations. But in addition one nation in the NATO system is known to have restricted travel for its citizens in the sense that the passports were not validated for such travel. Thus, the United States travel ban. In the East, travel restrictions are less explicit, and must be inferred from the extremely low level of tourists in the period referred to. The data have no clear relation to the basic hypothesis, however.

for travel to	was imposed		and lifted	
Hungary	January	1950	June 1	1953
Bulgaria	February	1950	September	1957
Czechoslovakia	July	1951	June	1953
Hungary	February	1956	April	1960

4.5.3. Tourist volume

Tourist statistics are rather unreliable and we present our data with many warnings as to their quality; although the gross information that can be derived from the data probably is valid. We have used data supplied directly by embassies, foreign ministries or national tourist offices. Except for Albania, for which we have no information at all as a receiver of tourists, the Warsaw Pact nations seemed to have much more accurate information about incoming tourists than the NATO countries provide — partly because the tourist volumes handled by the NATO powers are enormous (in 1961 12.5 million tourists to Italy, in 1963 5.3 million to USA and 4.2 million to Germany, in 1962 3.8 million to Belgium, and so on), and partly because the tourist traffic is less centralized (the national tourist offices play a less dominant role in the tourist industry). Thus, we shall use the information on tourists from the NATO and Warsaw Pact countries received in the Warsaw Pact countries — since we do not have information from Belgium, Canada, France, Greece, Italy, Luxembourg and Norway as to tourists received from the Warsaw Pact countries.

Data are shown in Table 7.15 with the countries in alphabetical order. In a sense, these data are interesting because they are so different from most of the other patterns we have found and which turned out as predicted by our hypothesis. And the immediate thought is that this is not strange: tourists travel to tourist-worthy countries within their reach geographically and economically speaking — and very often decide for themselves so that they can break with the pattern of the international system.

257

TABLE 7.15 *Tourist flow from the East-West system to the Warsaw Pact countries, Albania excluded. Data from 1963, Czechoslovakia 1961 and Poland 1962*

	Bulgaria	Czecho-slovakia	GDR	Hungary	Poland	Romania	USSR
Belgium	2075	1571	1698	1853	1538	1956	4079
Canada	366	756	—	1273	1689	—	—
Denmark	1068	1898	7075	908	1337	1179	see Norway
France	9415	8184	2853	8407	9271	3446	51700
GFR	26533	1046	2390	31772	8828	11076	29700
Greece	2534	25	4	483	243	—	—
Iceland	15	—	—	23	47	—	—
Italy	3825	1526	106	4808	1822	—	19338
Luxembourg	59	—	—	77	21		—
Netherlands	1638	940	538	2167	1573		8313
Norway	250	362	90	229	383	—	17310
Portugal	31	—	—	44	20	—	—
Turkey	94943	—	—	284	144	—	—
UK	8806	4007	2420	5733	8406	2034	31402
USA	4471	4362	344	9620	8910	2513	22533
Sum NATO countries	156029	24677	17518	67681	44232	22204	164385
Albania	48	—	—	45	—	—	258
Bulgaria	—	2202	2956	6031	3314	18227	60443
Czechoslovakia	43876		86406	147477	244268	35887	64507
GDR	48934	87959		53586	54340	33112	90810
Hungary	534	38577	18843		17552	5327	46549
Poland	25394	18646	34800	35510		23183	138341
Romania	28412	2483	2618	72191	2135		63545
USSR	30480	27172	8634	88453	25604	10100	
Sum W. P. countries	182465	177039	154257	403293	347213	125836	464453
Total of visitors NATO & W.P.	338494	201716	171775	470974	391445	148040	628848
NATO % of total	46.09	11.73	10.19	14.38	11.28	14.90	35.4
W.P. %	53.90	88.27	89.20	85.62	88.70	85.10	64.6
Sum	99.99	100.00	99.99	100.00	99.98	100.00	100.00

The tendency to overselect big powers will probably be there, but it may be overridden by other tendencies. Thus, let us test the hypothesis that the Warsaw Pact countries attract tourists from the NATO countries proportion- ately to their (the W.P. countries') population. In that case, the rank correlation between population and tourists received should be 1.0. In fact it is only 0.18. But perhaps tourists from Warsaw Pact nations would select the nations that way, on the assumption that they would know more people and hence go most to the nations where there are most people to know? Even less so, the rank correlation is 0. And we get corresponding findings if instead of population we use any one of the other rank-dimensions; all correlations are rather low. This applies to tourists from either bloc, the rank correlation between their choices is 0.86 so there is little doubt that we are dealing not only with another factor, but also with a factor about which there is consensus across blocs. A look at the table tells one the reason immediately: countries famous for their tourist resorts like Bulgaria and Hungary are heavily overselected particularly by the Warsaw Pact nations. Less scenic countries like the German Democratic Republic and Poland get fewer tourists than they should, but this tendency is less pronounced for tourists from the NATO countries, who are probably also going to the East out of political curiosity and, consequently, choose the bigger countries.

In other words a complete refutation of the hypothesis: but then it may be maintained that the hypothesis is about international relations and not so much about individual choices as they are reflected in the data on tourist traffic. So by and large it appears that when people are left to themselves, much of the feudal nature of the international system is countered. And this in turn means that to be a tourist nation has great potentialities as a compensatory dimension in the international ranking system.

Finally it should be noticed that a sizeable proportion of the total tourist volume, from East or West, in the Eastern countries is made up of people from the West. This is not reciprocated; the percentage of tourists from the East never exceeds 1% for the countries in the West.

4.5.4. Flight connections

Finally in this connection let us look at the number of flights per week between the most important cities in the NATO countries and the most important cities in the Warsaw Pact countries, as an indication of the travel possibilities between the countries. The *ABC World Airways Guide* (November 1965) was used for this purpose, and 173 weekly flights were found, distributed as follows among the countries (Table 7.16).

We have omitted the data about within-bloc flights since they are less interesting for our purposes here. As can be seen from the Table the ordering of the countries is quite different from the ordering we obtained for trade relations between blocs. In fact, the rank correlations between trade volume and flight volume to the other bloc was for the NATO countries .37 when based on import data and .43 when based on export data, and for the Warsaw Pact countries .90 when based on import data and .86 when based on export

TABLE 7.16 *No. of weekly flights between capitals (or biggest cities) in* NATO *countries and Warsaw Pact countries*

	1 Czecho-slovakia	2 Poland	3 USSR	4 Hun-gary	5 GDR	6 Bul-garia	7 Roma-nia	8 Alba-nia	Sum
1. Denmark	8	6	5	3	6	2	2	0	32
2. France	7	8	8	2	2	2	2	0	31
3. Netherlands	8	5	4	4	2	2	1	0	26
4. Belgium	4	4	4	6	2	0	3	0	23
5. UK	5	5	5	3	2	1	0	0	21
6. Greece	2	2	0	4	0	5	2	0	15
7. GFR	6	0	1	2	0	1	1	0	11
8. Italy	4	2	1	1	0	0	0	1	9
9. US	3	0	0	0	0	0	0	0	3
10.5 Portugal	1	0	0	0	0	0	0	0	1
10.5 Turkey	1	0	0	0	0	0	0	0	1
13.5 Canada	0	0	0	0	0	0	0	0	0
13.5 Iceland	0	0	0	0	0	0	0	0	0
13.5 Luxembourg	0	0	0	0	0	0	0	0	0
13.5 Norway	0	0	0	0	0	0	0	0	0
Sum	49	32	28	25	14	13	11	1	173

data. This indicates heavy correlation between a major rank variable and centrality in the communication structure for the Warsaw Pact countries and important discrepancies from this among the NATO countries. There are several reasons for this low correlation.

First of all, there is a distance factor. United States ranks very low, but is also the country most removed from the scene together with Canada, which ranks even lower. United States has three flights with Czechoslovakia — that is all. However, we doubt that this can be explained in terms of geography alone. A direct flight New York-Moscow-New York is an important symbol that would be dissonant in many people's minds with norms governing behavior in a major conflict. For in a sense flights are among the most visible forms of interaction, in a sense even more visible than diplomacy and trade.

Secondly, there are all kinds of special factors that have to do with the air communication network in the world. For instance, Denmark ranks highest and Norway lowest in the Table, not because of any basic difference in their East-West philosophy but for the simple reason that Scandinavia's major airport is Kastrup, Copenhagen, from which transfer flights (and some direct flights) connect with Oslo and Stockholm. And many flights to Eastern Europe would stop in Prague and Warsaw — they are important cities, and on the way further South or East.

Nevertheless, in spite of all this, the major hypothesis is verified on the flight data (Table 7.17).

TABLE 7.17 *East-West weekly flight connections, 1965,* %

	big East- big West	big East/West- small West/East	small East- -small West	Total
No flights	33	48	62	58
1—6 flights	34	45	36	38
7 flights	33	6	2	4
Sum	100	100	100	100
(N)	(3)	(33)	(84)	(120)

But the percentage differences are smaller than, for instance, for the diplomatic relations East-West — partly due to the factors mentioned above.

5. Discussion

What, then, does all this add up to ? In one sentence: *that international politics (not non-governmental interaction) is big power politics, for good and for bad, between friends and (particularly) between enemies, in the past, at present and in the foreseeable future, probably to some extent as long as nations exist.* However, the circumstance that a structural arrangement is lasting does not necessarily make it laudable or unavoidable. To mention some of the less laudable consequences:

1. *Initiative is concentrated on the big and taken away from the small,* because "if you think it over, it's only the USA and the USSR that really count, the other countries are of little or no importance". This type of thinking stands in a positive feedback relation to the kind of structure we have shown: the more people think like this, the more will they act accordingly and direct interaction upwards; and the more this happens, the more will they feel they are right and express themselves accordingly. This will stabilize the idea of letting everything important happen through the big powers, thereby reinforcing the structure of feudality and polarization. Another source of reinforcement is how dear this idea must be to many members of the biggest powers, the idea that they and they only count; and to decisionmakers and others in smaller powers who seek pretexts and excuses for not taking independent initiatives.

2. *There is an overexploitation of people in the big powers and an underexploitation of people in the smaller powers.* Assuming that the human

material is by and large of the same quality in all nations, big powers easily get into so central positions in the interaction networks that they will have difficulties staffing adequately all the programs they engage in internationally. After all, we have shown that there is an overlap in the size of populations, which would mean that it is, say, much easier for a Frenchman than for an Italian to get into an important job in some kind of international network. To the extent that this is the case, and we would like a direct verification of this hypothesis, the result is a waste of manpower in the smaller countries, but also a reservoir that may serve to staff international organizations properly.

3. *The system is vulnerable in periods of conflict.* It follows from our findings that conflicts and negative interaction also will tend to concentrate on big powers, just as positive interaction will be concentrated there. But negative interaction, e.g. destructive behavior, will tend to lead to rupture of positive interaction — which means that even big power positive interaction will be reduced, perhaps down to zero. And, since there is little or no positive interaction at lower levels, this means that there is little or nothing to absorb the shock of a conflict in the two-bloc system. Since we have shown that the same type of relation applies between the representatives in the United Nations, the shock will necessarily be absorbed through interaction in international organizations.

The last point can be made more clear by efforts to spell out what more independent small power interaction might imply for the capacity of the total system to absorb conflicts. More particularly, there seem to be four important mechanisms at work — although we do not claim to understand fully or know the conditions that would favor or impede their effective functioning:

Improved communication. If big power communication between the blocs breaks down, as it almost did during the Cuba crisis, there are still big to small, and small to small communication channels to rely upon, provided there is sufficient training in using them, provided they have a sufficient degree of autonomy, and provided intra-bloc communication has not broken down with member nations that have contact with the other side.

Split loyalties. If between bloc communication is increased, the probability is strong that there will be some points in the total structure where split loyalties may accumulate. One reason for this is the simple circumstance that smaller powers are less self-sufficient and hence often have more needs that can be satisfied by the big power(s) on the other side (which, indeed, is a source of jealousy for the smaller powers' own big brother). With need-satisfaction some element of split loyalty may enter, and this will serve to subdue behavior in a conflict, reducing the escalation factor. Personal friendships between small-power decisionmakers are probably important here, for which reason one may assume that big powers are very jealous of such contacts.

The model factor. The idea that small power interaction, if successful, may prove a stimulus for the big powers. Thus, initiatives by small powers may become meaningful in terms of the present feudal structure through imitation. This is mirrored in:

The testing ground factor, the idea that big powers may try out types of relationships, disarmament proposals, coexistence proposals, etc., at a lower level without committing themselves too much, and leaving to speculation whether what happens at a lower level has been learned at the top or not.

Thus, to the extent that these four factors are operative, one would probablly be right in assuming that some benefits would derive from increased smal power interaction in terms of making the system less vulnerable to conflicts· Essentially, increased small power interaction would reduce the degree of feudalism and polarization in the structure. But, according to the system of propositions presented in section 1, increased small power interaction between the blocs will also have the effect of increased big power interaction (proposition 1.1.2.). Thus, if this proposition is true, the result might well be a new division of the East-West system with the 19 small pitted against the four big in a class conflict instead of the East-West conflict we are accustomed to. The likelihood of this is perhaps not very high, but we nevertheless predict that in the years to come big powers will feel forced to cooperate in efforts to maintain their hegemony over smaller powers. The obvious countertactic would be for the small powers to seek cooperation with the big power(s) on the other side in addition (and according to the diagonal homology propositions, some efforts in this direction would pay off with high dividends).

Thus, we assume, essentially, that the East-West system would be most stable if 1. interaction rates of all three kinds (big-big, big-small and small--small) are high and 2. interaction rates are relatively even, so that the system is not too vulnerable in case of big power conflict. However, it would be foolhardy to believe that interaction dependence on rank can be reduced down to zero — that would run against all ideas about what rank implies. Rather, there will always be some tendency for the high to interact more among themselves, partly because interaction with high rank units may be more rewarding, and partly because units with high rank often are more receptive to new types of interaction, are more innovators. Thus, we assume essentially the same theory as to how propagation of types of interaction will depend on total rank as we have developed for how attitude propagation depends on social position.

Hence, the problem is not to equalize completely the interaction frequencies but to make them more even, at the same time as the general level of positive interaction is increased. And the second problem is how to do this without transforming the system from an East-West conflict to a class conflict between nations. To discuss this let us look at some concrete policy implications.

6. Some policy implications

We shall now give specific content to these general ideas, and at this point it would have been useful to have a good typology of types of positive interaction between nations so that a theory could be developed, but no such typology exists to our knowledge. However, two basic axes in the set of types of positive interaction should be singled out for further attention.

The first axis is the distinction between bilateral and multilateral forms of interaction, depending on whether two or more nations take part. The multilateral forms may take place within or without a supernational organization. We shall, however, continue to limit ourselves to bilateral types of interaction, and postpone the analysis of multilateral interaction to later occasions.

The second axis is more important for our purpose.

Interaction is exchange of value; and positive interaction, hence, exchange of positive value (Table 7.18). A trade relation is the typical example, or an exchange of exhibitions. In both cases exchange takes place, we assume, because of differences in utility: both parties "gain" because what they receive has more utility to them than what they send. This is the general principle behind *exchange* relations: no value is created in the process, but the utilities of both parties increase.

TABLE 7.18 *Different types of positive interaction*

	total value constant	total value increased
both utilities constant	no basis for interaction	supernational interaction
both utilities increased	international exchange	international cooperation

For simplicity we have assumed symmetry between the two parties.

264

But forms of interaction also exist whereby value is *created* so that the world as such contains more value than before. Norwegian and Polish scientists may cooperate in the field of disarmament research, Norwegian and Polish firms may enter into agreements about co-production. This does not necessarily imply that the utilities of either party will increase: the Norwegian-Polish team of scientists may decide to keep their findings to themselves or give them to some formal supernational agency; and correspondingly for the co-production arrangement. Thus, we get these possibilities:

If we assume that no interaction will take place unless both parties expect some kind of utility gain from it, only the bottom line has to be considered, and we can proceed with a dichotomy called *exchange vs. cooperation*. Thus, we assume that positive international exchange or cooperation always leads to some type of utility increase. But, we assume also that the best incentive for international exchange or cooperation is found when these types of interaction are not only sufficient but also necessary conditions for the utility increase. In other words, for exchange and cooperation to take place, they have to lead to some kind of gain, and if they are the only way of obtaining this gain, then they will take place particularly easily.

Let us then proceed to a short list of such forms of interaction [33], some of the exchange type and some of the cooperation type, for instance 5 of each type, and examine them for their possible effects. We have not included in the list in Table 7.19 the typical war-horses (peace-horses?) of most cultural agreements, such as exchange of exhibitions, scholars and artists, students, sports teams of different varieties, and tourist travels — in short, not the types discussed in the analysis above.

In this Table, no proposal is included that presupposes any change in domestic ideology or structure in any participant nation, or change in existing levels of armament. The proposals are value-free where these factors are concerned, not because status quo in these fields is considered desirable, but because proposals that do not touch upon these variables are more easily accepted, and nevertheless of considerable potential effect as sources of integration between the two blocs. However, there are other conditions that also have to be satisfied; we hypothesize:

— that the exchange or the cooperation take place on an equal basis, i.e. that there is no exploitation,
— that the exchange or cooperation take place over some time,
— that the exchange or cooperation yield substantial utility increases, and
— that these utility increases could not be obtained more easily by other means.

TABLE 7.19 *A short list of proposed types of positive reaction*

Exchange items	Cooperation items
1. *Exchange of newspaper columns* in newspapers to provide for more local news, news that does not make headlines	1. *Cooperation in education*, by providing facilities for children and adolescents from East and West for summer courses and full year courses
2. *Exchanges between a maximum number of organizations*, trade unions, professional organizations, hobby organizations, etc., of persons and of objects	2. *Cooperation in science and culture*, by providing facilities so that scientists and artists can work together
3. *Roundtable discussions* between various members of the elite of the two countries to provide for maximum exchange of opinion and information	3. *Cooperation in peace research and peace proposals* by establishing permanent research and proposal groups on such problems as disarmament and peaceful coexistence
4. *Exchange of heads of state and heads of government*, again to provide for maximum exchange of opinion and information at top level	4. *Co-production, i.e. economic cooperation*, by mixed staffing and investment in factories and other enterprises
5. *Establishment of a "hot line" between the foreign ministries*, to provide for exchange of information in periods of crisis and to facilitate direct communication	5. *Cooperation in the field of technical assistance*, by a) sending TA experts in pairs, one from a country in the East, one from a country in West to a country in "South"
Obviously, all of these five types of exchange will easily spill over into cooperation, in the sense that more comes out of the exchange than just transfer of values. Information will lead to new ideas that would otherwise not have arisen, etc.	b) having mixed East-West peace corps teams, with volunteers in "middle-level" manpower, sent to a country in "South" c) cooperation in a capital-requiring project (particularly for big power cooperation).

Thus, we do not assume that the utility of "peace" will be considered sufficient for engaging in such activities, for two simple reasons; first of all, the gains in terms of peace, if any at all, are long term and not easily demonstrated; and secondly, since we have (negative) peace between the two blocs today, there is no immediate gain in positive utility, rather a stronger guarantee against negative utility. But this is hardly as strong a source of motivation as some gain in positive utility.

Thus, if in general we have two systems, S_1 and S_2, with m_1 and m_2 small power members, and n proposals for positive, bilateral interaction, then the total number of peace proposals is $m_1 \times m_2 \times n$ — in our special case $12 \times 71 \times 0$, or 840, peace proposals. This is on the assumption that each pair of countries, one from East and one from West, carries out the whole gamut of positive interaction. A practical objection against this would probably be the lack of skilled manpower needed to staff all these schemes of cooperation; another objection, that not all of this is needed to obtain the positive effects described above. Where the latter is concerned, it is difficult to say what the minimum of cooperation is, and we do not even know whether the amalgamating effect is a continuous or discontinuous function of the degree of interaction.

Two reasonable minimum conditions might be

— All nations in one system shall have at least one type of interaction with all nations in the other system, and
— All nations shall have experience with all types of interaction.

Thus, a simple pattern would be for one nation in S_1 to distribute the patterns of interaction on all the nations in S_2. If $n = m_2$, this is easy; if $n < m_2$, some patterns will have to be repeated; if $n > m_2$, some ideas will not be used. This is also the case for the next nation in S_1, but it will have to distribute its pattern of interaction in such a way that the S_2 nations do not engage in the same type of interaction with the second nation as with the first. Again, if all S_2 nations shall engage in all n activities once and only once, then we must also have $n = m_1$. In other words, we get the simple case with $n = m_1 = m_2$. Imagine that they are all equal to 5, and that the forms of interaction are called A, B, C, D and E. We get, for instance, this pattern.

	S_2 nations				
S_1 nations	A	B	C	D	E
	B	C	D	E	A
	C	D	E	A	B
	D	E	A	B	C
	E	A	B	C	D

This kind of square, where the symbols are distributed in such a way that there are never two equal symbols in the same row or the same column, is known as a Latin square. It has the desirable properties: All nations interact with all nations and all nations practice all types of interaction. But instead of the 125 interaction patterns a maximum scheme would presuppose, 25 are sufficient for this minimum scheme. In general, $m_1 \times m_2$ or m_2 (since we assume that they are equal) would do; we do not need m_3.

Of course, this scheme and this way of thinking do not belong to practical politics: we cannot assume two blocs to have the same number of small powers, or that human inventiveness shall produce exactly the same number of forms of interaction as there are small powers in the blocs. In the actual case with 12 and 7 small powers, respectively, and say, 10 proposals, there would be some duplication; moreover, there is no law in human affairs saying that one nation shall choose only one form of interaction with any other nation. But what would be the minimum form of cooperation in this "rectangular" case? 84 would not do, for this would mean that the NATO nations would not be trained in all forms of interaction, since there would not be enough Warsaw treaty nations to practice them on But 120 would do (12 NATO nations engage each in 10 forms of cooperation, and distribute them on the 7 Warsaw treaty nations) since they can always be distributed in such a way that all nations on either side get practice in all forms of interaction. In general, we get the minimum scheme by multiplying the two highest of the numbers m_1, m_2 and n, and the maximum scheme by multiplying all of them. This means that any existing arrangement can be evaluated in terms of how far it is on the road between minimum and maximum, using the coefficient:

$$\frac{N - \min(N)}{\max(N) - \min(N)}$$

where N is the number of forms of interaction in the total system. Of course, min (N) may be equal to 0, in the case of complete polarization, in which case the formula reduces to $N/\max(N)$.

As mentioned, we have very little concrete information as to what will happen when this coefficient increases in value, or when more specified coefficients measuring types of interaction grow. But the general hypothesis, by no means tested by our data, that a system will become more resistant to violent conflict when the general level of positive interaction is higher and less dependent on rank (whether this is done by new initiatives of the type outlined above or by correcting the distributions in section 4) appears not only reasonable, but also highly plausible. To the extent this is true, increase and uniformity in positive interaction may appear as a very attractive road to peace because the process itself is so positive.

IV.8. Norway in the World Community

From N. R. Ramsøy (ed.): *Norwegian Society.*
(Oslo: Norwegian University Press, 197). PRIO publication No. 21—8.

Notes on page *705.*

1. Introduction

We shall deal with Norway's relation to the world community of nations in two ways here: first, by comparing Norway with other nations, finding out whether Norway ranks high or low on several variables; and second, by viewing Norway as a part of the world community, as one nation among many, in constant interaction with others in her efforts to realize central values.

In the following, therefore, we shall first attempt to draw a complete picture of Norway's place in the world community, how she is situated in relation to other countries: the *comparative* aspect of Norway's relation to the world community (sections 2—6). From this we may draw some conclusions that will form the basis for various viewpoints as to how we might expect such a country to act in relation to other countries (section 7): the *relational* aspect (sections 8—15). We shall view the relational as a function of the comparative — and here we hasten to add that such a picture may easily become one-sided. True, a country's position may to a great degree have a decisive influence on its politics, but the converse may also apply: through various forms of interaction a country may attempt to establish a certain position in the world; and this we shall keep in mind during our presentation here.

2. With whom does Norway compare herself?

Norway is a member of a world community consisting, at the present, of about 135 nations (of which 122 are members of the United Nations); in addition there are some 80—90 areas with about 50 million inhabitants without national status. Altogether, this is a large group indeed, and it is only in the last few decades that communications have brought most parts of the world in close contact with each other. Therefore we can

269

hardly expect a small country to attempt to compare itself or interact with the entire world community. Such ambitions are still the province of the great powers.

With whom, then, does Norway choose to compare herself in the world community? One way of finding this out is by exploring who Norway's 'models' are. The expression 'the countries it is natural to compare ourselves with' plays an important role in motivating proposals in Norway, both official and private. In a small, young, and somewhat hesitant country, proposals for change will be met with skepticism — unless it can be shown that larger, older, and seemingly more assured countries — or at least countries of the same kind — have already carried out similar proposals. This is so not because this necessarily provides experiences for study, but because the initiator does not run the risk of standing alone — or, even worse, standing *above* the reference group, endangering group solidarity by pretending to 'be something'. Any initiator has a stronger position if he can show that his proposal is not just a product of his or his group's special value orientation, but an expression of a general tendency in 'our part' of the world community.

To get an idea of which nations 'it is natural for us to compare ourselves with' we reviewed 36 government reports to the Storting from the period 1962—1968 and noted the frequency of references to other countries. The average frequency was then computed: the results are presented in Table 8.1.

TABLE 8.1 *'Countries it is natural for us to compare ourselves with'**

Rank	Country	Relative frequency
1	Sweden	27.2
2	Great Britain	13.4
3	USA	12.7
4	Denmark	9.2
5	Germany (West)	7.9
6	Finland	7.0
7	Italy	4.7
8	France	3.8
9	Netherlands	3.4
10	Canada	1.9
11	Austria	1.5
12	Switzerland	1.5
13	Belgium	1.1
14	Luxembourg	0.3

* Other countries had frequencies too low to be included.

Thirteen of the 14 countries on the list — the exception is Italy, which has not infrequently been used as a negative comparison — ('Anyhow, we must be better than Italy') are among the 19 richest in the world, as measured in GNP per capita. Obviously, Norway's base for comparison is in the world upper class. Norway's reference group in the world community has these qualities: rich, completely Western, and North Atlantic. At the top are the Scandinavian countries, together with the three Western great (economic) powers. And at the very top are Norway's two former overlords (Denmark and Sweden), together with the greatest of the Western great powers. The Latin countries all rank rather low on this scale, while the socialist and the developing countries do not appear at all. Judging from this list alone, we would say that *Norway compares herself with that which is near, rich, Western, and, first and foremost, Germanic; next come the Latin and the more distant countries.* It is thus characteristic that Germany ranks far above France, and the Netherlands far above Belgium as reference countries. The rest of the world, especially the socialist and the developing countries, would seem to serve to same extent as a 'negative reference group'.

These are the countries it is 'unnatural' for Norway to compare herself with, which in turn would mean that these are countries Norway would rather not see ranked above herself in important international statistics.

We might say it is not bad for so small a country as Norway to have such great models as Great Britain and the USA, numbers 2 and 3 on the list. But, on the other hand, Sweden ranks much higher than either of these, and much higher than Denmark. Sweden's position is probably due not only to her geographical proximity, but also to her comparable economic structure.

A survey of the largest firms in Scandinavia reveals that Sweden ranks far above the others, thereby serving as a model for other countries also interested in industrialization; Denmark, on the other hand, ranks much lower, and this would be a more natural model if Norway were more interested in trade and agriculture (see Table 8.2).

Denmark's largest industrial concerns are number 35 (Danish Sugar Refineries) and number 42 (Burmeister & Wain), while the largest Norwegian concerns are number 12 (Borregaard) and number 30 (Norsk Hydro). A certain asymmetry in relation to Sweden and Denmark is thus a recurrent phenomenon in comparisons with Norway's closest neighbors in Scandinavia.

The reference group holds true for the upper strata in Norway: *official Norway*, government departments and committees referring to other countries in their reports to the Storting and its committees. Let us now compare this picture with countries the *average Norwegian* seems to rank high-

TABLE 8.2 *Largest concerns in Scandinavia, by country*

Country	No. of the 233 concerns with turnover > 100 million Sw. kr.	Rank among largest in industry	Rank among largest in trade
Denmark	18	35, 42	1
Finland	46	9, 18	2
Norway	21	12, 30	—
Sweden	148	1—8, 10—11 13—17, 19—29	—

Source: *Ekonomen* 1965.

est — for example, which countries he could think of settling down in (Table 8.3).

TABLE 8.3 *Which countries can Norwegians imagine settling down in?*

Rank	Country	%
1	USA	24
2	Sweden	17
3	Italy	7
4	Denmark	7
5	Australia	7
6	Canada	5
7	Spain	5
8	Great Britain	4
9	Switzerland	4
10	West Germany	3
11	France	3
12	Argentina-Brazil	2

Source: The Week's Gallup, *Aftenposten*, 27 June 1966.

Finland, which occupied sixth place in Table 8.1, has now disappeared from the picture. This illustrates the contrast between the political concept of 'Nordic countries' and that existing in the popular consciousness. Otherwise, however, there is fairly good consistency in the picture. But we have a distinct climatic factor in Table 8.3: Australia, Spain, and Argentina-Brazil owe their position on this list, to some extent at least, to the fact that climate was the second most important reason for the 33 % who would think of settling abroad.

Let us draw another variable which also illustrates our choice of reference group: Which nationalities can Norwegians conceive of having as *sons-in-law?* (Week's Gallup, *Aftenposten*). Five countries were listed, and opposition to the countries *in* the reference group was, as expected, very low: only 6 % were against having a son-in-law from Sweden, 8 % against one from the USA. Opposition to our marginal countries and countries *outside* the reference group was, on the other hand, *high:* 28 % against a son-in-law from the USSR, 29 % against an Italian, and 45 % against a Negro. Therefore, we regard Table 8.1, especially the upper part, as a fairly good expression of what we are interested in understanding.

An important consequence of the arrangement in Table 8.1 is that it is only a small part of the world with which Norway in practice compares herself. In other words, while there is nothing to prevent our presenting statistics placing Norway in the *total* world picture, it is improbable that this placement would have much influence on how political leaders or Norwegians in general evaluate Norway's position in the total picture. Norway's position is, for the most part, evaluated relative to the quite small number of countries indicated in Table 8.1; and, *Norway's position is, on the whole, at the bottom of this part of the world community.* Norwegians appear to have selected a basis for comparison which makes Norway the smallest among the great, instead of the greatest among the small. If the basis for comparison had been more modest, Norway would have ranked otherwise; but as it stands, Norway has more than enough to look up to, look forward to, and be motivated by.

But the world does not consist solely of these countries. The reference group was perhaps fairly valid as a world picture in the period of colonialism prior to World War II, but not today. The total placement is important, because it indicates to what degree Norway has placed herself in relation to the older world picture without developing a position in the new one, and without capturing phenomena typical of the rest of the world. And since every passing day brings the entire world closer and closer together, such a limited reference group may increasingly lead to new consequences. We must therefore evaluate a country like Norway both in the total picture and in relation to its own comparison countries — and then have a look at how these comparisons work in relation to each other.

3. Norway's position in the world community: A bird's-eye view

Here we shall study Norway's position in the world community on the basis of data in *World Handbook of Political and Social Indicators* (Russett et al., 1964). Even though many variables have been excluded, the choice is comprehensive enough to give a good total picture of a nation. (For some of the variables, however, the data are a bit old.) Altogether, there are 75 variables for a highly varying number of nations (ranging from 12 for degree of equality in income after taxes, to 133 for area and population), depending on how complete and reliable is the available information. Only four variables were lacking for Norway, a good indicator of the extent and efficiency of its national socioeconomic bookkeeping system, and ability to report to international organizations.

To place is to compare, to find out how Norway stands in relation to others. That is to say, rank, more than absolute values, is of interest here: whether Norway is among the upper 10%, next 10% etc., down to the bottom 10%. Such a 10% group, or *decile* of the distribution, will therefore be our measure of Norway's position.

We are immediately struck by how Norway changes decile from one distribution to another: *Norway shows an extremely uneven profile*, probably one of the most uneven in the entire world community. To get a more exact impression of this, we have compared Norway's position with that of the two uppermost countries in the reference group, Sweden and Great Britain (Table 8.4).

TABLE 8.4 *Norway's, Sweden's, and Great Britain's distribution on deciles*

I, X	12	24	27
II, IX	14	12	16
III, VIII	13	13	12
IV, VII	16	9	10
V, VI	16	13	8
Total distribution	71	71	73

There is a marked difference. While Sweden and Great Britain have a clear tendency towards the extreme deciles, Norway shows an even distribution. Norway is to be found everywhere possible in the distribution: in other words, Norway occupies highly different positions in the world community, and is thus in marked rank disequilibrium. (It should be remembered that rank is sometimes found in the top decile, sometimes in the bottom decile.)

In concrete terms, this means that, as far as some variables are concerned, Norway ranks as an average country, a very ordinary country, in a world perspective. This is true for, for instance, the three most important variables concerning national size: Norway is number 55 (of 133) on area, number 93 (also of 133) on population, and number 34 (of 124) on GNP. If everything else about Norway were in accordance with this middle position, there would indeed be little to make Norway distinctive in a world perspective.

But the distribution in Table 8.4 shows that Norway is extreme in a number of cases, and this forms a part of Norway's profile in relation to other countries. These cases may be divided into the seven areas that follow.

3.1. Norway is a developed country

Norway belongs to the world upper class: she lies at the bottom of the first decile as number 11 (of 122) on the criterion most frequently employed to show level of development: GNP per capita. Like other developed countries, Norway, has, to a large extent, created an economic system not based on agriculture: her rank is number 79 (of 98) on 'fraction of working population in agriculture'; number 62 (of 75) on 'fraction of total production value derived from agriculture', and number 15 (of 78) on 'percentage of population employed in secondary sector'. However, Norway's tertiary sector is not very highly developed; more highly developed countries have already come much further in conversion of secondary to tertiary employment (e.g. conversion of industrial workers to office workers). We ought to mention that one main reason for the weak position of agriculture in Norway is geographical: Norway is one of the countries with most inhabitants (number 18 of 155 countries) per 1,000 hectares *cultivated* land (1 hectare = 2.47 acres).

3.2. Norway has a high standard of health

Norway is clearly one of the developed countries with respect to birth rate and mortality: both these are very low (respectively, 76 of 86, and 44 of 56 countries). The average life expectancy for women is the world's second highest (after Sweden): 75 years, according to these data. (This may well fall with increase in automobile traffic: 14 countries were above Norway in traffic deaths, of which 13 were in the reference group.) Norway is equally low on infant mortality (number 47 of 50 countries), number of inhabitants per physician (number 101 of 126), and number of inhabitants per hospital bed (number 115 of 129). Norway's standard of health is clearly high on a world scale.

3.3. Norway has a high standard of general education

Norway is one of the countries with least illiteracy and has a very high enrolment in elementary and secondary schools: number 17 of 125 countries. *But this picture is much weakened* when we view education at university and technical college levels: here Norway is only number 44 of 105 countries, far below the other Scandinavian countries (which are numbers 12, 17, and 25), and with a number of developing countries ahead of her. In amount of funds spent on research (in percentage of GNP), Norway is, generally speaking, at the bottom of the reference group (data from *Forskningsnytt* 1967, pp. 66—69).

3.4. Norway has a high level of equalization of social benefits

While international statistics are somewhat incomplete on this point, they still give some bases for our purposes. Let us take size of farms in the agricultural sector: Norway is number 11 (of 50) on degree of *equality*. This is also reflected in the tendency for the greater part of farms to be privately owned: Norway is number 44 (of 55) in agriculture on a tenant basis. Income distribution also exhibits strongly egalitarian features on a world scale: on income before taxes Norway is only number six of 20 with respect to equality; but on income *after* taxes Norway is number 2 (true enough, only of 12 countries; here more data are needed), *after Australia*.

3.5. Norway has a high standard of internal communications

Norway is number 7 (of 125 countries) on number of printed copies of newspapers per day per inhabitant (and undoubtedly number 1 on number of newspapers per inhabitant). On radios Norway is number 12 (of 118 countries), but is far behind with respect to television sets (although growth rates are high). It might be objected that newspapers and radios are, first and foremost, media the *elite* employ to communicate with the population; but people in Norway also communicate a lot with each other: Norway is number 12 (of 76 countries) on internal mail per inhabitant. However, on mail to foreign countries per inhabitant Norway is lower, number 23 of 74 countries. This is probably connected with Norway's *relatively* high degree of urbanization — number 32 of 120 — but this degree is low in relation to other developed countries. And the statistics on mail probably ought to be viewed in light of the high standard of general education. Norway ranks below the other Scandinavian countries on number of telephones and television sets per inhabitant, and below Denmark and Sweden on number of automobiles per inhabitant.

3.6. Norway is a highly homogeneous country

In homogeneity Norway ranks not only among the highest, but in part as the very highest: as number 1 (of 66) with respect to percentage of population speaking the country's dominant language ('Norwegian' — although many Norwegians would undoubtedly place more emphasis on the differences between various 'Norwegian languages' than would international statistics), and as one of the lowest countries on the list with respect to percentage of Roman Catholics and Moslems. This homogeneity manifests itself in various ways: where there are no marked group dividing lines on the basis of racial or ethnic criteria, there will, as a rule, be little organized violence between groups: Norway ranks lowest of 74 countries. Also, at the present, Norway has very low immigration and emigration rates: practically everyone in Norway is Norwegian, and most Norwegians are in Norway (although not all those of Norwegian descent). Thus, immigrants will have few of their own countrymen to turn to, and emigrants will seldom find large Norwegian colonies abroad. This is probably also an important factor behind the relatively low rate of mail exchange with foreign countries.

3.7. Norway is a highly static country

We have seen that Norway has a high standard of development: but this reflects, to a great extent, a development *which has taken place already*. Norway's population is increasing very slowly (Norway is here number 97 of 111 countries). She has a very high growth rate with respect to capital formation, but GNP per capita changes only slowly — here Norway is number 34 of 68 countries, with a number of socialist and developing countries ahead of her. This may of course be seen as expressing the fact that the higher a country has come, the harder it is to develop further — while the lower a country is, the more it has to catch up.

We find the same saturation phenomenon in other growth rates as well. Percentage engaged in agriculture is decreasing, but not particularly rapidly: Norway is number 25 (of 49) in rate of decrease. Furthermore, a criterion such as number of inhabitants per hospital bed, which ought to decrease in a developed country, is indeed decreasing — but here Norway is only number 49 (of 90 countries) in rate of decrease.

Another indicator pointing to Norway as a relatively stable country (i.e. great changes should not be expected in the future) is David McClelland's index of 'achievement-orientation' (also reproduced in Russett 1964, Table 56). This is compiled on the basis of the content of school children's books, to what degree these books depict men who through work and toil and ambition attained great results. The theory is that such tales will give children attitudes which will be transformed into creative activity when they grow up. The opposite is books emphasizing luck or moral qualities. Here the Norwegian folktale figure Espen Askeladd as a *motif* would certainly seem to indicate the second type — Askeladd is cunning, all right, but he is first and foremost good, and considerate for others. Indeed, Norway is number 26 of 41 countries, while *above* Norway we find a great many developing countries, socialist countries, and European countries Norway usually does not compare herself with (e.g. number 1: Turkey). Great Britain and Sweden follow directly after Norway. And Denmark — which in many respects should be considered a highly cultivated, developing country with intensive agriculture, by geographical chance placed in Scandinavia — comes almost at the bottom (number 38). Incidentally, all the top countries on this list are republics.

We do not wish to put too much emphasis on this discovery, although it does indeed fit in in several connections: such data can be somewhat coincidental. But if this can be said to be a valid discovery, it is compatible with the many low growth rates Norway has, and it reinforces the image that rapid development in the world community is now taking place in many countries outside Norway. This is of course connected with the fact that Norway is, to some extent, *arrivé*, judged by current criteria. Norway has attained a form which makes possible continued rapid economic growth; but in the social structure itself, in institutional expansion, the data do not indicate that Norway today represents a high degree of dynamism.

McClelland, however, has an interesting side perspective on this. According to him, various factors promote achievement-orientation, one of them being the father's absence from the home setting, such that the father cannot dominate his children to any great extent. Two conditions favor such long-term absence: frequent warfare, and a large merchant navy. And Norway, although not ranking high on the first, certainly ranks all the higher on the second factor. In building up her merchant navy in the last century, Norway thus — according to McClelland — got more than she originally bargained for: the merchant navy brought in revenue, while the absence of author-itarian fathers created a fund of achievement-orientation which in turn could be converted into entrepreneurial activity in industry and elsewhere later on in the century and indeed on into the twentieth century as well. This development generating factor, however, is weakened: with increasingly higher standard of living, fewer persons (and especially those who have already started a family) will want to be, or have to be, separated from their children for long periods of time, so that the merchant fleet is increasingly manned by foreigners; Norwegians stay at home with their families — and achievement-orientation is weakened. We only present this reasoning for what it is worth — an interesting side perspective worthy of more investigation.

These then are the seven characteristic features presented by this particular source. However, we ought to mention some other data on Norway's position in the world community, because they differ from what many believe.

Norway ranks very high in percentage of election votes for socialist parties — number 5 (of 58 countries; Communist parties are here not classified as socialist). This is connected with the total picture of Norway drawn above, but there are two conclusions we ought *not* to draw from the fact that Norway was for a long time under a Labor Government *(Arbeiderpartiet)*:

First, Norway is right in the middle on indicators of size of public sector in the total, overall picture: neither very high nor very low, whether on state expenditures, state revenue, or labor force employed by the state. Second, Norway is not particularly high on amount of national product utilized for welfare expenditure. Ten other countries are ahead of Norway here: among them five members of the EEC (all except Luxembourg) and the three other Scandinavian countries (Iceland is generally not included in statistical surveys (UN *Statistical Yearbook* 1958)). At the top is Germany, among other factors thanks to Bismarck's policies, having a standard of welfare almost three times that of Norway (as measured by this indicator); Austria ranks as number 2.

But all this does not mean that Norway is not marked by 'state-ism'; that is, the state is not a fundamental factor on the national scene. We shall now take a closer look at this special feature of our picture.

4. Norway as an extremely anti-pluralistic country

An important factor in evaluating a country's social and political structure is the degree of pluralism in that country. By degree of pluralism we mean whether all the country's inhabitants are subjected to the same type of influence from institutions, or whether the population is divided into groups, each with its own institutions. In short: Is the population cut from the same pattern, or has the society various patterns to offer? Does the population express its wishes and feelings in the same institutions, or in various different institutions?

Our immediate impression is that Norway must be an extremely anti-pluralistic country. It is dominated by one school system, one set of institutions for higher education, one church denomination, one national broadcasting system for radio and television; and all four of these are, in addition, state controlled. Such a first impression is not at all weakened by confrontation with such indicators of pluralism as percentage of population born abroad, organization of the school system, organization of religious life and organization of radio/television. For all these indicators we have compared Norway with several other countries, both far and near — a sufficient number to shed light on the general picture of Norway's extreme position.

4.1. Percentage of population born abroad

This is an important factor in this connection, as pluralism is strengthened if a large percentage of the population has been born and brought up abroad.

Table 8.5 presents a survey of percentage of population born abroad for several countries, in decreasing order. (Unfortunately, we have no data on how long the stay abroad was, and thereby how much these persons could have been influenced by the foreign country before leaving for Norway.)

TABLE 8.5 *Percentage of population in selected countries born abroad, 1950—1966*

Rank	Country	%
1	Australia	16.9
2	Canada	14.7
3	France	7.4
4	Switzerland	4.4
5	Sweden	4.0
6	Turkey	3.4
7	Great Britain	2.9
8	Brazil	2.3
9	Thailand	1.9
10	Norway	1.7
11	Finland	0.7
12	USA*	0.5

Sources: Statistical Yearbooks and Census Reports for the respective countries, 1950—1966.
* USA has, however, 19% of the population registered as of 'foreign stock',

At the top we have two typical immigration countries. We see furthermore that many of the countries in the reference group rank higher than Norway: Norway's position is low, as mentioned earlier, but not extremely so.

4.2. Percentage of pupils attending private schools

Most of the school system is, in the majority of countries, a state concern, so that any pluralism in this area will generally take the form of private schools. Of course, we must recall that this is not an unproblematic indicator: within the public school system itself there can in reality be great variations (from district to district, between types of schools, between various courses and subject divisions); and there can be built into the system a form of decentralization and freedom of choice for the individual teacher, both of which tend to increase pluralism. Likewise, private schools may be rather similar to each other — indeed, rather similar to those in the public system as well. All the same, we feel this is a valid indicator worthy of notice. In Table 8.6 the countries are arranged in descending order for the primary schools — primary schools because we felt these to be most important in any socialization process.

TABLE 8.6 *Pupils in private schools in selected countries, 1950—1966 (percentage)*

Rank	Country	Primary School	Secondary School	Remarks
1	Chile	25.9	34.1	
2	Ecuador	19.3	31.7	
3	France	15.1	22.8	
4	USA	15.0	11.2	
5	England	8.3	29.5	
6	Denmark	7.4	16.4	
7	Canada	(4.3)	(4.3)	Primary and secondary combined
8	Austria	2.2	7.9	% of *classes*
9	West Germany	0.83	32.7	% of schools
10	Japan	0.50	3.21	
11	Norway	0.36	3.1	

Source: See Table 8.5.

There are in the world many countries ranking higher or lower than Norway on this list; but in this connection Norway is found to be lowest on both dimensions, with quite a few of the countries from the reference group above her. Also above Norway, however, are several countries Norway would not ordinarily compare herself with, except negatively, such as Chile and Ecuador — both of them countries marked by a strong but small upper class which desires and gets its own school system. Thus, we might perhaps say that Norway, in rejecting this class-dominated form of pluralism, not based on free choice, has also rejected the more elective forms of pluralism found in some of the countries in Table 8.6.

4.3. Distribution of population as to religious denomination

A nation's capacity for maintaining peaceful co-existence between two or more religious denominations is probably also a fairly good expression of pluralism — although it may instead simply indicate indifference. In the countries presented in Table 8.7, however, there is no special reason to prefer the latter interpretation. Countries are arranged in order of increasing percentage for the largest denomination.

281

Here we see Norway in a rather different perspective than the usual one: Norway is found together with countries strongly dominated by *one* denomination, although not necessarily Christian. The Evangelical Lutheran Church is thus even more strongly dominant in Norway than the Roman Catholic in Brazil or the Buddhist in Thailand, although it is not so strong as the Moslem faith in Turkey.

TABLE 8.7. *Religious denominations in selected countries, 1950—1966*

Number*	Country	% in largest religious denominations	% in two largest religious denominations	No. of religious denominations with 1 % or more of population
1	USA	25.7	45.4	8
2	Korea	27.0	49.7	5
3	Australia	34.9	88.8	8
4	Netherlands	40.4	86.7	3
5	Canada	43.3	63.8	9
6	Japan	50.0	96.2	2
7	Switzerland	52.7	98.1	2
8	Austria	89.0	100.0	2
9	Finland	92.4	97.9	2
10	Brazil	92.5	96.9	3
11	Thailand	93.6	97.5	2
12	Norway	96.3	97.2	1
13	Turkey	99.0	99.4	1

Sources: See Table 8.5.
* Order of increasing percentage for highest denomination.

4.4. Television and radio

The socialist countries excepted, ownership and actual control of newspapers is pluralistic in most countries — at any rate, more so than institutionalization of religion, for example. But television and radio are considered by many as at least equally important, if not more so, as influential factors. Ownership of these media is therefore absolutely fundamental.

Table 8.8 presents data on 17 countries, arranged at random, as the data give no basis for clear ranking in most cases. We find Norway at the bottom with respect to pluralism, but joined there by several other countries in the reference group.

To sum up then, Norway is, to begin with, an unusually homogeneous country with respect to race and ethnic conditions (especially language). Only a small percentage of the population were born abroad and are thus

TABLE 8.8. *Television (TV) and radio corporations in selected countries, 1964-1965*

Country	No. of television corporations	Remarks on control etc.	No. of radio corporations	Remarks	No. of languages
Denmark	1	State, US Military TV on Greenland	1	State	3
Finland	1	State, sends commercial programs	1	State	2
France	1	State	1	State	2
Norway	1	State	1	State	1
UK	2	State — ITA commercially controlled and financed	1	State	1
Greece	none		1	State	1
Iceland	none	US Military TV	1	State	1
Italy	1	State	1	State	1
Netherlands	5	Private	1	Private	1
Portugal	1	State	23	State/Private	1
Spain	1	State	12	State/Private	1
Switzerland	1	State, some commercial broadcasting	1	State	4
Egypt	1	State	2	State/Private	6
Ethiopia	none		2	State/Private	3
USA	several	Private, commerc. educ. broadcasting	9	State	11
Nigeria	several	Commerc., educ. broadcasting	1	Private	1
Japan	70	State/private, one non-commerc., TV. several commerc., US military	59	State/Local govt.	17
				State/Private	1

Sources: *The Europe Yearbook 1965*, and *The Middle East and North Africa 1965*.

potential culture carriers. True, we find a great many tourists (although most of them may be found to be Swedish automobile tourists), but their cultural message is more fleeting, not a lasting source of pluralism. This homogeneous population passes, for the most part, through the same school system, much more so than in other countries, and belongs, to a great extent, to the same religious denomination, also here much more so than elsewhere. To the extent that the population is exposed to radio and television, it is the same corporation which carries the message of a homogeneous Norway to them — a state corporation, which, moreover, works in close contact with both the state school system and the state church. In other words, the country itself, the state school system, state church, and state radio television system have no sizable competitors within the national boundaries. Even though all four do possess a large degree of tolerance and scope, we must conclude that Norway is a highly protected country where sources of pluralism have dried up — if indeed there ever have been any there in modern times.

A glance at the Tables gives the impression that Norway must hold something like the world's record in anti-pluralism, at any rate in the non-socialist part of the world. This at once raises the question: Why has the country turned out like this ? We shall only indicate some possible answers and interpretations.

First ,a 'monolithic', 'unitary' system might simply be a logical consequence of a small, poor country's difficulties in making its scanty resources sufficient for competition with other countries. But such a view presupposes 1. that this is the result of logical thinking, and 2. that the logic holds. It cannot, however, be proved that a pluralistic system necessarily wastes resources or functions as less productive of resources than does a monolithic system.

A second, more attractive interpretation is connected with the concept of justice and universalism: everyone shall be treated equally, from Kirkenes in the extreme north to Lindesnes in the south; and this is best achieved by having all benefits extended by the same institutional framework. But, we might ask, where does this idea come from — and a possible answer might be found in the great degree of equality which seems always to have prevailed in Norway as compared with other countries: Norway never had a truly feudal upper class; the peasants and farmers to a large extent owned their land themselves.

It is the third interpretation, however, which we shall concentrate on. A social pattern does not appear from nowhere; it can be the result of an intense struggle, but it may also be an expression of continuity, simply an uninterrupted continuation of earlier patterns. And the anti-pluralistic pattern in Norway, marked by a high degree of state domination, is not a new Norwegian phenomenon. Instead, it is a natural successor to the system prevailing during Norway's period as a colonial land: several hundred years before 1814, perhaps up until 1905 — for that matter, also during the 1940—1945 German occupation. Most colonies are administered through a strong, local state administration controlling central organs (e.g. precisely such features as we have noted: immigration, school system, religion, mass media); this administration has its center of gravity outside the colony's borders (in Copenhagen, Stockholm, Berlin), and the local population (the 'natives') are accustomed to regard the state as a source of authority, as the legal ruler in a multitude of connections. To contest its legitimacy is not to deny its significance, on the contrary. Thus, in practice Norway has a socio-political system in many ways reminiscent of developing countries, not because Norway is poor, but because developing countries also are young as nations and are marked by administrative patterns from colonial times. In this respect, then, we may view Norway as an old developing country, rather than a young, developed one.

Another perspective of the same theme is presented in Harry Eckstein's *Division and Cohesion in Democrary, A Study of Norway*. Eckstein's point is that Norway's stability is *not* due to the country's homogeneity, or that she again and again has one institution where many other countries have a more pluralistic solution. For Eckstein, *congruence* is a main point: an administration is stable to the extent that its way of exercising authority is reflected in other parts of the society: in organizations, economic life, school, the family. Eckstein distinguishes between countries where all such relationships to authority are *similar* (e.g. all democratic, or all authoritarian) and countries where they are *dissimilar*; and, according to his theory, a regime is most stable in the first case. Intuitively this seems reasonable indeed. The individual receives a kind of pattern for decisionmaking and social interaction in general; this pattern is then reinforced in other connections, eventually building a foundation for general attitudes to authority — a foundation which will stand the administrative authorities in good stead if they exercise power in the same way.

Eckstein views congruence as typical for Norway — and this explains Norway's stability. Much of his data help confirm this, especially data from Norwegian organizations. But it is difficult to see that the Norwegian family, school, or economic life is particularly democratically organized. There is a movement towards more democratization in these areas today, but Norwegian stability has been a long-lasting phenomenon. On the other hand, it might be maintained that most decisions made in Norway are semi-democratic: the people in control (whether parents, teachers, industry leaders, foremen and members of the board, or the Storting and cabinet) receive a kind of mandate from their subordinates which may be withdrawn to some extent; that those in control listen to their subjects without actually putting the issues to a vote among them; that they are semi-authoritarian, but in a friendly and consensus-oriented manner.

However the case may be, there is something about Eckstein's analysis that corresponds to our impression of Norway as a country with minimal internal variation. Congruence simply means similarity on a slightly more abstract plane: similarity in structure, in power relations and forms of social intercourse in general. But to find out whether Norway really stands out among many other countries in being exceptionally low on structural pluralism, we need comparative investigations not yet carried out. In general, however, we believe it justifiable to view this minimal internal variation as one of Norway's main characteristics, especially because she stands out among other countries in the reference group in this respect. This seems to hold true for rates and averages (homogeneity) as well as for more structural characteristics (monism and congruence), if we accept the somewhat scanty data presented here.

5. Norway as an exceptionally peaceful country

Another area where Norway holds an extreme position is absence of internal violence, although Norway shares this low level with 15 of the total 74 countries Russett covers. Therefore we need more refined data to distinguish Norway's position from the other countries, especially from the positions of the other 15 in the same class.

An investigation carried out by Jonathan Wilkenfeld (1968), based on data collected by Rudolph Rummel (1963), is useful here. Wilkenfeld makes a distinction between two main forms of conflict behavior), domestic and foreign (i.e. inter- and intranational conflict behavior).

Domestic conflict behavior is then divided into three main groups, 'turmoil', 'revolutionary', and 'subversive'. Foreign conflict behavior is also divided into three main groups, 'warlike', 'aggressive diplomatic', and 'belligerent'. 'Belligerency' defines an actively hostile mood, including such behavior as severance of diplomatic relations, negative sanctions, and anti-foreign demonstrations. Wilkenfeld's study includes, then, six forms of conflict behavior in all.

The study shows that *Norway is lowest on all six*. This study includes 75 countries; Table 8.9 shows the ten countries who head the list in absence (therefore the minus sign) of these forms of conflict behavior.

We see that 'countries it is natural to compare ourselves with' are well represented here. We ought to add that such investigations are necessarily burdened with some weakness, both in data collection and in data presentation. But the results are in accordance with other data: nine of the countries

286

TABLE 8.9 *The ten 'most peaceful' of 75 countries, 1955 — 1957*

Rank	Country	Index of peacefulness
1	Norway	—.924
2	Ireland	—.919
3	West Germany	—.918
4	Sweden	—.918
5	Australia	—.917
6	Netherlands	—.914
7	Denmark	—.907
8	New Zealand	—.906
9	Finland	—.901
10	Switzerland	—.870

in Table 8.9 are, for example, included in the group of 16 mentioned above.

Another measure of peacefulness within a country is the number of working days lost in conflict — although the interpretation can be extreme suppression (either physical or psychological) just as well as extreme ability to solve conflicts by arbitration. Unfortunately, it is difficult to obtain good data on this point as number of working days lost is alone not sufficient as an indicator: the number must be viewed in relation to the total number of working days. We have, therefore, in Table 8.10, carried out such a comparison only between Norway and the country highest in the reference group, Sweden. While both countries are very low in number of working days lost, Norway is the lower of the two, therefore leading in this form of peacefulness.

TABLE 8.10 *Working days lost because of conflict: Norway and Sweden*

Year	% working days lost	Working days lost	Total no. of working days
Norway:			
1930	41,877,300	204,797	0.5000
1951—1955	787,709,400	204,007	0.0300
1956—1960	813,829,200	862,878	0.1000
Sweden:			
1930	166,036,800	979,586	0.5800
1951—1955	2,022,605,100	1,081,282	0.0530
1956—1960	2,168,068,500	56,433	0.0028

It might be objected that we here have dealt only with 'peace at the macro-level' — between countries, and between the large groupings within the country. What about 'peace at the micro-level' — within the family, within the individual human being? Here we could draw in many forms of social disorganization and many countries, but the problem of statistical comparisons would become overwhelming. Therefore we shall confine ourselves to placing Norway in relation to the other Scandinavian countries on two forms of 'peace at the micro-level' (see Table 8.11).

Table 8.11 further reinforces our impression of Norway's extreme position. The main thing, however, is to combine this picture with that we get from Table 8.9 and the data underlying it: this gives a total impression of a country where violent forms of aggression are unusually well controlled. But aggression is often connected with performance orientation, so let us now turn to an indicator of performance.

TABLE 8.11 *Frequency of divorce and suicide in Scandinavia, 1960*

Country	Divorces per 1,000 inhabitants	Suicides per 100,000 inhabitants
Denmark	1.46	20.3
Finland	0.82	20.4
Sweden	1.20	17.4
Iceland	0.71	8.0
Norway	0.66	6.4

6. Norway as a producer of science and scholarship

Since Norway ranks low in higher education, we might expect that research in general would have a modest scope. In a world where at least 90 % of all researchers and scholars who ever lived, live today — where their number is doubled every 15 years — in such a world, the mass effect of science and scholarship is important. There exist critical minimums in many branches of science, both with respect to quality and quantity of researchers, and with respect to equipment. To exceed these minimums requires a scientific and scholarly structure which is *a priori* difficult for a small country to build up, especially when college and university enrollment is so low.

To get an impression of Norway's position in the world-wide scientific picture ,we have employed the statistics on the Nobel Prize's distribution by country and scientific field since its beginning in 1901. A usual criticism of using the Nobel Prize as an indicator of what a country achieves is that the Prize is Western, more precisely North-Western, dominated. By this is meant not so much that it is awarded in 'our' part of the world (Stockholm and Oslo) by persons who, like everyone else, are most easily attracted by that which is nearest to themselves. Rather, and more important, it is especially those performances which our part of the world values highly that are rewarded. Another criticism is that the Nobel Prize rewards only performances in certain fields, and not in social sciences, in music, in architecture, etc. But once these limitations are taken into consideration, the Nobel Prize is clearly of great value as a general direction indicator of which societies perform the 'best' within the framework of the Prize's five fields. Norway's position here is extreme in a double sense. Five Nobel Prizes have been awarded to Norwegians, three in literature, and two Peace Prizes. Only the USA, Great Britain, Germany, France, and Sweden rank higher in total number of Nobel Prizes in these two fields; and if this were calculated per inhabitant, Norway would *rank highest on the two fields put together* (Norway's Prizes, however, were all awarded quite some time ago). But now Norway's imbalance enters the picture. In physics, chemistry, physiology, and medicine — in science as such — *no Norwegian has achieved a performance deemed worthy of a Nobel Prize.* In 1969, however, Norwegians shared the prizes in chemistry and economics. Interestingly, the nine countries highest in Nobel Prizes for science are also among the 12 uppermost 'countries it is natural to compare ourselves with'; this would seem to indicate a dilemma for Norway in the world community.

7. Norway in the world community — some theoretical considerations

Let us now sum up some of these impressions from comparisons between Norway and other countries. Norway generally compares herself with those countries which perform *most* in those directions which large parts of the world today have selected as important; furthermore, she ranks very high in those fields which do not require a highly developed scientific infrastructure, fields which first and foremost deal with inner human qualities or with the efforts of individual persons. But, in scientific fields where distribution of general abilities and intelligence plus high general education are indeed necessary but hardly sufficient in themselves, Norway falls behind.

However, we also feel it reasonable to view this in relation to Norway's homogeneity, egalitarianism, moralism, and anti-pluralism. Norway is an extremely egalitarian country; and to maintain this egalitarianism, the main emphasis must lie on something which all can attain, regardless of social class, whether the country has certain aristocratic or certain meritocratic tendencies besides the egalitarian ones. This 'something' cannot be intellectual development, as this would tend to divide and separate, rather than to unite. In more heterogeneous and more pluralistic societies such a division would be more natural, as it would be one division among many; but in a homogeneous and anti-pluralistic society it would stand out. It therefore seems reasonable to believe that the country would emphasize morality rather than intellect, *emphasize being 'good' rather than being 'bright'* — and, to a certain extent, emphasize religion rather than science. The good man who has just found redemption is no threat to equality in the same way that a bright, creative man is. Indeed, he can function as compensation in a society, which, because despite everything else it is highly developed, to some extent must be built upon abilities of the 'bright'. The bright person is regarded as 'somebody who thinks he is something': his attempts to find new approaches, new forms, will often appear disturbing, and it becomes important to put him in his place through informal social pressure. Elite schools for exceptionally gifted children — indeed, even strong university sectors that emphasize esoteric research and studies — these are viewed as 'un-Norwegian' institutions that either are rejected or come into being only with difficulty.

Anti-pluralism enters this picture in that the initiator, the creative person, rejected in one place, will often be rejected elsewhere, because elsewhere the same norms are also followed. Thus, experiments with new ideas seldom succeed: the initiator does not have the pluralistic society's 'second chance'. *Congruence* enters the picture in that the initiator is in practice often confronted with a network of institutions built up in the very way he is attempting to alter. Thus, an experimenter trying to alter at *one* point may appear as if he were out to alter Norway herself. Clearly, the limited social experiment is *not* Norway's form.

But this does not mean that change cannot take place, only that such change will often occur on a national scale, legitimized by outside references to 'abroad' rather than to successful experiments within the country. It is in this perspective that we must view the entire *concept of reference group* introduced earlier. And the present low achievement-orientation, if we are to stress McClelland's work, subdues tendencies which might break down the egalitarianism in society and strengthen the meritocracy too much. This in turn is directly connected with the low suicide rate: Hendin has indicated that when Norway ranks so much lower than Sweden, this is connected with the fact that Norway also ranks lower on ambition-oriented education and upbringing.

Norway can thus be described as a country that has achieved extreme peacefulness and equality by the help of homogeneity, anti-pluralism, and congruence. What Norwegians experience as contrasts (for instance on questions of language, religious views, sex/alcohol, all according to where one comes from in Norway) are very weak dissensions compared with what other countries have. In the effort to build up its system, Norway has developed considerably, but the system has now attained a degree of stability which may actually inhibit further development. At the same time, one of the prerequisites for rapid change based on own resources is lacking, namely, extensive investment in the scientific sector. In order to 'keep up', Norway must therefore become highly dependent on other countries, become an imitator rather than an initiator, thereby becoming extremely sensitive to other countries' evaluation. This introduces the entire question of the relational and not merely comparative position of Norway. Of the many distinctive features we have discussed in connection with Norway's position relative to other countries, one appears especially decisive for what the country is attempting to achieve on an *international* scale: characteristic of Norway is not that the country is developed, but the *extreme imbalance* in her total profile. Most of the indicators related to development are, as we have seen, very high (especially Norway's merchant navy fleet), whereas indicators of *size* are completely ordinary (this is true of military potential as well); on the other variables Norway ranks very low, even on a global scale. In general, Norway is an 'overachiever' on a global scale, in relation to her resources. This has both its causes and its consequences.

The *causes* of imbalance probably lie in one factor: the country has, to an almost extreme degree, managed to turn its many disadvantages into advantages — for only recently did Norway rank very low in almost all respects, in relation to its neighbors. For example:

— Norway lacked a true upper class of feudal extent. (In part, this was also true of the cultural upper class). But on this basis the country built up a highly egalitarian society which encouraged mobilization of talent from the entire population, and not just from a small upper class.

— Norway is geographically placed on the fringes of the world, with a disadvantageous climate. For that reason, she was mostly left in peace by her stronger neighbors, at the same time as these neighbors were sufficiently near enough to form a reference group which stimulated her longing for development. The population was not threatened by immigration, so that the density was and remains low.

— Norway lay on the periphery with respect to communications, and her coast faces the open and often fierce sea. Thus the country converted to seamanship. Far-ranging ships sailed undisturbed in the peripheral waters of Northern Europe — a thing impossible in the Mediterranean. (Had Norway been placed there, she would have been kept in check by her neighbors, and would hardly have developed.) What was a *peripheral* position, with respect to communications, Norway managed to convert to a *central* one through navigation and the shipping industry. While other countries, in getting high rank, thereby attracted communications, *Norway made herself a central position in the communications system, thereby obtaining high rank*. Norway converted central position into rank, and not the usual reverse.

— Norway was exceptionally poor in resources which could form the basis for industry and agriculture (except for water power.) Instead, the population concentrated on fishing, shipping, and commerce, which then formed a basis for expansion and strong bonds with other countries, which the country in turn became completely dependent on.

As to the *consequences* of imbalance, we would in general expect a high degree of aggression from a nation which has made more out of its resources and possibilities than would be expected. We would not expect either the natural superiority — and status quo — orientation of the more balanced nation on the top of the world society, or the more servile attitude of the balanced nation at the bottom of world society. Instead, we would expect a general attitude of 'there must be something about us Norwegians, since we've managed to get so much out of so little'. Such a feeling will easily turn into self-righteousness, into an injured attitude if others attempt to question its validity, and into a feeling that Norwegians have something to offer that others need. In other words: that Norwegians would be a blessing for others, and that Norwegian ways of being and of doing things ought to benefit others.

This basic principle may combine both Norway's and Norwegians' *attitudes* and *actions* on the international plane. But how is a country that ranks so low as Norway on such pure power variables as GNP, population, and size — all factors necessary for military power — how is she to be aggressive ? Aggression need not mean use of power in the sense of 'violence': aggression here is used to mean the attempt to change others, and it may be directed both inwards (as in suicide or apathy) or outwards (as in murder, other crimes, or creative behavior). A nation or individual which has managed to make *more* out of its resources than one might expect, will on the whole direct its aggression outwards, while a nation or individual which has got less out of its resources, will direct it inwards.

Thus we believe that if Norway had not 3.7 million but 37 million inhabitants, and a GNP ten times greater than what she has, but the same location, the same area, and the same neighbors — then the way would be paved for strong aggression on the part of Norway. Self-righteousness, the feeling of being unjustly treated in being so low on certain variables, the feeling of being entitled to change this: all these would be present. Inner homogeneity and stability, institutional anti-pluralism, tendency towards congruence, equality within the country — all these would make it comparatively easy to mobilize the population under the banner of a national ideology and a central leadership, and under the promise of immediate rewards.

But Norway is not this fictive country, but only one tenth of it, and therefore no real threat to her neighbors. Thus she must find quite different ways and means for any use of power on an international plane. Norway's neighbors are more powerful and rich than herself; she cannot do as Israel (a country which, incidentally, Norway somewhat resembles and with which she also identifies rather strongly). The solution must lie on another plane than direct attempts at controlling other nations. And the international system of today does indeed offer several other possibilities for influence than classical territory-oriented warfare.

For one thing, the desire for influence can find fulfilment through active participation in international organizations, both IGOs (international governmental organizations) and INGOs (international non-governmental organizations). Norwegians can again do what they did with their merchant navy fleet: not only man the international community's moving company, but be its managing personnel as well. By maximum Norwegian participation in a maximum number of IGOs and INGOs, both in permanent secretariats and in delegations and conferences, as consultants and experts, Norway will be able to assert herself, let her voice be heard, and influence decisions favorable to the country's interests. Just as we speak of 'imperialism' when one country advances on anoher (military, politically, economically, culturally), we can also speak of a kind of 'infiltration' in international organs.

We would therefore expect certain attitude patterns among Norwegians and certain action patterns for Norway with respect to the international community. To this we now turn. But 'aggression', as defined above, is of course not the only basis for Norway's interaction patterns. It is a pattern we can expect in addition to the obvious one: namely, that Norway, as a hesitant, outward-oriented nation, will have a strong tendency to act like the majority of countries in the reference group, in order to further and insure what the country defines as her interests. It is, for example, rather clear that Norway will attempt to join international organizations where the reference group is represented poorly or not at all.

8. Norwegian opinion on Norway and the world community

There are three investigations of Norwegian opinion on international relations as shown by the many surveys conducted by the Norwegian Gallup polls.

The first is from Ingrid Eide's examination of these in *Norway and the Norwegians* (in Alstad 1969). In one survey, the inhabitants of various countries, among them the Scandinavian, were asked personally to rank countries in respect of scenic beauty, quality of food, national patriotism, female beauty, etc. All these countries showed a tendency for the majority to emphasize their own country's superiority. Norwegians, however, did so to a much greater degree than any others. And, indeed more important, only Norwegians ranked *Norway* highest on the list, while other countries received varying degrees of support from abroad in their self-glorification. It must be mentioned that Swedes considered Norwegians as ranking very high with respect to patriotism!

The second one is from Galtung's investigation of surveys on international cooperation (in Alstad 1969). The conclusion from many such surveys is this:

The level of knowledge is low, sometimes very much so—and it appears to rise only through conflict and debate, and over time. Compared with other countries, however, the level of knowledge is not so very bad.

Attitudes to other peoples, especially other races (and gipsies) show marked negative tendencies, at the same time as there appear certain tendencies to self-glorification. This, however, does not hinder a generally very high degree of acceptance concerning international cooperation — it is the personal contact that seems to create difficulties.

Attitude towards cooperation appears to become more positive, the more extensive the cooperation is: There is greater interest for UN than for European cooperation, and greater interest for European cooperation than for Nordic.

In other words, we seem to see an expansive nation, in the sense that Norway opens up in relation to the world, but more from interest to go out to the world than to allow the world to approach her very closely. Thus Norway was, together with the Netherlands, the Western country under German occupation — aside from the Slavic countries — with the lowest percentage of surviving Jews. This was in part due to particular policies of the German administration in Norway — but it was probably also due to the low integration of Norwegian Jews into the population, which again can be traced to homogeneity and lack of training in true (not merely verbal) tolerance.

These features are also evident from Galtung's investigation of Gallup surveys on war, peace, and defence (in Alstad 1969):

There is no doubt that the general orientation is Western. The West is preferred to the East, the USA to the USSR, NATO to the Warsaw Pact, etc.

There, are however, nuances in the picture:

A general skepticism towards great powers causes many critical attitudes to the USA. In several situations, evaluation of the USA and USSR is almost symmetric, and Norway ranks very high in the reference group on this symmetric attitude.

There are also many positive features in the Norwegian attitude to the USSR: the USSR is the winner, the powerful, clever, mighty one.

There is no unqualified acceptance of all Western countries: great skepticism is found towards Germany, France, and, to a certain extent, Spain.

Generally, Norwegians are positive in respect of military defence: any critical attitudes are directed towards its individual national aspects. This, combined with the Western orientation, leads to a positive attitude to Nordic defense cooperation and to European defense cooperation (but in both cases there are many DK/NA).

The long-range perspective is generally optimistic, the short-range more pessimistic, but this depends on external events and crises. With lessened external pressure, worries about international events and relations disappear. Interest level is therefore low in periods when peacebuilding tactics can most easily be put into effect, and high in periods when a more threatening peace policy (military policy) may be easily launched. A strongly moral attitude lies behind many opinions. War is wrong; the aggressor shall be punished; he is not to be trusted. And if one's faith in a nation is violated, one ought to condemn that nation and turn against it.

In one comparative investigation of foreign policy opinion with Norway among the participants (the so-called Tri-nation survey of France, Norway, and Poland carried out in 1964), some of the findings place typically Norwegian attitudes in an international perspective.

Norway ranked above the other two countries in positive attitude to the UN: 48% wished to base a world order after disarmament on the UN, as against 25% in France and 29% in Poland.

In Norway, 64% wished to spend less on military defense, as against 40% in France, and 32% in Poland.

Norway was the highest of the three (45% as against 33% and 24%) in agreeing to place a part of the country's military defense under UN leadership.

Norway was the highest of the three countries in giving the UN an important role as a peacekeeping factor.

Norway was the highest of the three in interest in disarmament proposals and international news in general.

Norway was the highest of the three in level of knowledge on international affairs — e.g. there were more people in Norway than in France who knew that France was a member of NATO (*The UNESCO Courier 1967*).

In general, then, we get the impression of a country whose people are internationally 'committed' and feel that it makes a difference that they are committed. The people have an image of how the world ought to be — *and that image requires first and foremost that the world be a larger edition of Norway.* This identification becomes even easier because the UN is in many ways congruent with the Norwegian authority structure.

We get an even better impression of this if we turn to another investigation which attempts to clarify Norwegian 'peace philosophy', i.e. how people believe peace may be achieved (taken from the *Images of the World in the Year 2000* study). The five most important factors, according to a sample of 500 persons, are shown in Table 8.12.

We see no references to balance of power, alliance politics, or power at all. Instead, we find the concept of 'realizing Norwegian conditions all over the world', in that relationships between nations in the world community shall become like relationships between people in the Norwegian community. In these five peace philosophies we thus find moralism, the idea of active support to international interaction — all of these supported by the idea that these will serve the cause of peace.

TABLE 8.12 UN *voting agreement. Norway and other countries, 1964—1966*

Level of acceptance*	Peace philosophy: 'in order to achieve peace . . .'
0.92	hunger and poverty must be abolished throughout the world
0.84	we must increase trade, exchange, and cooperation, also between countries who do not have friendly relations with each other
0.82	we must improve the UN, so that it will become more effective than today
0.80	it must be possible for people all over the world to choose their governments freely
0.75	the gap between rich and poor countries must disappear

Source: International Peace Research Institute, Oslo: Norwegian Peace Philosophy (unpublished tables) 1967.

* Level of acceptance is an average based on a 3-point scale. It may vary between + 1 and — 1.

9. Norway in the UN

Norway's general position in the world community is also reflected in the form of action in the UN. Since this organization is universal, the country is confronted with not only the entire reference group, but practically the entire world. What then does Norway try to achieve in the UN, what are her aims?

We shall attempt to approach the problem by seeing who it is that Norway votes *most* and *least* with in the UN. The UN is more a sort of market for voting on ideas in the international community than a forum making real decisions of a fundamental nature, which then are put into action. 'Tell me whom you vote with, and I'll tell you who you are', therefore, seems to be a good clue to understanding a country's behavior in this organization.

Kurt Jacobsen has analyzed voting in the UN over a 20-year period, and some of the results of his investigation are shown here. Who Norway identifies herself most and least with can be seen from Table 8.13.

TABLE 8.13 UN *voting agreement, Norway and other countries, 1964—1966*

Rank	Most agreement	USA/ Great Britain* percentage	Least agreement	USA/ Great Britain* percentage
1	Denmark	90 L	Mongolia	26 L
2	Sweden	86 L	Byelorussia	31 L
3	Iceland	83 L	USSR	32 L
4	Ireland	81 L	Ukraine	32 L
5	Canada	76 H	Poland	32 L
6	Austria	76 L	Czechoslovakia	32 L
7	USA	74 H	Albania	33 L
8	New Zeland	74 H	Romania	33 L
9	Trinidad/Tobago	73 L	Hungary	33 L
10	Japan	72 H	Bulgaria	34 L
11	Italy	72 H	Mali	36 L
12	Netherlands	71 H	Algeria	37 L
13	Jamaica	71 H	Guinea	38 L
14	Turkey	70 H	Jordan	39 L
15	Finland	69 L	Saudi Arabia	40 L
16	Nicaragua	69 H	Afghanistan	41 L
17	Great Britain	69 H	Libya	41 L
18	Luxembourg	68 H	Morocco	41 L
19	Australia	67 H	Yemen	41 L
20	Brazil/Chile/ Panama/Peru	67 H	Egypt/Syria	43 L

Source: Kurt Jacobsen, *Voting Patterns in the UN*, International Peace Research Institute Oslo.

* USA's and Great Britain's percentage of voting agreement with each country has also been calculated. 'L' indicates that their voting agreement with the country is lower than Norway's, 'H' indicates that it is higher.

Norway votes least with the Comecon countries and the most radical African and Arab countries. In other words, Norway does *not* associate herself with the countries in the world which today are most fundamentally change-oriented, and this is what we would expect of a country which is both stable and highly developed.

Who it is Norway votes *most* with can be summed up briefly. First of all, *Scandinavian countries*, with Finland far behind the others as we would expect due to Finland's special relationship to the USSR, and with Denmark ahead of Sweden, as we would expect, since Sweden is outside NATO. After these, however, do *not* come all the other NATO countries: of the 12 remaining NATO countries, only seven are among the top 20. Especially we notice that France and Belgium are not high (with 61 % and 63 % respectively), which would mean that Norway has a qualified solidarity with the EEC countries. As usual, the borderline is drawn between the Germanic and Latin countries.

But stronger than the NATO elements are those from several smaller countries, *of which six are members of the British Commonwealth and belong to its moderate, more Western-oriented wing*. These elements are so strong that if we had only this Table and were to guess the basis of it, we would have guessed that Norway belonged to the British Commonwealth (average agreement: 73) rather than to NATO (average agreement: 70).

The fourth element in this picture is the Latin American countries. If we go as far down in voting agreement as to 66% we get 10 of them, i.e. one half (with Cuba as the lowest of the remaining, 51%). In one respect this is Norway's way of approaching developing countries — through the old, 'white' developing countries in Latin America, who generally vote in agreement with the USA. Of the *new* developing countries which are not members of the Britsh Commonwealth, Norway has highest voting agreement with Rwanda and Laos, 50%. But with such an important spokesman for the Afro-Asian bloc as India, voting agreement is only 50%. With Uganda, the other country (in addition to India) to which Norway has sent considerable technical aid, Norway shows likewise only 50% voting agreement.

Again, Norway appears as a North-Western nation, but not extreme in that direction. As we see from the Table, Norway rejects the Eastern Bloc and the South-Eastern countries, but not so much as do the USA and Great Britain. And Norway's agreement with the Scandinavian countries, neutral Austria and Ireland, and the more radical Commonwealth countries Jamaica and Trinidad-Tobago is *higher* than that of the USA and Great Britain. In return, Norway's voting agreement with the more conservative Commonwealth countries, European countries, and Latin American countries is lower than that of the USA and Great Britain. In other words, Norway seems to have placed herself in a bridge-builder position between East and West and between South and North.

The list of 'countries we cooperate with in the UN' is not identical with the list of 'countries it is natural for us to compare ourselves with'. True, we do find most of the same countries; aside from Germany and Switzerland, not members of the UN, only the Latin countries Belgium and France are missing. But there are great differences in the order of countries within the lists. Probably the reason is that in the UN, geographical and cultural proximity are much less important, so that ideology, working companionship, and even purely personal factors enter the picture. *It may be that in the UN, Norway ventures forth more in the world community, and as a bridge to the 'new' world Norway uses the system of nations that England has built up.* Here Norway's one-sided concentration on English as a second language and her traditionally pro-British sentiments are of course important. In the UN, we see that Norway partly separates herself from her close contact with the USA and Great Britain, instead identifying herself with other countries which are also small, but also fairly rich. On a purely political-technical basis Norway concentrates on cooperation with the other Nordic countri es (this cooperation was for a long time coordinated from Oslo) and on Ireland and Canada — who have also played very active roles in the UN.

How far this policy will take Norway is another matter. We might note that it takes her into the right-wing branch of the 'world community's Labor Party', to coin a phrase — but nowhere near into the 'world community's Socialist People's Party' (i.e. the party to the left of the Labor Party. Translator's note). In other words, Norway's UN policy is a true copy of her domestic policy, aside from the fact that she, through her UNCTAD policy, seems to have a more negative attitude to the less-privileged countries than she has to her own less-privileged citizens.

10. Norway as a contributor to the world community

Because Norway attempts to become attached to international organizations, especially to those that are universal and where her reference group is best represented, we would expect Norway's contributions to *development aid* to favor strongly the multilateral organs, because Norway could thereby help strengthen her own position within these organs. There is, naturally, also a negative reason: Norway, as opposed to many other countries in the reference group, has not had colonies in recent times and has therefore not established a set of interaction channels through which bilateral aid can flow naturally and easily (see Table 8.14).

Norway ranks lowest (together with Denmark and Japan) on total contributions to developing countries, and it is not lack of private transactions that pulls Norway down. But on contributions to the most important multilateral organs in this field, Norway rises sharply again, with her typical imbalance. A measure of imbalance has been calculated in the far right-hand column (although the time references do vary somewhat), and the countries ordered accordingly. This shows how Norway, together with Den-

TABLE 8.14 *Ranking of 14 countries, according to per capita contributions in* US *dollars to developing countries*

Country (rank order)	a Private transactions 1956—1962	b Total transactions 1956—1962	c UN Development Program contrib. 1966	d International Development Agency contrib. 1966	Difference*
Norway	11.5	13.0	3	5	9.0
Denmark	11.5	13.0	2	6	9.0
Sweden	8.0	9.0	1	1	8.0
Canada	11.5	10.5	5	3	6.5
Netherlands	6.5	5.5	4	4	1.5
Japan	11.5	13.0	14	13	—0.5
Austria	9.0	10.5	11	11	—0.5
Belgium	14.0	7.5	9	10	—2.0
Great Britain	5.0	4.0	8	2	—3.0
Switzerland	1.0	2.0	6	—	—4.0
West Germany	6.5	5.3	10	9	—4.0
USA	3.5	3.0	7	7	—4.0
Italy	3.5	7.5	13	12	—5.0
France	2.0	1.0	12	8	—9.0

Sources: For *a* and *b*, OECD 1964; for *c* and *d*, Norwegian State Department (*Utenriksdepartement* 1967, p. 107).
* Column 2 minus columns 3 and 4 added together and divided by two.

mark and closely with Sweden and Canada, leads in policy favoring the UN in development aid (but with Sweden clearly above on all dimensions, as usual). As a contrast we see France, who follows diametrically opposed politics with a clear predominance of bilateral forms of aid, both private and state.

We ought to mention in this connection that Norway was nation number 2, after the USA, in launching a government peace corps whose aim was to send low-paid volunteers to work in developing countries. Like other Norwegian bilateral aid projects, this has been marked by strong geographical concentration as to host countries.

We have mentioned morality, and the great emphasis placed on international organizations, like the UN, as basic characteristics of Norwegian orientation in the world community. We would therefore expect Norway's contributions to the world community via the UN's *refugee aid* programs to be especially high, because both characteristics are in a way united here. And this is indeed the case (Table 8.15). Norway ranks at the top of a group of 'small, good countries', a milieu which also corresponds with most of our reference group.

TABLE 8.15 *Contributions to and via* UN *High Commission for Refugees, 1959—1963*

Country	Dollars per inhabitant
Norway	0.54
Netherlands	0.40
New Zealand	0.36
Denmark	0.26
Sweden	0.22
Iceland	0.20
Belgium	0.12

Source: Unpublished information from UN High Commission for Refugees, 1967.

Finally, let us take a look at Norway's contribution to the world community through Christian *missions*. This form of contribution ought to suit Norway especially well: here practically all the good reasons to go outside the national borders are united. Contributions may be made from individual to individual, instead of being abstracted to a relationship between nations; that is to say, contributions may be made in a way more in keeping with the Christian ethic dominant in Norway. The contributions may be combined with a fundamental value in Norway: Christianity. This message may be joined to concrete actions and a concrete way of life — the missionary's — which is also a way of carrying to others the Norwegian social structure.

To get a closer view of this we have employed two measures of degree of missionary activity *from* a country: number of missionaries per 100,000 inhabitants, and voluntary donations to missions, per inhabitant (Table 8.16).

Among the countries closest to Norway, it is clearly Norway who has the leading position in missionary activity. This is also true if we extend the framework of comparison.

TABLE 8.16 *Missionaries sent and contributions collected for missions*

Country	Missionaries sent per 100,000 inhabitants	Total contributions, per inhabitant
Norway, 1965	27.4	9.3 N.kr.*
Norway, 1963	25.0	5.7 N.kr.
Sweden, 1963	19.0	3.7 Sw.kr.
Denmark, 1962	6.4	1.4 D.kr.

Sources: Mission statistics from the respective countries.
* Norway is much higher in 1965 than in 1963 because the 1963 statistics exclude various administrative expenditures included in 1965.

11. Norway in other international organizations

The world community has other international organizations than the UN: about 600 IGOs and 1,600 INGOs. Norway belongs to a great number of them, thereby increasing her possibilities for influence, indeed, far more than would be expected from Norway's tiny size. Thus, Norway is a member of the UN's special organizations, of GATT, OECD, EFTA, Council of Europe, and NATO. In general Norway has the same pattern of membership regarding these important organizations, as have most of the upper countries in the reference group — with important exceptions. Norway differs from Sweden in belonging to NATO, from the Common Market countries in belonging to EFTA, and from Great Britain in that the latter has a 'bridge to the continent' via membership in the Western European Union, to which the Common Market countries also belong. Otherwise, the reference group is clearly the same membership group, and the few points of difference are also some of the most explosive debate topics in Norway. And this leads us to modify our reasoning a bit: while it is doubtless true that Norway most often follows the countries in the reference group on questions of membership, it is also true that being together with other countries in an important international organization gives a basis for comparison which may lead to expanding the group.

The extent of Norwegian penetration into (and by) the system of international organizations can to some extent be judged from Table 8.17.

TABLE 8.17 *Norway and the international organizations, non-governmental (INGOs) and governmental (IGOs) (1964, last columns 1954)*

INGO/capita	IGO/capita	International officials/capita
1. Israel	1. Panama	1. Switzerland
2. Norway	2. Costa Rica	2. Belgium
3. Switzerland	3. Nicaragua	3. Netherlands
4. Denmark	4. Mauritania	4. Denmark
5. Finland	5. Liberia	5. Sweden
6. New Zealand	6. Paraguay	6. France
7. Panama	7. Central African Republic	7. Norway
8. Ireland	8. Israel	8. Great Britain
9. Uruguay	9. Norway	9. Italy
10. Austria	10. Honduras	10. North America

The first two columns will naturally favor the small countries since there are many international organizations today of which most if not all nations almost have to be members. Thus Norway is number 14 in the world when it comes to number of IGOs, but number 9 when it comes to number of IGOs per capita. Together with Norway are many of the reference countries except in the second column, where more or less compulsory membership gives high position to a number of small countries in other parts of the world.

In short, the non-territorial sphere, the field of international organizations, is an area where Norway may be said to compensate for what she lacks in territorial status. Of course, the crowning achievement in this little-noticed race came when the first position as a UN Secretary General was accorded to a Norwegian.

12. Norway in bilateral diplomacy

Norway has had her own foreign service only since 1905 and is thus a young country in this form of international interaction. The number employed in foreign services has, however, grown quite rapidly, from 55 in 1910, to 100 in 1939, and 201 in 1960. An increasingly larger part of the activity has been centred in the Ministry of Foreign Affairs, in Oslo: in 1910, 23% of those employed in foreign service were stationed there, as against 35% in 1960. And some of them are at all times available for delegations, etc. But about two-thirds are still permanently abroad, in the diplomatic or consular service.

Table 8.18 presents well-known features in twentieth-century world politics: we see the central European great powers' relative decline, the USA's progress, the anti-Soviet front accentuated by the Cold War, the emergence

TABLE 8.18 *Location of personnel in Norwegian diplomatic and consular services*, %

Location	1910	1920	1930	1939	1951	1960
Scandinavia	10	8	12	12	9	9
European Great Powers	40	31	28	23	20	18
Other European states	12	17	12	15	17	20
USA	12	17	16	19	20	19
USSR	12	5	9	6	3	3
Asia, Australia	10	6	12	12	11	13
Africa	0	3	2	4	3	2
Latin America	5	14	9	9	10	7
Delegations to international organizations	0	0	0	0	8	9
Total	101	101	100	100	100	100

Source: Galtung and Holmboe Ruge 1965, Table 6, p. 114.

of Afro-Asian countries, Latin America's steady decline in relative prestige, and, finally, international organizations as actors on the world stage. *Norway has kept up with these fluctuations*, has reacted to them adequately but slowly. A fairly constant factor is the approximately 600 Norwegian consulates abroad which naturally play an important part in connection with shipping and help diffuse a certain amount of Norwegian influence over the entire world community.

Bilateral diplomacy is in general symmetric: if Norway has diplomatic relations with a country, that country also has diplomatic relations with Norway. This then connects Norway to a number of countries, and an important question is this: How many such contacts has Norway, in relation to the net of contacts other countries have built up? Singer's investigation (Singer & Small, 1966) of the international diplomatic network shows the position of Norway and other nations according to number of diplomatic relations up to 1940 (Table 8.19).

Norway's position in diplomacy corresponds more or less to her general position in standard of living and level of development. Most of the reference

TABLE 8.19 *Countries with greatest number of diplomatic relations, 1909—1940**

Country	1909	1920	1930	1940
USA	1	3	3	1
France	3	2	1	2
Great Britain	2	5	2	3
Belgium	10	6	7	4
Italy	4	4	5	5
Netherlands	7	7	8	6
Argentina	11	8	11	7
Germany	5	20	4	8
Sweden	15	10	13	9
Brazil	13	15	15	10
Switzerland	19	9	9	11
Norway	20	14	16	12
Denmark	23	11	17	13
Cuba	—	—	—	14
Portugal	14	13	19	15
Mexico	12	19	28	16
Chile	18	16	27	17
Uruguay	16	21	22	18
Spain	6	1	6	19
Hungary		50	12	20

Source: Singer & Small, (1966).

* A weighted average was used to calculate the number of diplomats from each country. For details, see source.

group were above her in 1940, with Denmark under. If the list were extended to cover the next decade, there would be several changes in the picture,
but hardly in Norway's position: it is the new countries' and the socialist
countries' rise, and the Latin American countries' decline that are the
marked new features.

In this connection it is interesting to note one form of diplomatic relations Norway does *not* have: with the Vatican State. One might say that
this is due to the low number of Roman Catholics in Norway, but of the
59 countries accredited the Vatican State, 12 have less than 2 % Roman
Catholics (one of these is Finland). This lacuna should rather be seen in
light of many of the factors mentioned earlier, such as homogeneity, missions and their message, etc. It is also quite possible that Norway loses
more by not having this communication channel than does the Vatican.

Table 8.18 presenting data on where Norwegian foreign service personnel
are stationed, shows clearly that most activity is concentrated around the
North Atlantic area. But the Table is not particularly detailed; to clarify
this feature further, it may be useful to supplement Table 8.18 with data
on one of the classical expressions of bilateral diplomacy: the bilateral
agreement (see Table 8.20).

In the order Table 8.20 presents, then, we recognize the reference group —
but we also see how Norway's largest neighbor, the Soviet Union, enters
into Norway's international dealings even though the country is not included
in the reference group. However, we should also remember that an agreement does not necessarily express a positive tie; it may just as easily express
the necessity of regulating a conflict.

TABLE 8.20 *Norway's bilateral agreements, 1962*

Sweden	65	Finland	29
USA	55	USSR	28
Great Britain	49	West Germany	23
Denmark	42	Austria	22
France	41	Portugal	22

Source: *Utenrikskalenderen.*

13. Norway's trade partners

After viewing Norway's position in bilateral diplomacy it is natural for us
to turn to Norway's choice of trade partners. The most important ones,
measured in percentage of Norway's total export and import, are shown
in Table 8.21. We have data from two different years, as this item is among
the most important in determining Norway's international position.

TABLE 8.21 *Norway's main trade partners, percentage of import and export, 1963 and 1966*

Country	1963 Export	Import	Country	1966 Export	Import
Great Britain	18.7	17.8	Great Britain	18.8	13.7
Germany (West)	14.8	17.9	Sweden	15.3	18.8
Sweden	14.1	17.6	Germany (West)	13.3	16.1
USA	9.4	9.6	USA	8.9	17.5
Denmark	8.8	5.1	Denmark	7.1	5.8
France	3.7	3.8	Italy	3.1	3.2
Italy	3.2	2.0	France	3.0	3.1
Netherlands	3.1	3.8	Netherlands	2.8	4.4
Finland	1.8	0.9	Finland	2.1	1.1
Belgium/Luxembourg	1.9	2.7	Greece	1.9	0.1
Canada	1.7	4.1	Belgium/Luxembourg	1.9	2.2
Switzerland	1.2	2.3	Liberia	1.3	

Sources: 1963: NOS XII 107. Table 165, pp. 146—148, 1966: NOS XII 218, Table 175, pp. 136—139.

We see that Norway's most important trade partners are practically all the 'countries it is natural for us to compare ourselves with', and in practically the same order (rank correlation 0.87 for 1963, 0.88 for 1966). This seems to indicate that these concepts are closely adjusted to fit each other: that Norway's reference group in the world community is primarily adjusted according to her trade relations.

But the most important factor in the trade picture is not shown in this Table: the degree of dependency between the country's economy and trade. The value of Norway's export and import in percentage of GNP is high: Norway is number 19 of 81 countries, with a rate of 51 %. More important, however, is that of the 18 countries ahead of Norway in dependency, only three are at Norway's level of development — Belgium, Luxembourg and Denmark. Directly after Norway come four developing countries. In addition comes the fact that Norway, like so many developing countries, is highly dependent on one commodity, shipping, and that other Norwegian products show relatively little processing before sale. *We may therefore say that Norway's economic structure has many features in common with that of developing countries, in that the country is not self-sufficient, but dependent on international trade.* Norway, however, is not alone in this, but shares her situation with five small, Western European countries, who seem eager to participate in the Common Market — of which three (Benelux) are already members. The logic on this point in Norwegian foreign policy is thus shared very much by other countries in the same position.

14. Norway and international tourism

Do foreign visitors come from 'countries it is natural for us to compare ourselves with' or from other countries? What is the relationship between the two images which Norwegians form of the world community in this respect?

The number of foreign visitors to Norway (not all are tourists) is, first of all, very high; second, it shows an enormous rate of increase. In 1930 there were 80,000 visitors; by 1939 this had risen to 239,295. In 1946 this had sunk to 195,201, but even the next year, 1947 surpassed the pre-war level, with 303,326 visitors. The million mark was passed ten years later — in 1957 there were 1,019,614 — and in 1963, 3,970,000. This last figure is well over the total Norwegian population, in itself a typical indicator of the increase in world tourism. Naturally, many of these visitors stay only one day (in 1958, 35% of the total,) and the total figure counts separately many who return several times.

Furthermore, 83% in 1963 were Swedes (74% in 1961; of them, 96% came by car); but all the same, the figures give a good impression of the flood of foreign visitors and thereby of stimuli from the world community which Norwegians are being exposed to.

However, we are dealing with a very limited part of the world community, even when we have corrected for the high percentage of Swedes (Table 8.22).

TABLE 8.22 *Ranking of countries by number of visitors to Norway*

Rank 1930	1937	1947	1957	1960	1963
1. Sweden	Sweden	Sweden	Sweden	Sweden	Sweden
2. America*	Denmark	Great Britain	Denmark	Denmark	Denmark
3. Great Britain	Germany	Denmark	Great Britain	Germany	Great Britain
4. Germany	America	Germany	America	USA	USA
5. Denmark	Great Britain	America	France	Great Britain	Finland
6. France	Finland	Finland	Finland	Finland	Germany
7. Netherlands	France	Netherlands	Netherlands	France	France
8. Finland	Netherlands	France	Switzerland	Netherlands	Netherlands
3. Switzerland	Switzerland	Switzerland	Germany	Switzerland	Switzerland

Sources: *Landslaget for reiselivet i Norge* ('Norwegian Travel Association') 1964, and NOS XII, 100.
* Until 1955 all Western Hemisphere countries were designated 'America': by far the majority of these visitors were from the USA.

Sweden's position has at all times been the leading one, which is not in the least unusual when we remember geography. World War II put Denmark in second place, and then follow Great Britain and the USA. Germany's position is interesting: that the country sank immediately after the war is hardly surprising, but it is only since around 1957 that Germany has re-attained, more or less, her position as number four. Since German currency and the standard of living were quite strong in the early 1950s, it may be well to interpret this as an incidence of a mutual feeling of what is 'fitting': which again may be interpreted as an incidence of Norwegian moralism.

These nine countries are all among the top 12 in the reference group, and the internal order by number of tourists in 1963 is practically the same. The USA and Great Britain, great powers that they are, rank a bit higher on the comparison list than on the tourist list. Otherwise, this high correlation is hardly coincidental, but indicates the importance the pressure from tourists can have in creating standards for comparison. In general, then, there is harmony between the various sources of world images.

At the same time, Norwegians are great travelers. This was investigated by the International Peace Research Institute, Oslo, by asking a sample of Norwegians: 'Have you ever been abroad? If so, where?' Only 27% answered 'No'; 38 % have visited Norway's neighbors: 20 % have been to countries in Western Europe, only 2% to countries in Eastern Europe, USSR included, 5% to the USA, and 5% to Asia, Africa, or Latin America. Such high figures as these can be explained only by the great numbers of Norwegians who, at one time or another, and probably for short periods, have taken jobs aboard Norwegian ships calling at foreign ports.

But having been abroad is not the same as having developed international attitudes. The reason is not so much the brief time spent abroad as it is the type of contact most often made: with the lower, highly commercialized levels of the tertiary sector. Such contact can easily form the basis for contempt and generalizations that the foreigners are all out to make money, barter, and cheat.

Only seldom does tourist contact go further than to this superficial level which most countries show to foreigners. It is easier to give an impression of dignity and integrity when one is not dependent on some kind of trade with the tourists — but these levels in the population are hard for the tourist to find or have contact with.

15. Norway in the international sports picture

Let us conclude our survey of Norway's international interaction with data from a rather different field: international sports (Table 8.23). Norway's imbalance — or leitmotif — turns up again here: she is low in the Summer Olympics, high in the Winter ones. A main factor for high position in the Winter Olympics is the amount of snow in the country, but still, Norway's position is quite incontestable. If we were to calculate position per inhabitant,

Norway would move up on the list for Summer Olympics as well as on the total score.

However, the statistics are somewhat misleading, because Norway's high position in the Winter Olympics seems to be declining. In 1924 she won 83% of the total points awarded in the Nordic branches of the Winter Olympics, but in 1956 only 15%. In speed skating Norway reached a top in 1928, with 53% of total points, but received only 16% in 1956 (Andersen 1957). It is not so much that Norway is receding as such, but that the other countries are advancing. Moreover, the results of the 1968 Olympics tend to modify the picture.

TABLE 8.23 *Ranking of countries in Olympic Games, by scores achieved*

Summer Games 1896—1960	Winter Games 1924—1960	Total 1896—1960
1. USA	1. Norway	1. USA
2. USSR	2. USA	2. USSR
3. Great Britain	3. Finland	3. Sweden
4. Sweden	4. Sweden	4. Great Britain
5. Germany	5. Austria	5. Germany
6. France	6. USSR	6. Finland
7. Italy	7. Switzerland	7. France
8. Hungary	8. Germany	8. Italy
9. Finland	9. Canada	9. Hungary
10. Australia	10. France	10. Norway

Source: Andersen 1957.

We have given so many statistics on this point because sports is a form of placement in the world community and a form of international dealing which for many is highly important, perhaps most important, in that much personal experience and feeling are connected with it. The image of the world community is also formed on this basis, and there are many important impressions to be gained from such comparisons. First, that a small country such as Norway can do so very well, even become the world's best. World rank order is *not* constant; it *can* be changed, Norway *can* come at the top — ahead of the great powers, even ahead of all the 'countries it is natural for us to compare ourselves with'. Second, that such a position must be protected and defended, and that natural advantages (snow, long winter, mountains) do not represent any guarantee in a development-oriented world. Third, that people become accustomed to rank disequilibrium as characteristic of Norway, typical of the country. People become accustomed to the idea of being able to compensate for low performance in one field by high performance in another, and people may well become frequent users of mechanisms (of the type 'Well, what really counts is the Winter Olympics') which attach interest especially to those variables where Norway ranks high. Fourth, that a whole set of new countries is brought to the public consciousness through sports relations. The developing countries are still missing, but we see that the socialist countries have come quite far. Norway is thereby put in a slightly different connection than the purely Western, put in a framework where the competition is regulated according to international norms — and this probably helps increase openness towards such countries.

16. Conclusion

At this point we stop. The reason is not that we place so much importance on the international sports picture as such, but rather because this picture indicates new possibilities in the international pattern. Norway's position in the world community is not a given quantity; nor is any other nation's. Her position may be changed by her own growth and efforts — it may be strengthened, and it may be weakened if her resources are used without talent and imagination.

But Norway's position may also be changed in quite different ways: if the very criteria for a nation's position are changed, or if the importance of nations as actors in the international game is changed. Until now, nations have mostly been ranked according to political and economic power — a great power has been and is a country which ranks high on both these dimensions. But there is no reason to believe that the future may not bring new patterns. Koestler once wrote a play where the leitmotif was a ranking of nations according to average degree of happiness per inhabitant. Now, it is perhaps not so clear just what this happiness is, and definitely not clear how it is to be measured for use in international statistics. But it is hardly improbable that, in the not too distant future, well-being among a nation's inhabitants will be more emphasized than the nations' military and economic potential in the world society. Nor it is so improbable that we, in the not too distant future, will witness the decline of nations and the rise of international organizations as main actors in the international game. We have seen this develop — on the national level — where the local districts have gradually been overshadowed by organizations — and there is little reason to believe that the communications revolution will not have similar consequences on the international level.

And with that, everything in this article will seem a voice from the past — with its emphasis on political and economic variables, its emphasis on Norway as a unit. But the future has not yet begun on this point; and in the meantime this survey may perhaps provide a picture of Norway's position — from a bird's-eye view.

Appendix

Some theses about Norwegian foreign policy

If one should summarize Norwegian foreign policy one might profitably first try to locate Norway in the global structure, then try to look at some of the immediate consequences of this location, and finally look at the ideology, the official Norwegian foreign policy thinking that might come as a consequence of Norway's position in the world community.

Of course, Norway is *small, rich* and *Western*, but these three characteristics do not tell us enough. They serve to classify Norway, but not to specify Norway's relations with other countries. *If that should be done we would rather emphasize Norway's intermediate position in the world hierarchy of nations, especially where vertical division of labor — exploitation — is concerned.* More particularly, this means that whereas Norway is to some extent exploited by others (a good example would be the Norwegian aluminum industry where Norway contributes at the lower end of the degree of processing, not with cheap manpower but with cheap electric power), and to a large extent culturally (particularly scientifically) dependent on others, Norway also exercises more than her share of the total world exploitation, particularly through her participation in world trade with sophisticated shipping services. In official Norwegian foreign policy ideology, however, both these aspects can be forgotten and what is emphasized is the smallness (and hence Norway's vulnerability), the richness (and hence Norway's "responsibility") and Westernness (and with that Norway's natural belongingness to certain nations).

However, Norway's intermediate position, together with these three characteristics, has two very simple implications.

First, it gives Norway a chance as an arbiter in international relations, between countries that are *big*, rich and Western and those dominated by them, particularly Third World countries. Norway can present herself as the Western world with a human face. Relative to her more powerful reference group she looks leftist, at times even radical — relative to the world's spectrum as a whole she is solidly anchored on the right end. There is a certain political currency to be gained from this third party role as Norway counts very little when she is one among the big on the Western side, and very big when she is one among the very many small nations of the world. This creates a vested interest in such conflicts, and in seeing them as symmetric with Norway as impartial, disinterested, in-between.

Then, there is a second consequence of Norway's intermediate position: *the search for a master.* The thesis may be advanced that there has been, during the last 600 years of Norwegian history at least, a master giving clear signals, or even directing Norwegian foreign policy. As the master declines the Norwegian elite changes masters, and as Norway develops and grows the new master has to be stronger than the preceding one. There can be some overlap in time between masters, but only if they are consonant with each other, if their directives are not incompatible. The succession of masters looks something like this:

Denmark	Sweden	Great Britain	USA	and then the
till 1814	till 1905	till 1945—49	till 1968—73	effort to join the EEC

The relations have been complex and changing. Under Denmark, for all practical purposes, Norway was ruled as a colony. Under Sweden there was a personal union at the top, but it is fair to say that the point of gravity in foreign policy decisionmaking was located in Stockholm, and not only in the sense that the joint foreign office was there. With the union broken Great Britain became the natural leader and still serves, to a large extent, as a source of information and behavior to imitate. With the decline of Great Britain the United States surged to the forefront, as the Western nation that together with the Soviet Union not only won the war, but also the peace — or at least so it seemed. But the United States suffered a decline of colossal importance in the Vietnam war — a decline which was gradual but has here been dated from 1968 — keeping in mind Lyndon Johnson's speech on 31 March that year — ending with the withdrawal in 1973. That the US decline is related to the upsurge of the European Community, for the Six as well as for applicant countries in that period, including Norway, is rather obvious.

Needless to say all four cases are different, and motivations on either side of the relation to Norway also differed from case to case. But the focus here is not on motivation, but on the factual relationship. There has been increasing autonomy, it seems, on the Norwegian side when it comes to entering into the relation, from virtual subjugation under Denmark to application for membership in the European Community. Whereas Sweden was imposed upon Norway, this was not the case with the EC: there were alternatives available, and these alternatives had to be destroyed by a Norwegian decisionmaking elite wanting to enter into that kind of relationship.

One may ask: why this search for dependency? To be small and in the neighborhood of the big does not explain it fully, for the same pattern is not found in Sweden — and in a sense not in Finland either. Rather, one explanation would be in terms of habit formation: it has been that way for several centuries, it would be too much to expect that the Norwegian elite all of a sudden should declare itself independent, engage in complete and novel thinking about foreign affairs, derive models of behavior from nowhere but themselves, stand up and speak clearly and loudly in international organizations instead of playing a silent intermediary role in the corridors if any role at all. For Norway is often remarkably silent internationally.

So much for the intermediate position in the world community, although it should be emphasized that it is "intermediate" to the right, and towards the top. What kind of ideology would develop, partly as a consequence of the position, partly as a rationalization of actions taken?

Westernness in the Norwegian case also carries with it a connotation of Christianity, particularly in its Lutheran version. This is important because it has to do with a very pronounced profile Norway has with regard to direct and structural violence in the world. Neither of them is rejected — the Norwegian foreign policy elite is neither pacifist, nor revolutionary. Nor could they be rejected for Norway has been leaning on the military protection by powerful masters and has not been against the structural exploitation she herself engages in. But neither of these two items stand in any contradiction to what seems to be a basic Norwegian attitude: *a profound sympathy with the victims of either form of violence.* Wherever Man or Nature has caused a major calamity with people suffering and in distress, wherever exploitation has reached such proportions that famine is rampant — in short, whenever there is trouble or starvation in the streets and in the fields — Norway is present with medical teams, woolen blankets and food. This is a part of the role as an intermediary, an important ingredient in the third party "objective" profile. It is tied to fundamental Christian values and is only a way of putting into action the humanitarian face of Lutheranism, and since this particular face is very widespread in Norway such actions will never encounter any resistance and can always be counted on as a basis for consensus building. A disaster is seen as such, as a calamity, the quest for deep-lying causes will soon be overshadowed by the mobilization for remedial action.

And this brings out the second point: there has never been any strong *theoretical* tradition in Norwegian foreign policy thinking. One reason for this, probably, has to do with Norwegian general egalitarianism. Theories have a tendency to stratify people into theory-producers and theory-consumers; fundamental values do not have that effect. Values can be shared through allegiance, theories have to be understood, and that gives the producer the upper hand. The same actually applies to the "expert", who is also a theory-producer: he can of course form the consciousness of others by selective presentation of facts. But the facts are more generally available, they do not originate in the expert, and for that reason have less of a stratifying impact on society. Hence, Norwegian foreign policy argumentation will tend to be in terms of fundamental values backed up with non-controversial (which is not the same as objective) facts, not by complex theories. In this the Norwegian tradition would be very similar to — and indeed is derived from — British pragmatism: practical, "realistic", also moralistic (when facts are judged by values), but not forward looking. For that purpose theory is needed — to build bridges into the future.

A third and important item in the foreign policy ideology lies in the tendency, by no means limited to Norway, to see Norway as a *model* and as a *center*. There will be an instinctive identification with those features in the world community that are similar, even isomorphic to what is found in Norwegian society. In Norwegian society there are the traditional liberal institutions for the articulation of conflicts of *interest*, for their *transformation* in conflicts of *goals* that are concrete and easily understood (for instance salary, working hours), and *resolution* through compromise. Similar institutions in the world community at large will be welcomed by Norway as a world actor. Autocratic institutions where no articulation is permitted and there is no compromise, only dictates from above, will be as much resisted as revolutionary processes from below with a view to changing the total structure. In this there is a high element of ethnocentrism combined with simple class interests in the world community at large, or perhaps rather some kind of "morphocentrism," a tendency to project from one's own structure onto all other countries and the world in general.

It is hard to blame Norwegians for doing this since Norway is among the more well-functioning countries in the world today. It may fall short of ideals, but relative to others it passes many tests — as indicated in the first half of this chapter. The missionary zeal of Norwegians, sacred or secular alike, draws upon experience as well as rich motivation — the latter possibly linked to Norway's rank disequilibrium in the world setting. Thus, Norway becomes a mini-center with some ideological radiation, penetrating shells of concentric spheres, finding confirmation in the inner circle of the Nordic countries, something to learn, to comment on and to criticize in the next shell of NATO—OECD nations, and much preaching and teaching to be done to the rest of the world: the socialist countries, the developing countries in Asia, Africa and Latin America. The idea that there should be much to *learn* from these countries is as inconspicuous among today's development missionaries as yesterday's Lutheran missionaries.

In conclusion, let us try some speculations about the near future of Norwegian foreign policy. Thus, there are two factors that are rather important in this connection: the referendum about the European Community, frequently referred to in the text, whereby the search for a new master with more or less ready-made foreign policy models and a role written out for Norway in advance was thwarted, *and* the radicalization of a new generation of Norwegians to whom the *imperialism paradigm* with national and people's wars of liberation seems better suited to understanding world affairs than the *balance of power paradigm* between the forces of good and those of evil, adhered to by the past and present generations. Nowhere is this so clearly demonstrated recently as in the uproar

313

against the decision by the majority of the Nobel Peace Prize Committee to award a prize to Kissinger and Le Duc Tho for the negotiated Vietnam settlement (January 1973), an uproar that also found an organizational outlet in the initiative to award a People's Prize to Dom Helder Camara. It should also be noted how well the *Norwegian* model of foreign affairs can be recognized in both cases: the past generations, the Establishment's tendency to see the Indo-China wars as a symmetric war between more or less equals (the balance of power paradigm) and also to congratulate itself because Norway played a certain (not too big) role in bringing about negotiations; and at the same time the strongly Christian, moralistic strain underlying the choice of the Archbishop of Recife-Olinda as an exponent in the fight against imperialism.

If one looks at the succession of Norwegian masters there are two points that easily become apparent: Norway spent 400 years under Denmark, 100 under Sweden, about 40 years under Great Britain's tutorship, 25 years (say) under the moral leadership of the United States. The masters grow bigger and bigger, the period of subservience shorter and shorter. As Norway grows bigger the master also has to become bigger, and there is no doubt that the European Community was ideal from this point of view: including two of the old masters (Denmark and Great Britain) and with reasonably equitable relations to the other two (Sweden and the United States). In fact, it fits so well that it was almost miraculous (and even so only barely) that the referendum came out against — and this can only be explained in terms of the combined operation of center arrogance of power with unexpected strength of periphery organization against membership inside Norway herself.

Nevertheless, if a fundamental threat of war should emerge again in the old Cold War context the new equilibrium keeping Norway out of the European Community might prove its instability. Failing this, there is an alternative: allegiance to the *superpower condominium*, keeping a Norwegian self-image as bridge-builder between the two. But this is also likely to be relatively shortlived as a relationship: as our little list of figures above indicates changes are rapid in this century and likely to remain so. The Norwegian foreign policy elite might also for a short while find protection in adherence to the *big power concert* (the United States, the European Community, the Soviet Union, China and Japan) as an ordering factor in the world community, but this is likely to be even more shortlived, if it gets off the ground at all. Moreover, neither the superpower condominium nor the big power concert are extrapolations from Norwegian social structure, which means that they cannot draw upon explicit or implicit political ideology. Even at this point the European Community was far better with inequality at the top.

Hence, it is quite possible that Norway will become a more autonomous country, not because of internal changes inside Norway or new thinking, but simply because the world scene changes. Under no circumstance will Norway accept domination by a Nordic neighbor, those days are past. With no suitable big powers, singly or in combination, available for the master role she may be forced into autonomy. No doubt this will lead to a search for other countries in a corresponding position, even for the establishment of a union of those that are "small, rich and Western", from Canada to Finland, down in Europe to Switzerland and Austria. Since these external changes take place at the same time as there is a change of climate of opinion in Norway and a new generation coming up, the transition might be relatively smooth, towards a Norway that is less big power-oriented and less Western in its general outlook. And in that case Norway might no longer exchange mediation services for protection services, but be able to side more unambiguously with the underdog in the world community rather than being a fig leaf for the topdogs.

314

If there are changes within Norway in a more radical direction, away from liberal, social democracy towards a more egalitarian, less production/consumption-oriented society, then this will also influence Norwegian world cosmology. There will be more understanding for the socialist countries in the Third World, less preoccupation with being a mediator between the strong and the weak, less scope for the role as the Good Samaritan, changing rather than mediating power relations as such. Again the thesis would be that Norwegians — like most others — would single out for support and acceptance those features in the world that correspond to those they understand and even accept or at least condone at home. But the thesis is also that such social theories will only be preferred provided they do not upset the social order at home; hence, they will either be applied sectorially to very remote corners of the world, or become the guiding doctrine for general Norwegian foreign policy *after* some changes have taken place and the population have grown accustomed to them, inside Norway.

IV.9. International Relations and International Conflicts: A Sociological Approach*

From *Transactions of the Sixth World Congress of Sociology* (International Sociological Association, 1966). PRIO publication No. 21−7.

Notes on page *705*.

1. Introduction

Most analyses of internal affairs are concerned with the dimensions of power and economy, whether they are conceived of as properties of the individual nation or as relations between two or more nations. Analyses in these terms are indispensable, but the basis is nevertheless limited relative to the whole spectrum of dimensions that can be brought to bear on international relations. One such framework will be presented in the following, based on the conception of a *rank-dimension,* and efforts will be made to explore this type of analysis as extensively as possible. The claim will be made that this presents us with a very comprehensive scheme for analysis of international relations, and particularly of international conflicts. But there is of course no claim to the effect that all conflicts, in the international or inter-human system, can be conceived of as struggles for scarce rank.

A rank-dimension is a variable, and like all other variables its values, called ranks, are mutually exclusive and exhaustive in the system of units (individuals, nations, etc.) for which it is defined [1]. Unlike many other variables, however, a rank-dimension is ordered [2] (it has the properties of the ordinal scale) and there is a clear meaning given to 'high rank' at one end of the dimension and 'low rank' at the other end. Thus, one should only speak about rank-dimensions to the extent there is consensus in the system for which it is defined that high rank is to be pursued and low rank to be avoided. A somewhat less restrictive definition would be as follows: there shall at least be consensus in the system to the effect that high rank is not to be avoided and low rank is not to be pursued − for if these two conditions do not obtain one should clearly abstain from talking about a rank-dimension, and rather refer to the dimension as a general variable.

Thus, whether and to what extent a variable is a rank-dimension is a question that can only be decided empirically, although one may of course have more or less well-founded hypotheses. One way of testing this would

316

be as follows. Imagine that the dimension has three values which we shall refer to as T (for 'topdog'), M (for 'middledog') and U (for 'underdog') and that all N units are classified according to where they belong and where they want to belong:

TABLE 9.1 *The empirical testing of rank-dimensions*
         Units would like to belong

Units do belong	T	M	U
T	T → T	T → M	T → U
M	M → T	M → M	M → U
U	U → T	U → M	U → U

Thus, as in any table of this kind: in the lower left hand corner are the three frequencies that correspond to upward mobility, the diagonal corresponds to satisfaction and the upper right hand frequencies correspond to downward mobility wishes. One can now define the criteria above operationally:

Strong criterion of rank-dimension: $T \to T + M \to T + U \to T = N$
Weak criterion of rank-dimension: $T \to M + T \to U + M \to U = O$

Thus, the strong criterion implies the weak criterion but not vice versa: if the weak criterion is satisfied it is still permissible to wish to stay where one is (M → M and U → U different from O).

In general neither of the conditions will obtain perfectly, so there will be a need for a measure of the *degree* to which a variable is a rank-dimension. One such measure is as follows:

$$G = \frac{(M \to T + U \to T + U \to M) - (T \to M + T \to U + M \to U)}{N - (T \to T + M \to M + U \to U)}$$

This measure reflects the weak condition of rank-dimension. It is equal to $+1$ when the weak criterion obtains, and, of course, also when the strong criterion is satisfied. It is equal to -1 when there are no units that wish upward mobility. In this case we clearly have a rank-dimension, except that there is a wish to turn the dimension upside down. The measure is equal to O under a set of conditions that have one thing in common: there is an equal number who want upward mobility and downward mobility, which seems to be a reasonable definition. Finally, if all units want to stay where they are, then the measure becomes indeterminate. We think it should not become O in this case. The rank-dimension may become completely ascriptive (sex in Norway, caste in India, natural resources for a nation) so that a unit cannot imagine any change and for that reason prefers to stay where it is. Thus the measure is only meaningful for dimensions where mobility is to some extent permitted, or at least imagined. For ascriptive dimensions one will have to study the differential distribution of rewards or the evaluation of others rather than self to get at data to classify the dimension.

We shall refer to the measure G as the *gradient* of the rank-dimension. Its meaning is very easily seen when the rank-dimension is a dichotomy with the two values T and U:

$$G = \frac{U \to T - T \to U}{N - (U \to U + T \to T)}$$

It is simply the difference between those who want to move up and those who want to move down, evaluated relative to the maximum number possible when we 'permit' units to stay where they are. If we do not, the denominator would of course be N — and in some cases this may be preferable. At any rate, we shall say that the rank-dimension is *steeper*, the higher the numerical value of G. A *flat* rank-dimension (G = O) is evidently no rank-dimension at all, but where the borderline should be drawn can only be established after more theory has been developed and empirical experience been gained.

2. Fundamental categories of rank analyses [3]

We can now proceed with a more systematic analysis of a system of units S, in terms of its set of rank-dimensions D. To see what can be done in general we shall proceed systematically, starting with one unit and one dimension, and then add units and dimensions. For our purposes Table 9.2 exhausts all interesting combinations.

This system should be relatively exhaustive, and at the same time suggests a standardization of the wildly fluctuating terminology in this field [4]. More particularly, we have avoided the use of the words 'status' and 'inconsistency', the former because we want to make it completely explicit that we are concerned with *rank* and not with other characteristics of the status of a unit, the latter because 'inconsistency' can mean so many things. Thus an individual may have 'status inconsistency' because of conflict among the statuses he has, or because of difference in style — he may combine some modern with some very traditional statuses (which probably would only be a subcase of conflict). Since conflict does not necessarily

TABLE 9.2 *The dimensions of rank analysis*

No. of units	No. of dimensions		
	one	two	several (n)
one	I Rank	II 1. Total rank, unit 2. Rank congruence, rank disequilibrium	IV 1. Total rank, unit 2. Rank equilibrium, disequilibrium
two	III 1. Total rank, pair 2. Rank equality, rank difference	VI 1. Rank equivalence, rank inequivalence 2. Rank congruence, rank incongruence	VII GENERALIZATION
several (n)	V 1. Total rank, m-tuple 2. Difference	VIII GENERALIZATION 1. Rank agreement 2. Criss-cross	IX GENERALIZATION 1. Concordance

involve rank, we prefer to use this more generic term of status inconsistency in a more general context [5].

We shall now comment on all the dimensions of rank analysis in Table 9.2 and indicate how they can be operationalized. To do so we proceed cell by cell, in a zig-zag pattern.

I. One unit, one dimension

The only thing to be done here is to assign to the unit its rank, and we assume that can be done unambiguously. If this is not the case, one will have to collapse rank-values and simplify the dimension until ambiguity is sufficiently reduced — this will probably lead to a trichotomy or a dichotomy. In the following we shall assume that this has been done.

II. One unit, two dimensions

Conceptually there is little difficulty connected with the two concepts mentioned:

total rank of a unit: the rank of the unit in two-dimensional space, reduced to one dimension.

rank equilibrium: the degree to which the ranks of the unit along the two dimensions correspond to each other.

319

To operationalize these two concepts we may assign values 0, 1 and 2 to the three ranks U, M and T (or 0 and 1 to the two ranks U and T) and assume that this can be done according to standard methodological prescriptions. We get Fig. 9.1.

FIGURE 9.1 *Operational definitions of total rank and rank disequilibrium*

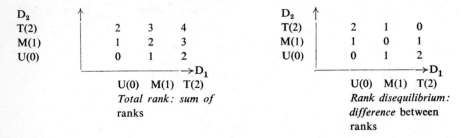

In the first case all that has been done is to construct an additive index, in the second case the absolute value of the difference between the ranks has been computed. These operations both presuppose that the two dimensions for the same unit are comparable, that it somehow makes sense to give them the same weight. One way of ensuring this would be to require that their gradients have (about) the same strength.

We can now refine these dimensions of rank analysis:

Total rank: low, score 0-1
               medium, score 2
               high, score 3-4

But this subdivision will, of course, depend on the statistical distribution. We also get

Rank disequilibrium: *equilibrium,* score 0
                            weak disequilibrium, score 1
                            strong disequilibrium, score 2

If the dimensions are dichotomies no distinction can be made between weak and strong disequilibrium [6].

III. Two units, one dimension

This case is actually completely parallel to the preceding case. Conceptually, we have:

Total rank of pair: The combined rank of the pair, reduced to one dimension.

Rank equality: the extent to which the ranks of the two units are the same.

To operationalize these two concepts we do exactly the same as above, and get a table that corresponds completely to Fig. 9.1. Formally Figs. 9.1,2 are completely equal, but there is this difference between them: in Fig. 9.1 the unit is a unit and the two axes refer to two different dimensions, whereas in Fig. 9.2 the unit is a pair and the two axes refer to the same dimension, but there is one axis for each unit in the pair.

FIGURE 9.2 *Operational definitions of total rank of pair and rank diffe-rence*

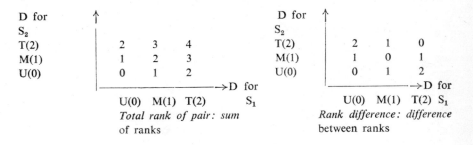

D for				D for		
S_2				S_2		
T(2)	2	3	4	T(2)	2	1	0
M(1)	1	2	3	M(1)	1	0	1
U(0)	0	1	2	U(0)	0	1	2

U(0)   M(1) T(2) S_1

Total rank of pair: sum of ranks

U(0)   M(1)   T(2) S_1

Rank difference: difference between ranks

Or, in a more refined version:

Total rank of pair: *low*, score 0-1   *medium*, score 2   *high*, score 3-4
Rank difference: *equality*, score 0
minor difference: score 1
major difference, score 2

If the dimensions are dichotomies no distinction can be made between small and big differences. It should be noted that if the dimension is power and the units are nations, then rank equality is often referred to as 'balance of power' [7].

Thus, by means of these measures meaning is given to the total rank of a pair, which then can serve as an independent variable for relational analysis [8]. But it does not discriminate too well, like all additive indices. Thus, the total rank of 2 may be obtained by two units of rank 1 each or by two units, one with rank 2 and the second with rank 0. But if, in addition, rank difference is made use of, one can discriminate between the two: the rank difference is 0 in the first case, and 2 in the second.

Imagine now that one had not made use of trichotomies for the rank-dimensions but instead had used a scale with, for instance, 11 points, such as the deciles from 0 to 10. In that case the rank of the pair would vary from 0 to 20. Would one get the same results if one trichotomized this in 'low', 'medium', 'high' as one would get by first trichotomizing the basic variable and then proceed as indicated above? No, but nearly the same. It is a weakness of the methodology that it is not invariant of the order of the operations, but the difference will usually be insignificant, both theoretically and empirically.

IV. One unit, several dimensions

In this case total rank can be computed extending the method in the left hand part of Fig. 9.1 to n dimensions. We recommend the additive index since it is by far the simplest procedure and, when properly executed, can yield very good results [9]. The index may be tested to see whether it is cumulative (Guttman scale) or not. If it is cumulative or nearly so it may be indicative of some internal structure between the dimensions in the sense that a unit first has to get into the top category of one dimension, then it can start conquering dimension no. 2, then dimension no. 3, etc. However, all this is actually meaningless before one has several units, so that a discussion of this really belongs to case IX.

But this does not apply to the next two dimensions. One unit with a rank score on n dimensions has a *profile*, and since we assume that the dimensions are comparable this profile can be collapsed to a distribution that gives the number of U-statuses, the number of M-statuses and the number of T-statuses — with a total equal to the number of dimensions n. This distribution has a central tendency, which may be measured in terms of the mode, the median or the arithmetic mean (or any other measure of central tendency). If we use the arithmetic, then we get exactly the same as we would get by dividing the total rank of the unit with the number of dimensions. Often the mode may be just as useful, however — it tells which rank is the most frequently found rank in the rank profile of the unit. The arithmetic mean makes less sense because there is usually nothing in sociological theory that corresponds to it.

It was easy to extend the idea of total rank to several dimensions since addition is equally well defined for n as for two elements. The difficulty comes when we extend the definition of rank disequilibrium to n dimensions. Rank disequilibrium for two dimensions was simply defined in terms of a difference between the two ranks. But subtraction is only defined between two elements, not between n at the same time. One suggestion here would be to make use of one of the standard measures of dispersion, such as the standard deviation, of the distribution of ranks in the profile of the unit. But there are two objections against this measure. First of all its formula of calculation is so remote from sociological theory — there is nothing in that theory that corresponds quite to the calculation of sums of squares of differences, particularly since the differences are relative to the mean which is almost equally artificial. And secondly, it would not reduce to our simple and attractive measure of rank disequilibrium in the case of n = 2. One might try with a simpler measure of dispersion, such as the percentage of ranks that fall in the modal category. Obviously, if the percentage is very high there is (almost) rank equilibrium, if it is low there is rank disequilibrium. In this case the first objection would disappear. But the second objection would still be valid, and in addition there would be a third objection: the measure would not be sensitive to the difference between, say 3 T's, 1 M and 1 U; and 3 T's and 2 U's. Internal distance would not count — only whether the rank is in the modal category or not.

The measure we shall suggest is as follows:

Rank disequilibrium:
$$\frac{\text{Sum of all distances for all pairs of ranks}}{\text{number of pairs} = \binom{n}{2}}$$

With n dimensions, hence n ranks for the unit, there are $\binom{n}{2}$ or $1/2n(n-1)$ comparisons to make if all ranks are to be compared with all others. For each pair a difference can be calculated since only two elements are involved, and the expression is nothing but the average value of these differences — where we, of course, always use the absolute value of the difference, the distances. If we compare units for the same number of dimensions it is unnecessary to divide by the number of pairs.

When all ranks are equal all differences will be equal to 0, which means that the degree of rank disequilibrium becomes 0 — as it should in the case of rank equilibrium. The measure is sensitive to all rank differences, and is not too artificial. Thus, it does not involve the mean, for all ranks all *other* ranks are used as bases of comparison — and it does not involve squares of differences, only absolute values. Moreover, for n = 2 it reduces to the measure introduced above of rank disequilibrium.

Thus, the situation of one unit in n-dimensional rank spaces is clarified operationally, and we can proceed to the corresponding case, with dimensions and units reversed.

V. Several units, one dimension

This case is so similar that there is no need to spell out everything. The total rank of an m-tuple is measured in exactly the same way as for two units. The distribution of the m units on the dimension offers no conceptual difficulties since this is an ordinary frequency distribution. Measures of central tendency have obvious interpretations whereas the standard measures of dispersion are indicative of equality when they are (near) zero and of much internal rank difference when they are different from zero. However, the following would be much better than these measures:

Rank difference:

$$\frac{\text{Sum of all distances for all pairs of units}}{\text{number of pairs}} = \binom{m}{2}$$

Hence, to arrive at a measure of total internal distance in the sense of rank difference one would compare all units, two at a time, add the distances and divide by the number of pairs, which is $\binom{m}{2} = \frac{1}{2}m(m-1)$. Actually, the latter is unnecessary if we compare dimensions for the same number of units.

In the case of complete rank equality between the units the measure is equal to 0, in all other cases it is positive. And in the case of $m = 2$ it reduces to the measure introduced above of rank difference. Hence, we can consider this case also to be completely clarified operationally, and turn to a much more difficult case.

VI. Two units, two dimensions

In this case something quite new is introduced, and the additional complexity calls for great caution. We have now two different units on two different dimensions, so that all concepts and all operations from cases 1, 2 and 3 are meaningful. But in addition we need

Rank equivalence: the extent to which the ranks of two units are the same, with two-dimensional rank.

Rank congruence: the extent to which the two units stand in the same or in different relation to each other on the two rank dimensions.

These very brief descriptions actually say very little; the concepts will acquire meaning through operationalization alone.

One could approach the problem of rank-equivalence by saying: *two units are rank-equivalent if they are rank-equal on both dimensions.* But this is trivial; if rank-equivalence comprised only this, we would not need the concept since it would be enough to say 'rank-equality on both dimensions'. Obviously, there is the sense in which two units may add their ranks and come up with the same result and find out that they are 'rank-equivalent', which leads to this operational definition:

Rank inequivalence: the difference between the total ranks of the two in two-dimensional space.

Rank equivalence: the two units have the same total rank in two-dimensional space, the difference is zero.

Thus, one would locate the two units in the left hand part of Fig. 9.2 and then calculate the difference between their total ranks. If they should happen to be rank-equal on both dimensions then they would both have the same total rank and consequently be rank-equivalent, which means that our more tolerant operational definition of rank-equivalence includes the stricter definition as a special case — as it should. Of course, how good this definition is can only be ascertained after some empirical experimentation.

We then turn to the more difficult problem of rank congruence. To arrive at a rationale for its operationalization, consider the combinations of rank-profiles in Fig. 9.3.

FIGURE 9.3 *Some combinations of rank-profiles*

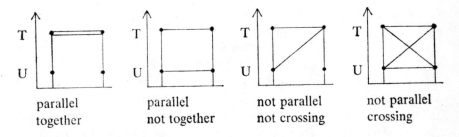

| parallel | parallel | not parallel | not parallel |
| together | not together | not crossing | crossing |

Here we have different degrees of rank incongruence, where for simplicity we have used dichotomized rank dimensions. In the first case there is equality on both dimensions, in the second case there is not equality but something else is equal: the rank difference between the two units is the same for both dimensions. This actually also applies to the first case, except that the differences are equal to zero. In both these cases the two units can meet

325

in the context of both dimensions in the same relationship; in the first case as equals, in the second case in the same superior—inferior relationship. In the third and the fourth cases we do not have rank congruence since the differences are not equal; in the third case one of the differences is positive and the other is zero, in the fourth case the differences have different signs. We use this for the following operational definition:

Rank congruence: rank differences between the units are equal.
Rank incongruence: rank differences between the units are not equal.
  weak case: differences do not have different signs.
  strong case: differences have different signs.

In the case of strong rank incongruence the relative position of the units is reversed when one moves from one rank-dimension to the other. As is immediately seen, the definitions correspond to the four cases in Fig. 9.3 (we have not singled out for special attention the case of rank equality under rank congruence, however, because it is trivial). Also, the introduction of a third rank for each dimension will offer no difficulty — but the definitions become meaningless unless each rank dimension has the same number of ranks.

The operationalization has the virtue of simplicity since all that is needed is an inspection of the rank differences, always obtained by subtracting the ranks of one unit from the ranks of another unit so that the signs have a clear meaning. Thus, in this case, unlike in all preceding cases, we cannot use distances without losing important information. We can then proceed to the next case.

VII. Two units, several dimensions

All we have to do is to see to it that nothing has been introduced so far that cannot easily be generalized.

The total rank of either unit offers no difficulty, since the generalization has already been carried out under IV above, and this means that rank inequivalence can be calculated. Since we can form the differences between the two units on each of the n dimensions we shall have no difficulty with rank incongruence either. All one has to do is to inspect the set of rank differences; if they are all equal we have rank congruence; if they are different but not of different sign we have the weak case of incongruence, and if they are different and with different signs we have the strong case of incongruence.

The only objection is that this is inelegant — one would like to express the degree of incongruence by means of one numerical characteristic alone. But this is not so easy. If one calculates the dispersion in the set of differences one may discriminate between congruence and incongruence, for the dispersion is obviously zero in the case of congruence and positive in the case of incongruence. But it does not discriminate between the weak and strong cases, and there is little doubt that there is a borderline there: one thing is to be below in varying degrees, another thing to be below in one context and above in another. The ideal would be an index that not only reflected the magnitude of the discrepancy from the case of rank congruence, which dispersion measures in the set of differences would do, but in addition made a discontinuous jump or changed sign when strong incongruence occurred. The trouble is that one may have strong incongruence in our sense for relatively low values of dispersion. Hence we are actually dealing with two different dimensions of incongruence: *magnitude*, and *kind*. The latter can be decided by inspection, to see whether all signs are the same or whether signs are different. And where magnitude is concerned we propose to proceed in analogy with cases IV and V. In the set of n differences all possible comparisons are made: there is a total of $\binom{n}{2}$. For each pair of differences the distance is computed, the sum is calculated, and the average is computed.

Rank incongruence, magnitude: $\dfrac{\text{Sum of all distances for all pairs of diff.}}{\text{number of pairs of diff.} = \binom{\binom{n}{2}}{2}}$

Thus if one has three dimensions and the differences for the two units are $2, 0, -2$ (corresponding to the two profiles TMU and UMT) the three distances between the differences will have to be taken into consideration. The sum is 8 and the average is 2.67. Hence there is rank incongruence, and inspection of the differences reveals that this is a strong case of rank incongruence. When there are only two dimensions there is only one pair of differences, hence only one distance to compute. If the distance is 0 we have rank congruence, for the distance or sum of distances is 0 when — and only when — all differences are equal. The operationalization above is therefore completely consistent with what we have done in VI above.

One may now ask whether there is any new concept that can be introduced here, but we have not found any fruitful dimensions that apply to this case in addition to what we have already done.

VIII. Several units, two dimensions

Again, the problem is the same: have we introduced something so far that we cannot easily generalize? For any *single* unit total rank and disequilibrium can still be computed, and for any *pair* of units rank inequivalence and rank incongruence will offer no difficulty. Since we have m units and

327

hence $\binom{m}{2}$ pairs we can also find the distributions of the m units on total rank and on disequilibrium, and the distribution of the $\binom{m}{2}$ pairs on rank inequivalence and rank incongruence. From these distributions some evaluation of the total situation can be obtained, but the problem is whether other, more global, measures would be of interest.

As to total rank, the total rank of an m-tuple has already been introduced. Since this can be calculated for either dimension the set of units can be compared with itself to see where it scores highest, on D_1 or on D_2. This, in other words, would be a measure of the extent to which the m-tuple is in equilibrium or disequilibrium where its total rank is concerned. This is already a rather abstract concept, and although it is obvious that we would analyze the m-tuple with regard to disequilibrium exactly as we did in case II for one unit, it is not obvious that the theoretical harvest would correspond to the empirical investment.

Does it make sense to generalize rank disequilibrium? Strictly speaking, rank disequilibrium is the property of *a* unit, and although it makes sense to speak about the central tendency, for instance the arithmetic mean, of the distribution of rank disequilibrium in the set of units — as an aggregate measure — it does not make sense to generalize in some other way. But it does make sense to generalize rank incongruence to more than two units. Thus, to return to Fig. 9.3: if the profiles of m and not only 2 units were represented it would still make sense to talk about parallelism or not, about profiles touching each other or crossing each other; just as it made sense in the preceding case to talk about parallelism etc. between two profiles involving more than two dimensions.

To develop a measure of total rank incongruence one should proceed by comparing the units two at a time. Interaction between units, individuals or nations, is mostly and essentially between two units at the time (with others as a context) and this applies particularly to rank incongruence. Since there are $\binom{m}{2}$ pairs all one has to do is to proceed as in the preceding case. For each pair of units the two rank *differences* are calculated. Then they are compared by computing the *distances* between them, which is simply the magnitude of the rank incongruence for that pair. If one wants an aggregate measure of the total rank incongruence, then the central tendency of the distribution of distance should be found. But it may also be interesting to calculate the dispersion of this distribution, since it would tell something about whether the rank incongruence found between pairs varies much in magnitude, or is of the same magnitude. Thus one would calculate:

Rank incongruence, dispersion:

$$\frac{\text{Sum of all distances between distances for all pairs}}{\text{Number of pairs of pairs}} = \binom{\binom{m}{2}}{2}$$

Thus, if one has three units and the patterns on the two dimensions are UT, MM and TU respectively, then one would proceed as follows:

TABLE 9.3 *An example of the calculation of central tendency and dispersion*

	differences	distance (incongruence)	pairs of distances	distances
$S_1 - S_2$	−1, 1	2	2 4	2
$S_1 - S_3$	−2, 2	4	2 2	0
$S_2 - S_3$	−1, 1	2	4 2	2
Sum		8		4
average		2.67		1.33
		(central tendency)		(dispersion)

In this case the average rank incongruence is 2.67 and the dispersion in the distribution of rank incongruence is 1.33 — by our measures.

That concludes the generalization and we now turn to two new concepts that are characteristic of case VIII, but would have been meaningless or almost meaningless in all preceding cases:

rank agreement: the extent to which rank-dimensions agree in their ranking of units.

lack of criss-cross: the extent to which rank-dimensions divide the units in the same groups.

It should be noted that these two concepts are by no means identical:

FIGURE 9.4 *Examples of perfect rank-agreement and perfect lack of criss-cross*

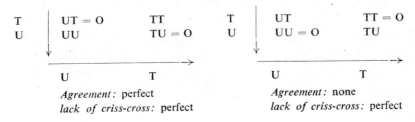

```
T  │  UT = O      TT          T  │  UT          TT = O
U  │  UU          TU = O      U  │  UU = O       TU
   ↓                             ↓
   ───────────────────→           ───────────────────→
     U           T                  U           T
```

Agreement: perfect   *Agreement:* none
lack of criss-cross: perfect   *lack of criss-cross:* perfect

Since we have no criss-cross in two situations where the agreement is respectively perfect and perfectly absent the two concepts evidently do not coincide. We then proceed to operationalization.

The problem of agreement between two variables has been analyzed extensively elsewhere. We have agreement when, and only when, each unit is given the same rank on both dimensions. Thus agreement is a subcase of correlation, but much narrower; one can have correlation without agreement (as when all units are given one rank lower on the second dimension than on the first dimension). This means that all cases where the ranks are different should be treated as deviations from rank agreement regardless of whether the disagreement is by one or two steps. Thus, we get this very simple operational definition:

$$\textit{Rank agreement:} \quad \frac{\text{No. of units given same rank on both dimensions}}{\text{No. of units} = m}$$

The maximum value of 1 corresponds to perfect agreement, the minimum value of 0 to perfect disagreement.

But there is another way of defining operationally rank disagreement which is much more in line with the kind of thinking we have developed here. For any one unit one would simply calculate the distance in his ranks on the two dimensions, in other words his disequilibrium — and then add the disequilibria for all units:

$$\textit{Rank disagreement:} \quad \frac{\text{Sum of the rank disequilibria for all units}}{2m}$$

When all units are in rank equilibrium the numerator will be 0, which corresponds to complete agreement, and when all individuals are in maximum disequilibrium (all with profiles UT or TU) the numerator will be equal to 2m and the disagreement measure will attain its maximum value. We prefer to use this measure.

We then turn to criss-cross. Its rationale is more involved and will not be developed here [11]. Suffice it to say that in the case where both rank-dimensions are dichotomies and we have m units operationalization has been solved giving this expression (Table 9.4).

This formula is developed at length elsewhere, as well as its generalization to the case of three ranks, and there is no reason to repeat all that here [12]. In the case of perfect agreement we have $b = c = 0$ and consequently 0 criss-cross; and the same obtains if we have $a = d = 0$ (when agreement $\frac{a+d}{m}$ would also be 0), all in agreement with Fig. 9.4. The maximum

TABLE 9.4 *The operationalization of criss-cross*

| | | First dimension | |
		T(1)	U(0)
Second dimension	T(1)	a	b
	U(0)	c	d
Criss-cross	$\dfrac{(a+d)\ (b+c)}{\dfrac{m^2}{4}}$		

of the criss-cross coefficient is 1, which is attained when the units are equally divided between the two diagonals.

Using the symbols of Table 9.4 we can now make a complete list of formulae for the concepts we have introduced. This makes sense because the case of two dichotomous rank dimensions and m units, although a special case of case VIII, is fairly general and frequently encountered in the literature. Thus, we get:

Total rank of m — [tuple on first dimension:

$$1\cdot(a+c) + 0\cdot(b+d) = a+c]$$

Total rank of m — [tuple on second dimension:

$$1\cdot(a+b) + 0\cdot(c+d) = a+b]$$

Rank-disequilibrium of m — [tuple: $\qquad 1\cdot(b+c) + 0\cdot(a+d) = b+c]$

Rank incongruence:

types of pairs	*differences*	*distance*	*to calculate dispersion*
TT—TU	0, 1	1 ac = *ac*	here are 6 distances, i.e.
TT—UT	1, 0	1 ab = *ab*	15 pairs of distances. They
TT—UU	1, 1	0 ad = *0*	can all be calculated, add-
TU—UT	1, −1	2 cb = *2bc*	ed and divided by the
TU—UU	1, 0	1 cd = *cd*	number of pairs.
UT—UU	0, 1	1 bd = *bd*	
SUM		(a + d) (b + c) + 2bc	

Rank incongruence average: $\quad \dfrac{(a+d)\ (b+c)+2bc}{m}$

Rank agreement: $\quad \dfrac{a+d}{m}$

Rank disagreement: $\dfrac{b+c=1=a+d}{m \qquad m}$

Criss-cross: $\dfrac{(a+d)\,(b+c)}{\dfrac{m^2}{4}}$

And that brings us to the final case.

IX. Several units, several dimensions

In this case the ranks of m units on n dimensions are given. We can calculate the total rank for each unit (case IV) and the total rank for each m-tuple (case V). We can calculate the total amount of rank disequilibrium for *each unit*, of rank difference for *each dimension* and rank incongruence for *each pair of units* and also for *each pair of dimensions*, and even for all units for each pair of dimensions. But what about rank incongruence for all m units and all n dimensions, what about rank agreement and what about criss-cross? And, will not all these concepts somehow meet in one master concept that measures the degree of order or disarray in the total configuration? We shall see that there is something to this, but it is not so simple. To illustrate this, let us take an example with four units and three dimensions (Table 9.5).

TABLE 9.5 *An example with four units and three dimensions: differences*

			$D_1 - D_2$	$D_1 - D_3$	$D_2 - D_3$	Disequilibrium
To calculate	S_1	UTM	−2	−1	1	4
disequilibrium	S_2	TMT	1	0	−1	2
for each unit	S_3	MMM	0	0	0	0
and disagreement	S_4	UUT	0	−2	−2	4
for each pair						
of dimensions		*Disagreement*	3	3	4	10

		D_1	D_2	D_3	Incongruence
To calculate	$S_1 - S_2$	−2	1	−1	(4) 3, 1, 2 6
incongruence	$S_1 - S_3$	−1	1	0	(2) 2, 1, 1 4
for each pair	$S_1 - S_4$	0	2	−1	(3) 2, 1, 3 6
of units and	$S_2 - S_3$	1	0	1	(2) 1, 0, 1 2
distance for	$S_2 - S_4$	2	1	0	(3) 1, 2, 1 4
each dimension	$S_3 - D_4$	1	1	−1	(3) 0, 2, 2 4
	Distance	7	6	4	(17) 26

In Table 9.5 we have computed all differences; for each unit and each pair of dimensions, and for each dimension and each pair of units. In three cases we have simply added the absolute values of all these differences, so as to get the total amount of disequilibrium for each unit, the total amount of disagreement for each pair of dimensions and the total amount of internal distance for each dimension. We have also done it for each pair of units. But for rank incongruence we have proceeded as otherwise indicated: we have calculated the distance between each pair of differences, and then added these distances, and it can be seen at a glance that it discriminates better.

We have not averaged the sums, nor have we divided by their maximum values which are not so easily found. The maximum for all differences is always 2 or −2, which means that the maximum distance is 2. But since the distances are interdependent, not all can attain the maximum value. The maximum sum is therefore not more than twice the number of elements to be added. The case of rank incongruence is more complicated, however, if one uses the correct formulae.

The problem is now whether the numbers 10 and 17 can be given any meaning, and it is obvious that they can. Thus, 10 is the total amount of intra-unit difference, and thus a measure of the total amount of disequilibrium or disagreement there is in the total system. Correspondingly, 17 is a measure of the total amount of intradimension distance, but not a measure of the total amount of rank incongruence present in the system, since it does not involve the dispersion of the differences. These measures should then be compared with their maxima, which can be computed once one knows more about the particular system, how free the variation is, etc. And this is the only sense we shall give to the generalization of these concepts.

Since we have m units and n dimensions it is tempting, however, to see whether the concept of rank concordance can be of any use here. By this we mean

rank concordance: the extent to which all m units are ranked the same way on the n dimensions.

One way of operationalizing this would have been to proceed as we have done above and to find the degree of disagreement for each pair of dimensions; then one could easily compute the average or divide it by its maximum attainable value. This is more or less what we do when we calculate the figure 10 above, and it is not satisfactory because it is time-consuming. A more direct method would be preferable, but we shall see that it is hardly possible.

The obvious model would be Kendall's famous *coefficient of concordance* [13]. But the difficulty is that we have no basis for determining what would correspond to Kendall's 'maximum sum of squares'. First of all we have only two or three ranks at our disposal — not as many as there are units. Secondly, there is no rule that the units will be evenly distributed on each dimension. On one dimension all units may have the same rank, on another they may be evenly distributed. And then: to calculate the 'sum of squares of the actual deviations' from the arithmetic mean would bring us far away from the principle of staying close to the concepts. Hence, it looks as if the best we can do actually is to do as we did in the top part of Table 9.5, and we define:

Rank discordance:

$$\frac{\text{Sum of sums of distances for each unit and each dimension}}{\text{Maximum sum of sums}}$$

The denominator should only be calculated if it is meaningful, often it is not necessary. Obviously the rank discordance is zero when and only when all distances for each unit and each pair of dimensions are zero; in this case we have rank concordance. *In general we have that rank concordance, complete rank agreement* (for *all* pairs of dimensions) *and complete rank equilibrium* (for *all* units) *imply* each other and are implied by each other because they all refer to the same condition. This means that the conditions are equivalent, which simplifies the system considerably.

This set of conditions, which we can now refer to as concordance, *also implies rank congruence.* For if any unit is classified the same way by any pair of dimensions, then any pair of units will have the same rank differences on any one of these dimensions. But the converse is not true; one may have rank congruence without equilibrium as evidenced by the two profiles MTM and UMU. A system where all units had one or the other of these two profiles would be completely congruent but no unit would be in equilibrium, nor would there be complete agreement and hence not complete concordance.

The only thing that remains now is to say something about criss-cross. The formula we have given for the special case under case VIII is not easily generalizable, unfortunately, for the concept is much more complicated than the other concepts right now, for one particular reason. The concept refers to the systemic level, but no unit as such is the systemic level. We can build a theory around the concept of disequilibrium or incongruence or all the other concepts because they involve one unit or a pair of units at the time — for that reason we assume their motivating power to be strong. Unless criss-cross is internalized as an ideal no unit or no pair of units will be motivated to increase or decrease criss-cross because it is not a property of the unit or of the pair of units. This does not imply that the search for a fruitful generalization will be given up, however, for it is obvious that analysis should also be carried out at the systemic level.

That concludes our operationalization of variables that are indispensable for any serious analysis of multidimensional rank systems. Starting with the concept of the rank of one unit on one dimension, the matter was quickly complicated, the definitions were generalized and at the end the concepts found a fairly harmonic meeting ground in the most general case, where m units are ranked on n dimensions.

3. Propositions in multidimensional rank analysis

We can now present some of the basic propositions in multidimensional rank analysis because all concepts we are going to use have been conceptualized and clarified through the operational definitions. Thus, when propositions are presented they are given a precise meaning through the definitions and there is also implicitly a set of clear prescriptions as to how to test the propositions.

The set of propositions we shall use is as follows, where we make use of Table 9.2 and present the propositions in the order of the presentation of the concepts:

P_1: *Units seek to maximize their ranks on all dimensions*
  $P_{1,1}$: *Units seek to maximize their total rank*
P_2: *Units try to avoid rank disequilibrium and obtain rank equilibrium*
  $P_{2,1}$: *If efforts to obtain rank equilibrium are frustrated, aggression will result*
    $P_{2,1,1}$: *The aggression will be directed to self if ascribed ranks are higher than achieved ranks.*
    $P_{2,1,2}$: *The aggression will be directed to others if ascribed ranks are lower than achieved ranks.*
P_3: *The higher the total rank of a pair (or m-tuple), the more interaction there will be between the units in the pair (or m-tuple), and the more associative the interaction.*
P_4: *The lower the rank difference in the pair, the more interaction there will be between the units, and the more dissociative the interaction will be.*
  $P_{4,1}$: *The lower the rank inequivalence in the pair, the more interaction there will be between the units, and the more associative the interaction will be.*
P_5: *The higher the rank incongruence in a pair, the less interaction there will be between the units and the more dissociative the interaction will be.*

$P_{5,1}$: *If possible, interaction between incongruent units will be avoided.*

$P_{5,2}$: *If interaction cannot be avoided, interaction between incongruent units will be aggressive.*

$P_{5,2,1}$: *In case of work incongruence the most aggressive will be the unit in strongest disequilibrium.*

$P_{5,2,2}$: *In case of strong incongruence the most aggressive party will be the unit in disequilibrium with achieved ranks highest.*

$P_{5,3}$: *The higher the average rank incongruence in a set of units, the higher the probability of zero or aggressive interaction in pairs of units.*

$P_{5,4}$: *The lower the dispersion of rank incongruence in a set of units, the higher the probability of institutionalizing the incongruence.*

P_6: *The higher the criss-cross, the higher the probability of finding mediators and in-betweens in a conflict between two- or n-dimensional rank-groups.*

P_7: *The higher the concordance, the higher the probability of the emergence of generalized rank-roles.*

Since we have, essentially, seven concepts — (total) rank, rank disequilibrium, (total) rank of m-tuple, rank difference and rank inequivalence, rank incongruence, criss-cross and rank concordance — we have seven major propositions, one about each concept. Then there are sub-propositions, and in the case of rank disequilibrium and rank incongruence also sub-sub-propositions. In addition to this comes the mathematical theorem propounded in connection with rank concordance: that concordance, complete agreement and complete equilibrium imply each other, and that any one of the three implies rank congruence, but they are not implied by rank congruence.

We shall now present some comments on these propositions. They are empirical propositions; they say something factual about human behavior, whether that behavior is organized at the individual level or at the national level. As such, these seven propositions with sub-propositions should be distinguished from the purely mathematical theorem repeated above.

What the first proposition says is actually a tautology, since we have made use of the proposition to operationalize the concept of a rank dimension. A rank dimension is a variable that can be used to classify individuals, and on that variable the values on the one end are what units seek to obtain and the values on the opposite end are what units seek to avoid. Since this holds true for all rank dimensions, it also holds true for the total rank, since total rank is a simple additive function of the ranks on any single dimension.

The second proposition with its sub-propositions is based on ideas that have been developed in detail elsewhere [14].

The third proposition uses as dependent variable both amount of inter-action between units and quality of interaction, What the proposition says is that there is more and more positive interaction at the top of a social structure than at the bottom. This will be elaborated much more in connec-tion with the theory of feudal systems developed in the following section.

The fourth proposition is the well-known proposition about rank equality or rank equivalence as a condition that favors both quantity and quality of interaction.

The fifth proposition involves the more complicated concept of rank incongruence. For rank incongruence to obtain, at least two units must be involved, but at least one of them must be in disequilibrium. What the theorem says is that rank incongruence contributes either to disintegration of the system because of interaction avoidance, or to conflict in the system because of aggression. Just as it is hypothesized that disequilibrium will lead to aggression if it cannot be reduced through equilibrium, incongruence will lead to aggression if it cannot be reduced by interaction avoidance. We cannot here asume the mechanism that would correspond to equilibra-tion, because this would mean that the two units should agree between themselves that they should make their patterns congruent to each other. But this would be a highly improbable agreement that would almost pre-suppose a sort of dyadic motivation. For that reason what corresponds to equilibration in the theory of rank disequilibrium is interaction avoi-dance in the theory of rank incongruence.

The propositions about where the strongest or more probable sources of aggression will be located are relatively obvious, and so is the proposition about the effect of high average rank incongruence. More interesting is the proposition about the dispersion of rank incongruence: the lower it is, the higher the probability of arriving at some kind of solution. If the dispersion is very high it means that many different degrees of rank incon-gruence are represented among the pairs of units, which in turn means that there are many types of rank incongruence. But if the dispersion is very low, the number of units being the same, there will be more of a tendency for the rank incongruence to be of the same type so that *patterns* of accom-modation to rank incongruence can be developed. The general theory of rank incongruence and the reason why it should lead to effects in terms of interaction avoidance or aggressive interaction has been explored elsewhere [15]. Here the general theory of criss-cross has also been presented, as well as the development of the operationalization that was presented in the text above.

The seventh and final proposition concerning concordance is something new which is not already included in the propositions above. Concordance means that there are several dimensions and that not only the pairs of units find themselves at the same relative distance on these dimensions, but any single unit also finds itself in the same position on each dimension. Thus, the society is divided into three groups of people: one group that is topdog on all dimensions, one group that is middledog on all dimensions and one group that is underdog on all dimensions (or in two groups only if the middledog status is not included). The implication of this again is that all structural conditions are present for training in generalized topdog roles, middledog roles and underdog roles. The same individual will not have to face any change in rank when he moves from one interaction context to the other, which means that general patterns of behavior that correspond to his rank can be internalized as a permanent part of individuals: since they are in perfect rank congruence their role relations can be generalized so that the top person always can play a todog role towards the bottom person and the bottom person always an underdog role towards the top person. There is no need for any individual to train in playing roles appropriate to different ranks, nor is there any need for any pair of individuals to change their relationship when they move from one interaction context to another. The content may differ according to the dimension, but the general style will be the same; the patterns of reference etc. will be constant [16].

4. Types of rank systems

Our procedure in this paper is synthetic. We have started with the idea of the rank of one unit on one dimension and gradually generalized to m units on n dimensions, introducing concepts on the way, operationalizing them, and then a system of propositions has been presented. We shall now combine some of these ideas in such a way that something empirically recognizable emerges.

To do this imagine that we have a system of m units and n dimensions, and that the system obeys the propositions in the preceding section. What will happen to the system in that case? This depends on a number of factors, and among them is the ease with which mobility can take place. If we imagine that mobility is possible, then the result will be equilibration upwards, by virtue of propositions 1 and 2. In other words, the system will tend to become rank concordant and rank congruent. This means that the system will be divided into equilibrated *classes*, with within-class interaction facilitated and between-class interaction impeded by the rank-equality or rank equivalence in the first case and rank-difference or rank inequivalence in the latter. But at the same time, by virtue of proposition 3, there is (much) more interaction between the topdogs than between the underdogs, with the interaction of topdogs with underdogs as an intermediate case.

In this kind of system there will, by virtue of the mathematical theorem, be no rank incongruence and no criss-cross in addition to no disequilibrium. This means that there will be no built-in source of intrapersonal conflict due to disequilibrium (possibly acted out as aggression) or interpersonal conflict due to incongruence (possibly acted out as withdrawal) — but neither will there be any built-in protection against disruption due to the criss-cross effect. Typically, generalized rank roles will be formed.

Let us then consider the case where mobility is frustrated, as it usually is, for reasons of scarcity or 'ascription' or both. The tendency will be in the direction described above, but at some points in the social structure disequilibria will remain, producing aggression directed to self or to others, and there will be cases of incongruence, weak or strong, possibly leading to interaction avoidance and the split of the system into subsystems. Within these subsystems the structure mentioned above may emerge, but the system will be more complicated, more true to life, one may say. Thus, there will not be perfect rank congruence, the tendency for generalized rank roles to emerge will be less pronounced, and there will be some units that can function as mediators and in-betweens in a possible conflict between all topdogs and all underdogs by virtue of having some topdog ranks and some underdog ranks.

However, the pure case that will emerge under conditions of perfect mobility is so important that we want to give it a special name, and have chosen to call it a *feudal system*. In order to identify it we make use of two of the variables used in the formulation of the propositions, *viz. degree of rank concordance*, and the degree to which the amount of interaction depends on the total rank of the pair. For short, we shall refer to the latter as the *degree of interaction-dependence*. Thus, a feudal system is characterized by being high on rank concordance and high on interaction-dependence. The perfectly feudal system is a system completely divided in two classes, one topdog class and one underdog class (or in three classes, including a middledog class, if that status is present), and with all interaction that exists in the system between topdogs and no interaction at all between underdogs or between underdogs and topdogs. On the other extreme would be the completely defeudalized system, which would show a maximum of rank discordance and no dependence at all of interaction on the total rank of a pair. In this system there would be just as much interaction per pair whether the pair was of the TT-type, the TU-type or the UU-type (for simplicity we disregard here and in the following the middledog rank, since it is unlikely to occur in the kinds of feudal system we are talking about).

To understand the feudal system and to develop a more comprehensive system of multidimensional rank analysis we have to vary systematically

339

the two variables we have focused on, and arrive at the simple typology in Table 9.6.

TABLE 9.6 *Four basic types of rank systems*

		Interaction-dependence	
		high	low
Rank concordance	high	I. feudal systems	II. class systems
	low	III. mixed systems	IV. egalitarian systems

The egalitarian system is referred to above as the defeudalized system. The other two are intermediate cases. In the class system there is still rank concordance, but the interaction frequencies are much less dependent on the total rank: interaction between underdog nations or underdog individuals has been brought up towards the level of the interaction between topdog nations or individuals. It is obvious how this can be brought about: by energetic efforts to organize the underdog groups (trade unions, emancipist organizations, rural leagues, youth clubs, Bandoeng conferences, UNCTAD, etc.). However, in the mixed system we do not presuppose that this equalization of interaction levels has taken place. Characteristic of the mixed system is the absence of rank concordance, whether this is because the system does not permit sufficient mobility to become a feudal system, or whether it is because it has been feudal in its structure and is in a state of flux with some units in positions of disequilibrium and pairs of units in positions of incongruence.

No doubt, one could have cut into this system of thought using other variables than the two we have focused on, *viz.* degree of rank concordance and degree of interaction-dependence but we shall try to justify in the remaining sections the choice that has been made. Also, one might perhaps have chosen terms that are less overused. However, these terms, we feel, can also be justified by their usage in the following sections.

5. A dynamic theory of rank systems

We shall now turn to the relationship over time between these four structures, these four types of rank systems, and to do this we shall start with a more detailed analysis of the feudal system. More particularly, we shall develop further the theme touched on above, that almost any system if 'left to itself' will tend to develop towards a feudal system by showing 1. that the two properties of feudal systems are self-reinforcing, and 2. that they

340

reinforce each other. If this can be shown, then it is obvious that not only does the feudal system have stability, but there will also be a tendency for other systems with one of the properties to develop towards feudal systems.

Rank concordance is a very strong condition. It implies, as has been mentioned many times, both complete agreement, complete equilibrium and complete congruence. With the equilibrium a source of motivation for mobility as well as a source of aggression has been eliminated. With the congruence another source of aggression has been eliminated, and with concordance itself a factor that may contribute to a considerable amount of stability has been introduced: the generalization of rank roles. This means that provided the system is 'left to itself' in the sense of no external interference with the system (no change that it will have to cope with by institutionalizing new statuses and possibly bringing disequilibrium, incongruence, disagreement and discordance into the picture), then the system will be in a state of rank concordance forever. For every single unit there is a sort of intra-unit harmony, based on equilibrium and generalization of role expectations, and for every pair of units there is a similar harmony based on congruence and generalization of role patterns.

The important point here is that rank concordance, once it has started, will tend to develop further. If one unit already has three topdog statuses and is used to associate with a unit that has three underdog statuses, then both of them will learn roles that they will easily generalize. For the topdog unit this is an asset, a resource that he may use to conquer other topdog statuses; for the underdog unit it means a kind of inhibition, a general pattern of behavior that will not only prevent him from conquering topdog statuses but also make him more likely to accept more underdog statuses. Every disturbance brought into this system in terms of disagreement, disequilibrium or incongruence can be dealt with precisely as a disturbance, and be eliminated by bringing the elements in line again. The more concordance there is, the more facilities will be available to bring about conformity to the general pattern.

We then turn to the second condition, the condition about interaction-dependence. This condition obtains in small groups that are formed in laboratories with no prior social structure. The tendency is, as reported again and again, for small groups to develop interaction patterns so that most interaction is found at the TT-levels, then follows the TU-combination, then the UT, and finally the UU [17]. If we disregard the difference between TU and UT, which is not found in all investigations and which also assumes that the interaction is of an asymmetric kind, then one result of the small group studies can be summarized as follows: the higher the total rank of the pair, the higher the amount of interaction. And this is exactly feudal condition no. 2, and also proposition no. 3.

That this condition is self-reinforcing is easily seen. Once a differential in amount of interaction has been introduced interaction will be most rewarding at the points in the social structure where there has been most interaction. Interaction will generally mean experience, and it will work like money in a capitalist economy: the more a person has of it, the more he will get, for the more he will become trained in rewarding patterns of interaction both for himself and for others. In the small group, the person who has participated much will also be a person trained in capturing the interest of others, trained in rewarding them and in getting rewards from them. And the person who is very low in general interaction participation will not develop his potentialities and for that reason lose in competition with others. This presupposes an interaction market with relatively free choice, a condition which is present in the laboratory small group, but not necessarily in the international system. However, we assume that the *tendencies* will be present.

We now have to show that the two conditions are interrelated by positive feedback, and start by pointing out reasons why a system in rank concordance will be a system displaying the interaction pattern mentioned in condition no. 2.

Rank is a kind of resource, and rank concordance means a heavy concentration of resources among the people who are high on all dimensions and a similar deprivation of resources from the units that are low on all dimensions. Interaction will often presuppose resources just as much as it will beget resources; for that reason there will be more interaction, the more resources are present. But, in addition to that, the topdog unit will prefer to interact with another topdog unit for the simple reason that he can get more rewards from a topdog than an underdog. The topdog unit will at times want to interact with an underdog unit to get the kind of services the underdog can give him, and the under dog will certainly want to interact with the topdog unit. But to the extent that we assume that any unit will try to interact with the top because that is most rewarding, two topdog units will be at an advantage because their wishes correspond to each other, whereas the wishes of two underdog units will never correspond to each other and the wishes of one topdog and one underdog unit only sometimes. And from this simple reasoning the proposition about how total rank of pair is related to amount of interaction is a necessary consequence.

But just as interesting is the opposite proposition that the more a unit interacts, the higher its rank will become. Again the findings on small group studies are illuminating: we are thinking particularly of studies by Bavelas and others [18]. These studies tend to show that if a person or a unit in our general language is put in a communication structure that directs interaction to it or from it more than to or from other units, then this unit will tend to get increased rank from the interaction. There seems to be a kind of principle of 'justice' involved here, a kind of generalization of rank from what might be referred to as interaction-rank. This may also be result of incomplete induction: people are so used to the topdog being high on interaction that they wittingly or unwittingly attribute to people high on interaction topdog status. At any rate, it is interesting and highly significant that units distributed at random get their rank to some extent decided according to their structural position in an interaction network. In this context the significance is that the second condition of a feudal system will reinforce the first condition perhaps just as much as the first condition will reinforce the second condition.

With this pattern of circular causation between and within the two conditions we have established the feudal structure as not only a very stable structure, but also as, in a sense, a 'natural' structure. The general thesis resulting from this is that *if one does not want systems to become feudal, then something has to be done, something active, otherwise they will develop in that direction.* And the implication of that direction is the general interaction pattern of any feudal system: between the tops, and bilaterally from one top to one underling but not between the underlings.

We have already indicated above what this 'something active' may be: organization of the underdogs to strengthen them relative to the topdogs, leading to the class system with two classes pitted against each other, one favored by society and one not but more equal in strength because of the organization of the underdogs. The underdogs can now use this strength for one particular and important purpose: to increase the price of the values they contribute to the top dogs. Trade unions become instruments of a better price for the unit of labor force, organizations of developing or poor countries become instruments for a better price for their raw materials, emancipist organizations become instruments for equality between men and women (which means more similarity and hence equality in the role definitions).

But from the feudal system there is also another possible road of development in terms of our variables: towards the mixed system where there is still interaction-dependence, but the rank concordance has been broken down. This system offers a large variety of possibilities because of the imbalances built into it, but the underdogs are still exposed to exploitation (in the sense that they yield much more than they receive, according to the value standards) and without the organizational instruments to achieve more equitable treatment. The high degree of interaction-dependence splits the underdogs, makes them dependent on their particular topdogs, but the clear structure of the feudal system is broken up by all the disequilibrated individuals and rank incongruent parts that can be found in the system.

Looking at Table 9.6 it is clear how the transition from the two interme-diate systems to the egalitarian system can take place. From the class system, what is needed is a breakdown of rank concordance. Generally this takes place if more mobility is introduced into the system: talents kept down by a rigid system are permitted to move up. Agents of such changes are manumission and literacy campaigns and welfare state policies at the level of individuals and independence movements and economic development at the level of nations: they introduce differentiation between former slaves, serfs, low class members or colonies and poor countries respectively. The worker may still be a worker, but he is nevertheless an educated man; the nation may still be 'developing' but it is nevertheless independent.

Thus, we are brought into systems of types II and III in Table 9.6 — and the next step is the step to type IV, the egalitarian system. From the class system this will take place when the improved bargaining position of the underdogs leads to a change in the system. This again may take place in an evolutionary or revolutionary fashion, but in either case the result is that some former underdogs drift upwards and some former top dogs down-wards, reducing the degree of rank concordance considerably. From the mixed system it will take place by gradually increasing the interaction levels for the pairs, triples etc. with relatively low total rank. And this again is probably often brought about by means of voluntary associations, not of the trade union type referred to above, but of the usual criss-crossing type found in modern societies.

This whole set of social processes may be illustrated diagrammatically as follows, where the circle is one rank dimension, the distance from the center another (Fig. 9.5).

The diagrams correspond to the definitions given in Table 9.6. In the first phase high rank concordance and interaction-dependence make the under-dogs dependent on their top dog; each top dog has *his* underdogs (the slave-owner relative to his slaves, the factory-owner relative to his workers in early capitalist society, the feudal lord or modern *latifundista* relative to his peasants; the colonial powers relative to their colonies, the big powers relative to their 'sphere of interest'). Within this system the underdogs may protect themselves against excessive exploitation on the part of the top dogs by forming vertical associations of the underdogs belonging to that particular topdog (workers' associations, cooperation between Latin Ameri-can countries to strengthen their bargaining position relative to the topdog, the United States, cooperation between Eastern European countries for the same purpose relative to the Soviet Union). But this is not the same as the situation depicted in the upper right-hand corner: here all underdogs unite in the common cause against the common class enemy and we get the *horizontal* trade unions uniting workers of the same kind all over the

FIGURE 9.5 *An illustration of the four types of rank systems*

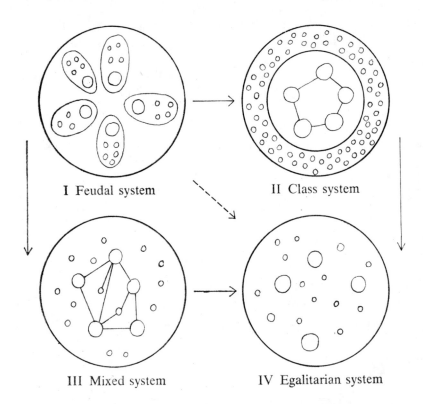

I Feudal system   II Class system

III Mixed system   IV Egalitarian system

country — eventually all over the world. The international parallel would be the (so far not realized) trade union of all small nations, pitted against the five big powers. For this to happen there must be a change of focus and loyalties from the sphere dominated by the top dog to other underdogs in similar positions all over the world; and the conditions under which this change takes place are not too well understood.

Then, finally, there are the third and fourth cases where top dogs and underdogs are mixed. In the figures the big and small circles are mixed, and there is no clear pattern of big circles in the center and small circles in the periphery. However, in the third case interaction is still most pronounced in the center of the system — only in the fourth case has this, the last of the feudal characteristics, disappeared.

Needless to say, all these types are ideal types; they are baselines with which empirical systems can be compared. Such investigations are currently being carried out at the International Peace Research Institute in Oslo, both for international systems and interindividual systems, and over time so as to test the dynamic theory here developed [19].

Two important questions in this connection remain to be discussed in this section: is there no direct line of transition from the feudal system to the egalitarian system? And what about the egalitarian system? Is that the end of the story — is there no further development from that stage on?

As to the first question, empirical investigations along these lines will probably reveal many processes of gradual transition from type I to type IV systems that do not go via types II or III. Thus, the heavy arrows in Fig. 9.5 are there to indicate the two *components* of this process — viz., decrease in interaction-dependence and decrease in rank concordance — and there is no principle according to which the process from I to IV cannot take place along any road in the two-dimensional space shown in Fig. 9.6.

FIGURE 9.6 *The rank concordance interaction-dependence space*

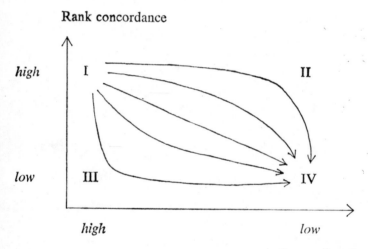

Since the two extreme cases — the process via type II and the process via type III — are so different (the former seems more likely to be of a revolutionary nature, the latter of an evolutionary nature) an important topic of investigations in this field is precisely the conditions that favor and impede one or the other of the two types of transition from feudal systems to egalitarian systems.

The second question: *after egalitarianism, what?* is easily discussed, if not necessarily answered in a satisfactory way, within the framework of this model. The answer is given in terms of the analysis in the preceding section, where reasons why the feudal system seems to be more stable than the others are outlined. In the egalitarian system rank-concordance

346

and interaction-dependence are not reinforcing each other since they are both absent. But rank has not been abolished, and we know of no system pursuing values (which action-systems by definition do) where units are not differentially evaluated (i.e. ranked) in terms of their ability to realize the value(s) of the system. This means that the egalitarian system will break down for one or both of two reasons: either units will start equilibrating and avoiding rank incongruence relative to the old rank dimensions, or else some new rank dimension is introduced or emerges. Thus the system tends to slide back to a high level of rank-concordance, and according to the general theory in the preceding section interaction-dependence will then easily follow. And this means that one is back at the point of origin again: the feudal system, but usually stratified by some new variable(s). To take the much discussed case today of interindividual systems: they used to be stratified according to the occupational position of the father in highly rank-concordant and interaction-dependent systems with the wealthy, well-educated and powerful on top, and the poor, illiterate and powerless on the bottom. Then transitions towards egalitarian systems take place, partly through the mechanism of underdog organization, partly through the mechanism of mobility facilitated by such processes as expanding economies, expanding educational systems and expanding parti-cipation in the political systems. And then the new stratification emerges, according to achievement rather than ascription, according to intelligence and merit rather than father's position [20]. And the result is (or may be) a new feudal system where the clever are the top dogs, with their less clever underdogs referred to as employees, with the clever interacting at a very high level in their self-styled elite, and the less clever doing so considerably less. According to the model what would follow would be the organization of the less clever to arrive at a better bargaining position, or the introduction of new rank dimensions along which the less clever can drift upwards and the more clever downwards — or both [21].

Thus we see the development of systems as a pendling process with the feudal system and the egalitarian system as extremes, and the feudal system as the most stable point. But all feudal systems will in the long run lead to their own destruction because of their built-in contradiction — the exploi-tation that results so easily from the combination of rank concordance and interaction-dependence. There will be a claim for egalitarianism, but once that has been arrived at the system will tend to slide back to more feudal varieties, whether they are organized around the old stratification variables or around some new ones.

And this circling or spiraling process, depending on whether the old or new rank-dimensions are used, is what is referred to as *history* [22].

6. Some further elaborations

So far we have only discussed the case of *one* system of actors, individual or national, ranked by a set of dimensions and interacting with each other. To give more perspective to the theory, let us indicate how these ideas may be extended to more complicated structures, without going too much in detail. The problem is: what if we have *two* systems, in the same or different phase on the road from feudal to egalitarian structure, and in interaction with each other? It seems fruitful to distinguish between three cases:

1. There is *no overlap* between the two structures: a unit belongs to one or the other,
2. There is *some overlap* between the two structures: some units belong to both and some to one but not to the other, and
3. There is *complete overlap* between the two structures: all units of one belong to the other.

As an extreme case of the latter one might include the case of identity between the two structures.

As an example of the first, we may cite the East-West system consisting of the 15 NATO nations, headed by three topdog powers, the United States, the United Kingdom and France, and the Warsaw treaty system consisting of one big power, the USSR, and smaller powers [23]. Both structures have feudal characteristics in themselves insofar as there is both rank concordance and interaction-dependence, and the rank-dependence is even more pronounced between the two structures. It should be noticed that this interaction-dependence is highly compatible with the doctrine of conflict-polarization: when there is conflict between two structures the tendency is to break off interaction, starting with underdog interaction so that interaction becomes the monopoly of the topdogs. Thus in the feudal interaction pattern between two feudal structures there is already built into the structure a readiness for conflict, the kind of 'stripping for action' [24]. This should be remembered in connection with Fig. 9.5: it is actually a feudal system with five feudal subsystems, and although we assume concentration of interaction on the top, we do not assume in any sense that the interaction is always positive. There may also be conflicts and destructive behavior, and the theory is then that this will be between the topdogs more than between the underdogs (although the topdogs may let the underdogs do the fighting) from different structures. Since there is little interaction at the bottom, this means that the total structure is highly vulnerable to topdog conflicts: there is little or no underdog interaction that can cushion the effect of topdog struggle and keep the system interacting.

What will then happen if the underdogs of the two structures neverthe-less start interacting and form an underdog organization? One probable consequence is that it will unite the topdogs to fight better for common topdog interests, for instance in efforts to preserve their status as big powers. The obvious individual level analogy can be taken from the theory of em-ployer-employee relationships: it is not unreasonable to postulate that trade unions have made economic competition and conflict between em-ployers less bitter and less pronounced since the 'capitalists' have been forced into positions of cooperation to withstand better the pressures from united labor unions [25].

As an example of the third case above, we may cite the whole world if we look at it as in Fig. 9.7.

FIGURE 9.7 *The Chinese boxes' model of the world*

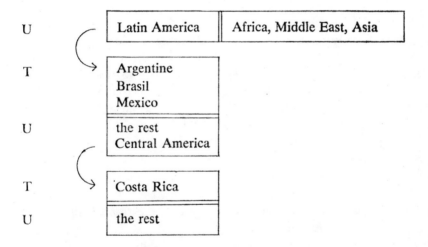

The whole world has its top dogs (the big powers, the OECD countries, the 'rich' countries, depending on what criterion is used) and its underdogs, with rank concordance and interaction-independence. Thus, whereas there are 440 flights a week between North America and Europe, there are only six flights a week between Latin America and Africa. And this pattern reappears if one studies the Western Hemisphere as a subsystem, reappears again if one studies the Latin American system as a subsystem of the Western Hemisphere, and reappears again if one studies the Central American system as a subsystem of the Latin American system [26]. Thus, to be an underdog in the latter (the case of Honduras) is to be the underdog in an underdog system in an underdog system in a feudal system which is a subsystem of the total world. On the one hand, this may be said to be a sad position, on the other hand it has the virtue of being consistent: here is a kind of equilibrium between levels.

For, obviously, one can now start again with the theory of rank disequilibrium, but this time apply it to systems and subsystems that relate to each other as Chinese boxes. If we assume that all units want to maximize their rank and want to interact with other units of maximum rank, then we get the following propositions:

P_1: *A unit which is consistently top dog will press for interaction that gives it widest influence, i.e. the most comprehensive system.*

P_2: *A unit which is consistently an underdog will press for interaction that leads to contact with the highest topdog, i.e. the most comprehensive system.*

P_3: *A unit which has an inconsistent pattern will press for interaction in the system where it ranks highest.*

From this an interesting proposition about the community of interests between the top-top-topdog and the under-under-underdog can be deduced: they both want to interact in the most comprehensive system, the former to reach a maximum of underdogs, the latter to reach the highest topdogs. Thus a corollary of this kind of thinking is the pattern of cooperation between the biggest and the smallest, over the heads of the middle powers, well known from many systems [27].

The whole system can now be complicated further if we no longer assume that the rankings are made according to the same criteria in the structures, whether they are collateral or inclusive, and if we introduce the second case with partial overlap. However, these themes will not be developed here.

But there is another development which is worth mentioning: the relation between systems of different types, one at the national level and the other one at the individual level. Imagine that there is only one rank-dimension in each: what would then be the relationship between, for instance, an underdog in a topdog nation and a topdog in an underdog nation? Both are in rank disequilibrium, so both will have an incentive to equilibrate. They are also rank-incongruent to each other, which means that they should have a particularly uneasy relationship (the poor white settler and the colored political leader), leading to aggressiveness or mutual isolation. Equilibration may take place in many ways: the topdog in the underdog country may migrate to a topdog country to obtain equilibrium (permanently, or as a diplomat or representative of some other kind); and the underdog in the topdog country may migrate to an underdog country and establish himself as a topdog over the natives (the colonizer, the lower-rank members of technical assistance or diplomatic missions, etc.). Then

350

there is the more active underdog nation topdog who tries to make his nation a topdog nation so that it can become a more worthy stage for himself, whereas the underdog who wants to move his own topdog nation downwards seems to be a merely speculative by-product of the general theory.

This can now be elaborated further by introducing more rank-dimensions on each level, and be combined with the more complex structure developed above. Moreover, we have only so far touched the case of *two* systems — collateral, inclusive or parallel, to introduce some useful terms — and the obvious generalization would be to n systems.

7. Conclusion

We have presented a system for analysis of rank systems, with operationalization of the concepts of the system. Connected with the system is a set of propositions and a general dynamic theory of change, which is presented as a paradigm for the analysis of social systems, since all social systems will have to be rank systems, or tend towards rank systems. The whole theory is centered around such simple ideas as the mobility postulate, the equilibration postulate, and so on. It is claimed that this system has a considerable explicative power.

But its power is, of course, not unlimited. Many conflicts are not about rank but about other scarce values. Nevertheless, the system of analysis has its heuristic value in addition to its explicative and predictive values, and has already proved fruitful in empirical investigations.

IV.10. Big Powers and the World Feudal Structure

PRIO — publication No. 21—34.

Notes on page *707*.

1. The feudal analogy

The point of departure for this discussion of world structure is a very general scheme of what feudalism means, and what a feudal system is (Fig. 1).

FIGURE 1 *The feudal pyramid*

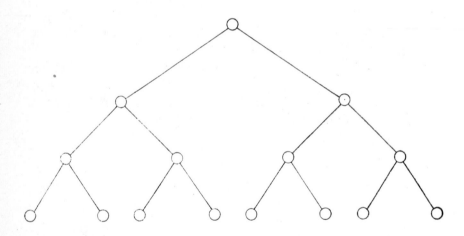

A perfect feudal system as it developed in Europe in the Middle Ages looked somewhat like a pyramid. The king was on the top, then came the lords, the vassals and finally at the bottom the serfs [1]. More importantly, "interaction", as the social scientist would say, was essentially *vertical*, so if an underling wanted some contact with somebody at a distance but at his own level, the system was set up in such a way that he had to go via a superior.

International analogy: let us say that you want to make a telephone call from Kenya to the Central African Republic. You have to place the call in Nairobi, it then goes to London, for there is a link there (the higher up in the pyramid, the more *horizontal* interaction), it goes on to Paris, then down to the Central African Republic. This is feudal interaction; controlled by those high up, the top integrated and the bottom not.

In the perfect feudal system there is a unification on the top, the structure converges into something. But very often this is not the case; often we have what we may call a truncated feudal system [2]. There is no king. It looks like Fig. 2: two power blocs, themselves feudally organized. Let us call one of them West and the other East.

FIGURE 2 *Two feudal pyramids*

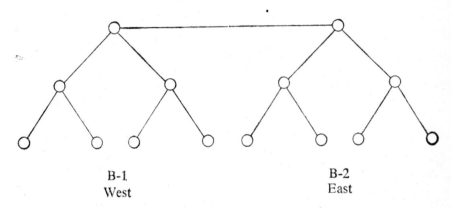

B-1
West

B-2
East

Here there are two basic dimensions: the horizontal dimension between the two feudally organized blocs, and the vertical dimension inside the blocs. As an example may serve the relationship the Soviet Union has to her satellites in Eastern Europe, similar to that the United States has to her satellites in the Western hemisphere. What happened in the Dominican Republic in 1965 is almost exactly the same as what happened in Czechoslovakia in 1968, the Brezhnev doctrine and the Monroe doctrine could have been written by the same man; the defense Adlai Stephenson gave the United Nations after the Dominican Republic incident is almost identical to the speech given 3 years later by the Russian Ambassador to the United Nations after Czechoslovakia [3].

But why is this so? Because there is a fundamental structure underneath it all, a structure with which we all seem to be firmly imbued, a structure that haunts us. The structure is often defended by people and nations on the top, and it had better be so, because they get the net benefits of the structure. The structure is compatible with "law and order"; and there is little noise in the system, for at the bottom there is fragmentation, disintegration, lack of mutual visibility and contact. The contact which exists is, as mentioned, channeled through the top, and also controlled by the top. Net result: *split and conquer*.

353

Let us now reinstate the King for a moment, and go back to feudal Europe. In 1789 something happened. Of course, it is nonsense to claim, even if we are taught this in some history books, that the whole world changed its features in 1789. Very much of what happened had already happened before, and very much of what was before indeed persisted after. But something happened: there was, for instance a certain increase in transparency — the total structure became more apparent to people. And the belief in the feudal system as something God-given was seriously shaken.

That scheme had been seen as sanctified by God himself, and the King derived his power by the grace of God. Through the commanding lines of the feudal system the power of God drizzled down to the humble son, and crystallized at the bottom of the hierarchy in a heavily ideologized religious orientation, saying more or less: "You cannot ever hope to change this world. To try to change it only betrays your vanity. The best thing you can do is to change your own soul so as to become as God-like as possible. By doing so you can go straight to God, and you don't have to bother about the social structure".

In the capitalist system this is done more systematically. There are mechanisms for extracting the surplus from what is produced at lower levels, sending it upwards. But the feudal kings were also fabulously rich, their palaces were conspicuously different from the village in which their serfs lived. Those who had the job of sanctifying it, the priests, did not live too badly either. The cathedrals they built were at the same time built to the glory of God, as a measure and instrument showing at a large distance what the structure was all about: to the glory of the Lord and the lords.

Towards the end of the 18th century, however, all this seems to have become more transparent, and consequently it was more evident to people what this was all about. Protest emerged due to many factors. The growth of a parallel structure with merchants on top could not easily be accommodated within the system. The merchants wanted political power commensurate with their economic power, leading to what we now know as co--decision. Through the initially very narrow concept of "citizen", a feeling of "general belongingness" was created, excluding workers and women. The feeling that the rest all belonged led to some sense of shared responsibility.

Nobody would say that everything that happened in 1789 lasted, nor that what lasted was in any sense sufficient. But 1789 was important — it was in a sense a breakthrough to defeudalization. But it was certainly a very partial one: man conquered power and co-decision at the middle level of social organizations, and feudalism survived at the level above and the level below: the macro and micro levels. Feudalism survived in the international systems and remained, for instance, in the universities:

the feudal pyramids with the deans, the professors and at the bottom, the students. What happened in Europe in 1968, and what is going on in the world today, is to a large extend to extend 1789 to the micro level in spite of all the Marxist slogans that one has to start with the social level. It is a question of achieving *at least* 1789, some kind of transparency of what happens at the university, a sharing of decisionmaking, a general sense of belongingness, a sharing of responsibility. The idea, for instance, that there are overlords who can decide over others by means of something they call examinations with no reciprocity at all, belongs to the feudal syndrome. It will take time to change the micro level, but changes will come.

If we look at the international system, we can see that the logic of the system still derives from pre-1789, with the added comment that there is no unifying structure at the top. To make the world a perfectly feudal world, all you need is actually to realize the program of some World Federalists: to put on top of it a centralizing, authoritarian world government. But in our world there are (at least) two blocs, B-1 and B-2; there are also two axes, one called East-West, between the blocs, and the other North-South, within the blocs. To see this one should use both the bourgeois concept of underdevelopment and the Marxist concept; they are both important. The bourgeois-liberal concept of underdevelopment leads to the idea of low GNP per capita, or more sophisticated versions, with several indicators at a time, developing some complex system for saying that a country is underdeveloped or not. The Marxist concept is more structural: if a country is in the position that what it produces of surplus is being extracted and sent higher up, then it is underdeveloped by definition regardless of how high its GNP per capita is. Even if Venezuela grows much more in GNP per capita it is still an underdeveloped country because it does not have autonomy. It is not the master of its own fate, it is being exploited. There is a correlation between the two concepts: countries at the bottom of such exploitation pyramids also have a tendency to be countries far down on indicators selected to measure development. But there are exceptions on both sides. There are poor countries that are autonomous (China), and there are indeed rich countries that are not autonomous (Canada).

On the top of the international system, then, are the so-called big powers, under them the middle powers, and at the bottom the small powers. These countries are small, not in geographical size, nor in population, nor necessarily in GNP per capita, but in terms of their structural position. In fact, there are two such strongly related pyramids in the international system: one headed by the big economic powers with other rich countries in the middle and the Third World at the bottom; the other headed by the superpowers with lesser military powers under them. In this perspective it is

355

quite interesting how much one can say about big powers; they are conspicuously similar to the feudal lords of the Middle Ages.

2. Ten characteristics of big power dominance

First of all, big powers have a part of the world they call "theirs". They refer to it as a "sphere of interest", a euphemism for a sphere of control, and it is *theirs*. Big powers use personal possessive pronouns, and the usage of such personal possessive pronouns works both ways, "It is our super-power". As feudal lords in the Middle Ages did, the big powers have a certain type of sovereign, "and don't you, other big brother, intervene". Sometimes these spheres of interest overlap, in which case there is conflict. Sometimes countries manage to stay outside such spheres, in which case they are referred to as a "vacuum". In extreme cases the spheres of interest are the whole world.

To protect this concept there are juridical doctrines, referred to as the Monroe Doctrine, the Brezhnev Doctrine, and so on [4]. There are also agreements like those emerging through the Tehran-Yalta-Potsdam-system, chopping up Europe for instance, or the agreement implicitly or explicitly formulated in connection with the Western Hemisphere after the emergence of socialist Cuba, a highly complicating factor. But the sphere of interest, it should be noted, is not necessarily a geographical characteristic. In feudal Europe the sphere of interest was usually geographically contiguous, or almost that. The feudal lord presided over what he could reasonably control given the means of communication he had at hand. That was not much, and it was only after the 18th century that man could move with more than a maximum speed of 20 km/h. The steam engine "came" in the 1780's, but it took some 40—50 years to put it into a boat and call it a steam-ship or and into something on rails and call it an engine. After that there has been an upward curve in the speed of locomotion, and in our age contiguity is certainly not as important as it once was. And this means that the feudal structure is often less visible, more difficult to detect.

Long-distance calls were used above as one example; flight connections could be used as another one. As a matter of fact, the first time I started thinking about this structure was while working for UNESCO, and having to go from Bogotá in Columbia to Caracas in Venezuela. These are neighboring countries, but there was only one flight a week between them, and I had to be there the next day. I was informed that the way to do so was to go Panama-New York-Miami-Caracas. But then, the feudal interaction pattern is the way the world to a large extent is organized.

Next on the list of what it means to be a big power is the right to have *foreign bases* within your sphere of interest, using others as outposts and warring stations. Technically speaking this is violation of foreign territory, and the big powers are the only ones who can have it, and get away with it. When a new country is born, the big powers are the first to violate its territory with their foreign bases. This is not unlike the "ius primae noctis" in the feudal times: when one of the daughters of the serfs was going to be married the lord had the right to the first night. The big powers have the right to the first base.

Regionalism, one of the many terms used for this system, is spun like a protective cocoon around that part of the world which belongs to the feudal power. It may be a security regional organization; it may, of course, be a technical assistance organization; or it may take on such strange and peculiar forms as one finds in the Western Hemisphere and Eastern Europe: an organization for internal security, so-called *peacekeeping, with the big powers as self-appointed policemen*, jealously guarding against any kind of subversion, making use of a supersystem that tries to encompass the whole. It is some kind of incarnation of both King and God in one, turning the head when the police activity goes from patronizing benevolence to direct terror.

In the case of the Dominican Republic, and in Eastern Europe, the same happens again and again: Big Brothers jealously, eagerly, see to it that the UN does not obtain primary jurisdiction. They see to it that little Norway votes with the United States when it comes to handing the case of the Dominican Republic over to the "appropriate organization", OAS (Organization of American States), which is like seeing to it that the Hungary case of 1956 was handed over to the Warsaw Pact, or that the Czechoslovakia case of 1968 was handled by the same "appropriate organization".

In order to coordinate this, including the use of the UN, one needs good communication between the two big brothers — which is, of course, the "hot line". One could imagine the following communication between the two, taking place the 20th August, 1968:

Big brother 2 calling big Brother 1:
— Are you there Big brother?
— Yeah, what is it??
— Well, we are performing some little surgical operation of the same type as you did in 1965, you remember the Dominican Republic?
— Oh yes, Go ahead, what do you want?
— Well, you can organize a little demonstration outside our Embassy in Washington tonight. Not more than two hours, please. Then we'll have to have a debate in the United Nations this fall, shall we take one week? — I think we can use the old speeches.
— We'll have time for that. Go right ahead!

What is suggested by this is the joint, mutual interest in preserving the system that big brothers have. More particularly: B-1 will want to protect a B-2 prerogative in his sphere of interest in order to use it as a precedent when he is in the same situation. To preserve B-1 is more important than to protect B-2 underlings. This is in a sense trivial, but explains why lawyers of the State Department in the United States were eagerly collecting the evidence of the 1956 Hungary case, and could use it in the case of the Dominican Republic. It is indispensable for them in order to preserve the regionalism.

Let us move from these very overt political factors to more subtle aspects in this connection. Thus, *the big powers are the definers of the international system*. They define what a problem is: a real problem is a big power problem. When the small powers have a quarrel, right now there is one between Argentina and Chile, then it is referred to as "irresponsible", showing that they have not grown up. If the quarrel is on the top, then it is a real conflict to which serious men must pay attention. But one could also argue just the opposite: exactly because we are all so indoctrinated with this respect for big powers, we should pay much less attention to them. We should not accord to them the right to define what are real problems, accepting that big powers by definition deal with big problems, and that if one has a big problem in the world, it can better be handled by the big powers. Thus, Middle East crises are handed over to the big powers, and the interesting thing is the way and the degree to which this is accepted all over the world, in spite of their failure and egoisms. The big powers are expected to take the initiative, others are expected to stand by and wait, immobilized and immobilizing themselves.

This is important, and in a sense more so than the other aspects mentioned above. Here we come down to psycho-cultural sub-stratum: what we do when we pay so much attention to the big powers is, psychologically speaking, to act out some patterns imbibed in a very early childhood. We become like small children watching our parents when we are doing big power watching in the international scene, thereby supporting them in their arrogance. This is also reflected in the newspapers. Material in this field compiled by UNESCO a few years ago revealed the following in Argentinian and Brazilian newspapers: Argentina devoted something like 4% of their news columns to the big neighbor Brazil, Brazil something like 2% to Argentina. Close to 90% of all the foreign news columns was about the big powers. In other words, one jumps across neighbors, watching upwards. Why? Because one is trained by family and religion in watching upwards, reflecting what happens there.

Then there is the case of *the spy-organizations*. In a sense the most interesting thing about them is that we let it happen, telling ourselves that it is "normal" that big powers do such things. If Norway had a spy organization in Sweden, not to mention in the US, it would be somewhat phony, not because our friendly relations, but because it is not our prerogative to have such things. The big powers have that prerogative. They have certain ways of behaving in which they can indulge; their agents will be expelled when behaving too openly, but we expect them soon to be back in operation.

Next: one would expect big powers to have big weapons because they are big. The perfect fulfilment of this is the nuclear club, and as long as nuclear proliferation only takes place within the big power circle, from one to two, from two to three, from three to four, from four to five, it is as if one were fulfilling laws of nature by giving unto the lords what belongs to the lords. Beyond that discussion about nuclear non-proliferation treaties really gets going. Big powers should have *big* weapons and small powers *small* weapons, so this is the moment where rank concordance has been obtained. The world is as it should be; at ease. The mountains are standing with their tops up and bottoms down, not the other way round. Things are as they should be according to the law of social gravity. And the rationalization of the system is the same: there will be a lot of talk about big power responsibility and small power irresponsibility in nuclear matters, their problems not being considered real, only apparent.

It goes without saying that the languages big powers speak are called *world languages* and it is obvious that their cultures are *world cultures*. A world power can use its language and culture to penetrate small countries, and even have cultural organizations for doing so: USIS is one, the British Council another, Alliance Française still another, and so on. If small countries should try to do the same, they better not have more than a modest, poorly paid cultural attaché with some slides and pamphlets, and nothing really serious, because we do not have world cultures, just cultures. The self-fulfilling rationale would be that due to the imperial constructions by the big powers, these languages and cultures *are* in fact world encompassing — more or less — and it would be stupid not to pay attention to that fact.

That countries of this stature also have *veto* in the United Nations and their own club, the (permanent members of the) *Security Council*, goes without saying. It is the feudal court of the international system, with the difference that there is no king — they are the King.

3. On the theory of defeudalization

Let us now try to see more in detail how this works in real situations of conflict where the feudal structure is put to a test. Thus, imagine one of the serfs trying to go over to the other side, or at least trying to leave its own system. The system is then in a crisis, as when the Dominican Republic

·might have gone "communist" in 1965, or Czechoslovakia might have gone "neutral" in 1968. These are the crucial moments where one can see the system naked, laid bare so to speak. And if we look at this from the point of view of the small countries at the bottom of the pyramid "protected" by the big ones, we cannot help concluding that they need some protection against protection. Thus, with the Dominican Republic at the bottom of the B-1 pyramid and Czechoslovakia at the bottom of the B-2 pyramid, it is obvious that those who believe very much in Big Brother 1 would say that countries under B-2 are different from those under B-1, and those who believe very much in Big Brother 2 would say that countries under B-1 are completely different from those under B-1, and that any similarities are purely formal; what matters are the capitalist/socialist and parliament/party rule distinctions. But positionally these countries are rather similar, so why don't these two countries join together (the Dominican Republic and Czechoslovakia) and form an alliance for protection against protection? There are many reasons for this, and the basic reasons are, of course, that they are far apart and not permitted to by their big brothers. But it is not so much the distance from the Caribbean to Central Europe that matters as the social distance, because there is no direct channel of interaction between the two. Whether one looks at flights, at international trade, at telephone connections, at letters written, at any kind of indicator for international interaction: they all follow the same basic pattern — from the bottom of one pyramid and upwards until you can find a horizontal bridge, usually passing through one or two big powers, and then down again to the bottom of the other pyramid [5]. This means that it is in the power of the big powers to interrupt interaction. When they interrupt it, it has repercussions lower down in the pyramid. There is almost nothing at the bottom to sustain it, no direct interaction, it is all at the mercy of the big powers. Obviously this type of situation cannot be permitted to continue.

What does one do about such a system? How does one try to defeudalize it? How does one try at least to bring 1789 into it as a modest beginning? There are many answers, and they can all be organized on an axis from an evolutionary to a revolutionary pole.

Let us begin by finding out what the revolutionary in changing the international system pole is: it is to organize all small powers into one sixth big power, and then go to war against the rest. This is the big war approach. It is implicitly and explicitly suggested by Lin Piao when he says, more or less, the following. What happened in feudal ages in China was that the small cities exploited the villages and the big cities the small cities. The Chinese communist revolution was a revolution of the village against the town. Much can be said about this, but let us accept that in part it was village against town. Then Lin Piao says that there is something called the world village and the world city. The world city is the big monopolies, the big metropolies of the world, whether in the imperialist or the revisionist camps. The "world village" is the third world and exploited parts of the first and second worlds. The sixth big power is exactly the world village against the world city. (Incidentally it will have to be the fifth power, because China obviously wants to be the leader of the village revolting against the others and overthrowing the whole structure.) There we have one extreme on the defeudalization continuum.

Let us then in order to put it into perspective consider the most modest other extreme: to "change interaction rates", in the terminology of a sociologist. It simply means trying to have more diplomacy among the small countries, more flights, more direct postal connections and telephone links among them, more trade. In other words, more horizontal interaction at the bottom, less looking upwards at the overlords for permission, letting interaction pass through them, or at least, not without their permission.

Much of this evolutionary change is going on today, but it is only going on in times of peace and quiet. Looking at it statistically and systematically, one can construct a measure, showing to what extent interaction is saturated at the top of the pyramids, in vertical connections within each pyramid at the bottom, and in the horizontal connections between pyramids. Usually the saturation levels are decreasing in that order with the tops having complete sets of embassies with each other, with much less interaction between countries at the bottom of one pyramid, and almost nothing horizontally between the lower brackets of the two pyramids. The steepness of the decrease in saturation is a measure of the amount of work to be done.

What happened in Europe before the Czechoslovakia "incident", to put it in a neutral way, was exactly that this discrepancy was being evened out. There was an increasing tendency for small powers in the West to interact as much with small powers in the East as they interacted with the topdog on the other side, and as the topdogs interacted with each other. In other words, there was a defeudalization of interaction rates. That, the socialist scientist would say, is a change in structure which may serve as a very fruitful basis for the next step, organization formation.

To gain perspective, let us change the example for a while. Let us call the top "the establishment" and place lower down, on one side, the students, and on the other, the workers. One basic point which any student revolutionary anywhere in the world will know fairly well, is the difficulty in getting students and workers together. This is not because they cannot meet; in a so-called free society one can meet anywhere. But that meeting has to be *ad hoc*, it is not built into everyday work interaction. One has to make an effort to carry it out over and above work interaction; it may even look artificial. It is exactly the same on the international scene: there is nothing linking the Dominican Republic and Czechoslovakia, and there is as little tying Norway to, let us say, Nepal. Increased interaction will raise political eye-brows. In this situation, with a lack of institutionalized interaction, organization formation is difficult. What one has to do first is somehow to build those bridges of interaction, and then let organizations grow as a result — unless, of course, the situation is so extreme that it calls for immediate action.

Between the two extremes, the big war and the change of interaction patterns, there is a spectrum which by and large can be referred to as *trade union policies*. They can be soft or they can be tough, there are different kinds of trade unions. There is a world of difference between Japanese trade unions and British trade unions, for instance. Let us just indicate three different stages in trade union policies.

The first is *the voting caucus*. This would have to be within the international organizations, because that is the only place where one can vote. Hence the tremendous importance of having a unifying structure for the whole world system so that there is somewhere a united front can be expressed. That something is the United Nations. However feeble, a fantastic potential in the defeudalizing direction because it permits playing multilateral interaction up and bilateral interaction, dominated by big powers, down.

It is puzzling, humiliating, sad, intriguing, to see how long it took in human history to establish this. From Pierre Dubois, who in 1306 in "De Recuperatione Terrae Santae" published his first proposal for the United Nations of Christian Nations, via the various attempts to stem the tide from the Turks and Russians, it took six centuries of thinking before we got the League of Nations. It had to go through such stages as the Vienna Conference and the 'concert of Europe', with the idea that the princes understand these things better than others, and if only princes from the big powers could be friends, like a big family, then they could decide things among themselves. There were five of them and they tried to do that, and so we know the system worked to a large extent to avoid war, but not to avoid repression. A further development was the idea of extending the European concert to a world concert, but retaining big power hegemony. Today the Security Council is the aftermath of the structure which emerged. Such a structure was perhaps necessary to beat Napoleon, and the threat. of a new Napoleon is to a large extent at the roots of the Security Councilt The role of the big powers is certainly there, but not so much the role of the big persons.

The real small power voting caucus has not yet emerged, but we have had other types of voting groups in the United Nations. There are East/West groups and to some extent North/South groups but they are not the same as the voting caucus we have in mind; this is an axis which does not divide the world into socialist, capitalist and neutral camps, or into the 77 countries of the Charter of Algiers versus the other UNCTAD members. It divides it into essentially the five big and the 130 small powers. The world is still split into feudal fiefs. All one can say is that the voting caucus will come; it is, so to speak, implicitly on the agenda. There is a need to extract the remaining teeth of the big powers.

The second stage is the *bargaining trade union*, not only in the sense that it puts forward collective demands, but a trade union which places some kind of power behind its claims. This would be a trade union of small countries saying that "we are sick and tired of you all, of your espionage, your tricks, your intrusions, your sickening paranoia, your primadonnaism, your desire to attract all attention to yourself. We are sick and tired of it all, we are just as real as you are, our conflicts are just as real as yours, we do not want to be supervised by you, we want to supervise our own conflicts, and if we do something which you call subversion, then you, indeed, do something we might call "subversion".

One idea at this stage would be to sell raw materials at higher prices, even to "one's own big power", trade unions function in order to 'sell' man-power at higher prices, by means of strikes or by threats to stop exports. This is an old idea, and it may even be too late now, because the ability of the developed countries and the big powers to construct synthetically what one can get from raw materials probably is increasing at a faster growth rate than the organization potential of the smaller countries. It is a question of two growth curves, both positive, but the wrong one may be faster, meaning that one has missed the train in a certain sense.

This, then, brings us to the third possibility: the idea of *separate organizations*. Just as it was indispensable for the 77 countries to meet, in Algeria, it was also indispensable for them to meet without the rich countries present. It may one day be necessary for the 130 to meet without the five present. In a sense this would mean a break-up of the United Nations.

That would be no catastrophe. One could still have the UN, and it would still be very useful as a umbrella organization. But it may also well be, and this is seen everywhere in human history, that those far down have to go through a phase, often called a revolutionary phase, of withdrawal in order to liberate themselves and become truly independent. I will call this a phase a *dissociation*. That is what happens when a teenager leaves home: the only way to become independent of one's parents is to live outside one's parents' home, not necessarily for a long time. Some people have a puberty crisis which lasts through their whole life and never get to a reasonable, egalitarian relation with their parents. Other people can do it quickly.

But at some point, some kind of dissociation seems to be indispensable. Of course, the top dogs will always say: look, you lose so much, you will go down in GNP per capita, you will no longer be protected by us! And this is exactly the point: better independent and poor, than rich but on one's knees, to quote both Sekou Toure and Julius Nyerere.

All of this is completely compatible with the idea of the United Nations, just as UNCTAD survived the idea of a separate meeting of the Algerian nations. What is wrong with UNCTAD seems to be that the group of 77 were too modest, that they should have gone much further along this line and that they were having a separate *meeting* only, agreeing on how to vote. This is not enough; much more is needed, and by separate *organizations* to see to it that what one needs is organized by oneself and does not come handed down on a platter from the big powers.

To take another example: look at the news agencies in the world. The 5 big news agencies are the following: Tass is Russian, AP and UPI are American, Reuter is British, AFP is French. Where is the news agency of the world village?

Thus there are many different possibilities, and later on in this century they will emerge. What is said here is in a sense a combination of prescription and prediction: it is a good thing, *and* it will happen, probably with many oscillations around this line, the line between the moderates and the radicals.

But these are not the only possibilities in defeudalizing a structure. What has been said so far essentially amounts to one thing: the idea of strengthening the power positions of those who are low, relative to those who are high.

But there is also another approach: the idea of strengthening the super-structure surrounding it all so that it penetrates into the big powers' spheres of interest. The question of creating a UN which is able to vie with the big powers as a focus of attraction would be an example of that approach. An example is found in the UN resolution to the effect that the moon should belong to everybody. The moon belongs to humanity, nobody can plant a flag and claim it. They cannot do as Cook did in New Zealand in 1770, the first to come will have to do it in the name of humanity [6]. But it is not so certain that the Big Two will do so in the name of UN or humanity when they land. The UN flag was conspicuously absent from Charlie Brown and Snoopy. I do not see it on the Vostoks either. There is usually relatively little talk of humanity, and much, much talk about the USA and the Soviet Union.

Much worse is the situation at the other extreme, at the bottom of the ocean, on the ocean floor, where we now have the US Navy vigorously protesting efforts to ban all military establishments on the ocean floor. There is serious talk about trip-wire mechanisms on the ocean floor to get the other one into some kind of mesh where he will trigger a cascade of all kinds of explosives, possibly nuclear, if he goes too far. This is the logic of the bloc policy, of the balance of deterrence: it knows no geographical limits.

The sad fact is that the UN has acted too slowly, and the small countries have not been radical enough to see the necessity of such measures. Very often they have been uniquely concerned with immediate problems, and it took one very particular person, Ambassador Pardo of Malta to really put the ocean floor issue effectively on the agenda.

The idea of UN ownership of outer space, of international waters, of the ocean floor, of the atmosphere above the oceans, of the remaining unpopulated areas; the idea of UN taxation of communications satellites, of proceeds from the ocean floor; the idea of UN revenue for renting outer space when one uses a satellite, of revenue for exploitation of the ocean floor, of the atmosphere and the unpopulated areas: all these ideas have been circulating for some time and are all important. They would strengthen the UN, because they would give independent sources of income which could be used to redistribute resources in the world, and thus implicitly weaken the power position of the two Big Brothers. But just as important as this is a system of security which penetrates into and through the regional cocoons which today are so effectively built around the interests of the big powers.

4. Conclusion

Internationally the feudal system is still very viable and visible, it is here; the world has not yet had its 1789, the UN is a meeting place, effective and efficient as such, but it is not a place which has seriously changed or even challenged that structure. Some pessimists would even say that maybe the structure will just appear and reappear again under other guises.

There may be something to that, and it may be that the historically best period is the period between two feudal structures; the period when we fight against one and still have the illusion that the other one will not come, like the period between aristocracy and meritocracy when aristocracy was out, old-fashioned, and meritocracy not yet quite in.

But even if this is the case we still have not even come to that point internationally. 1789 did much to change the old feudal system and make the nation-states more visible to us. But the international systems above, and the intra-national systems, remained basically feudal inside. We therefore have a solid revolution in the making, not only in schools, universities, prisons, mental hospitals, industries, and incidentally in the family — but also in the international system, against the big powers.

We do not have that revolution yet. It is not really showing up on the horizon.

But it will come.

IV.11. A Structural Theory of Integration*

From *Journal of Peace Research* IV/4 (1967). PRIO publication No. 25—6. Notes on page *708*.

1. Introduction

This article has grown out of a feeling of dissatisfaction with the general state of affairs in the theory of integration. More particularly, I feel that this basic concept in the social sciences has not been given the prominent place it deserves, and that authors, instead of trying to develop anything like a general theory of integration, focus on very special cases (such as integration of nations), and on integration as a rational, egalitarian, and legitimate device with explicit goals (and not, for instance, as the result of even irrational conquest).

But the most general weakness in contemporary theories of integration, I feel, is the tendency to confuse the *definition* of integration on the one hand, with *conditions* promoting integration and *consequences* resulting from integration on the other. Of course, anyone may be free to define 'integration' as he deems best, but we shall prefer to see the following as conditions rather than as definitions:

I. *Integration as value-integration*

1. *Egalitarian model.* This is integration of values in the sense often found in international relations theory: actors are seen as having 'coinciding interests'. In general, the actors are coupled together in such a way that a higher state of value for one actor is also a higher state for another actor — as opposed to the conflict-coupling where higher values for one exclude higher values for the other. In the case of nations this means that they are coupled together in such a way that they are either 'low' on the value-dimension (e.g. prosperity) together; or 'high' together [1], the combinations 'low-high' and 'high-low' are excluded. Translated to the integration of actors this is the case where actors can be united and conflicts solved because there are no conflicts: there are no (or only a few)

states of the world so that high value for one actor excludes high value for the other. Thus, this is a way of obtaining egalitarian integration, because no actor need prevail over any other.

2. *Hierarchical model.* This is 'integration of values' in the sense often found in psychology and sociology, and perhaps particularly often in social psychology: values are arranged in a hierarchy so that dilemmas can be solved by picking the value highest in the hierarchy. If the hierarchy is *linear*, then all such conflicts can be solved; if it is only *pyramidal*, then no priority relation is given for some pairs of values. Translated to the 'integration of actors': this is the simple case where actors are ranked or stratified, and all conflicts are 'solved' according to the principle that the actor with higher rank prevails over the actor with lower rank [2].

II. *Integration as actor-integration*

3. *Similarity model.* Here integration is seen as a process of increasing *similarity* between actors. There are many kinds of similarity: similarity of rank, similarity in demographic composition, in economic structure or in political structure. The last cases are usually referred to as *homology*, a similarity in structure so that each member of one actor can find his 'opposite number' in the other actor. Another aspect of homology, or perhaps of cultural similarity, would be *harmonization* of laws and regulations. In the literature on the East-West conflict this is usually known as the 'convergence thesis', with the implicit assumption that the greater the similarity, the more peaceful the relation.

4. *Interdependence model.* Integration is here seen as a process of increasing *interdependence* between actors. There are many kinds of interdependence: cultural, political, economic — but the last is probably that most usually thought of in this connection. Interdependence is often referred to as 'symbiosis'; the idea being that actors are integrated to the extent that they are coupled together so that what harms one also harms the other, and what is to the benefit of one also is to the benefit of the other. But the coupling need not be so perfect as in the 'coincidence of interests' case.

III. *Integration as exchange between parts and whole*

5. *Loyalty model.* Here the idea is that the integrated whole can only come into being and continue if it is supported by the component parts. This support may be seen as an *input* from parts to whole, as when individuals pay allegiance or loyalty to the nation-state, or nations allocate resources to regional or universal organizations.

6. *Allocation model*. Here the idea is that the integrated whole can only come into being or continue if it has something to offer to the component parts. This offer may be seen as an *output* from whole to parts, as when a nation provides individuals with identity, protection, sense of purpose, etc., and the regional or universal organization serves as a multilateral market-place for persons, goods/capital/services or information, effectively redistributing these resources where they can best be put to use.

There seems to be general agreement that the existence of a new organization, a secretariat or something of the kind, is neither a sufficient nor a necessary condition for integration. And there is also agreement that the six concepts referred to above (and many more could be mentioned) are empirically interrelated. Thus, loyalty and allocation obviously stand in a relation of positive feedback to each other, whereas the egalitarian and hierarchical models can be easily combined both with the similarity and interdependence concepts, respectively — which in turn may be combined with the loyalty and the allocation models [3].

But our point here is that all six constitute *conditions* of integration, and probably also conditions that are neither necessary nor sufficient for integration to take place. It is difficult to identify any of them as *the* criterion of integration, since it is so easy to find counter-examples. Hence, against this background we start our search for a definition that can be used at all levels, regardless of conditions and consequences.

We want a concept of integration that can be used at all possible levels where at least two actors can somehow get together and form something that is more than simply interaction, more than just a social system. *How much* more will have to be decided by *fiat*. But the definition should be applicable to couples, to boys' clubs, to fusion of municipalities, to political unification of nations, to the formation of a world state — but should presuppose as little as possible or even nothing about *how* this process takes place and what the consequences are. To this we now turn.

2. A definition of integration

Integration is integration of something; we assume that the units to be integrated can all be referred to as actors, and that actors can be divided until we reach the social atom, the *individual*. Under what conditions, then, would we say that actors are integrated, that a process of integration has been completed? Our definition is as follows:

Integration is the process whereby two or more actors form a new actor. When the process is completed, the actors are said to be integrated. Converse-

ly, disintegration is the process whereby one actor splits into two or more actors. When the process is completed, the actor is said to be disintegrated.

Integration does not yield a *set* of actors, but a set that can act, a new actor. The employees of an organization eating in the cafeteria do not constitute a new actor, but the staff association, meeting at night in the same place, may do so. Evidently, 'actor' and 'act' are then taken as even more fundamental concepts, but we shall not here enter into the complexities of defining or explicating these terms.

Our definition has one immediate, undisputable virtue: it is short. But its usefulness has to be judged by other criteria. For instance, does it help us in locating important problems? We think it does, and shall give some examples.

Integration is here seen as a process, a gradual build-up with a discontinuous end result: *a new actor is born,* and the original actors are then said to have become integrated. Since the new actor is supposed to act in some context, he must be launched in a system where he has at least one contra-actor [4]. And this immediately points to three important dimensions of integration.

First, we should distinguish between integration whereby a new actor of the *same* kind is created, and integration that leads to a new actor of a *different* kind. When two municipalities coalesce completely and form a new municipality, a new actor of the same kind, only bigger, has been born. This is generally the case when the original actors are no longer discernible. This particular case of integration may be referred to as *fusion* (with *fission* for the corresponding disintegration). But when two individuals, man and woman, form a *couple*, an actor of a different kind has been created.

Second, integration as defined here obviously has its *internal* aspects concerning the changing relations between the original actors needed to integrate them, and its *external* aspects concerning the relations of both the original and the new actor to other actors. From the internal point of view this is a question of *capability*: are the original actors, in fact, capable of producing a new actor? And from the external point of view it is a question of *recognition*: does the environment, in fact, deal with the new unit that pretends to be integrated, or does it still operate as if the integration had not taken place? This leads to the fourfold table presented in Table 11.1. In case 1 there is full-fledged integration, whereas in case 4 there is clearly only a pretence. The borderline cases, 2 and 3, are particularly interesting. Case 2 is reminiscent of the relation between the EEC and the socialist countries in Europe: there is certainly a measure of capability, e.g. coordination, but the socialist states still — by and large — refuse to deal with the Community as such (e.g. by not having diplomatic representations), preferring

369

TABLE 11.1 *Internal and external aspects of integration processes*

| | | External aspect | |
		new actor recognized	new actor not recognized
Internal aspect	new actor capable	1	2
	new actor incapable	3	4

to deal with the six constituent actors. Case 3 is the opposite of this: the environment sees more unity than there is, as when the 'imperialists' or the 'communists' or the 'third world' are treated as if they were one actor. In both cases, the discrepancy between the internal and external perspectives may lead to quite interesting consequences and this in turn, leads to some more refined distinctions [5] building on well-known concepts in integration theory:

domain: the number of *actors* involved in the integration — and here we should distinguish between *internal domain* (the number of actors the new actor has been capable of absorbing) and *external domain* (the number of actors recognizing the new actor).

scope: the number of *functions* involved in the integration — and here we should also distinguish between *internal scope* (the scope of the internal interaction necessary to maintain the capability) and *external scope* (the scope of the interaction with external actors).

It may be fruitful to lay down as a precization of the definition that the integration process is not fully completed before external and internal domains coincide. Hence integration should be seen as a process involving not only the constituent actors but also their environment. Only when the new actor is so firmly integrated that the images formed by self and by others coincide, is the integration process completed.

So far we have talked very generally about integration: let us now be more specific. At the level of individuals: on what basis do individuals integrate at all and form new actors? Which are the principles of integration that tie them together?

A first distinction is obviously between *geographical* and *functional* or *social* principles of integration. In the *geographical* case, actors are integrated by virtue of the fact that they are found within the same contiguous (or nearly contiguous) territory. The actors are tied together before integration by the relation of simple *spatial proximity*, and integration is then spun around this relation. Of course, for any integration to take place in anything but an abstract way *temporal proximity* is also needed; the actors have to coexist in time, not only in space. But we regard that as a trivial category since we are dealing with concrete integration, not — for instance — with feelings of closeness or coexistence with ancestry and posterity.

In the *functional* or *social* case, actors are also related to each other before any integration takes place, but this time by social relations. Social relations can be of two kinds: *concrete* relations of *interaction* and *interdependence* whereby actors exchange something, and *abstract* relations where nothing need be exchanged between them; actors are only somehow compared. Examples of the former are the relations inside a factory between management, white collar, and blue collar workers; examples of the latter are such relations as *similarity* (e.g. same sex, same occupation) or *dissimilarity* (e.g. inferiority, superiority). But we shall cut through this variety and state simply that there are two social bases for integration: *interdependence* and *similarity*; and discuss them at greater length.

In the case of *interdependence*, we are simply dealing with actors interrelated by exchange: in other words, with actors interacting. In sociology this is usually referred to as a *social system*, but when the patterns of expected interaction are crystallized into interrelated statuses a certain permanence is achieved, and this is dignified by the term *organization*. Thus, an organization is a set of statuses filled with actors mutually interdependent, so that if one status is emptied completely (e.g. by all status-incumbents going on strike), the organization is no longer the same. But this does not necessarily mean that the organization perishes: it may continue because some of the functions of that status may be carried out by others, etc. Characteristic of an organization is only that there is a *division of labor*: not all members perform the same work. The net result of this interdependence is some kind of product, and sociologists analyze these products by institutional realms. Thus, in the economy *goods* are produced, in policy *decisions*, in science *knowledge*, in religion *salvation*, and so on.

In organizations two important dimensions seem to be the degree of *indispensability of a status*, i.e. how necessary a given status is to the continued operation of the organization, and *insubstitutability of an actor*, i.e. to what extent a given actor can be replaced by another actor filling the same status. Thus, the worker as a *status* is completely indispensable in a factory, but the individual worker as an *actor* is usually highly substitutable the way most production processes are set up in modern, industrialized societies, whether capitalist or socialist. What one worker does could just as well be carried out by somebody else — the work-product is invariant under substitution of status-holder (often referred to as 'rationalization'). But this is not true for many intellectuals: they often have a relation to their work-product that is intrinsic in the sense that no other person could do exactly the same. Characteristically, the intellectual's name usually appears on the book he turns out, whereas the worker's product is anonymous [6], even when it is not an assembly line product, but the product of one man.

To tie this in with another important concept: substitutability seems to be one, or perhaps *the*, structural basis of *alienation*. But alienation can also be generalized: just as the individual *actor* is alienated by a high level of substitutability even if this substitution is not, in fact, carried out, the *status* as such will also be alienated by a high level of dispensability, or expendability. And both indispensability and insubstitutability can now be seen as two factors related to the ranking of statuses in an organization. On top, in general, are (almost) indispensable statuses (e.g. the manager) whose status-incumbents are (almost) insubstitutable — permitted and even prescribed to leave a personal imprint on the way they fulfill their status obligations. At the bottom level, in general, are the highly substitutable actors in highly dispensable statuses (the messenger boy), with the insubstitutable actors in dispensable statuses (the servant), and the substitutable actors in indispensable statuses (the workers) in between. Thus, to account for organizations we have to study *both* how statuses relate to the organization as a whole, and how individual actors relate to their statuses.

We now turn to the second basis for social integration: *similarity*. The mechanism used here is not interdependence of the kind described above, but likeness: the actors are like each other in one or more respects. Again, it may be fruitful to distinguish between two basic types of similarity around which integrative attempts can be built and an *association* formed: similarity in the sense that actors have the same *status*, and similarity in the sense that actors have the same *values*. In the first case, actors come together because of similar positions in comparable social structures and for that reason have shared perspectives and interests; in the latter case, they come together because of shared values. Of course, the two do not exclude each other but may empirically be found together and reinforce each other, as in the case of socialist trade unions.

A very basic distinction between organizations and associations can now be made clear: the former tend to be more vertical, the latter more horizontal. In organization, by definitions based on division of labor, *statuses* tend to be ranked; and degree of indispensability and insubstitutability seem to have much to do with this ranking. This does not [7] mean that *actors* are necessarily also ranked — they are only implicitly ranked if they are very firmly tied to one status. But at the status level there seems to be a vertical dimension in organizations, even though there are very many ways of reducing its impact. And this vertical dimension is not found in associations — at least not in the same way. For whereas *organizations* by definition are based on *dissimilarity*, by virtue of the division of labor principle, *associations* are by definition based on *similarity*. This similarity is contradictory to a strictly vertical organization, but highly compatible with a horizontal pattern.

On the other hand, associations take some of the characteristics of organizations by introducing an element of division of labor, such as a distinction between members, board, and executives — a division of labor with clear rank implications. But there is a rather basic distinction between the president of an association and the director of an organization: the former is 'one of us', is usually elected for a limited period with rotation built into the pattern, whereas the latter is usually appointed for life or an indefinite period. In general, organizations and associations, built on division of labor and on similarity respectively, obviously serve as models for each other in the sense that associations (especially the big ones) tend to imitate the structure of organizations and to become similarly rigid, whereas organizations (especially the small ones) may tend to imitate the structure of associations and, for instance, introduce rotation schemes. For that reason we cannot simply say that 'organizations are vertical, associations are horizontal': they are both in-between, with organizations generally more on the vertical side and associations generally more on the horizontal side.

Thus, we have distinguished between the following types of integration shown in Fig. 11.1. We shall not make much use of the last distinction, since it is both less sharp and less basic. But the trichotomy in *territory*, *organization*, and *association* is basic, and *we claim*

FIGURE 11.1 *The basic types of integration*

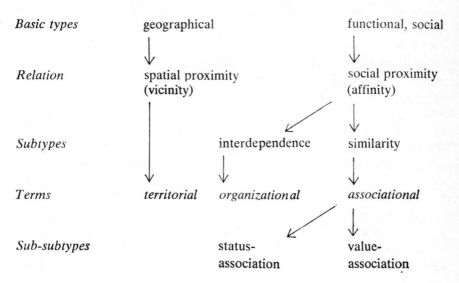

Basic types	geographical		functional, social
Relation	spatial proximity (vicinity)		social proximity (affinity)
Subtypes		interdependence	similarity
Terms	*territorial*	*organizational*	*associational*
Sub-subtypes		status-association	value-association

that these are the three basic elements in human integration. Of course, a given case of integration may not have the purity of the typology in Fig. 11.1, but be based on a mixture. For instance, a village may at the same time be a production community and have similarity built into it, at least by virtue of the fact that the individuals are all members of the same village.

These three basic elements in human integration can now also be seen as three basic modes of human existence. We all live in spatial contexts, in organizations and associations, but different individuals, different societies, different eras and areas may be particularly strong on one and weak on one or two of the others. The mixture ratio is by no means fixed; there are wide ranges within which variety is possible. For this reason it is interesting to explore how the three principles of integration relate to each other, and efforts in that direction will be made in subsequent sections.

3. Toward a calculus of integration

Integration has been defined as 'the process whereby two or more actors form a new actor'. Formally, it can be represented as an operator I, operating on a set of actors, A, creating a new actor A^*. But what has happened once can happen twice: the integration operator can be applied to the outcomes of the first integration process and yield integration of a higher order, and theoretically this may go on and on. Thus, by stepwise integration, military hierarchies are formed: soldiers are integrated into a troop, troops into a company, companies into a battalion, battalions into a regiment, regiments into a brigade, brigades into an army, yielding a six-fold application of the integration operator (and more could be added, for instance by integrating army, navy, and air force into a national defense, by integrating the defense of various nations into an alliance, etc.).

The three basic types of integration posited in Fig. 11.1., viz. territorial, organizational, and associational integration, can now be brought into this 'calculus' as three operators — T,O, and A respectively. Single application of these operators to a set of individuals yields well-known results: $T(i)$ is an actor based on all individuals found within the confines of a given, contiguous territory: $O(i)$ is an actor based on individuals tied together in an organization by a relation of interdependence, in a production community, and $A(i)$ is an actor based on individuals tied together in an association by virtue of being somehow similar.

Multiple applications of those operators yield more interesting results. Obviously, n applications yield 3^n different types of actors since there are three archetypes, and for $n = 2$ we get the following types with examples shown in Table 11.2. Clearly, the integration operator is not commutative.

There is considerable difference between the pairs TO and OT, TA and AT, and AO and OA. At the same time the operation can be defined as associative, and an 'identity integrator' (leaving the set of actors intact) and 'disintegrator' (reversing the process, reviving the original actors) may be introduced. Thus, the set of integration operators may be said to have the mathematical group structure, but this is a very weak structure that does not seem to produce interesting insights in and by itself.

TABLE 11.2 *Nine types of actors resulting from double integration*

No.	Symbol	First integration	Second integration	Example
1	TT(i)	territorial	territorial	nation, seen as an integration of municipalities, provinces
2	TO(i)	organizational	territorial	nation, seen as an integration of organizations
3	TA(i)	associational	territorial	nation, seen as an integration of associations
4	OT(i)	territorial	organizational	commonwealth type of integration of nations, with a mother country
5	OO(i)	organizational	organizational	clans integrated into super-clan
6	OA(i)	associational	organizational	race-societies, based on hierarchy of races
7	AT(i)	territorial	associational	associations of cities
8	AO(i)	organizational	associational	associations of factories in the same branch
9	AA(i)	associational	associational	unions of trade unions

More promising are efforts to use these simple tools as the fundamental concepts in a language in which numerous problems can be expressed. We shall look at some of these problems.

3.1. *Nation-building*

How does one build a nation? If we assume that the nation has the average size of nations today, around 3 million inhabitants, there will usually be some actors interspersed between the top national level and the lowest micro-level — which we take to be the level of the individual. Some immediate results of the application of the three integrators at this bottom level are shown below:

Micro-level integration

territorial	*organizational*	*associational*
(extended) *household*	(extended) *family*	*peer group*

The family is probably primordial here, with its spatial integration into a household and its structure with similar and dissimilar actors, yielding a basis both for production and consumption organization and for associations of peer groups that are collateral (e.g. siblings, parents). Thus, the family gives training in all three, in territorial, organizational, and associational integration as well. And this is probably one major reason both for the strength and the prevalence of the family as a social unit: it is small enough to combine. all three principles. This is not so easy at higher levels of organization, and the family is also threatened when or if one of these three bases is weakened.

Using the three integrators at intermediate levels we now arrive at three ways, in principle, of building a nation. The classical way is through repeated application of the *territorial* integration process: e.g. individuals are tied together in municipalities, municipalities in provinces, and provinces in nations.

But this is not the only way. We could also imagine the basic unit to be the *organization* and the nation to be set up through them. Thus, we could create associations of all organizations with the same output (all farms, all factories, all firms in the same branch, all universities), and then integrate these associations vertically and/or horizontally. The nation in the world that comes closest to this is probably Japan.

And then there is the third way: to base the nation on *associations*. We could imagine two basic models: the status-association, which would lead to a *corporate state*; and the value-association, which leads to the *party-state*. In practice, parties unite not only people with the same values but also people with the same status, although neither unification is perfect. In either case, the result would be some kind of association of associations expressed in a national assembly of representatives of status- and value-associations. The closest example of the former would be some aspects of the systems found in Mussolini's Italy, in Vargas' Brazil, in Mexico under Partido Revolucionario Institucional, and in Argentina under Peron. And the typical example of the latter is found in most parliamentary democracies.

However, we should add that empirical systems, as usual, show a mixture of the forms discussed here. There is an interpenetration, or transgression, of the geographical foci into the organizational and associational structures. Most concretely this is found in the form of local chapters of associations, including parties, at municipal and provincial levels. Elections are broken up by territorial units. And here there is a distinct asymmetry: there is nothing quite corresponding to the way in which geography chops up associations: associations do not subdivide geography the same way.

Thus, nations can be built in many ways, and we have so far only considered some varieties. If we introduce two integrative levels, more nuances can be captured. Thus, at the lowest level would be individuals; then at the next level organizations or associations, or both. They could then be linked together in territorial subdivisions, simply by virtue of proximity, and these geographical units could then form the nation together. Or, we could start with the geographical units, e.g. at the level of the municipality, and combine them in associations or even organizations — the latter with division of labor and some element of stratification, e.g. in districts that specialize in the primary, secondary and tertiary sectors of the economy respectively. The net result would still be a nation, but the internal structures would be entirely different.

3.2. *World-building*

All these ideas can now, *mutatis mutandis*, be applied to the task of world-building. In principle the task is not too different from nation-building, the structure of the building blocks being essentially the same, but since the scale is different the relative prominence given to the three principles of integration is bound to differ considerably.

Using nations as building blocks there are in principle three ways of proceeding further:

Territorial integration: joining together nations by the principle of *vicinity*, because they are located close together. This is usually referred to as *regionalism*.

Organizational or vertical integration: joining together nations by the principle of division of labor into an interdependent system. This is usually referred to as (neo-)*colonialism*.

Associational or horizontal integration: joining together nations by the principle of *affinity*, because they have some kind of similarity. This is usually referred to as *functionalism*, and leads to an international, governmental organization, an IGO.

A given case of integration will usually display elements of all three principles of integration. One simple reason is the cost of transportation and communication: with the distances in international space, geography will of necessity play a considerable role and there will be a tendency to give some prominence to territorial integration — in other words, to regionalism. Thus, in principle we could repeat the maneuvers from nation-building and start with territorial integration *or* with organizational/associational integration.

But for world-building the matter is somewhat different. To start with world-wide associational integration, e.g. according to profession/occupation or according to ideological preference, and then use these associations as building blocks would be to build a house on sand. Transportation and communication are still dependent on distance, which gives prominence to contiguity and vicinity, not to interdependence, and absolutely not to similarity. Hence, first level integration will probably still be dominated by the territorial principle; and this being said, it is clear that there is at present less leeway in world-bulding than in nation-building. But this is highly dependent on the state of transportation and communication. And every change will disfavor territorial integration, since innovations in the field of communication and transport, once made, are hard to lose.

The other two types of integration, organizational and associational, are nevertheless distinguishable even if they are not so prominent. Characteristic of an *organization* of nations is division of labor, for instance between producers of primary goods and producers of manufactured goods. And the criterion of a vertical element is also included: nations may be military, political, economic or cultural powers, dominating others. In the colonial systems, and in the modern power-bloc systems, all four tend to go together; in the neo-colonial system the structure is carried over inside universal, apparently 'democratic' organizations.

The *association* of nations, or horizontal integration, would be exemplified by the international governmental organizations where nations join on the traditional basis of 'one nation, one vote'. Like associations consisting of individuals, there is here an element of built-in division of labor, but this time between the member nations on the one hand and the international secretariat on the other. Moreover, there is usually an assumption of rotation in the secretariat, at least in principle — so as to reduce the dominance of many nations by a small group of very powerful nations. Clearly, however, nations may increase their power by controlling the secretariat, or by controlling votes of other nations, etc., so the distinction between associational and organizational integration in the field of nations is certainly not a very sharp one — nor is it very sharp in the field of individuals, as already pointed out. These must be regarded as ideal types, relatively well approximated in the colonial empire on the one hand and in some of the UN specialized agencies on the other.

At any rate, it is clear that the term 'vertical' means two very different things in the theory of world-building: the dominance exercised by one nation over several others (in organizational integration) and the dominance exercised by an association over its members (in associational integration),. The second case, however, is not a case of vertical integration, but of horizontal integration where the autonomy and identity of the individual actors are about to disappear completely with the emergence of the new actor, the IGO.

Thus, in world-building as seen today the first step is generally territorial, and the second step may be territorial, organizational or associational — leading to three well-known principles of integration that may be combined in several ways. Today the territorially contiguous tends to be more horizontal; for vertical integration to occur, territorial non-contiguity seems to be a condition. To maintain an explicit hierarchical order relative to close neighbors seems today to be difficult but there are still remnants of the old tradition from colonial times of having subordinate nations 'overseas'.

This being said, we should emphasize that with a longer time-perspective there is no reason why nations should be the major building blocks in a future world order. Given the size of the world and the principle of limited control, we might perhaps hypothesize that between three or five levels of integration would be needed to build a world [8]. This gives many possibilities of combining the integration principles, particularly since the principles do not exclude each other. One might start all over the world with organizational integration, just to ensure that products are, in fact, produced. Out of these vertical organizations horizontal associations are bound to emerge, reflecting interests and values in a vertical structure. Due to the principle of geographical transgression these horizontal organizations are still quite likely to be based on national and even local 'chapters'. But just as geographical integration comprises everybody regardless of social position, associational integration could in principle comprise everybody regardless of geographical position — as long as these international, non-governmental organizations (INGOs) differ according to whether they are based on direct individual membership or the membership is indirect, mediated through interspersed levels of geographically determined integration.

Taking INGOs, of the direct or indirect kinds, as building blocks we could then proceed further. There would be no sense in more geographical integration, since the INGO has already been extended all over the world. But, they could still be vertically or horizontally integrated. Thus, to take the latter, which is simplest: INGOs with a certain similarity can group together in super-INGOs — as when international councils of scientific unions are formed. But this development can take place parallel to a similar development using geographical integration as building blocks. Nations can be brought together in super-nations or other types of systems, and so on, with the net result of a very complicated world integrated in a criss-crossing fashion, and in many different ways, at the same time. In such a world there would no doubt be important problems of loyalty, but at the same time a complexity in the integrative principles that would more or less eliminate clear-cut, simple borderlines between integrated actors.

4. Changes in principles of integration

So far we have presented the tripartite conception of integration based on a very simple definition of integration. The question is now the following: why do the principles of integration change? Why does a system not remain content, stabilize around the formula T^3, or TAT, or TAO, or any other way of building a nation? Why all these changes, all this 'messing around'? The answer seems to be that these types of integration satisfy different needs. To account for such changes — or for any social change, for that matter — we have found a particular combination of structural-functional and dialectical thinking to be useful. The argument is, roughly, as follows.

Imagine a social system with a set of values to be fulfilled/satisfied — we shall refer to them as *functions*, f_1, f_2, ...f_n. To fulfil these functions the system has a number of devices — like schooling for the function of education. We shall refer to them as *structures*, s_1, s_2, ...s_m [9]. In general there is no simple correspondence between functions and structures. Of course, we could imagine social systems with m = n and a one-one correspondence, so that each structure satisfied one and only one function. But in general one structure contributes, positively or negatively, to more than one function, and vice versa: one function has inputs, positive or negative, from more than one structure. Thus, schools also serve the functions of national integration, of indoctrination in a common culture, of diffusing standards with regard to health and behavior in general — and all of these functions also have inputs from other structures in modern societies.

The net result is a matrix, which we call the structural-functional matrix or sf-matrix for short. This is shown in Fig. 11.2.

FIGURE 11.2 *A structural-functional matrix*

	f_1	f_2	.	.	.	.	.	.	fr
s_1	+	−	.	.	.	.	.	.	+
s_2	−	+	.	.	.	.	.	.	0
.	.	.	.	.	.	.	.	.	.
.	.	.	.	.	.	.	.	.	.
s	0	+	.	.	.	.	.	.	−

Here pluses, minuses, and zeros can be distributed according to whether the input of structure s_i to function f_j is positive, negative, or zero. In structural-functional jargon, the structure is then referred to as eufunctional, dysfunctional, or non-functional respectively, *with respect to that particular function* — the latter qualification is often forgotten.

Within this matrix, a number of propositions about social change can now be formulated. Obviously, each minus is like a warning light, like a signal of coming change. One could now imagine, for each structure and for each function, a figure expressing the average contribution of that structure to the total system, and a figure expressing the average level of fulfillment of the function. This could be done by means of a weighted additive index, where the weights would reflect the relative importance of structures and functions; and technically the simple devices of pre-multiplication with a row vector filled with weight for the structures, and postmultiplication by a column vector giving the weights for the functions could be used. The idea would then be that something will happen to/has to be done with (depending on whether one is engaged in predictive or prescriptive activity) the structures and functions ranking negatively when ordered according to these indices. What this readjustment should consist in, however, is not so obvious.

In general, some rearrangements will take place, increasing the number of pluses and reducing the number of minuses. But this can be done in many ways. For instance, a function that most structures contribute negatively to is obviously not fulfilled. But from this it does not follow that all structures have to be changed: another approach would simply be to give up the function (e.g. pre-, extra- and postmarital sexual abstinence) and simply strike it out from the value-repertoire of the system. And similarly: if a structure has merely negative contributions to make, the response would probably not consist in changing all functions, but rather in eliminating the structure.

Thus, social change can be seen as a continuous striving, an effort to adjust the matrix. The task derives its character of being perpetual from the simple circumstance that whenever new structures replace old ones — in order to fulfill new functions or eliminate minuses in connection with old functions — new minuses are likely to appear and often at very unexpected places.

However, it can be argued that this is immaterial so long as at any given point in time, pluses sufficiently outweigh minuses. The assumption would then be that as long as the overall picture for a structure or a function is positive, that structure or function will be able to survive. In other words, we assume also that given the configuration of structures and functions and the sf-matrix at a given point in time t, with good, positive balances for all structures and all functions, the best prediction we could come up with would be that there need be *no change*.

This is about as far as the structural-functional principles carry us, and this is useful as a heuristic device pointing to the interdependencies between m structures and n functions. But it is not satisfactory, *for it assumes a symmetry between pluses and minuses that is probably unrealistic.* The reasoning so far assumes that if pluses compensate for minuses at one point in time, they will also do so at a later point in time, if there have been no changes in structures and functions. But this assumes that the interior of the matrix is only a function of the entries. *What is forgotten is the changing nature of these relations over time when pluses are increasingly taken for granted, and frustration due to the minuses accumulates.* If human beings had the same ability to perceive and to appreciate a well-functioning relationship as they have to perceive and deprecate a badly functioning relationship, then the model above might be a close approximation to social reality. But with time, the functions fulfilled by the structure tend to be, if not forgotten, at least taken for granted, as a part of social nature much like the air around us (appreciated only when it disappears in smoke or under water). And there is a quantitative accumulation of frustration due to the negative inputs from the structures. Less and less will be said, written, or at least felt about the functions fulfilled; more and more about the functions not fulfilled. In this sense, each structure bears within it the seeds of its own destruction.

But what if we had a structure with no minuses at all? Would this structure also be self-destroying? This is less obvious, but it may be argued that since ideologies, value-patterns, etc., are constantly changing, 'sooner or later' functions will appear according to which even the most functional structure will appear as negative. Moreover, sf-matrices usually have an internal logic, in the sense that ideologies that make some structures look dysfunctional also have a tendency to extend this evaluation to a cluster of structures. Hence, unless the system is very simple and isolated, with a very limited number of functions and a limited number of structures that have a simple and clear and well-integrated (in the usual sociological sense) relation to the functions (as in many monasteries) — unless these conditions are fulfilled, the system is bound to develop some minuses in its associated sf-matrix sooner or later, if only in the minds of some participants. That raises the question of what kinds of system might escape this fate and persist in some kinds of blissful innocence; the answer would be: very small communities like kibbutzim, perhaps some village systems, and above all: utopias. The sf-matrix without minuses is one of the criteria by which all utopias seem recognizable. And this seems to underline even further how unrealistic that idea is; it seems to underestimate the extent to which man is 'looking for trouble', or, in our language, to have minuses in his perceived sf-matrix.

Let us now apply these principles to the relation between the three principles of integration by asking: what are the major functions these principles fulfill? There are at least four such functions; production or output, variation or heterogeneity, security or homogeneity, and equality or justice. By and large, the functions seem to relate to the three principles of integration in the way shown in Table 11.3.

TABLE 11.3 *An sf-matrix for the three principles of integration*

	production, output	heterogeneity, variety	homogeneity, security	equality, justice
territorial integration	0	+	+	0
organizational integration	+	+	—	—
associational integration	—	—	+	+

As we have put it here, each type of integration satisfies only two of the four functions. To start with organizational integration: its *raison d'être* is to produce some kind of output; so far, we do not seem to know any way this can be done without an element of division of labor, or a way of dividing labor without also introducing an element of stratification of *statuses* (not of actors). This means that organizations, except at a very primitive level with very simple output, not only produce output, but also satisfy the requirement of variety and heterogeneity. But this variety is vertical, it is variety bought at the expense of stratification and curtailed by social distance — hence the minus for equality. At the same time this heterogeneity also usually represents a challenge and a threat — from which follows the minus for security.

Associational integration is the answer here. It is supposed to provide the individuals with a setting of equality and with the type of security derived from homogeneity, whether this homogeneity is due to sharing status or sharing value (ideology). Thus, associations, having a membership criterion, are in principle designed to counteract heterogeneity; but this is a question of degree, depending on how many membership criteria are employed. And associations do not produce: they are precluded from doing so by having built into them a measure of equality and homogeneity hard to reconcile with most production processes.

Territorial integration combines heterogeneity and homogeneity — as in the nation-state where everybody is a citizen, yet different from most others on many other criteria. Of course, the nation-state more resembles the association as to principles of equality and homogeneity defining the roles of the citizen; and more resembles organizations as to production and heterogeneity. But by and large we cannot say that the territorial unit produces. True, most factories today show territorial contiguity, but that is merely due to our poor means of transportation (of materials, goods, people) and communication (of messages, for control purposes [10]). But that organizations tend to have a territorial basis does not mean that any territorial unit *can* be used for production, or *is* used for production: countless numbers of villages around the world are not *organizationally* integrated, even if they are *territorially* integrated.

We now assume that human beings need production/output to survive, that they need some measure of heterogeneity/variety to be stimulated, that they need some measure of homogeneity/security to thrive, and that they need contexts with an atmosphere of equality and possible justice. But this means that a focus on only one of the principles of integration will lead to accumulated frustration; the minuses will be ever more heavily felt, and the net result will be some kind of rupture, and the emergence of a new focus of integration.

Thus, we could put the three principles down as a triangle:

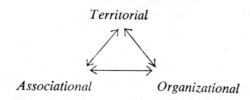

Territorial

Associational   *Organizational*

The transitions can probably be in all directions, but just to indicate a clockwise cycle:

1. *Territorial integration yields to organizational integration,* simply because of a demand for higher output. Territories do not produce: organizations do, and the more so the more people identify with them and the more people perceive them as sources of gratification.

2. *Organizational integration yields to associational integration,* because of a demand for equality and justice, and a highly felt need to be closer to people similar to oneself. Autonomy and dignity are derived from such memberships; visions of change likewise — even realization of such visions. The focus of identification with the organization is gradually reduced; the focus of interest is on the associations.

3. *Associational integration yields to territorial integration,* because of a need for some type of unification that can offer heterogeneity and variety again. Life in an association becomes too limited, too one-sided; it appeals to only a small segment of the personality. Territorial integration offers a possibility for renewed union, for sewing together what is kept apart

or within bonds, behind the lines drawn around trade unions, classes, races, etc.

Thus, there are sufficient forces present in any social system to maintain processes from any basis to any other basis. But this does not mean that one has to pass through phases with only one of the integration principles prevailing at a time:

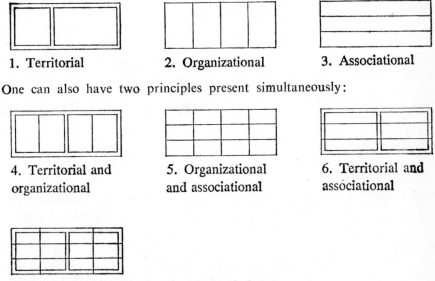

1. Territorial   2. Organizational   3. Associational

One can also have two principles present simultaneously:

4. Territorial and   5. Organizational   6. Territorial and
organizational   and associational   associational

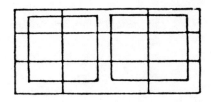

7. Territorial, organizational and associational

Not to mention that all three principles can be present at the same time:

Essentially, the figures give us three different ways of constructing a nation, mentioned in the preceding section; with the first three of many African nations, of Japan and of India, (as a set of castes), respectively, and the last one more typical of Western societies. Here we shall not develop this in any detail, but rather turn to the major topic: dynamism in the principles of integration. We shall formulate this dynamism in a certain sense dramatically, in terms of *crises*.

The crisis in territorial integration. This crisis is mainly negative, due to increasingly keen competition from organizational and associational integration. By and large we would put most emphasis on the transportation/communication revolution, constantly reducing the role played by continuity. What this means is, essentially, that whatever territorial bond is defined (unless it is universal) communications is likely to transcend it and to create new ties — partly because organization transcends territorial units (creating *interdependencies* across borders), partly because associations transcend territorial units (creating *identification* across borders). This pattern of outgrowing any territorial units is evident all over the world, but more so the more developed the networks of transportation and communication are — which usually means the more developed the nations are in general. Thus, the crisis will be more evident the more developed the territory is; *the territory is abolishing itself, so to speak.* But in this process the great virtues of territorial integration are easily lost sight of. Territorial integration can combine homogeneity: an individual can surround itself with its kith and kin (e.g. in the household, in the neighborhood, in the village) and then surround that protective unit with other units providing heterogeneity in life experience. The condition is, of course, that the total system regulates intra- and inter-unit interaction such that each individual can find a ratio between the two that suits his capacity to digest heterogeneity — and this capacity seems to be extremely variable.

The crisis in organizational integration. This crisis is best known of the three, and by many identified as *the* social crisis. Actually there are two very different aspects: the conflicts arising *between* organizationally integrated actors, and the conflicts arising *within* them. To describe these conflicts the simple paradigm shown in Table 11.4 is useful.

TABLE 11.4 *A paradigm for the analysis of the organizational conflicts*

| | Organizations | |
	O_1	O_2
Topdog level	T_1	T_2
Underdog level	U_1	U_2

The conflict *between* the two organizations O_1 and O_2 may be for markets, for the share of the consumption of the products or the organizations — assuming that O_1 and O_2 are producing the same goods. But O_1 and O_2 may also be political machines competing for voter allegiance; economic organizations (farms in the primary sector, factories in the secondary sector, and firms in the tertiary sector) competing for consumer inclinations; producers of knowledge (universities) competing for intellectual dominance; producers of art competing for their type of dominance; and so on. Best known and best analyzed are the conflicts between economic organizations, but the others can usually be analyzed using the same type of models. Principles of supply and demand regulating prices; principles of elasticity; or of perfect and imperfect competition — not to mention monopoly — are usually immediately translatable.

More important for our purpose are the conflicts *within* the organizations. The conflict is here usually structured around a phenomenon that can be described as *the law of feudalization of stratified system* [11]. By this we mean simply the combination of two tendencies: rank-concordance and *rank-dependence of interaction*. The result is a structure where topdogs tend to be topdogs on many dimensions, and underdogs to be underdogs on many dimensions — and where the interaction is between the topdogs, with some interaction between topdog and 'his' underdogs, and very little interaction between the underdogs. This structure so facilitates organization control by the topdogs that they need not total more than 5%, or even 1%, of the total number of individuals in the organization [12]. The thesis then is that even if the structure is not set up like this from the beginning, it will tend to develop in this direction, unless strong counteracting forces are present. The net result is *exploitation*, very often combined with a high level of substitutability at the bottom of the organization (for instance substitution by foreign immigrants), and with efforts to make the bottom levels expendable (for instance by means of automation) if they cause too much 'trouble' (often referred to as 'social unrest').

There will, sooner or later, be a reaction against this tendency, and the thesis is that *the crisis in organizational integration is conductive to associational integration*. Exploitation has its limits, there will be forces calling for restraints or for revolution. Altogether we can distinguish between five types of integrative moves that take the form of associations, and are outcomes of the crisis in organizations. These are shown in Table 11.5.

We are not saying that all possible associations are the reaction to the internal conflict in organizations; that would be saying that *all* associations have a *class* character. Even more far-fetched would be the idea that all associations can be seen as expressions of conflict in *economic* organizations. But many can be analyzed in this light, and all we are saying in Table 11.5 is that there are six very important types of associations of this kind. These types depend heavily on each other and can be seen as reaction-formation to each other. Let us look more closely at that using Fig. 11.3 as a point of departure.

TABLE 11.5 *Reactive association-formation due to organizational crises.*

	Intranational examples	*International examples*
1. $A(U_1)$, $A(U_2)$	shop unions	union of colonies under same colonizer
2. $A(T_1)$, $A(T_2)$	shop managment unions	big power executive committee in alliances
3. $A(T_1, U_2)$, $A(T_2, U_2)$	total staff association	horizontal commonwealth
4. $A(U_1, U_2)$	nationwide trade union	'trade unions' of colonies, of poor nations, of small powers
5. $A(T_1, T_2)$	nationwide employers' association	worldwide rich nations' club
6. $A(O_1, O_2)$	integration of factories	United Nations

FIGURE 11.3 *Diagrammatical presentation of organizational reaction-formation*

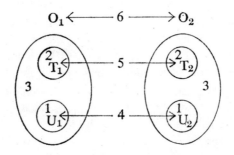

Two types of association-formation can be seen as underdog strategies: the effort to integrate, horizontally, the underdogs in one organization; and the effort to extend this integration (usually territorially) to underdogs in other organizations but in similar positions. The purpose is clear enough: to combat substitutability and expendability, usually under the leadership of some particularly disequilibrated members. Solidarity makes both substitution of actors and elimination of statuses difficult or even impossible, this raising the rank of lower statuses through power to disrupt completely the functioning of the organization. Obviously, extension of the underdog associations makes it more difficult for the topdog in one organization to come to terms with its own underdogs, and also increases the domain of solidarity. This not only increases, but also standardizes the price demanded in bargaining — but usually within territorial confines, thus reinforcing territorial integration.

The most obvious topdog strategies as a reaction to this are obviously nos. 2 and 5: the formation of associations of topdogs. But nos. 3 and 5 can and should also be seen in this light: associations incorporating 'all' very often become associations dominated by the most powerful and most skillful, and the actors with most training in interaction — and in a feudal structure this will almost by necessity have to be the topdogs in the organization. Thus, one typical cycle here would be to start with association no. 1 followed by no. 2 so that the topdogs can better contemplate how they can extend it to no. 3. When there is sufficient capacity to overcome the communication difficulties, all this will then be repeated at a higher level, with the underdog initiating no. 4 and the topdogs responding with nos. 5 and 6. If there is first a period of polarization based on nos. 1 and 2, or on nos. 4 and 5, the gap in bargaining position is much smaller, perhaps even zero or reversed. By that time, strategies nos. 3 and 6 will lose much of their character of being topdog strategies — but not until then. Thus, the wisest underdog strategy is probably not to be absorbed in frameworks involving the 'total personnel', or 'all nations' before they have increased their bargaining position or even changed the organization completely through association-formation and polarization in general.

The net result of all these moves towards association-formation is not easily predictable. When there is consciousness about exploitation, association-formation is a response but not the only one. Apathy, withdrawal, isolated outbursts of violence, etc., may also be among the responses. And association-formation may lead to stronger bargaining positions, and to new formulas for cake-sharing; but it may also lead to revolutions that may change the system or preserve it, in either case at the expense of violence. The present paradigm does not enable us to say when we are likely to get one or the other of these results.

The crisis in associational integration. This crisis is perhaps least frequently identified as such, although there are constant indirect references to it. Thus, a major feature of associations, pointed out above, is their failure to produce. They may induce changes in social structures or at least changes in allocation patterns within social structures, but that is not production. Hence, associations may often be seen as integrative foci tapping organizations for allegiance energy. The best known example is, of course, modern trade unions insisting on demands that 1. not only decrease the profit that could be expended on luxury consumptions but also the savings that could be turned into investments, and 2. impede modernization and rationalization through feather-bedding (practices) etc.

The interesting new element brought into social life by means of truly comprehensive status-associations (at least within the boundaries of a nation-state) is their *total power*. In principle many of them have the power to paralyze society, since they have the power to vacate a status completely, to empty it of actors. In so doing they can deny the society the services of one status; and with the degree of interconnectedness found in modern societies, this means that they can often obtain very high prices for offers to abstain from carrying out such threats. And this factor is increasing rather than decreasing in importance the more interconnected society becomes and the more 'rational' it becomes, i.e. the less expendable any status is.

A third weakness in connection with associations is their lack of heterogeneity, as pointed out above. They provide equality within, but polarization between; homogeneity within, but at the expense of putting all heterogeneity between so as to lead to a polarization that offers little challenge and stimulus. For that reason, and because of the potentially destructive nature of associations (especially when they lead to the formation of contra-associations and consequent polarization), we can with equal right talk about a crisis in association-formation.

5. Conclusion

Thus far, we have tried to show the inherent weakness in all principles of integration; how they satisfy some basic needs but to the exclusion or even denial of others. As one type of integration has been used for some time the functions it satisfies are gradually taken for granted and lose in importance: whereas the functions that remain unsatisfied or even are counter-acted stand out as increasingly important. The accumulated frustration may, then, lead to a 'change of horses in the middle of the race' — but then any society is always in the middle of *some* race, so that is perhaps less important. What does matter is the *frequency* and *amplitude* of these pendular movements from one type of integration to the next, and finally back again — for it seems reasonable to assume that there is an optimum point here. Too frequent changes may have highly disruptive consequences, while on the other hand no change at all in the proportion of integrative strategies deprives society of a chance to get a new start, some kind of discontinuity in its history that may have a very beneficial effect.

But the probability of finding some kind of mixture which would yield stable equilibrium over a prolonged period is probably negligible, if for no other reason than the dialectic elements in these processes: the dys-functions that will dominate more and more as time passes. Hence integrative foci change, and new actors are born — and they are born for structural reasons, because of structural fatigue within the existing order. For this reason the present theory is structural; it does not presuppose anything about motivation or ideology. Rather, it assumes that motivation and ideology will emerge, given the structural basis presented in Table 11.3.

The most important consequence of our theory, however, lies in one important asymmetry between the three types of integration. Thus, we see no reason why the dialectical changes from organizational to associational integration and back again cannot go on for some time, but there are many reasons for believing that territorial integration is fading out of the total picture. Thus, our general model where the relative importance of the three foci of integration is concerned would be the picture in Figure 11.4, next page. By and large we assume territorial integration to be decreasing and the other two to be increasing, and in a complementary manner. But this has a very important consequence, which can be seen by comparing two points in social time in Fig. 11.4; t_1 and t_2. At t_1 there is territorial integration keeping units together. Inside, there is very little going on of the type modern societies carry out by means of organizations and associations; the society is 'underdeveloped'. At t_2 all this is changed. The faunas of organizations and associations are both rich, but the territorial focus is decreasing in significance. The society is 'overdeveloped' relative to the traditional borderlines defined by the nation-state. Between t_1 and t_2 there are intervals where the territorial focus serves very well to integrate the organizational actors and even the associational actors; they are all developed to the national cause, for instance. The nation serves as an overriding focus of identification. But what about the situation at t_3? What can then serve to keep the associations together, or the organizations together, depending on which phase the system finds itself in? It is well known that this is a very real problem, and there are many tentative answers, none of them quite satisfactory.

Thus, one answer would be that territorial integration will still take place, but with increasing domain and decreasing scope as time passes on. Organizations spin webs of interdependence and associations webs of identification that both transcend classical nation-states; hence, the argument would run, territorial integration has to expand so as to comprise the domain integrated by interdependence and/or identification. Hence, all that happens is that the borderlines of territorial units are pushed outwards, in concentric circles as interdependence and identification are pushed outwards, eventually encompassing the whole world.

The difficulty with this is first of all the time needed for such extensions, and secondly the conflicts that are bound to emerge if two territorial centers of interdependence and identification are both pushing outwards, as in the current superpower confrontation. Organizations and associations tend to grow faster than territories, especially in a world where there are no longer vacant territories to speak of. Both objections point to the type of difficulties our world is experiencing at the moment.

FIGURE 11.4 *The relative significance of the three integrative foci as a function of social time*

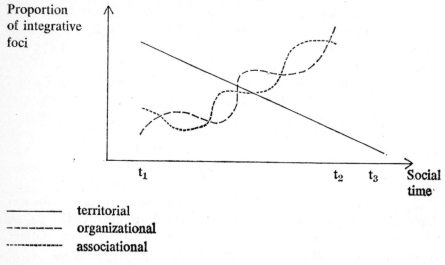

territorial
organizational
associational

But the other answer is also problematic: to integrate organizations and associations by means of a second level of organizations and associations. One may organize a nation as an association of status-associations. This presupposes that everybody is meaningfully allocated to at least one such association, but that can probably be arranged. However, associations of that kind will tend to be homogeneous and provide members with a poor social environment. They have risen in periods when territorial integration was always present as a dominant or at least a variant theme, as a source of richer social experience. And associations will change their meaning completely when this source of variety vanishes, when people no more see their neighbors but only their fellow status- or value-holders, or their fellows in the work organization. And then we are back to the old argument again: the crisis in associational or organizational integration.

And this is where we leave the argument. The point is that the changing focus of integration seems to confront humanity with a kind of total crisis to which we do not as yet have the answer: *the problem of an adequate substitute for territorial integration.*

IV.12. Non-Territorial Actors: The Invisible Continent*

PRIO-publication no. 22-44.

Notes on page *709*.

1. Territorial and non-territorial actors: A comparison

Geographers may debate how many territorial continents there are in the world: five, six, maybe more. Since the Great Discoveries increasingly adequate maps have been made available to create an image of the world in terms of territory. From this elementary school indoctrination generations have been trained to see the world in terms of territorial actors, in conflict and cooperation. What is left out of that image is the forgotten continent, *an invisible continent of non-territorial actors*, the international organizations. Of course, everybody talks about them today, but still mainly as an adjunct to the territorial system, with insufficient emphasis, to our mind, on the system of non-territorial actors as also being a system in its own right, *sui generis*, with its own logic, contradictions and structure [1].

Such actors have been in existence for a very long time [2], in a sense during most of human history, but in a different way from what we are experiencing today, not to mention from what we probably are going to experience tomorrow. Thus, for the first time in human history, we are entering a stage where we may soon see the emergence of an international system with the center of gravity in the political game, so to speak, in the hands of non-territorial rather than territorial actors, particularly in the richer part of the world. This is of course not to say that territorial actors will disappear completely, only that they may gradually recede into the background and that various types of non-territorial actors will be located increasingly at the forefront of the political stage [3]. To understand these processes, and particularly to discuss whether any real change is involved, typologies of international organizations are needed.

For the purpose of this discussion we need some definitions: what do we mean by the term actor, and what precise meanings should be given to "non-territorial" and "territorial"?

Both types of actors have in common the ability to mobilize resources in order to pursue their goals. But whereas these resources are usually found within a contiguous territory in *geographical space* in the case of the territorial actor, they are not located in any easily defined spatial region in the case of the non-territorial actor. The territorial actor has a territory over which he has political control in the sense that he has power over the power-relations inside that territory, to the exclusion of other territorial actors. The non-territorial actor commands no such territory. But this does not mean that his power is not defined in some space, only that in this case the space is not geographical. The power of the non-territorial actor is defined in a *functional space*, or, if one prefers a more general term, in a *social space*. Thus, a UN specialized actor agency may have a certain political monopoly over certain types of relations defined in a particular region of functional space, e.g. health, to the exclusion of other non-territorial actors.

When defining the two actors so symmetrically we are, of course, not implying in any sense that a state, a nation, a UN specialized agency, an international hobby association and an international business corporation are similar where degree of autonomy or degree of power over resources they can command are concerned. All we are saying is that they exist, so to speak, in their own right, that they can command resources, that they can pursue goals; in short: that they are actors. But the regions over which they have some degree of monopoly and autonomy are very differently defined, as is to be expected given the difference between the simplistic, two-dimensional (or three-dimensional) geographical space that has given rise to our metric concepts, and the complex, many-dimensional, non-metric social spaces.

Most easily defined are the territorial actors, simply because geographical space is so easily defined. One may say that geographical space has a structure, even a metric, that has colored our entire conception of what an actor is. The concept of collective actor is structured so as to fit the possibilities given by geographical space rather than vice versa. Thus, just to give a very brief list of important characteristics usually attributed to geographical space:

1. Geographical space is *constant*, i.e. in limited time spans geological and geographical changes are so slow or so small or so limited that they do not in any really significant sense extend or contract the geographical space available — with the exception of major land reclamation schemes (there are, of course, also some islands that disappear and appear or reappear, but these are minor events; and the movement of glaciers is too slow relative to the life span of geographical actors, not to mention the life span of human beings, to have important effects of a more short range nature).

2. Geographical span can be clearly, unambiguously (with minor exceptions) *subdivided* in such a way that a one-one mapping between actors and regions is possible, meaning that ownership of a region excludes ownership by other actors.

3. A corresponding *one-one mapping is possible between regions and human beings,* for instance defining a person's citizenship according to the place where he is born. Since locomotion takes place at restricted speed, it is always possible at any given moment in time to pin down a person to a specific region and use that as a criterion for belongingness, and one such point in time is obviously the point of birth. But, as the theory of citizenship shows, there are also other possibilities — the point here is only that it is *meaningful* to define it so that to each person there is one and only one citizenship.

4. Consensual, *clearly defined borderlines or demarcations between territorial regions can be obtained,* often making use of highly visible lines in the topography such as the coast, rivers, mountain ranges, etc. But even if borderlines are drawn as lines in a completely homogeneous desert, consensus may be obtained; not in the sense that there are no disputed territories, but in the sense that all parties concerned know where the disputed borderline runs.

All these properties have been important for the emergence of the territorial state. Let us now compare them with the structure, or lack of structure, in a functional or social space.

In this case one cannot talk about constancy, nor of constant expansion; for societies to develop, new functions are constantly amalgamated into the structure and old functions may die out — the net result being that functional space is changing and shifting, expanding here, contracting there.

Further, in the territorial case, one has generally not accepted joint ownership over the same territory, but has regarded this as an anomalous situation leading to a type of instability that may even escalate into a war. In functional space one very often has the case that several actors are defined as having competence over the same functional region; sometimes leading to conflict, sometimes forcing them into cooperation because subdivision may be impossible or very harmful [4].

Then, it is not true that an individual can belong to one and only one non-territorial actor. The circumstance that he does not have infinite speed of locomotion, enabling him to be in several positions in geographical space at the same time, does not prevent him from occupying several positions in social space at the same time, multiplying memberships in value, and interest-organizations, for instance.

As to borderlines between regions: they are usually well defined in geographical space, but highly nebulous in functional space. Thus, where does health end and education start, or education end and labor relations start? What about training in hygiene; or the working situation of teachers, and so on, and so forth.

Let us now imagine efforts to make the two spaces more similar, partly because such efforts may be politically highly meaningful, and partly as a heuristic device to develop more insight. Obviously, there may be two kinds of efforts, making social space look more like geographical space, and making geographical space look more like social space.

As to the former it is easily seen what this would mean in principle. One could imagine some high council of theologically, metaphysically, legally, sociologically, etc., oriented "high priests" trying to define once and for all what the functions of the general and total human enterprise are. With the clarity of a constitution or a penal/civil code, or a sociology textbook, they would try to describe human society in such a way that all its functions, forever, were clearly listed [5]. Having done this, they would make, once and for all, a list of non-territorial organizations deemed by them to be necessary. These organizations would be given a well-defined existence, and complete monopoly over the function(s) would be given to them by decree. This can be done in such a way that human beings would also by definition fall under one and only one organization. Just as their *place of birth* might be used to define their geographical belongingness and hence their belongingness to a territorial actor, their *occupation* could be used to define their social belongingness and hence their belongingness to a non-territorial actor. There would be an implicit assumption about uniqueness here, at least in general: just as a person is born in one and only one place, he would be supposed to have one and only one occupation, or at least only one major occupation [6].

If this assumption is satisfied, then the definition of borderlines should not be too difficult: much work would have to be invested in elaborations of borderline cases so that it is clear on what side of the water-shed each case would fall. For geographically defined actors this is not only a question of clear patterns of belongingness where geographical points are concerned, but also a question of where human beings belong: if they very often belong to more than one geographical actor, then the borderlines become less sharp because they become too porous. And correspondingly for the non-territorial actor: it is not only a question of clear rules as to where the most minute sub-sub-sub-functions belong, but corresponding rules as to the belongingness of persons charged with the articulation or implementation of these functions

Both systems can stand a certain ambiguity, but there are upper limits [7].

It is easily seen that a social space of the type described here, structurally similar to geographical space, is of a type one would most easily associate with highly stable social structures where the leading political and scientific hierarchies have tremendous power. In other words, it might be associated with utopias, with preindustrial societies of several types, and with totalitarian states. This is also clearly seen in the directives implicitly given to human beings: you shall have one and only one occupation, you shall belong to one and only one organization. One might perhaps add that there is only one field of organizational behavior where these principles have been really approximated: the field of trade unionism, not to mention the caste system. Here one has a social space corresponding to the list of occupations, changing over time as that list changes but constant at any point in time; there is a clear autonomy of one trade union over a class of occupations, a clear pattern of belongingness for the individual worker, and clearly defined borderlines. The same seems to some extent to be the case for professional associations, traditionally accustomed to mirror the structure of higher education as it has been crystallized into faculties, departments and institutes in the traditional universities. And much of this is then reflected in the corresponding international organizations, but only partly. In general functional, social or oganizational space has a much more complicated structure, most easily appreciated by performing the corresponding experiment of imagining geographically defined actors structured in the same way as socially and functionally defined actors in complex and dynamic societies as we know them today.

If geographical territory should behave in a similar way, it would be changing all the time, expanding in some directions, perhaps contracting in some other directions, making a mockery of any permanent or "final" pattern of subdivision. Some geographical actors would have command over several regions, some over one, and some would have to share their control with several others — in addition there would be unclaimed regions. The limits of space would be unknown, and would defy exploration — in fact, it would change by being explored. Human beings would be the citizens of zero, one, or several territorial actors; very much according to their own decision. For all these reasons borderlines would be highly volatile, regions would intermesh and interconnect, and their patterns of interpenetration would change over time, making it very dificult to say where one country ends and the other starts. This is far beyond the problem of a river bed changing with seasonal variations, with excessive precipitation and changing sedimentation, etc., making the river less than suitable as a baseline for a clear definition of the borderline between two nations. Rather, it bears some similarity to many people's image of the world prior to the era of the Great Discoveries and the system of nation states, as it may have appeared to peripatetic intellectuals, to traders, to pilgrims. And — perhaps also an image of a world of tomorrow [8]?

It may now be a question of personal taste what one prefers: a concept of nation-states patterned according to what today may be said to be the case for social space, or a concept of non-territorial actors patterned according to what today may be said to be the case for geographical space, or the co-existence we have today of the two types of actors. If our concern is with, for instance, peace theory, it is not easy to see what is more peace productive. According to one such theory messiness, lack of clarity, what in general is referred to as high level of entropy, is conducive to peace because of the difficulty in obtaining the clear borderlines that can serve as a baseline for a major war between two well-defined and completely polarized actors [9]. But that is only one theory; there are others in the field, such as the idea that messiness may lead to uncertainty which may lead to fear and anxiety and to destructive conflict behavior.

However that may be, let us try to use the parallels between the two systems to see how one can learn from the other in the field of two important problems, one of them related to the potential for direct violence, the other to the potential for structural violence [10].

First, we mentioned that in functional space there is much more experience with joint authority than in territorial space — except at the local territorial level (port authorities, lake authorities, etc.). Thus, there is a joint ILO--UNESCO Commission precisely to handle the problems of the teacher in his work situation; but there is not yet a joint Chile—Peru—Bolivia commission to handle the problems of the Arica-Tacna region — presumably because each party would consider this a weakening of their claim to unrestricted sovereignty. From this, it seems that one may draw the conclusion that experiences made in functional space could serve as a good model for territorial space.

Second, we mentioned that in territorial space there is a one-to-one mapping, or pinning down, of a person to one place in space; where he is born, where he lives, where he works, etc. There is one obvious advantage to this in any system based on voting: since a person cannot be two places in space at the same time, it is easier to see to it that he votes only once. If he can vote through his associations his vote will be weighted with a factor that increases with the number of memberships he has. And this experience or pattern is not so easily transferred because it is one thing to pin down a person in functional space (e.g. by his education), quite another to require that he shall be pinned down to only one point (have only one type of education). The problem of double voting or multiple influence could, conceivably, be handled by having a special category for the *pluralists*, those with multiple education, multiple career lines, membership in opposing parties, or what not. There is some similarity here to the special voting arrangements for those who move much across borders, e.g. sailors and foreign workers. In other words, it seems that one may draw the conclusion that experiences made in geographical space may serve as a good model for functional space; in other words that both systems may learn from each other.

2. A theory of non-territorial growth; and a first typology

After these excursions into the similarities and differences between the territorial and the non-territorial system, let us now look at the phenomenon of non-territorial growth in a more dynamic perspective. We have mentioned above that the non-territorial continent is more flexible than the territorial one — more dimensions, less metricized, not only non-finite but ever-expanding, ever-contracting and ever-changing. To explore this imagine a set of territorial actors; they could be countries but could also be local communities, districts, regions, for the concepts to be developed are general enough to cover several cases, and we do not have to make any particular assumption about size distribution, distances, communication potential and so on. The only thing we need for the theory is the idea of some kind of need for interaction, in at least some pairs of actors, that their geo-political system is not sufficient to contain their socio-economic needs [11]. If there is interaction, then it does not seem unreasonable to assume that sooner or later the need for regulation of patterns of interaction will arise. There will be a need for some kind of coordination, for some kind of machinery to settle conflicts, for revisions of terms of exchange in general and terms of trade in particular.

Our simple theory is now based on a four-fold table in which this can be discussed [12]. We assume that such discussions or exchanges can take place between two actors only and hence be termed *bilateral*, or between more than two actors and be referred to as *multilateral;* and we assume further that these discussions may be *ad hoc* or *institutionalized*. And this leads us immediately to Fig. 12.1.

FIGURE 12.1 *The IGO machine: phases in organizing governmental interaction*

	ad hoc	institutionalized
bilateral	I envoy	II resident diplomacy
multilateral	III international conferences	IV international organizations

In Fig. 12.1 there is ambiguity with regard to the second axis. Thus, the negation of "ad hoc" is relatively rich in structural alternatives. "Ad hoc" means actually three things: there is no *emerging suprastructure* to handle these negotiations; there is no *permanent session* of conference in which the actors participate even without having any superstructure, and there is not even any way of *predicting* when these non-permanent conferences do take place, like "every second year".

This means that at the extreme of institutionalization one will find the permanent suprastructure, then follow various forms of permanent sessions of countries negotiating with each other but without what today is known as a "secretariat", and at the lowest level of institutionalization there is only the periodical or otherwise predictable, repeatable meeting with nothing happening in-between. It may actually be disputed where the cutting point between "ad hoc" and "institutionalized" is located, but it can hardly be doubted that there is a continuum rather than a dichotomy involved here.

The arrows in Fig. 12.1 indicate an hypothesis as to temporal succession. This should not be taken too seriously: there are many examples where one or even all of the arrows could be turned around. But in general we would assume that the bilateral, ad hoc form is the most frequently found starting point, e.g. the diplomat visiting the country to which he is accredited at intervals, for instance once a year, and usually from a neighboring country in which he is stationed. From this lowest level it can be developed further into a pattern of resident diplomacy where the embassy is permanently located in the capital, close to the centers of power of the host nation. But one could also extrapolate from this to a third form that does not seem to have become part of contemporary diplomatic practice: a form whereby the embassy of nation X in nation Y would amalgamate so effectively with the nation X desk in the foreign ministry of nation Y that the two would be virtually inseparable and constitute some type of international organization, although only at the bilateral level. That these people know each other, negotiate and meet frequently, and even may share political tastes and practices almost completely (if the countries are not too separated by dissimilarities and disharmonies) is not the same as saying that a new structure has emerged. It should be noted that this kind of superstructure seems to exist in trade and commerce: the existence of joint (bilateral) chambers of commerce beween nation X and nation Y testifies to that.

There is something rather trivial about the transition from "ad hoc" to the various levels of "institutionalized". It can be discussed in terms of *costs:* there is a certain break-off point where permanent contacts become less expensive than often repeated ad hoc contacts. There is the question of *control:* permanent contact increases the predictability and stabilizes patterns of influence. And there is the problem of *communication:* permanent, close contact makes feedback of information and decisions more rapid and speeds up interaction in general. To this one could then add quite a number of other elements, such as, for instance, the permanence of contacts as a sign of *recognition*. In fact, the very axis from ad hoc to the highest form of institutionalization, not yet really clarified systematically, is in itself one of the best indicators of the degree of proximity between countries. Countries need some indicator of how distant or close they are to each other; if this one did not exist something else probably would have to be invented [13].

Let us then look at the other axis, the transition from *bilateral to multilateral* forms of interaction; conferences and organizations. Of course, one can again look at it from the point of view of *costs* and argue that a multilateral meeting of n countries may be a highly efficient substitute for $\binom{n}{2}$ bilateral meetings. Or, one can discuss it from the point of view of *control* and argue that multilateral forms make for a higher degree of mutual visibility than the corresponding number of bilateral forms, and this is undeniable. There is also the point frequently made by big powers that this will increase small power influence since they not only will have a chance to speak for a large auditorium but also to aggregate and pool their voices for joint articulation; and there is the collateral argument, frequently heard from smaller powers, that the multilateral form of organization is a major instrument of *big power manipulation*. And then there is the argument of *communication:* no one can deny the rapidity and the efficiency that can be attained with face to face contact, particularly when the services of a loyal and efficient secretariat are available. The arguments for multilateral institutionalization are about the same as at the bilateral level.

However, the matter is not quite that unproblematic. First of all: it does not really explain why multilateral forms of contact come into existence at all. For just as every nation is unique every dyad is also unique. As is painfully obvious in the world today some dyads are further advanced in positive interaction than others; no two dyads seem to be at exactly the same level [14]. This means that efforts to break up the interaction monopoly held by bilateral relations and tie it together again in a multilateral form presupposes considerable ability to unify what is already highly diverse. In fact, it presupposes some of the same standardization of international relations that at the level of human interaction is associated with industrial, "modern", Western societies and the capitalist rather than artisan mode of production. For there is a real transcendence implicit in the multilateral form of social existence once this step has been taken. The sum of bilateral agreements, or treaties, is never quite the same as a multilateral agreement, or a convention. And this is a discontinuous transition, completely unlike increasingly frequently held ad hoc, but bilateral, conferences that gradually develop into permanence and end up in bilateral institutionalization. Needless to say, the transition is smoothed by keeping all four forms at the same time [15].

There is no necessary logical connection between movements along the two dimensions; all four forms are completely conceivable, and indeed empirically found. And Fig. 12.1 can now be seen as an X-ray photo of a social mechanism, *where the inputs are national actors and the final output is an intergovernmental organization,* an IGO [16]. It is like a sausage machine: one puts in countries and gets out an IGO. However, the machine is hardly very efficient: it took something like, say, 500 years to enter into efficient production of this end product, from ad hoc bilateral diplomacy by envoys among Italian city states to the IGO proliferation of today [17].

But what has been done once can be done twice. So, why not regard the IGO output of this machine as the input to a new machine, with exactly the same structure, but producing super-IGOs and linked together in a coupling that looks something like Fig. 12.2.

FIGURE 12.2 *The super-IGO machine*

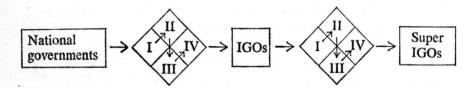

This is what is quickly taking place today: we are rewriting the last five centuries of human history, but this time with IGOs as the units upon which this superstructure machine works. How this takes place concretely is obvious enough. Two IGOs are in need of some kind of mutual control and communication, very often referred to as "coordination". Misinformation, jealousies and potential conflicts are operating and propelling enterprising individuals into action. The first step is obviously the ad hoc contact: the sending of envoys in either direction for information collection. There may easily be a ranking variable at work here: the smaller IGO has to send an envoy to the bigger IGO before the latter condescends to reciprocate [18]. The institutionalization of this ecxhange usually takes the form of exchanges of members on councils or executives, after an initial phase where these persons are referred to as "observers", and often only admitted to open sessions, to the general assemblies, or conferences. One can now easily imagine the extrapolation from this: the permanent representatives from other IGOs are given separate offices in the host secretariats, and not only observe and report and give feedback as resident diplomacy in its bilateral form would do, but participate actively in the work of the IGO [19]. In that case a bilateral IGO structure would have emerged, a super-IGO with two members.

Multilateralization could then take the same forms as for country actors. There would be an initial phase with conferences on an ad hoc basis, then these conferences would be institutionalized and held at regular intervals, for instance annually, as "consultations", paving the way to the final step: the erection of a multilateral super-IGO of which the " bilateral super-IGO" mentioned above would be the simplest case.

We are probably today mostly in the first and second phases of this development. But what we have seen so far, seems to indicate one rather obvious thing: this second machine in the superstructure generation works much more effectively than the first one. If we should venture a guess it might be that what the first machine was able to produce in 500 years, the second machine may be able to do in 50 [20]. And the reason for this is not only the increased communication and transportation facilities of our age, but also to a large extent that the individuals in command of the end product of the *first* process, the IGOs, are already trained in this type of superstructure creation. In other words, although we are by no means minimizing the extent to which they may be as jealously safeguarding the functional autonomy of their IGOs as any president, king or prime minister the territorial interests of his country, they may relatively easily engage in super-IGO creation, exactly in order to protect these interests. That structure is already thoroughly imprinted on their minds, they have considerable training in the verbalization and the activities needed, and they have the pleasure of having as their opposite number in other organizations people with the same kind of training.

What now has happened twice can also happen three times: we can easily imagine one more machine of the same kind coupled in *series* with the others as to produce super-super-IGOs. But we are not quite there yet, this is still for the future. More important would be to look at the corresponding machines operating in a *parallel* fashion to what we have described, producing inter-nongovernmental organizations, INGOs and super-INGOs, or producing business INGOs, BINGOs and super-BINGOs. The first one obviously feeds on national non-governmental organizations and amalgamates them into (B)INGOs, and the second one correspondingly feeds on (B)INGOs and produces super-(B)INGOs on that basis.

Let us now complicate this general image of future growth even further by introducing the ideas of parallel coupling and coupling in series of these machines, at the same time (Fig. 12.3).

The vertical arrows stand for liaison organizations, at all three levels of organization, and in all three pairs. Thus, one of them would be the link

FIGURE 12.3 *Parallel coupling between the IGO, INGO and BINGO machines*

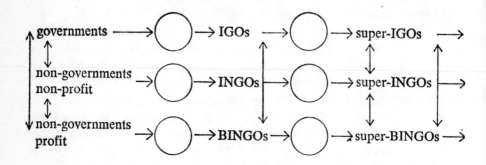

between INGOs and IGOs — e.g. as it is found in the institution of the "consultative status" of certain INGOs with certain IGOs — or between two IGOs, e.g. between OPEC and the IEA. To take another example: the possible link between a super-INGO (e.g. a Council of Scientific Associations) and a super-BINGO (e.g. a combine of international business in the oil field). There is no upper limit to how far the complexity can develop. Moreover, the more complex the network, the longer the chain of machines coupled in series and the denser the network of parallel coupling, the more power can be obtained from certain positions in the total network. In fact, most heads of governments may be left somewhat behind at the left hand end of the scheme relative to the tremendous power that ultimately develops to the right, although there is a limit to how far one can go in complexity. And this power should not be measured by means of such crude indicators as the amount of *capital* they handle, but rather by taking the network context and the amount of *information* they handle into account [21].

Moving towards the right in Fig. 12.3 there will probably also be another significant development: the transition from the use of permanent organizations with secretariats and staff to the use of instant ad hoc communication, e.g. via telesatellite, as the "logical" solution to the problems of extremely complex networks of organization [22]. The whole system will be so complex and its needs will change so quickly as to make the classical response, one new organization and one new office whenever there is a need, impracticable.

So far, we have looked at growth from the point of view of *integration and meta-integration* etc. [23]. But growth in the non-territorial system can also come about by other means. Thus, *there is the tendency for each IGO, INGO and BINGO to foster through the usual social dialectics, a counter-IGO, -INGO, -BINGO in competition with it,* vying with each other for political, socio cultural and economic markets among the territorial actors (an example would be international trade unions relative to transnational corporations). In fact, they may often cancel each other out, like matter and anti-matter, leaving behind a lot of noise [24].

Then, there is the equally dialectical *differentiation in the non-territorial system along class lines.* As it is now, masters and servants are already emerging in the NT system and although the smaller, younger and less powerful NTs are badly organized it will hardly last long before they see the need for some kind of trade union formation. A stratification system may sooner or later crystallize into a class system, e.g. pitting the prestigious IGOs against the less prestigious INGOs, and the result can easily be gigantic super-IGOs, super-INGOs and super-BINGOs, pitted against each other, just as for territorial actors. Thus, the upper class among the IGOs is probably the UN organizations and the IGOs of the most powerful countries — these may be pitted against each other, or together against all others.

Finally, and most significantly: *new non-territorial actors form in socio--functional space at any time,* simply because there is a need for them. If they are neighbors in that strange space they may perhaps easily fuse together, integrate, like various types of social scientists. Correspondingly, if they are built over too much internal distance in that space, covering too diverse functions, they may undergo fission and disintegrate, like international student unions in the late 1950s. But the tendencies towards disintegration are hardly that important, and the net result would be an increase in the number of NTs anyhow.

One particular source of growth of this type is the principle of *growth by intersection:* if there is union of esperantists and a union of nudists there may be basis for a union of esperanto-speaking nudists [26]. As time goes on one could imagine increasing complexity also along this dimension: organizations based on the intersection not only of two but of three or more organizations [27]. There is no introduction to new functions but of functions of a higher order, once more telling us something about the flexibility and expandability of this socio-functional space. In other words: *the invisible continent will grow and continue to grow,* and unlike the visible continents there is no upper limit, no limits to growth except, perhaps, the number of human beings and the time they have available to make their organizations meaningful [28].

In order now to understand this phenomenon better, the question must be asked that can be asked in connection with all dynamic phenomena: where is the growth most pronounced? One way of answering would be to look at the location of headquarters, in Table 12.1.

The general conclusion is clear: more than four-fifths of the non-territorial machinery is controlled from the North-West of the world, making the entire structure relatively similar to the colonial pattern. There is a slight

TABLE 12.1 *Location of headquarters of international organizations, 1906—1968*,* %

Year	North-West	Latin America	Arab countries	Western Asia	Socialist Asia	Eastern Europe	Black Africa	Rest	Total	N
1906	97.0	.6	0	0	0	2.4	0	0	100.0	169
1912	97.3	.7	.2	.2	0	1.6	0	0	100.0	437
1921	98.4	.6	.3	.3	.3	0	0	0	99.9	321
1926	98.2	.7	0	0	.3	.7	0	0	99.9	397
1029—31	97.9	.6		0	0	1.6	0	0	100.1	·524
1938	96.1	.7	.1	.4	0	2.7	0	0	100.0	705
1950	95.1	2.6	.5	.2	0	1.4	.1	·0	99.9	804
1954	93.2	3.1	.4	1.3	0	1.3	.5	.3	100.1	1,198
1958	92.0	3.7	.5	1.5	0	1.6	1.6	.1	101.0	1,257
1962	90.8	3.7	.5	1.8	0	1.8	1.2	.1	99.9	1,549
1964	89.4	4.4	1.1	1.7	0	1.8	1.4	.1	99.9	1,758
1966	88.7	4.8	.9	1.7	0	2.1	1.5	.1	99.8	2,207
1968	87.1	5.4	1.1	2.1	0	2.1	1.9	.2	99.9	2,663
1972	87.8	4.8	1.3	2.3	0	2.1	1.7	.1	100.1	3,185
1974	86.6	5.1	1.4	2.6	0	2.1	2.2	0	100.0	2,904

* Sources: *International Associations*, 1954, no. 11, pp. 548—49; 1954, no. 11, pp, 548—49; 1959, no. 6, p. 446; 1965, no. 2, pp. 86—89; 1976, no. 2, pp. 166—69.
Yearbook of International Organizations, 12th edition, 14th edition.

trend towards some redistribution, but a very slow one indeed, and lagging far behind the pattern of political decolonization from World War II onwards. The reason is partly structural — the North-West has the monetary and human resources — and partly cultural — the North-West combines expansionism with individualism and non-territorial actors are very much based on detachable, mobile individuals and expand very easily by establishing local chapters anywhere once the actor is born. This leads to an hypothesis to be explored in the next section: non-territorial actors constitute a mechanism for neo-colonialism just as territorial actors did for colonialism.

But there is also another aspect to this pattern that should be pointed out. In the rich and capitalist North-West there is one group of countries that probably benefits particularly from the development of the invisible continent: the *small* countries. If we calculate INGO and IGO membership per 1 million population, and exclude territories with less than 1 million inhabitants, the ranking list in 1964 was as follows (Table 12.2):

TABLE 12.2 *The first nations in terms of* INGO/*capita and* IGO/*capita, 1964*

Rank	INGO/capita	IGO/capita
1	Israel	Panama
2	Norway	Costa Rica
3	Switzerland	Nicaragua
4	Denmark	Mauritania
5	Finland	Liberia
6	New Zealand	Paraguay
7	Panama	Central Africa Rep.
8	Ireland	Israel
9	Uruguay	Norway
10	Austria	Honduras

The two lists are quite different and the reason is simple. There are many IGOs in the world today to which a country simply has to belong in order to be a country; hence the countries on top of the list are above all the very small countries regardless of level of development. That does not mean that we do not have the same neo-colonial pattern in the IGO system, even for UN agencies. only one of which (UNEP) has a headquarter in East or South — headquarters are either in the militarily organized West — the NATO countries — or in countries "neutral to West". But it does mean that the whole world is taken in, in a way that is not the case for the INGOs. INGO membership seems to presuppose a certain social structure, above all that the country is "developed" and/or capitalist, and this is clearly reflected in the INGO/capita list, especially when compared with the other list.

It may be argued that the absolute number of memberships is more significant than the relative number per million inhabitants, but they both are significant. Thus, it is not unreasonable to assume that with a constant number of memberships the smaller of two countries is more penetrated because proportionately more people are involved: *the invisible continent becomes more visible.* And this brings us to the important perspective that *the invisible continent is (except for* BINGOs) *the continent the small, developed and capitalist states try to colonize; particularly since all territorial continents have to some extent been colonized by the big powers, capitalist or socialist.*

The significance of this factor, and the validity of this general hypothesis, can be further appreciated by studying Table 12.3.

Although the *site* of the organization definitely is an important factor here, it is another important indicator of the extent to which small, rich countries have made use of this resource.

But it is also quite obvious that numbers are not good enough here; it is only an indicator. Thus, the growth in *number* of cars would not in itself be sufficient as an indicator of how dominant cars are as cultural themes:

TABLE 12.3 *Number of international officials per million inhabitants, 1954* [29]

1. Switzerland	86	6. France	22
2. Belgium	55	7. Norway	19
3. Netherlands	42	8. United Kingdom	16
4. Denmark	25	9. Italy	9
5. Sweden	23	10. North America	4

socio-psychological investigations would also be needed to say something about the grip cars have on people's minds. Correspondingly for the non-territorial actors: we do not know to what extent there is real identification with them. This is probably a function (but not a simple linear one) of the extent to which they satisfy perceived needs, and even can start competing with the territorial system in so doing. And if this competition gets off the ground to the extent that the latter is threatened, how will they, the countries, hit back in efforts to control and possibly stifle non-territorial growth? There is no doubt that they are hitting back at the TNCs, but when will that be generalized to other non-territorial actors [30]?

All we can say where this is concerned is the rather trite conclusion that for the year 2000 there will be three possibilities when it comes to the relative salience of the two systems, NT and GT [31]:

1. NT weaker than T in salience;
2. NT equal to T in salience;
3. NT stronger than T in salience.

The point here is merely that anyone concerned with images of future worlds would do well to take the invisible continent into account. Nobody would today analyze a country only in terms of its territorial subdivisions — states, prefectures, departments, provinces, counties, etc.; they would bring into the analysis organizations and associations, e.g. business corporations and trade unions, particularly when they are national, spanning across the subdivisions of the geographical space held by the country. The same applies today to the world, and increasingly so, it seems. On the other hand, social systems are dialectic systems, there are movements but also counter-movements. How they will add up in the year 2000 we simply do not know.

3. Relations between territorial and non-territorial actors: A second and third typology

Let us now combine points made in the preceding sections into a scale of increasing non-territoriality depending on what kind of units are members of the "international organization":

— Members are national governments, and the organization is *inter-govern-mental*.(IGO);
— Members are other national organizations or associations than governments, and the organization is *inter-nongovernmental* (INGO);
— Members are individuals, and the organization is a *transnational* (non-governmental) association (TRANGO).

We prefer not to use the term "international" for any one of these, for the term "international" in our view does not necessarily imply any organization or actor at all. The international system is simply the system of nations (actually, the system of states, or countries), in cooperation and conflict — nothing more, nothing less. For that reason we interpret IGO to mean inter-governmental (and not international, governmental), INGO to mean inter-nongovernmental (and not international nongovernmental), and we add to this well-known distinction the transnational (or, really, trans-nongovern-mental) organization, the TRANGO, which relates directly to individuals whereever they are found. In the TRANGO there are no "national chapters" or similar arrangements filtering the direct relation between individuals.

Then there is that vitally important special case of the INGO: the *business* inter-nongovernmental organization (BINGO). It links together nongovern-mental business organizations in various countries and is better known today as the "multinational corporation". However, the latter may be an unfortunate term for at least three reasons. Firstly, "multi" connotes more than two nations, but often there are only two, and in that case the term "cross-national" may, perhaps, be preferred to "multinational". Further, the term "multinational" conceals how asymmetric these corporations are, usually being dominated from one country. And, finally, "corporation" may not be broad enough, for there may be many other ways of organizing international business than in corporations. (Incidentally, one of these ways would be governmental, as an IGO, which in that case — when it is for business — would be termed a BIGO.)

Let us now try to make this over-used typology more meaningful by exploring two important phenomena located at the interface between the territorial and the non-territorial systems. These two systems are by no means unrelated, particularly since one, the territorial, preceded the other by thousands of years and consequently must have set its stamp on the latecomer, however efficiently the latter uses transportation and communication.

We have found it useful to discuss the relation between the two systems under the headings of *isomorphy* and *homology*. The propositions are simple:

Proposition 1: The non-territorial actors tend to be isomorphic with the territorial system.

Proposition 2: The non-territorial actors tend to induce homology among territorial actors.

Proposition 3: The propositions above are most valid for inter-governmental organizations, (usually) less for inter-nongovernmental organizations, and (almost) invalid for transnational organizations. They are also highly valid for transnational corporations.

Let us spell this out.

Characteristic of the two lowest types of non-territorial actors, the IGOs and the INGOs, is that the *world territorial structure, the nation-state structure, is still entirely visible.* When governments are members this is obvious, but it also applies to the typical "international organization" built as an association of associations (e.g. an association of national associations or dentists, longshoremen, stamp-collectors). An association or organization at the national level becomes a "national chapter" or a "mother, sister, or daugter company", depending on the position in the hierarchy, at the level of the non-territorial actor.

But there is not only a clear relation in the sense that the states of the world are reflected as components of the non-territorial actor. Not only the *elements* of the territorial system, but also the *relations* between them can usually be rediscovered; and that is why the stronger term "isomorphy" is used. Relations of power (both resource and structural power) and inter-action frequency are often mirrored faithfully. The most powerful chapter comes from the most powerful country — in terms of location of headquarters, recruitment of staff, general perspective on world affairs; frequencies of interaction in the territorial system are mirrored in frequencies of interaction in the organization, and so on [31]. In other words: the territorial system is reproduced inside some non-territorial actors *which for that reason are not truly non-territorial.*

This way of thinking carries us quite far analytically. Non-territorial actors with national components — governmental or nongovernmental — can be seen as governed primarily by the principle of isomorphy. This is the baseline, as implemented in the United Nations, when the major victors among the "united nations", the Allies fighting against the Axis power, appointed themselves to permanent Security Council seats, even with a veto. Isomorphy is called "realism" in the plain language of power; and it means that to those who have power in the territorial system, power shall also be given in the non-territorial system. And it may also be partially true that the more an inter-governmental organization departs from this isomorphy, the less attention will be paid to it, because its decisions will be seen as not reflecting the "real world" — meaning the territorial system with its bilateral relations — to which decisions will then be referred.

But it is only a partial truth. A non-territorial actor that is 100% isomorphic with the territorial system is in a sense only a replication of that system, except that it makes multilateral interaction possible. But small deviations from strict isomorphy will take place when countries are represented by persons, making these organizations a medium in which the smaller powers *can* more easily express themselves, can be listened to, and perhaps can make some impact on the territorial system. It is not merely a medium in which they can be more easily bossed.

But then, again, the opposite view: that this is precisely the medium in which the territorial system is kept alive and even reinforced. For instance, Nationalist China had for a long time a power excess because of its position in the UN Security Council. The argument would be, however, that this was not because of too much isomorphy, but because of lack of isomorphy, that the UN was not up-to-date, but served to freeze the *past*. One might also extend that argument to the case of the UK and France, and even to the United States, for all practical purposes defeated by what was often referred to as a "fifth rate power", Vietnam. So, imagine the UN brought up-to-date, in an effort to mirror the territorial system. The argument would then be that any distinction between veto and non-veto is too sharp, too absolute relative to the power distinctions in an increasingly subtle and complicated territorial system. Moreover, if war is used to decide who has veto, then the US and Vietnam should at least be on a par, viewing Vietnam as an effective challenger of a former heavyweight champion.

Of course, over time the internal workings of a non-territorial actor will acquire complex facets never contemplated by its social architects, the lawyers. There will be informal structures in addition to the formal ones. But the power differentials *may* actually be magnified rather than reduced in an intergovernmental organization.

In the INGO, all of this becomes much less important, except for the BINGO, of course. Non-governments may feel less *obliged* to act in the name of the national interest, and more free to find the pattern of action and interaction that fits the values of the organization. Thus, one would assume in general that INGOs have national elements — by definition — but that the relations between them are different, for instance much more egalitarian. The world has come to accept the idea of a big power veto in the UN, whether this reflects adequately or even exaggerates territorial power — but it would hardly accept it in an international philatelic association. Needless to say, however, all shades and gradations can be imagined here.

When it comes to transnational organizations isomorphy would break down completely: there would be neither the national elements, nor the relations of the territorial system. Transnational ties uniting individuals across territorial borders might even be stronger than common citizenship. The classical example here is, of course, *nation membership* as opposed to *state citizenship*. The nation, defined as a group of human beings having in common some characteristics, referred to as ethnical, is the most important of all transnational organizations. (Here the unfortunate consequences of the double meaning of "nation" becomes particularly obvious!) Time and again it proves to be more important than territorially defined state citizenship, but the two are often confused because the nation-state is taken as a norm, and sometimes also as a fact in our world. Thus, Jews form such a transnational group, although a much better expression would be "transgovernmental" — a TRAGO — since they are found under the protection (or abuse) of various governments. The extent to which Jews would identify themselves as "Soviet" Jews, "US" Jews, and so on would then be a test of the extent to which this is an INGO or a TRANGO.

More recent examples would be international scientific unions where the dissolution of national organization has gone quite far [18]. Of course, people in the same discipline from the same country may know each other better, and their interaction is usually facilitated by speaking the same language, but the search for significant colleagues, for meaningful persons with whom to work, to converse, to exchange ideas will not be restricted by such borders. Only few and particularly repressive countries would imagine organizing their citizens so as to act as a bloc in a transnational organization

Then there are, of course, the political parties and pressure groups that are transnational, such as the World New Left and the Vietnam solidarity movement. The fact that there may also be cooperation at sub-national and national levels does not detract from the transnational character of such world movements, for national identities are usually successfully washed out. Good cases in point are the world hippie movement — or any movement for new life styles in defiance of the various versions of vertical success--oriented, power-oriented societal orders.

For these reasons we see the transnational organizations as the real non-territorial actors of the future. Only they deserve the epithet *global* actors, since only they (like states) are based on individuals as their units, *and* are global in their scope.

To summarize: the idea of isomorphy splits into two: are the territorial *elements*, the countries, present in the "non-territorial" actor? and are the territorial *relations* present (Table 12.4)?

TABLE 12.4 *Three types of non-territorial actors*

Territorial elements	Territorial relations	Non-territoriality
present	present	low (IGOS, most BINGOS)
present	absent	medium (INGOS)
absent	absent	high (TRANGOS)

Let us then turn to the problem of *homology;* in other words, a focus on the non-territorial organizations as giant mechanisms for making all states as *similar* to each other as possible. Just as a state tries to find its appropriate place (often called its "natural" position) in a non-territorial organization, so a non-territorial organization is a vehicle facilitating the search for an *opposite number* inside any state. Whether members are governments, non-governmental associations, organizations, or simply individuals, any non-territorial actors will look for like-minded or like-positioned elements in all states around the world. For that is their task: *to organize all of their kind,* wherever they may be found. And if they do not exist they can be created, for instance by inviting observers to international conferences who then return to their country with the message imprinted on their minds: *solch ein Ding müssen wir auch haben.* But this means that non-territorial actors become giant mechanisms through which the stronger states, the states that started these organizations, can imprint a message on weaker states: you must have this profession and that profession, this hobby and sports association and that ideological movement, you must produce this and that — in order to be full-fledged members of the World. Active membership in IGOS, INGOS, etc., is taken as an indicator of how deeply embedded the country is in the world system — without questioning who started all these organizations, on what social basis, for what purpose, in what image. Having said this it becomes obvious that the reasoning also applies to regions: the weaker regions will tend to imitate the stronger regions and import the IGO/INGO machinery they have.

Thus, international conferences become giant markets where isomorphy and homology can be checked; the former for inter-state, the latter for intra-state relations. They become giant reproduction mechanisms. Power relations in the non-territorial organization will be compared to power relations in the territorial system, to see to what extent T is reflected in NT. And individuals from any country will compare notes to find to what extent that particular NT is reflected in their part of T — whether it is present at all, and whether their government pays as much attention to it in terms of subsidy and deference as other governments are reported to pay to sister chapters, and so on.

This entire presentation may now gain in depth if we tie it to a simple four-country model of the world with two Center and two Periphery countries (Fig. 12.4).

FIGURE 12.4 *Non-territoriality as an elite concept*

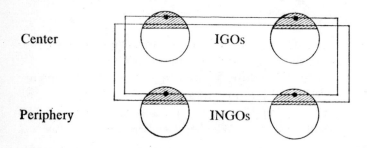

We have added a little dot on top of each circle for the governments, the nuclei of the centers. Obviously, the IGOs connect these dots in various ways. The INGOs do not necessarily connect only the center of countries — they *may* also tie periphery elements together. But chances are they do not: chances are that the masses are tied to their territorial units because they do not have the resources, *that the whole concept of non-territoriality is fundamentally an elite concept.* Even such grandiose concepts as "Europe", yes, even the nation-state is very much of an elite concept because of the way in which such means for developing consciousness as literacy, reading beyond primary school, knowledge of foreign languages are badly distributed, not to mention all the other inequalities and inequities, access to transportation and communication. Hence, even though we do not have good data on national participation in the type of associations and organizations that also are multinationally organized, we can safely say that those individuals who participate internationally, in conferences and in secretariats, etc., generally belong to the center of their countries. They are the individuals who serve as links between countries, not the non-participant member and the even less participant non-members, hidden behind the national screen.

Thus, if non-territorial actors (and this includes the transnational ones) essentially link governments and other elite groups together, then there are, in principle, and refering to Fig. 12.4, four types of international organizations:

1. connecting Center countries (horizontal lines, top);

2. connecting Center and Periphery countries in the same bloc (vertical lines);

3. connecting Periphery countries (horizontal lines, bottom)
   in same bloc
   in different blocs

4. universal organizations (the whole rectangle).

The first three may be referred to as "regional" organizations as long as we keep in mind the distinction between horizontal and vertical regions, and are not really non-territorial actors. In the real world. however, a particular organization is often too complex to permit classification in any single one of these classes.

Thus, the secretariat of an organization may often be different from the rest of the organization and be transnational even when the rest is inter-governmental or intra-governmental. Much of the history of the big inter-governmental organizations is the story of how the secretariat has tried to transnationalize the national delegates (meeting in conferences/assemblies, in councils or in executive boards), teaching them "to think in terms of the world as a whole" (the "world" usually meaning the organization, meaning the secretariat) — *and* of how the national delegates try to internationalize the secretariat by such methods as secondment, short tenure, return to governmental posts rather than a career in another transnational secretariat, and so on.

The net conclusion of all this is that the two systems, T and NT, are not independent of each other — nor is there any reason why one should expect them to be. The NTs of today are instruments in the hands of the territorial units who know how to use them, and that, as mentioned, is not only the big powers. But this is less true for the transnational organizations, since they are not organized in national chapters, and since the loyalty is to the world level and the individual level, not to the intermediate nation-state level. Their members become less concerned with "organizing something similar at home" after they have been exposed to patterns in other nations through the medium of transnational conferences. For them an institution found or founded in one country is already a world institution — not some-thing to be used by that country alone and copied elsewhere.

4. Conclusion

We have tried to conceive of international organizations as a modern, post-nomadic, form of non-territorial actors. They have their own peculiarities, particularly emphasized in the first section of the article; and they are conditioned by the still more important territorial system, particularly emphasized in the third section of the article. In short, the international organizations are ambiguous phenomena, capable of being analyzed from several and partially contradictory angles, giving rise to several different typologies, using as raw material the basic distinction between the inter-governmental, inter-nongovernmental and transnational organizations (IGOs, INGOs, TRANGOs).

The first typology offered was based on *the idea of the international organization as a super-actor*, and a distinction was made according to the level of organization depending on how many steps it was removed from the territorially based unit (a governmental organization, a nongovernmental organization or an individual — all of them non-profit or profit). Thus, there is the first order organization, the second order or super-organization, the third order or super-super-organization, and so on. On the other hand there is also the possibility of mixed liaison types, creating new actors out of different types of international organizations, and liaisons between territorial and non-territorial actors.

The second typology takes as its point of departure *the degree of isomorphism an international organization has with the territorial system*, making a distinction between three types depending on whether both territorial elements and relations are reproduced inside the international organization, only the elements or none of them. It is postulated that the IGOs are more of the first type (together with the BINGOs), the INGOs more of the second type and the TRANGOs (with individuals as members) more of the third type.

The third typology takes as its point of departure the obvious circumstance, today, that most international organizations connect elites, governmental or nongovernmental, profit or non-profit, around the world. The question is *what kind of countries are brought together*, and a first distinction would be between horizontal organizations (Center-Center, or Periphery-Periphery) and vertical organizations (Center-Periphery). A second distinction would be between universal (open to all of the same kind) and regional (restricted to a geographical region) organizations.

In addition to this, all kinds of distinctions could be made depending on the purpose of the organization — but we have been more interested in characteristics that relate to structure and process so as to better see which role these organizations play in the total world system, which in turn is a combination of the territorial and the non-territorial systems. For

416

this purpose it may be useful to make a distinction between the "least non-territorial" and the "most non-territorial" within the present typology, positing against each other a first order IGO that reflects faithfully the territorial system and essentially brings together Center countries, and an nth order TRANGO bringing together individuals from all over the world. Do they have enough in common to be referred to as international organizations? By definition, yes. But in terms of non-territoriality the former is so little removed from the territorial level as to make little difference, and the latter so much removed from the territorial level that it probably also has little impact.

This might indicate that it is the in-between types that are the carriers of the most dynamic and interesting aspects of the processes of change in the non-territorial — and thereby the world — system. One may even talk about processes of penetration into the deeper recesses of the non-territorial continent, creating higher levels, less isomorphic, less centristic and more universal organizations, all the time trying to liberate the non-territorial system from constraints placed upon it not by the territorial system as such, but by the particular territorial system that was shaped by Western oxpansionism during the last five centuries. And that places the international erganizations in today's political context in the struggle for a new international economic, political, military, cultural and social order.

A Survey of International Nongovernmental Organizations *

1. Introduction

Above a general theory of the "invisible continent", the nonterritorial actors, has been presented. In this second part some data will be given relating to one particular group of people: the Secretaries General of the nongovernmental organizations, the "chief executives". In 1967 the International Peace Research Institute in Oslo (PRIO) mailed a long questionnaire to Secretaries General of all IGOs and INGOs listed in the eleventh edition of the *Yearbook of International Organizations* (1966—1967) and its three first supplements. The response rate was satisfactory, and parts of the data have been used in several different publications (cf. the bibliography). However, the respondents were also promised a simple and concentrated presentation of the data that were derived from the questionnaire. This article serves that purpose.

2. Representativeness

The questionnaire was mailed to 2196 organizations all over the world. Twelve of these were reported dissolved or inactive at the time they received the questionnaire. Nine hundred and eleven of the remaining organizations returned completed forms. The percentage answers for the various main categories of organizations are as follows:

Intergovernmental organizations	31.3%
INGOs (proper)	45.6%
National organizations in consultative status with ECOSOC	13.3%
EEC and EFTA business and professional groups	23.7%
Total	41.7%

A thorough comparison was made of the set of INGO respondents and the total sample of INGOs as reported in the tenth edition of the *Yearbook* which we had coded. The differences were small indeed. Here are a couple of examples: In the total sample the mean number of national representations per INGO from the Nordic countries was 10.18, and across the respondents the percentage was 11.04. Of all INGOs in the *Yearbook*, 82.6% reported that English was one of their official languages, compared with 85.6 % among the respondents. It was therefore concluded that the INGO

---

* This part was written by Kjell Skjelsbaek in 1972.

respondents made up a sufficiently representative group for serious analysis and conclusons abut INGOS in general. The other categories of international organizations did not meet these requirements and have been excluded from the subsequent discussion.

3. Foundation, past and future splits and mergers

Most of the INGOS, 52 %, were founded at the national level, that is, various national organizations came together and formed an international one; 24% started at the international level, and then national chapters were founded; 23% were founded as international organizations and have remained that way without national organizations. In other words, about a quarter of all INGOS do not have national member organizations.

Sometimes INGOS merge or split, and they were asked whether this had happened in the course of the previous three years and whether they expected splits or mergers to take place in the foreseeable future. The percentages are:

	Splits	No change	Mergers
Past three years	3	92	5
The foreseeable future	2	89	9

There seems to be slightly more fusion than fission in the world of INGOS, and more change anticipated in the future than reported from the past.

4. Membership patterns

A parallel question was asked about gains and losses of national branches.

	Loss	No change	Gain
Past three years	4	41	55
The foreseeable future	2	37	61

There are many more gains than losses, and the proportion of gains is expected to increase. In other words, most INGOS are expanding their domains in terms of member organizations, and they believe that they will continue to do so.

This does not preclude that many organizations are small. According to the criteria set by the Union of International Associations (UIA), a minimum of three countries must be represented in an organization if it is to be considered international, and the average number of national "representations" in INGOS is about 26 (1966). The questionnaire contained questions about the dispersion of the membership, financial support, etc., and the answers were (in percent):

	One country	Two countries	More countries
The majority of members came from	7	10	83
The secretaries general tend to come from	43	17	40
The location of the international secretariat tends to be in	59	26	15
The staff of the secretariat tends to come from	52	19	27
The board tends to come from	4	3	92
Most of the revenue comes from	9	9	81

The questions fall into two distinct groups. General membership, revenue, and the membership of the board are very seldom limited to less than three countries only, while this is the rule rather than the exception in the case of the location of the international secretariat, the staff of the secretariat and the position of the secretary general. It is understandable that headquarters seldom are moved, and that the staff usually is recruited from the host country, but it is not so obvious that the nationality of the secretary general does not change more often. One possible explanation is that many of these organizations are quite young and simply have not changed secretaries general often. Besides, most secretaries general serve for quite a long period of time.

Those organizations that had a low dispersion of membership were also asked to name up to three countries that provided the majority of members, income, etc. France, Belgium and UK were most often mentioned, followed by the remaining EEC members and the Scandinavian countries.

As a corollary to the question about the way in which the organization was founded we asked how individuals could become members. Fifty-two percent answered that individual membership was possible through national organizations/chapters only, while 23% checked the opposite alternative, only direct affiliation with the international secretariat. In 24% of the INGOS both forms of individual membership are possible. These figures match well with those reported about the way in which the organization was founded.

Most INGOS set limitations on their membership in one way or another. Only 35% of our respondents checked the alternative that in principle every person in every country could become a member. Two percent admitted all kinds of persons provided they came from a certain geographical area. Thirty-six percent of the organizations were in principle universal, but their members must meet certain functional requirements (have certain interests, beliefs or positions), while the remaining 26 % restricted their potential membership both geographically and functionally.

When the membership is functionally restricted, which criteria are used? The questionnaire offered four different alternatives, and the distribution of answers was as follows:

Members become members on the basis of what they *are* or *do* (for instance, professional organizations)	75
Members become members on the basis of what they *think* or *believe* (for instance, ideological organizations)	9
Both	12
Neither	4

In a broad sense, most INGOs seem to be professional organizations.

Given these membership restrictions, we were interested in the extent to which potential members actually joined the various organizations. Forty-three percent of them claimed that they had more than half the maximum possible membership. Although this figure is quite impressive, there is definitely room for expansion.

5. Goals

The goals of INGOs are so varied that it is impossible to list them all. For our purposes the secretaries general were presented with a list of twelve rather general objectives and asked to check all those that applied to their respective organizations.

Goal no. 1 was the most popular, which is no surprise since it expresses the *raison d'être* of almost any organization. A factor analysis of these goals reveals that they can be reduced to four factors. We called the first factor "Peace and Development" because the three last goals (and no others) were associated with it. Goals 4, 5 and 6 made up another group, termed "Member cooperation". The next three goals loaded on the third factor, which was called "Influence others". Finally, the three first goals correlated with a factor given the label "Member Protection". Thus these four factors seem to reflect four general concerns of INGOs, but they receive different emphasis in different kinds of organizations. Generally speaking, ideological organizations are more outward-oriented (scoring high on an index made up of the six last goals) than professional organizations, but the correlation is far from perfect. Actually, the great majority (or 70 %)

	% who checked this goal
1. To improve communication between members in the special field of the organization so that they can do a better job	87
2. To work for the interest of the members, such as salaries, rights, social prestige, etc.	26
3. To strengthen members in their relations with non-members	27
4. To improve communication between the members also outside their common field of interest	32
5. To promote general cooperation and friendship between the members	79
6. To make members know each other so that they have contact in other countries for travel, correspondence, etc.	56
7. To convince those who are not members to join the organization	41
8. To disseminate information to non-members so that they think and/or act differently in some respect	37
9. To make non-members understand better what the members stand for	38
10. To improve general cooperation and friendship between all human beings	48
11. To work for peace between all nations and peoples in the world	45
12. To work for social and economic development in the world	51

of our respondents checked the alternative that their organizations worked not only for the interests of their own members, but also wanted to exercise an influence on non-members.

6. The decisionmaking structure

Most INGOs have a rather centralized decisionmaking structure. Although as much as 65 % of the secretaries general report that they share the initiative with the board of the organization, 62 % nevertheless think that most of the activity of the organization is initiated by the secretariat, cf. the table below.

Those organizations that have branches usually have a very hierarchical or feudal structure: inter-branch communication is negligible compared to the amount of communication with the secretariat. When asked about the importance of the direct communication between the branches, the respondents gave the following answers:

of major importance:	13 %
of minor importance:	39 %
there is no such communication:	47 %

The establishment of bilateral contacts seems to be of relatively little interest to most INGOs.

The Secretary General acts mainly on his own initiative	He acts equally much on his own initiative and at the request of the board	He acts mainly at the request of the board	Sum	(N)
22	65	13	100	(765)

Most of the activity of the organization is initiated by the secretariat	About equally much is initiated by the secretariat and the branches	Most of it is initiated by the branches	Sum	(N)
62	29	9	100	(722)

The branches communicate more with the secretariat than with each other	There is about an equal amount of communication between the branches as between the secretariat and the branches	The branches communicate more with each other than with the secretariat	Sum	(N)
76	21	3	100	(685)

Because contacts between the secretariat and the various branches is of such importance in the organizations, it is interesting to note how often it takes place:

at least once a fortnight:	15 %
at least once a month:	27 %
at least once a quarter:	37 %
once a year:	17 %
less often:	4 %

On the basis of these figures it is probably fair to say that most of the secretariats are not very often in contact with the member organizations.

7. Budget and staff

Most INGOs operate on very small budgets. In fact, some of them do not really have a budget at all. This is partly due to extensive reliance on volunteers to get the work done. The distribution of the size of the budgets is as follows:

less than $ 10 000	52 %
$ 10 000 — $ 100 000	37 %
above $ 100 000	11 %

The percentages correspond well to the information given about the size of the paid staff of the INGOs:

No paid staff	35 %
One employee	16 %
Two or three employees	23 %
Four to seven employees	12 %
Eight to fifteen employees	8 %
More than fifteen	6 %

Many INGOs have a small number of unpaid workers, often in addition to the paid ones:

No unpaid staff	32 %
Two or three unpaid workers	61 %
More	7 %

Even the secretary general is often partly or exclusively paid from other sources:

No salary from the organization	64 %
Receiving a salary, but also salaries from other sources	11 %
Receiving a salary, but in addition other sources of income (honoraria etc.)	18 %
Receiving a salary as practically only source of income	7 %

From one point of view, the executive staff of INGOs has a low level of "professionalization", but that is in no way equivalent to lack of professional or administrative competence.

8. Sources of income and priority of money-spending

Although most INGOs operate on very small budgets, they have to get money from somewhere. The sources are different for different types of organizations, but most organizations rely on a relatively small number of sources of income.

The table shows that contributions from national branches are by far the most important source of revenue for INGOs. Contributions from individual members come in second, and this is simply a reflection of the different membership structures of INGOs as described above. There is no doubt that membership fees in one form or another make up the better part of most INGO budgets. Proceeds from sales of publications are, generally

Sources of income and priority of money-spending

	Most important	Less important	No such income	Sum	Score*
Contributions from national branches	43	15	42	100	1
Contributions from individual members	29	20	51	100	—22
Proceeds from sales of publications	1	33	66	100	—65
Contributions from private organizations	7	19	74	100	—67
Contributions from national governments	5	12	83	100	—78
Contributions from INGOS	5	11	84	100	—79
Contributions from IGOS	2	9	89	100	—87
Proceeds from commercial activities other than publication	2	9	89	100	—87

speaking, far less important. Contributions from the governmental sector, whether on the national or on the international level, play a minor role. A few INGOS are subsidized by other INGOS. These are presumably super-INGOS, i.e. organizations with other INGOS as members.

The respondents were also asked what their priorities would be if their organization should happen to get some extra money, that is, money beyond what is stipulated in the budget. The answers are quite interesting:

	Highest or second highest priority	Lower priority	No interest	Sum	Score
Doing research on how to promote the goals of the organization	46	17	37	100	9
Having more conferences in the organization	37	19	45	99	—8
Hiring more personnel in the international secretariat	29	16	55	100	—26
Subsidizing poor national branches	14	17	69	100	—55
Creating more national branches	13	14	72	99	—59
Things other than those mentioned above and below	17	5	78	100	—61
Buying more office equipment in the international secretariat	9	19	72	100	—63
Contributing economically to plans against hunger and poverty	6	13	81	100	—75

"Doing research on how to promote the goals of the organization" is given the highest or second highest priority in 46 % of the organizations. The second most important priority is "having more conferences in the organization". "Hiring more personnel in the international secretariat" seems to be more important than "subsidizing poor national branches", which in turn is more important than the "creation of new national branches". The general impression one gets is that the secretaries general think it is more important to improve the quality of the work of the organization than increasing its size, that is, the number of members. Buying more office equipment scores low, presumably because most INGOs do not need office equipment, or because many INGO headquarters are parasites inside other offices, usually the one in which the secretary general is employed full-time. Finally it is worth noticing that very few INGOs would spend extra money on development of aid programs.

9. The contacts of INGO secretariats

We were interested in mapping parts of the interaction structure that surrounds INGO headquarters and asked therefore the respondents to order their contact partners with whom they stay in touch by way of mail, conversations, etc.

Contact partners	Highest or second highest rank	Lower rank	No contact	Score
National branches of the organization	69	6	25	44
Individual members of the organization	64	13	23	41
Other INGOs	28	39	33	—5
IGOs	15	35	50	—35
National governments	4	27	69	—65
Others	6	9	85	—79

The ranking of the contact is quite similar to the ranking of different sources of income. The members of the organization, whether individuals or associations, constitute the most important contact partners, and this comes as no surprise. What is a little surprising is that the contacts are so infrequent. There are fewer contacts with IGOs than with other INGOs and still less with national governments. Fifty percent of the organizations had no contacts with IGOs. This is reasonable in view of the fact that roughly one third of all INGOs have consultative status with one or more IGOs. Some interaction is also likely to take place outside the system of consultative statuses.

Almost 70 % of the INGO headquarters have never had contact with national governments. Most of their attention is directed at the international level. Contacts with national governments are taken care of by national branches.

Contacts with national governments	%
Mainly through the national branches	47
Mainly directly	14
Both ways	13
Those contacts are not performed at all	26

We guess that in the few cases that INGO headquarters make direct contact with national governments, the organization does not have chapters in that particular country. Unfortunately we have not asked any questions about the extent to which INGOs try to influence national governments through IGOs.

The questionnaire also contained some questions about what kinds of very frequent contacts INGO secretaries general had with other international organizations, whether governmental or nongovernmental.

The table below gives the percentage of INGOs that had a particular kind of contact with one or more other international organizations:

Personal friendship between secretaries general	54%
Joint meetings and conferences	50%
Exchange of observers at board or council meetings	39%
Sharing international secretariat facilities	21%
Exchange of members at the board or the council	12%

Many organizations also mentioned other kinds of contacts. It seems as if informal contacts are at least as important as formal ones.

Some INGOs are members of more inclusive organizations. Twenty-eight percent of our respondents reported that their INGO was member of one super-INGO, while 11 % were members of two or more. This is a relatively large number of organizations and includes many trade unions, scientific unions, etc., that have their umbrella organizations.

10. Frequency of meetings

It is difficult to find good indicators of the intensity of the activity of INGOs, but one that deserves mention is the frequency of meetings within the organization. We have asked about two kinds of meetings, those of the board of directors, and conferences open to all members:

Frequency	Board	Conferences
Once a month	5	1
Once a quarter	23	5
Once a year	56	41
Once every second year	8	24
Less often	8	29
Sum	100	100

Naturally the board meets more often than the rank-and-file members. Of the latter, almost 30 % see each other less often than once every second year. On the other hand, almost one half of the number of organizations arrange conferences once a year or more often. Only 16 % of the boards meet less often than once a year.

11. The secretaries general: their background and education

The remaining part of this presentation will be devoted to the secretaries general, their background, careers and attitudes. They make up an interesting category of "international men". As demonstrated above, quite a few of them are personal friends, and many others see each other often and do business with each other. Some of them have long experience in international work.

Ninety-two percent of the secretaries general are males. In other words, practically all secretaries general of INGOs that are not special women's organizations, are males.

The majority of the secretaries general are middle-aged people:

30 years and below	5 %
31—40 years	14 %
41—50 years	29 %
51—60 years	32 %
61—70 years	16 %
71 years and above	3 %

Eighty-two percent of the respondents were married at the time they completed the questionnaire, while an additional 7 % had been married earlier.

The rank ordering of nations in terms of the nationality of secretaries general correlates highly with the rank ordering of nations in terms of national "representations" in INGOs. About 18 % of our respondents were French, 14 % Belgian, 14 % British, 10 % from the USA. Seven percent of the secretaries general had changed nationality once or several times during their lives, and about 1 % had double citizenship. Eight percent of those that were married, had spouses of a different nationality.

Most secretaries general command an impressive number of languages:

One language	9 %
Two languages	23 %
Three languages	28 %
Four languages	25 %
Five or more	12 %

Sixty-five percent of them know at least three languages. This high figure is not so surprising considering the long education most of them have gone through. Eighty-seven percent have completed university or equivalent forms of education, and only 1 % have no formal education after primary school. In terms of years, the distribution is as follows:

8 years or less	4 %
9—10 years	3 %
11—12 years	8 %
13—15 years	16 %
16 years or more	70 %

Those with university education cover a number of different fields of study: 18 % have studied law, 20 % business administration and economics, 13 % physical and natural sciences, 15 % medicine, veterinary sciences and odontology, 9 % agricultural sciences. As many as 11 % have studied at least two different disciplines at the university level.

12. The secretaries general: their careers within the organization

In some organizations it is not necessary for the secretary general to be a member. However, 73 % of our respondents reported that they in fact were members, and most of them had been members for quite a long period of time:

0— 5 years	21 %
6—10 years	26 %
11—15 years	22 %
16—20 years	15 %
21 years and more	16 %

Some of them have also served in the position of the secretary general for an impressive number of years:

2 years or less	25 %
3— 4 years	22 %
5— 6 years	13 %
7— 8 years	9 %
9—10 years	9 %
11 years and more	20 %

Twenty percent of them have been the executive leader of their organizations for more than a decade. Many INGOs in fact do not put any limitations on the term a secretary general may serve. In response to a question about the period of time they were elected or appointed for, the secretaries general answer as follows:

2 years and less	16 %
3 years	18 %
4 years and more	20 %
indefinitely	39 %
As long as he wants himself	9 %

Fifty-two percent of the secretaries general had been elected by their organization, while another 36 % were appointed by the governing body of their INGO. Three percent had applied for the post, and 2 % had volunteered. The remaining 4 % had got the post by other means, and many of these had actually founded the organization of which they were in charge.

However, most of our respondents had had other positions in the organizations before they became secretary general. The table below gives an overview of the positions held:

24% became secretary general when the INGO was founded
13% were not members before becoming secretary general
17% were members of the national section only
13% were or had been on the board of a national section
8% were or had been the president or chairman of a national section
19% were or had been the secretary general of a national section
18% were or had been on the national board
3% were or had been international president or chairman
13% were or had been working in the international secretariat

13. The secretaries general: careers in other organizations

Many of our respondents have been and are active in other organizations than the one in which they serve as secretary general. They are "organizational men" with extensive administrative experience, often in addition to professional competence in science, medicine, economics, etc. We first asked them about positions in other national nongovernmental organizations with no international affiliation (including business firms) before they became secretaries general:

No position	27 %
Only member	13 %
Member of board	17 %
President	14 %
Secretary General	29 %

A large proportion have been in leading administrative positions.

The next question concerned participation in national governmental organizations:

No position	80 %
Low-ranking governmental employee	3 %
High-ranking governmental employee	15 %
MP	2 %
Member of government	1 %

As much as 80 % have had no governmental position, and three fourths of the remaining have served as high-ranking employees.

Membership in other INGOs is not infrequent, either on the national or on the international level:

No membership	73 %
Member only	11 %
Member of board on the national level	7 %
National President	3 %
National secretary general	6 %
Member of international board	10 %
International president	4 %
International secretary general	8 %

It is of course possible to serve in both the national and international sections, and therefore the sum of percentages exceeds one hundred. No less than 22 % of our respondents had served in other INGOs on the international level, and this means that experiences from one organization are often communicated to and used in another.

A few secretaries general have served in IGOs before they became administrative heads of INGOs:

No position in IGOs	94 %
Low ranking employee	1 %
High ranking employee	3 %
Secretary general	1 %

In addition, 11 % of those who answered our questionnaire had been members of one or more national, governmental delegations. As I shall show below, some INGO secretaries general expect to transfer to IGOs, so there is a certain amount of exchange of personnel between the two categories of international organizations.

14. The position of the preceding secretary general

In order to get some more information about the careers of secretaries general, we asked about what happened to their predecessors, and what plans they themselves had for the future. These questions were not answered as completely and consistently as most of the others. The data are therefore not as reliable as we should like them to be, but they nevertheless give some indications of trends.

We shall first deal with the fate of the predecessor. Twenty-seven percent of our respondents had never had one. This figure corresponds well with the 24 % who had become secretary general when the organization was founded. Seventeen percent of those who had a predecessor, reported that he was no longer alive, while another 23 % reported that he was not working any more. Only 8 % of the predecessors were women.

Let us first look at the position of the predecessors within the organization they had been heading:

No position	63 %
Rank-and-file member of a national section	20 %
Member of a national board	6 %
National president/chairman	4 %
National secretary general	7 %
Member of international board	18 %
International president	10 %
Working in the international secretariat	5 %

It is possible to hold positions at both the national and international levels. Therefore the sum of percentages exceeds one hundred. The figures in the above table are surprisingly low, which probably means that the secretaries general often withdraw from active participation in their organization when their term is ended.

Some of them remain or become active in other nongovernmental organizations on the national level, organizations without any international affiliations;

No position	54 %
Member only	15 %
Member of board	12 %
President	7 %
Secretary General	11 %

Some join national, governmental organizations; but there are fewer of them:

No position	85 %
Low ranking employee	1 %
High-ranking employee	10 %
MP	2 %
Member of government	1 %

It may of course be important for INGOs to have insiders in national governmental structures, particularly insiders with first-hand experience with the particular problems of INGOs.

Then there are some predecessors who have gotten or maintain positions in other INGOS:

No position	80 %
Rank-and-file member of a nation section	13 %
Member of a national board	5 %
National president/chairman	0 %
National secretary general	2 %
Member of international board	7 %
International president	4 %
International secretary general	4 %

The figures again add up to more than one hundred, but the total percentage of those who are active in another INGO is low, only about 20 %.

Only 2% of the predecessors were working in IGOs, and the majority of those had positions as high-ranking employees. About 3% is reported to have become members of national governmental delegations, but the data are not very reliable.

The secretaries general were also asked about which positions *they* expected to get in the future when *their* term was over, and they were given alternatives identical to those used for their predecessors. The distribution of answers is also almost identical. The only figure that stands out a little, is the 11% that expected to serve on national, governmental delegations.

In conclusion, previous secretaries general most often withdraw from active participation in organizational life, but to the extent they are active, they are more likely to be so in the nongovernmental sector. This is hardly surprising.

15. Some attitudes and preferences of secretaries general

Finally, some data about how the secretaries general look upon their organizations and their role. We first asked: In general, if *a friend* asked your advice about his professional career *in organizations*, which of the following would you recommend to him?

National nongovernmental organizations (private business or non- lucrative organizations)	27 %
National governmental organizations (ministries etc.)	6 %

International nongovernmental orga-
nizations   34 %
International governmental organi-
zations (UN, or any of the specialized
agencies)   33 %

The international level is beyond a doubt seen as more interesting than
the national ones. Furthermore, the governmental sector is deemed less
attractive on the national level, while the difference on the international
level is negligible. Despite the frequent complaints from INGO officers about
IGOS, quite a few of them are prepared to advise friends to work in such
organizations.

In order to get a better impression of how strong the preference for
work on the international level is, the respondents were confronted with
two alternatives and asked which one they would choose:

— To work in an *international organization* that has no connection with
your personal goals and membership, or
— To work in a *national organization* that is related to your personal goals
and membership.

Only 65 % of the respondents answered this question, but of those that
answered, 66 % preferred the first alternative. There would seem to be
a strong motivation for international work regardless of relatedness to
personal interests and goals.

In order to get some indication of whether the attitudes of secretaries
general are predominantly national or transnational (global), we confronted them with the hypothetical situation that they were going to work
for the UN in New York and asked in which capacity they would like
to serve there:

Work in the UN secretariat   46 %
Work in the UN mission of your
country   18 %
Be a member of a delegation from
your country to the UN   36 %

Almost one half of the respondents wanted to work in the transnational
part of the UN, the secretariat. To be a member of a delegation from one's
country is checked twice as often as working in the UN mission of one's
country. This may have to do with the short-term nature of appointments
to delegations, as opposed to missions. But it is also possible that respondents would see themselves representing certain professional or other transnational rather than national interests if appointed to national delegations.

Having established that our respondents generally prefer international to national work and the nongovernmental to the governmental sector, and that transnational loyalties seem to play an important role, we shall lastly look at the relative importance, as they see it, of being a good administrator, of being committed to the goals of the organization, and of having good knowledge about the issues the organization is concerned with. The method used is paired comparison of answers to the following question: If you were asked about who should be your successor, what kind of person would you prefer?

	a person who is a good administrator	36%
or	a person who has a deep commitment to the goals and values of the organization	64%
	a person who is a good administrator	29%
or	a person who has good knowledge about the issues the organization is concerned with	71%
	a person who has a deep commitment to the goals and values of the organization	53%
or	a person who has good knowledge about the issues the organization is concerned with	58%

Commitment is preferred to knowledge about the issues, and knowledge about the issues is preferred to administrative skill. On the basis of this rank ordering of preferences one would have expected that more respondents would have preferred commitment to administrative skill than knowledge to administrative skill, but the opposite is the case. The reason is that some secretaries general have not checked these alternatives in a consistent manner. However, the number of cases of inconsistent rank-ordering of alternatives is not large enough to blur the general trend: Strong emphasis on commitment to the goals and values of the organization, and relatively little stress on administrative skill. This is not so unreasonable in light of the remuneration of these persons. Most of them receive very little money, and a strong dedication to the organization and its objectives and values is a prerequisite for doing a good job.

16. Concluding remarks

We shall make no attempt to summarize all the findings reported here. The questions in our form were worded with various theoretical concerns in mind, and the information gathered has been used for different purposes (cf. the bibliography). Nor shall we try to relate these data systematically to the first part of the present chapter: the tendencies are in agreement with the general theory, what this part purports to offer is some measure of quantity, how much.

Bibliography

Publications in which the INGO-questionnaire data have been used:

BROGDEN, MIKE: "Integration and the International Community." Unpublished M. Phil. thesis, University of Leeds, 1972.

GALTUNG, JOHAN: "Non-territorial Actors and the Problem of Peace." Revised version of a paper presented at the World Order Models Meeting, 1969 in Saul H. Mendlovitz, ed., *On the Creation of a Just World Order*, New York: Free Press, 1973.

JUDGE, ANTHONY J. N.; and SKJELSBAEK, KJELL: "Transnational Associations and Their Functions." *Functionalism: Theory and Practice in International Relations*. A.J.R. Groom and Paul Taylor, eds. London: University of London Press, 1975.

KRIESBERG, LOUIS: "Centralization and Differentiation in Nongovernmental Organizations." *Sociology and Social Research*, LXI, No. 1 (1976).

SKJELSBAEK, KJELL: "Peace and the Systems of International Organizations." Unpublished Magister thesis, University of Oslo, 1970.

SKJELSBAEK, KJELL: "Development of the Systems of International Organizations: A Diachronic Study." *Proceedings of the International Peace Research Association Third General Conference*. Vol. II: *The International System*. IPRA Studies in Peace Research, No. 4. Assen: van Gorcum, 1970.

SKJELSBAEK, KJELL: "The Growth of International Nongovernmental Organization in the Twentieth Century". *International Organization*, XXV, No. 3 (1971). This issue is also published as: *Transnational Relations and World Politics*. Robert O. Keohane and Joseph S. Nye, Jr., eds. Cambridge, Mass.: Harvard University Press, 1972.

SKJELSBAEK, KJELL: "Peace and the Structure of the International Organization Network." *Journal of Peace Research*, IX, No. 4 (1972).

YOUNG, LAWRENCE: "Secretaries General in International Nongovernmental Organizations." *International Associations*, No. 7, 1971.

IV.13. A Structural Theory of Imperialism*

From *Journal of Peace Research* VIII/2 (1971).
PRIO publication No. 27—1
Notes on page *712*.

1. Introduction

This theory takes as its point of departure two of the most glaring facts about this world: the tremendous inequality, within and between nations, in almost all aspects of human living conditions, including the power to decide over those living conditions; *and* the resistance of this inequality to change. The world consists of Center and Periphery nations; and each nation, in turn, has its center and periphery. Hence, our concern is with the mechanism underlying this discrepancy, particularly between the center in the Center, and the periphery in the Periphery. In other words, how to conceive of, how to explain, and how to counteract inequality as one of the major forms of *structural violence*. [1]. Any theory of liberation from structural violence presupposes theoretically and practically adequate ideas of the dominance system against which the liberation is directed; and the special type of dominance system to be discussed here is *imperialism*.

Imperialism will be conceived of as a dominance relation between collectivities, particularly between nations. It is a sophisticated type of dominance relation which cuts across nations, basing itself on a bridgehead which the center in the Center nation establishes in the center of the Periphery nation, for the joint benefit of both. It should not be confused with other ways in which one collectivity can dominate another in the sense of exercising power over it. Thus, military occupation of B by A may seriously curtail B's freedom of action but is not for that reason an imperialist relationship unless it is set up in a special way. The same applies to the *threat* of conquest and possible occupation, as in a balance of power relationship. Moreover, *subversive* activities may also be brought to a stage where a nation is dominated by the pin-pricks exercised against it from below, but this is clearly different from imperialism.

Thus imperialism is a species in a genus of dominance and power relationships. It is subtype of something, and has itself subtypes to be explored later. Dominance relations between nations and other collectivities will not disappear with the disappearance of imperialism; nor will the end to one type of imperialism (e.g. political or economic) guarantee the end to another type of imperialism (e.g. economic or cultural). Our view is not reductionist in the traditional sense pursued in Marxist-Leninist theory, which conceived of imperialism as an economic relationship under private capitalism, motivated by the need for expanding markets, and which bases the theory of dominance on a theory of imperialism. According to this view, imperialism and dominance will fall like dominoes when the capitalistic conditions for economic imperialism no longer obtain. According to the view we develop here, imperialism is a more general structural relationship between two collectivities, and has to be understood at a general level in order to be understood and counteracted in its more specific manifestations — just like smallpox is better understood in a context of a theory of epidemic diseases, and these diseases better understood in a context of general pathology.

Briefly stated, imperialism is a system that splits up collectivities and relates some of the parts to each other in relations of *harmony of interest*, and other parts in relations of *disharmony of interest*, or *conflict of interest*.

2. Defining 'conflicts of interest'

'Conflict of interest' is a special case of conflict in general, defined as a situation where parties are pursuing incompatible goals. In our special case, these goals are stipulated by an outsider as the 'true' interests of the parties, disregarding wholly or completely what the parties themselves say explicitly are the values they pursue. One reason for this is the rejection of the dogma of unlimited rationality: actors do *not* necessarily know, or they are unable to express, what their interest is. Another, more important, reason is that rationality is unevenly distributed, that some may dominate the minds of others, and that this may lead to 'false consciousness'. Thus, learning to suppress one's own true interests may be a major part of socialization in general and education in particular.

Let us refer to this true interest as LC, *living condition*. It may perhaps be measured by using such indicators as income, standard of living in the usual materialistic sense — but notions of *quality of life* would certainly also enter, not to mention notions of *autonomy*. But the precise content of LC is less important for our purpose than the definition of conflict of interest:

There is *conflict*, or *disharmony of interest*, if the two parties are coupled together in such a way that the LC *gap* between them is *increasing*;

There is *no conflict*, or *harmony of interest*, if the two parties are coupled together in such a way that the LC *gap* between them is *decreasing down to zero*.

Some points in this definition should be spelled out.

First, the parties have to be coupled together, in other words *interact*. A difference between mutually isolated parties does not in itself give rise to problems of interest. There was neither harmony, nor disharmony of interest between the peoples in Africa, Asia, and America before the white Europeans came — there was *nothing*.

Second, the reference is to *parties*, not to actors. In the theory of conflict of *interests*, as opposed to the theory of conflict of *goals*, there is no assumption that the parties (better: categories) have crystallized into actors. This is what they may have to do after they see their own situation more clearly, or in other words: the conflict of interest may have to be transformed into a conflict of *goals*. Thus, if in a nation the center, here defined as the 'government' (in the wide sense, not the 'cabinet') uses its power to increase its own LC much more than does the rest of the nation, then there is disharmony of interest between government and people according to this definition. This may then be used as a basis for defining the government as illegitimate — as opposed to the usual conception where illegitimacy is a matter of opinion, expressed in the legislature or in the population. The trouble with the latter idea is that it presupposes a level of rationality, an ability of expression and political consciousness and party formation that can only be presupposed at the center of the more or les; vertical societies in which human beings live. It is a model highly protective of the center as a whole, however much it may lead to rotation of groups within the center, and hence protective of vertical society.

Third, there is the problem of what to do with the case of a *constant gap*. The parties grow together, at the same rate, but the gap between them is constant. Is that harmony or disharmony of interest? We would refer to it as disharmony, for the parties are coupled such that they will not be brought together. Even if they *grow* parallel to each other it is impossible to put it down as a case of harmony, when the distribution of value is so unequal. On the contrary, this is the case of disharmony that has reached a state of equilibrium.

Fourth, this definition has the advantage of enabling us to talk about *degrees of harmony and disharmony* by measuring the angle between the two trajectories, perhaps also taking speed into account. Thus we avoid the difficulty of talking simplistically in terms of polar opposites, harmony vs. disharmony, and can start talking in terms of weak and strong harmony and disharmony.

Fifth, there is an implicit reference to *time* in the two terms 'increasing' and 'decreasing'. We have not been satisfied with a time-free way of operationalizing the concept in terms of static LC gaps. It is much easier with conflict of goals, as we would then be dealing with clearly demarcated actors whose values can be ascertained, and their compatibility or incompatibility likewise: there is no need to study the system over time. To understand conflict of *interest* it looks as if at least a bivariate, diachronic analysis should be carried out to get some feeling of how the system operates.

But we should obviously make a distinction between the *size* of the gap, and what happens to the gap over time. If we only had access to static, synchronic data, then we would of course focus on the magnitude of the gap and talk about *disharmony of interest if it is wide, harmony of interest if it is narrow or zero.*

As a first approximation this may not be too bad, but it leads us into some difficulties. Thus, how do we rank these combinations in terms of increasing disharmony of interest? (Table 13.1).

TABLE 13.1 *Four types of harmony / disharmony of interest*

		gap decreasing	increasing
gap	narrow	A	C
	wide	B	D

As we see from the Table, the only doubt would be between combinations B and C. We would favor the alphabetical order for two reasons: first, becoming is more important than being (at least if the time-perspective is reasonably short), and second, the diachronic relationship probably reveals more about the coupling between them. For example the gap in living condition between Norway and Nepal in 1970 is not significant as an indicator of any imperialism. If it keeps on increasing there may be a bit more basis for the suspicion, but more evidence is needed to state the diagnosis of imperialism. The crucial word here is 'coupling' in the definition. The word has been put there to indicate some type of social causation in interaction relation and interaction structure which will have to be demonstrated, over and above a simple correlation.

Let us conclude this discussion by pointing out that a gap in living condition, of at least one important kind, is a necessary, if not sufficient, condition for conflict or disharmony of interest. If in addition the gap can be observed over time, a more satisfactory basis for a diagnosis in terms of imperialism may emerge.

And then, in conclusion: it is clear that the concept of interest used here is based on an ideology, or a *value premise of equality* [2]. An interaction relation and interaction structure set up such that inequality is the result is seen as a coupling not in the interest of the weaker party. This is a value premise like so many other value premises in social science explorations, such as 'direct violence is bad', 'economic growth is good', 'conflict should be resolved', etc. As in all other types of social science, the goal should not be an 'objective' social science freed from all such value premises, but a more honest social science where the value premises are made explicit.

3. Defining 'imperialism'

We shall now define imperialism by using the building blocks presented in the preceding two sections. In our two-nation world, imperialism can be defined as one way in which the Center nation has power over the Periphery nation, so as to bring about a condition of disharmony of interest between them. Concretely, *Imperialism* is a relation between a Center and a Periphery nation so that. [3]

1. there is *harmony of interest* between *the center in the Center* nation and the *center in the Periphery* nation.
2. there is more *disharmony of interest* within the Periphery nation than within the Center nation,
3. there is *disharmony of interest* between the *periphery in the Center* nation and the *periphery in the Periphery* nation.

Diagrammatically it looks something like Fig. 13.1.

FIGURE 13.1 *The structure of imperialism*

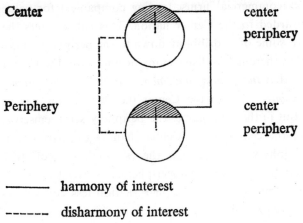

Center center
   periphery

Periphery center
   periphery

———— harmony of interest

------ disharmony of interest

441

This complex definition, borrowing largely from Lenin [4], needs spelling out. The basic idea is, as mentioned, that the center in the Center nation has a bridgehead in the Periphery nation, and a well-chosen one: the center in the Periphery nation. This is established such that the Periphery center is tied to the Center center with the best possible tie: the tie of harmony of interest. They are linked so that they go up and down, even under, together. How this is done in concrete terms will be explored in the subsequent sections.

Inside the two nations there is disharmony of interest. They are both in one way or another vertical societies with LC gaps — otherwise there is no possibility of locating a center and a periphery. Moreover, the gap is not decreasing, but is at best constant. But the basic idea, absolutely fundamental for the whole theory to be developed, is that *there is more disharmony in the Periphery nation than in the Center nation.* At the simplest static level of description this means there is more inequality in the Periphery than in the Center. At the more complex level we might talk in terms of the gap opening more quickly in the Periphery than in the Center, where it might even remain constant. Through welfare state activities, redistribution takes place and disharmony is reduced for at least some LC dimensions, including income, but usually excluding power.

If we now try to capture in a few sentences what imperialism is about, we might perhaps say something like this:

In the Periphery nation, the center grows more than the periphery, due partly to how interaction between center and periphery is organized. Without necessarily thinking of economic interaction, the center is more enriched than the periphery — in ways to be explored below. However, for part of this enrichment, the center in the Periphery only serves as a transmission belt (e.g. as commercial firms, trading companies) for value (e.g. raw materials) forwarded to the Center nation. This value enters the center in the Center, with some of it dribbling down to the periphery in the Center. It is important that there is less disharmony of interest in the Center than in the Periphery, so that *the total arrangement is largely in the interest of the periphery in the Center.* Within the Center the two parties may be opposed to each other. But in the total game, the periphery see themselves more as the partners of the center in the Center than as the partners of the periphery in the Periphery — and this is the essential trick of that game. Alliance formation between the two peripheries is avoided, while the Center nation becomes more and the Periphery nation less cohesive — and hence less able to develop long-term strategies.

Actually, concerning the three criteria in the definition of imperialism as given above, it is clear that no. (3) is implied by nos. (1) and (2). The two centers are tied together and the Center periphery is tied to its center: that is the whole essence of the situation. If we now presuppose that the center in the Periphery is a smaller proportion of that nation than the center in the Center, we can also draw one more implication: *there is disharmony of interest between the Center nation as a whole and the Periphery nation as a whole*. But that type of finding, frequently referred to, is highly misleading because it blurs the harmony of interest between the two centers and leads to the belief that imperialism is merely an international relationship, *not a combination of intra- and international relations*. [5].

However, even if the definition given above purports to define the pure case of imperialism, we may nevertheless fruitfully think in terms of degenerate cases. Thus, the first point in the definition about harmony between the two centers is obviously the most important one. If the second point does not hold and consequently not the third point either, it may still be fruitful to talk about imperialism. But in this degenerate case the two peripheries may more easily find each other, since they are now only kept apart by geographical distance (assuming that the two nations are nation-states, often even located far apart), not in addition by disharmony of interest. Thus, if the relationship between the two peripheries and their centers should become more similar, periphery alliance formation might easily be the result, and the two centers would have to resort to more direct means of violence rather than, or in addition to, the delicate type of structural violence that characterizes the pure type of imperialistic relationship.

But what if there is no distinction between center and periphery in the two nations, what if they are completely horizontal societies ? In that case, we should not talk about the dominance relationship whereby the Center nation extracts something from the Periphery nation as an imperialistic one, but rather as something else — looting, stealing, etc. Where there is no bridgehead for the Center nation in the center of the Periphery nation, there cannot be any imperialism by this definition.

From this, an important methodological remark may follow. Imagine we now start from the other end and discover that over time some nations increase their living conditions more than other nations — the' increasing gap' so often referred to today — and that there seems to be some kind of structure to this, some kind of invariance. As mentioned, this does not in itself constitute proof of any diagnosis in terms of imperialism, but should prompt the researcher to look for data in that direction. More particularly, we should try to study the precise nature of the interaction between the nations or groups of nations, and see whether the nations can be differentiated in terms of center and peripheries that relate to each other in the way indicated. But to do this in at all a concrete manner, we must make our definition of imperialism much less abstract. To this we now turn, in successive stages, exploring two *mechanisms*, five *types*, and three *phases* of imperialism.

4. The mechanisms of imperialism

The two basic mechanisms of imperialism both concern the *relation* between the parties concerned, particularly between the nations. The first mechanism concerns the *interaction relation* itself, the second how these relations are put together in a larger interaction structure:

1. the principle of *vertical interaction relation,*
2. the principle of *feudal interaction structure.*

The basic point about interaction is, of course, that people and nations have different values that complement each other, and then engage in exchange. Some nations produce oil, other nations produce tractors, and they then carry out an exchange according to the principle of comparative advantages. Imagine that our two-nation system has a prehistory of no interaction at all, and then starts with this type of interaction. Obviously, both will be changed by it, and more particularly: a gap between them is likely to open and widen if the interaction is cumulatively asymmetric in terms of what the two parties get out of it.

To study whether the interaction is symmetric or asymmetric, on equal or unequal terms, *two factors* arising from the interaction have to be examined:

1. the *value-exchange between the actors* — inter-actor effects,
2. the *effects inside the actors* — intra-actor effects.

In *economic* relations the first is most commonly analyzed, not only by liberal but also by Marxist economists. The inter-actor flow can be observed as flows of raw material, capital, and financial goods and services in either direction, and can literally be measured at the main points of entry: the customs houses and the national banks. The flow both ways can then be compared in various ways. Most important is the comparison in terms of *who benefits most*, and for this purpose intra-actor effects also have to be taken into consideration.

In order to explore this, the interaction budget indicated in Table 13.2 may be useful. In the Table the usual exchange pattern between a 'devel-

TABLE 13.2 *An interaction budget*

	A ('developed')		B ('developing')	
	inter-actor effects	intra-actor effects	inter-actor effects	intra-actor effects
positive (in)	raw materials	spin-offs	manufactured goods	little or nothing
negative (out)	manufactured goods	pollution, exploitation	raw materials	depletion, exploitation

oped' nation A and a 'developing' nation B, where manufactured goods are exchanged for raw materials is indicated. Whether it takes place in a barter economy or a money economy is not essential in a study of exchange between completely unprocessed goods like crude oil and highly processed goods like tractors. There are negative intra-actor effects that accrue to both parties, indicated by the terms 'pollution' for A and 'depletion' for B, and 'exploitation' for either. So far these negative spin-off effects are usually not taken systematically into account, nor the positive spin-off effects for A that will be a corner-stone in the present analysis.

It is certainly meaningful and important to talk in terms of unequal exchange of asymmetric interaction, but not quite unproblematic what its precise meaning should be. For that reason, it may be helpful to think in terms of three stages or types of exploitation, partly reflecting historical *processes* in chronological order, and partly reflecting types of *thinking* about exploitation.

In the first stage of exploitation, A simply engages in looting and takes away the raw materials without offering anything in return. If he steals from pure Nature there is no human interaction involved, but we assume that he forces 'natives' to work for him and do the extraction work. It is like the slave-owner who lives on the work produced by slaves — which is quantitatively not too different from the land-owner who has land-workers working for him five out of seven days a week.

In the second stage, A starts offering something 'in return'. Oil, pitch, land, etc., is 'bought' for a couple of beads — it is no longer simply taken away without asking any questions about ownership. The price paid is ridiculous. However, as power relations in the international systems change, perhaps mainly by bringing the power level of the weaker party up from zero to some low positive value, A has to contribute more: for instance, pay more for the oil. The question is now whether there is a cut-off point after which the exchange becomes equal, and what the criterion for that cut-off point would be. Absence of subjective dissatisfaction — B says

445

that he is now content? Objective market values or the number of man-hours that have gone into the production on either side?

There are difficulties with all these conceptions. But instead of elaborating on this, we shall rather direct our attention to the shared failure of all these attempts to look at *intra-actor* effects. Does the interaction have enriching or impoverishing effects *inside* the actor, or does it just lead to a standstill? This type of question leads us to the third stage of exploitation, where there may be some balance in the flow between the actors, but great differences in the effect the interaction has within them [6].

As an example let us use nations exchanging oil for tractors. The basic point is that this involves different levels of processing, where we define 'processing' as an activity imposing Culture on Nature. In the case of crude oil the product is (almost) pure Nature; in the case of tractors it would be wrong to say that it is a case of pure Culture, pure *form* (like mathematics, music). A transistor radio, an integrated circuit, these would be better examples because Nature has been brought down to a minimum. The tractor is still too much iron and rubber to be a pure case.

The major point now is the *gap in processing level* between oil and tractors and the differential effect this gap will have on the two nations. In one nation the oil deposit may be at the water-front, and all that is needed is a derrick and some simple mooring facilities to pump the oil straight into a ship — e.g. a Norwegian tanker — that can bring the oil to the country where it will provide energy to run, among other things, the tractor factories. In the other nation the effects may be extremely far-reaching due to the complexity of the product and the connectedness of the society. There may be ring effects in all directions, and in Table 13.3 we have made an effort to show some types of spin-off effects. A number of comments are appropriate in connexion with this list, which, needless to say, is very tentative indeed.

First, the effects are rather deep-reaching if this is at all a correct image of the situation. And the picture is hardly exaggerated. It is possible to set up international interaction in such a way that the positive intra-actor effects are practically nil in the raw material delivering nation, and extremely far-reaching in the processing nation [7]. This is not in any sense strange either: if processing is the imprint of Culture on Nature, the effects should be far-reaching indeed, and strongly related to development itself.

Second. these effects reinforce each other. In the nine effects listed in Table 13.3, there are economic, political, military, communications, and cultural aspects, mixed together. Thus, the nation that in the international division of labor has the task of providing the most refined, processed products — like Japan with its emphasis on integrated circuits, transistors, miniaturization, etc. (or Eastern Europe's Japan: the DDR, with a similar

TABLE 13.3 *Intra-actor effects of interaction across gaps in processing levels*

Dimension	Effect on center nation	Effect on periphery nation	Analyzed by
1. Subsidiary economic effects	New *means of production* developed	Nothing developed, just a hole in the ground	Economists
2. Political position in world structure	Central position reinforced	Periphery position reinforced	International relationists
3. Military benefits	*Means of destruction can* easily be produced	No benefits, wars cannot be fought by means of raw materials	
4. Communication benefits	*Means of communication* easily developed	No benefits, transportation not by means of raw materials	Communication specialists
5. Knowledge and research	Much needed for higher levels of processing	Nothing needed, extraction based on being, not on becoming	Scientists, technicians
6. Specialist needed	Specialists in *making*, scientists, engineers	Specialist in *having*, lawyers	Sociologists of knowledge
7. Skill and education	Much needed to carry out processing	Nothing needed, just a hole in the ground	Education specialists
8. Social structure	Change needed for ability to convert into mobility	No change needed, extraction based on ownership, not on ability	Sociologists
9. Psychological effects	A basic psychology of self-reliance and autonomy	A basic psychology of dependence	Psychologists

emphasis) — will obviously have to engage in research. Research needs an infra-structure, a wide cultural basis in universities, etc., and it has obvious spill-over effects in the social, political, and military domains. And so on: the list may be examined and all kinds of obvious types of cross-fertilization explored.

Third, in the example chosen, and also in the formulations in the Table, we have actually referred to a very special type of gap in processing level: the case when one of the nations concerned delivers raw materials. But the general point here is the *gap* which would also exist if one nation delivers semi-finished products and the other finished products. There may be as much of a gap in a trade relation based on exchange between textiles and transistors as one based on exchange between oil and tractors. However, and this seems to be basic: we have looked in vain for a theory of economic trade where this gap is meaningfully operationalized so that the theory could be based on it. In fact, *degree of processing*, which is the basic variable behind the spin-off effects, seems absent from most thinking about international exchange.

This, and this is observation number *four,* is not merely a question of analyzing differences in processing level in terms of what happens inside the factory or the extraction plant. It has to be seen in its social totality. A glance at the right-hand column of Table 13.3 immediately gives us some clues as to why this has not been done: academic research has been so divided that nowhere in a traditional university set-up would one come to grips with the totality of the effects of an interaction process. Not even in the most sophisticated intercross or trans-disciplinary research institute has that type of research been carried so far that a meaningful operationalization has been offered. Yet this is indispensible for a new program of trade on equal terms to be formulated: *trade, or interaction in general, is symmetric, or on equal terms, if and only if the total inter- and intra-actor effects that accrue to the parties are equal* [8].

But, and this is observation number *five:* why has the idea of comparing the effects of interaction only at the points of exit and entry been so successful? Probably basically because it has always been natural and in the interest of the two centers to view the world in this way, not necessarily consciously to reinforce their position in the center, but basically because interaction looks more like '*inter*-action only' to the center. If the center in the Periphery has based its existence on being rather than becoming, on ownership rather than processing, then the inter-action has been very advantageous to it. What was formerly Nature is through the 'beneficial interaction' with another nation converted into Money, which in turn can be converted into many things. *Very little effort was needed:* and that this was precisely what made the exchange so disadvantageous, only became clear after some time. Japan is, possibly, the only nation that has really converted the absence of raw materials into a blessing for the economy.

Some implications of the general principle of viewing intra-actor in addition to inter-actor effects can now be spelled out.

One is obvious: *asymmetry cannot be rectified by stabilizing or increasing the prices for raw materials.* Of course, prices exist that could, on the surface, compensate for the gap in intra-actor effects, convertible into a corresponding development of subsidiary industries, education industry, knowledge industry, and so on (although it is hard to see how the psychology of self-reliance can be bought for money). Much of this is what raw material producing countries can do with the money they earn. But this is not the same. One thing is to be *forced* into a certain pattern of intra-actor development in *order to* be able to participate in the inter-actor interaction, quite another thing to be free to make the decision without having to do it, without being forced by the entire social machinery.

The second implication is also obvious, but should still be put as a question to economists. Imagine that a nation A gives nation B a loan L, to be repaid after n years at an interest rate of $p\%$ p.a. There is only one condition in addition to the conditions of the loan: that the money be used to procure goods at a high level of processing in A. Each order will then have deep repercussions in A, along the eight dimensions indicated, in addition to the direct effect of the order itself. The value of these effects is certainly not easily calculated, but in addition A also gets back from B, if B has not gone bankrupt through this process in the meantime, $L(1+p)^n$ after n years. If procurement is in terms of capital goods rather than consumer goods (usually for consumption by the center in the Periphery mainly) there will also have been intra-actor effects in B. In all likelihood the intra--actor effects of the deal in A are more far-reaching, however, for two reasons: the effects of the interaction process enter A at a higher level of processing than B, and A has already a socio-economic-political structure enabling it to absorb and convert and redirect such pressures for maximum beneficial impact.

Imagine now that n is high and p is low; the loan is said to be 'on generous terms'. The question is whether this generosity is not deceptive, *whether it would not have paid for A to give L for eternity, at no interest,* i.e. as a grant. Or even better it might even have paid for A to persuade B to take on L with negative interest, i.e. to pay B for accepting the loan, because of all the intra-actor effects. The situation may be likened to a man who pays some people a certain sum on the condition that they use the money to pay him for an article on, say, imperialism. By having to produce, by having obligations to fulfil, the man is forced to create and thereby expand, and consequently forced to enrich himself [9].

In short, we see vertical interaction as the major source of the inequality of this world, whether it takes the form of looting, of highly unequal exchange, or highly differential spin-off effects due to processing gaps. But we can also imagine a fourth phase of exploitation, where the modern King Midas becomes a victim of his own greed and turns his environment into muck rather than gold, by polluting it so strongly and so thoroughly that the negative spin-off effects from processing may outstrip all the positive effects. This may, in fact, place the less developed countries in a more favourable position: the lower the GNP, the lower the Gross National Pollution.

But this phase is still for the (near?) future. At present what we observe is an inequality between the world's nations of a magnitude that can only be explained in terms of the cumulative effect of *strong* structural phenomena over time, like the phenomena described here under the heading of imperialism. This is not to deny that other factors may also be important,

FIGURE 13.2 *A feudal center-periphery structure*

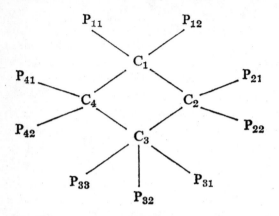

even decisive, but no analysis can be valid without studying the problem of development in a context of vertical interaction.

If the first mechanism, the *vertical interaction relation*, is the major factor behind inequality, then the second mechanism, the *feudal interaction structure*, is the factor that maintains and reinforces this inequality by protecting it. There are four rules defining this particular interaction structure [10]:

1. interaction between Center and Periphery is *vertical*
2. interaction between Periphery and Periphery is *missing*
3. multilateral interaction involving all three is *missing*
4. interaction with the outside world is *monopolized* by the Center, with two implications:
   a) Periphery interaction with other Center nations is *missing*
   b) Center as well as Periphery interaction with Periphery nations belonging to other Center nations is *missing*

This relation can be depicted as in Fig. 13.2. As indicated in the Figure, the number of Periphery nations attached to any given Center nation can, of course, vary. In this Figure we have also depicted the rule 'if you stay off my satellites, I will stay off yours'.

Some important *economic* consequences of this structure should be spelled out.

First and most obvious: the *concentration on trade partners*. A Periphery nation should, as a result of these two mechanisms, have most of its trade with 'its' Center nation. In other words, empirically we would expect high levels of *important concentration* as well as *export concentration* in the Periphery, as opposed to the Center, which is more free to extend its trade relations in almost any direction — except in the pure case, with the Periphery of other Center nations.

Second, and not so obvious, is the *commodity concentrations:* the tendency for Periphery nations to have only one or very few primary products to export. This would be a trivial matter if it could be explained entirely in terms of geography, e.g. if oil countries were systematically poor as to ore, ore countries poor as to bananas and coffee, etc. But this can hardly be assumed to be the general case: Nature does not distribute its riches that way. There is a historical rather than geographical explanation for this. A territory may have been exploited for the raw materials most easily available and/or most needed in the Center, and this, in turn, leads to a certain social structure, to communication lines to the deposits, to trade structures, to the emergence of certain center groups (often based on ownership of that particular raw material), and so on. To start exploiting a new kind of raw material in the same territory might upset carefully designed local balances; hence, it might be easier to make a fresh start for that new raw material in virgin territory with no bridgehead already prepared for imperialist exploits. In order to substantiate this hypothesis we would have to demonstrate that there are particularly underutilized and systematically under-explored deposits precisely in countries where one type of raw material has already been exploited.

The combined effect of these two consequences is a *dependency* of the Periphery on the Center. Since the Periphery usually has a much smaller GNP, the trade between them is a much higher percentage of the GNP for the Periphery, and with both partner and commodity concentration, the Periphery becomes particularly vulnerable to fluctuations in demands and prices,. At the same time the center in the Periphery depends on the Center for its supply of consumer goods. Import substitution industries will usually lead to consumer goods that look homespun and un-chic, particularly if there is planned obsolescence in the production of these goods in the Center, plus a demand for equality between the two centers maintained by demonstration effects and frequent visits to the Center [11].

However, the most important consequence is political and has to do with the systematic utilization of feudal interaction structures as a way of protecting the Center against the Periphery. The feudal interaction structure is in social science language nothing but an expression of the old political maxim *divide et impera*, divide and rule, as a strategy used systematically by the Center relative to the Periphery nations. How could — for example — a small foggy island in the North Sea rule over one quarter of the world? By isolating the Periphery parts from each other, by having them geographically at sufficient distance from each other to impede any real alliance formation, by having separate deals with them so as to tie them to the Center in particular ways, by reducing multilateralism to a minimum with all kinds of graded membership, *and by* having the Mother country assume the role of window to the world.

However, this point can be much more clearly seen if we combine the two mechanisms and extend what has been said so far for relations between Center and Periphery *nations* to relations between center and periphery *groups* within nations. Under an imperialist structure the two mechanisms are used not only between nations but also within nations, but less so in the Center nation than in the Periphery nation. In other words, there is vertical division of labor within as well as between nations. And these two levels of organization are intimately linked to each other (as A. G. Frank has always emphasized) in the sense that the center in the Periphery inter-action structure is also that group with which the Center nation has its harmony of interest, the group used as a bridgehead.

Thus, the combined operation of the two mechanisms at the two levels builds into the structure a subtle grid of protection measures against the major potential source of 'trouble', the periphery in the Periphery. To summarize the major items in this grid:

1. the general impoverishment of pP brought about by vertical division of labor within the Periphery nation, and particularly by the high level of inequality (e.g. differential access to means of communication) and disharmony of interest in the Periphery nation;

2. the way in which interaction, mobilization, and organization of Pp are impeded by the feudal structure *within* Periphery nations;

3. the general impoverishment of the Periphery nation brought about by vertical division of labor, particularly in terms of means of destruction and communication;

4. the way in which interaction, mobilization, and organization of the Periphery nations are impeded by the feudal interaction structure *between* nations
   a. making it difficult to interact with other Periphery nations 'belonging' to the same Center nations,
   b. making it even more difficult to interact with Periphery nations 'belonging' to other Center nations;

5. the way in which it is *a fortiori* difficult for the peripheries in Periphery nations to interact, mobilize, and organize
   a. intranationally because of 1 and 2,
   b. internationally because of 3 and 4,

c. in addition: because the center in the Periphery has the monopoly on international interaction in all directions and cannot be counted on to interact in the interest of its own periphery;

6. the way in which pP cannot appeal to pC or cC either because of the disharmony of interest.

Obviously, the more perfectly the mechanisms of imperialism within and between nations are put to work, the less overt machinery of oppression is needed and the smaller can the center groups be, relative to the total population involved. *Only imperfect, amateurish imperialism needs weapons; professional imperialism is based on structural rather than direct violence.*

5. Types of imperialism

We shall now make this more concrete by distinguishing between five types of imperialism depending on the *type* of exchange between Center and Periphery nations:

1. *economic*
2. *political*
3. *military*
4. *communication*
5. *cultural*

The order of presentation is rather random: we have no theory that one is more basic than the others, or precedes the others. Rather, this is like a Pentagon or a Soviet Star [12]: imperialism can start from any corner. They should all be examined regarding the extent to which they generate interaction patterns that utilize the two *mechanisms* of imperialism so as to fulfill the three *criteria* of imperialism, or at least the first of them.

The most basic of the two mechanisms is *vertical* interaction, which in its modern form is conceived of as interaction across a gap in processing level. In other words, what is exchanged between the two nations is not only not the same things (which would have been stupid) but things of a quite different kind, the difference being in terms of where the most complex and stimulating operations take place. One tentative list, expanding what has been said in section 4 about economic interaction, might look like Table 13.4. The order of presentation parallels that of Table 13.3, but in that Table cultural imperialism was spelled out in more detail as spin-off effects from economic imperialism.

TABLE 13.4 *The five types of imperialism*

	Economic	Political	Military	Communication	Cultural
Center nation provides	processing, means of production	decisions, models	protection means of destruction	news, means of communication	teaching, means of creation— autonomy
Periphery nation provides	raw materials, markets	obedience, imitators	discipline, traditional hardware	events, passengers, goods	learning, validation — dependence

The vertical nature of this type of *economic* interaction has been spelled out in detail above since we have used that type of imperialism to exemplify definition and mechanisms. Let us look more at the other types of vertical interaction.

The *political* one is clear: the concept of a 'mother' country. The Center nation is also an indication of how the decisionmaking center is dislocated away from the nation itself and towards the Center nation. These decisions may then affect economic, military, communication, and cultural patterns. Important here is the division of labor involved: some nations produce decisions, others supply obedience. The decisions may be made upon application, as in 'bilateral technical assistance', or in consultation — or they may simply emerge by virtue of the model-imitator distinction. Nothing serves that distinction quite so well as unilinear concepts of 'development' and 'modernization', according to which Center nations possess some superior kind of structure for others to imitate (as long as the Center's central position is not seriously challenged), and which gives a special aura of legitimacy to any idea emanating from the Center. Thus, structures and decisions developed in the 'motherland of liberalism' or in the 'fatherland of socialism' serve as models by virtue of their place of origin, not by virtue of their substance.

The *military* implications or parallels are also rather obvious. It cannot be emphasized enough that the economic division of labor is also one which ensures that the Center nations economically speaking also become the Center nations in a military sense: only they have the industrial capacity to develop the technological hardware — and also are often the only ones with the social structure compatible with a modern army. He who produces tractors can easily produce tanks, but he who delivers oil cannot defend himself by throwing it in the face of the aggressors. He has to depend on the tank-producer, either for protection or for acquisition (on terms dictated by the Center). And just as there is a division of labor with the Center nation producing manufactured goods on the basis of raw materials extracted in the Periphery nation, there is also a division of labor with the *Center nations processing the obedience provided by the Periphery nations into decisions that can be implemented.* Moreover there is also a division of labor with the Center providing the protection (and often also the officers or at least the instructors 'in counter-insurgency') and the Periphery the discipline and the soldiers needed — not to mention the apprentices of 'military advisors' from the Center.

As to the fourth type, *communication* imperialism, the emphasis in the analysis is usually turned towards the second mechanism of imperialism: the feudal interaction structure. That this largely holds for most world communication and transportation patterns has been amply demonstrated [13]. But perhaps more important is the vertical nature of the division of labor in the field of communication/transportation. It is trivial to say that a high level of industrial capacity is necessary to develop the latest in transportation and communication technology. The preceding generation of *means of communication/transportation* can always be sold, sometimes second-hand, to the Periphery as part of the general vertical trade/aid structure, alongside the *means of production* (economic sector), the *means of destruction* (military sector), and the *means of creation* (cultural sector). The Center's planes and ships are faster, more direct, look more reliable, attract more passengers, more goods. And when the Periphery finally catches up, the Center will already for a long time have dominated the field of communication satellites.

One special version of this principle is a combination of cultural and communication exchange: *news communication.* We all know that the major agencies are in the hands of the Center countries, relying on Center-dominated, feudal networks of communication [14]. What is not so well analyzed is how Center news takes up a much larger proportion of Periphery news media than vice versa, just as trade with the Center is a larger proportion of Periphery total trade than vice versa. In other words, the pattern of partner concentration as something found more in the Periphery than in the Center is very pronounced .The Periphery nations do not write or read much about each other, especially not across bloc borders, and they read more about 'their' Center than about other Centers — because the press is written and read by the center in the Periphery, who want to know more about that most 'relevant' part of the world — for them.

Another aspect of vertical division of labor in the news business should also be pointed out. Just as the Periphery produces raw materials that the Center turns into processed goods, *the Periphery also produces events that the Center turns into news* [15]. This is done by training journalists to see events with Center eyes, and by setting up a chain of communication that filters and processes events so that they fit the general pattern.

The latter concept brings us straight into *cultural* imperialism, a subtype of which is scientific imperialism. The division of labor between teachers and learners is clear: it is not the division of labor as such (found in most situations of transmission of knowledge) that constitutes imperialism, but the location of the teachers, and of the learners, in a broader setting. If the Center always provides the teachers and the definition of that worthy of being taught (from the gospels of Christianity to the gospels of Technology), and the Periphery always provides the learners, then there is a pattern which smacks of imperialism. The satellite nation in the Periphery will also know that nothing flatters the Center quite so much as being encouraged to teach, and being seen as a model, and that the Periphery can get much in return from a humble, culture-seeking strategy (just as it will get little but aggression if it starts teaching the Center anything — like Czechoslovakia, who started lecturing the Soviet Union on socialism). For in accepting cultural transmission the Periphery also, implicitly, validates for the Center the culture development in the center, whether that center is intra- or international. This serves to reinforce the Center as a center, for it will then continue to develop culture along with transmitting it, thus creating lasting demand for the latest innovations. Theories, like cars and fashions, have their life-cycle, and whether the obsolescence is planned or not there will always be a time-lag in a structure with a pronounced difference between center and periphery. Thus, the tram workers in Rio de Janeiro may carry banners supporting Auguste Comte one hundred years after the center of the Center forgot who he was.

In science we find a particular version of vertical division of labor very similar to economic division of labor: the pattern of scientific teams from the Center who go to Periphery nations to collect data (raw material) in the form of deposits, sediments, flora, fauna, archaeological findings, attitudes, behavioral patterns, and so on for data processing, data analysis, and theory formation (processing, in general) in the Center universities (factories), so as to be able to send the finished product, a journal, a book (manufactured goods) back for consumption in the center of the Periphery — after first having created a demand for it through demonstration effect, training in the Center country, and some degree of low level participation in the data collection team [16]. This parallel is not a joke, it is a *structure*. If in addition the precise nature of the research is to provide the Center with information that can be used economically, politically, or militarily to maintain an imperialist structure, the cultural imperialism becomes even more clear. And if to this we add the *brain drain* (and body drain) whereby 'raw' brains (students) and 'raw' bodies (unskilled workers) are moved from the Periphery to the Center and 'processed' (trained) with ample benefits to the Center, the picture becomes complete.

6. The phases of imperialism

We have mentioned repeatedly that imperialism is *one* way in which one nation may dominate another. Moreover, it is a way that provides a relatively stable pattern: the nations are linked to each other in a pattern that may last for some time because of the many stabilizing factors built into it through the mechanism of a feudal interaction structure.

The basic idea is that the center in the Center establishes a bridgehead in the Periphery nation, and more particularly, in the center of the Periphery nation. Obviously, this bridgehead does not come about just like that: there is a phase preceding it. The precise nature of that preceding phase can best be seen by distinguishing between three phases of imperialism in history, depending on what type of concrete method the center in the Center has used to establish the harmony of interest between itself and the center in the Periphery (Table 13.5).

TABLE 13.5 *Three phases of imperialism in history*

Phase	Period	Form	Term
I	Past	*Occupation*, cP physically consists of cC people who engage in *occupation*	Colonialism
II	Present	*Organization*, cC interacts with cP via the medium of *international organizations*	Neo-colonialism
III	Future	*Communication*, cC interacts with cP via international communication	Neo-neo-colonialism

From the Table we see that in all three cases, the Center nation has a hold over the center of the Periphery nation. But the precise nature of this grip differs, and should be seen relative to the means of transportation and communication. No analysis of imperialism can be made without a reference to these means that perhaps are as basic as the means of production in producing social dynamics.

Throughout the overwhelming part of human history, transportation (of human beings, of goods) did not proceed at a higher speed than that provided by pony expresses and quick sailing ships; and communication (of signals, of meaning) not at higher speed than that provided by fires and smoke signals which could be spotted from one hilltop to another. Precise control over another nation would have to be exercised by physically transplanting one's own center and grafting onto the top of the foreign body — in other words, colonialism in all its forms, best known in connection with 'white settlers'. According to this vision, colonialism was not a discovery of the Europeans subsequent to the Great Discoveries: it could just as well be used to describe great parts of the Roman Empire that through textbooks and traditions of history-writing so successfully has dominated our image of racial and ethnical identity and national pride [17].

Obviously, the quicker the means of transportation could become, the less necessary would this pattern of permanent settlement be. The break in the historical pattern came when the steam engine was not only put into the factory to provide new *means of production* (leading to conditions that prompted Marx to write *Das Kapital*) but also into a vessel (Fulton) and a locomotive (Stephenson): in other words, *means of transportation* (the book about that is not yet written). This gave Europeans a decisive edge over peoples in other regions, and colonialism became more firmly entrenched. Control could be accurate and quick.

But decolonialization also came, partly due to the weakening of cC, partly due to the strengthening of cP that might not challenge what cC did, but want to do so itself. Neo-colonialism came; and in this present phase of imperialism, control is not of the direct, concrete type found in the past. It is mediated through the means of transportation (and, of course, also communication) linking the two centers to each other. The control is less concrete: it is not physical presence, but a link; and this link takes the shape of international organizations. The international organization has a certain permanence, often with physical headquarters and a lasting general secretary in the mother country. But above all it is a medium in which influence can flow, with *both* centers joining as members and finding each other. Their harmony of interest can be translated into complete equality within the international organization, and vice versa. Their identity is defined relative to the organization, not to race, ethnicity, or nationality. But with differential disharmony *within* nations, this actually becomes an instrument of disharmony *between* nations.

These organizations are well-known for all five types of imperialism. For the economic type, the private or governmental multinational corporations (BINGOs) may serve [18]; for the political type, many of the international governmental organizations (IGOs); for the military type, the various systems of military alliances and treaties and organizations (MIGOs) [19]; for communication the shipping and air companies (CONGOs?), not to mention the international press agencies, offer ample illustration; and for cultural imperialism, some of the international non-governmental organizations (INGOs) may serve as the conveyor mechanisms. But this is of course not to say that international organizations will necessarily serve such purposes. According to the theory developed here, this is an empirical question, depending on the degree of division of labor inside the organization and the extent to which it is feudally organized.

Next, the third phase. If we now proceed even further along the same line of decreasingly concrete (but increasingly effective?) ties between the two centers, we can envisage a phase where even the international organizations will not only fall into disrepute, but dissolve. What will come in their place? *Instant communication*, whereby parties who want to communicate with each other set up ad hoc communication networkers (telesatellites etc.) that form and dissolve in rapid succession, changing scope and domain, highly adjustable to external circumstance, guided by enormous data-banks and idea-banks that permit participants to find their 'opposite numbers' without having them frozen together in a more permanent institutional network that develops its own rigidities [20].

In other words, we envisage a future where very many international organizations will be threatened in two ways. First, they will be exposed to increasing criticism as to their function as a tie between two centers, communicating and coordinating far above the masses in either country, which will in itself lead to a certain disintegration. Second, this does not mean that the centers, if they are free to do so, will cease to coordinate their action, only that they will do so by other means. Instead of going to ad hoc or annual conventions, or in other ways instructing a general secretary and his staff, they may simply pick up their videophone and have a long distance conference organized, where the small group of participants can all see and talk to each other — not like in a conference, but in the more important adjoining lobbies, in the coffee-houses, in private quarters — or wherever they prefer to carry out communication and coordination [21].

To penetrate more deeply into the role of international organization as an instrument of imperialistic dominance, let us now distinguish between five phases in the development of an international organization. As an example we take one economic organization, General Motors Corporation (GMC) and one political organization, the International Communist Movement (ICM) — at present not organized formally as an international organization. The stages are indicated in Table 13.6. Needless to say, these two are taken as *illustrations* of economic and political imperialism — this is not a *study* of GMC and ICM respectively.

In the beginning the organization exists only within national boundaries. Then comes a second phase when it sends representatives, at that stage usually called 'agents', abroad. This is a critical stage: it is a question of gaining a foothold in another nation, and usually subversive, from below If the other nation is completely new to this economic or political pattern the 'agents' often have to come from the 'mother country' or the 'fatherland' on the invitation of dissatisfied individuals who find their own mobility within the system blocked *and* who think that the present system does not satisfy the needs of the population. But this phase is not imperialist,

TABLE 13.6 *Stages in the development of an international organization*

	General Motors Corporation (GMC)	International Communist Movement (ICM)
Phase 1: National only	in one country only ('mother country')	in one country only ('fatherland')
Phase 2: National goes abroad	*subsidiary*, or branch offfce, established by 'agents'	*subversive* organization, established by 'agents'
Phase 3: Multinational, asymmetric	other national companies started, with 'mother country' company dominating	other national parties established, with 'fatherland' party dominating
Phase 4: Mutinational, symmetric	total network becomes symmetric	total network becomes symmetric
Phase 5: Global, or transnational organization	national identities dissolve	national identities dissolve

for the center in the mother country has not established any bridgehead in the *center* of the offspring country — yet.

The agents may be highly instrumental of social change. They may set into motion patterns in economic life that may reduce significantly the power of feudal landlords; or they may set into motion patterns in political life that may reduce equally significantly the power of industrialists and introduce socialist patterns of production. Both activities are subversive of the social order, but not imperialist, and are, consequently, examples of other ways in which one nation may exercise influence over another [22].

But in Phase 3 this development has gone a significant step further. The agents have now been successful, so to speak: national companies/parties have been established. Elites have emerged in the Periphery nations, strongly identified with and well harmonizing with the Center elites. The whole setting is highly asymmetric; what we have identified as mechanisms and types of imperialism are now discernible.

There is *division of labor:* the 'daughter' company in the Periphery nation is particularly concerned with making raw materials available and with securing markets for the mother company in the Center nation. If it enters into processing, then it is often with a technology already by-passed by 'development' in the Center country, or only leading to semi-finished products. Correspondingly, the company/party in the mother country makes more decisions and the parties in the Periphery provide obedience and secure markets for the implementation of orders. Thus, in both cases the implicit assumption is always that the top leadership of the international organization shall be the top leadership of the company/party in the Center country. Headquarters are located there and not elsewhere; this location is not by rotation or random choice [23].

Further, the *general interaction structure is clearly feudal:* there is interaction along the spokes, from the Periphery to the Center hub; but not along the rim, from one Periphery nation to another. There may be multilateral meetings, but they are usually very heavily dominated by the Center, which takes for granted that it will be in the interest of the Periphery to emulate the Center. And this then spans all five types of interaction, one way or the other — in ways that are usually fairly obvious.

We have pointed to what seem to be basic similarities between the two international organizations (GMC and ICM). Precisely because they are similar, they can do much to impede each other's activities. This similarity is not strange: they both reflect the state of affairs in a world that consists of 1. nation-states of 2. highly unequal power and level of development along various axes, and is 3. too small for many nation-states to stay within their bonds — so they spill over with their gospels, and patterns are established that are imperialist in nature. *For phase 3 is clearly the imperialist phase;* and because so many international organizations are in this third phase, they at present stand out as vehicles of asymmetric forms of center-center cooperation [24].

This is the present state of most international organizations. Most are extensions of patterns developed first in one nation, and on assumptions that may have been valid in that country. They are usually the implementation in our days of the old missionary command (Matthew 28: 18—20) 'Go ye all forth and make all peoples my disciples'. This applies not only to economic and political organizations, but to the other three types as well. Typical examples are ways in which cultural patterns are disseminated. In its most clear form, they are even handled by official or semi-official institutions more or less attached to the diplomatic network (such as USIS, and the various cultural activities of the Soviet and Chinese embassies in many countries; and to lesser extent, the British Council and Alliance Française). But international organizations are also used for this purpose by Center nations who firmly believe that their patterns are good for everybody else because they are good for themselves.

However, the Periphery does not necessarily rest content with this state of affairs. There will be a dynamism leading to changes towards Phase 4, so far only brought about in very few organizations. It will probably have its roots in the division of labor, and the stamp as second class members given to the Periphery in general, and to heads of Periphery companies and parties in particular. Why should there be any written or unwritten law that GMC and ICM heads are located in the United States and the Soviet

461

Union, respectively [25]? Why not break up the division of labor completely, distribute the research contracts and the strategic planning evenly, why not rotate the headquarters, why not build up interaction along the rim and build down the interaction along the spokes so that the hub slowly fades out and the resulting organization is truly symmetric? This is where the Norwegian GMC president and the Rumanian ICM general secretary have, in a sense, common interests — and we predict that this movement will soon start in all major international organizations following some of the very useful models set by the UN and her specialized agencies. It should be noted, however, that it is not too difficult to obtain equality in an international organization where only the elites participate, since they already to a large extent harmonize with each other.

But this is not the final stage of development, nothing is. The multinational, symmetric form will always be artificial for at least two reasons: the nations are not symmetric in and by themselves — some contribute more than others — and they form artificial pockets relative to many of the concerns of the organizations. Any multinational organization, however symmetric, is a way of reinforcing and perpetuating the nation-state. If nation-states are fading out in significance, much like municipalities in many parts of the world, multinational organizations will also fade out because they are built over a pattern that is becoming less and less salient. What will come in its place? The answer will probably be what has here been called a hypothetical Phase 5 — *the global* or *world organization*, but we shall not try to spell this out here.

7. From spin-off to spill-over: convertibility of imperialism

We have now presented a theory of imperialism based on *three* criteria, *two* mechanisms, *five* types, and *three* phases. In the presentation, as is usually done in any presentation of imperialism, economic imperialism was used for the purpose of illustration. However, we tried to carry the analysis further: for economic imperialism, exploitation was not only defined in terms of unequal exchange because A gives less to B than he gets from B, but also in terms of differential intra-actor or spin-off effects. Moreover, it is quite clear from Tables 13.3—4 that these spin-off effects are located in other areas in which imperialism can also be defined. Vertical economic interaction has political spin-offs, military spin-offs, communication spin-offs, and cultural spin-offs; and vice-versa, as we shall indicate.

For that reason we shall now make a distinction between *spin-off* effects and *spill-over* effects. When a nation exchanges tractors for oil it develops a tractor-producing capacity. One possible spin-off is a tank-producing capacity, and becomes a spill-over effect the moment that capacity is converted into military imperialism, for instance in the form of *Tank-Kommunismus* or *Tank-Kapitalismus*. Of course, this does not become military imperialism unless exercised in cooperation with the ruling elite in the Periphery nation. If it is exercised against that elite, it is a simple *invasion* product of cC—cP cooperation.

A glance at Tables 13.3—4 indicates that the road from spin-off to spill-over is a short one, provided that there are cooperating or even generalized elites available both in the Center and the Periphery nations. It is not necessary for the same person in Center and Periphery to be on top on the economic, political, military, communication, and cultural organizations — that would be superhuman! Many would cover two or three such positions, few would command four or five. But if the five elites defined through these five types of exchange are *coordinated* into generalized upper classes based on a rich network of kinship, friendship, and association (not to mention effective cooperation), then the basis is laid for an extremely solid type of *generalized imperialism*. In the extreme case there would be rank concordance in both Center and Periphery, which means that there would not even be some little disequilibrium present in either case to give some leverage for a revolutionary movement. All groups would have learned, in fact been forced, to play generalized roles as dominant and dependent, respectively.

For this rank concordance to take place, gains made from one type of imperialism should be readily convertible into the other types. The analytical instrument here could be what we might call the *convertibility matrix*, given in Table 13.7. The numbers in the first row correspond to the spin-off effects for vertical division of labor in economic transactions, as indicated in Table 13.3. A more complete theory of imperialism would now try to give corresponding spin-off effects, convertible into spill-over effects, for the other four types with regard to all five types. We shall certainly not engage fully in this taxonomic exercise but only pick one example from each row.

Thus, it is rather obvious how political imperialism can be converted into economic imperialism by dictating terms of trade, where the latter are not seen so much in terms of volume as of trade composition [26].

TABLE 13.7 *Convertibility of types of imperialism*

	Economic	Political	Military	Communication	Cultural
Economic	1	2	3	4	5—9
Political					
Military					
Communication					
Cultural					

Correspondingly, military imperialism can easily be converted into communication imperialism by invoking the need for centralized command over communication and transportation facilities. It is no coincidence that the capital in so many Center countries is located inland and well protected, whereas the capital in most Periphery countries is a port, easily accessible from the Center country, and with a feudal interaction network inland facilitating the flow of raw materials to the capital port and a trickling of consumer goods in the other direction (most of it being absorbed in the capital port itself). Precise command of territory may be necessary to establish a communication network of this type, but once established, it is self-reinforcing.

Similarly, to take another example: communication imperialism may be converted into cultural imperialism by regulating the flow of information, not only in the form of news, but also in the form of cheaply available books etc. from the Center country.

Finally, cultural imperialism is convertible into economic imperialism in ways very common today: by means of technical assistance processes. A technical assistance expert is not only a person from a rich country who goes to a poor country and stimulates a demand in the poor country for the products of the rich country [27]. He is also a man who goes to the poor country in order to establish a routine in the poor country, reserving for himself all the benefits of the challenges of this entrepreneurial activity. He *writes* the SOP (Standard Operating Procedure); it is for his 'counterpart' to *follow* the SOP. That this challenge is convertible into more knowledge (more culture) and eventually also into economic benefits upon the return of the technical assistance expert is hardly to be doubted in principle, but it is another question whether the Center country understands this and fully utilizes the resource.

Convertibility could now be studied at two levels: the extent to which the nation as such can use such spin-offs from one type and direct them towards consolidation of another type, and the extent to which an individual may do so. If an individual can, the result is some type of rank concordance; if the nation can, we might perhaps talk of imperialism concordance.

But the only point we want to make here is that the convertibility matrix seems to be complete. It is hard to imagine any cell in Table 13.7 that would be empty in the sense that there could be no spill-over effects, no possibility of conversion. If everything can be bought for money, obtained by political control, or ordered by military imposition, then that alone would take care of the first three horizontal rows. Correspondingly, most authors would talk about economic, political, and military imperialism, but we have added the other two since they seem also to be primordial.

Perhaps the first three will build up more slowly along the lines established by division of labor in communication and cultural organizations, but it is very easy to imagine scenarios as well as concrete historical examples.

The completeness of the convertibility matrix, more than anything else, would lead us to reject the assumption of one type of imperialism as more basic than the others. It is the mutual reinforcement, the positive feedback between these types rather than any simple reductionist causal chain, that seems the dominant characteristic. If economic, political, and military imperialism seem so dominant today, this may be an artifact due to our training that emphasizes these factors rather than communication and cultural factors. Belief in a simple causal chain is dangerous because it is accompanied by the belief that imperialism can be dispensed with forever if the primary element in the chain is abolished, e.g. private capitalism. The more general definition of imperialism presented here directs our search towards the two mechanisms as well as the particular criteria of exploitation within and between nations.

In order to talk about imperialism, not only economic inequality but also political, military, communication, and cultural inequality should be distributed in an inegalitarian way with the periphery at the disadvantage. Are they? We think so. The, not so blatantly, unequal access to acquisite power, to some *political* power through voting, to some control over the *use of violence* (through political power, through civilian control of the military and through equality of opportunity as access to ranking positions in the military), to *communication* (usually via access to acquisitive power, but also via denser, less feudal communication networks linking periphery outposts more directly together in Center nations), and to *cultural* goods (through widespread literacy and equality in access to educational institutions) — all these are trademarks of what is referred to as a liberal democracy. And that form of socio-political life is found in the Center rather than the Periphery of the world.

This leads to an important point in the theory of imperialism. *Instead of seeing democracy as a consequence or a condition for economic development within certain nations, it can (also) be seen as the condition for exercising effective control over Periphery nations.* Precisely because the Center is more egalitarian and democratic than the Periphery, there will be more people in the Center who feel they have a stake in the present state of affairs, since the fruits of imperialist structures are more equally shared on the top than on the bottom. And this will make it even less likely that the periphery in the Center will really join with the periphery in the Periphery against the two centers. Rather, like Dutch workers they will oppose the independence of Indonesia, and like US workers they will tend to become hardhats over the Indo-China issue.

It is now relatively clear what would be the perfect type of imperialism. In perfect imperialism, regardless of phase, we would assume all three criteria, both mechanisms, and all five types to be completely operative. This would mean complete harmony between the centers with the elites in the Periphery nations almost indistinguishable from the elites in the Center nations where living conditions are concerned; much better distribution in the Center nations than in the Periphery nations; a perfectly vertical division of labor along all five types of exchange, and a perfectly feudal interaction network.

Where in the world, in space and/or in time, does one find this type of relations? The answer is perhaps not only in the colonial empires of the past, but also in the neo-colonial empires of the present using international organizations as their medium. To what extent it is true is an empirical question, and all the factors mentioned above can be operationalized. In other words, what is often called 'positivist' methodology can be brought to bear on problems of structuralist or even Marxist analyses. A crude and limited exercise in this direction will be given in the following section.

Suffice it to say that no system is perfect, and no system is a perfect copy of some ideal-type model. It may be that the neo-colonial empire the United States had in Latin America in the 1950's and into the 1960's was a relatively perfect case [29], and that this also applies to the relation between the EEC countries and the Associated States [30]. But it does not apply to the United States in Western Europe, nor to the Soviet Union in Eastern Europe, to the Soviet Union in the Arab World or to Japan in Southeast Asia. This is not to deny that the United States in Western Europe and the Soviet Union in Eastern Europe are at the summit of military organizations that seem to satisfy all conditions, although the parallel is not entirely complete. But both of the superpowers are peripheral to the communication networks, their cultures are largely rejected in Western and Eastern Europe respectively, and where economic penetration is concerned there is a vertical division of labor in favor of the United States relative to Western Europe, but in favor of Eastern Europe (in general) relative to the Soviet Union — with Soviet Union as a provider of raw materials for, for instance, high level processing in the GDR. But it may then be argued that what the Soviet Union loses in economic ascendancy it compensates for in a political organization with strong feudal components [31].

Similar arguments may be advanced in connection with the Soviet Union in the Arab World, and with Japan in Southeast Asia. Where the latter is concerned there is no doubt as to the economic imperialism, but there is not political, military, communication, or cultural ascendancy [32].

And this, then leads to the final conclusion in this section. Imperialism is a question of degree, and if it is perfect it is a perfect instrument of structural violence. When it is less than perfect something must be substituted for what is lost in structural violence: direct violence, or at least the threat of direct violence. This is where the military type of imperialism becomes so important, since it can be seen as a potential to be activated when the other types of imperialism, particularly the economic and political types, show important cracks in the structure. This does not, incidentally, necessarily mean that direct violence only has to be applied in Periphery nations; it may also be directed against the periphery in Center nations if there is a danger of their siding with the periphery in the Periphery. The structural conditions for this would be that criterion no. 2 in the definition does not hold, in other words that there is not less, but possibly even more, inequality in the Center than in the Periphery [33].

8. Some empirical explorations

The theory developed above is too complex in its empirical implications to be tested in its entirety. But some data can at least be given for economic imperialism, not because we view this as the basic type of imperialism, but because it is the type for which data are most readily available.

Everybody knows that there is the gap in GNP per capita, that there are rich nations and poor nations. From one point of view this gap poses a problem, the answer to which is in terms of *redistribution*. But from the structuralist point of view taken here the gap poses a problem that can only be answered in terms of *structural change*. It may be that redistribution can contribute to this change; but it may also be that it only serves to postpone the solution because symptoms rather than the disease itself are cured.

The claim, therefore, is that when some nations are rich and some nations are poor, when some nations are developed and some nations are underdeveloped, this is intimately related to the structure within and between nations. To explore this in line with the theory developed above we shall make use of the following seven variables [34].

Development variables:	1. GNP/capita
	2. Percentage employed in non-primary sectors
Inequality variables:	3. Gini index, income distribution
	4. Gini index, land distribution
Vertical trade variable:	5. Trade composition index
Feudal trade variable:	6. Partner concentration index
	7. Commodity concentration index

The first two variables place the nation in the international ranking system using two types of development variables that are, of course, highly but not completely correlated. The next two variables, the Gini indices, say something about the internal structure of the nation, whereas the last three variables say something about the structure of the relations between them. Of these three, the first one (5) relates to the first mechanism of imperialism and the other two (6, 7) to the second mechanism of imperialism. More precisely, the trade composition index is based on the following formula [35].

Trade composition index

$$\frac{(a + d) - (b + c)}{(a + d) + (b + c)}$$

where
  a is value of raw materials imported
  b is value of raw materials exported
  c is value of processed goods imported
  d is value of processed goods exported

There is no doubt that this index is a crude measure, among other reasons because the variable *degree of processing*, so crucial to the whole analysis, has here been dichotomized in 'raw materials' vs. 'processed goods' neglecting completely the problem of degree, *and* because the basis for dichotomization is the division made use of in UN trade statistics. However, despite its shortcomings it serves to sort nations apart. The highest ranking nation on this variable is Japan with an import consisting almost entirely of raw materials and an export consisting almost entirely of processed goods. Correspondingly, at the bottom according to this index are the nations that export raw materials, and import processed goods only; but the relative position of several countries in between may certainly be disputed.

As to the last two variables, they are simply the ratios between the proportion of the export going to the *one* most important partner, or consisting of the *three* most important commodities relative to the total export, respectively [36].

According to our general theory we should now expect some countries to be developed (see Fig. 13.3) and to be on top of the vertical trade index but low in terms of inequality and position on the feudal trade index — whereas other countries would be underdeveloped and low on the vertical trade index but on the other hand high in terms of inequality and position on the feudal trade index. The correlation structure should be something like Fig. 13.3 where the solid lines indicate positive relations and the broken lines negative relations,

FIGURE 13.3 *The correlation pattern according to the imperialism hypothesis*

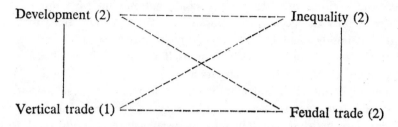

and the numbers in parentheses are the numbers of indicators for each dimension.

Thus, of the twenty-one bivariate correlations we predict six positive and twelve negative correlations. In addition there are the three correlations between indicators of the same dimension: we expect them to be positive, but not too positive since that would reduce the usefulness for independent testing of the hypotheses.

Because of the grave doubts as to the validity and reliability of all variables we decided to dichotomize them, either at the point where there is a 'natural' cut (a large interval between one country and the next) or at the median cut. The correlation coefficient used was Yule's Q and the results were as shown in Table 13.8.

TABLE 13.8 *A test of the hypothesis of economic imperialism (Yule's Q)*

	1	2	3	4	5	6	7
1 GNP/capita		0.79	—0.90	—0.80	0.89	—0.52	—0.89
2 % non-primary			—1.00	—0.83	0.77	—0.72	—0.87
3 Gini income				0.20	—0.83	0.80	0.86
4 Gini land					—0.95	0.21	0.85
5 Trade comp.						—0.69	—0.97
6 Partner concentration							0.35
7 Commodity concentration							

All correlations are in the expected direction, most of them rather substantial. There are only three low correlations, and two of them are between indicators or the same dimension. Hence we regard the hypothesis as very well confirmed.

Of course, this is only a test of a theory along the edges of that theory; it does not in itself prove that the system is in fact working as described above. But if these findings had not come out so strongly as they do, we would have been forced to conclude that the imperialist model cannot possibly be a good model of the world system today. Hence, as a test of the hypotheses the findings provide positive confirmation, but as a test of a theory there is only the negative support that a theory would have to be rejected if the findings had been in the opposite direction [37].

We should also add that the theory in itself is so rich in implications that it provides ample basis for empirical research, within liberal and Marxist schools of thought, and employing synchronic statistical methods as well as diachronic case studies. It would be sad if ideological and other types of conflicts between adherents of different schools should lead to any systematic neglect as to mobilizing general social science for a deeper understanding of how this system works.

9. Further theoretical explorations

Let us then make use of the results of the theoretical and empirical explorations to go somewhat more deeply into four problems.

9.1. Defining 'center' and 'periphery'

We are now in a better position to define our basic terms, 'center' and 'periphery' (loosely introduced in section 2), whether they refer to relations between or within nations [38]. Actually, implicit in what has been said above are three approaches when it comes to defining these terms:

1. in terms of *absolute properties* (e.g. development variables): center is high on rank dimensions, periphery is low
2. in terms of *interaction relation* (e.g. trade composition index): center enriches itself more than the periphery
3. in terms of *interaction structure* (e.g. partner and commodity concentration index): center is more centrally located in the interaction network than the periphery — the periphery being higher on the concentration indices.

Empirically it may not matter that much which of these three dimensions is used to define center and periphery, since Table 13.8 shows them highly correlated — at least today. According to one type of theory this is because (1) above is primordial, and basic: the richer, more educated, stronger nation (individual) is able to place itself in the world structure (social structure) so that it can be on top of a vertical interaction relation and in the center of a feudal interaction structure. According to another type of theory (2) or (3) is basic: if an individual or nation is able to place itself on top of a vertical relation, and possibly, in addition, in the center of a feudal interaction structure, it will also be able to climb higher on the dimensions on which nations (individuals) climb — whatever they might be.

We find it difficult to be dogmatic about these two theories. Rather, they seem to complement each other. One nation (individual) may have gained an edge over another in one way or another, and been able to convert that into an advantageous interaction position, as the Europeans did after the Great Discoveries. Or it may have come into an advantageous interaction position by some lucky circumstance, e.g. in a communication network, and been able to convert this into some absolute value for itself, and so on.

In general, we think there are reasons to say that the relative significance of the three *aspects* of the center-periphery distinction varies with time and space, with historical and geographical circumstances. For that reason we would prefer to view them precisely as three different *aspects* of that distinction. Thus, we define center vs. periphery as nations (individuals) that satisfy (1) *or* (2) *or* (3); 'or' taken in the usual sense of and/or. This may lead to confusion, but since both theories above would lead to the same conclusion we do not worry so much about that. Rather, the definition should be accompanied by a warning to the analyst: he should always be sensitive to possible cases of divergence, that a nation (individual) may be in the center relative to one aspect and in the periphery relative to another, and so on. That this in itself would provide rich sources for theories about dynamism, about how a center position of one kind can be converted into a center position of the other kind, is obvious. And in that connection the second aspect, the relation itself, may perhaps be more basic, since it provides, through accumulation, a constant flow of resources towards the center. The advantage of this aspect is that it is so *concrete*. According to this aspect the sorting into center and periphery is not only an operation carried out by the analyst, it takes place, *in concreto*, in the interaction process itself. The two actors 'sort' themselves away from each other by participating in vertical interaction, and become increasingly unequal in the process [39].

9.2. *Generalization to three nations and three classes*

So far we have operated with a simple scheme involving two nations and two classes; the time has now come to break out of that limitation. Here we shall only offer some remarks in that connection, not carry through the analysis in detail.

Thus the introduction of a middle class between center and the periphery would be entirely consistent with thinking in most social science schools. Whether the center is defined in terms of economic, political, military communication, or cultural interaction, a strict dichotomy between center and periphery will often be too crude. The alternative to a dichotomy may be a continuum, but on the way towards that type of thinking a trichotomy may also be useful. Strict social dichotomies are usually difficult to obtain unless hedged around by means of highly visible and consensual racial, ethnic, or geographical distinctions. A country composed of three races may therefore provide a stable three-class structure; if there is only one race, the conditions model may be more useful.

However, it is difficult to see that this should significantly affect our theory. Whether there are two or three classes or a continuum from extreme center to extreme periphery does not invalidate descriptions of the nation in terms of averages (such as GNP /capita) and dispersions (such as Gini indices). Nor will it invalidate the comparisons between the nations in such terms. In fact, there is nothing in this theory that presupposes a dichotomous class structure since the theory is not based on a dichotomy like owner vs. non-owner of means of production.

More interesting results can be obtained by interspersing a third nation between the Center and Periphery nations. Such a nation could, in fact, serve as a go-between. Concretely, it would exchange semi-produced goods with highly processed goods and semi-processed goods with raw materials downwards. It would simply be located in between Center and Periphery where the degree of processing of its export rpoducts is concerned. Moreover, such go-between nations would serve as an intermediate layer between the extreme Center and the extreme Periphery in a feudal interaction structure. And needless to say: the intranational center of all three nations would be tied together in the same international network, establishing firm ties of harmony of interest between them.

In another version of the same conception the go-between nation would be one cycle behind the Center as to technology but one cycle ahead of the Periphery [40] in line with its position as to degree of processing. This would also apply to the means of destruction and the means of communication.

If the United States is seen as *the* Center nation in the world (with Japan as an extremely dangerous competitor precisely in terms of degree of processing), then several such chains of nations suggest themselves, as shown in Table 13.9.

Just as for the generalization to three classes, this could also be generalized to a continuous chain which would then serve to make for considerable distance between the extreme Center and the extreme Periphery.

TABLE 13.9 *Some hypotheses about go-between relations*

Center	Go-Between	Periphery
USA	Western Europe	Eastern Europe
USA	Canada	Anglo-America (Trinidad etc.)
USA	Mexico, Argentina Brazil	Central America
USA	Japan	Southeast Asia
Japan	South Korea, Taiwan	Southeast Asia (and North America)
Western Europe	Eastern Europe	Soviet Union

9.3. *Generalizations to more than one empire*

So far all our thinking has been within one empire, except for passing references to countries outside the empire that the Periphery is prevented from interacting with. But the world consists of more than one empire, and any realistic theory should see an empire in its context — especially since direct violence is to relations between empires what structural violence is within empires.

Clearly, relations between empires are above all relations between the centers of the Centers; these relations can be negative, neutral, or positive. Two capitalistic empires may be in competition, but they may also sub-divide the world between them into spheres of interest so peripheral that relations become more neutral. In this first phase one empire may fight to protect itself in the competition with another capitalistic empire, but in a second phase they may join forces and more or less merge to protect not this or that particular capitalist empire, but the system of capitalism as such. And we could also easily imagine a third phase where non-capitalist empires join with capitalist empires in the pattern of 'united imperialism', for the protection of imperialism as such.

All this is extremely important from the viewpoint of the Periphery nations. A world with more empires, which above all means a world with more Center nations, is at least potentially a world with more possibilities. To explore this in more detail, let us assume that we have Center and Periphery nations, vertically related to each other. For each type of nation there are three cases: one nation alone, two nations either very low on interaction or hostile to each other, and two nations in such friendly cooperation as to constitute one actor. The result is shown in Fig. 13.4 which

473

permits us to recognize many and politically very important situations (the arrows in Fig. 13.4 stand for relations of vertical interaction). Here, situations *a, b*, and *c* take place within one empire and lead to a situation with a certain element of defeudalization: horizontal interaction has been established between the two Periphery nations.

FIGURE 13.4 *Possible relations in a multi-empire world*

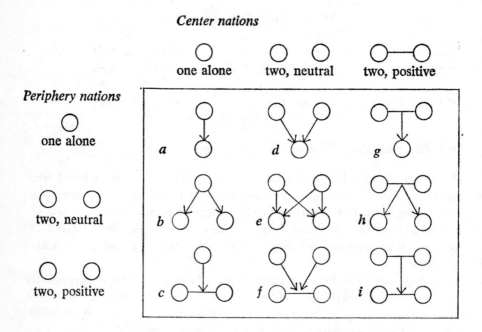

In situations *d, e*, and *f* Periphery nations are able to interact with more than one Center nation, possibly even play one against the other because of their hostile relationship. In this situation the Periphery will have a vested interest in protracting the Center conflict, and may even join forces (model *f*) to make optimum gains from the conflict.

In situations *g, h*, and *i* it is the Center side that cooperates, for instance by establishing a 'consortium' whereby several rich nations join together to help one or more poor nations, singly or combined [41].

Importantly, none of these strategies will lead to any changes in the vertical interaction *relation*, only to some changes in the feudal interaction *structure*. As such they attack only one aspect of imperialism, not the other, possibly more important aspect. And if we look more closely at model *i*, this is nothing but model *a* writ large, as when the EEC rather than France alone stands in a relationship of vertical interaction with 18 Associated States rather than with one of them alone. It is difficult to see that imperialistic relationships become less imperialistic by being established between super-Center and a super-Periphery rather than between the original Center and Periphery nations (we should add that *h* rather than *i* is a more correct model of the relationship between the EEC and the Associated States).

This factor notwithstanding, there is no reason to deny that a multi-empire world not only creates more bargaining possibilities, but also is a more realistic model of the world in which mankind lives — at present.

9.4. Generalization to non-territorial actors

We have defined non-territorial actors above, in Table 13.5, phases 3, 4, and 5 where phases 3 and 4 refer to multinational or international non-territorial actors and phase 5 to transnational actors. These are collectivities, they consist of human beings, they have more often than not a vertical division of labor within, and there is little reason why they should not also often have vertical division of labor between and be chained together in imperialistic relationships. Thus, there may be a division of labor between governmental and nongovernmental international organizations, with the more far-reaching decisions taken by the former and some of the implementations carried out by the latter. For this system to function well, the governmental organizations will have to harmonize the policy-making centers of the nongovernmental organizations with themselves, and one concrete way of doing this would be to have a member on the Council or Executive Committee. This article is not the occasion to spell this point out in any detail or with empirical examples, but we should point out that imperialism as a structure is not at all tied to territorial actors alone [42].

10. Conclusions: Some strategic implications

From a general scheme, we cannot arrive at more than general policy implications that can serve as guidelines, as strategies. Something more concrete is needed to arrive at the first tactical steps. But theory developed in peace research should lead to such guidelines; if it merely reflects what is empirical, not what is potential, then it is not good theory.

Our point of departure is once more that the world is divided into have's and have-not's, into have and have-not nations. To decrease the gap [43], one aspect of the fight against structural violence, redistribution by taking from the have's and giving to the have-not's is not enough: the structure has to be changed. The imperialist structure had international as well as intranational aspects and will consequently have to be changed at both levels.

However, let us start with the international changes needed, for a point of departure. Following closely the analysis of the mechanisms of imperialism in order to establish anti-mechanisms, we get Table 13.10.

TABLE 13.10 *Strategies for structural change of the international domi-nance system*

I. HORIZONTALIZATION

1. *Horizontalization Center-Periphery*

   a. *exchange on more equal terms*, either by reducing the divison of labor or by more horizontal division of labor that would equalize spin-off effects. Concretely this would mean that Center nations would have to start importing processed products from Periphery nations, and engage in intra- rather than inter-sector trade, and even intra- rather than inter-commodity trade.

   b. *reduction of vertical interaction*, down to total de-coupling in case exchange on more equal terms is unacceptable or does not work.

   c. *self-reliance* [44] partly in order to develop important substitutes, and partly for Periphery nations to define themselves what products they need rather than adapting the preference scales developed in the Center.

II. DEFEUDALIZATION

2 a. *exchange on equal terms*, intra- rather than inter- sector, but obviously at a lower level where degree of processing is concerned than under 1a. above. It may imply exchanges of raw materials, or exchanges of semi-processed goods. Obviously, which Periphery country should interact horizontally with which other Periphery countries would depend on the nature of the economic exchange and the concrete geo-political situation.

   b. *development of viable organization of Periphery countries for international class conflict.* Such organizations seem to depend for their viability not only on commitment to an ideology (rejection of past and present as well as visions for the future), but also seem to function better if they are built around an exchange relation of the type indicated in 2a. The exact purpose of the organization would be to force Center nations to change their policies in the direction of 1a, also to command a better redistribution of capital and technology from the Center. This would also be the organization that could organize a strike on the delivery of raw materials in case Center nations do not conform with these types of structural changes, as an analogy to the denial of human manpower typical of intranational strikes.

2. *Multilateralization Center—Periphery*

   a. *multinational, symmetric organization should be established wherever possible*, the system of international organizations should be taken out of phase 3 and moved towards phase 4. These organizations would serve as concrete instruments for horizontal relationships between Center and Periphery, and between Periphery and Periphery.

   b. *destruction of multinational asymmetric organizations* if they do not change in the direction of 3a above by withdrawal of Periphery participation.

   c. *self-reliance with the Periphery itself building multinational symmetric organizations*, retaining some contact with the Center for conflict articulation. This pattern might also apply to the UN and the UN Agencies unless they pursue policies of the types indicated above.

d. *establishment of global or transnational organizations* that could serve to globalize the word's means of communication and means of production in order to establish a universally accessible communication network and a production system that would give top priority to the needs of the periphery of the Periphery.

4. *Extra-bloc activity*

a. *Periphery-Center contacts extended to other Centers*, but in accordance with the program indicated in 1a and 1b above.

b. *Periphery-Periphery contacts extended to other Periphery countries*, but in accordance with points 2 and 3 above. For the latter the Algiers Group of 77 would be an important, although weak, model, and the conferences of nonaligned states another. At the first conference in Beograd in 1961 there were 25 participants, at the second in 1964 in Cairo 47 participants, and at the 1970 Lusaka conference there were 54 participants (the number of observers was 3, 10, and 12 respectively).

Again at this general level it is impossible to indicate the first steps that would lead from vertical, feudal interaction towards horizontalization and defeudalization. These are guidelines only. And their implementation should certainly not be seen as a sufficient condition for a process of genuine development to start in the Periphery, with the possible result that the gap between Center and Periphery may be decreasing again, but as a necessary condition. Very many of the findings in 'liberal' development theory may become valid precisely when today's periphery nations become autonomous through structural change. Hence, the basic formulas of horizontalization and defeudalization are necessary conditions, not panaceas.

But another question that certainly has to be asked is what this presupposes in terms of intranational strategies. In one sense the answer is simple: Table 13.10 also applies to the relation between center and periphery within a nation, not only between nations. As such it gives four general guidelines for a revolutionary process that would abolish the exploitation of the Periphery by the Center.

But this is too abstract, so let us return to the question in more concrete terms. The major difficulty with the international strategies in Table 13.10 is obviously that these would not be in the interest of the center in the Periphery. Nothing in these strategies would guarantee them the living conditions they already enjoy, very often on par with (or even above) the living conditions of the center in the Center. They would have all reasons to resist such changes. In fact, from a purely human point of view this group is perhaps the most exposed group in the whole international system, on the one hand the pawn and instrument of the center in the Center and on the the other hand the exploiter of the periphery in the Periphery. In such a cross-pressure it seems reasonable to expect that the group will sooner or later have to choose sides. Either it will have to relocate and join the center in the Center, or it will have to stand in solidarity with the periphery in the Periphery.

We can now, building on the *criteria* of imperialism, formulate a new set of strategies that would have more immediate domestic implications and support the international strategies of Table 13.10, as is shown in Table 13.11.

TABLE 13.11 *Strategies for structural change of the intranational dominance system*

I. REDUCED HARMONY BETWEEN THE CENTERS

1. *Reduction to neutral or no relationship*
This type of situation arises often when there is a crisis in the center of the Center, for instance due to internal war in the Center or external war between two or more Center nations. In this situation the Periphery attains some kind of autonomy because the Center can no longer exercise minute control — as seemed to be the case for many countries in Latin America during the Second World War.

2. *Change to negative relationship between the centers*
In the general theory it has been postulated that there is 'harmony' between the two centers, but social relations being complex such a harmony is hardly ever complete. There may be some privileges that cC reserve for themselves (such as taxation *without* representation) or some privileges that cP reserve for themselves (such as the right to remain a slavery or racist society). In general, tensions may arise precisely because the model of complete harmony and similarity is not realized. The result may be a *nationalist* fight for liberation from the Center country, and this fight may even attain a populist character if cP can manage to intepret the conflict as a threat to the Periphery nation as a whole, not only to its centre. If the Center engages in destructive behavior against the Periphery, such as economic warfare (with economic sanction as a special case) or even military warfare, a homogenization of the Periphery may occur, sufficient to conceal the disharmony of interest built into the Periphery.

II. REDUCED DISHARMONY IN THE PERIPHERY

3. *Violent revolution in the Periphery*
According to this formula the internal disharmony of interest is eliminated by eliminating cP as a class, by using means of force. This can be done partly by killing them, partly by means of imprisonment and partly by giving them the chance to relocate, for instance by using their ties with cC so as to settle where they really belong — in the Center [45]. A new regime is then introduced which perhaps may have its center, but certainly not a center that is tied by relations of harmony to the old cC.

4. *Non-violent revolution in the Periphery*
In this approach cP are not eliminated as persons, but as a part of the Periphery structure because the rest of the Periphery nation refuses to interact with them. They become non-functional socially rather than eliminated in a physical sense. To give them new tasks in a new society becomes an important part of the non-violent revolution.

5. *Cooperation between the peripheries in the Periphery*
Since international relations are so dominated by the centers in the Periphery, more of international relations has to be carried out by the people themselves in patterns of

nongovernmental foreign policy. The Havana-based *Tricontinental* (OSPAAAL) is an important example.

But in general we would believe more in Periphery-generated strategies than in the Center-generated ones, since the latter may easily lead to a new form of dependence on the Center.

III. CHANGES IN THE CENTER

6. *Increased disharmony in the Center*
In this case pC may no longer side with cC as it should according to nationalist ideology in the Center, but may find that the Periphery nation in general and pP in particular is the natural ally. It is difficult to see how this can have consequences that could be beneficial to the Periphery unless the two countries are contiguous, or unless this might be a factor behind the types of development outlined in I.1 and I.2 above.

7. *Changes in the goals of the Center*
In this case there is no assumption of changes in the level of internal disharmony in the Center. The Center might itself choose to stop imperialist policies, not because it is forced to do so from below (the Center by the Periphery or cC by pC as above), but out of its own decision. Thus cC might see that this is a wrong policy to pursue, e.g. because of the exploitation it leads to, because of the dangers for world peace, because of relations to other nations, etc. Or, there may be internal reasons: the Center might reduce its economic growth and change towards a politic of justice. Anti-centers or the periphery in the Center might decide to boycott further economic growth because of its consequences in terms of negative spin-off effects (pollution, exploitation of man). There are many possibilities, and they may combine into quite likely contributions towards a disruption of the system. But in general we would believe more in Periphery-generated strategies than in Center--generated ones, since the latter may easily lead to a new form of dependence on the Center.

At this point we choose to stop. These strategies will be explored in much more detail elsewhere. They are only presented here in brief outline in order to indicate what to us seems to be a crucial criterion against which any theory should be tested: is it indicative of a practice, does it indicate who the actors behind that practice could be? A theory should not only be evaluated according to its potential as a reservoir of hypothesis implications to be tested against present reality (data), but as much — or perhaps more — as a reservoir of policy implications to be tested against potential reality (goals, values). What we have tried to do here is an effort in both directions.

Appendix on page 480

Appendix

Some data on economic relations within and between nations

Nation	1 GDP/cap.	2 Non-primary %	3 GINI (i)	4 GINI (1)	5 Trade composition index	6 Partner concentration	7 Commodity concentration
Argentina	670	82.2	0.45	0.863	—0.667	16.5	51.5
Australia	2035	90.6	0.35	0.929	0.576	18.4	50.9
Austria	1287	79.9	—	0.740	0.021	20.1	29.2
Belgium	1761	94.5	—	0.587	0.175	22.4	34.1
Brazil	273	48.4	—	0.837	—0.510	32.0	59.3
Canada	2505	87.9	—	0.497	—0.258	57.5	26.7
Ceylon	145	51.1	0.50	—	—0.375	29.3	93.4
Colombia	305	52.8	0.50	0.849	—0.710	47.3	84.8
Congo, D. R.	85	86.4	—	—	—0.062	32.3	65.5
Costa Rica	421	50.9	—	0.892	—0.989	50.0	65.1
Denmark	2109	83.4	0.42	0.458	—0.270	22.5	34.8
Ecuador	223	44.4	—	0.864	—0.766	54.7	75.2
El Salvador	273	39.7	0.45	0.828	—0.529	25.7	68.3
Finland	1747	64.5	—	0.599	—0.039	20.8	60.5
France	1922	83.4	—	0.583	0.158	18.7	23.8
W. Germany	1977	90.0	0.44	0.674	0.418	11.3	24.7
Ghana	288	42.0	—	—	—0.750	22.0	78.1
Guatamala	322	34.6	0.48	0.860	—0.659	32.9	68.0
Guyana	—	70.4	—	—	—0.675	—	—
Honduras	225	33.2	—	0.757	—0.759	56.9	67.9
India	102	27.1	0.57	0.522	—0.044	19.0	54.8
Iran	270	53.1	—	—	—0.812	17.3	92.8
Ireland	951	69.2	—	0.598	—0.322	70.7	42.3
Israel	1407	88.0	—	—	—0.076	14.9	52.4
Italy	1100	76.7	0.40	0.803	0.384	20.1	22.5
Ivory Coast	285	13.6	—	—	—0.703	37.5	83.1
Jamaica	516	63.9	—	0.820	0.480	37.4	76.5
Japan	870	79.4	—	0.470	0.707	29.7	36.1
Jordan	237	64.7	—	—	—0.241	15.0	59.9
S. Korea	99	48.2	—	—	—0.114	27.3	26.8
Kuwait	—	98.9	—	—	—0.486	—	—
Liberia	280	19.1	—	—	—0.754	38.7	91.2
Libya	705	64.3	—	0.700	—0.871	19.0	98.8
Mexico	482	45.2	0.53	—	—0.608	55.0	35*)
Morocco	196	43.7	—	—	—0.335	42.8	45.2
Netherlands	1532	91.7	0.43	0.605	—0.077	27.2	18.5
New Zealand	2025	86.9	—	0.772	—0.733	46.4	81.0
Nicaragua	325	40.3	—	0.757	—0.783	29.5	65.2
Nigeria	91	3.1	—	—	—0.688	—	—
Norway	1907	81.5	0.39	0.669	—0.207	18.9	26.4

Nation	1 GDP/cap.	2 % Non primary	3 GINI (i)	4 GINI (1)	5 Trade comp.	6 Part. conc.	7 Comm conc.
Pakistan	97	31.2	0.38	—	—0.337	12.8	61.7
Panama	517	53.8	—	0.737	—0.524	55.9	89.4
Peru	372	50.3	—	0.875	—0.545	41.8	58.7
Philippines	156	47.3	—	0.564	—0.608	43.1	72.7
Poland	—	52.3	—	—	0.037	—	—
Portugal	400	66.5	—	—	—0.068	—	25*)
Sierra Leone	159	25.2	—	—	—0.108	65.7	82.7
S. Africa	590	70.5	—	—	—0.386	—	—
Spain	600	67.2	—	0.780	—0.131	—	35*)
Sudan	103	14.2	—	—	—0.718	14.4	69.7
Sweden	2487	89.9	0.42	0.572	—0.012	13.8	28.6
Switzerland	2301	92.5	—	0.498	0.152	15.8	28.5
Syria	228	43.0	—	—	—0.449	36.5	64.9
Thailand	129	18.0	—	—	—0.606	19.4	56.3
Turkey	279	28.8	—	—	—0.705	17.2	38.2
UAR	159	43.4	—	—	—0.275	50.8	63.0
UK	1790	96.9	0.38	0.710	0.424	10.8	22.2
USA	3536	95.0	0.36	0.705	0.101	20.2	15.6
Venezuela	971	67.7	—	0.909	—0.893	35.5	99.6
Yugoslavia	—	43.1	—	—	—0.045	—	—

* Estimate

Sources:

GDP/cap.: Hagen & Hawlyryshyn, 1969: Analysis of World Income and Growth, 1955 — 65, *Economic Development and Cultural Change*, Vol. 18, No. 1, part II, 1969.

%Non-primary: The PRIO Nation Data File. Compiled from ILO and OECD sources. Year: 1967.

GINI (i): Weisskopf, T.E. 1970: *Underdevelopment, Capitalistic Growth and the Future of the Poor Countries.* Preliminary Draft, (Harvard University, April 1970).

GINI (1): Russett, B. et al., *World Handbook of Social and Political Indicators.*

Trade comp.: Computed from UN *Yearbook of International Trade Statistics*, 1967.

Partner conc.: Weisskopf, op. cit.

Comm. conc.: ibid. This variable and no. 6 are three years' averages 1964—66, computed on the basis of data in the UN *Yearbook of International Trade Statistics*, 1967.

IV.14. Cultural Contact and Technical Assistance as Factors in Peaceful Relations

PRIO publication No. 25-4.

Notes on page *720*.

1. Introduction

"Cultural cooperation" and "peaceful relations" are among the major slogans and values of our time, so it is not so strange that there is an effort to tie them together both in theory and in practice. Man wants to justify his actions; and if he has two goals, then it is tempting to construct a theory that one of them leads to the other, that they facilitate each other, or at least are highly compatible with each other. If they are seen as competitive or even as completely inconsistent with each other, then this complicates both thinking and actions.

In the present connection, this simple principle from the psychology of knowledge [1] leads to two propositions:

1. *Cultural cooperation will facilitate peaceful relations*
2. *Peaceful relations will facilitate cultural cooperation*

In other words, one is seen as a condition of the other. However, "condition" is a difficult term, since one may immediately ask: "Does it mean necessary or sufficient condition? Does it mean an absolute condition (deterministic) or a weaker one (probabilistic)? Does it mean that the consequence will obtain immediately or after some time? Does it mean under all conditions or only under some?" We shall assume in the following that it means neither necessary nor sufficient — that is, in proposition (1) above, we do not assume that peaceful relations cannot be obtained without cultural cooperation, nor that cultural cooperation leads with certainty to peaceful relations. What we shall discuss is rather the proposition, as stated, that when one of them is present then the probability of obtaining the other (in case, after some time) increases — even strongly. We shall explore the conditions under which these probabilities seem particularly high or low — since it is rather obvious that the proposition does not hold unconditionally.

The second proposition above seems less interesting, being more of a truism. When peace obtains there is less polarization in relations between nations, and all kinds of positive interaction become more easy — or at least so one should believe. However, even this is not necessarily true. In a state of cold war or uneasy peace between two nations, cultural cooperation may be facilitated precisely by the lack of peace — simply because decision-makers believe in proposition (1) and see cultural cooperation as a way out of the dilemma. Cultural cooperation is innocuous, and is therefore often seen as a good way of starting a process of depolarization [2]. When peace comes closer, the cultural cooperation is deemed less necessary, and the result may be a decrease, not an increase. Thus, it is conceivable that the current honeymoon in cultural cooperation between countries in Eastern and Western Europe in itself can be interpreted as a sign of deep, latent conflict, and that rates of exchange and cooperation will decrease when or if relations become more normal, the curiosity value as well as the political gains imagined dominate less, and cultural cooperation has to be judged on its own merits alone. These merits may of course be high enough, but they would have to stand on their own feet.

However, in general the second proposition is probably correct, as long as one remembers that we are not dealing with a necessary or sufficient condition in the strict sense. For example, relations between Norway and Nepal are extremely peaceful, but it is hard to discover any cultural cooperation between these two countries that seem to be close neighbours only in the alphabetical sense. But if we assume both propositions to be valid, then they can be combined into one at a higher level of complexity:

3. *There is positive feedback between cultural cooperation and peaceful relations,*
cultural ———→ peaceful
cooperation ←— relations

which is already an interesting fragment of social theory. The problem is, of course, whether the propositions on which it is based are empirically tenable — and that is what we shall look into in some detail. But first let us return for a moment to our point of departure.

If the propositions were tenable, under a wide variety of conditions, then we would possess a button that could be pushed, starting a machinery with peace as its output — and there is a high premium on such machines these days. Moreover, the machine would be close to a perpetuum mobile since it would use its own output as an input (proposition no.3 above). Even if we assume a lot of friction in the machinery, this is clearly too good to be true. But precisely for that reason, the theory stands out as particularly tempting. The agent of cultural cooperation becomes also an agent of peace. Moreover, the good goal of peace is obtained by way of good means (more culture) — means that are positive in themselves by most value standards —

and not by using means that are at worst negative or at best neutral, such as military force used for the purposes of belligerence or deterrence. It is like the theory about sex, love, and marriage: all three are considered laudable, and a considerable amount of human mental energy has gone into proving, showing, prescribing and idealizing to the effect that the three are each other's necessary and sufficient conditions. But much energy has equally gone into demonstrating, elaborating, and prescribing that this simply is not the case, that one can have marriage without love, love without sex, and sex without marriage, etc. Similarly, anybody would agree that one can have peace without cultural cooperation and cultural cooperation without peace. This all goes to show that human life in general and social life in particular are complex, and that our formulae to reflect this complexity are usually far from adequate. It also goes to show that there is some kind of structure to human variety, since such propositions usually are at least somewhat more right than wrong, under a variety of conditions. The problem is to specify these conditions and try to sort out elements of wishful thinking that are demonstrably wrong, or at least highly dubious.

2. Some definitions

We shall conceive of "cultural cooperation" in a fairly broad sense. It is not only concerned with "culture" in the sense of *belles lettres*, but includes science and education — in short, anything that has to do with standards of what is true and false, right and wrong, good and bad, beautiful and ugly, even sacred and profane. By "cooperation" we shall mean any kind of transnational cultural activity such as cultural exchanges of persons and objects between nations (the standard content of cultural agreements) and cooperative activities (such as regional nuclear research centers, international organizations with a cultural purpose, etc.). However, in agreement with current usage of these terms, we shall not interpret "exchange" and "cooperation" between nations in such a way that they necessarily take place on equal terms. Thus, there is an important difference between cultural "cooperation" in the sense stipulated in a cultural agreement between nations A and B, both developed, where A sends a professor of linguistics to B and B sends one of philosophy to A — or they exchange nuclear physicists or economists — and cultural cooperation between A and C, underdeveloped, where A sends a professor (now called an "expert") to C and C sends nothing back (because it is "technical assistance"), or sends back a student to study with the professor's colleagues in A. This pattern is also often referred to as cultural cooperation, but is clearly of a different kind.

Thus, we get essentially four different kinds of patterns, all referred to as "cultural cooperation":

	Exchange	Cooperation
Symmetric	cultural agreements, "cultural tourism"	international, non-governmental and governmental organizations, or ad hoc arrangements
Asymmetric	technical assistance, experts, students abroad	cooperation on unequal terms

Fundamentally, one may conceive of cultural cooperation as a kind of exchange in all four cases. All nations yield something and receive something. If in the process no extra cultural value is created, but simply transferred across national borders — as when a professor gives his lectures in Moscow instead of in Oslo — we shall talk about *exchange*. If something new and additional is created, we shall talk about *cooperation*, as when they engage in a research project together, or in a cultural restoration project. Further, if the nations participating receive about as much as they contribute, then the arrangement is said to be *symmetric*, if there are gross discrepancies between what they receive and what they contribute, the relationship is *asymmetric*. In the table above we have put in some terms to illustrate what the combinations stand for, but they should be seen as examples only, and the correspondence with the table headings is never perfect.

If the concept of "cultural cooperation" is problematic, "peaceful relations" is certainly not less problematic. For our purposes it should be sufficient to define it in the negative sense, more or less as "absence of organized group violence". There is also a more positive definition of peace that would be in terms of patterns of absence of exploitation, justice, cooperation, harmony, etc., but that would make proposition (1) above a tautology. Hence, it is the "absence of violence" that interests us, and where this is concerned one might perhaps also add the "absence of threats of violence". This would exclude deterrence and balance of power policies from the idea of peace; and it is probably this kind of peace obtained by peaceful means most people think of when they want to relate cultural cooperation and peaceful relations. On the other hand again, to add this meaningful clause to the definition of peace implies a rather pacifist or at least nonmilitary conception of peace.

The concepts have been made more precise, and the proposition is now the following: "Take bilateral relationships between all nations. If there are N nations, then there are $\frac{1}{2}N(N-1)$ such relationships. By and large, the more cultural cooperation one is able to introduce into these relationships, the more peaceful they will be". This is certainly no tautology. If the exchange of guest professors or cooperation in cultural restoration of objects damaged by floods and earthquakes, or threatened by dams and

485

wars should be related to absence of violence it cannot be said that this conclusion follows from an analysis of the meaning of these terms alone. The tenability of the proposition, in the final analysis, will have to be decided on the basis of empirical evidence.

At this point one should have tried to present some data on the correlation between the two variables. However, such data may be grossly misleading unless elaborated more than the data masses we know of would be able to stand. Hence, we shall try to assess the tenability of the proposition on the basis of what seems reasonable in the light of some conceptual analysis, some common sense, and some social science theory — and indicate rather than demonstrate This is not an ideal procedure; we would have liked to be able to present empirical evidence. But as we shall try to show, the relation between the two key concepts is so problematic that any theory about how they "facilitate" each other will have to be tested at a number of points. More precisely, it is doubtful whether the hypothesis can be tested at all with one sweeping empirical operation. Rather, the hypothesis has to be split into a system of interlocking hypotheses with a number of specifications of the conditions under which they are valid, so that one can proceed with empirical tests at crucial points in this structure. Much of this empirical evidence already exists in the literature, but much of it will have to be collected, and this will be done on a later occasion. In the present article, however, we shall only try to clarify the structure of this network of hypotheses, and to indicate conditions under which we would say that the hypotheses seem *reasonable*. We shall try to apply a social science microscope to the general proposition that cultural cooperation leads to more peaceful relations and report what we see — remembering all the time that what one sees depends not only on what there is to be seen, but also on the eyes that do the seeing.

3. Ten arguments considered

We shall now examine a list of ten reasons why cultural cooperation (C) should lead to peaceful relations (P), to arrive at a better basis for assessing the tenability of the proposition. The general structure of this type of thinking is as follows. Since $C \rightarrow P$ is certainly not self-evident one would in general have that C leads to a condition X, which in turn increases the probability of P. This immediately makes the argument more tenuous, for if C leads to X only with a certain probability and X to P only with a certain probability, then the probability linking C to P may become quite small. But apart from that, it is clear that there are other points at which counter-arguments against a relation of the type $C \rightarrow X \rightarrow P$ may arise.

Thus, one may ask whether it is really true that $C \rightarrow X$, and that $X \rightarrow P$?

And even if both are true under certain conditions, could it not be that C, or X, also has other effects that are less laudable? Or that one has to insert more factors, for instance that X leads to Y which in turn leads to P so that the relation becomes even more attenuated if the links are less than sure? Or that C leads to X only under conditions that are very different from (and even incompatible with) the conditions under which X leads to P? There are plenty of problems, as is usually the case with social analysis — particularly when the point of departure, as in this case, is a proposition between common sense categories and not between categories chosen by the social scientist himself. When he himself can choose his categories and make his own definitions, then both can be adapted to his methodologies and his data, and the problem is simplified into one of testing fairly uncomplicated relationships.

We shall consider ten such "intervening" factors, X. No doubt there are more, and other authors would have put the emphasis differently. One have deliberately excluded: the diffusion of culture that in itself, by its very content, leads to more peace. Many missionaries of various types through the ages have proclaimed this as a special virtue of their creed or ideology — but we find it difficult to handle this argument in this context, it is another problem and equally important. Rather, we have put the emphasis on the ideas of contact, cooperation, and assistance rather than on the cultural content itself, to see what kind of thinking might confirm or deny the general proposition.

3.1. The "increased knowledge" argument

This argument is probably the one that immediately comes to mind for most people who give any thought to the general problem of the relevance of cultural cooperation to peaceful relations. The argument is clear enough. Through cultural cooperation, both parties gain more knowledge of the culture of the other party. This knowledge may now turn into a reservoir for peacebuilding via three mechanisms.

First of all, there is the idea that knowledge may lead to liking and friendship, which then serves as a protection against violent disruptions. This mechanism works on the lines that through knowledge one gains an insight into the other culture and that this makes its proponents appear in a better light because one is more able to judge them on the basis of *their* own cultural standards, not as deviants from one's own culture. One becomes more of a cultural relativist by knowing other cultures. "*Tout comprendre c'est tout pardonner*" is a negative way of formulating this, but there is also the more positive idea that human beings are basically friendly to each other and basically imbued with a capacity to like and love each other —

487

a capacity which a deeper understanding of their background will stimulate more fully and translate into action, and a capacity which ignorance and misunderstandings serve to mystify and mask.

In other words, one may learn to like people *in spite of* the fact that they are different, if one only gets to know them. One may even like them *because* they are different, simply by being attracted by them as sources of new experience, revealed through knowledge.

Secondly, there is the idea of *tolerance*. By this we do not mean friendship and liking or other positive evaluations of representatives of other cultures, but simply the idea of live and let live, of peaceful existence between different systems. In slightly different terms: the attitude one has when it no longer seems important to convert other people and change other cultures, at least not completely and at least not as long as they do not try to change oneself. This attitude should not be confused with liking them because they are different, as mentioned above. Tolerance means to tolerate: nothing more, nothing less. It is supposedly bred by knowledge much in the same way as in the mechanism mentioned above. Possibly, it may also be the result of indifference, and the rationalization of powerlessness. One learns to see other cultures from the inside, and in so doing realizes that it would be impossible to change them even if one wanted to do so. And so one translates this insight into the ideology of tolerance. Obviously, this may remove one source of violent conflict behavior: coercive efforts to change others.

Thirdly, there is the idea that knowledge of other cultures facilitates prediction, and that prediction — whether one likes the other culture or not — facilitates positive interaction and makes it easier to avoid negative interaction. When one knows what to expect then one fears it less, and what one does not fear does not so easily stimulate threat-orientation, defensive postures, and other types of sentiments and behavior that may be highly productive of violent behavior. This third idea implies nothing about change in evaluation, as the first idea did. There is only a change in the cognitive ability to predict what is going on in the world.

Are these theories reasonable? Our answer will have to be ambivalent. It should be noted that they are actually somewhat more complicated than the C — X — P pattern, since three steps are involved:

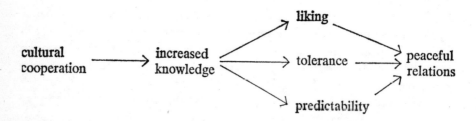

We shall look at all three steps.

First of all, it cannot be assumed in general that cultural cooperation leads to more knowledge about other cultures. We have the proverbial technical assistance expert who transmits much culture but lives in such a way that all stimuli that might have increased his insight in the other party's culture are filtered away. There are well-known structural arrangements like "the golden ghetto" that foster this, and also attitudes of the "I-am-here-to-teach-not-to-learn" type. In general, asymmetric types of cultural cooperation are quite compatible with minimal gains in knowledge by the sending side of the relationship — and such gains as are made are likely to be superficial, of the kind made by tourists and people who collect impressions as they might collect stamps or photos. It is also quite possible that the cooperative type of cultural cooperation, as opposed to the exchange type, serves *less* to stimulate knowledge and insight into other cultures, because the participants become so concerned with the common goal and the culture surrounding that goal (which is likely to be the culture of one of the parties more than the others, or some generalized technical culture). The symmetric type of exchange is probably the type of cultural cooperation that most easily leads to an increase in knowledge. However, even if we assume that knowledge is increased, its effects are not certain. The safest proposition is probably that concerning increased predictability, since it involves no attitudinal change. But it presupposes a high level of insight into human affairs, whether it is of the professional social science type or the more generalized type of empirical evidence accumulated by, say, the trained and experienced diplomat. In other words, knowledge certainly does not automatically lead to higher predictability, but it does facilitate it.

The same applies to the other two mechanisms. Obviously, it is not enough to *know;* much also depends on whether one *likes* what one knows. It is hard to believe in any automatic transfer from knowledge to liking — from *kjennskap til vennskap* as it is said in the Scandinavian languages. All research on *prejudice*, even the concept itself, is centered around the idea that human beings are capable of maintaining patterns of negative or positive evaluation of others, individuals or categories, in spite of the most glaring evidence contradicting their assumptions. Of course, they may protect their negative evaluation by systematically avoiding occasions that might present them with data to the contrary — but human beings also seem capable of absorbing a good amount of contradictory data and ideology and of working on it so as to produce a relatively coherent pattern in the end. The scientifically minded person will perhaps respect the data more and the prejudiced respect them less and pick what confirms his ideas — but the difference is one of degree and not a strict dichotomy. The net result of increased knowledge may therefore easily be neither liking, nor tolerance, but reinforcement and even growth of negative evaluations. On the other hand, against such a background as that provided in the 1950s by the Cold War, there was hardly anything to lose. Attitudes were so overwhelmingly negative that any change would seem to be in a more positive direction. Under such conditions even a little bit of cultural cooperation can probably contribute a great deal towards tolerance and even friendship — because the prevailing conditions were so artificial.

But even if it is hard to believe in any automatic transfer of negative attitudes to positive ones through the mediation of increased knowledge, it is not so hard to believe in a transition from negative evaluation to indifference — called "tolerance" above. Insight into the complexity of the world around one may lead to a decline in missionary fervour that otherwise would give rise to threat-orientation in others. The road from negative to neutral is shorter than the distance from negative to positive, and implies less in terms of directives for actions. Liking releases positive actions, whereas "tolerance" only impedes negative ones and is compatible with low activity levels. On the other hand, these negative actions, springing from negative sentiments, are exactly the material out of which wars are made — so if tolerance is the result it is certainly a very meaningful result in our context.

Thirdly, there is the step to peaceful relations. Again it is problematic, since liking may lead to more positive relations if there is a chance of translating positive sentiments into action. But it may also lead to a feeling of betrayal and to extreme emotions and even actions if conflicts nevertheless develop despite, not to mention because of, cultural cooperation and bring about negative interaction. A deeply internalized pattern of liking may represent no danger; but superficial, positive attitudes may crumble at the first shock they receive and be translated into anger and aggression. The fight between former friends, lovers, fellow party members is always the toughest. The more indifferent type of attitude called "tolerance" is probably more reliable here, since there will be no basis for feeling betrayal and yet restraints against negative interaction. As to predictability: there is no guarantee that insight into the other party's behavior can be used only to facilitate *positive* interaction — it can equally well be used for the opposite purpose. On the other hand, if the *will* to positive interaction is present, then *knowledge* of the other party will facilitate it to some extent.

Thus the balance sheet is mixed, and the net result depends not only on the nature of the cultural cooperation, but on the input of personnel into it. The most negatively prejudiced person will probably not be changed

490

much even by the most successful type of cultural cooperation designed today — and even a highly unsuccessful experiment in cultural cooperation may well fail to eliminate the reservoir of goodwill in the positively prejudiced person. But much depends on the project of cultural cooperation itself. If it works well, then cultural cooperation has in itself, at the level of the persons that meet or are exchanged or of the small human groups or enterprises involved, become a model of what it is supposed to stimulate. The person who participates and likes the people he meets, from the other culture, will probably generalize this experience in his mind and want to repeat it afterwards. And the person with the more modest framework of tolerance, who finds that it is *possible* to work together with representatives of other cultures in a pattern of peaceful coexistence, may also generalize *his* experience. Since attitudes are born through experience and fed into new experiences, this will create a possibility for positive feedback cycles that may gradually enlarge, involve more people and more fields of cooperation, and translate into peaceful relations at a more comprehensive level. But this said, one should be reminded that exactly the opposite can be said about the humanly *unsuccessful* cultural cooperation — it may stimulate negative feedback cycles that may feed on preexisting attitudes in the culture and have disastrous effects for broader cooperation. The problem then concerns the dimensions of successful cooperation, touched upon in the next section.

3.2. The "successful cooperation" argument

This argument is very simple: As long as cultural cooperation is really cooperation it serves in itself as a model of peace, and this model may have a certain contagious effect. The parties may convince themselves that they are able to cooperate in one field, hence why not also try another field? The cultural field may serve as a point of attack on frozen lines of communication and postures, and if successful a broader attack may follow.

This argument is probably valid only insofar as one is dealing with genuine cooperation on a symmetric basis, and not only exchange. This is based on some general research findings to the effect that cooperation has to satisfy the three following conditions if it is to lead to more lasting positive relations [3].

— that there is full *equality* between the partners,
— that it is *functional* in the sense of producing something that could not be obtained equally well without the cooperation,
— that it *lasts over some time* so as to lead to patterns of cooperation, to institutionalization.

Of course, what is called "exchange" may also satisfy most of this, but the typical paradigm seems rather to be that of cooperation in the more narrow sense. Simple exchange is not functional enough; it yields benefits too similar to what the nation might have obtained on its own — or at least believe that it might have obtained. It is different from advanced know-how and capital consuming projects with international participation and financing; they constitute a kind of archetype of cooperation. But some of these do not fulfill the first principle above because of the lack of equality. Thus, cooperation of the type where one country supplies the capital and the know--how and the other the unskilled labor (the typical colonial enterprise) is not symmetric, not even when capital and know-how are supplied as buying power by the country that also supplies the less skilled labor (the typical car plant cooperation pattern). It is quite conceivable that all such asymmetries will lead to less rather than more peaceful relations and hence be counterproductive, because the asymmetry, rightly or wrongly, is perceived as some kind of exploitation.

But let us imagine that the conditions for successful cooperation have been satisfied. The parties cooperate in an egalitarian fashion (not with the colored as private soldiers and the whites as officers); cooperation produces something (it is not fake, like some student-volunteer road-building projects where it is obvious to everybody that the cooperation becomes not only excessively expensive but also excessively time consuming), and the cooperation lasts long enough for the organization to take on definite shape and the role-expectations to be institutionalized and internalized (not like the volunteer summer camp). The theory now rests on the assumption that there will be rings in the water, that there will be a tendency for people to generalize this experience. As a rule this is certainly true. To the extent human beings are rational one must assume that they generalize from successful experiences and that they later on and under other circumstances try to imitate what is essential in them, *in casu* the cooperative elements. And it is also reasonable, in general, to assume that many links of positive cooperation will serve as a bulwark against large scale violence.

One should, however, warn against excessive belief in the contagion effect. Human societies seem remarkably compartmentalized. True, it is a common social science dogma that if one changes society at one place, in one institution so to speak, other changes will follow because of the coupling of social institutions. But changes may also *not* follow, or they may be very different from what one intends or hopes. Resistances may build up, inertia effects are strong and only very few such carry-over effects seem automatic. This may depend very much on the differentiation inside societies [4].

However that may be, even one positive link of cooperation is a protection against easy and total disruption. It serves to symbolize communality of purpose, it trains personnel in peaceful cooperation — personnel that may later be channelled to other positions along the contact surface between two nations; and it serves as a possible line of communication between the two nations. If this line of communication is located high up in the two societies, close to the decisionmaking nuclei, it may even have important functions as an extra-diplomatic source of communication in periods of extreme conflict. Thus, in general this argument seems to have a high level of plausibility.

3.3. The "development" argument

This argument is well known but also remarkably weak. The idea is that the more developed a nation is, the more it will be able to satisfy the needs of its citizens, and the less internal frustration there will be that might turn into internal cleavages and might escalate into international wars, not to mention efforts by leaders to conceal and reduce such cleavages by engaging in international wars. In addition, there is the idea that social and economic development also leads to internal institution-building that in turn leads to more mature nations which will not engage in adventures on the international scene, or which have built-in safeguards against such adventuring. In short, this is where the *general* argument in favor of the thesis that development leads to peace enters the debate on the effects of cultural cooperation. Since development and peace are perhaps the major values of our time [5], the tendency to view them not only as compatible but also as mutually supporting would be particularly strong.

The first part of the argument, that cultural cooperation leads to development, seems relatively indisputable. Of course, the exchange of two professors in numismatics or number theory or in *belles lettres* will hardly directly speed up social and economic growth, but when we look at the entire range of cultural cooperation as it exists today there is no doubt that much, even most of it, is highly productive of development. Growth is to a considerable extent based on knowledge, and knowledge is based on exchange and cooperation — unless one would assume that everybody could and should make the same cultural inventions over and over again. But we have included technical assistance in our concept of cultural cooperation. Besides, we have defined "culture" so as to include technology with all its prescriptions as to the right thing to do to obtain material goods, and science with all its formulae as to what is true and what is not.

But the second part of the argument, that development leads to peace, is more difficult to agree with. For one thing, there are many different kinds of war. It may well be true that developed nations, since they are more interested in the rank structure of the status quo, do not engage so often in wars to alter the existing conditions in international society: but they may certainly engage in wars and other types of aggression to preserve them — as amply evidenced in the post-war period. Thus what developed nations call "maturity" may to others look like conformity, paternalism, neo-colonialism and the like; and what they call "immaturity" may to others look like acts of social justice, wars of liberation, etc. In this connection it should also be remembered that a social structure may represent a huge quantity of "frozen aggressiveness" — even when there are no overt acts of violence whatsoever. An obvious example is the rigid caste structure or slave society based on a power structure — internalized in the lower levels or not — which must be taken into consideration when aggressiveness in general is discussed. Otherwise one ends up with a concept of aggression with a very heavy bias in favor of the power-wielders.

Thus, the argument is weakened *a priori* by simple conceptual analysis of peacefulness and aggressiveness. But then there are all the empirical arguments showing that development not only constitutes no guarantee for peacefulness, but even seems correlated with belligerence.

First of all, the kind of development fostered by cultural cooperation is likely to upset some kind of internal equilibrium. It will usually be translated into education which in turn usually leads to a class of people over-educated relative to what the occupational structure can absorb. This then leads to a strong rank disequilibrium [6] which may be converted into heavy internal disorder, taking the form, for example, of the many revolutions triggered by students or half-educated proletariats in urban slums. Thus, far from decreasing the probability of internal cleavage and violence, development will probably increase it because of the introduction of new, rank-disequilibrated groups. Another important recipe for violence here is the group of *nouveaux riches* who find that their wealth is not matched by their power.

It may be objected that internal disorder does not necessarily lead to external aggression, which is true. But there will always be a strong probability of escalation because other nations' interest may be threatened in the process. And this, after all, is the basis of the whole argument that development should lead to more peaceful relations.

Then it may be objected that development will have to be "harmonious", so that tensions are avoided by means of rapid absorption of new groups of wealth and wisdom into the occupational structure and the power structure, or adequate changes of these structures. Experience seems to show that this is more easily said than done; it is easy to create a certain amount of wealth in a few hands, and to promote some degree of literacy, health, and education — compared with the difficulties of obtaining economic and political growth.

By the same mechanism, economic development may upset equilibria — however unjust, cruel and artificial — existing among nations at the international level. A nation that sees its educational level and per capita income increase much above what it used to be may feel that its position in the international power structure does not correspond to its newly attained educational and economic ranking — and might be tempted into feeling that some adjustment would be appropriate. In some cases this is provided for (as when the Security Council is expanded to accommodate the mobility wishes of new nations) — in other cases it is not. Then such nations might feel very tempted to convert the new resources of capital, goods, and material, as well as organizational skill, into military technology and organization to rectify the situation by threat or by action. Of course, it is also possible that development might produce more equilibrium — but since the point of departure in the world seems to be a structure dominated by some few big powers at the top and a small "middle class" of nations, "development" of the large group of poor nations will almost always lead to more disequilibrium. And nations that move into the upper class will develop more vested interest in the status quo. Hence less, not more, peaceful relations are to be expected, *ceteris paribus*.

The point here is not that cultural cooperation does not lead to development (for it is probably among the most important necessary conditions), but that development alone hardly can be said to lead to peace. Economic development does not easily translate into that kind of development. Of course, when certain conditions are met (for instance, that the development takes place under the auspices of a supranational organization) [7] then development may certainly be compatible with increases in the probability of peaceful relations — but in general this cannot be said to be the case. That point will be developed further under section 3.10.

3.4. *The "hostage" argument*

So far we have looked mainly at changes brought about by cultural cooperation inside the participant countries — such as changes in opinions, attitudes and beliefs, changes in their interaction patterns relative to nationals from other cultures, and changes in the level of development. We now turn to an argument that is truly *relational*, applying to the relations between two or more nations. The idea is as follows. Countries enter into cultural cooperation; the net result may be the transfer of a lot of citizens from one country to the other, on a temporary or more permanent basis. As long as they are there, they may serve as a protection against attacks, for

495

the simple reason that nation A does not want to be responsible for killing its own compatriots located in nation B. The result will be a gain in peaceful relations.

The argument has a certain degree of plausibility, but not a very high one. First of all, it only applies to some types of cultural cooperation, and mainly to the bilateral exchange type. Here the idea would be that nation A has its students or professors in nation C and hence refrains from attack. But if an attack from nation A is to be considered at all, then nation A is probably the militarily stronger of the two, which usually means that it has more resources, which again usually means that it has a cultural level that makes it more a sender of cultural goods than a receiver. Thus, although nation A may have a couple of professors in nation C, large numbers of students from C are likely to be in A, and may protect A against a second strike from poor nation C instead of impeding it from launching a first strike against C itself. In this way the factor actually works the other way. And if there is cultural *cooperation* between A and C the center is likely to be located in one country only, not in both — and a neutral country like Switzerland is often chosen as the location (among other reasons precisely because of the hostage argument) and so that it can carry on in spite of conflict between A and C.

On the other hand, it is probably true that hostages give some sort of protection especially if they are located close to important targets (e.g. if they are studying at a university close to an atom bomb target) and are of sufficiently high status in their home country. For that reason it has often been suggested that the first to participate in cultural exchanges should be sons, daughters, and other relatives of foreign ministers, joint chiefs of staff, and other top decisionmakers. If these conditions are fulfilled there would probably be a considerable deterrence effect. But only few nations would be willing to run such risks, for hostages may also be used for reprisals.

But what is easily underestimated in this connection is the process of polarization. Wars rarely start all of a sudden: they have usually a history of bad relations crystallizing around some conflict issue. In the process of polarization contacts like cultural cooperation patterns are broken, and the function of this is to "strip for action", to make the enemy appear so completely purged of everything that has to do with oneself that there are no ambivalences to impede one from striking. Exchange students are simply withdrawn, called home, cultural cooperation agreements are abrogated, etc. It may be argued that this proves how cultural cooperation may be peace-productive precisely because it gives the parties some negative action to engage in short of war (and not only, as argued in the introduction, some positive interaction to engage in short of peace) — and this is probably a good point. But the major effect of the hostage institution does not seem to come through easily, simply because it is too easy to get away with it. Even if polarization processes do not clear the board, there are still very often provisions made for the repatriation of foreign nationals, and belligerent governments may decide that the few that are left are easily expendable. In short, the argument seems relatively untenable.

3.5. "Insurance" arguments

These arguments are somewhat similar to the hostage argument. They have to do with cultural cooperation in the asymmetric sense, where there is a flow of value in one direction, but no counterflow or only a very minor one. Technical assistance is one typical example; cultural exchange between a cultural superpower and a cultural satellite (where the professor from the former comes to teach, from the latter to study) is another. The idea is that the flow of value into the poorer nation is like money paid into the bank, or rather to the insurance company. It is there so that one can get something back, under particular conditions. The assumption is that one builds up goodwill by yielding more than one receives, and that this goodwill is an asset that may be drawn upon in cases of emergency.

There are now two versions of this argument. There is the *direct* argument, where the idea is that the goodwill accumulated will serve to protect oneself against any attack from the direct recipient; and the *indirect* one, where the idea is that the recipient will come to one's assistance if somebody else launches an attack, or even that this somebody else will refrain from doing so for fear of losing goodwill invested in the recipient. The whole point here is *asymmetry*: by yielding technical assistance one protects oneself. Cooperation characterized by *symmetry* would be of no use, since there would be no accumulation of assets, the flow of value already having been balanced by a counterflow.

Again, there may be some truth in this argument. One can probably buy friends, to put it cynically, or at least bribe one's enemies into more peaceful behavior. But there are also contra-arguments. Thus, even if objectively the assets seem to pile up, subjectively, from the point of view of the recipient nation, this may not be the case. The recipient may feel, on the contrary, that technical assistance is an effort by the rich nation to pay off on an old debt from the days of colonialism (paying back what he took away in raw materials, unfair prices, or as exploitation of local labor). Or he may feel that what he receives as technical assistance is going to be paid for in ways other than political support — for instance by having to acquire tools, spare parts, etc., from the rich nation. In short, he may figure out the balance in a way that differs from what was intended

497

in the richer nation — and may easily come to the opposite conclusion, that *he* is the one who has assets to cash in on.

This leads to the second type of counter-argument. In this situation the result may be the opposite of peaceful relations because the two nations may have completely irreconcilable images of what they expect from each other. They may both expect the other nation to yield something "in return", and accumulate frustration in the waiting period. This may also be a period of constructive cooperation; but if so, the mechanism is different from the one mentioned here.

There is another argument, which also applies to the hostage argument. Is it morally correct to pretend that something is a gift and nevertheless expect something in return? Should it not then be done explicitly, by preference, as in an agreement between the nations to the effect that A gives B so much cultural value and B openly gives A a promise of friendship and help? And is it not reasonable to believe that this will make the "direct insurance" argument more valid because of the explicitness of the assumptions? But if cultural cooperation is just made a part of an ordinary international bargain, it is one value more that may enter in any kind of negotiation. And since cultural cooperation is considered positive by most, it can help resolve conflicts by giving negotiators more to trade with. This will be elaborated further under section 3.7.

But even with these provisos there clearly remains some validity to the argument. The nation that yields something is experienced as a source of satisfaction and will probably receive some loyalty and identification in return that may pay off politically, *in casu* also as a protection against violence — but of course equally well as an incentive to join the yielding nation in a violent encounter with a third party. Thus, if the receiving nation accepts that it owes the yielding nation something, then the argument seems valid — but that condition seems only rarely to be satisfied.

3.6. The "similarity" argument

This argument would run as follows. The more cultural cooperation, the more similarity there will be between the nations. Not only will there sooner or later develop a similarity between the two cultures but there will also, partly as a cause, partly as a consequence, develop a similarity in the social structure of the nations engaging in cultural cooperation; they will become homologous. They will learn about each other's way of doing things, and like a set of communicating vessels they will eventually borrow from each other what they like and in the process become more similar. This similarity, in turn, will facilitate positive interaction, since a common culture (with the world culture as the extreme case) facilitates communication (like money facilitates trade). The same applies to common social structures. A person in nation A finds his "opposite number" in nation B, and interaction flows more easily because of this. The net result is increased empathy, and with that reduced propensity to engage in violent behavior.

All this immediately raises a great number of problems. We shall touch on only some of them. First of all, it is not that certain that cultural co-operation really leads to a total increase in homogeneity or similarity in the world culture. It may be correct to say that the world's nations look more similar today than they did, say, one hundred years ago; but hardly more than they did during *pax ecclesia*. That they are built largely according to the same model, and that diffusion rates for cultural elements are so high that isolated cultures are increasingly rare, is probably true. But this may also mean that all nations are converging towards the same *mixture* of cultures, that they are similar in their dissimilarity, so to speak, because they all harbor highly divergent cultures within themselves. To take a concrete example, there is considerable difference between the lawyers' and the sociologists' approach to the problem of crime, much in the same sense as when C.P. Snow talks about two cultures. Today both approaches are found in most nations, with ratios usually more in favor of the lawyer in the less developed nations and less in favor of the lawyer in the more developed nations. One day the ratios *may* become almost similar, in quality, quantity, and in power. But that does not mean that total similarity has increased — it may mean just the opposite. Today it is highly unlikely that lawyers and sociologists should go to war over their divergent conceptions of deviant man. But only some hundred years ago people in the same nation went to war over divergent conceptions of The Holy Family. In other words, the similarity argument, to be valid, would call for examination of intranational dissimilarities as well.

Even between nations it is doubtful whether the role of cultural cooperation necessarily is in the direction of increased similarity. It makes cultural resources available on a world scale and thus enlarges the range of cultural stimuli. But the cultural response is not necessarily one of imitation. It may be just the opposite: such as rejection, or innovation. If the result of diffusion were by necessity, imitation, and similarity, then we would have it in the world already. But societies are complex; they are not like a bathtub of cold water with the warm tap turned on. Diffusion rates are uneven in different directions. Small cells of "cold water" may remain completely untouched. In some cases the hot water is turned into ice, and so on. It should not be forgotten that the Reformation with consequent warfare was also a result of cultural cooperation.

However, even if it were true that exchange and cooperation lead to more similarity, both within and between nations, it is difficult to see that this constitutes any guarantee for peace. That communication becomes easier — but perhaps also less interesting because of the lack of stimulating discrepancy — is probably true. But it does not follow from this that the lines of communication are used for positive interaction; they may just as well be used for the opposite. As a trivial example, similarity in dimensions of railway material may facilitate tourism and international marriages — but also invasions. Knowing one's opposite number means also knowing better how to hurt and harm, not only an individual, but also the whole structure in which he is found. Most wars have been fought between nations that speak languages belonging to the same general group; similarity constitutes no guarantee for peacefulness.

What seems more plausible is the idea of *increased empathy*. Again it can be used both ways, but it is probably true that increased *empathy*, based on similarity, also leads to increased *sympathy*. Man seems, in general, to surround himself with people like himself, and the double meaning of the word "like" — likeness and liking — is sociologically meaningful. Similarity is seen as less of a threat, as more of an invitation to spin webs of positive affiliation.

But it may also well be that this is only at a relatively high level of similarity. It may be that before one reaches that level, cultural cooperation leads to similarity in a limited sense only. This may be a double-edged sword: There are more points of contact, which mean more points of communication and bargaining, but also more points of friction and conflict. If the relationship between the two nations is really well cemented, so that one might use the word "integration", then there will probably be mechanisms for handling such conflicts. But if this is not the case, then it may well be that the conflict level will increase and not decrease with increasing similarity — as well as the potential for violent encounters. In short, the argument seems problematic, and the conditions under which it is valid do not seem too well known.

3.7. The "interdependence" argument

This argument is closely related to the "similarity" argument. Through cultural cooperation, ties are established between two nations; the nations are "sewn together", to use the old metaphor. Across the lines of scientific cooperation countless interdependencies arise, in the literal sense that somebody or something in nation A depends on somebody or something in nation B. A student in A cannot go ahead without advice from a professor in B, the professor in B needs the stimulus provided by a conference in which he meets his colleagues from A, and so on. But this interdependence, then, becomes a condition for continued existence — and the more so the

500

more numerous the lines of interdependence that are woven between the two countries. This, in turn, means that A will hardly attack B, because this means to attack herself. Like a cell in a human body it depends on other nations to such an extent that it cannot start destroying others without being self-destructive. Everybody's investment in everybody else makes any attack an attack against oneself.

This sounds convincing, but there are the same gaps in the reasoning here as elsewhere, although perhaps somewhat less so. First of all, it is not certain that cultural cooperation leads to interdependence. It may also lead to self-sufficiency, like the son who tells his father: "OK, you have taught me all you know about the trade, thank you, I am now leaving you and setting up my own business". Nations may absorb from others what they want, and then continue on their own. Some cultural cooperation may lead to interdependence, but more of it may lead to less, even with the result that the initial cultural cooperation disappears. Norwegian sociology was largely the creation of United States technical assistance in the field, using the Fulbright scheme among others. However, *interdependence* in the sense that Norwegian sociologists *need* the help and advice of their us colleagues (which is more than mere interaction) has probably diminished since the early 1950s when this development started.

Secondly, even if it does lead to interdependence, this is no guarantee for friendly relations. There is an assumption of rationality here to the effect that nations under no condition want to hurt themselves. But if this assumption were warranted we would have few wars or threats of war at all with the high level of present-day world integration. Rather, it seems that nations sometimes go to war well knowing that they will harm themselves in some sense, but hoping nevertheless that a. they will make some important gains from the war along some other dimensions, and b. they will be able to hurt the other nation even more than that nation will hurt them. Moreover, nations are willing to sacrifice and adapt to hardship — and most nations would probably be willing to sacrifice temporarily some benefits derived from cultural cooperation.

Moreover, interdependence is always bought at some cost. To put it in one simple formula, the more interdependent two nations are, the more values they exchange. And the more values they exchange, 1. the more can they engage in "horse-trading" as a way of solving conflicts, and 2. the more can conflicts generalize and aggravate and the more chances there are for conflict to arise. Thus, there are both positive and negative effects of increased interdependence from the perspective of conflict theory; and since conflicts may become dangerous when they lead to violent conflict behavior, the final conclusion is by no means clear. It probably depends on to what extent a conflict-resolving machinery can be set up more quickly than the rate of which interdependence is built, so as to preempt conflict generalization and build on "horse-trading" potential.

3.8. The "equality" argument

Here the idea is that cultural cooperation is a way of distributing more evenly, over the world's surface, the cultural heritage of all mankind. It should not be confused with the development argument, where the major point is that culture is used to develop each single society; or the similarity argument, where the idea is that societies become more similar through cultural cooperation. The idea is one of equity and justice, of providing equal opportunities. It is like the welfare state ideology about schooling: everybody should have the same opportunity. This does not imply that they end up being completely similar, because of different ability and different inclination to use the opportunity. The argument here is that cultural cooperation serves as a diffusion channel for culture — the communication vessels model — thus providing equal chances of benefiting from human culture. This equality of opportunity, in turn, is translated into peaceful relations mainly in a negative way. Gross inequalities of opportunity can easily produce aggression and action to change the distribution of opportunities.

We assume without further discussion that cultural cooperation in fact has the effect of diffusing knowledge of cultural patterns in such a way that the culture of the developed countries becomes more evenly distributed. This seems almost to be true by definition. The same does not necessarily apply to the culture of the countries that are on the receiving end. In a sense they come out richer since they gain insight into another culture without having to share their own — and this may in the long run have some interesting consequences. But we shall not develop that theme here. We shall assume that unequal opportunities may be disruptive for peaceful relations, and that completely equal opportunities may be more peace-productive.

The difficulty with the argument lies in the assumption that what may apply to *equal* opportunities also applies to the process of *equalizing* the opportunities. In other words, that what applies to the end result also applies to the process. Briefly expressed, the goods of culture are distributed more evenly in the process of *equalizing* the opportunities (e.g. resources such as textbooks in all languages, transistor radio education, literacy campaigns, multiplication of libraries, exhibitions) — what applies to the end result also applies to the process. But some countries will make use of this more than others and translate it into some kind of growth. This inequality in growth potential will change the relative rank and standing of the nations of the world. Some of them may become more equilibrated in the sense that they use the cultural resources to adjust their low standard of living to their large size and population, whereas others may become less equilibrated so that they outgrow economically and socially the more humble role they play in the world community of nations. The former may become more peaceful with their neighbors, the latter less. At any rate, there will be changes, old equilibria and disequilibria will be upset and inverted, and the net result may well be less, not more, peaceful relations.

This argument is similar to the development argument, but it should be pointed out that here it is the international context that is being considered. A nation may be *developed* or not in absolute terms, regardless of other nations, since development can be measured in relation to the possibility the nation has of satisfying the needs of its citizens. But a nation can be *equilibrated* only relative to other nations, by looking at the whole set of nations to find the average patterns of correspondence, since there is no other way of finding out which level of education corresponds to which level of per capita income [8]. The same applies, of course, to such a concept as equality of opportunity. In short, we encounter the same difficulties as we find in connection with the development, similarity, and interdependence arguments. If all nations were equal, developed, similar, and interdependent then we might get peaceful relations; but in the process towards this goal there seem to be serious danger spots — many of them still ahead of us.

3.9. The "power distribution" argument

This argument would set cultural cooperation in the general analytical framework of the distribution of power among the nations of the world. As is well known, the distribution of military power is extremely uneven, as seen when a superpower is compared with one of the smallest and poorest nations of the world of today. At the same time there is the idea of balance of power as a mechanism to preserve peaceful relations. To translate this idea into social reality there is need for alliance formations of different kinds. Such alliances are, of course, an important feature of international reality, especially if one also counts the more tacit, implicit alliances. They create borderlines in the world community of nations, freezing interaction at some points and increasing it in other directions.

But "power" can be regarded as a general potential for influencing others, not only by means of military force or threats of force but also, for instance, by means of cultural diffusion as well. To propagate and internalize one's own cultural framework into others is to open a channel of manipulation, particularly in the period before the neophyte becomes sufficiently well versed in the intricacies of the new culture he is trained in. The diffusion of one's own language is good enough as an example; the same applies to the diffusion of science, ideology, etc. Since cultural cooperation also is a means of cultural diffusion, this means that cultural cooperation can be and should be analyzed in a power context.

There are now two lines of reasoning. According to the first, cultural cooperation will serve to reinforce military power patterns, and to the extent that these patterns facilitate peaceful relations they will be reinforced by cultural cooperation. According to this model, some powers, notably the big and the bigger ones, are seen as the guardians of the rest. They are guardians not only by virtue of their superior military power, but also because all five big powers today speak a world language and hence possess a world culture (only one world language, Spanish, does not correspond to a big power but is split between about a score of nations that together might constitute a big power). Thus, to the extent the world is protected by the big powers that are then seen as guardians of their own spheres, cultural cooperation will maintain this structure — by means of such agencies as USIA, Soviet friendship societies, Alliance Française and the British Council. Cultural power seems to flow easily along the same lines as political and economic power.

According to the second model, cultural cooperation is seen as a corrective to the powerlines of military force. The idea is that superiority in culture does not necessarily go together with superiority in military power, which gives the lesser powers a chance to compensate for their military inferiority and to make themselves heard in the world at large. It creates a more complex pattern of power, so complex in fact that the unequal distribution of military power becomes more tolerable. And then there is the idea that a nation under the influence of one superpower may develop cultural cooperation with another superpower and create a certain bridge that also makes the total pattern more complex, less polarized, more amenable to local solutions of conflicts.

Of course, it is to some extent an empirical question how closely cultural superiority is correlated with military superiority. But the structure of international relations will reinforce any existing correlation because 1. a "superior" culture may have been used in the past to build the kind of technological and organizational basis on which military power rests, and 2. military power may have given a nation a leading position so that its culture by definition becomes superior and worthy of being pursued. This last point is illustrated by the large numbers of students from former colonial countries who go to their former metropolitan country for their studies. And 3. military alliances are often built around cultural similarities, so that the lesser power in the alliance is particularly receptive to the kind of culture offered inside the alliance. Thus, there should be good reasons why the first model is correct in the sense that cultural cooperation tends to reinforce existing power structures. But this does not rule out the second model, which in a sense covers all the exceptions to the pattern of the first model. Thus, we can assume some validity in both models.

However, from this it does not follow that cultural cooperation will be productive of peace because of its implications with respect to the power distributions of the world. On the contrary, it is as open to criticism as all other models of power distribution seem to be. We shall examine only part of that criticism here.

First of all, to the extent the first model is valid it may explain peaceful relations *within* the sphere controlled by the nation that is a big power both in the military and in the cultural sense. This long seemed to be the case in spheres dominated by the present big powers. But it has little to offer in terms of peace *between* these spheres, except in the one sense that it contributes to a kind of polarization, which in turn contributes to predictability which in turn makes balance of power policies more meaningful. But this is a peace that rests on threats of war, and the kind of peace that is exclusive, not inclusive of all nations or even as many as possible. It is "peace" against somebody. In the long run it may also lead to exactly the opposite of peaceful relations at the world level, since it may breed regional ethnocentrism; and the pattern of cultural cooperation that unifies within may also be the pattern that prepares for aggressive action against the outsider. Moreover, the nation that is a military satellite also becomes a cultural satellite, with a resulting net loss in cultural variety.

At this point the second model enters the scene, making claims in terms of factors that preserve variety and cut across borders between military alliances. In short, it claims to be a corrective. To be effective in this regard, cultural cooperation will have to be developed in a way that will give the lesser powers good opportunities to act as cultural senders, and so as to bridge gaps between military groupings. It will have to be set up against the forces favoring big power domination and conflict polarization — and this can probably be done only within a framework of international non-governmental or governmental cooperation. If successful, it seems very meaningful as a peacebuilding agent, except to the extent it disrupts successful balance of power structures. In so doing it may also rock the boat too much, or at least more than ethnocentric policymakers with a low level of tolerance for ambivalence are able to stand. And this may produce less peaceful relations — which brings us back to the point of departure. However, we mentioned in passing that this may change somewhat if the cultural cooperation is sponsored by international organizations.

3.10. The "supranational" argument

This argument would focus attention on one particular way in which cultural cooperation may be carried out: through the creation, or good offices, of a supranational organization. The argument would then run as follows. Since cultural goods are pursued for their value in their own right and for their usefulness in promoting other goals, and since they are scarce, there is competition for access to such goods. An organization providing such cultural facilities will then be seen as a provider of something good and valuable, and the result is likely to be identification and loyalty, as pointed out in connection with "insurance" and "power" arguments above. This identification/loyalty can then be transferred from the supranational organization providing cultural goods to other supranational organizations. The net result will be a general inclination to accept peacebuilding policy advice from that supranational organization. There is also the more negative argument that identification with a supranational level of human organization reduces the propensity to identify sufficiently with lower levels such as the nation-state, or to engage in violent behavior on their behalf. Thus the structure of the argument is as follows:

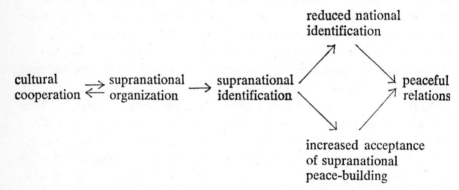

Because in general this is one of the arguments we would believe in most, let us be particularly careful in the more critical phase of the examination. First of all, the idea that cultural cooperation leads to supranational organization is of course most tenable in the case of real cooperation; exchanges can very well be organized on a completely bilateral basis. However, when there is transnational cooperation, there seems to be a tendency towards integration, i.e. the emergence of new foci for the allocation of resources. Since the cooperation is international, these new foci will by necessity be supranational. One is thinking of the numerous international cultural associations, of nuclear research establishments and other cooperation endeavors in the fields of science, and so on. They tend to develop a life of their own; and this *may* also be true for a bilateral commission that meets regularly to negotiate the pattern of cultural cooperation between the two nations, especially if there is some permanence and scope about the arrangement.

But one may also turn the argument around, as indicated by the double arrow in the figure, and assume that there is already a supranational organization in existence, which then assumes the role of facilitating cultural cooperation. To the extent it does so successfully, this will probably contribute to its own growth. There will be more cooperation and more supranationalism until perhaps one or more major powers feel that their use of cultural diffusion as a general instrument in the power struggle between nations is threatened. From that point on, it becomes a question of relative power between the supranational organization and the major power(s) — which may incidentally produce most unpeaceful relations, such as when the cultural superpowers compete for cultural satellites (the "insurance" and "power" arguments above, with nations as yielders of cultural goods).

However, let us assume that a supranational organization has emerged, as an instrument or as a result of cultural cooperation. Does this necessarily lead to identification with the organization? If it does good work and the values it stands for are commonly accepted, the answer will be affirmative. But we should at once note that this would apply only to the people immediately affected by the organization — for instance the direct recipients, such as the wage-earners in the organization, the institutions that get contracts or see their own goals promoted by using the organization, and so on. The degree of change in identification for people who are less affected is probably quite low. Thus, to sit in a library and read about other cultures hardly increases supranational identification much, even if the word UNESCO is printed on the books. However, repeated exposure to such experience can probably be meaningful in these terms. Thus, one has to be realistic and admit the probability that relatively few people are directly affected by such a supranational organization. But if the number of such organizations is multiplied, this will also multiply the number of people affected, unless these are only the same people reappearing in different contexts.

The next steps in the argument are more difficult. Does increased identification with supranational agents of cultural cooperation lead to generalization in the senses indicated in the figure? For instance, is there any reason to believe that the total potential for loyalty is constant, so that increasing supranational loyalty means decreasing national loyalty? Probably not, but it seems reasonable to assume that if there is a conflict of loyalty, in the sense that action directives from one's own nation and from the supranational organization are in conflict, then increased supranational loyalty will increase the chances that one will follow the supranational organization. Or put differently, leaders at the national level will refrain from suggesting action violently opposed to supranational directives, since they will know that people in their countries have a high level of identification in the supranational direction.

It may be argued that some leaders are not very sensitive to the hurt feelings of their subjects. But even if this is so, there is another argument which is more direct and does not presuppose the mediation of public opinion: the supranational organization may use its services in the field of cultural cooperation as a reservoir of positive and negative sanctions. Thus, the peace-loving nation that behaves well may get more, and the aggressive, naughty nation may get less — it may lead to activities being suspended, as happened in Southern Rhodesia after the "Unilateral Declaration of Independence". Cultural cooperation in the hands of a supranational organization is also a tool with which international behavior can be conditioned — if used with care.

The most problematic element here, however, is the idea that loyalties are easily transferred from one supranational organization to another. In concrete terms, if UNESCO is identified as a provider of cultural goods and there is a feeling of loyalty towards UNESCO among the people affected by UNESCO, will this attitude be transferred to the UN as a whole? To a resolution of the General Assembly or of the Security Council? To the command of a UN peacekeeping operation? This will probably depend a lot on symbolism and information. The more the service-yielding specialized agencies of the UN insist on a presentation of themselves as detached from the policy-making organs of the UN, the more will this transfer of identification be impeded. A good question to ask is whether the many benefits the nation-state provides, such as schooling, the idea of domestic and international security, roads, insurance schemes, etc., make the police more acceptable. The answer is probably in the affirmative, in general. But this depends on the level of irritation with red tape and bad services, and of course also on the style of police behavior.

Least problematic in this chain of reasoning is the final idea of transition from changed levels of identification to peaceful relations. This is almost by definition, since there is, after all, some correspondence between human attitudes and their patterns of action. But then there is the assumption that the supranational level is somehow more oriented towards peace than the national level, and this is not necessarily valid. At present there is an image in most countries of the United Nations as the major actor at the supranational level; but this image is not universally valid and may also be less valid in the future. What seems tenable is only that human beings in conflict tend to follow the directives that come from the source with which they identify most, and that they tend to identify more with sources of grati-fication than with sources of frustration, other things being equal.

Thus, with all these provisos there seems to be some validity to this argument. It should be noted that it is also compatible with the structural arrangement that most easily facilitates symmetric patterns of cooperation, and this is also an argument although of a different kind. The argument here expressed can actually be re-formulated as follows. If cultural co-operation of any kind is successful, then it produces a fund of identification and loyalty with the agency that has provided the means of cooperation, unless the nations benefiting from cooperation feel that what they receive is no more than repayment of old debts. Then, if such a fund of identifi-cation and loyalty is produced somewhere, benefits in terms of peacebuilding potential will probably be highest if identification and loyalty are directed towards supranational agencies that also have a direct role in peacebuilding. In other words, this is an argument — and in our mind an important one — in favor of multilateral cultural cooperation in general and multilateral technical assistance in particular.

4. Conclusion

The conclusion from this essay in ambivalence will necessarily have to be rather ambivalent itself. There is no clear conclusion: not because the proposition as originally stated is wrong, but because it is right only under so many conditions that the general picture becomes very confused.

Let us try to summarize what we have said so far:

Argument No.	Cultural cooperation in the sense of	Peacebuilding factor, X	$C \to X$ relation	$X \to P$ relation
1	Symmetric exchange	Knowledge	strong	weak
2	Symmetric cooperation	Cooperation	strong	strong
3	Asymmetric (exchange)	Development	strong	weak, even negative
4	Exchange (symmetric)	Hostages	strong	weak
5	Asymmetric (exchange)	Insurance	weak	strong
6	All types	Similarity	weak	weak, even negative
7	All types	Interdependence	weak	weak, even negative
8	Asymmetric	Equality	weak	weak, even negative
9	Asymmetric	Power distribution	strong	weak
10	Symmetric	Supranationalism	strong	strong

This table is no more than tentative, and only indicates the major results. Usually either one or the other or both of the two links ($C \to X$ or $X \to P$) are weak, meaning that many conditions will have to be satisfied. And propositions will usually apply only to particular types of cultural relations.

Moreover, when something can apply to all types of cooperation, then both links are weak (the similarity and interdependence arguments above). It should be pointed out, however, that this serves more as an illustration than as anything definitive. On the other hand, the table also points to some very positive conclusions, some of them well known, others easily reached on a commonsense basis, still others perhaps more novel.

The following is a summary of the major points that seem to have emerged in the course of the article.

1. *One should never assume that cultural cooperation fosters peaceful relations in any automatic sense.* It may facilitate them, but under adverse conditions it may also impede them. Rather, one should ask: "How can cultural cooperation best be carried out so that both cultural goals and goals in terms of peace are achieved?" If the choice is between two cultural cooperation policies that produce different degrees of cultural value and different degrees of peace, with one policy strong on the side of culture and the other strong on the side of peaceful relations, then it is a clear question of priorities. But if the amount of cultural value obtained is about the same, then it seems obvious that the more peace-producing pattern would be preferable.

2. *All four types of cultural cooperation (exchange vs. cooperation, symmetric vs. asymmetric) have their place and mission in the total picture of cultural relations today.* The interesting thing about this type of analysis is that all of them seem to have peace-building properties under certain conditions, which means that one should try to reinforce these properties as much as possible. Thus, if one has to engage in asymmetric exchange then one should see to it that this is done in such a way that the persons from the donor countries get a real increase in their knowledge of the culture of the receiving country.

3. *The strongest peacebuilding factor is probably cultural cooperation, particularly via supranational organizations* (arguments (3) and (10)). But this holds only if it can compete successfully with other agents of cultural transfer, such as the organizations of nation-states — otherwise there wil hardly be a loyalty transfer. Badly organized supranational activity at la lower level than bilateral cooperation may decrease rather than increase supranational identification, since the output probably is comp ared with other outputs, not to output zero.

4. If one wants to use cultural cooperation to counterbalance the world structure induced by the military power distribution, then one must remember

that an *overrepresentation of militarily weak powers as senders of culture is needed*, and that an overrepresentation of cultural cooperation across conflict borders is needed. Simple proportionate representation will not be enough, since so much asymmetry and polarization is already built into the social structure of the world. And cultural cooperation between countries already very friendly to each other (although such cooperation is important for other reasons) should not be given high priority as a peacebuilding measure.

5. The strength of cultural cooperation as a peacebuilding factor lies not only in the selection of one mechanism described above, but also *in the composition of a variety of strategies so that they may reinforce each other*. Supranational and bilateral cultural cooperation can be combined, although not all types. Thus, cultural cooperation as a weapon in a cold war may tear down much of what is built up by means of supranational strategies: but bilateral cultural cooperation to change the power pattern may perhaps more easily be combined with supranational activities.

IV.15. Peace Corps:
Structure and Function*

PRIO publication No. 15—2.

Notes on page *721*.

1. Background and definitions

1.1. The forerunners

Almost every work about the peace corps starts with a sentence saying more or less this: *the peace corps is not a new idea,* so we can just as well start that way ourselves. The statement is certainly neither true nor false as it stands. There are forerunners, and then there are not: there has been nothing like the American Peace Corps before in human history, nor does it seem likely that Gandhi's satyagraha brigades were copies of an ancient tradition.

For anything to be called a peace corps it should preferably have an intended peace relevance, so as to exclude any group of voluntary workers, masons or students out to construct something or to do good. This being said, it seems correct to see the present peace corps as something that was found in embryonic form in the rightly celebrated essay by William James, *The Moral Equivalent of War* [1]. Let us give a collection of quotations from this essay which was originally written for the Association for International Conciliation in 1910:

"The war against war is going to be no holiday excursion or camping party. The military feelings are too deeply grounded to abdicate their place among our ideals until better substitutes are offered than the glory and shame that come to nations as well as to individuals from the ups and downs of politics and the vicissitudes of trade" [2].

"War is the *strong* life, it is life *in extremis;* war-taxes are the only ones men never hesitate to pay, as the budgets of all nations show us" [3].

"It may even reasonably be said that the intensely sharp competitive preparation for war by the nations *is the real war*, permanent, unceasing; and that the battles are only a sort of public verification of the mastery gained during the "peace"-interval" [4].

"It would seem as though common sense and reason ought to find a way to reach agreement in every conflict of honest interests. I myself think it our bounden duty to

512

believe in such international rationality as possible. But, as things stand, I see how desperately hard it is to bring the peace-party and the war-party together, and I believe that the difficulty is due to certain deficiencies in the program of pacifism which set the militarist imagination strongly, and to a certain extent justifiably, against it". [5].

"In my remarks, pacifist though I am, I will refuse to speak of the bestial side of the war-regime (already done justice to by many writers) and consider only the higher aspects of militaristic sentiment" [6].

"Militarism is the great preserver of our ideals of hardihood, and human life with no use for hardihood would be contemptible. Without risks or prizes for the darer, history would be insipid indeed; and there is a type of military character which every one feels that the race should never cease to breed, for everyone is sensitive to its superiority" [7].

"So long as anti-militarists propose no substitute for war's disciplinary function, no moral equivalent of war, analogous, as one might say, to the mechanical equivalent of heat, so long they fail to realize the full inwardness of the situation" [8].

"All these beliefs of mine put me squarely into the anti-militarist party. But I do not believe that peace either ought to be or will be permanent on this globe, unless the states pacifically organized preserve some of the old elements of army-discipline. A permanently successful peace-economy cannot be a simple pleasure-economy" [9].

"If now — and this is my idea — there were, instead of military conscription a conscription of the whole youthful population to form for a certain number of years a part of the army enlisted against Nature, the injustice would tend to be evened out, and numerous other goods to the commonwealth would follow. The military ideals of hardihood and discipline would be wrought into the growing fibre of the people; no one would remain blind as the luxurious classes now are blind, to man's relations to the globe he lives on, and to the permanently sour and hard foundations of this higher life" [10].

"We should get toughness without callousness, authority with as little criminal cruelty as possible, and painful work done cheerily because the duty is temporary, and threatens not as now, to degrade the whole remainder of one's life. I spoke of the moral equivalent of war. So far, war has been the only force that can discipline a whole community, and until an equivalent is organized, I believe that war must have its way" [11].

The next to the last quotation points directly to the present peace corps, although the tasks suggested are somewhat different from the ones offered in the era of the developing countries:

"To coal and iron mines, to freight trains, to fishing fleets in December, to dishwashing, clothes-washing, and window-washing, to road-building and tunnel-making, to foundries and stoke-holes, and the frames of sky-scrapers, would our gilded youths be drafted off, according to their choice, to get the childishness knocked out of them, and to come back into society with healthier sympathies and soberer ideas. They would have paid their blood-tax, done their own part in the immortal human warfare against nature; they would tread the earth more proudly, the women would value them more highly, they would be better fathers and teachers of the following generation" [12].

513

Today we would certainly doubt that the tasks suggested by William James would have such far-reaching effects on those who carry them out. But his perspective is domestic, it is clear that such an "obligatory service to the state" is geared to solving problems in one's own country. It is a kind of community service on a higher level. It seems that today's offer of tasks has better chances of making for all the effects envisaged by James — including that "the women would value them more highly". Clearly, this is a reflection of the growing world consciousness, a growth not even the imaginative mind of William James foresaw.

However, the list of possible tasks and the theories as to the effects they may have on the actors themselves are hardly central to James' thinking. The idea is very clearly put forward in the last quotation of the selection given above. Sociologically speaking, it is the question of functional equivalence — the question of finding something that can take care of the positive functions of the "war-*regime*". This central thesis is simply that some kind of service for and to the nation would be a step forward towards this aim and that "it would be simply preposterous if the only force that could work ideals of honor and standards of efficiency into English or American natures should be the fear of being killed by the Germans or the Japanese" [13]. This idea is considerably less applauded today, one finds frequent references to James' idea of something corresponding to a *Service Civile Nationale*, but not to his sociological proposition.

One difficulty with his proposition and his way of thinking, however, may lie precisely in its non-sociological nature. James is thinking of the wonders wrought in the human mind by this kind of service (by dish-washing for the state?) — not of what it might mean if the idea was extended in the modern fashion to a Service Civile *Internationale*. Psychologist as he was, it was natural for him to look for intra-personal rather than international integration as a possible consequence. The optimism he expresses at times, thus, seems to presuppose a relatively atomized model of society where individuals are autonomous to a high degree and capable of waging peace as long as their wishes for manliness and the good, hard life are fulfilled to some extent. Contemporary thinking would perhaps emphasize this less and more automatically working factors on the more international level of analysis more.

Another interesting feature of the James article is his inability to stretch his idea just one more step in a certain direction. He points out the need for an institution where brave men can still perform deeds, but not for an institution where this need is coupled with the need for an institution to solve conflicts. In other words, although he anticipated the German *Arbeitsdienst* and the Soviet voluntary or conscripted service in distant Asiatic regions, he did not really anticipate the technical assistance peace corps and much less the ideas implemented by Gandhi in his satyagraha brigades.

We shall not deal with the many forerunners of the technical assistance youth corps between the wars and after the last world war, nor shall we discuss the interesting transitions from intra- to international services (to a great extent paved by the work of the various missions), or the transition from private to governmental service-organizations (paved by the depression and the recognized need for governmental initiative in the field of technical assistance). Our purpose is to give to "peace corps" a much wider significance, much more in line with the audacious ideas forwarded by William James.

1.2. A definition of "peace corps"

We have tried to outline some of the background for the present peace corps, ideologically and organizationally speaking. We shall now extract what seems to be a necessary and sufficient core to provide criteria for what we shall consider to be a peace corps. We suggest:

By a "peace corps" we mean a body designed to further peaceful relations between peoples and countries, provided that:

1. the personnel is sent to other countries,
2. it includes low-level person-to-person contact,
3. it is ideologically neutral,
4. it is unarmed.

Condition No. 1 rules out technical assistance in terms of capital goods and equipment and domestic police or non-violent self-defense, No. 2 rules out diplomacy and the technical assistance expert, No. 3 rules out directly religious and political missionary efforts to convert people or to be "at their disposal" in case they ask for affiliation, and No. 4 rules out such enterprises as UN peacekeeping forces, and military forces in general. Note that the definition is phrased with regard to *intentions*, not *consequences;* thus the definition does not stipulate that the organization shall be successful in its ambitious attempts, only that it shall be designed to promote peace. The three organizations mentioned in the preceding section can be seen to satisfy the criteria in the definition, provided the US peace corps cannot be said to engage in partisan political propaganda. We would tend to agree with the many who emphasize the distinction between knowing how to answer a factual question and being indoctrinated with regard to ideological questions, not to mention the distinction between answering questions

515

and participating in unsolicited propaganda. At the same time, nothing is completely politically neutral.

The definition leaves unanswered a number of questions. First of all, it is organizationally ambiguous, and these ambiguities will be outlined in the next section. But secondly, it is ambiguous as to philosophy of peace. This does not only concern the choice of "which road to peace", but also the choice of "which peace" — although we shall take the latter to mean first of all absence of violence in conflict resolution, secondly some kind of "harmonious interdependence", which we prefer to leave unspecified, since it is not central to this discussion. What is needed is a broad classification of peace corps with regard to how the problem of peace is attacked.

Since the problem of peace is also the problem of conflict, we can take as a schematic point of departure the three phases of any conflict: *genesis*, *dynamics* and *resolution*. A peace corps should be concerned not with the prevention of conflict in its broad sense, but with the prevention of violence and the creation of harmony, and here there seem to be three schools of thought depending on which phase is emphasized:

1. *genesis* — a peace corps may prevent a conflict from developing by attacking *selected causes* of the conflict.

2. *dynamics* — a peace corps may be an effort to fight conflicts without violence by direct participation as a *second party* to the conflict.

3. *resolution* — a peace corps may try to bring about a conflict resolution by acting as a *third party* to the conflict.

Historically it is interesting and important that Gandhi's peace corps, his satyagraha-brigades, worked very consciously along all three lines at the same time. This means that not only do we have experience on which the world can draw in all three fields, we also have some experience, however unsystematic and conditioned by particular circumstances, as to possibilities of combining the three kinds of peace corps in one institution. At present, there is little doubt that the US Peace Corps adheres to the first school of thought, as do the plans for a Norwegian peace corps; while the peace corps contemplated by the World Peace Brigade Committee seems to be more along the third line, with elements of the second idea. There are, no doubt, also many other possibilities compatible with our definition both in pacifist and non-pacifist debate, but we shall limit ourselves to these three. It should be noticed how entirely different they are.

The first one, which corresponds best to the popular concept of a peace corps, takes as its point of departure the situation prior to some kind of difficulty and aims at doing a concrete job removing some causes of evil or supplying some causes of good. It is almost implicit in the conception that the philosophy is "if it works, it works; and if it does not work, we did our best to prevent what happened"; which means that the peace corps will have to withdraw if some kind of violence breaks out.

Whereas this first kind of peace corps has as its goal to attack the very conditions leading to conflict, the second and third kinds see conflict itself as manipulable. But the philosophies behind are different. To participate in a conflict as one of the parties, although non-violently, must be seen as an effort to redefine the conflict in non-violent terms, thus decreasing the amount of violence. The emphasis is not so much on removing causes, nor on finding a solution, as on the way in which the conflict itself is fought.

This will also be central to the third school of thought where reduction of violence is of paramount importance. But the goal is, supposedly, to be obtained not by direct participation in the conflict but by presence as a third party that can try to bring about a resolution acceptable to both antagonists.

Thus, the three schools of thought attack the problem of peace from different vantage points, which at once might lead one to the conclusion that a combination of the three might yield an optimal solution to the problem of "how to make a peace corps". The analysis of this will be taken up in the following chapter, where the three schools of thought will be outlined in detail and possible combinations examined. At this early point it should only be noticed that they are all compatible with the conditions in the definition, but that the definition will have to be restricted considerably if one wants to use the term "peace corps" with reference to one of the schools of thought only.

1.3. Some organizational dilemmas

What we have said so far puts almost no constraints whatsoever on the structure of the peace corps, it only points out the very broad function it shall serve: it is a "corps" designed to serve "peace". In the preceding section, the latter is specified in three directions. But organizational choices must also be made, and since the peace corps, according to the definition, involves the sending of personnel from one country to another, some important organizational choices will be outlined under the headings below. A full discussion of the possible consequences of these choices will be deferred to the section 3; what will be attempted here is only to show the variety that is covered by the single term "peace corps", a variety that sooner or later will lead to a more or less corresponding variety in terminology.

1. *The organization in the sending country.* The basic choice is between *governmental* or *private* organization, with the possibility of some compro-

mise between the two extremes. A governmental organization with the aim, implicit in the name "peace corps", of contributing to peace by sending citizens to other nations will automatically be a functional part of the foreign policy of the sending country, and the second dilemma is whether this shall be made explicit by organizational links, or total integration, with the *Foreign Ministry*. There is a continuum of possibilities if these choices are made bases for further choices:

integrated in Foreign Service at home and abroad	integrated in Foreign Service at home, not abroad	govt. insti- tution	private, with govt. support	private, with govt. tolerance	private, with govt. opposition

The last case is included because the situation may very well arise that a private group organizes peace corps activities in spite of governmental regulations, for instance because of highly diverging conceptions of what is "peace". Integration in Foreign Service abroad means simply that peace corps activities are channeled through embassies etc.

2. *The organization of the transfer*. International transfer of goods and services can be characterized in many ways, but the most important one seems to be in terms of the number and organization of sending countries and receiving countries. It makes a great deal of difference whether there is one, more or a collectivity of sending countries — and one, more or a collectivity of countries that receive peace corps [14]. At one extreme is the bilateral arrangement between *one* sending and *one* receiving country; at the other extreme is an international pool under the auspices of the United Nations where all countries are both senders and receivers, in the sense that they contribute personnel to the pool according to supply and demand, and get personnel from the pool according to demand and supply. This also introduces the problem of one-way vs. two-way vs. clearing system in the flow of Peace Corps and services.

3. *The organization in the receiving country*. Again, the basic choice is between receiving *governmental* or *private* organization, or some combination of both, as a receiver of the services offered by the peace corps. As a special case comes the possibility of no organization at all; that the peace corps simply lands and starts carrying out its objectives. However, there is another dimension that ties in with the preceding distinctions, and much more important.

It is the choice between attaching the peace corps to organizations (located in the receiving country) belonging to the *sending* country (s) or collectivity or to the *receiving* country (s) or collectivity, or to some *international* organization including both. It makes a lot of difference whether a technical assistance peace corps works with a Norwegian mission, a bilateral project, a Scandinavian project, a UN project, an East African organization, or the Tanganyika government or a private group in Tanganyika. The choice must be made for each single project.

4. *The local organization.* We are, now, no longer thinking of the country-to-country level, but of the person-to-person level, where the peace corps is in the receiving country and its task is to transmit its skills, whether these are in the generalized technical assistance category, or in the field of non-violent techniques, or in the field of conflict resolution. It is in the definition of the peace corps (see section 1.2) that whatever is transmitted by means of a peace corps is transmitted from one person to another. Direct contact across national divisions is the *conditio sine qua non*, and the question is how this contact is organized. Again, it makes a lot of difference whether there is one, more or a collectivity of people on the sender and receiver sides.

However, even more important is the amount of organizational integration. At the extremes are a peace corps with no contact between senders and receivers (excluded by definition) and a peace corps with complete "equality" in the sense that senders and receivers do the same kinds of jobs, together; in, other words, they do not work in a parallel fashion, but along the same line. Between these two forms are forms with hierarchical subordination of the receivers, or forms where contact is less than maximum because senders and receivers do the same jobs in different settings, at different places and hours.

5. *The participants.* We have outlined the main dimensions of the organization; it remains to say something about the participants. This can be phrased very simply by asking the following for any dimension that human beings can be classified according to: do we want the participants to come from one category only, or from more, or from all; and in the last case, do we want equally many or proportionately many? This question can be asked meaningfully with regard to *sex, age, class, educational level, skill,* geographic origin *intra*nationally, geographic origin *inter*nationally, *occupation,* ideological *orientation, personality* variables, etc. In addition to all these there is the question of recruitment based on *volunteers* or *conscripts.*

Of course, although all these questions have to be settled before any specific project can be initiated they will almost never be dealt with in the empirical practice in the way we have listed them. Rather, total models of organization will be used and choices will only be made where models differ, not where they coincide. Administrative decisions will be made on the basis of the range of the decisionmakers' acquaintance with models they can imitate more or less, and their decisions will hardly be facilitated if they have to scrutinize a fairly exhaustive list of possibilities, with all the hidden constraints and impossible combinations inherent in it. For our purpose, however, this list is useful as a background for the presentation of the concrete projects as well as for the analysis in the following sections.

2. Three kinds of peace corps

2.1. Peace corps as technical assistance

This is the first and so far the most important school of thought. We have chosen to emphasize the word *peace*, and see it as an effort to prevent conflicts from developing by attacking selected causes. Others see it primarily as a branch of technical assistance, still others see it as an instrument of international public relations. What is clear to all is the common nucleus of technical assistance, what is less clear is how technical assistance is conducive to "peace".

Technical assistance can be defined as a one-way flow of values from one government to another, necessary for technical and economic construction, maintenance and/or reconstruction. Since this is among the purposes of the peace corps, there is no doubt that it can be classified as a branch of technical assistance as long as it is clear what kind of value is transferred: it is not capital, nor technical equipment, nor expert advice and know-how but what had been described by Sargent Shriver, the first director of the American Peace Corps, as "middle-level man-power", as "doers" on a level between the untrained and the expert, low enough to comprise levels of training attainable by youths in developed countries yet high enough to consist of levels of training in high demand in the developing countries. This does not necessarily mean kinds of manpower that are virtually absent, but rather skilled manpower that is not present in sufficient degree. In other words, the peace corps is an institution for the transmission of "middle-power"; in that sense it is a novelty in the technical assistance field.

The question is how "middle-power" can be transferred, since it is clear that it requires a different organizational setting from the setting provided for the TA expert. If the latter is to inject his skills successfully what is needed is probably a high level, central institution where there are recipients able to benefit from his knowledge and problems that really require his talents. But he who has only "middle-power" will need a medium level or low level setting for his contact with people. Since "skill" is exported for two purposes — 1. to be utilized and 2. to be copied — the ideal setting for the peace corps member will be one where he can function in a dual capacity — 1. as "doer" and 2. as "teacher". This way he will do both, perform a job and teach counterparts who can take over when he leaves. In other words, the teacher of English shall not only teach English to youngsters, but at the same time teach the teaching of English to teachers and impart to them the skills necessary for progress in the language.

We shall not discuss whether this is asking too much, and whether "middle-power" in fields such as agriculture, health, mechanical maintenance work, etc., is also by necessity "middle-power" in didactic techniques [15]. The important structural consequence is the organizational arrangement. Since the peace corps members in most cases will teach by performance, they will have in their role-set one set of persons to whom they are possessors of skills that are used and from which they may benefit *and* persons who are present as imitators, if also in the capacity of being colleagues. This is an interesting combination, much like the professor in the university clinic who performs an operation for the benefit of the patient as well as for one hundred pairs of student eyes. It means that the peace corps member quite often must perform his job in a very visible way, visible to the imitators, and even more important: the objects of his job, if it is person-centered, must accept the presence of other natives as observers. The ideal might be coincidence between these two types of persons, but such cases (e.g. the patient who is himself a student of medicine and watches the operation in a mirror, under local anesthesia; or the student at the teachers' training college who can learn English and the teaching of English simultaneously), are so rare that they cannot be counted upon.

This, then, leads to an organizational problem. How does one provide the peace corps member with a setting germane to both purposes? Let us try a cross-tabulation of the two dimensions mentioned in section 1.3. as possible ways of handling the administrative problem in the receiving country (Table 15.1). Examples could be mentioned for all six possibilities,

TABLE 15.1 *Possible settings for peace corps members in receiving country*

	with sending country organization	*with international organization*	*with receiving country organization*
private	service-organizations	SCI	local service-organization within the
governmental	bilateral TA-projects	UN TA-projects, assistants for technical experts	local administration

either from practice or from blueprints for peace corps, and all of them will have an attractive flavor to various groups of people. It is interesting to note that of the first 25 us peace corps projects all but five (East-Pakistan, Colombia, Chile, Brazil, and St. Lucia) are within governmental organizations in the receiving countries, and of these five, four are with private American organizations, and one with a private organization in the receiving country (Chile). As stated in an interview with the *New York Times* [16]: "participation by private voluntary agencies had been far less than expected, for a variety of reasons"; and this "variety" seems to include the difficulty in finding "agencies which have been conducting non-religious activities abroad for a number of years". In other words, even though the geographical distribution of receiving countries is meticulously even between the three major regions (Latin-America, 9; Africa, 9; and Asia, 7;) the organizational distribution shows a marked bias in favor of one special arrangement and the total exclusion of three possibilities.

Whatever the reasoning may have been it seems safe to say that this distribution is skewed in favor of an arrangement that permits access not only to people as objects of skills, but also to people as imitators of skills. Organizations in the receiving country will be at an advantage here, with governmental organizations having the additional advantage that they shorten the distance from the governmentally negotiated agreement to the organizational setting. Since there is a long tradition for un projects this should not prejudice against the use of international, governmental organizations; but the possibility of using the peace corps within bilateral projects has so far not been exploited. One major reason may be the fear of too successful images, that the peace corps should build up its own positive image and not be associated with other bilateral attempts. The unfortunate thing about the present distribution is its incompleteness as an experimental design.

We shall return at some length to the problem of transfer of manpower as an efficient form of technical assistance, and turn now to the general problem of technical assistance as a means of peace-promotion, with special regard to the peace corps. To the extent the argument is valid, that *absolute material deprivation* in terms of calories, raw materials, consumer goods or what not are causes of international wars, it will also be an argument for the peace corps, as technical assistance, to the extent it can contribute to a better standard of living. But the distribution of wars in the past seems rather to suggest the importance of *perceived relative deprivation*, relative to "significant others" among countries, to one's own perceived *past* or even to the perception of what one feels should be the *present*. We believe this feeling to be particularly important in really developing countries, both as a cause and as a consequence of their economic "better-off". Lord Boyd Orr's dictum to the effect that wars start in the empty barrel suggests the "absolute deprivation" theory, which again is compatible with the general humanitarian *ethos* that has permeated technical assistance, but it may be highly unrealistic if the manifest purpose is to prevent wars.

The difficulty in choosing the "relative deprivation" theory as a basis for the administration of technical assistance, however, is that it will involve highly controversial political arguments that frequently will run counter to more consensual humanitarian arguments. Besides, it is difficult to find objective standards for needs. A country's calorie level can be demonstrated but it is harder to convince people what its level of average relative frustration is. Politically it might be wise to assist a well-to-do country which is aggressive because other countries have even more. This can be done by impersonal devices such as transfer of capital and expert advice, but is hardly sufficient as motivational basis for the transfer of "middle-power".

There is, of course, a more psychological-political line of reasoning which runs something like this: provided A has assisted B without too much humiliation or too many political strings, then the chances that B will join in an attack on A decrease. A friendly act is long remembered, as indicated by Stuart Dodd's research in the Near East: Armenian students in the 1930s were greatly influenced in their views concerning the us by the positive image they had of us relief for Armenians after the First World War [17] (it is the present author's experience from Soviet Armenia that this also applies to Norway, because of the role played by Friedtjof Nansen). But the difficulty is that this argument, however valid it may be, only has practical validity as long as technical assistance is administered to potential enemies and not, as happens in most cases, within a bloc of countries generally friendly to each other. The question is whether there is anything in the peace corps which makes it likely that it can transcend borderlines that technical assistance so far has not transgressed; conflict polarization is not easily compatible with giving and receiving aid. But politicians have been disinclined to treat the peace corps differently in this regard from other kinds of us technical assistance. The peace corps' way of administering TA may also be particularly unpopular with unfriendly and even neutral countries because of suspected espionage; the personnel transferred is less easily controlled, and less visible than e.g. the technical expert. The political difficulties with this argument of "direct insurance" are great, like the difficulties with the "relative deprivation" argument, if not unsurmountable.

But there is a second, more refined argument along these lines. If A has assisted B, and C cares about the public opinion of B, then this will probably decrease the chances of aggression from C to A. This may be called the *argument of indirect insurance*, and it does not presuppose that technical assistance transcends conflict borderlines, only that it reaches into a bloc of neutrals (if it reaches countries already committed to one's own side chances are that a potential aggressor will not care so much about lost goodwill — he will probably not have much to lose anyhow). So far the majority of host-countries for US Peace Corps projects are more or less non-aligned countries, and there are reasons to believe that the peace corps is particularly valuable from this point of view. Moreover, the "indirect insurance" argument is highly compatible with the "absolute deprivation" argument because they cover so many of the same countries — and both arguments are relatively compatible with humanitarian ideas prevalent in Western ethics: "help where help is needed" and "do good for the good's own sake". Indirect insurance makes the good act instrumental, but after all only "indirectly" and this is less objectionable to many. Correspondingly, the arguments of "perceived relative deprivation" and "direct insurance" also cover many of the same countries — but both of them are relatively incompatible with the humanitarian basis of TA and the particularities and peculiarities of the peace corps. On the other hand again, the "absolute deprivation argument" is probably, as already argued, relatively unrealistic if the goal is peace-making.

Since all those arguments are by no means unknown to politicians, they may serve as bases for predicting which countries will be selected as host-countries (Table 15.2).

TABLE 15.2 *Potential host-countries as seen by the sending country*

deprivation argument	Insurance argument		
	direct (unfriendly countries)	*indirect* (neutral nations)	*unnecessary* (friendly nations)
absolute (underdeveloped countries)	1	2	
relative (developing countries)	3	4	
little or no (developed countries)			

It should be emphasized that "deprivation" refers only to very concrete technical-nutritional matters, and that its relation to the trio "underdeveloped-developing-developed" should be taken with more than a grain of salt. There are four possibilities of practical importance (1—4); for the other five possibilities the political gain would hardly warrant the expenses and/or there would be insufficient legitimate basis for assistance. This applies particularly well to the bottom righthand cell, whereas the other marginal cells form interesting unbalanced combinations.

Our reasoning has led to a preponderance of host-countries in (2). But the politically most important discrimination has probably not been made; between neutral countries seen as drifting into the other bloc, remaining stable, or drifting into one's own bloc. There may be some reasons to believe that chances of alignment with the Socialist bloc increase with development, and then decrease with even more development. At any rate, strain will inevitably result if aid is given into (1) ("why help people who are against us", the case of wheat to China) and (4) ("others need it more", the case of Mexico).

2.2. The peace corps as second party to a conflict

To be second party to a conflict is to *participate* in a conflict, to act in favor of one of the parties more than the other, to wish one state of affairs to obtain more than the other. There is nothing "objective" or "impartial" about this kind of activity. Hence, it is an aspect of the peace corps highly different from what has been treated in the preceding section — so different that it raises problems that will be discussed in section 2.4. The difference is of such an order that it may be debated whether it should not be reflected semantically, in choosing another term than "peace corps" for this kind of activity. When we have not done so it is to be in accordance with the usage in circles interested in the kind of initiative described in section 1.6.

There is no reason to go into any detail where this kind of peace corps is concerned. The main point is simple enough: the functional need of any social system for a nondestructive way of acting out conflicts, and the structures so far proposed, do not depart significantly from the Gandhi satyagraha-brigades model. It simply means helping, nonviolently, one of the parties — persumably the dominated one — nothing more, nothing less.

2.3. The peace corps as a third party to a conflict

It is not difficult to reason about a non-existing organization; it is in fact extremely easy since there are no burdensome facts to take into consideration. What we shall do is to outline a number of functions that may be relevant for the peaceful resolution of conflicts, and try to find out whether a structure as defined in section 1.2 has any bearing upon the solution of these functional problems.

As stated in the heading, this peace corps idea presupposes a bipolar conflict with the peace corps added on as a third party, whose functions we are going to outline. To write a program for a peace corps with tasks of this kind is impossible without a theory of human conflict, at least in embryonic form. Such theories exist today. They must have a fair degree of generality so that the peace corps can obtain a fair degree of permanence — a theory with no invariances would lead to a peace corps working completely *ad hoc*, and hence to a peace corps with insufficient organizational stability.

Another condition for a peace corps of this kind to be relevant is the absence, or insufficiency, of other third parties, such as supranational organizations, federal authorities, community organizations, clans, tribes, etc. The task of the peace corps, briefly stated, would be to take over some or all of the functions that would ordinarily be met by other third parties. Since these third parties usually prevent conflicts from developing into extreme phases it is clear that this kind of peace corps should be called into action in the early phases of a conflict.

There is no single formula that expresses what third parties do or can do. There are many answers, and all of them provide us with clues for a peace corps program (Table 15.3).

TABLE 15.3. *Functional needs and third party tasks*

Functional need	Third party tasks
1. Objective definition of the situation according to lasting standards	To describe the conflict accurately and impartially, to prevent false rumors from developing, to issue reports
2. Assessment of the nature of the conflict, of the goal-states of the conflict groups	To record and make public the positions of the two parties so that positions are known to all three parties
3. New ideas concerning solutions of the conflict	To suggest and make public to both parties new ideas
4. Contact and exchange between conflict groups, to avoid polarization	To serve as media of interaction, indirect or direct, between the groups
5. Active efforts to bring about compromises	Mediation, bordering on the more compulsory arbitration
6. Continuation of parts of system not directly touched by conflict	See to it that no essential function of the system is discontinued
7. Reconstruction of damage to body and property	Continuous repairs and impartial treatment of wounded, etc.
8. Decisions concerning postconflict value-distribution	Courts etc. that render verdicts generally held to be impartial
9. Distribution of sanctions	Enforcement of decisions, distribution of negative and positive value
10. Termination of conflict	Binding definition of conflict as solved

Of course, no claim is made for completeness — the list only suggests some important functions normally attributed to third parties, particularly to the state.

Items 8—10 differ from the rest in that they involve or may involve the use of authority that very often is accompanied by force. The three can to some extent be treated together under the general heading of "resolution mechanisms", and the best contemporary example is the function of the judiciary: whether the case belongs to civil or criminal law, a future state is decided upon and there are mechanisms to ensure that this state of affairs obtains. Characteristic of the judiciary is also that, in principle, it is endowed with so much authority that the conflict is terminated because the future state of affairs is accepted. However, third parties are very often also given power enough to freeze conflicts and define them as dead. This means that the conflict is not allowed to manifest itself — not that the latent aspects of the conflict vanish.

The argument against these three third party tasks, of course, will be directed at the "what price life?" question. In other words, how much violence are we willing to use to destroy violence, how many wars are we willing to use to end war, how many executions to end murder, etc. Since the peace corps is defined as a non-violent force, it seems obvious that it will have to start at the other end of the list, *trying to create more normal relations between conflicting groups by carrying out as many of the first seven third party tasks as possible.*

2.4. The problem of compatibility

The three schools of thought have now been outlined, and it is quite clear that they represent conceptions of peace corps that are different in form as well as in content. As a matter of fact, they have nothing more in common than the nucleus we have extracted and presented as a definition in section 1.2. The question is whether they are "compatible", whether they can be combined. Three organizationally completely autonomous peace corps specializing in each method would present no problem, especially if they came from different countries and operated in different countries and were dispatched by means of different organizations. In a world of countries no corps etc. that come from the same countries, go to the same countries, or are transferred by means of the same organization will be regarded as completely independent of each other, but it is not this trivial kind of combination we shall attempt to examine.

There are actually many interpretations, depending on the *level of organizational combination.* One extreme would be a central peace corps administration with three fairly independent divisions, much like army, navy and air-force, with inter-service rivalries and problems of coordination, but also with a considerably autonomy. One can also imagine the other extreme: one administrative body with personnel on *all* levels trained for all three purposes. And to carry it even further, one can imagine the corps trying to engage in all three activities simultaneously or at least within the same "space-time context" — at the same place and the same time. Obviously, the problems of coordination and combination vary depending on which level of organizational combination the analysis concerns itself with.

There is also a second variable which has to do with the *location of strain*, or even the location of incompatibility. Strain or incompatibility means that one action or set of actions seem to exclude or make difficult another action or set or actions, *for some people*. The problem is *for whom*. It may be quite possible for a peace corps *member* to combine technical assistance and Red Cross work with civil disobedience, but for the objects of both activities his participation in a conflict as a second party will probably detract considerably from the acceptance of his technical assistance work. Other actions may be completely acceptable by others but impossible to perform together for one individual, i.e. the emotional involvement in second party intervention and the detached objectivity in third party mediation. Actually, the strain can be located in *outsiders*, in the *individual peace corps member, between peace corps members*, etc., but we shall limit ourselves to these three locations of strain.

To start out: imagine an *outsider*, not participating himself in the peace corps activities but rather an object of them, observing different kinds of combinations of the three types of activities. To what extent will they be "associative" or "dissociative" in his mind? To be systematic, let us make a complete Table (Table 15.4; symbols in parentheses are efforts to catch the evaluation given in the text).

TABLE 15.4 *The problem of compatibility*

What are the consequences of/for	Peace corps as technical assistance	Peace corps as second party	Peace corps as third party
Peace corps as TA		(+)	(+ +)
Peace corps as second party	(—)		(— —)
Peace corps as third party	(+)	(+)	

Since the diagonal cells are unproblematic, there are essentially six "effects" we have to consider, and we start in the upper righthand corner: what

528

effects does the peace corps as technical assistance have on the peace corps as a third party in a conflict?

By and large, it seems that a very fundamental part of the *pacifist* belief can be expressed as follows: the institution that has been of sincere service to both parties in a conflict, provided it has acted in a non-partisan way, is also the institution best fit to enter a conflict as a third party. Expressed in one sentence: *by means of services rendered, technical assistance yielded, and aid in distress, a good-will and general aura of invulnerability may be created that can be drawn upon in times of conflict.* There are some very practical and quite valid arguments that seem to favor this proposition. First of all: technical assistance *legitimizes contact* of the kind needed for future work as a third party in a conflict. There is a limit to the number of ways in which citizens of one country may legitimately enter another country. *Tourism* is one, but often very limited in the scope of contact and also relatively limited when it comes to the number of countries or places accessible. *Diplomacy* has a tendency to focus on high level contact. One of the principal shortcomings of a *military* force is exactly that there is no legitimate way in which it may already have been on the spot, if not to establish good-will, at least to establish contacts. *Technical assistance* provides the present generation with a gate through national and local barriers, right into the deepest hinterland.

Further, technical assistance means *contact* if it is done in the way the peace corps is supposed to do it, and it means relevant, functional contact; not the kind of contact established during the tourist season with a low degree of relevance for situations of crisis. The TA peace corps member will have developed a feel for the web of work-relations and have a number of personal friends whose evaluation of the situation he can evaluate. Equally important is the local population's knowledge of him, and the positive image they will have of him if his mission has been of any value to them. In other words, in a situation of conflict he will know some very basic facts and he will be known, and may thus better understand and see possible solutions. Thus, it seems that the proposition above is relatively tenable: peace corps as TA does facilitate peace corps as a third party in a conflict, since legitimate access and intimate knowledge down to the grass-roots are prerequisites.

This looks so obvious that it may be worthwhile pointing out some difficulties. First of all, there is a danger involved in the way TA activities have so often been presented, as instrumental to something different from welfare in the local community. For the recipient, TA will above all be a *bene per se* if it is of any value at all. If it shall serve as an instrument to facilitate intervention in future conflicts (or for any other political purpose like a guarantee against attack, a way to fight "communism" or other undesirable political factions, etc.) it may fail for lack of acceptance and response: people will probably often resent efforts to use their distress as a pawn in a political game, and the more so, the more clearly it is expressed. This may be an argument against too close an organizational combination, but it may also well be that it has more to do with the *way* in which TA is given than the presence of possible functions (in addition to the welfare function) the peace corps may serve in the minds and speeches and articles of some administrators and members.

Second on our list of objections: is it necessarily true that to know and be known is instrumental to efficient mediation and arbitration? It may be detrimental to a certain kind of objectivity, and it is quite possible that the many primary relations that have developed during TA work will catch the peace corps members in a web of loyalties and allegiances that may cause a number of difficulties. Probably, one answer to this lies in the way we have indicated that third party activities should be carried out by peace corps members: as assistants and workers on the immediate human level of interaction, more than as real arbitrators. The latter would have to be very experienced people, and thus beyond the age range usually considered for peace corps personnel. This touches on the old problem solved in so many countries (e.g. Italy, Egypt) by the statute that a policeman shall not serve in his native village or in the village he has married into. What one loses in direct insight due to personal contact is supposedly gained in terms of impartiality and efficiency — but then those peace corps people are not supposed to act as policemen, they shall suggest and serve, not coerce.

Thirdly (and this is not really an objection, but has to do with the more exact nature of the relationship between the first and third kind of peace corps activities): in the gandhian school of thought the idea of *community service* would be regarded as both a necessary *and* a sufficient condition of conflict intervention. Only through services does one gain a moral *right* to intervene, but the ties thus created will also lead to a moral *obligation* to intervene. The disinterested outsider is not the right person because of his lack of sincere concern, and the concern will have to be proved and tested for its true quality and endurance. Although the moral stand here does not concern this kind of analysis, the empirical factor of importance is the relevance of TA *as a kind of testing ground* for recruitment to the even more difficult work in times of crisis. But this presupposes even *a low level organizational combination*, in fact, most of our argumentation does. In most cases it will *not* be sufficient for *some* people in the organization to have participated in TA activities and for others to participate in third party activities: although the former may transmit a lot of their experiences to the latter, and the local population may transmit a lot of their positive attitudes to the former unto the latter; there is no real substitute for personal experience and no real substitute for friendship between one person and another. There is an attenuation effect in the transfer of good will; the longer the chain, the more will probably get lost. Identity at the governmental level may be good; at the organizational level, backed up by powerful symbols like the Red Cross, even better; but personal identity is probably best, particularly within the framework provided by the other two.

If we assume that this kind of combination is conducive to more efficient third party work, the question to be answered at once becomes: does this also work the other way round? What effects will third party intervention have on the organization's efficiency as an agent of TA? We have already touched upon the problem of being *too instrumental*, and it seems that this is the main difficulty. Both forms of activity require devotion to the total community, not only to fractions of it. Both forms require *contacts* with the total community. And contacts made in one context will be of value for the other context, since people important in a conflict also are likely to be important for social change. They will be people who are "influentials", but not necessarily of high social status from the total community point of view.

So far, we have mostly studied the relation between the first and third kind of peace corps from the onlooker's point of view. We shall now try to look at it from the peace corps member's point of view. As just pointed out, no fragmentation of loyalty should be necessary. But there is certainly a diversity of skills; the person who is a good member of a TA team may not necessarily be so good on personal relations that he can make a valuable contribution in times of conflict. And even though his technical and human skills are considerable., the simple factor of human *courage* may make a man who is suitable for the most intricate problems of human relations in connection with social change useless in a physically or ethically dangerous conflict situation. This may actually be more important than the differential in skills needed for the two purposes, particularly inasmuch as the peace corps member in a TA team is seen more as an expert on human relations than on technical matters. For the latter purpose there is the *technical assistance expert*, already a well-known person on the international scene.

Let us then move to the second pair of problems related to peace corps as TA and peace corps as *second* party in a conflict. Here there seems to be a distinct asymmetry: TA experience will be useful very much as it was useful for the case of third party intervention, but the deliberate participation on one side in a local issue, however justified it is by local and other standards, is hardly conducive to general TA work. The TA work will, and not quite without reason, be seen as a trick, as a way of gaining access for other, less consensual, purposes. But even if such access is possible, there is the difficulty inherent in the tremendous change in perspective. TA addresses itself to the total community or ought to do so; its acceptance will depend on this in many cases. To participate as a second party means to be a party to the conflict, it means that one side is seen as more "right" than the other. And even though the non-violent approach in conflict behaviour is distinctly different from the violent approach in the way in which it takes account of and incorporates the goal of the adversary, who is seen less as an enemy than as a member of a whole to which all belong (although he has a different approach and point of view), there will be an asymmetry in the way the peace corps enters the conflict. Its knowledge of the local scene, its contracts, its reputation for objective, constructive and self-sacrificing behavior may have had a great impact on both sides — there will nevertheless be a difference between being of equal service to both sides and furthering the cause of one side more than the other.

For the individual peace corps member there is the serious psychological question of how loyalty to one party can be combined with loyalty to the totality needed when TA is administered. The traditional solution to this problem is the idea that the other party *does not belong*, that he is the enemy, the intruder, the traitor, the exploiting upper class, the imperialist, the colored, etc. [18]. Services rendered to them are not seen as rendered to the society but to somebody outside it who by fault or accident happens to live on the same territory. Thus, a force that enters the scene to help the side of its choosing in a nonviolent way *may* not experience any difficulty if it has given (or later on will give) TA: they may sincerely feel both services go to the entire society, only not to the *alien* element in it. But there may also be situations like in the Congo, where most outsiders did not have immediate sympathies with local groups but waited for others to take sides so that they could get their cues that way. In such situations the ideology of"TA to the whole of Congo and non-violent support to one group only" seems unstable, and likely to yield to a number of more stable ideologies like "both to all sides" or "both to one side only".

On the other hand, TA administered to both sides before a conflict breaks out in the open, or TA evenly administered to both sides during the conflict will give obvious advantages in a conflict. It will facilitate the acceptance by the party one is helping of the peace corps army, and it may also tend to weaken the adversary's front. Nonviolent assistance to one side by a group extending its technical services to *both* parties may represent a moral challenge. The difficulty with this theory, however, is that conflicts are very likely to be between groups of different rank (as in all the examples listed above), in which case there may be difficulties in finding goods or values both parties need, or goods and values that the peace corps knows how to deliver. A TA peace corps will very likely have its expertise linked to the kind of activities that are highly relevant in underdeveloped countries (only under that condition will young people possess scarce skills), but of considerably less relevance to the present or former colonial power. Some kind of functional equivalent of the TA rendered to one of the parties must be found, if TA is to be truly non-partisan. This will hardly be easy, since the value most desired by the colonialist will be some kind of basis to stay in power, and this is exactly the value he will be denied. Much political acumen is needed to find such an equivalent, if it is at all possible — "spiritual values" of any kind will hardly be sufficient in the long run to make a defeat more bearable. This does not mean that the local population could not or should not try nonviolent means in a struggle, nor that TA should not be given, only that it seems very difficult for a peace corps that also wants to extend TA to combine the two activities.

These difficulties are increased even further when one examines the possibilities of *combining second party with third party work*, the last pair of problems, although the situation is also here very asymmetric. Experience in third party work may add considerably to the kind of experience and detailed knowledge that is valuable in a conflict, particularly if the activity has been in the same area. It may also add to the probability that the adversary will accept one's position, although there is the distinct chance that he may come to regard it as treason and opportunism. But it seems highly unlikely that a force known for partisan participation in conflicts will have much chance as a source for mediation in conflict. The acceptance of the judiciary in any country is highly, but negatively, correlated with the degree to which it is seen as an instrument of special interest-groups; its acceptance depends on its reputation for impartiality in deeds, not only words, relevant to the legal case at hand. Thus, a peace corps which has participated as party to a particular kind of conflict may still be engaged as mediators in conflicts of an entirely different kind; particularly as mediators in an *intra*-group conflict in the group they have helped — whether it is by TA or by non-violent assistance. But if there is a clear resemblance between a conflict where they have participated and the conflict where they offer their services as mediators, it seems highly unlikely that both parties will accept.

Even if they do accept, there is an important asymmetry where transfer of training is concerned. As mentioned, third party training may be useful for second party participation in a conflict — but it may also have a negative influence unless the participants are very well trained in the gandhian philosophy, or in an equivalent which teaches and prepares for little or no difference in attitudes whether one participates in the conflict or acts as an go-between. Otherwise, the training in objectivity and balanced perception of both parties' point of view may be detrimental to the minimum of singlemindedness so often found to be functional in a conflict, and under a variety of cultural, social, and personal conditions thought to be necessary for active and devoted participation — just as much as a record of strong and partisan views and actions may serve as a basis for distrust and suspicion! When "objectivity" is needed a record of impartiality may be a reason for exclusion from highly partisan activities, if they include more drastic means. Members of conflict groups may doubt one's loyalty, predict low efficiency; or they may prefer to preserve a source of objectivity, immaculate and uncontaminated, for later use.

Singlemindedness, subordination to the general polarization of the human mind and the social group during conflicts are *normal* phenomena; the preservation of objectivity and development of attachment to *all* human beings regardless of their stand in the conflict are not so easily fostered. It seems to be an essential part of peace corps thought that it should be international in its composition, and absolutely indispensable if it shall work as a third party in a conflict. Thus, it seems that *if* the two types of activities we are discussing here should be combined at all, then the individual participant should learn the proper all-embracing attitude from third party activities first, and then possibly transfer them to work *in* a conflict — but not start with work in a conflict in order to attempt a transfer later to work *on* a conflict. The latter seems so much more difficult, though it may certainly also be argued that only he who has lived in a conflict himself is endowed with the capacity to empathize with parties he shall try to mediate between.

Even with the relatively few factors we have considered the picture has become quite complex. And we have not even touched on the difficulties that can emerge between different members or branches of a peace corps that tries to embrace all three kinds of activities. Very likely there will emerge a differentiation according to skills and experience in the different activities, and according to ideology as to where the emphasis should be. The old rule that "everybody thinks what *he* knows is most important" will probably hold here as in other organizations, and a consequence of this may be rivalries and jealousies and great importance attached to theories and information about possible difficulties arising from the diversity of activities. The classical solution to this organizational problem is the introduction of *branches* in the organization, like the services in the military institution, where antagonisms and rivalries are institutionalized and even utilized deliberately for the common goal. Specialization will decrease many of the difficulties referred to, but it will also tend to reduce such possible positive consequences as immediate transfer of experience, knowledge, and reputation. This, in turn, can be partly counteracted by excellent communication and transfer of knowledge and experience between the branches of the organization, and the creation of a *symbol*, of a peace corps as one and undivided in people's minds so that prestige accumulated in the most grateful activity, TA, can be transferred to its function as a third party or even as a second party, in conflicts.

It seems possible that the difficulties in combining TA and third party activities can be overcome, and that the two will actually tend to strengthen each other, be "associative" if a suitable organizational combination is found — but the work as a second party in conflicts does present the entire organization with difficulties. The possible harm done to its mediation potential is considerable, and perhaps so important that a choice must be made between the two. This does not mean that a nonviolent organization primarily designed for defense or for the aid of another group could not or should not also engage in the other two types of activities, but an organization designed primarily for TA and for third party intervention should not engage in second party activities as well, because of the "dissociative" effects indicated.

In part, this is a question of semantics. As mentioned before, words like "peace corps" and "peace brigade" have caught on and very much so — mainly because of their appeal as an extension of TA in a direction that may lay the foundations much more effectively for good interpersonal relations, across international borders. It seems that some activities can be added to this without causing much friction and even with the possibility of strengthening the institution considerably — but other activities may cause so many difficulties precisely because of the effort to combine them with TA and mediation, not because they are not valuable in themselves. Since the symbolic value of an institution is so closely linked to its name, it is a question of whether activities that for many people would mean conflict, trouble, difficulties and possibly defeat should properly be labeled "peace corps activities".

IV.16. Notes on Technical Assistance:
The Indo-Norwegian Project in Kerala

PRIO publication No. 2—3.

Notes on page *722*.

1. The general case: some aspects of technical assistance

1.1. The concept of technical assistance

It can safely be said that so far no general theory of technical assistance has emerged from the vast literature ranging from the common-sense comments in newspapers and political magazines, via reports made by technical experts, to the relatively few social science contributions in the field. But it can also safely be said that comprehensive theories with technical assistance as their field will arise, due to the necessity of thorough thinking in this vast and expanding field. Any such theory would have to be inter-disciplinary in character, because of the strange mixture of psychology, sociology, anthropology, economics, political science, international relations, etc., that applies. In this section no attempt in this direction will be made, but efforts will be made to call the attention of the reader to some crucial factors in the area of technical assistance — as seen by an observing sociologist, not by the political expert. We shall give the presentation a fairly general form, but at the same time try to characterize and single out for comment some problems for research with particular relevance to the Indo-Norwegian Project in Quilon, Kerala, India. Essentially, what we are aiming at is a general framework for a better understanding of public opinion concerning technical assistance.

What is "technical assistance", or TA, to use a suitable abbreviation? We shall take the expression to be an abbreviation for "technical and economic assistance". To arrive at some criteria for the usage of this term, imagine a system of nation states, or of some other social units for that matter. Between these units exchange of values may take place, dependent on the degree of interaction between them. In general, it seems fruitful to work on the assumption that value is always exchanged in the sense that there is never a one-way flow. Whoever gives something, gets something in return sooner or later — or expects at least something. The *basis* for exchange is partly the factor of differential subjective utility: an object may

536

have different utility for different units, for different persons — and hence both parties to an exchange may report that they are better off although the values exchanged are "equal". And secondly there is the obvious factor of differential scarcity; what is abundant in one system may be scarce somewhere else.

Of course, it is not always meaningful to look for an "equally big flow of value in the opposite direction" whenever value is observed to pass from one social unit to another. There may, perhaps, be cases of pure gifts where no counter-value is ever expected, or rendered, at least not from the receiver of the gift. In cases of coercion it is difficult to see what the coerced party gets out of the "bargain" — except, perhaps, a moral status that can be drawn upon later. Extortions, like gifts, may lay the foundation for a reservoir of future benefits — but in the long run many things may happen and confuse the pattern.

The perspective given by the term "value-exchange" stimulates research in the direction of what is expected, and what is actually rendered as counter--value when technical assistance is offered. There seems to be no readily available cue to this. To mention some possible counter-values: priorities in competition for future economic expansion, provision of public opinion pressure in cases of direct attack or attack by third party, non-aggression against self or others, atonement for wrongs committed during colonialism, denial of the right to yield technical assistance to other nations, political alliance, voting in the United Nations, favored treatment in the most general terms, reinforcement of self-image as peace-loving nation, control via cultural contact, surrender to "cultural imperialism", efficient cooperation so as to make the TA project and the donor nation a "success", etc. Political situations may easily arise, and have to some extent already arisen, *where there is more TA supply than really manifest demand* (the latent demand is always tremendous in a world with such catastrophic technical and economic differentials as ours has). In this case the counter-value may be precisely the extension of the privilege to yield technical assistance: "you offer us TA, and we permit you to do so!"

Thus, what is typical of technical assistance is not the absence of any counter-value, but rather the absence of technical and economic counter-value [2]. But this is not a sufficient condition, as it may also be true in the case of coercion, booty, etc. The basic fact is that this absence is hedged around by a shared expectation by both parties to the assistance. If we define "goods and services" so that this simple dichotomy covers everything that falls under the heading of "technical and economic assistance", then both parties know that there will be no economic compensation for what is given (if the compensation is to be given over time, and is stipulated in economic terms, we shall talk of "loans" rather than assistance or aid). To this, however, we should perhaps add that technical assistance is yielded between *nations*, and is of a non-military character. Thus, we shall make use of this definition:

By "technical assistance" we mean a process where
a. there is a one-way flow of goods or services from one nation to another,
b. the goods or services are of a non-military nature,
c. neither party expects economic compensation to be made for the goods or services, or at least not full compensation.

"Technical cooperation" is also a frequently used term, and we shall use it to denote technical assistance projects where both parties cooperate on the project, whether it is in terms of manpower, capital in any other form, or both [3]. Though it is obvious, it should be pointed out that technical cooperation is only one among many ways in which technical assistance may be administered — and this does not detract from the fact that goods or services are yielded without compensation. The semantics of TA is complicated by the political reasons for changing the term "aid" to "assistance" and the latter to "cooperation" — not unlike the change from "backward" via "underdeveloped" to "developing" countries.

One also encounters the idea that technical assistance should be given without any ties, strings or obligations. We shall take these expressions to mean that there shall be no explicit or implicit expectation of non-economic compensation — for instance of all or some of the kinds suggested above. Although this is socially almost meaningless unless specified to mean for instance "explicit, political ties", it plays an enormous role in the culture of technical assistance.

At this point the word "expect" should be commented upon. Imagine a country A has given assistance to a smaller country B, and does it out of a sense of moral obligation, as a kind of charity. B may still expect A to expect some compensation, and thus feel under a certain pressure. And to go one step further: A may even expect B to expect A to expect some compensation — and thus be under a pressure to expect it, and even to allude to it as time passes on. Thus, out of lack of sufficient communication or explicitness tensions may emerge that can draw on the rich reservoir of suspicions and fears so prevalent in international relations. For this reason, we have emphasized in the definition that *neither* party should expect economic compensation.

The concept of "technical assistance" certainly invites taxonomies preferably based on social theory and not on administrative or political circumstances. A basic, if not very subtle, distinction should be made between technical *aid*, *maintenance* and *development*. For our purposes we shall make use of these definitions:

"Technical development" is the effort to develop new institutions in an existing social order so that the production output can be *increased*.

"Technical maintenance" is the effort to assist in such a way that the production output can be *maintained*.

"Technical aid" is the effort to *reconstruct* what has been destroyed because of external causes such as natural or social catastrophes.

We shall use the term "technical assistance" to cover all three, but the reference will in most cases be technical development only.

Graphically, we can illustrate the three ideas as in Figure 16.1.

FIGURE 16.1 *Three types of technical assistance*

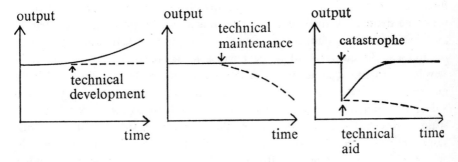

(the dotted lines represent the future development without technical assistance)

From the administrative, the technical, the economic and even the political points of view these three forms of technical assistance may look quite equal, but their social psychology differs. Technical development is a step into the uncertain with no preexisting model in the community where the assistance is injected. There is a preexisting model somewhere else, however, presumably in the donor country. This factor makes comparisons between what is happening in the developing nations and the industrial revolutions in the West a century or two ago unsatisfactory. The amount of human audacity required may be the same, but relevant models, even if they are in other countries, facilitate the proper selection of means. This, of course, is even more true for technical reconstruction.

Maintenance and aid aim at the preservation or reestablishment of the *status quo*. Thus, the latter two are in a sense a reaffirmation of the existing

539

order. The very fact that these kinds of technical assistance are yielded symbolizes the validity of what *is*, and the very fact that technical assistance in the sense of technical development is yielded symbolizes the opposite: *the invalidity of the existing order*. Aid and maintenance thus have a certain conservative effect, whereas technical development represents an open challenge of the old order, and particularly of everybody with vested interest in this order. One may try to delimit the challenge by minimizing the envisaged change, but some challenge will always remain.

Thus, we would expect aid and maintenance to meet with considerable support, but aid more so than maintenance. A catastrophe due to extrinsic factors may reduce the level of social interaction considerably, but if it is defined as ill fate, misfortune, etc., it carries no connotation of devaluation of the victims (except within a theory that connects misfortune with God's moral judgment). The need for maintenance of what exists *may* have such a moral significance, because the inference to be drawn could always be that "these people are not able to take care of what they have themselves". A maintenance operation, hence, will probably be more easily accepted if it can be defined as an operation of technical aid, by pointing out extrinsic and exculpatory circumstances (such as unfavorable climatic conditions or political difficulties held to be beyond local control).

What is intended as technical development and perhaps most objectively described as such may sometimes be perceived or interpreted as technical aid or maintenance, however. The idea of a golden past may turn any assistance into aid, belated aid, where the aim is to restore what was, with some minor adjustments. This interpretation should be particularly acceptable if it is combined with the idea that colonialism destroyed what *was*, and that assistance is reconstruction, by the wrongdoers.

Under what conditions is technical *development* accepted in spite of the challenge it, however inadvertently, implies? Some hypothetical factors are:

1. Under the condition of some kind of *direct reciprocity*, either by a (trade) counter-flow of economic goods (in which case it is not technical assistance) or by means of some other kind of value. This compensation may already have been given as colonial exploitation, at least according to the receiver.

2. Under the condition of some kind of *indirect reciprocity*, for instance by yielding technical assistance to other countries so that the net sum approaches zero, or if the *donor* country receives technical assistance from other countries.

3. Under the condition that a similar development without any assistance is seen as "impossible" for other than human or cultural reasons, for instance "because of" lack of raw materials or "because of" climatic conditions.

4. Under the condition that the superiority of the donors in this respect can be defined as due to other than human or cultural reasons, for instance, presence of raw material, absence of wars or famines or colonization, by invoking some version of the climatic theory, etc.

5. Under the condition that the yielding of goods is seen not as an act of benevolence or charity, but
   a. as a disguise for other kinds of motives,
   b. as the lavishness of a nation so rich that the flow out of the country in terms of technical assistance is hardly noticeable.

In other words, there must be some kind of *local theory* that can lead to the acceptance of the fact of technical assistance for development. We have distinguished between three kinds of such theories: the notion of *full or at least partial compensation*, directly or indirectly, in the sense that the receiver yields or that the donor receives or both, *theories that "explain"* why it is possible that this kind of value-flow is in only one direction and explains it in an easily acceptable way, and theories that *reduce the image of the donor as a giver*. Of course we do not claim that such theories will necessarily arise, only that they will be readily accepted. The need for *some* such theory will be present among politicians as well as in the public opinion, as we assume only few people to be able to harbor theories with *no* such element. To what extent the theories are true or not is an entirely different, but certainly not unrelated, question.

1.2. TA *as international interaction*

Technical assistance has now been defined as a one-way flow of economic, non-military goods or services between nations, with a possible counter-flow of some noneconomic value. We shall call nations from which these economic goods or services come, *donor nations*, and nations to which they go, *receiver nations*. The term "host-nation" suggests the idea of technical cooperation, but that is not essential in technical assistance. The terms "giving" and "receiving" should be interpreted relative to specific projects. A nation may be donor in one context and receiver in another, India is an important example, and the sum total may even be zero judged by some "objective" measure of value given or received. Typical of technical assistance is the absence of expected compensation from the receiving nation, not the absence of expected economic compensation from somewhere. Thus, an international system where technical assistance is exchanged in such a way that all nations end up with non-negative balances is quite conceivable, for reasons already mentioned. But it is not easily realized in this world because of universal scarcity of some demanded commodities, a decreasing differential in subjective utility, due to increasing similarity between nations, and the many impediments to a free flow of value.

At this point a simple trichotomy may be introduced on both sides of the technical assistance relation as defined by a project or a "plan" (Table 16.1).

TABLE 16.1 *The macroscopic structure of technical assistance*

		receiving party one nation	more nations	collectivity [4]
donor party	one nation	Indo-Norwegian project, Kerala	U.S. Marshall-aid	USA assistance to Latin-American countries via OAS
	more nations	All bilateral yielders vis-a-vis India	the general case, no structure	no example known
	collec-tivity	Scandinavian hospital in Korea, UNKRA, consortium idea	EEC economic and technical assistance	UN *programs*, technical assistance, OPEX, EPTA, Special Fund, UNICEF and specialized agencies

The distinction is often made between "bilateral" and "multilateral" assistance, but this distinction seems to be based on the nature of the donor party only. Thus, *bilateral* assistance defines a relation between one donor and one receiving nation, and if there are more donor nations one usually talks about *multilateral* assistance [5]. The distinction is valid, but the distinction between assistance given to *one* national unit and to *more* national units, under the same general program, is also valid. The nature of the Norwegian fisheries development project in Kerala would change completely were it to be extended to other Asian nations. Marshall-aid administered to Norway alone would be a totally different thing, even if the value received in Norway were exactly the same.

When more nations are involved as donors or receivers of technical assistance, collectivities of nations may more or less automatically be defined by nations with the same position in the technical assistance relation. This may take the shape of some kind of supranational organization, which enters in the channel of communication and value-flow needed for technical assistance to be administered. Such an organization may be introduced on the donor side or on the receiving side or on both — and as a special case the two collectivities may even coincide as an international clearing center for technical assistance: e.g. under the auspices and supervision of the United Nations. In that case receiving nations may participate in making decisions concerning TA and this will probably contribute to its acceptance [6]. The basic distinction between assistance given to "more nations" or to a "collectivity" is that in the latter case the decision as to how goods or services shall be allocated to the participant nations lies with the collectivity, i.e. on the receiving side. On both sides, however, the difference between "more nations" and "collectivity" may be a minor one, depending on how much additional institutional framework has been created.

Gunnar Myrdal [7] sees five reasons why assistance through the UN is preferable: 1. less suspicion as to motives, 2. sufficient resources to permit an efficient administration of TA, 3. international organizations less vulnerable to pressures from yielding or receiving nations, 4. it is easier to take advice and orders from a supernational organization than from another nation, and 5. the receiving country has much more of a choice in programs and experts. Of course, the points 2 and 5 depend on how much money and support in general the international organizations have; after all, it is hard to compete with the United States or the Soviet Union in these matters. And as to the other points it may certainly be objected that they depend on how UN and its organizations are perceived by the receiving country. If it is perceived as a power instrument of one big power, these points may easily be reversed. But the importance of a TA structure that permits active participation on behalf of the receivers, control over political pressure (bilateral agreements can be made more secretly) and legitimation of authority by reference to something "beyond" is obvious. The point about avoidance of secrecy is also mentioned by V.K.R.V. Rao [8] as well as "no political strings" [9], coordination with receiving country's own plans, local administration by receiving country, avoidance of propaganda effect for the yielding country, etc. Many similar lists exist.

The pros and cons of bilateral vs. multilateral assistance on both sides are many, but we shall limit ourselves to point out some that follow almost immediately from the few and very general concepts we have introduced. We can analyze it from the vantage point of *success vs. failure* — and for the moment disregard the difficulties in assessing what constitutes a success and what constitutes a failure in this field. If we start with the donor, the main point is his interest in protecting himself against failure but not against a possible success. From this follows, as a first approximation:

1. For important projects where *success* is expected, the donor will prefer to be the only yielder.

2. For minor projects or projects where there is a chance of failure, the donor can protect himself in either or both of two ways,
a. by sharing the status as yielder with others, and thus sharing the responsibility,
b. by giving the assistance multilaterally, to more than one nation, to increase the chance of *some* success and as a protection against *total* failure as when everything is yielded to one nation.

We do not claim that the donor will always act according to these principles, only that there will be forces in these directions. An interesting question is whether we may postulate that "where success is expected, there will also be a tendency to yield all assistance to one unit". This, of course, depends on the amount of economic goods available for the purpose — and it seems likely that small nations giving assistance will try to concentrate on *one* receiving nation. The receiving nation will probably be picked on the basis of implicit, non-economic counter-value it can yield, and on the basis of the expected probability of success, rather than on the basis of technical and economic needs, and the expected success will be in terms of a complex combination of technical success for the project and the extent to which these counter-values appear.

So far we have tried to study this from the point of view of the nations yielding assistance. What are the pros and cons as seen from the other side of the relationship ? They will have a corresponding interest in terms of the success/failure variable — but in addition there will be the incentive to find some form of protection against expected counter-values. One of the most important counter-values is *gratitude*, and the need for a protection against gratitude derives partly from the nebulous, never ceasing nature of this expectation, partly from the negative self-image it implies. How is this protection best accomplished ? There are many ways, and we can only point out some of them [10]:

The receiver can protect himself against expected counter-value

1. by preventing success of the technical assistance project (we feel there will always be *some* motivation present of this kind),

2. by means of multilateral TA-*giving*, preferably from a diversity of nations so that the implicit counter-values expected may be contradictory,

3. by means of multilateral TA-*receiving*, preferably to a diversity of nations, so that the implicit counter-values that can possibly be offered will be contradictory,

4. by technical assistance administered via one or more supernational organizations, so that there is less immediacy in the link between yielder and receiver to the point where the goods received bear no sender address, are "anonymous".

With all these structures combined, the receiver should be well protected. The central point is the protection against concentration of "gratitude" from *one* receiver directly to *one* giver after a successful project. It is in the giver's immediate interest to concentrate success around himself, and in the receiver's immediate interest to protect himself against such a concentration of the cause of success. More indirectly, it may be argued that the donor will try to protect his future status as donor by avoiding situations that are too difficult for the receiver, and it will be in the interest of the receiver to try to protect his future status as receiver by granting the donor the remuneration stemming from at least an open flow of gratitude value [11].

Thus, the situation is more than complex, and it is further complicated by these hypothetical principles:

1. The donor will be motivated to yield to
   a. *one* nation because of the increased return expected from a concentrated investment of scarce goods and expertise,
   b. *more* nations because of the demand and the desire to behave in a universalistic way when assistance or aid is given. The main function of the international organization is precisely to regulate the flow of supply and demand.

2. The receiver will be motivated to be
   a. the *only* receiver, because of the demand within the nation and the perception of the resources as scarce,
   b. *one among many* receivers, for the same reasons as (1b) above.

Within this sphere of argument, dealing with the purely human aspects and the technical aspects of success it seems reasonable to expect that the *donor will pick only one receiver and that the receiver will prefer to be the only one picked* — particularly if there already exists a well-defined relationship between a potential donor and a potential receiver where technical assistance may easily be administered. This is the idea of *adoption*, especially as a relation succeeding classical colonialism. We have outlined above some other arguments and sources of strain that will be important, and they tend to point out structures quite different from the above as stable: the donor will prefer more receivers, at least the number within his means, and the receiver many donors — or even to be one among many receivers.

From what we have said it may look as if we believe the donor always to be zealously watching all moves taken by the receiver and evaluating them in terms of their possible content of gratitude. Although this undoubtedly will often be the case, there will also be cases where the donor will try to protect himself against open expressions of gratitude directed towards him personally. Gratitude may be a source of strain, particularly when it is confronted with one's own less honorable motives, or perceived as a way of soliciting more assistance. But it is our thesis that some kind of compensation *is* expected, not necessarily in terms of gratitude, and that the donating nation may be watching the development very closely even when the line of communication has been made more complex through the intervention of international organizations for the administration of technical assistance. Like welfare boards, community chests, etc., these organizations have the additional function of keeping donor and receiver apart so that they are both protected from additional expectations. But, not unlike welfare boards and community chests, the further the two parties are kept apart, the less immediate is the possibility of reinforcing the motivation through the numerous possibilities of communication and control inherent in the direct relation [12].

Collection of private funds in the donor country is probably considerably more easy for bilateral than multilateral projects. The fund drive for the Norwegian project in Kerala in 1953, in connection with "Folkeaksjonen" (the "People's Action") was not a success, but nevertheless suceeded in making almost four million kroner available for the project. A fund drive for Norwegian participation in a UN program would hardly have elicited much support unless the role of *Norwegian* experts was so heavily stressed that the multilateral nature of the project was obscured. From the point of view of the public opinion in the donor country, a complete "multilateralization" of TA will mean a loss in terms of support.

Bilateral assistance appeals more to the imagination of the public — it takes a very cosmopolitan orientation to fully comprehend the importance of multilateral assistance. For a successful project this means more support, but for a project in crisis the price is bitter criticism. Gleditsch notes [13] as "strange" how much more criticism the Indo-Norwegian project in Kerala has been exposed to as compared with Norwegian contributions via the multilateral programs. This is partly a function of the simple economic fact that Norway has contributed more to the bilateral project in Kerala than to all multilateral programs Norway participates in. But the main impact of the bilateral assistance to India (where the UN, strictly speaking, is a partner, in a "tripartite" agreement, but a sleeping partner, not even represented in the Standing Committee of the project) has been to stir imagination and cause praise as well as criticism. The latter has been more pronounced in later phases of the project, only partly because of lack of imaginative ways in presenting the successes.

These arguments run in all possible directions, and rarely permit an unambiguous, stable and mutually accepted arrangement where the structure of technical assistance is concerned. Thus, great political skills are needed to assess the pattern of expectations in concrete cases and find the most appropriate form of organization. Our main purpose in indicating some of the problems is not to make an attempt in the direction of a really satisfactory analysis, however. *The point is that technical assistance is a form of interaction in the system of nations, characterized by an exchange of values which is of an explicit, technical/economic nature in one direction, and of an implicit, political/cultural nature in the other direction.* This relation defines a kind of international social system with its statuses and roles, its system of mutual rights and obligations — and any theory of technical assistance will have to account for the web of normative expectations pertaining to this relation.

Since TA is international interaction it must also be related to foreign policy [14], for good or for bad. However much TA may be blamed for inefficiency, corruption, etc., it has the distinct advantage over other forms of international relations of being non-violent [15], which makes TA a challenging field for peace research.

Finally, let us give some information about the sums of money so far allotted to the most important UN TA-programs, and Norway's part (the information is taken from *Engenutvalget*) (Table 16.2).

TABLE 16.2 *Money appropriated to* UN TA *in Norwegian kroner* (*1961 included*)

	UN TA-total	Norway's part	
TA, regular programs	188,269,000	927,860	0.49%
EPTA (Expanded Program of Technical Assistance)	2,216,750,000	25,350,000	1.01%
Special Fund	849,960,000	9,965,000	1.04%
UNICEF	2,120,718,200	5,055,000	0.21%
Fund for the Congo (as of February 6 1961)	115,481,545	3,503,000	3.04%
Total	5,491,178,745	44,800,860	0.82%

In addition, Norway has yielded an additional N.kr. 20 million (about) to other TA programs under the UN. That makes the total Norwegian contribution via UN about N.kr. 64.8 million. In addition, 52.5 million kroner have been appropriated to the Indo-Norwegian Project in Kerala, and

18.45 million kroner to the Scandinavian hospital in Korea. Thus, Norway has so far yielded N.kr. 135.8 million, out of which

35% directly to UN as shown in Table 16.2
12% to other UN agencies
39% for bilateral TA to India
14% for Scandinavian TA to Korea
———
100%

This gives an impression of how important the Indo-Norwegian Project is in the total picture of Norwegian TA. And this is one more reason why we have made it our special concern in the next section.

1.3. TA as intergroup interaction

We have made use of the distinction between goods and services and shall now proceed further along that line. It is quite conceivable that TA may be given in the form of "goods only", a ship load with some kind of cargo, but the current argument seems to be that this may be possible for technical *aid*, but not for technical assistance in general. In the case of technical *aid* a model of what shall be constructed already exists, for the construction is *re*construction, but in the case of technical development this is no longer true. Hence, the services of people with an intimate knowledge of such models, from their own country, are called upon, and in this way the *expert* enters the stage. Technical development means transplantation of elements of one culture in another culture, and the job of the expert is to facilitate this process. Thus, *technical assistance may be regarded as a communication process where cultural elements are communicated, with the donor country as the sender and the receiving country as the receiver.* The role of the technical expert is, more specifically, to facilitate this process of communication by being present at the receiving end, and making the "message" communicable by interpreting it to the receivers.

This is not enough, however. Bitter experience has led to the systematic introduction of "counterparts" as interpreters and intermediaries between the experts and the local receivers (Figure 16.2) [16].

FIGURE 16.2 *The* TA *communication channel*

donating party   receiving party

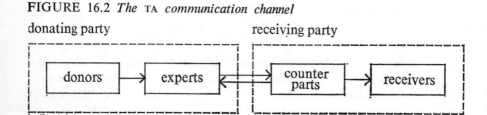

It should be noticed that counterparts can also be receivers, but their main function in this connection is as a means of implementation of expert advice and techniques. The focal point in this figure is the interaction between the experts and counterparts. Geographically, this interaction may be located in the donating country (fellowships, scholarships, study tours) or in the receiving country (TA experts, TA projects) or somewhere else (conferences, training centers). We shall confine ourselves to the second case only.

The expert is not there to "give" goods or services, in the same sense as a man may give alms to the poor — rather, his *services* are "given" as a part of the total technical assistance [17]. The role of the technical expert is to make himself superfluous by teaching local people to act as receivers and users of the communicated cultural element. But in practice, and this is a crucial point, there will always be the need for identification and concreteness. The abstract relationship between one or more donor nations and one or more receiving nations will remain meaningless to many people, whereas the concrete day-to-day interaction between the "experts" and their "counterparts" is full of crucial meaning and often easily understood. The experts are identified as Norway, and they themselves are seen as the donors, they are not merely a medium [18]. Correspondingly, the fishermen of the Malabar coast become "India", and they are the receivers — to the technical experts. From a greater distance, grosser units will be used to describe the assistance; for the common Norwegian this is still the assistance to "India" or to "Kerala", not to fisherman N.N.

Naturally, the interest centers around the very spot where technical assistance is carried out — and here technical development is sociologically far more interesting than technical aid, precisely for the reason that an international process of communication has its focus in an on-the-spot interpersonal relation with at least three main statuses: the "expert", the "counterpart" and the "receiver". Occasionally, the "donor" may also be present, as in the case of visiting senators, journalists, tourists — not to mention visiting social scientists. The three statuses serve as a basis for group formations, and the sociology of technical assistance is to a large extent precisely the study of the interplay between these three groups, with the possible coalition formations that may reduce the pattern to a relation between two parties. A coalition on the receiving side between the receivers and their agents, the counterparts, may be built on the theme of cultural distance or extortion — "get as much as possible"; a coalition on the top level between experts and counterparts may get its ideological fuel from recurring and increasingly irritating resistance in the local population, from a shared perception of the "backwardness" and lack of foresight, etc. [19]. And the third coalition between experts and receivers, in a sense the most interesting combination, may appear as an effort to combat local bureaucracy — "if it were not for the "counterparts", our assistance would have been efficient", not to mention the ever present dogma of "corruption among officials".

In all three groups there will probably be individuals who have enough political acumen to sense these possibilities, and this makes a study of how each group tries to maneuver so that the other two will not find a coalition rewarding. It lies in the logic of Figure 16.2 that the group of counterparts is at an advantage here: they are already defined as intermediaries and can, because of their high status in the receiving country, request that all communication between experts and receivers go via them. On the other hand, the experts may be able to exploit existing internal controversies, and legitimize their claim to direct access by reference to the functional necessity of intimate knowledge of the receivers' situation. This, in turn, will probably be met with the: "you may be good as an expert, but we know this people". Mutual respect, loyalty, a common jargon, close contact due to work partnership, etc., will, however, usually make the top coalition of experts on both sides quite likely — and the net result will easily be an expert vs. lay conflict which the receivers may easily interpret as a continuation of colonial patterns.

This at once leads us to one of the most frequently mentioned aspects of the arrangement of technical assistance, viz. the pattern of interaction between experts and counterparts. When assistance is yielded a new social relationship, even a new social structure, will often be indispensable in the receiving country. Mechanized fishing and modernized methods of fish distribution presupposes gadgets, but also adequate social relations. Training in social relations is usually of a less codified and more diffuse nature than the training in the use of "ironware". For this reason, it is often argued, technical assistance should be communicated by means of a collectivity of experts, who through their working relationships may serve as a model of the adequate social relationships for the particular project. There are two extreme ways in which this can be done (Figure 16.3).

FIGURE 16.3 *The structures of* TA *extreme cases*

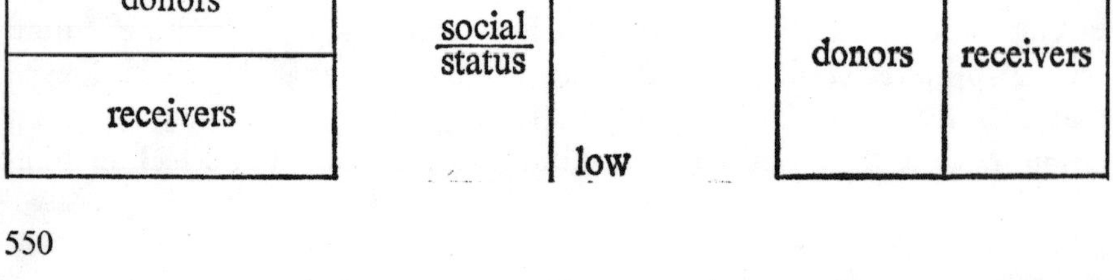

In the first case, all top positions in the hierarchy of communication are given to the foreign experts, all lower positions to the local population — which then does not, strictly speaking, appear as counterparts, but as subordinates. In the second case, there is a certain homology between the collectivity of experts and the collectivity of counterparts. Empirically, the former corresponds to the classical pattern of teaching in the colonial tradition, and the latter to the novel idea of the peace corps. In contemporary practice there are all sorts of compromise between these two extremes (Figure 16.4).

FIGURE 16.4   *A compromise structure*

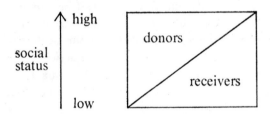

The argument against the first possibility is partly ideological and partly even practical, for the short term: if all experts have high status, the group experts can never serve as a model of the social relations to be established for lack of personnel in the lower positions. If this personnel is taken from the local population, the top layer of foreign experts will hardly ever be able to make itself superfluous — and the social structure gives reason for doubts whether this is actually the intention. Clearly, the degree of "horizontality" in the borderline between foreigners and natives will be an important factor of friction.

One difficulty with the second pattern (Figure 16.3) is its element of utopia. The experts are there precisely because of a lack of native skill, and a proportionately equal representation on all levels in the TA hierarchy can hardly be based on equality in competence. Status equivalence must be obtained on some other basis, for instance by means of a complicated, and frequently problematic, pairing off of a top engineer with a top politician or local administrator, or a recent graduate from an engineering college. To find an acceptable basis for equivalence between the hierarchies is as essential as it is difficult, because of the lack of similarity between the two nations that has led to the TA project. The last of the three patterns will probably represent a relatively unstable compromise [20].

Although the principle often is that TA shall be under local administration, in practice there may very well arise a power struggle between experts and counterparts. If the expert legitimizes his claim for power by referring to the scarcity among the counterparts of the kind of knowledge he possesses, and the counterpart by referring to the scarcity among the experts of the kind of political skill and local know-how he has, then we may postulate that both parties will try to exclude people with their own skills in the other camp. This does not mean that donors will try to exclude all local experts, but they will define the situation so that they come out on top in the sense of always having *some* scarce knowledge. Nor will the counterparts try to exclude all "politicians", but they will easily claim that knowledge of local conditions is "unnecessary" — "we are here to take care of that". The conflict material latent in this is obvious.

Under what structural condition is the communication in the TA project optimal? We do not know, only that it depends on *what* shall be communicated, and that this field abounds with dilemmas. One may argue that effective *teaching* depends on some kind of legitimacy, on the authority of the teacher — and this should lead one to the first pattern with the donors on top. One may also argue that although some teaching from status-superiors will always be needed, the transfer of novel ideas between status-equals will facilitate the internalization, because of the broader contact and the greater ease with which imitation of a status-equal may take place.

But the most important argument in favor of the second model of culture contact for technical assistance has to do with the nature of the learning process. Not only individual skills, but social relations shall be taught and the argument that they are best taught when a complete system of receivers try to learn from a complete system of donors seems quite valid. Thus, although teaching from a position of status superiority may be excellent for transmission of routine skills to be exercised individually, it may not be suitable for the transmission of skills to be exercised in social contexts, teams, production relations, etc. It should also be remembered that although it may be easier to listen to and accept the instructions of a superior, it may be easier to ask and demand explanations from equals.

The kind of communication envisaged in the second figure, which takes place on many status levels, will inevitably force a certain homology between the systems, not only because this is, in a sense, the ultimate goal of the teaching process itself — *but in order for the teaching to take place*. In the process of finding out "who corresponds to whom" small adjustments will take place, often unnoticed, and they may serve to give the systems a more similar structure. How this happens we do not know, not even that it does happen, but we believe that the drive to be able to orient oneself in the social labyrinth of a foreign social system will force some similarities. One inevitable question that must arise from this is: does this process of mutual adjustment change the yielder system into a new system that may be better suited for communication purposes but less suitable for the technical task to be done ? Or, translated into power terms: who wins the power struggle, the technical expert or the public relations expert ?

Let us then turn to the question of cultural differences. It is well known from many findings that there is a positive correlation between cultural distance and social distance, in the sense that the more culturally distant two persons are, the less probable is a primary relation between them. It is also well known that there is, in general, a positive correlation between social distance and rank distance — the greater the difference in rank, the less probable is a primary relation. *For these two reasons there is a certain initial stability in the first pattern above* (Figure 16.3), because of the coincidence of two kinds of distances. The second pattern implies a certain amount of strain: on all status-levels the rank-equality should imply a social nearness the cultural distance does not warrant. On the other hand: if the second pattern is established, then it should be very stable, because of the crisscrossing effect of the two differentiating factors. In the first pattern a conflict between high and low is at the same time a conflict between donors and receivers (and hence in most cases also a conflict between white and colored) — in the second pattern the first of these two correlations is at least very low. Although we feel this pattern may be difficult to establish, it should be very stable if it survives the initial phase. But for the reasons mentioned, cultural difference should lead to the first pattern, cultural similarity to the second pattern — other factors being equal. Since, in general the greater the cultural difference, the more will there be to transmit via such channels as technical assistance, it is not strange that the first pattern is so frequent, even with no prior tradition of colonialism.

The most important factors in connection with cultural differences in the discussion so far, however, have not centered around the differences as sources of distance, but as sources of negative evaluation. The cognitively different easily becomes different in value, as is well known, and the single quote that comes to one's mind is "The Ugly American". If this seems to be almost inevitable, it may serve as a valid argument for the extension of technical assistance over relatively minor cultural differences only, where A can give value to its cultural neighbor B, B to C and so on until the flow reaches the culturally very distant country Z. On the other hand, we have reasons to believe that assistance to development is more easily accepted over a considerable cultural distance, especially if it is filtered through supernational organizations. Again, a culturally distant donor *may* sometimes make use of culturally close experts, and thus diminish the cultural friction. Finally, there remains always the problem of whether cultural friction is necessarily completely bad, or whether it can possibly have positive functions. We shall not try to embark upon an analysis of that problem.

The figures do not express a distinction that is of crucial importance: whether the model project carried out in the initiation of the TA work is manned entirely with foreign personnel with the counterparts as *onlookers* (later to become copiers) — or else manned with personnel from both camps, *participating* on as equal a basis as possible. For both purposes the first structural arrangement is hardly commendable. The second way of implementing the idea of technical assistance should develop somewhat as shown in Figure 16.5.

FIGURE 16.5   *Withdrawal of donating party*

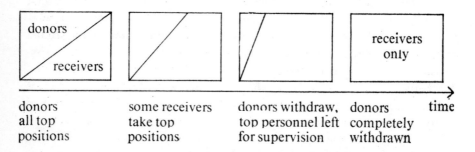

| donors
all top
positions | some receivers
take top
positions | donors withdraw,
top personnel left
for supervision | donors
completely
withdrawn | time |

Other patterns are possible. Thus, the withdrawal of experts may be from the top rather than from the bottom, for instance because of a serious need for higher personnel somewhere else. This poses the interesting problem of subordination. Figure 16.3 shows (to the left) a complete rank--equilibration between status as superordinate in the project and status as citizen from an "upper class nation". The righthand pattern has no correlation at all. Figure 16.4 is one of compromise. In none of the cases is there a direct negation of the principle of rank-equilibration, but extraction of top personnel may easily lead to a situation where lower foreign personnel will be under direct leadership of natives who have risen in the hierarchy because of the TA project, and with an insufficient basis of authority as judged by the standards of the donating country. This may be a source of rather serious conflict — and makes one wonder what evidence exists concerning the best way of withdrawing foreign personnel.

The counterparts will always have one argument of some importance when it comes to the incessant human game of comparing bases for authority: "we *know* this region, these people, their customs, desires, values . . ." One way of defending this source of authority is precisely to deny the experts systematic access to this kind of information, which can easily be obtained by institutional arrangements such as an excessively high standard of living for the foreigners. The direct contact may always be a source of concern for the local counterparts, partly because of the challenged authority, partly because of the jealousy when the local population embrace the foreigners with gratitude and answer their questions much more readily than local officials are used to and appreciate — partly because of the fear of all kinds of slander and negative comments, which may abound in such situations, and partly because of the danger of a lasting coalition. The basic difficulty lies in the possible narrowness and provincialism in the counterparts' "knowledge", which may be intimate but restricted to what was relevant for the *ante*-TA order.

We have dealt at some length with sources of strain between experts and counterparts, and turn now to a more systematic account of the relation between experts and receivers. In a sense, this is a projection on the local sense of the international system; the TA project is an international microcosm with its connotations of upper-class vs. lower-class nations etc. And it seems that the distinctions made above in Table 16.1 for the international interplay are quite valid, in the sense that there is a strong isomorphism between these two levels of thought and political reality (Table 16.3).

TABLE 16.3 *The microscopic structures of technical assistance*

| | receiving party | | |
	one receiver	more receivers	collectivity
donating party one expert			
more experts			
collectivity			

Which are the pushes and pulls away from and towards these possible combinations? Which solution is the most stable one, under given conditions? We do not know the answer, but can point out some of the stresses and strains inherent in the system. First of all, we assume parallel forces of the kind we have already indicated for the international system. Thus, we believe that an expert will like to monopolize a success about as much as he wants to share a failure. Instead of saying, like President Kennedy after the Cuba invasion April 1961 that "success has many fathers, failure is an orphan", we believe that fatherhood for a success is readily admitted, and fatherhood for a failure readily shared with others. Further, to pick another example: we believe that the receivers may prefer to multiply the experts in order to be able to spread gratitude thin, just as the expert will ask for colleagues in order to spread the aggression directed against him relatively thin — in case of a failure, that is.

But there is another opening in the system in addition to the manipulation of numbers: the counterparts. In a successful project the experts have the possibility of seeking as direct a contact with the receivers as possible, in order to get some personal compensation in terms of expressive, human values for the goods and pleasures they have forsaken by being away from their home country. If the project is a failure, there may be a similar incentive to use the counterparts as a buffer and decrease interaction with receivers accordingly, to the point of even moving from the project area and settling somewhere else (usually in the capital). The international analogy lies in the use of UN or its agencies as intermediaries. The main source of strain between experts and counterparts lies precisely in the latter's motivation to do the opposite — and this can only be studied by simultaneous consideration of all three groupings. In this situation of latent conflict and lack of lasting stability, there are great possibilities for politically talented natives.

Just as assistance given to one nation may arouse the jealousy of other nations, and assistance given to "more nations" may arouse the jealousy of the remaining nations in a given, well-defined collectivity of nations — so also with individual receivers. To give TA to one person in the village will look like nepotism, to give it to more than one person may look like group nepotism — the only solution may be *to administer it in such a way that the whole collectivity is perceived as the ultimate receiver*. By using the word "ultimate" we emphasize the fact that some people may be the immediate receivers of the assistance yielded, such as technicians, plant-owners, etc., and then serve as media for the development of the total community.

But the problem, indeed, is not solved by the simple means of assisting already existing communities only. On a higher level, for instance, the level of the *village*, one village assisted will create jealousy among the others, and to add more villages will probably be to no avail unless all villages in an existing unit are taken. Somehow, something must be done to alleviate this pressure, if it is not possible to assist all units at the same time. Formulas must be found, structures must be introduced that can somehow serve to justify the selection of the given unit. We shall have occasion to delve into this later on, and shall only mention one of these formulas here: that of the *model* project, that a unit is assisted not for its own sake, but to serve as a model for the development of other units of the same kind. Thus, one may have a pilot *village* for irrigation or a pilot *family* for hygienic practices, etc.

The advantage in assisting a total community, however, is not only the avoidance of internal friction because of differential assistance yielded, but also the possibility of a less direct relationship between receivers and donors

that is less permissive of streaks of paternalism. Interaction between collectivities serves as a filter for the intensity of human interaction, and softens
both positive and negative outbursts because of the definition of lines of
communication, as already indicated earlier. The distinction between "more
counterparts" and "collectivities" is precisely the distinction between
single, relatively unconnected units and an organized social entity — just
as for the case of nations discussed above. On the whole, we assume *mutatis
mutandis* the propositions put forward in section 1.2 to be equally fruitful
on this microscopic level.

Finally, let us illustrate the importance of what has been mentioned
in this section as well as in section 1.2. by reference to American and Soviet
TA in India. India is in a position where it is true that "the cold war is our
fortune, we have been wooed by both parties and they compete for our
allegiance" [21]. The American contribution has by far exceeded the Soviet
contribution to India's development, however. In a public opinion poll
with 793 respondents drawn from the cities of Delhi, Calcutta, Bombay,
Madras, Kanpur and Lucknow attitudes to foreign aid were studied [22],
and the results were quite interesting.

Before we present the important Table 16.4, which has to do with a
comparison of the two parties to the cold war, it is interesting to note
that when the sample was asked "Do you favor aid from all countries or
only from some?" 51% answered "all countries" (except Pakistan was
added by some) and 26% answered "some countries". This may be taken
as an indication of popular preference for many countries, or collectivities,
as donors.

The main results can be summarized as follows (Table 16.4).

TABLE 16.4

	USA	Soviet Union	UK	others, all countries	self-sufficiency	DK	Sum
Kindly name the country which is assisting India most on the Plan	34%	19%	1%	1%	—	45%	100%
Which country do you favor most for aid to India	7%	13%	1%	14%	1%	64%	100%

The DK-rates are substantial as was to be expected, but it is interesting to
note that they are higher for the evaluative than the cognitive question.

Two facts stand out: almost one fifth have been so impressed by Soviet or Soviet aid that they believe they are "assisting India most on the Plan", and *more people prefer Soviet than the USA* "for aid to India". (This also comes out in the second preference given). In spite of the fact that USA has given more, the Soviet Union is preferred by more people. It turns out after closer inspection [23] that preference for the Soviet Union is particularly pronounced among males, aged 20—29, educated ("matrics"), poor and unemployed and above all among *students*.

What in the attitudes of Indian students makes it natural for them to answer this way? Fortunately, there has been a study of "Indian Student Images of Foreign People" [24]. The instrument used in the study was a sentence completion test, designed to get images of the "The people of America", "most Westerners" and "the Russians". The conclusions were as follows [25]:

"The image of the American is that of the wealthy, happy, friendly but dissolute person. The Westerner (presumably a European), on the other hand, is the epitome of culture and fashion, a true aristocrat, with all the charm and pleasure that goes with that status, but also with snobbery and arrogance. His physical beauty is often referred to and also his learning, but he is selfish and self-centered.

Our new data concern the Russian. He is a solid citizen with all the Puritan virtues: Hard-working, brave, strong, patriotic, honest; also progressive and peace loving. That is the Russian viewed as a person. Only a small minority reacted in terms of the regime *and most of that small group pointed to cruelty*. However, the individual is perceived not as a political figure, but as a constructive worker in a development program, a kind of hero of labor.

To the American author of this paper, our finding suggests that Americans have themselves promoted one important misconception in international propaganda by stressing their high standard of living, rather than the high level of work which produces it. In the eyes of the subjects whom we are studying, the highly regarded values are sacrifice, work and effort rather than leisure and status".

The last point is made even more strongly in the conclusion [26]:

"That makes it clear that industriousness and striving rather than comfort or success were the elements in a culture which would make its image appealing in the eyes of our respondents. Not wealth but work was the trait to be emulated. The images of foreigners accorded with a value system in which there is sensitivity to power but in which respect is bestowed for Puritan conduct."

Of course, "industriousness and striving" rather than "comfort or success" are things Indians can do *today*; that contributes to their acceptance. If technical assistance is to progress, regardless of which national interests it may serve, it seems clear that more research should be done in this field.

1.4. The "values to collectivities" principle

We have mentioned the principle of administration of assistance to *collectivities*, such as for instance villages, to counteract the negative influences of jealousies arising from differential distribution of goods among families or individuals. This principle is partly a question of administration, but to a considerable extent dependent on the nature of the values to be distributed. In this section, an attempt will be made to analyze the principle further.

It is easy to make a new road, or a village well, appear as a collective commodity, but not so easy to do so for fishing boats in a highly inidividualized economic order. In general let us make these important distinctions between the kind of values that can be given by means of technical assistance (Table 16.5).

TABLE 16.5 *A typology of values distributed by* TA

	receivers have equal access	receivers have unequal access
distributive values	food distribution	fishing boats
non-distributive values	new roads, health services, cooperatives	privately owned factory

By "distributive" we mean that the value (goods, community service or whatever is offered) *can* be divided into parts that can be owned in the sense of monopoly over its disposition, by small units such as individuals or individual households. A school building cannot be distributed to individuals, nor can a road, a pier or a health center, but they can be used or enjoyed by individuals. Correspondingly, toothbrushes, contraceptives or bicycles can easily be given to individuals, and be enjoyed by everybody.

The property of being distributive is not an intrinsic property in the sense that it can be derived from the nature of the valued commodity, or service, itself. Land, for instance, may be tilled individually or on a cooperative basis. In both cases vegetables may be distributed, but individual ownership is absent in the case of the cooperative: there is no correspondence between individuals and plots such that the individual has the monopoly to dispose over the plot. At the same time a highly important property of land is its divisibility — it *can* be divided into plots of almost any size so that a man can draw a line around it and call it "mine". In other words — a commodity may have properties such as divisibility that *permit* distribution — but whether or not it *is* distributed in the sense mentioned above is a social fact. In either case, however₂ the *access* to the values may be "equal".

If something of value *can* be distributed this does not mean that it *has* been distributed in a way defined in the culture as egalitarian. And if something valued is not distributed, this certainly does not mean that everybody has the same access to it. In the latter case it is important to distinguish between trivial cases of differential access (such as the childless family with no "access" to the new schoolhouse because of no need for it) and cases where a person, who by some generally accepted standard is eligible to make use of the commodity, still is prevented from doing so. The nature of these "generally accepted standards" will have to be explored in each concrete case. A waterpipe that cannot be used by people in a remote part of the village, boats that cannot be used by people living far away from the possible landing places, constitute examples.

The basic thesis in this connection is the rather trite:

Assistance given in terms of values, distributive or non-distributive, to which the access is unequal will arouse discontent, because of its disequilibrating effect on the local value-distribution.

The only thing in this sentence that makes it less tautologous than it looks is the word "unequal". Imagine a social order established through tradition with its unequal distribution in the sense that value is differentially distributed according to several kinds of rank orders. Then, imagine technical assistance with its flow of value into the community. Does "equal access" mean "same to everybody", or does it mean "proportionate to amount of value prior to the assistance"? What is equitable in this connection? More probable than not, the donors and the receivers will have different images of the ideal future distribution. But both will probably feel the difficulties that arise if individuals with legitimate claims to the new values are denied any access to them, whether they are distributed or given to the collectivity.

The crucial point in Table 16.5 given above, however, is not the two distinctions made but their interrelation. For instance, is it easier to secure equal access in any sense of this word by means of non-distributive or distributive values? This is probably dependent on the possibility of a transformation of value. Fishing boats given to individual households may help the families meet their day-to-day needs for food and furnish them with means of exchange. Fishing boats given to a suitable organization representing the collectivity may provide the whole collectivity with some kind of value that can be distributed so that everybody gets some kind of access to the goods. It may be necessary to spread the yield quite thin, but it seems possible to obtain more "equality" this way than by distributing the means of production, *in casu* the fishing boats. Generally, means of production are less divisible than the products. The crucial factor is that collective ownership implies or at least may imply collective decisions as to distribution, and hence makes possible an equal distribution. With individual ownership this is more difficult to obtain, although measures like progressive taxation and differential social welfare may even out unequal distributions.

We can now present a more precise version of the "values to collectivities" principle. As far as we can see there are three ways of obtaining relatively satisfactory results from the point of view of *short-term attitudes* (not necessarily from the point of view of what is potentially the best basis for further development):

1. *Non-distributive values with equal access*, i.e. "collective goods". This is probably the safest strategy, but a necessary condition is often the creation of new social institutions. The latter can be administered by foreigners who will then have to remain as an alien element in the local structure (the case of missionaries) or else be administered by local political bodies — thus extending their power. In either case problems will be created both political and ideological. In most cases it will probably imply collective ownership of means of production, to avoid jealousy etc.

2. *Distributive values with equal access*, where goods are given directly to individuals or households. This is simple because of the possibility of using the existing social structure, but its drawback also lies precisely here: there are limitations to what can be achieved with no new social institution. Typically, this is the pattern for technical *aid*, and less suitable for technical development than the pattern mentioned above.

3. *Values with unequal access*, provided this can be supported by means of readily acceptable ideas, such as
   "equal access in the long run",
   "priority to people in serious need"
   "extrinsic circumstances, such as geographic conditions",

The amount of hostility arising from an unequal distribution of goods coming from TA can be almost incredible, probably partly due to the conception that TA goods will give the local population a new deal. This introduces a new kind of conflict between experts and counterparts; the receivers who for one reason or another are denied access to the new goods, will easily put the blame on the counterparts, and believe that they have diverted value into their own pockets by way of corruption. The experts may similarly, tend to prefer this interpretation to an interpretation in terms of technical difficulties or social inequities that they themselves have not been able to master. Undoubtedly, the variables we have touched upon are of tremendous importance as sources of local conflict, and if it had not been for the demonstrable evidence of some, at least partially, successful TA projects the conclusion might easily be that TA is impossible. Where new social institutions are needed, political resistance will always be high because of the implied change in the power structure, and this has often been the case for cooperatives [27]. In a sense efforts to introduce cooperatives epitomize everything said so far, and deserve a closer study.

1.5. TA *as a means of integration*

Much has been said since the Second World War about the importance of TA as a means of integration, as a strategy in the struggle for peace, etc. So far we have not been able to locate empirical demonstrations of such effects, but this may be because of the almost complete neglect of TA as a field of serious research and the inherent difficulty in locating such effects at all. Theories in this field are usually of two kinds: that the *result* of TA is the removal of a cause of conflict, e.g. differential distribution of welfare, and that the *process* of TA has an integrating effect. The first theory presupposes that TA is technically and economically efficient, but makes use of no assumptions that do not apply equally well to the receiving nation's own effort to raise its standards of welfare. The basic assumption is that standard of living is a relevant factor (which, no doubt, is true when other factors of a more social and psychological nature are added to this), and at this point there may be two schools of thought: emphasizing *absolute* deprivation in poor countries, and emphasizing *relative* deprivation in poor countries, relative to the rich countries. In other words, does war originate in the empty stomach, or does it start when somebody sees that others have more food than they have themselves? Is an empty stomach more conducive to apathy than to manifest conflict, and what other factors are important in addition to perceived relative deprivation? Egalitarian ideologies? Notions of injustice, of treason, of exploitation?

Leaving all this aside, let us try to look for some crucial factors related to the possibility that the *process* of TA *may* be a factor leading to peace or reducing conflict. An extreme version of this theory is that the process alone matters, the results (at least as long as they are not negative) are of minor importance. Thus considered, any form of cooperation similar to TA may be an instrument of peace. More realistically, both *process* and *result* must be considered in order to arrive at a theory concerning TA as a means of integration — but at present, let us assume that the result judged in terms of some technical/economic data or criteria is considered good by all parties involved.

If we take bilateral assistance as a point of departure, three levels must be distinguished in both countries; viz. political elite, experts/counterparts and the public. Thus we get Figure 16.6.

FIGURE 16.6 *Lines of influence in the* TA *process*

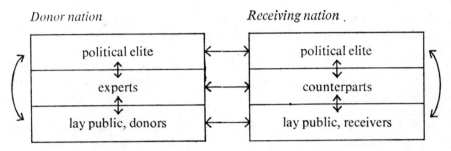

The double-arrows indicate channels of interaction and communication-with the focus on interaction between experts and counterparts. The relation between foreign and local leaders of a TA project is probably quite crucial. This is where the mode and speed and whole atmosphere of the interaction is decided. Personal conflicts at this crucial point may well be com municated as negative comments on the other party to the project upwards and downwards in their own systems. Hence, it seems obvious that anybody interested in the TA process as an instrument of peace will do his utmost to secure a good working relationship at this most central point in the whole machinery.

The question to be discussed is "what do we mean by integration" in this connection? On what level? How is integration on one level related to integration on the other levels? It is easy to assert that in the short run political elite integration is more important, in the long run, rank and file integration may be more important and that the integration of experts and counterparts is only a means to achieve these two goals and not important in its own right (they are so few, and do not necessarily have much power). But exactly how an image of a TA project is formed on all three levels is very difficult to ascertain, and we can only put forward some points. First, let us briefly recapitulate what has already been said about factors influencing evaluation of a project among the receivers. The ten most important points in this analysis were

1. The idea that the donor expects *some* kind of compensation, tangible or intangible.

2. The feeling that no compensation is necessary because the donor is so fabulously rich, or that compensation has already been given so that the debt can be written off (the donor first of all has no right to expect anything, secondly he has already received his compensation — colonial extortion, moral prestige, etc.).

3. The suspicion that his motives are less honorable (he may be a donor, but certainly no samaritan).

4. The idea that the differential wealth between donor and receiver is due to extrinsic factors only (climate etc.).

5. Whether the assistance given is reconstruction or construction, and to what extent the latter represents a challenge of a status quo in some kind of equilibrium.

6. The *macroscopic* structure of the relation between donors and receivers; whether there is one, many or a collectivity of donors and receivers (we feel it is impossible to give a general formula here).

7. The *microscopic* structure of the relation on the spot, and as a most important special case.

8. The "values-to-collectivities" principle.

9. The structure of the cooperation, whether it is horizontal or vertical, whether the cultural distance is bridged in any way or not, and whether it is real cooperation or only a pretense.

10. How the donors are introduced and withdrawn from the social structure of the project itself.

In a provocative article "Why Hasn't Foreign Aid Made Foreign Friends?" [28] by Frank E. Wolf, "sixteen principles are set forth as the minimum guideposts in evaluating our past and present foreign aid programs, and new bases for future foreign aid planning" [29]. We mention thirteen of them here (the remaining three are too specific for the US), with our own comments in parentheses and without necessarily agreeing with everything said. The points can all be seen as important specifications of our point 9, above.

1. The need for aid should be recognized and expressed by the recipient (but such recognition should be sincere and not feigned).

2. Planning should include lower echelons (for simple democratic reasons, for efficiency, and because lower echelons will at some point become higher echelons).

3. The cultural surrogate (technical or educational aid person) and the indigenous worker should meet as equals (if this is the future world we want, today is where we start — and this is the only way of securing a transfer of the project to indigenous personnel).

4. The artifacts of equality should be equal (because they are the symbols visible to third parties who immediately draw inferences from differences in standard of living, etc.).

5. International understanding should grow naturally from concerted efforts of the participants (project cooperation is the point from where cooperation may spread).

6. The professional host community should be oriented to the purposes and nature of foreign aid (this, essentially, means an extension and possible support of the technical expert's role-set when he is abroad).

7. A working knowledge of the foreign language should be achieved prior to departure (for practical reasons, and as Wolf indicates, as an expression of "respect for the host culture").

8. Current information, as well as historical information, should be available to and sought by the cultural surrogate (especially other experts' reports — a small investment here is probably worth the expense).

9. Demonstrations of democratic procedure and behavior in practical situations should be made wherever possible (but if they are only "demonstrations" and not sincere they will probably backfire).

10. An optimistic attitude may result in desirable outcomes (because of optimism as a mechanism of self-fulfilling prophecy).

11. Close association with indigenous personnel will tend to create confidence of the cultural surrogate (again, provided it is not a trick).

12. Cultural surrogates' reports, both written and verbal, should be assembled for analysis by policymakers (and by social scientists).

13. The masses of a population are permanent; the officials are transitory; therefore the surrogate's major efforts should be with the masses (which is also a good argument for peace corps).

Numerous other factors could be mentioned, singly and combined they will all contribute to the evaluation of the project and the international relationship in particular. The outcome may be that project personnel on both sides decide the project is a success or a failure — as the case may be. Very often it is in the power of a strong personality to lay down the official evaluation. The perception of the other party will be conditioned by all these factors, and the way in which the receiver solves the dilemma of being receiver will be an important determinant in how he likes the donor nation. A corresponding list can be drawn up for the donor and the way in which he solves the dilemma of being donor, including the right to yield, will be a determinant of his perception of the other nation.

However important perceptions at the central point in the interaction between personnel on both sides in the project may be, it is obvious that its importance is proportionate to the ease with which communication upwards and downwards from experts and counterparts takes place. If communication is blocked, the political elites may retain the honeymoon feelings when the agreement was signed, in spite of the complete failure of the project in practice — whether this is good or bad is a matter of taste. Project personnel may be under the obligation not to tell anything about the project to the press, radio or other means of mass communication till some time after their work is terminated; this may prevent communication to the lay public of secrets, frustrations well remembered or personal details — but it may also efficiently prevent the communication of success. Returning personnel may be so tired and "through" with the whole project that they prefer not to think of it. Politicians may be too busy or technically unskilled to understand the details — they may decide that information may be harmful to the relationship and the net result may be little or no communication to the public — as is the case with the Indo-Norwegian Project in Norway. Communication to the lay public in the receiving country may be complicated by such factors as illiteracy and absence of media of mass communication. But communication upwards is probably facilitated by the smallness and concentration of elite. A specialist who functions as a counterpart is more likely to have direct links to the political elite in a receiving than in a donor country, he will more often than not be a part of the elite himself. Misgivings may reach the top immediately and color relations between the political elites. But something will also filter down to the lay public, although the knowledge of the project will decrease rapidly with increasing distance from the project area.

What role does public opinion in the donor country play? TA can strengthen public conscience and awareness of problems in other countries, publicity about TA is also a reminder about other people in distress. But whether this strengthens solidarity and integration is difficult to know. It may easily serve as a foundation for a feeling of surprise and bitterness if the receiving nation does not behave properly. A feeling of being deceived is very detrimental to integration, and a complete equilibration of expectations so that the receiving nation pays back in gratitude value exactly what the donor expects is difficult to achieve. There are stories of Indians visiting Norway who report that they can hardly count to ten before "good Norwegian friends start throwing the Kerala project at us", and by the time they are supposed to say something on their own initiative, they have seen too many Norwegian eyes shining in anticipation of expressed recognition and gratitude.

Of course, most of these difficulties are avoided when assistance is administered by a supernational agency. But UN assistance raises two important questions: to what extent does such assistance promote any attitudinal change or any attitudes at all? And if it does, and the result is some kind of integration — then integration to what? Multilateral aid may cause changes locally. The villager who knows nothing of Norwegians may get a positive impression due to a nice Norwegian surveyor, or change his negative attitude towards the US because of an excellent American dairy expert. The basis for change will probably be in the *surprise*, in the discovery of unexpected acts from nations where they expect nothing or at least nothing positive. But if the assistance is given multilaterally with constant emphasis on the UN symbol, this surprise will be diluted and what is left is an organization surrounded with attitudes that also apply to the Red Cross. And it may be argued that there is no need to discover that cooperation with the Red Cross is possible; Red Cross threatens nobody.

On the other hand, a positive image of the United Nations and its divisions will provide the agency with a reservoir of goodwill it can draw upon in periods of crisis. Both bilateral and multilateral assistance can lead to *multiple loyalties* that may soften and prevent conflicts [30]. But the distinction implicitly made above, between new loyalties where one's own nation is a member is so important that a terminology is needed. We shall call the latter an *extended loyalty*, as it is essentially only a widening of one's own traditional loyalty, and very different from a loyalty created to another geo-political unit to which there is no tie via a supersystem. We shall call this kind of loyalty a *parallel loyalty:* it is a loyalty created to another system at the same level.

For parallel loyalties to be of real value, they should tie together potentially conflicting systems. However valuable it may be to create more friendship out of existing friendship, parallel loyalty is a better investment if it transcends conflict borderlines. It is very difficult to see that extended loyalty can replace parallel loyalty here. My fights with my neighbor do not cease because of my increasing respect for the police because of its social work — they may even become more bitter because of my moral judgment when I discover that he does not respect the police nearly as much as I do. To what extent one kind of multiple loyalty may be a psychological bridge to the other kind we do not know, but it is quite conceivable that they are so different in kind that one may even be a negative stimulus for the other, under some conditions. With the present level of knowledge it is difficult to maintain an either/or when it comes to a choice between what is customarily bilateral and multilateral aid — the answer should rather be both/and with the hope of achieving both kinds of loyalties.

Everything we have said so far in connection with the TA process as a means of integration has to do with attitudinal change — and intuitively we feel that the case for TA as an agency of change creating new loyalties is by no means obvious. But in conclusion it must be mentioned that there are numerous other ways in which TA may have an integrating effect than via the often dubious medium of attitudinal change. To mention some: contact in a TA project *breeds new contacts* (some of them will marry; in the wake of the project follow the politicians, journalists, tourists), a TA project will force a certain *homology* between the parties to the project in the sense that the receiving nation will become a little bit more like the donor country structurally, and this will multiply the possibilities for extended contact; interaction, especially economic interaction will lead to *interdependencies* that *may* lead to considerable interest in preventing conflicts. But these important factors would lead too far away from the concepts and ideas so far developed.

1.6. *The problem of research*

The scarcity of good research reports dealing with the social structure of technical assistance is heavily felt, and the present report is certainly no exception. What is available is much below what is needed as background material for decisionmakers, and also much below what should be expected if social scientists scattered their research interests randomly over the entire field of social relations. The answer, of course, lies in the absence of randomness in the choice of research problems, and this section is devoted to some reasons for the underrepresentation of this intriguing field of research.

A research project presupposes research motivation, available techniques, assistants, monetary and other resources, and access to data. We shall not discuss the amount of money available for this kind of investigation, nor the applicability of existing techniques — we feel reasonably sure that both would be forthcoming if motivation and access presented no problems. Let us first deal with the problem of motivation.

We have no exact knowledge about the quantity or quality of motivation in this field, and can only venture some speculations. What are the main *negative* incentives in this field, for instance? First of all, the field of investigation is *unchic* — at present. It has the unmistakable flavor of the *applied* and the theoretical gains from a study of technical assistance are not obvious. Traditionally, the sociologist studies human interaction in a more pure form if he wants theoretical insight: the frozen interaction in the total institution (the prison, the mental hospital, etc.) and the artificially contrived pattern in a small experimental group are typical examples. The anthropologist will, perhaps, frown upon studies of TA for similar reasons, particularly because of the impurity in culture and social structure [31]. But this was more true some years ago than today; by now there is a strong tradition for studies of cultural change. A study of technical assistance requires the skills of the sociologist *and* the anthropologist, and the barriers between the two sister sciences are not easily overcome in practical cooperation.

An even more important negative factor, perhaps, is the presence of the TA bureaucracy. The working social scientists wants autonomy and independence of powerful bureaucracies — he does not want to have his conclusions dictated. Nor does he want constant supervision and interference with his work, however legitimate the intention may be. Resistance for political or human reasons requires capabilities the scientist does not necessarily possess, and he is likely to interpret it as an expression of anxiety and not as legitimate for other reasons. And if he is *hired* to do research, he may suddenly discover that he has been hired to prove that the contractor is right.

The following are some reasons why resistance to research seems quite natural:

1. Quite a lot of the work with the local population in an underdeveloped country must by necessity be based on some theory as to how they are and how they behave. In other words, *the project officers must have something we can call their "private anthropology" and "private sociology"* in order to carry out the job at all. How this private social science is *acquired* is a most important research question, and how it is *preserved* represents a very important problem. Since work and investment will be based partly on this theory, quite a lot of prestige will necessarily be attached to it. To revise the theory may mean at least a partial admission that something has been done on an incorrect basis. Research that concentrates on this will therefore hardly be welcome, except in the initial phase, before too many investments have been made. This is particularly true for the local counterparts since their status to a consi-

derable extent is based on their knowledge of the local situation. For this reason alone we will expect more resistance to research in this group than in the group of experts.

2. Concomitant with this first idea is the second idea, viz. that *the project officers are the real experts*. They have been in the field often for a long time, they have met local people every day, they have their theories and since their techniques of testing the theories are hardly scientific, they will probably register more verifications then falsifications of their theories. If in addition they are politicians and always need some kind of private sociology, they will probably more than ever feel that they are the experts in this particular area. To the TA expert the sociologist and anthropologist may appear as not only intruders, but even as childish amateurs who cannot possibly know their job because they do not have the same data, nor do they collect information the same way as the technical experts do. The idea that "insight is proportionate to duration of stay" will easily gain popularity, and specific descriptive knowledge will be judged as more valuable than general analytic knowledge. Thus there will be a great deal of usually very elementary methodological criticism.

3. The *criteria of success* for a technical assistance project are many and diversified. They range from increase in stand of living and increase in hygienic standards to such evasive things as increase in goodwill and contributions to peace. All these standards, when used as yardsticks to measure success, can be ranked according to degree of intersubjectivity. For instance, there cannot be much discussion about how much fish was caught. What the exact rise in hygienic standard has been can perhaps be discussed, but infant mortality is a highly consensual measure. As it is in the interest of both the donor and the receiving countries that the net balance of the evaluation is positive, clear consensual measures will always lead to difficulties: there is no way of escaping from unpleasant conclusions.

If now the intersubjective criteria of success give a highly *positive* picture, an investigation of the more evasive aspects may be met with little resistance. But if the intersubjective criteria give a more mixed or even negative balance, then the resistance will be much higher. If research is carried out by people who cannot be controlled, one can never be quite sure what their findings will be. Of course, there is the possibility that their findings can be interpreted as positive, but they may also be interpreted as negative. And in the latter case the total picture will be even more negative. *As long as no research has been carried out there is always a possibility of doubt.* In such case knowledge may be seen as dysfunctional, and ignorance as bliss. And the more "objective" the knowledge, the fewer possibilities there are of interpretations, the more resistance will there be.

4. In addition to the last point there is also always the possibility that there may be some concrete features [32] the administration simply does not want to become known, and rather would see hidden or forgotten. More particularly, they may be afraid of publication, uncontrolled by them, of project results etc. — This will also apply to journalists.

5. *Research looks like inspection and supervision*, and evaluation research even more so. This impression can be counteracted by a research team with no administrative connection with the project, or even from a third nation (but the latter solution is often impracticable for the simple reason that so much extra knowledge is required when there is no national identity.) Many respondents and informants will see this as a great chance for reporting real or imagined harms done to them — and this will be resented by the administration. Nor shall it be forgotten that overworked people will resent additional burdens [33].

6. *To collect data is in itself a social act* and as such may have unanticipated consequences; some of them functional, some of them dysfunctional. Research will have a tendency to make the latent manifest, make the implied explicit — and research may also make what is only problematic to some people a shared concern — because of the public nature of research, however discreetly it is carried out.

7. *To publish the reports from an investigation is in itself a social act*, and may, like the collection of data, change the object of the investigation. We have already mentioned the possible effects it may have on local ideology, on the status of the local expert, on the evaluation balance for the whole TA project, on efforts to conceal less desirable features of the project — and shall only mention one additional effect. Facts and interpretations will always be seen as for or against a certain point of view, although the intention and interest of the researcher may be completely orthogonal to the local issues. In other words, a report will be seen as more for one point of view in local politics, and more against the other point of view, which is tantamount to saying that it will change the power balance between local groups or antagonists in the project itself. This may be interpreted as a serious intrusion, and above all as an unsolicited interference in other people's business.

8. *Research is in itself a kind of technical assistance*, and should meet with the same negative reactions. More specifically, when research is organized from the outside, there may always be the feeling that "they think we

are not able to do this job" — and the entire psychology of being defined as "underdeveloped" may be invoked [34]. There is another factor, however, which is more directly related to social research. To study human beings may be interpreted as an expression of the idea that they are strange, that "they think there is something abnormal about us, but they have the same problems at home, even more so — not to mention the additional problems they have — why don't they study all this at home if they take so much interest in it". Although this may often be true, there are some counter-arguments that should not be forgotten. Social science considers social action in its full variety its legitimate field, and to study a phenomenon abroad does not imply a denial of its existence at home. On the contrary, it is entirely within the generalizing tendency in modern social science to test hypotheses under as varied conditions as possible. Further, there is another argument pertaining to technical assistance. TA is basic to changes most people consider important, and knowledge of how to extend TA should also include the kind of evaluation the social scientist may contribute. It is not true that research done in the receiving country has the same effect — though the publication may be the same, the donor country needs research experience *in corpore* at home if the results shall be really valuable.

Other functions of research, real or imagined, with this much in common, that they are seen as negative by the administrator, could be mentioned. It goes without saying that these effects can be minimized by the experienced investigator, but some of the anxiety will always remain and part of it will even be valid, and serve as a verification for the initial level of anxiety. This makes the problem quite intricate, since the politically acceptable solution — that the administrators do the research themselves — is hardly recommendable from a scientific point of view.

Finally, instead of mentioning the (to us) obvious positive functions research of this kind may have for the implementation of the idea of technical assistance, let us mention the importance the research can have for social science. At first it may well be that research on TA will have the unmistakable flavor of the *applied*, and that it will not give an occasion for the development of new insights. But it will open the whole world of mankind to a sociology which has so far concerned itself mainly with industrialized societies, and as a part of the bilateral ties established between nations under the TA programs, it may be a real eye-opener to social scientists. Experts on fisheries, on health, on administration learn a lot from their participation in TA programs, so why not also social scientists? That social scientists have much to learn in a changing world is at least beyond doubt, and that they must learn more before they can teach more to anyone who wants to be taught is as true as it is often neglected [35].

2. The special case: report from a pilot project

2.1. The project area: some intuitive impressions

If one approaches the Indo-Norwegian Project (INP) area by ship, the Malabar coast looks like a tiny stretch of sand covered with palms. It is beautiful, but in a sense very monotonous — everywhere the same beach, the same palms and the same small huts with thatched roofs. At one point there is a gap in the coastline flanked by two white churches. The churches belong to the Catholic community of Sakthikulangara and the gap is the inlet to the Ashtamudi lake, which is a part of the backwaters that run continuously along the coast, protected from the ocean by a stretch of land that varies in breadth from a couple of hundred meters to a couple of miles. Over the gap passes *the bridge*, the Neendakara bridge, and along the coastline and over the bridge there is a road, National Highway no. 47, which runs down to Cape Comorin.

This inlet is central to the project both geographically and technically. To the south is the village of Sakthikulangara, which is Catholic, and to the north of the inlet is the village of Neendakara, which is mostly Hindu. A part of Neendakara is called Puthentura, and the project camp itself is located just about where Puthentura starts. Thus, there is a natural geographic borderline *between* the two villages that form or make up the project area, but at either extreme to the south and to the north the borderlines are considerably less clear. Although it was frequently denied by the population, it seems that communication between the two villages is far below what one would ordinarily expect from two villages that close, and that this has one of its roots in the religious distinction, among other possible areas of dissimilarity and conflict [36].

When asked what villagers in the other community were like, the stereotyped answer "they are just like us" was sometimes given, but even more frequent was some kind of theory as to how the others were different. This was not done in derogatory terms, however — but religious distinctions were very clearly pointed out.

Religious belongingness is also correlated with the difference in last names. Thus, the Catholics very often have European sounding names of Latin origin (Portuguese) and these family names are quite often what Westerners ordinarily would recognize as biblical first names, such as Sebastian, Jacob, John, etc. Villagers in Neendakara have Indian names. Another distinction which seems quite crucial in any analysis of this project area lies in the authority structure: in the Catholic community there is a priest, a Father, and he is a most central figure. He is at the same time in charge of the secondary school and, as far as could be ascertained, in

573

practice in charge of most municipal work. Orders emanating from him bear a degree of authority that few other orders except from persons even higher up in the Catholic hierarchy can possibly have. In the Hindu community there is nothing quite similar to this, no such central figure with the same kind of powerful spiritual sanction a Catholic priest can have.

The whole project area covers 10 sq.miles (out of which 6.8 sq.miles are covered by the Ashtamudi lake) and has something like 14—15,000 inhabitants. According to the last census undertaken by the statistician of the project, there are 2,414 households in the area [37]. The number indicated in the population figures from the area is often spuriously high, as there are reasons to believe that some people have smuggled names of relatives into the files of the health center in order to benefit from the free health service provided for residents of the area.

Most of these 2,414 households live under rather primitive conditions; small huts (where palm leaves seem to be the main material) with mud floors and little light make up most of the villages. There is hardly anything like streets, pavements, etc. The huts are rather scattered in a seemingly random way among the palm trees [38]. Most households have a number of cocoanut palms on their little ground; and in this climate the cocoanut-palms are said to be harvested 6 times a year, or almost continuously [39].

One immediate point that can be made and that carries a lot of weight is this: *Everything is highly visible in this community.* There is no hill that can protect one part of the community from the eager eyes of the other part. The houses are so tiny, and so much of the household activity takes place outside the house, that most families very easily can get all the information they want about most other families. It is true that an abundance of trees decreases visibility but people seem almost always to be walking around. They make the roads look extremely much more crowded than Norwegians are used to, and the flow of information about what somebody is doing seems to be rapid.

In such communities not very much can possibly be kept secret, and it is interesting to speculate a little bit about this. Imagine a community where everybody is hidden behind a high wall and rarely moves outside the wall. Uncertainty will be tremendous and the community will try to satisfy its curiosity by means of the few cues that will always be available. As an extreme case, one can imagine a community where the isolation is so perfect that it is almost impossible to get information at all. In this community there should perhaps be *less* curiosity, just because of the impossibility of satisfying the curiosity. On the other hand, in a community with as high degree of visibility as this community seems to have, one might also conjecture that there should be little curiosity because there is so little to be curious about. But the easy access to information will also facilitate control of others, based on highly relevant information.

In the midst of all this visibility the Norwegian camp is located. The first thing that may strike one is how different the camp with the about thirty Norwegians is from the surroundings. The buildings are clean, white, recently painted, relatively low and do not look particularly luxurious. On the other hand, they look like wealthy and upper class dwellings against the background of very poor huts. The second impression is the fence. The fence is high enough to keep people out. On the other hand, it is not massive, so it is easy to peep through it, which means that it does not prevent the usual kind of visibility. Probably it would have been very unwise to have a tight stone wall, so as to prevent any kind of visibility in both directions, this would stir curiosity more than anything else. But there are some important dysfunctional consequences of this arrangement too. For instance: Whenever Norwegians relax, engage in tennis, do their swimming, lie on the beach, take a drink in the evening sitting on the verandahs of their bungalows, they are engaged in activities that are unusual by the common standards in the neighborhood. Most visible is the inactivity of the wives of the project personnel, and the general separation of their children from the village boys and girls. This is noticed, everybody sees it and everybody is free to comment on it [40]. Here is one comment, not necessarily typical:

"You see, these Norwegians are always sitting in their small bungalows. They can sit there all evening through and perhaps they take a drink. They never come out to us in our huts. Whenever they leave the gate, leave the camp, it is always in a car and always with some dignitaries. It didn't use to be in this way, some years ago it was all different. A Norwegian could come into the humblest hut, he would talk with us, he was one of us. Of course we knew that when he was a Norwegian, he needed better conditions to live in, because he was not used to this place, otherwise he couldn't work. But the Norwegians who are in the camp today, never leave the camp. Some of them don't even talk English. Quite a lot of them we don't even know. They come, they stay for a time and then they move, and nobody knows them."

The difference in living standard is as mentioned, highly visible. On the other hand it is interesting to see from the quotation above that if a person gets out of the camp and into the village and behaves in a certain way that perhaps only few people are able to, then the villagers are quite willing to have a very mild view of his high standard of living, *it is seen as instrumental to his good deeds*. On the other hand, if the actions of the Norwegians are restricted to the technical field alone, their standard of living can easily be perceived as mere indulgence and be turned against them.

If one leaves the camp through the gate, passes the guard and puts one's feet on the road, the almost immediate thing that happens to the stranger is that a couple of boys run towards oneself and start begging. Usually they say something like this: "Saipe, saipe, I want one rupee, I am *very* hungry", and then they put the hand on their bellies to indicate how hungry they are. With a dozen of such boys in front of oneself it is quite easy to get irritated and annoyed. One immediate and premature reflection is that there must have been important lacks of control or lacks of communication when after a stay of eight years it has not been possible to convey to the villagers that *this just isn't done*. The second reflection brings to one's mind that many of these people live on or below that most important of all borderlines: between sufficient nutrition and hunger bordering on starvation in some periods. Which of these reflections will win out in the long run is another question, dependent on personality characteristics — but the first one is less difficult to harbor. We shall see, however, that there is another solution to this problem than that of choosing interpretations.

A walk around the area is an enticing experience for a visitor. At dawn or sunset the colors have a certain pastel quality that renders the landscape extremely attractive — when the sun is scorching in the middle of the day it is easier to remember the problems of the area. We have mentioned what to Norwegians looks like extreme overcrowding (to quote a leading official of the project: just like the main street of Oslo after the National Day Parade [41] and visible poverty — although the visitor does not have to face anything similar to the urban slums of India.

Scattered all over the area are the visible signs of the Indo—Norwegian Project (here as elsewhere we concentrate all attention on the part of the project located in what we have called "the project area", and say nothing about the ramification of the project to Ernakulam and elsewhere). Most impressive, perhaps, is the landing place for the fishing boats, at the inlet to the lake, where fishermen bring in their catch in the old *valloms* or the new mechanized boats and market the fish right there, on the beach. On either side of the inlet are the ice factory and center for distribution of fish, and the boatyard. And further away, along the road, is the waterpipe factory for the pipeline that shall furnish Quilon town and the district with fresh water. And there are the breakwaters, the tackle and the nets and gadgets, the clinics, the latrines, the maternity ward, etc., inside and outside the camp — signs of initiative and development, all functioning, all subjects of conversation and attention.

But all over the place, among the palmtrees, by the road side, close to the beach or the backwaters are the humble huts and smiling, friendly, but impoverished people. And to remind one of the harsh reality, this naive observation can be mentioned: "But why are there only *young* people to be seen on the roads, under the trees, on the beach?" Answer: "Not because the old people stay at home, but because they are not there — the life expectancy is half that in Norway . . .".

2.2. *Why did the Norwegians come?*

An important social fact, this Norwegian presence in a tiny community far away, requires explanation in terms that are not only understandable but also acceptable. We have given (section 1.2) a number of reasons why technical assistance constitutes a challenge and these reasons can easily be conceived of as reasons why a functional perception is necessary. Instead of premature theoretization, however, let us present some examples of how the leading question in this section was answered by some of the local people, with no claim to a full understanding or knowledge of the diffusion of such images in the local culture.

The immediate impression was the rather trite observation that the closer the local people were related to the project, the more did their theory as to why this whole project was ever undertaken look like official Norwegian theory. From a functional point of view, the observation becomes less trite if we ask the question: what if the relationship were the opposite — the more intimate the knowledge, the more discrepant the perception. No doubt, in the vast field of TA projects this phenomenon is empirically represented — even if attempts to counteract it by limiting contact to selected and "loyal" local people are made. A discrepancy between official donors' motivation and the receivers' perception of this motivation is a good indication of bad contact, or even of serious conflict — but not necessarily of hypocritical pretenses on the part of the donors — they may also have been seriously misunderstood. Thus, the correlation we feel holds between closeness and correctness is a positive sign. It does not mean that the official Norwegian motivation is internalized, however; it is often merely recited, in the manner of the clever pupil.

More peripherally located villagers had ideas that, perhaps, are quite typical and serve to illustrate the points we have made. To get at this, we asked several fishermen what Norway was like, and the idea of Norway immediately led to the idea of the project and how it was incepted. Needless to say, the level of information about Norway was very low as was to be expected, although one might also have thought that more information about Norway could have been disseminated during these eight years. A group of fishermen and some students gave this image in a collective discussion:

"Well, the population of Norway isn't very much. It's at the most something between one lakh and two lakhs [about 150,000]. It is ruled by a king and his name is Haakon the seventh. He is a socialist and that is also the case with the government. The country is big, it is very sparsely populated, so all Norwegians have plenty of ground. The country is rich and Norwegians are very rich, but not fabulously rich [42]. So one day **King** Haakon decided that something should be done about this, because he knew about the poverty in other parts of the world, and he dispatched a team of three wise men among whom was Mr. Lund [43]. They travelled all around, some people even say they travelled all the world, and finally they came to Kerala. Here they found the fishermen on the Malabar Coast and they found *us*. They saw that we were poor but they also saw that there were great possibilities of developing the area, and they liked us. So they decided that Norway should adopt Sakhtikulangara and Neendakara and this was done in 1953. All kinds of services were given to people living in this area at that time and in the years that followed. Particularly the health services have been very successful. Everybody in this area is for it. But now things are going to change".

There are three aspects of this image that are of a certain importance. First of all, whatever differences there are between Kerala and Norway they have certainly not been diminished in this image. Secondly there is the idea that Norway's motives first of all are pure and secondly are very benevolent, even paternalistic. It is a question of giving aid, not of receiving anything in return. And, as was mentioned very frequently by others, it is a question of giving out of a feeling of social conscience and an economy of abundance. Thirdly, there is the idea of adoption. Essentially, the idea is that people living in the project area have been *selected* because of their human qualities, not only because of the particular economic and technical conditions of the area. A particularistic relationship exists between the Norwegian population and its King Haakon the seventh, and the population in the area, and the relationship seems to be a little bit like an old feudal lord who picks a poor peasant and makes him his entrusted knight. It would be interesting to know how widespread such images are.

Clearly, the last part of this image will be of some importance when the project is extended to other districts. In purely economic terms, this is a question of sharing with others what people in the project area regard as rightfully theirs, because of the kind of implicit contract with "the Norwegians". In more psychological terms, it is a question of sharing love and a relation of the more feudal type already referred to with others, and true love is held to be monogamous, to extend it to others means to deny it to the project area.

For the people living *outside* of the area it is difficult to say exactly what this means; an extension of the project may also solve a problem that undoubtedly has troubled them for some time: the problem of exactly why the people in Neendakara and Sakthikulangara were chosen. To what extent a latent or manifest conflict between the insiders in the area and the outsiders exists, is not known, but some indications to that effect were easily found.

To get some more insight into the question of perceived motivation, quite a lot of questions were asked in connection with the perception of the Norwegians *when they first entered*. Fishermen were asked to describe what happened and here is a typical account:

"You know, when the Norwegians first came and nobody had given us any orientation about it we did not know exactly what to believe. So, quite a lot of people were suspicious, that is not strange. That foreigners should come and give something to us out of sheer kindness, is not what we are accustomed to. Some people thought perhaps they were Christian missionaries, but they very rapidly understood that this was not the case. (Why? Well, you know, they never engaged in any of the usual Christian practices, such as prayers, efforts to convert us, etc.) The Communists started a lot of rumours about why the Norwegians were here. First of all they said that they are probably *spies*. Secondly, that this was just another way of colonizing India, just 5 or 6 years after liberation had come and that one should be on guard against it . . . " [44].

A more specific version of the latter idea, and this is the third point, had to do with the *radioactive sand* which is found in the area [45]. This sand contains radioactive elements and metals; part of it is exported and the rest is used for domestic purposes. Some factories exist, located close to the Norwegian camp, and the idea was that the Norwegians had come in order to get hold of the radioactive sand and export it to the United States in order to make atomic bombs.

The fourth idea encountered was the idea of propaganda, that even though it looked like this was done in order to help India, the real reason why it was done was that Norwegians wanted to make some good propaganda for themselves. Contributing to this idea was the very well known fact that Norway was a NATO power.

"But the communists were not successful with their propaganda. It never really caught on, and by now we all know that there are no strings to it. We know that the Norwegians are idealists and the only thing they want is to help us help ourselves".

the informant concluded. A happy ending from the Norwegian point of view!

To what extent this is a shared image and to what extent it is a more private one, is not known. The fact that Norway is a NATO power was well known and very meaningful, but there also seemed to be a distinction made between Norway and the other NATO powers. Norway was somehow set apart as a more peace-loving country than the others, used by the colonial powers as a disguise. On the other hand, even down in these small villages the U-2 incident May 1960 and the role of the Bodö airfield in that connection were fairly well known and not a single positive comment was heard about it. It should be very interesting by means of more intensive interviewing to know how some of the people in the area are able to solve this dissonance. If the Norwegians for instance were representatives of a private firm or a private cooperation, they could invoke the usual difference between government and individuals. But in this case most people seemed to be quite aware of the fact that the Norwegians are government employees. So how could this Norwegian government at the same time be responsible for the Indo—Norwegian project and for a part of the U-2 incident ? One informant, a Communist, expressed the idea that "governments are not always of one mind, you know!" Actually, the impression was that he and others wanted nothing to spoil the image of the purity of the Norwegian motives for them, for in a sense, *Norway was theirs.*

This list of perceptions could be continued at length. Just to mention one : the idea that the *real* motivation behind blood samples for diagnostic purposes was the export of Indian blood to Norway even at the expense of the local population. Here the function of the perception is that of the less honorable motive that establishes a counter-flow of value, so that the brunt is taken off the assistance as *aid*. The same applies to the ideas of espionage, colonization, theft or export of radioactive material, and the more subtle (and certainly not completely true) idea of the propaganda effect. More interesting, in a sense, is the idea of paternalistic adoption, especially when combined with the frequently found feeling that Norway was about as affluent as a country can be — and that fifty million kroner out of the King's treasury chest was a drop in the ocean — hardly noticeable. To give from abundance is no longer to give, it is rather the idle, rich man's whim, or his effort to assuage his own conscience.

The variations on this theme are numerous indeed, and knowledge of their dispersion and relative frequency in different parts of the population will no doubt contribute to our understanding of the social psychology of technical assistance. Most interesting would be a dynamic account of changes in perception — but this will have to be done in retrospect as there are no such data available now.

2.3. *The problem of contact*

"You see, these Norwegians are always sitting in their small bungalows. They can sit there all evening through and perhaps they take a drink. They never come out to us in our huts ... "

This quotation, already given in section 2.1, may serve as an introduction. The absence of spontaneous contact between Norwegians and villagers is one of the first observations a visitor makes, which does not preclude either spontaneity or depth in the contacts that are established during work with office-mates, counterparts, personnel on board the boats and in the yards factories, etc., not to mention with patients and servants. We are thinking of contact that is not directly instrumental for the explicit purpose of the project, not instituted as a work obligation — just human contact for no specific purpose except, perhaps, that of having contact. As mentioned, there is the widespread idea of a different past, and consensus about this is so remarkable that we assume it to be a fact: there was more contact during the first half than during the second half of the project. Our task is to try and give some indications as to why this is so — which structural factors apart from intangible personality characteristics counteract the very natural tendency to seek contact — particularly at this period where ideas that have been fully expressed in the proposed peace corps have a considerable currency.

First of all, the typical Norwegian response:

"When work is over, then it *is* over. Remember, it is interesting, but also very tiring. The heat, the humidity, always unexpected problems, much waiting time which is frustrating, and, I must confess, the human problems are difficult. We are simply exhausted and feel we are entitled to relax completely. It may be wrong, but I simply feel I have done my share. After all, that is what I am here for and what I am paid for."

That the Norwegians define their job as mainly technical, is quite understandable. They have been selected on that basis alone, it seems, and they are paid for their technical qualifications. But some of them also feel that there is nothing technical to be gained from the stay. When asked whether he himself had learnt something in his own field, one of the experts answered:

"No. Not at all. I cannot say that. You see, I'm not here to learn, I'm here to teach. I'm here to teach the Indians the things I know, not to pick up the misunderstandings they have. The way they do things here is so primitive that there is nothing that can be learnt from it" [46].

This, however, was not an attitude shared by everybody. Others expressed that this had been a stimulating experience because everything they knew in their own field had to be looked at from a new angle, so to speak.

In other words, the routinization of the job, with explicit and well-codified rules and limits — where the "myth of the past" of the project contains elements like "unrelentless self-sacrifice", "working sixteen hours a day", "always seeking contact with the humblest villager", "learning our language", etc. The local explanation of this change, among Norwegians as well as among Indians, is very frequently in terms of personalities. Which other factors could be pointed out?

Eight years ago the whole project experience was new, not only to the individual newcomer, but to the whole team. There were no old-boys present to impress upon the newcomer their ideas of the project, the local people, etc. Everybody had to learn for himself, the land was virgin and unexplored and a new discovery was one's own discovery, not a rediscovery. This was clearly reciprocated by the villagers, who must have felt enthused by this chance to bring some variation into their daily life, when the initial suspicion (if any) was overcome. Today, there is no newness, no love at first sight, only new personnel to "take over": "and they come, they stay for a time and then they move, and nobody knows them".

Adding to this is the widespread rumor that the whole project is going to change, move to other places, even be discontinued — so that contacts and knowledge would be considerably less functional. Few people had precise ideas about this, but it is intuitively clear that the possibility of a termination does not motivate for better human relations. It is similar to the spontaneous contacts made during a bus journey, they are made after the departure, not immediately prior to the arrival, since they are perceived as valuable for the trip itself only.

It seems that many Norwegians have had the best intentions in the direction of having good contact. When they came to the project area *they* should be able to do what others did not do. What happens is that they may start doing what they interpret as some kind of service to some of the villagers. Immediately, they encounter two difficulties: the villagers "misunderstand" and do not display the kind of gratefulness the Norwegians had expected, and if a service is rendered to one family it is difficult to give good reasons why it was not rendered to the neighbor family, too.

Secondly, let us add a factor somewhat similar to the "when work is over, it is over" factor:

"You get to know this place after some time. During weekends, we want to see something more of India. After all, this is probably my only stay in Asia, and I feel it is better for me as well as for my work performance that I get a chance to see the project area from the outside, compare it to other places, etc. So we usually try to get as far as possible during weekends".

It should be mentioned that the weekend may not necessarily be a good time for contact because of the religious activities much of the population is engaged in. But sometimes it might perhaps have looked to the villagers as if a main preoccupation of the Norwegians was to collect all kinds of ivory, jewels, and the small pieces and souvenirs foreigners usually pick up in India — not to mention to utilize their heavy photographic equipment as fully as possible. The villagers did not fail to notice this, and it *may* have been an additional cause of friction. If combined with good contacts and knowledge of village life, it would probably not have been frowned upon — but the present setting may encourage the idea that the Norwegians are "just like other tourists". Of course, we do not say that this is good or bad or that the argument quoted is invalid. Taken together, the two arguments serve to justify the lack of contact after work and during weekends: in other words, *the leisure time is my own, I do only what I am under explicit obligation to do.* This, of course, does not mean that there is no informal contact. The importance of contact has probably been pointed out so often that it may even have been perceived as a part of the job proper and put within the strict working hours that are not always either enjoyable or enjoyed.

Thirdly, it is impossible not to mention once more the tremendous difference in standard of living, accentuated by the high degree of visibility both ways that may make the Norwegians uneasy and the Indians suspicious [47]. The life the Norwegians lead has most of the connotations of the overlord, and it must be difficult for the villager to differentiate between what he sees with his own eyes and what he may have heard about "rich Americans", the British colonial power, etc. That they eat Norwegian style food, some shipped from Norway (fish-balls, goat cheese, etc.), seems to be well known, but this is hardly crucial except as one among many elements that contribute to the idea that *Norwegians set themselves apart*. Essentially, the camp is a part of Norway, not unlike the resort culture found in parts of the Norwegian coast in summer time, transplanted into the traditional fishing village culture of the Malabar coast variety. It provides Norwegians with optimal conditions for some kind of efficiency, but at the expense of contact, for a number of reasons, out of which sheer geographic separation is one. The Norwegians are together and stay together, and the camp looks high class, although it is actually quite simple.

A tremendous, perceived differential in wealth is one of the conditions for the insistent begging encountered in the area. Caught between the dilemma "give and you get one hundred requests tomorrow" and "do not give, and you feel like a miser, a cold-hearted mercenary, etc.", there is little wonder that the solution lies in staying at home or leaving the camp "always in a car and always with some dignitaries".

"Whenever you get out of the camp these youngsters are around you. They start begging, and if you give them anything at all, then the day thereafter, you have one hundred of them. As a matter of fact, if you give in to any Indian when he asks you for a favour, then you are lost. For instance: N. N. out of his good heart, and after a fisherman had prayed and begged him several times, consented in doing something for him before he was able to pay the expenses. Usually they shall pay at a no-profit, no-loss basis. At this time the man obviously was in a miserable situation so our man out of his good heart did what he should never have done. The next day the rumour was all over the place and he received dozens of calls and letters and efforts to persuade him to do the same in other cases as well. And there are other cases of the same kind. One of the servants, for instance, complained how miserable his conditions were and after severe pressure he was given a little bit of money. The day thereafter they were queuing up to get money. Unfortunately they have so much better understanding of the immediate pleasures that can be gotten for a sum of money today than of the more remote but also much more lasting benefits that can be drawn from a continued effort to develop the fisheries".

It is awkward to be poor, but it is also awkward to be rich — it makes one feel bad in front of extreme poverty, and induces a certain uneasiness

[48]. The feeling that "we are here to help you, we do as well as we can" is natural and justified — and makes begging a constant source of irritation and isolation. "The many beggars who plague us in the villages and in our compound are another source of constant irritation" [49].

Fourthly, it would be extremely unrealistic not to mention the very human factor of *irritation*. We shall take up the problem of mutual perception later, and only touch on what the local conditions may do to the human mind. This is an old-timer speaking [49]:

"You can never tell how a person will behave down here from what you know about him at home. He may be the nicest man in Norway, and turn into a bore with fits of anger and bad temperament after some time in India — and vice versa: you may feel about a person that this will never result in anything good, and he may prove to be the nicest of them all. Conditions are so different, and they bring out new and unknown aspects of one's personality. Norwegians may try to keep the rhythm they are used to, only to find out that they lose too much time in frustration and irritation, anger and quarrels. After some time they either break down or relax a little, they learn from the local population to take matters less seriously. But in the meantime much harm may have been done to human relations."

The newcomer, whose tragic part it is to play the role of the eager reformer who is converted into the more easy-going style, is often commented on: "after some time, he became like the rest of us".

It should be noticed that this presupposes overlap in personnel, if there is a complete shift of personnel this factor will need time to get established. One may ask what this has to do with the absence of contact, and we suggest an answer along these lines: non-instrumental, voluntary contact presupposes motivation and a human involvement with other people that is not easily developed in a state of constant irritation. In the beginning open conflicts are shunned and there may be more of a honeymoon atmosphere, later on frustrations accumulate. There may, as a matter of fact, be restraining forces within project personnel and villagers that prevent contact in order not to expose the bad temper too openly to others. On the other hand, it may be argued that precisely under this condition should contact with the villagers be a suitable occasion for some renewal of the possibilities of human interaction. We need more insight into why this does not seem to be the case, and that must have something to do with the perception of and by the villagers. This will be the topic of the next section.

A factor of some importance here may be an element of displaced aggression. After an initial period of general support in press and parliament, the project and its officers have been violently criticized by some parts of the press. Norwegian personnel may have felt that Indians more than they themselves were to blame if anybody at all should be blamed. Many

Indians may be perceived as "trouble-makers" as time goes on and since association is so often interpreted as acceptance, there will be controls against association.

Fifthly in section 1.2 many reasons were given for local officials to intervene and institute themselves as intermediaries between, *in casu*, Norwegians and villagers. In the project area, one theory has been that the Norwegians should communicate via the Indian officials with whom they seem to have obtained a good working relationship. There are some reasons why this theory seems unfortunate, however.

Project officers, coming from the outside, have only general knowledge of these particular villages in the same sense that all Norwegians living in Oslo have some general knowledge of conditions at Svolvaer, Lofoten. They can be as wrong as to their knowledge and feelings as Norwegians who have lived in the villages for some time. Actually, it may be more a question of human intuition and experience than place of birth [50]. On the other hand, there is more to be gained than to be lost if this point has some bearing on the organization of the contact.

Then, Indian officials or project officers of importance are said to be of relatively high caste, mostly Hindu and mostly Congress Party [51]. These three characteristics alone are enough to create barriers of communication that the Norwegians perhaps could have penetrated because the Norwegians are 1. outside the caste system, 2. outside the religious distinctions, and 3. outside these particular political groupings.

Finally, the communication between important Indian officials and the fishermen does not seem to be the best either, at least as indicated by what one of them has to say about communication with the cooperative:

"Well, we have meetings and meetings and meetings evening after evening and quite a lot of the fishermen are present, and we present to them our plans. Now, when we present the plans we know that somebody will always stand up and criticize them, and they will go on arguing hour after hour after hour. Then at the end of the meeting late at night we will usually say, listen, you have to accept this, it is important, it must be passed, otherwise we cannot continue. And then they will pass it. So we could just as well have skipped the whole meeting, it seems only a waste of time and they are not really interested in contributing good ideas, they are mostly interested in quarreling, and of course they are interested in seeing to it that they personally do not risk even the slightest short-run loss from any scheme."

From one of the fishermen the counterpart of this story was obtained (as usual, the important point is not whether his points are all true, but that he believes them to be true):

"You see, they arrange meetings now and then, but you know all these cooperatives set up along the coast are not set up because they are wanted by the people, but because

585

of an order from above. They look nice on the paper, they are numbered, etc., and then the plans are read to us, but our opinion is never really taken seriously. In addition to this, they make no effort to explain beforehand, everything is presented when it is already too late for us to object. When the whole project was inaugurated, for instance, there was nobody who ever came to the villagers to explain what was going to happen. They could easily have arranged a meeting and tried to explain it to us. That was not done. They could have written articles in the paper, there is a paper that would be good for this purpose, but that was only done three years after the project had been started. The whole thing come as a shock to us, and if it hadn't been for the fact that some of the Norwegians in the beginning of the project went around and talked with us, we would never have been able to clear away some of the misunderstandings there were."

We do not say that Norwegians would have done better, although the famous "stranger effect", in addition to the reasons mentioned above, might have given them an advantage if forms of cooperation with their counterparts were found [52]. The important factor is the partial blocking of certain kinds of contacts and the specificity of the whole status of the Norwegian this entails. If they seek contact with the villagers, it may be perceived as additional threat to the rank of some Indian counterparts to the extent they see knowledge of the local scene as their main asset.

Sixthly, the difficulties in establishing contacts should be mentioned. There is an enormous cultural difference and only people with motivation and talents in the direction of bridging such gaps will have the courage to try. Relative to a situation where all Norwegians spoke nothing but Norwegian and all villagers nothing but Malayalam the situation is certainly conducive to contact: but few of the villagers and certainly not all of the Norwegians speak English well enough to make for fluent and easy exchange [53]. Interpretation is time-consuming and tiring. More important is perhaps the factor of having something to talk about:

"You cannot really talk to these fishermen, even if you make use of an interpreter, they are only standing there glancing at you and do not say anything sensible. But with the intellectuals, with the educated people in the villages everything is of course different and it should be possible to have a nice talk with them, However, I am so busy so my time really does not permit me to do it".

In this statement there is an unmistakable connotation of class difference, and there is little doubt that the combination of class and cultural difference impedes contact considerably. One source of contact, where the *class* difference is almost eliminated is the *boat club*. The club is located in Quilon, nicely situated at the waterfront, at the Government's Guesthouse, and serves as a meeting-place for the Norwegians and relatively rich Indians. But this is certainly not a place to meet the villagers, and not even a place to meet the rank and file Indians from Quilon town. For this reason it may even be that the boat club impedes contact with villagers because it may provide project personnel with the illusion that "good contact" is established. At a dinner in the boat club there is always an occasion to meet nice and important people in Quilon, with their wives, and to have interesting talks with them, but their knowledge of village life is not necessarily what a Norwegian can pick up quickly — with the only exception that it seemed to be of a more dogmatic kind than a foreigner in most cases would permit himself to express.

There is also the kind of contact where the *cultural* difference is almost eliminated, i.e. between Norwegians. Even in this field the "myth of the past" had it that there was more contact between high and low in the project in its first phase. Personality characteristics *apart*, this is to a large extent a function of the bureaucratization and routinization of the work that comes when the initial phase is overcome. Patterns are established, what charisma there is gets routinized, the pioneer spirit vanishes and the outcome is a kind of equilibrium where Norwegians bring into the organization what they are used to from Norway. But, however understandable this is, the villagers do not fail to notice it, and the class differences and distances they notice among the Norwegians partly serve as a counterargument when Norwegians argue that caste differences and rules impede progress, and partly serve to undermine the moral position of the Norwegians.

One factor that should be remembered in connection with cultural differences is the almost complete absence of any training of the personnel for this purpose [54]. There are many reasons for this, one of them being the general difficulty in getting personnel, and this is not conducive to additional requirements. The discontented old-timer, hence, finds fertile and unprepared soil when he starts his indoctrination of the newcomer and tries to imbue him with his scepticism. There is one reason why the discontented old-timer should be more outspoken than the contented one: he is more likely to get group support for the simple reason that all of them, more or less, will have encountered some of the difficulties. The negative indoctrination of the newcomer serves the function of preventing him from initiatives that will challenge the validity of their own positions and prejudices.

It is hard to estimate the importance of group living where cross-cultural contact is concerned. Probably, this is one of the major impediments, because it emphasizes the contrasts in standard and general culture and because it provides Norwegians with a handy reservoir of human contact: their own kind. But in addition to all this there is another structural factor. We postulate, in spite of all we say to the contrary, a motivation for establishing contacts, and we know from observation and many interviews that the ability to establish contact nevertheless is one of the main sources of prestige in the local community. "He is very clever undoubtedly, but has no contact at all with the fishermen — they just stay away from him"

587

— "Well, his work is very irregular, but he has a marvellous ability to make friends with the local people", etc., are very typical comments. In other words, we may postulate a certain competition, and even jealousy when others make good friends. In a physically close group as the camp itself the reward for success will probably be higher, but the price of failure will also be higher. The whole group will be witnesses to the first, clumsy approaches, and there will be less chance for the experimenting, unobserved by others, that scattered living permits. Thus, the group form that explains absence of contact serves at the same time as a protection against highly visible failures. In the camp pretenses to have more contacts than is actually the case are easily revealed — with scattered houses small exaggerations etc. might pass unnoticed.

A *seventh* reason: even among the Norwegians and the local counterparts off-work contacts are considerably less frequent than they were in the project's first phase — probably mainly for the reasons already outlined. It is less challenging, interesting and functional. In addition, as time goes on, conflict material may accumulate and sediment, thus creating fronts and issues [55]. Apart from a very few exceptions the two groups do not eat together (festive occasions excepted) — the Indians go by car to Quilon and return after lunch. For both parties interdining would mean talking English, which may be a hardship on both, climatic conditions at mid-day taken into consideration.

Eighthly: obviously, for administrative reasons there will be a tendency to negotiate with administrative units that constitute the whole project area. Negotiations with units making up only part of the area may look like a waste of time — the other units at the same level may disagree, local jealousies may greatly complicate the whole matter — whereas what super-units decide may be consequential to the whole area. Thus, there will be a tendency for administrative contact to address itself to higher levels in the hierarchy. The question, empirically, is this: how far up does one have to go? We disregard for the moment the frequent assertion made about developing countries by Westerners, that "you have to go to the top, everything else fails". It shows up that the Ashtamudi lake inlet serves as a border-line not only between the two *karas*, the residential villages Neendakara and Sakthikulangara, or the two administrative villages (with the corresponding panchayat council), but also between two *taluks* (Karunagapally and Quilon Taluk) so that the first unit to comprise the whole area is a *district, in casu* Quilon district, which is at the first level below Kerala state itself. As it is important to deal with the two *karas* symmetrically, one can imagine that this structural fact is conducive to high level interaction only. And this corresponds very well to the observation that whereas the Norwegians were fairly conversant with high level officers like the District

Collector in Quilon and governmental officers in Trivandrum, they did not seem to be so knowledgeable with regard to the local leaders. They rarely knew their names (only names of the old ones, presumably those who had been contacted in the first years, from the beginning on); they had not met them (as was for instance the case with the new Catholic minister three months after his arrival); and they knew little about the local administrative units such as the panchayat council. It seems safe to say that there is a preponderance of high level interaction at the expense of low level interaction.

This should in no way be perceived as a criticism of the selection of the project area [56]. To mention only one potentially very positive function of this arrangement: a borderline between two *taluks* in the very center of the project means that at least two *taluks* with their administrative personnel are involved, and this is turn means that there is less of a problem of paternalism and particularism. At the same time, the area comprises two religions so that the claim of religious favoritism cannot easily be made. Our point is only that the structural arrangement is conducive to high level contact and to legitimize the ideology that "it is only a waste of time to wait and start with the lower echelons". And this *might* have been one among other counterarguments in the selection of the project area.

To continue the list, we are now at number *nine*: *maximization of institutionalized rank* leads to top level contacts at the expense of low level contacts. Everybody knows that contact is more often between status equals. Ambassadors meet, and villagers meet — but ambassadors and villagers meet only rarely. The exact correspondence between Indian and Norwegian hierarchies has perhaps not been worked out, but it is tempting to draw the conclusion that one's own rank corresponds of the rank of the person with whom one interacts. It would be less than human not to prefer high rank interaction to low rank interaction for this very reason, and this may be particularly true for Norwegians who suddenly find themselves in a milieu where high status people are abundant and more accessible to them than ever before.

A certain amount of social insecurity may also lead to efforts to stay away from low status contacts after the job is finished — if you cannot get high contacts you can at least improve your position by staying away from the low ones.

And this brings us to the *tenth* and final reason on our list: Top level contact is by no means an unanticipated consequence of the development, but a deliberate instrument designed to speed up the work of the project. For this reason high rank foreign service personnel (an ambassador, a consul general) were recently called upon to serve as project directors [57] whereas the first directors were an engineer and specialist on fisheries. A former diplomat will probably feel that his particular talents are wasted if the *only* contacts are low order ones. Squatting in a panchayat house may be colorful and interesting, but hardly a setting for his particular talents and experience to be fully utilized. He will feel that his talents should be used at the level they are geared towards, which means high up. Upper class style requires upper class settings to unfold itself. And it can even be phrased stronger than this: it *may* well be that *trained capacity for high level contact at the same time is a trained incapacity for low level interaction*, for many reasons not to be elaborated here. The highlights for the project will be the top level meetings, and this will set a pattern for low level personnel as well. The leader of a group will be imitated, and the more prestige his activities have the more he probably will be imitated.

To sum up: we have tried to give a number of reasons why low level contact is not engaged in, and have, to some extent, explained it by the frequency and dominance of top contact. Contacts with New Delhi, Trivandrum, Quilon or local contacts by no means exclude each other logically, but they may be more or less compatible in a more empirical sense. Different phases in the progress of the project require different emphases, and different levels require different approaches, training of the project leader, and style. If low rank personnel try to emulate their leader, there is a limit to how far they can follow him on the road to New Delhi. But there is less constraint on how far they can follow him into the fishermen's huts.

This has two important consequences, both supported by the intuitive impressions and observations we have obtained so far. When low level contact is seen as most important, the contact between different levels of personnel is probably also better, because of the need for exchange of information and experience. The Norwegian fishermen become more relevant to a locally oriented director than to the New Delhi or Trivandrum oriented director. But the consequence of this is that contact between Norwegians of different rank will deteriorate when high level contacts dominate.

And secondly, when high level contact is the style, even at the expense of low level contact, low rank Norwegians will have to direct more of their interaction and need for social contact to fellow Norwegians. When high rank Norwegians are socially distant, and the experience of rank and file personnel is of less relevance to them, and when contacts with villagers are very limited, then interaction with colleagues is the only possibility left. The amount of friction and tension that may result from this is not hard to imagine — if the safety valves called weekend trips, vacations in Norway, etc., are not fully utilized.

Finally, let us repeat that we fully realize the value of high level contact as instrumental in terms of obtaining a license, or getting a job done. But if one distinguishes between *instrumental, task-centered contact* and the more *expressive, person-centered contact* the instrumental gain may certainly become an expressive loss — as we have tried to indicate. From the practical point of view, the dilemma lies in the problem of to what extent an expressive loss may mean a long-term loss also where practical tasks are concerned. Although this is probably the case, it may be more so in the beginning of a project than towards the end. Hence, if we are now approaching the end of the project, there is a certain logic to the phase movement we have indicated.

2.4. *The perception of each other*

If nations were to be placed on Sorokin's ideational-sensate continuum [58] "India" and "Norway" would have to be placed at quite a distance from each other. And this holds *a fortiori* for the Indians in the villages and the Norwegians in the camp; the general village culture contains so many elements incompatible with sensate culture, and the kind of Norwegians who would dominate a TA project would more often than not have ideological orientations incompatible with ideational culture. This will be the dominant theme in their perception of each other, where tendencies to description and evaluation in terms of the culture of one's own group and not of the other groups' culture, will prevail. Today, this psychological mechanism is so well known and recognized that the problem is to explain accurate perception, not ethnocentric perceptions. Actually, we have little to say that has any bearing on this — only some scattered notes.

The villagers were very willing to tell how they felt about Norwegians, even without being asked. Unfortunately, most of their comments were about specific people as perhaps is usually the case under such circumstances. However, a kind of general picture emerged: First of all, there was not much tendency to perceive the Norwegians in a stereotyped way. *Norwegians were seen as very different from each other*, a fisherman even pointed out that "there are as big differences between the Norwegians as between Norwegians in general and Indians". When this statement comes from a person who has not had direct contact with the project, it seems correct to interpret it as an indication that the total amount of contact cannot have been so bad as some other impressions may lead one to believe.

A second point is more trivial: *Norwegians are seen as tall and strong and energetic*. They work hard, but they do not take the climate too well. Some of them are fond of girls and liquor, but this, from one informant's point of view, was seen as a positive trait. Evidently, it proved that Norwegians were human beings, and hence that they could be treated as human beings. There was not a single rumor as far as could be ascertained within a short period to the effect that Norwegians were corrupt, made use of bribes or made use of other suspect ways of getting what they wanted. To what extent other traditional underdog stereotypes of topdogs hold in this area we do not know.

To the Norwegians the main puzzle was the factor of caste, of which the knowledge was relatively scant. Division of labor is found everywhere, but the division of labor implicit in the caste system is very different from what Norwegians are used to. The divisions are along lines such as dirty — not dirty, manual — not manual, and killing — not killing, and these factors correlate so that some people do dirty, manual work that even included killing, and other people do clean, nonmanual work that excluded killing. Fishermen, by the logic of their vocation, had to be in the first group, and hence of low caste. On board a ship, or in the medical office, these lines cut between people in the Indian society and exclude some work-combinations. To Norwegians, this creates difficulties, particularly in emergency situations — and stories about work that was not done for what was held to be caste reasons abounded, and never ceased to circulate. There were stories about how an assistant to the physician could do some kind of paper work, but not, for instance, carry boxes with medicine from the store room, etc. [59]. Similarly, it was observed that when a big sword-fish should be hauled on board a trawler, which meant some tension and even danger, the division of labor still held to some extent. When one of the wires broke, it did not seem to be a matter of course, as it might have been onboard a Norwegian ship, that everybody did as best he could regardless of what kind of work it would involve him in. Such incidents often created, partly due to the constant level of irritation that partly stems from the climate, certain outbursts that must be very disagreeable to all parties involved.

In a sense, this is one particular variation of the general theme that Norwegians do not adjust themselves to some Indian conceptions and attitudes towards *work*. For instance, Indian fishermen go to the job dressed in beautiful and clean *dhoti* and change when they are onboard the ship. A Norwegian in a similar situation would already have put on clothes at home that he sees as suitable both on the road to the work and on the job itself. A certain tension can easily arise also for this simple reason. More important, perhaps, is how the Indian perceives the situation, and the case can probably be made that he interprets the Norwegian as a person for whom everything is inferior in value to the value of work alone.

This is particularly interesting in conflicts between Family and Work. Here is a Norwegian speaking:

"You see, you can never quite tell what they are going to do. You have an appointment and the Indian tells you that he will come. But then suddenly he doesn't show up and the reason is that his brother is home on a vacation and everything has to yield for that brother. Or his son has fallen ill or has to go to the dentist's. In that case, of course the Indian has to accompany him but the obligation he has on his job goes down the drain."

But what do Indians say, what is their counterpart of this image? One of the villagers had this to say:

"Honestly I feel the Norwegians are very different from us. They are always working by the clock, they are slaves of the clock, so to say. I have seen cases of Norwegians who feel it is more important to go to a meeting than to take care of their family or their children if they are in distress. Whenever you meet them leisurely, they are always talking about the work. I am sure they even dream of it. It seems that the job fills their lives to an extent it would never do here in India. To us other things are equally and even more important. Or course a person must work in order to live, but what is the use of life if work is the only thing to do?

The symmetry in these two statements is almost perfect, and it would be extremely interesting to know how many Indians and Norwegians are able to go one step further and see themselves as the other party sees them. The impression was that this is not often the case, even after this culture contact of relatively long duration. Rather, it looks like the relative priority of Work in the Norwegian value-system and the relatively priority of Family in the Indian value-system in certain conflicts felt by them both was seen as self-evident to Norwegians and Indians respectively. There seemed to be one important difference, however; the Norwegians were perhaps more eager to express the resentment of the other party's value-system than vice versa, and in this particular social structure that seems legitimate because a value system that does not give a certain priority to Work can be interpreted as detrimental to the whole purpose of the project. If the impression of more resentment on the part of the Norwegians is true, it can probably be explained on the basis of a shared feeling of their cultural pattern as more legitimate.

The conflict-material in the project district is abundant. Just to mention some groupings: Neendakara vs. Sakthikulangara, which coincides partly with Hindu vs. Catholic, high caste vs. low caste [60], those who think they will lose more than they gain vs. those who think they will gain more than they may lose (or have nothing to lose), economically speaking, those with a "traditional" orientation vs. those with a more "modern" orientation, the population of the area vs. their neighbors, Norwegians vs. Indians, project personnel vs. villagers, those who have already gained something vs. those who feel they have gained nothing from the project, conflict between two (or more) generations of Norwegians, conflicts between project personnel who are thing-oriented (fisheries, waterpipes) and those who are person-oriented (health services); conflicts over economic distances in the Norwegian camp, etc. Fortunately, these potential or actual conflicts do not all organize people residing in the district along the same lines, so the stabilizing effect of having some, but by no means all, friends or enemies in common obtains. The possibilities of interesting analyses are manifold.

There is, however, another line of thought that is of some importance in this connection. Many of the conflicts mentioned above existed prior to the project, many of them are induced by the project — but the project has some relevance for all of them. Although conflicts of this kind are by no means unknown in other parts of the world, the conflict elements specific to the project are unique, and *contained within the area*. Since TA always means a disruption of *some* kind of equilibrium even in a situation of extreme frustration and disequilibrium, conflicts are bound to arise in the microcosmos of the project area. This does not mean that the conflicts will be projected on to the macrocosmos of the nation states, *in casu* in the relations between Norway and India. For one thing, they may simply not be known at the top level, where the administrative and political elites communicate. Hence, although it is quite possible and even probable, that a TA project creates more short-term discontent than it causes integration between donors and receivers in the project area, *the converse may be true higher up*. (For technical *aid*, the relation may well be the opposite of this again; with more integration in the area where the aid is injected.) This is a typical case of a possible positive function of bad communication between local and central authorities.

Control from above, over a distance of many thousand miles, as between Norway and Kerala, presents the project with an interesting problem. Says Sandven [61]:

"The Board considers it to be of importance that every Board member shall be given opportunity to visit Kerala as a member of a Board delegation in order to get a first hand impression of the Project. At least once a year a Board delegation goes to India, and whenever possible the delegation visits are timed to the meetings of the Standing Committee."

The Board, if substitutes for the chairman and the vice-chairman are counted, has 14 members — all of whom cannot possibly go at the same time. The policy is to use delegations with a nucleus that remains more or less permanent and add to it so that "every Board member shall be given opportunity to visit Kerala". The consequence of this policy is that the distribution of number of visits where the Board members have participated is U-shaped [62] (Fig. 16.7).

FIGURE 16.7 *The pattern of board member visits*

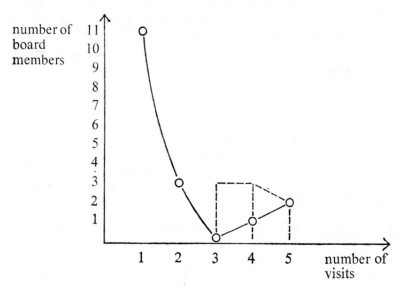

In other words: *two* board members have has as many as five visits, *one* has had four visits, *none* three visits, *three* two visits and finally: *eleven* members have had one visit each. This makes a total of 31 visits, out of which two persons "control" (32%). This pattern is interesting, and has important consequences. (In addition several other prominent Norwegians have been to the project area, including the Prime Minister and the Foreign Minister.) Given the economic constraint, the pattern makes visits by all Board members impossible. The three persons who have been on as many as four or five visits *ex officio* were present (one of them, or two of them) on nine of the twelve Board delegations up to date. This means on the one hand that they can save the newcomers from misinterpretations and from some of the difficulties involved in adjusting to a country where they have never been before — but there is also the possibility of, if not indoctrination, then the passing on of a certain perspective, of emphases, etc. To the newcomer to India everything is new and causes emotional and intellectual reactions, not only the project.

For anybody not very experienced in traveling etc. one trip will probably not be enough to understand what is India-specific and what is project-specific. Further, one trip gives only one point in time, and never the dynamics of the project. If there is a second turn this factor may be corrected, but only if the Board retains its composition — and that is not necessarily "democratic" either. Thus, the peripheral members have considerably less chance to control what happens than the two or three central members.

The nucleus will gain a superiority due to repeated visits that no opposition can beat. By adding one peripheral member at the time, the new member will probably "learn" to "understand" the central members' point of view. And, more likely than not, this *may* be a quite correct point of view.

Imagine the policy had been to send two people five times, three people four times and four people three times (total 31 visits as before). Economically it would have meant the same, but only nine people as against 17 would have had a chance to see the Project. As this visit is probably regarded as a reward, it would be hard to defend the monopoly on the reward, and the suspicion among the outsiders would increase. To be on a delegation may serve as an instrument of co-optation, and as a means of acquainting everybody with the project. On the other hand, the other policy would have given an opposition a chance to consolidate itself, at least if there were two disparate schools of thought in the Board from the beginning, each giving support and exercising pressure on its own delegation members. This structural condition is not met, however, since Board decisions are said to have been unanimous. So the problem is quite complex!

Let us finally point out again what we have already mentioned in section 1.5: the attitudinal consequence of a TA project is not only a function of how the people directly involved in the project from either country perceive each other, but also of how efficient communication is, upwards and downwards, in the donor as well as in the receiving country [63]. The more the central government knows of the many difficulties, and the more direct knowledge they obtain, the more likely is some measure of identification with their co-nationals, and adoption of their point of view. This *may* have consequences for the function of TA as an instrument of peace, but we do not know how — only that there have undoubtedly been occasions when insufficient or almost non-existing communication has been positive from the point of view of creating positive attitudes.

2.5. Conclusion

Repeatedly in this chapter we have made use of the idea that TA projects in general and the INP project in particular have *phases*, that the phases are the life-cycle of the project, and that they deserve closer study. Let us at this point collect most of what we have said about these phases and see what structures may emerge. For simplicity, we shall make use of the idea of two phases only, corresponding very roughly to the first and second half of the Indo-Norwegian project so far. First of all, let us point out the differences that have to do with the general factor of *time alone*, with no reference to the INP and regardless of whether the project is a success or a failure.

	first phase (beginning)	*second phase* (later)
general mode of work	exploratory, experimental	standardized, routinized
general attitude	waves of optimism and pessimism, strong feelings	"realistic" assessment, not so strong feelings
information about local population	obtained by personal explorations	handed over by old-timers
contact with local population	extensive, personal informal	limited, impersonal, formal
organization of work	informal, few regulations, much contact between experts and between experts and counterparts	formal, many regulations, less contact across class and nation, more with status equals from same nation
contacts outside project	limited, too much involvement in project	extensive, involvement in project not enough
conflicts	many latent but few manifest, tendency to shun open conflicts, "honeymoon" atmosphere, high degree of personal involvement	few latent that are not also manifest, conflicts handled in a prescribed and ritualized way, not much personal involvement
personnel are ranked	more on the basis of their achievements in their jobs.	more on the basis of how high jobs they have
social control	informal "talking it over"	formal or not at all
THE DREAM	to get established, to make things work smoothly, the myth of the future	back to the golden days when the project had more charm, the myth of the past

This is mere organizational theory and much of what is said can be derived from the simple fact that *time passes*. Thus, sooner or later patterns of social interaction that satisfy some of the more important functions will crystallize and be repeated, and that transition from the informal and exploratory to the formal and stabilized is precisely what is spelt out in these ten items. Particularly important is THE DREAM at the end, the relentless desire to be in the other phase — not that everybody will feel this way, we only postulate that it will be a recurring theme. Another important feature is the comparison with the "honeymoon", or the sociology of early love, when love is tender and human relations fragile and the partners are considerate to the extreme because they have not yet built up mechanisms and habits that make it possible to handle conflicts. An old couple may feel less of a romance, and still have the strength to take conflicts that would lead to complete rupture for young people recently fallen in love.

It goes without saying that the phase movement makes for considerable strain in the upper strata of the project. To be the leader of a project of this kind is not like stepping into an office job or a vacancy in a factory already established, because of the quickness with which the TA enterprise is supposed to pass through the first phase and get established. For that reason strains can be predicted when the project moves from the first into the second phase.

Let us then repeat some of the changes specific to the INP project that seem to have occurred:

	first phase (beginning)	second phase (later)
basis for salaries [64]	according to the person hired	according to the position needed
center of gravity for contact	local	higher up
background of directors	engineer, experts on fisheries	diplomats, administrators
focus of fishing experiments	beach-fishing, Quilon	ocean fishing, Cochin
focus of attention focus of local power	villages relatively to the second phase, with the Norwegians	extension of the project relatively to the first phase, with the Indians

Read vertically, we see the internal logic in the scheme: the villagers are no longer the only center of attention, the project is extended, due to many factors, new kinds of leadership are judged to be necessary. What is more interesting is not this change in project policy, *but how the change coincides with what we would expect from the phase movement policy.* Clearly, the more local and technical perspective of the first phase in the Indo-Norwegian project is more compatible with the first phase of any organization. Village level work is considerably less amenable to formalization than grandiose projects extending over several districts, and even nations, in Asia.

If we now compare the two lists, an interesting question that may be met with vehement denials from the project officers can be asked: *is it fruitful to regard the administrative changes in the second phase as an adjustment to the almost unavoidable organizational change that is more or less bound to take place?* In other words, were the leaders of the project in a sense directed by "an invisible hand" in addition to the undoubtedly good reasons for doing what they did? And another question which is more meaningful to people who know the project well: to what extent can personal hostilities be explained by difficulties in the transition from the first to the second phase? We do not know, but feel that this phase movement is a most important explanatory principle for the study of a TA project [65].

In conclusion, let us point out a consequence of this phase movement. If all foreign experts withdraw when the project is still in its first phase, speaking in terms of this organizational theory, the probability that the project will collapse under native control will increase. For in this phase the project is still a function of persons with personalities, not of positions with a high degree of substitutability of personnel. If substitutability among foreigners is not even obtained, there is, generally speaking, much less hope that natives can be substituted for all foreigners. But parts of the project may be ripe for change and give an occasion for the rest to have a visible model of the new conditions the project will have to adjust to. So the third phase is the take-over phase, and the project may look even more dull and run-of-the-mill to the villagers. It will have become a part of the local administration, just as intended, and perform its services with no glamor and no special excitement.

And that leads us back to where we started: in a boat, approaching the Malabar coast at a point where there is an inlet flanked by two white churches, a white beach with green palms, huts with thatched roofs and some modern-looking boats and installations. We can ask the same question as, no doubt, scores of Norwegians who have done their best to promote welfare in these two villages have asked: what will remain of all this twenty years after the Norwegians leave? Nobody knows, but it seems safe to say that the project has long since entered the second phase and that time for take-over is approaching. This is the meaning of technical assistance, as defined in the first chapter, and as intended by the Norwegian administration; Norwegians have come not to stay, but to leave. And to leave behind a piece of machinery and a piece of social organization, a couple of Norwegian words and expressions, and — after time has softened conflicts, frustrations and misunderstandings — some lasting human ties.

IV.17. European Security:
An Era of Negotiations?

From Adelphi Papers, No. 71.

PRIO publication No. 22—15.

Notes on page *728*.

In order to speculate on the international implications of social change in countries in all of Europe, from the more developed North to the less developed Mediterranean basin, from the most pure of the market economies in the West to the most centralized of the economies in the East, views are needed on at least three matters:

— the nature of international relations in Europe at the moment;
— the likely nature of social change in some major types of European countries in the coming years;
— a theory as to how social change in European countries will affect international relations.

I shall try to deal with these matters in this order, but would like immediately to anticipate a conclusion that to many may seem obvious: I do not think we are at the threshold of any golden era of peaceful relations in our peninsula of a continent. On the contrary, the last decades of this century may well prove to be extremely difficult, athough not necessarily in terms of the standard measure, the probability of what Europeans refer to as a Third World War, i.e. a war that not only originates in Europe, but also is fought in Europe.

All European powers, big and small, North, South, West and East, have declared themselves in favor of peace. However, there are two major philosophies contending for the minds of men when it comes to how peace can best be obtained. According to one, let us call it the *liberal* view, peace is obtained by suitable organization at the international or supranational, level, by building organizations that are viable, at those levels. The structure of peace is built at the levels between and above the nation state, it is not basically found in the nation state itself. Peace is a question of inter-

600

national organization, a view that contrasts sharply with the other view, the *marxist* view. According to that view the key to peace rests with the structure of the building unit, the nation-state. Only in a world of socialist nation states can peace be guaranteed, only in such states will the drive towards war be effectively extinguished.

It now seems relatively obvious to one who prefers a more eclectic position in the general liberal-marxist controversy, and who refuses to believe that these views are mutually exclusive, that there is some truth in both and that the validity of one or the other of these views may vary with historical circumstances. More concretely, the extreme versions of these views, that peace can be built using any type of nation state as a building block — democratic or fascist, for instance — *or* that peace comes as an extra gift as soon as the building blocks are the right ones (meaning socialist) regardless of how they are put together, are hardly worth being taken seriously — however frequently they may be found. A major challenge for peace research lies precisely in the effort to transcend the liberal-marxist controversy by trying to pave the way for some new thinking that can fill this gap, seeing the two views as mutually incomplete rather than as mutually incompatible. The structure of peace, even in the limited sense of absence of direct violence, seems to have subnational as well as inter- and supranational components, and this is a *fortiori* true if peace is also defined so as to include the absence of structural violence [1].

However this may be, the fact is that West and East in the twenty-five years since World War II ended have acted to a large extent from different social philosophies, and even when they have not, they suspect the other party of doing so. More concretely:

— the obvious implication of the *liberal* peace philosophy would be to try to integrate East together with West in a solid international and supranational framework so tightly woven that there would be little room for belligerent activity, above all because of the symbiotic nature of the relationship [2].
— the obvious implication of the *marxist* peace philosophy would be to try to contribute to the change of all European societies towards the type of society that contributes to peace, the socialist society [3].

It hardly needs any spelling out that the latter view, especially when it takes the form of support to Communist parties via the international Communist movement, is regarded as highly subversive by Western societies — and not only by governments in those societies, but generally by the great majority of citizens. The West does not seem to want to be saved from war by the East in this particular way, a fact that the East often fails to understand, or even pretends to deny by putting it down as one more case of false consciousness in the West, domination, economically, politically, militarily, culturally, of all Eastern countries bordering on the Soviet Union, one way or another, by the West (Britain, France, Germany — singly or combined). Of considerable importance is the extent to which international organizations starting with the UN are Western-dominated, one way or another (location, concepts, staff, finances, etc.). Finally, there is the Western economic offensive after the *détente* [4] especially when the way the EEC looks to the East, as well as the American economic penetration of Western Europe, are taken into account. Particularly important here would be the EEC's tendency to enter into treaties between united EEC on the one hand and separate nations on the other, to export technology and skills and import raw materials and to cater particularly to the consumer needs of the more privileged parts of the population. As is well known, several East European governments are currently negotiating treaties with the EEC. There are several interpretations of this: they are unaware of the possibility that this might decrease their autonomy and permit EEC domination, they are aware of it but think it can be controlled, or they are aware of it and hope for it — among other reasons to balance Soviet domination. I prefer the second interpretation, with some ingredients of the third.

Formulated very briefly one might perhaps say that the East fears the Western use of General Motors (and other multinational corporations) as much as, or more than, the West fears the Eastern use of the Communist Party — however pure the motives in terms of building a peace based on the *right* type of society in the latter case and the *right* type of international superstructure in the former. Both have good reasons for their anxieties although they also exaggerate and tend to see the other side as more clever, more cunning, more one-sided than it really is. But there is also a basis for a deal here: if we permit your Communist Parties, you permit our corporations.

Obviously, this image was more correct some years ago than today. Both parties today have softer versions of their views. Instead of outright subversive activity, the East has learnt to coexist with their own doctrine of *peaceful coexistence* between different political and economic systems. And the West has *perhaps* learnt that what is good for Western Europe is not necessarily considered good for Eastern Europe, particularly not *in* Eastern Europe, and that this applies to the majority of the population, not only to governments [5]. The West has *perhaps* learnt that *supranational structures have to be symmetrical*, that they will fail if they are used as instruments for Western hegemony one way or the other — as, for instance, when the EEC tries to establish deals with Eastern European countries one at a time. We say *perhaps* because we have the feeling that there has been more of a decline in Eastern efforts to subvert than in Western efforts to 'supervert', although this is hard to prove. One reason may be that this particular type of domineering activity is so essential to the capitalist system of the West in its present multinational corporation phase, whereas subversion in other countries is not in the same sense a *raison d'etre* of Eastern Communist states.

However, if one is generous and assumes a symmetry in the development here, East and West should now, ideally speaking, have arrived at a point in history where a basis exists for a more genuine East-West cooperation of a really symmetrical character. Symmetrical institution-building and active peaceful coexistence are concepts taken from different philosophies, but in their practical implications they may lead to about the same type of result: an effort to build peace in Europe on institutions like the ECE — the UN Economic Commission for Europe — vastly expanded in scope, and extended to include both Germanies as members. In a sense this type of development is a concession to the liberal view of peace based on the superstructure rather than on the infrastructure of the nation state. The Eastern initiative in the field of a European Security Conference can actually also be seen in this light, it is an effort to bring about a formalization of the *status quo*, which means a state of affairs where the East is truly independent of the West and there is no trace of pre-war domination. But this North-South aspect of East-West relations in Europe has never been well enough understood in the West, as domination is usually best understood by the dominated party.

We can now conclude this overview of East-West relations in Europe by distinguishing between the following aspects of what is often called the 'cold war':

1. *The North—South element in the East—West conflict*, the story of a dominated Eastern Europe that wanted to become truly independent, not only independent in the formal sense with an upper class tied to Western Europe (as in Latin America today, or Black Africa, to a large extent). For this historical process the Cold War was functional because it isolated East from West and gave it autonomy relative to the West. That domination by the Soviet Union was the result is another matter, and a separate problem: *it does not in itself make Western domination before the war or in a possible future more attractive*. Domination either by one party or by another is not seen as something constant, but as something of which to rid oneself; and the time will come for that process, too;

2. *The internal changes in feudal or precapitalist Eastern countries* with socio-economic and political systems very similar to many of the more

backward countries in the Third World today. In this process the upper classes, the ones with contacts in the West, suffered — and the sympathy for them crystallized sentiments and action in the West. Nobody had ever heard of the masses among the peasants in Poland and Hungary exposed to the whims and the whips of their landowners. They were as anonymous as the plantation workers in the Dominican Republic today — as opposed to the professionals, intellectuals and many others who are the main victims of the current suppression in Czechoslovakia. In my view these changes were *needed* in Eastern Europe and it is only to be regretted that they were not better understood by the West, but were seen only as a question of big power strategy. Also, I think two major mistakes were made: the East should not have engineered the coup in Czechoslovakia, a highly developed democratized country that has lost more than it gained, it seems, from a Communist take-over. Correspondingly, the West should not have maintained a conservative, even reactionary, regime in Greece but permitted a social revolution to pave the way for living conditions at least as high as in Bulgaria (not necessarily in terms of GNP/capita, but in terms of the level at which the lower part of the population lives); the argument is that these two countries are located wrongly, and many problems will still arise from this factor;

3. *Residues from World War II*, above all the division of Germany, Poland and the Berlin problems;

4. *problems arising from the military capabilities built up on either side.* The systems built up to keep the two sides apart so that they shall not trespass in any form on what the other side considers as his are so formidable that however strongly it can be argued that it may have averted violent encounters in Europe (apart from Greece, Cyprus, Hungary and Czechoslovakia) the cost is tremendous, the danger ever-present and likely to stay with us for a long time;

5. *and problems arising from the pursuit of associative policies* in a climate where the West still suspects the East of having subversive, and the East still suspects the West of having 'superversive', intentions — and both occasionally can pick up something that can be construed, rightly or wrongly, as evidence. The result is the well-known pendulum of 'on again, off again', swinging between associative and dissociative extremes, between *détente* and crisis, in a pattern to which Europeans have become fairly accustomed, even if they may not be very sophisticated at handling it. Neither side is sufficiently trained for this positive type of interaction with the other side.

Let us then turn to the speculations about social change in the various sectors of Europe so that we may later have some basis for an educated guess as to where these changes may lead us with regard to these five aspects of East-West relations. We would just like to emphasize once more the idea that right now the basis for East-West cooperation, ideologically as well as structurally, may be at an all-time high — for it may well be that both parties have learnt from Czechoslovakia in 1968 how the associative game has to be played, just as both parties learnt something about behavior in the nuclear age from Cuba in 1962. Since the basic theme of our speculations in connection with the future is that these conditions to a large extent are going to fade away, there is something tragic in the total picture. It is like two young persons, a man and a woman, who could meet each other in love and create fulfilment if it had not been for the circumstance that when they were closest to each other neither of them knew it, nor did they feel the closeness intensely enough, and both of them had other concerns on their minds.

Thus, an analysis of Western European politics today with the possible exception of the *Bundesrepublik* would certainly tell any observer that it is not East-West relations that weigh most heavily on the shoulders and the minds of foreign offices, parliaments, mass media and the public alike, but a mixture of intra-West European affairs centering on the EEC relations with the United States and relations with the Third World. The very negotiations and agreements between Bonn and Moscow which could herald the opening of a new age of cooperation seem to serve to make East-West relations even less important, among other reasons because there is no concrete program for the *au-delà* as there is a concrete program in connection with the EEC: to get the membership expanded from six to ten or some other number, and to add more functions. The *détente* and the ultra-stable character of East-West relations, in spite of pendulum swings and some ups and downs, make them in a sense uninteresting, and much more attention in Western Europe is focused on another front: the economic battle with the United States, a battleground where Right and Left somehow seem to join forces.

In a sense this is not strange. The West European nations are all liberal societies with varying degrees of personal freedom, and an essentially capitalistic economic system with varying degrees of state intervention. The game the United States is playing in Europe, of investment and systematic use of multinational corporations, is a game Western Europe can also play and is willing to play, although her ability to play that game has been seriously questioned. The game played in the Soviet Union and the East European countries, however one chooses to describe it, is definitely not a game chosen by the majority of the West European populations. Hence Western Europe is contained militarily by NATO and politically, economically and culturally by overwhelmingly dissociative policies, and that solves the problem for the time being. But this type of policy cannot be pursued with regard to the United States, an immensely powerful political and military ally. Here other strategies must be employed, such as the general European pastime of deriding and ridiculing American culture while heavily consuming it, and efforts to build an economic countervailing power of equal magnitude, capable of utilizing its own resources, including brains, and capable of doing to Black Africa what the United States has done to Latin America.

My major point is that this activity will prove satisfactory enough to West European politicians to distract attention from all-European problems. Politicians will continue to do as British politicians do, making themselves believe that they are engaged in politics at the all-European level when they discuss when, how, whether and why 'Britain should join Europe' when in reality what they do is to engage in a Western economic bloc formation that may or may not stem the tide of American dominance, but almost definitely will make symmetrical cooperation with Eastern Europe even more difficult than before. With EEC becoming the overwhelming part of Western Europe, the latter becomes so strong that any cooperative deal with the East is almost bound to be asymmetrical. The result, I predict, is that the East will abstain from such deals above a minimum and token level and become increasingly self-sufficient, so that the division of Europe may last for the rest of the century — unless EEC either gets into serious difficulties or includes all European states as members.

However, the extension and expansion of the EEC is not the only thing taking place in Western Europe at the moment. There are also other factors, all of them of great significance for future development. More concretely, we are thinking of the *subnational* independence movements, and of all the complex phenomena associated with the youth revolt of the late 1960s. They have one factor in common: the nation state, that impressive political structure that emerged out of events in the 17th, 18th and 19th centuries, has in a sense come to the end of the road. This does not mean that nation states will not continue to exist on the map; that there will not be parliaments, governments, prime ministers and such things — even national armies. What is meant is rather that the nation state in Western Europe, and particularly in North-Western Europe, is rapidly approaching the stage which municipalities have already reached. Borders will become like county borders, highly porous. Much more important: identity will become like county identity and recruitment into top positions will become increasingly unattractive to the more outstanding of the younger generation. To be a national parliamentarian or politician will have a tinge of the old-fashioned, of the person who did not quite understand what the end of the 20th century is about; like the blacksmith in the age of automobiles. Stated in different and quite chilling terms: *increasingly mediocre politi-*

cians will have increasingly far- and deep-reaching means of control and power at their conmmand, and will probably bring the nation state into an escalation of disrepute by committing increasingly colossal blunders. Having more and more to conceal, they may also become increasingly secretive. And they will also become increasingly irrelevant to the younger generation because they will continue enacting the programs that were built into them at an earlier stage, right after, during and even before World War II. Like some old-fashioned computers they may be unable to change their programs. The programs have to run their course, and the politicians with them. Constructing an EEC to solve the problems of the First World, at the expense of new problems with the Second and Third World.

Supranational structures like EEC will, of course, erode the nation state from above but do not constitute any fundamental challenge to the basic framework of thinking and acting. The super-state is merely the nation state writ large; based on internal cohesion and planning and a front toward the outside: *dissociation* towards the East, *domination* towards the South according to the well-known formulas of capitalist societies (alliance with a small upper class of entrepreneurs, a network of subsidiaries, creation of a market for consumer goods of interest for, say, 10 % of the population, and *competition* with the United States. As stated above: there is nothing new in this, old politicians can be recruited into what superficially look like new roles, but regardless of how much or how little they manage to create a central authority, the member nation states will gradually vanish into some kind of oblivion.

With the weakening of the nation state, it is only to be expected that *subnational* independence movements will gain strength: in Wales, Scotland and Ulster in several forms, Brittany, Catalonia, the Basque provinces, the regions of Italy, possibly among the Lapps across Norway, Sweden and Finland, and many more of whom we do not even dream today. They may never become nation states in the sense we use that term today, for part of their tragedy may, in a sense, be that as they approach some kind of autonomy the goal they are striving for has already declined in significance and changed its nature. In other words, I would not predict that all of these units would ever become separate politics with monopolistic control of what happens inside their own territories, but I would predict that they would have their own representatives in supranational organizations. The territorial nation state will be eaten up both from above and below, and the two currents will meet in a system of representation that is more decentralized and more sensitive to regional variation within today's nations than we have so far envisaged.

But all of this is of minor consequence, for it is all within the old paradigms of the territorial policy and the liberal society, with its emphasis

607

on individualism and a vertical social structure, and with its emphasis on success and social climbing as motivations for economic growth. All of these assumptions are so effectively challenged by today's younger generation that it is hard to believe that they will be able to survive this century in anything but a highly modified form. The younger generation seems to be *transnational*, and much more so than their parents. This should not be confused with *supranational*: they do not seem to be particularly interested in supranational institution-building, except, perhaps, groups like the Young Conservatives in Britain. The transnationalism consists in identification with similar and similar-minded persons in other countries, to the point where nationality plays no role at all. There are values and anti-values involved, they are directed against structures in their own societies and in favor of new structures. In relation to the basically marxist East their goal is social transformation and reconstruction, not inter- and supranational institution-building. Their horizontal loyalties across borders are stronger than the vertical identification upwards to their own establishments — and this seems to be true not only for a small, vocal and active group but increasingly also for the silent majority. Their efficiency is impressive: during the events of spring 1968 there was far better coordination at student level than at the university administration and politician level; and young peace researchers today, to take another example, cooperate far better across borders than their predecessors in more classical approaches to international relations were ever able to do.

What is their social goal? Here it should be remembered that the New Left is not identical with old marxism but is rather a mixture of updated marxism with strong elements of existentialism. The uniformity of certain autocratic regimes is rejected as strongly as the vertical, inegalitarian nature of liberal, capitalist society. State capitalism is not seen as a solution to the problems of private capitalism. The Soviet Union is rejected as strongly by some as is the United States. There is a groping, a search for a social form that permits basic equality, a democracy not only for the strongest who can survive and make themselves leaders and élites, but a democracy where the distinction between weak and strong is obliterated. At the same time, there is a search for a social form that permits self-realization and self-individuation through decentralization, even if it should be a much lower level of so-called standard of living than is found today. In general, there is a rejection of the politics of *growth* and a yearning for a politics of *justice* to substitute for it: a justice that encompasses all of mankind in world thinking and planning and acting, not only that particular patch of territory referred to as one's own nation state.

That there are rival groups among the young is well known, and much will depend on whether the groups that are most violently directed against the existing structure and want to revolt against it in their struggle for a more egalitarian structure will be able to join forces with the groups that are more interested in decentralization, and 'doing one's own thing'. If they are able to do so, the nucleus of new social forms may be forming before our eyes. But even if they are not able to do so, it is hard to believe that the imprint of this kind of thinking will not be considerable. To take some specific examples:

— it will be increasingly hard to mobilize young people for territorially defined, centralized political roles;
— it will be increasingly hard to mobilize young people for important roles in the technical-economic structure on which societies are built, for the roles in big corporations and governmental bureaucracies. Super-state bureaucracies will probably still attract many, but that may only be for some time, not for the rest of the century;
— the anti-establishment will be able to mobilize increasingly stronger forces, qualitatively and quantitatively, against establishment policies. This may take such forms as organized boycotts of establishment positions and professions (such as the foreign service, the military, many positions in the bureaucracy and so on) and organized actions against establishment policies (such as building of dams and power plants that may destroy natural beauty, anti-pollution actions, any military activity and so on). It is certainly not inconceivable that the younger generation may have it in their power to paralyze Western society as we know it, and very many of them would see this as preferable to its continued existence. Actions like coordinated tearing down of all billboards alongside roads in Europe because they are seen as an insult to the human mind and an affront to anybody's aesthetic sense, or the occupation of TV and radio stations that engage in excessive commercialism or dissemination of violence (on American TV there is an average of one sadistically performed murder per hour) will be nothing compared to what may be organized in the future.

In short, Western society is in crisis. This is extremely well-reflected in a large-scale public opinion study that was recently (1967—68) carried out in ten nations (eight of them in Europe, North and South, East and West, and two outside Europe, India and Japan). What the study shows is that the higher the level of technical-economic development, the higher the resistance to further advances of science and the higher the level of pessimism about development [7]. The feeling is that the future is full of the evil effects of development. There is even the feeling that development towards the end of this century will be retrogressive — a feeling that was particularly pronounced in Britain, Norway and the Netherlands. In short, there is what one might call a *development fatigue*. But it should immediately be pointed out that this did not apply to the less developed countries in this sample of European nations. Hence, it is not a phenomenon that applies necessarily to Western Europe but to the Northern part of it: *Spain showed as much optimism about development and enthusiasm for science as Poland, for instance.* Hence, this seems to indicate that it is North-Western European society that is in crisis, partly because of the negative effects of development, but more, we feel, *because of the feeling of having run out of a program.* The more developed nations need new goals since their means have already to a large extent satisfied their old goals — and this is, of course, precisely where the younger generation enters with their new values and insistence on the old. For the less developed nations new goals are not needed: there may be scarcity of means for the old goals, but at the same time there is the feeling that a program exists — that of technical-economic development.

The implication of this is probably that the future of East European societies must be seen in a completely different light from that of North--Western Europe. The study certainly revealed that no other countries have such high levels of feeling of *personal* powerlessnes as the two socialist countries, Poland and Czechoslovakia; but that is not the same as pessimism about development. There is faith in science and development — the evils of pollution, of family disruption, of narcotics, crime, alcoholism, mental disease, not to mention far more basic critique of vertical, growth-oriented society in general, have not (yet?) made their full impact. Hence the prediction might be that societies in the East, but also to some extent in the South of Europe, will continue along the old paths for many years to come.

The implication of this, in Eastern Europe, for the three-pronged attack on the nation state predicted for (North-) Western Europe — supranationalism, subnationalism, and transnationalism — is simple: there will be much less of this. The program of nation state building still has to run its course, there is much work to do within it that will capture the minds of men. More specifically:

— the trend towards *supranationalism* in Eastern Europe will continue to be weak. This is not only because of Soviet hegemonial tendencies, although these are more political and military than economic and cultural. Nor is it because of what in the West is loosely called 'nationalism'. Rather, it is because of a general and shared feeling that there are so many fascinating and attractive tasks and problems to be solved within the confines of one's own state, and capable of being solved within it, that the overwhelming proportion of political energy will be channelled in that direction. It should be noted that this is not the same as saying that there is popular support for the government in power. Precisely the desire to change governments is in itself a sign of the relevance of the nation state; it is the nation where people no longer care who is in power that is in real trouble. Nor is this the same as saying that there is virtue in poverty and vice in affluence. The point is that there is virtue, if that is the word, in having a goal in search of means, and vice in having plenty of means in search of a goal. The need for more consumer goods in the East also comes into this, and transnationalism will probably increasingly be seen as the means to achieve that type of satisfaction;

— the trend towards *subnationalism* will be weak. This is not because there are no minorities which could have aspirations in this direction; Eastern Europe is full of them. Rather, it is because the nation state is not so demoralized, so full of doubts about its own basic legitimacy, as in the West. Any such attempts will be weakened by internal doubts in the movement itself as well as by fierce repression. It will be easier to use the national armies against secessionist attempts in the East than in the West, and not merely because the regimes are more autocratic;

— the trend towards *transnationalism* will also be weak. This is partly for the same reasons as above, partly because of the many constraints on the freedom to associate, to move, to be stimulated, but mainly because of the feeling that there still is a basically valid program to follow; that of technical-economic development. That does not mean that there will not be more student and youth revolts (as in Warsaw in March 1968 and Belgrade in June 1968). But their goals will be different: they will aim at the preconditions for the Western youth revolt, the freedoms just mentioned. They will probably also argue in favor of more all-European institutions, more associative policies, since they see these as strengthening their own position internally against the more parochial, anti-cosmopolitan, classical Communist leadership that is now on top of everything else, becoming rather aged.

Thus we are in the strange position that the younger generations in the two parts of Europe are to some extent exchanging roles. Both are rejecting their elders, although more so in the West than in the East, but this is probably mainly due to the *repressive intolerance in the East* that, regardless of Marcuse's scholasticisms, may be more intolerant than the *repressive tolerance of the West*. The rejection in part takes the form of talking the opposite idiom to that of their parents — a Marxist idiom in the West, a more liberal idiom in the East — but with strong trends of convergence in the ideas of decentralization and equality mentioned above. However, there is one basic asymmetry in this picture: the Eastern nation states are fundamentally stronger, less demoralized, in spite of the opposition to their autocratic rule. For that reason, the youth revolt will, for the coming decade or two, be much more consequential in the West than in the East. In a sense this is tragic, especially for the biggest and most repressive of the Eastern states, the Soviet Union. In repressing its opposition so cruelly, it drives itself into a corner where it deprives itself of the major sources of its own renewal. It may very well be that the Chinese are right when they say that the Cultural Revolution saved them from a far more violent revolution against the vertical society that was emerging.

What, then, are some of the implications of all this, for East—West relations in Europe? Needless to say the future cannot be predicted, for the future can transcend any basis on which predictions are made. But one can present a *prévision* based on a number of *ceteris paribus* assumptions. In other words, let us assume that the domestic futures are roughly as envisaged here, and see what the implications could be for all-European relations. Broadly, our prediction is negative: we feel a chance was lost some years ago. Perhaps it was buried in Czechoslovakia, where both West and East went too far too quickly, and perhaps the total system has taken too long a time to overcome the effects of August 1968. However that may be, here is the *prévision*:

For the *first decade* to come the West will be busy building up its supranational structure of an EEC with all its proliferations; and the East will be busy building up its nation states. Both of them will have little time, resources or energy to devote to all-European efforts except on a bilateral basis. These efforts will always be placed low down on the scale of priorities, except in a crisis. Crises will come and go with a periodicity of a couple of years, but will not be fatal. There will be honeymoon feelings of short duration, quarrels and separations of longer duration — but the system will basically be under control. Western Europe will, incidentally, probably win its fight for some kind of parity with the United States, because of the effect of some elementary injections of professionalization and modernization in general in some fossilized European structures, in particular the structures for production and consumption of knowldge.

For the *second decade* to come, or maybe much before that, Western Europe will discover that it has lost more than it has gained. Instead of the economic warfare between US-dominated and EEC-dominated multinational corporations, the world will be groping to organize basically *global corporations*, catering to the needs of *mankind*. Only people left very far behind in their thinking will still act in terms of a balance of economic power between US- and EEC-produced cars. Others will ask how the world can produce the cars that man needs and wants, cars that are more economical, cars that are less dangerous, that do not pollute, that are not victims of policies of planned obsolescence, etc. They will ask for higher priorities for transportation for the underprivileged. Initiative for this may come from the UN and from new UN agencies, and will not call for (Western) European supranationalism, but for much more extensive types of identification. At the same time, the South will have revolted effectively against EEC penetration, South-East Asia against Japanese penetration and perhaps even the Middle East against Soviet penetration. At the same time, sub-nationalism and transnationalism will have grown so strong that the West will be caught up in all kinds of domestic struggles and crises of confidence, and will have to turn inward.

At this point the roles between East and West will be reversed. The East may become more ready for *supranational and international cooperation* of the old liberal variety, having run the full course of its program, whereas people in the West who are now still in their twenties and thirties will gain power and see the key to peace more in terms of basic social *transformation within Western societies*. They will press for transnationalism, decentralization, a society based on structural (not only distributive welfare state) equality, and a much higher level of individualism than is commonly seen today. They may even be afraid of the Eastern overtures towards more cooperation and may read, and make use of, speeches made by the East in the 1960s and early 1970s when they were warning against Western economic offensives.

If, at that point in time, the East should catch up and liberalize so much that a stronger expression of transnationalism were permitted, completely new structures might emerge in Europe towards the end of the century. These structures would require a degree of imagination of the same order of magnitude as that which brought parliaments into being or organized nation states with cabinets and ministries centuries ago. We do not see these structures today, that is certain, but they are not at all likely to be a simple extrapolation from past structures.

In conclusion, it may look as if the chances of all-European integration are slim indeed. This is not so much due to the five aspects of the 'Cold War' mentioned above. Of these the first, second and third are rapidly becoming less important — even the third one will soon dissolve and recede into oblivion. East Germany will be recognized, perhaps by supranational organizations before it is done by nation states, and by non-aligned nation states before Western nations do so, but in the end Bonn will hasten to follow the trend in order not to be isolated. The basis for structural symmetry will exist, not only between the two parts of Germany, but between the two parts of Europe. Security conferences, security commissions and SALT and its many successors will become permanent institutions to take care of the perils emanating from the military colossus on which the balance is based. There will be oscillations between dissociation and association.

All this will be managed. The real problem will be elsewhere: in the *asynchronous* development of the West and the East ideologically as well as structurally, in development-pessimism as opposed to development-optimism, in the withering away as opposed to the growth of the nation state, in the search for new goals in the West as opposed to the search for means in the East, in supranationalism and subsequent crisis in the West, as opposed to nationalism and subsequent supranationalism in the East. *These are the real gaps*, and to bridge them more than political craftsmanship and towering statesmen are needed. What is needed is what was written on walls in Paris during *les événements de mai*: *l'imagination au pouvoir!*

IV.18. On the Future of the International System*

From *Journal of Peace Research* IV/4 (1967). PRIO publication No. 25—6. Notes on page *729*.

1. Introduction

Our image of the international system is incomplete, subjective and un-certain, and the future is filled with possibilities none of which is certain — so the effort to indicate trajectories the international system may follow into the future must be a relatively hazardous enterprise. Some would claim it is not even meaningful [1], but we feel good meaning can be given to future-oriented research on the international system [2], as well as on any domestic system, if we split the task into three components:

1. *Value research* — the effort to establish not only basic values of the system, but also the conditions under which they are most likely to be realized.
2. *Trend research* — the effort to establish trends in the system, based on data from the past, and theories as to how extrapolations should be made.
3. *Exploitation of relations between trends and values* — in other words, efforts to find out whether the trends do or do not lead the system into the 'promised land': and in case they do, how to reinforce and stabi-lize them; in case they do not, how to change them.

Thus, future research has essentially three components or aspects, all of them well known in other connections. What is, perhaps, new in future research (but not new in planning) is the idea of rejecting the traditional division of labor between *ideologists* who establish the values, *scientists* who establish the trends, and *politicians* who try to adjust means to ends, by a more unified approach to the three fields. A consequence of this rejection is the rejection of any strict dividing line between values and trends, or 'facts'. Values are no longer seen as exogenous to the system, as given; but more as a part of the total system that also may emerge from the discovery of new, possible, trends — just as much as trends are seen as something that should be adjusted to existing values. In other words, a more symmetric relation between values and trends will probably emerge from this type of approach [3].

As the matter stands today, particularly with regard to the international system, where the planning approach is highly underdeveloped, the *ideologists* are likely to argue against the trend-makers' or prognosticians' saying that they make the future a prisoner of the past by their explorations, which are usually based on the assumption of continuity [4]. The *scientists* will argue against the ideologists' saying that they posit values that 1. are mutually inconsistent, so that they ask for non-viable social orders; 2. are so detached from trends that it becomes impossible to 'reach them from here' (to which the ideologist may answer: true, except by a discontinuous jump, e.g. a revolution [5]). Both scientists and ideologists will turn against the *politicians*, claiming that the latter pay attention neither to values nor to trends but are merely enmeshed in a jungle of details, intrigues, petty conflicts, and bureaucratic embroidery. The politicians will answer that this may be true, but such are the intricacies of the social order — very different from the views from the ivory towers of ideologists and scientists alike.

This debate is well known and is only dissolved, it seems, when politics becomes sufficiently technified. The conditions for this, in turn, seem to be 1. that the values become highly consensual; 2. that applied science develops sufficiently to offer a supply of acceptable means whereby the values may be obtained with fair certainty; and 3. this level of development is generally recognized. The argument in favor of a unified approach to the three components mentioned above is precisely that the unified approach is more likely to promote this kind of technification. We should, perhaps, add that this in no sense means 'the end of ideology': only that technification takes some issues out of the ideological sphere, which then can move on to absorb new issues [6].

Our task in this connection, then, is precisely to view all three components in that order, asking what are the basic values, what are the basic trends, and ending up with an exploration of the relation between them. To this we now turn.

2. Basic values of the international system

The world consists of 3.3 billion human beings organized in a complex network of criss-crossing groups, some of which are called nation-states; and there is no reason to assume that the values of such groups should be essentially different from values found within the groups, e.g. within nation--states. But that also means that the values are far from consensual. They may include such elements as *cooperation* (as opposed to isolation), *freedom from fear, freedom from want*, values of *growth* and *development, absence of exploitation*, and concomitant values of *equality* and *justice, freedom of action, pluralism* and *dynamism*. But for all such values it is easy to list important cleavages that we shall not enter into here; they are very likely to be values that divide mankind and mobilize groups against each other — at least at present, and depending on how they are made more precise. They should be contrasted with the basic value of (negative) *peace*, which we define simply as 'absence of organized, collective violence', where violence is defined in terms of bodily destruction as immediate consequences of action by some human beings against others. We assume that this value at present is relatively consensual, that it unites mankind rather than dividing it — although the unification is lost in the dividing split in the search for appropriate means [7].

Since peace research as a discipline tries to understand better how this value can be realized, and particularly how it can be realized if the system also tries to realize any combination of the other values mentioned above, we should require of a peace researcher that he be able to say something about the conditions under which negative peace is most likely to obtain. A highly abbreviated version of the present author's attempt to answer would run something like this [8]:

There are two basic approaches to peace, the *dissociative* and the *associative*. The former consists in keeping groups apart, e.g. by balance of power principles or any kind of polarizing or isolating measures. The latter consists in making peace by getting groups closer to each other, e.g. by various ways of integrating them by any kind of depolarizing and unifying measures. In other words, to get peace you must either keep groups (such as nations) well apart or well together — in between there is a very dangerous zone where the parties are neither mutually isolated nor sufficiently close.

There are two reasons why today we would gamble much more on the associative approaches. First, the general communication revolution works against all kinds of dissociative policies, making them look rather artificial and counterproductive. Second, most of the other values mentioned above can be better realized in an associative than in a dissociative world, provided a number of other conditions are fulfilled [9].

The associative conditions of peace we are thinking of can now be expressed under three basic headings:

1. *Symbiotic and symmetric cooperation between groups* [10]. Groups must stand in cooperative relations to each other, i.e. not be too self-sufficient. The mutual interdependence must be such that group A knows that to hurt and harm group B is also to hurt and harm itself. But this is only necessary, not sufficient; for such has also been the relation between masters and slaves during some periods. Hence, a maximum of egalitarianism must be worked into the cooperation, whether it is between nations,

between groups in the productivity system of any nation, between INGOS or IGOs (international nongovernmental and governmental organizations, respectively).

2. *High entropy between actors and in the system of interaction* [11]. In a very approximate way we may say that the major idea behind this condition is that there be no clear fronts in the total system. Members of two races should mix completely in terms of occupations they have, or districts where they reside. Or more precisely: since human beings have different capacities for the tolerance of ambiguity and storage and processing of information we may assume pockets of low entropy (e.g. where there is homogeneity with regard to race), but that these pockets should be mixed and stirred in such a way that the total system has very high entropy (low degree of order, high level of disorder, of 'messiness'). The same applies to the system of interaction: we should avoid systems with very clear, unique paths of interaction, and support systems where the interaction patterns are less clear, in many different directions.

3. *A high number of supragroup organizations.* For nations these are known as IGOs, but we are thinking in general terms that there should be a maximum of organizations bridging and facilitating communication between groups. Thus, INGOs should come together and form super-INGOs; IGOs should form super-IGOs; super-INGOs and super-IGOs may come together; and so on. This formation of increasingly complex systems should take place under the two conditions above, i.e. the members should enter on an egalitarian basis, and there should be high entropy — at all levels in the decision-structure, members of all member groups should be mixed together.

Without going into any detail, there seem to be excellent reasons to say that systems organized along such lines have high conflict-absorbing and conflict-solving capacities. The analytical point now is simply that these seem to be the conditions under which peace is most likely to be obtained. These conditions are phrased in system terms so that they can be compared with trends in the system; they are expressed in the same language, so to speak. Thus, if we merely looked at trends in system properties, we could not read the chances of peace or war out of them, without any theory as to how system properties can be related to the chances of peace and war. To this it may be objected that we could have looked at the trends in peace and war as such, to see whether they are increasing or decreasing, and then tried to extrapolate. But such an approach will easily make us blind to the underlying dynamics; no social phenomena can be viewed independently of their structural correlates.

We then turn to the trends, to see how they relate to the three system properties mentioned above.

3. Trends in the international system

3.1. The state-society incompatibility thesis

When we say 'trends in the international system', what we really mean is trends in the *global* system, for we do not assume that this system is to remain, essentially, an inter*national* system. But nations are going to remain dominant actors for some time to come, so we will also have to discuss trends in the relation between them on the basis of trends in what happens inside these nations of relevance to the interaction between nation-states [12].

To do this, it is obvious that *nations* cannot be discussed under one heading. They have to be subdivided into groups of nations; and for a suitable discussion of this a point of departure is the concept of a *society*, which we take to mean a self-sufficient social structure in the sense that it will remain essentially the same if the rest of the world is removed. Thus, for any given person in the world we could in principle find his 'circle of interdependence' by examining how much of the world could be removed before his life situation changed — and here we might distinguish between the *maximum* circle needed for complete maintenance of the satisfaction level, and the *minimum* circle needed for the satisfaction of basic values. We are thinking rather of the maximum circle.

In Table 18.1 [13] four societal forms have been outlined, the primitive, the traditional, the modern, and the neomodern; respectively. The indications of magnitude are very approximate indeed; they are rules of thumb, but like most rules of thumb more often right than wrong. In general, sociologists do not know enough about the number of people and occupations needed to make a social order viable at all. Read horizontally, the Table gives some of the basic factors in the general development of the human society; read vertically it gives some of the internal (socio-)logic of these societies. In this presentation agricultural productivity — i.e. the number of families one family doing farming can feed — and the general distribution of the population on the primary, secondary, and tertiary sectors of production have been taken as basic [14]. But behind these, in turn, are variables that have to do with technology, particularly the technology of production *and* of communication — the latter added to Marx's emphasis on 'means of production' as a factor of primary importance.

From this nothing follows in terms of changes inside or between nations. But if we introduce the following two assumptions, many consequences follow more or less immediately:

1. *The assumption of development* — that primitive societies tend to develop into traditional ones, traditional societies into modern ones, and

Table 18.1. *Stages of socio-economic development*

Term for the stage	Primitive (P)		Traditional (T)		Modern (M)		Neomodern (N)	
	Primary		High / Low (Primary | Tertiary)		High / Middle / Low (Pri-mary | Sec-on-dary | Terti-ary)		Tertiary (Post-tertiary education | Tertiary education | Secondary education | Primary education)	
Term for the transition		Urban revolution		Industrial revolution		Automation revolution		
Population profiles								
primary sector	100	90	80	75	50	20	5	0
secondary sector	0	5	5	10	20	30	5	0
tertiary sector	0	5	15	15	30	50	90	100
GNP/capita								
Agricultural productivity	1:1 and less		1:1.25	1:1.33	1:2	1:5	1:20 and higher	
Communication								
goods, persons	walking, running, rowing		animals, wheels, sailing		steam engine, combustion engine		jet rockets	
information	eye and ear		dispatches		post, telegraph, telephone		tele-satellite	
Economic system	subsistence economy		barter economy		money economy		credit economy	
Domain	group, clan, tribe		village, city-state		nation-state		region, world-state	
Magnitude	10^0–10^2		10^2–10^5		10^5–10^8		10^8–10^{10}	

modern societies into neomodern ones. This development may also take place in jumps, i.e. 'from the stone age to the electronic age'. The general move in this direction is not strictly linear, but more linear and in general more rapid the higher the level of communication between societies at different levels of development.

2. *The nation-state as a general pattern* — that the surface of the world is divided into generally contiguous territories called nation-states (about 135 of them; in addition there are some 85 territories with about 50 million inhabitants that do not as yet live in nation-states), and that some nation--states are composed of societies at various levels of development, and thus have dual or triple economies; others may coincide with one social order at a particular level of development, whereas other nation-states are segments within one society comprising more nation-states. The division is never thought of as final, but major changes by means of war are seen as illegitimate especially if a nation at a higher level attacks lower level nations.

These two assumptions now lead to what we see as the basic structural condition for change in the international, or global, system: *the consequences of the incompatibilities between state and society, between the nation-state and the social orders that it contains or is contained in.*

Let us first spell out some conditions under which there would be no such incompatibility. There are two such sets of conditions, depending on which assumption above we would negate. First let us assume that each nation-state coincided with *one* society, so that each nation-state would be self-sufficient, independent of the rest (e.g. it would not engage in any significant amount of trade or other forms of exchange). Some of these nation-states would be primitive, some traditional, some modern, and some neomodern, although the neomodern social order, strictly speaking, has not yet crystallized completely [15]. Needless to say, they would differ greatly in size, e.g. as indicated by the orders of magnitude in Table 18.1.

To make for compatibility we would have to assume that there should be no change in this situation, in other words that the societies should not develop further. For in this type of international system the societies that really started developing would soon outgrow the limits set by the nation-states, which means that they would have to interconnect some-how, and this would immediately create a different international system from minimum to increasing interdependence. But with stability there would be compatibility, possibly with interaction, but not with interde-pendence since all states would be self-sufficient.

There is also another way of obtaining compatibility. We could divide the world into a small number of nations, which might then be called empires, each of them self-sufficient and consisting of societies at highly different levels of development. Inside each nation there would be development in the sense that the primitive segment would be transformed into traditional segments, which would then be transformed into modern segments, and in turn develop into a neomodern society. The nation-states in this type of world would be highly heterogeneous and at the same time flexible and spacious (both geographically and socially) enough to permit the gradual transformation into neomodern social orders. This type of world was approximated by the system of colonial empires prior to the First World War — as the societies developed and grew, the nation-states expanded correspondingly by means of territorial acquisitions — as they had always done before — so as to obtain compatibility, even for future development. Nations like Brazil and the Soviet Union, even China and India, can also be seen from this perspective.

But neither of these two models of compatibility obtain in the present international system. Instead the two assumptions above seem to be generally valid: high value is attributed to development (almost) all over the world, with modern societies in general contributing to make traditional societies more modern, while they themselves are rapidly becoming neomodern [16]. At the same time the net of nation-states is thrown in such a way that most of them have segments representing societies in different stages of development, and some of these intranational segments are tied to segments in other nations and constitute cross-national social orders [17]. In other words, a highly complex picture, the consequences of which we have to examine.

Some reasons why the world looks like this and not like the two models with built-in compatibility above should now be spelt out. We may say that the reasons are not so much structural as cultural, due to the nearly universal prevalence of ideologies about development and national independence. The latter throws out the second model of compatibility, whereby modern and neomodern segments inside a large political unit dominate traditional and primitive segments; for the traditional and primitive segments organize themselves, get rid of the colonization, and declare their national independence. Experience shows that it is exceedingly difficult to achieve a form of cooperation between societies at different levels of development that is both symbiotic *and* symmetric. Instead, patterns of exploitation, whereby the more developed receive much more from the less developed than they pay back, easily develop — patterns referred to as *external* colonization if they are found between nations (not necessarily nation-states), and *internal* colonization ('colonización interna') if they are found inside a nation (typically in the form of the modern urbanized sector exploiting the lagging, traditional rural economy [18]). Whether this leads to wars of independence and liberation probably depends on the second peace factor in the preceding section: the level of entropy. Inside nations, entropy is usually higher than between nations, providing less clear fronts than between the peoples in the colonizing and colonized nations. In addition, the amount and nature of supragroup organizations play an important role. One gets anticolonial movements and wars, but domestic protests from the countryside are usually absorbed in the national machinery for conflict resolution — only rarely do they lead to revolutions.

Thus the net result is a collection of independent nation-states, all formed in principle according to the model appropriate for nations that are also societies, and particularly societies at the level of development characterized as 'modern'. Since these units, the nations, are in interaction, a certain amount of homology is impressed upon them. They have to be organized in a relatively equal manner at the top to respond to at least some of the demands made by international interaction, to participate in the international game. This will facilitate the emergence of modern and even neomodern segments at the top of many nations, which in turn has as a consequence that the 'internal development distance' between the least and most developed segments is greater, the less developed the nation is — in general — making the less developed nations less cohesive.

Since all nations, in order to participate in the international game, must have at least some modern segment, we shall translate our typology of four types of societies into two types of nation-states: type PTM, which has primitive, traditional, and modern segments and hence is *less* developed; and type TMN, which has traditional, modern and neomodern segments, and hence is *more* developed. There are, of course, also societies like Brazil, which would be PTMN, and this would to some extent also apply to the United States and the Soviet Union, but we would nevertheless put the first one in type PTM and the second ones in type TMN. Essentially, this typology can be operationalized by using the percentage not working in the primary sector as one indicator; and since this is highly correlated with GNP/capita, we have essentially the often-used division into poor and rich, developing and developed nations.

But this is not sufficient for our purpose, since we are concerned with the degree of compatibility with developmental level and the space provided by the nation-state. One measure of the latter would be in terms of size of population, as an indicator of the magnitude of the society the nation--state could house within its borders. This yields the typology in Table 18.2. Certainly, the level of development is the more important of these two dimensions, but it should also be related to size. The incompatibilities are clearly found in types II and III in Table 18.2; in the first case the societal units are too big for the nation-state, in the second case too small for the

TABLE 18.2 *A typology of nation-states**

	Big	Small
More developed (TMN)	I (34)	II (27)
Less developed (PTM)	III (32)	IV (24)

* Nos. in parentheses are no. of nations in each category. The correlation is only —0.03 with development expressed in GNP/capita.

nation-state. The consequences of this will now be commented on in detail, using for simplification the simple division in developmental levels.

3.2. Trends in the more developed part of the world

Characteristic of this part of the world, now, is the manner in which the societies with increasing development are *growing out of* their nation-states, which even become like strait jackets for them. A consequence of this is a certain general erosion of the nation-state, since it is perceived as being of decreasing relevance for an increasing fraction of the members of the nation. But there is a double process taking place: on the one hand, some layers of the population become identified with neomodern societies and grow out of the nation-state; while on the other, formerly traditional, peripheral segments become more modern, and hence arrive at a level of social identification compatible with the nation-state. But the net result will nevertheless be a decrease in loyalty, a decrease in nationalism, because the 'leavers' are on the top and the 'joiners' come from the bottom.

Specific consequences of this should then be observable at the level of very concrete participation on behalf of the nation-state: as members of parliament or government, and as soldiers 'giving their lives' for the country. The prediction would be that both decisionmakers [19] and people willing to act as soldiers [20] for their country will come increasingly from the periphery; or rather, that the strata and levels from which they come will look increasingly peripheral, since an increasing fraction of the population will be located in the segments typical of neomodern society which in turn will reject this type of participation: To participate in parliament or in government will look the way participation in the county council or administration today looks to many today — as slightly comical — even if the county is urban. This does not mean that they are disinterested in power, only that their orientation is towards other foci.

In other words, we predict an increasing gap between the neomodern makers of new civilizations and the people making decisions and fighting for the 'national interests'. But what then happens to the identification patterns of the disenchanted intellectuals? — for that is essentially what they are. There seem to be four basic types of substitute identification for the lost national identification; we shall refer to them as subnational, cross-national, transnational and supranational.

1. *Subnational identification.* Individuals disenchanted with the nation-state, yet less inclined or less able to identify outside the borders of their own nation-state, will find a variety of subnational foci of identification. This may coincide with a trend dealt with in domestic futurology: the tendency to feel that we now see the end of this long and painful transition from the 100-0-0 population profile to the 0-0-100 profile, from 'all in the primary sector' to 'all in the tertiary sector', and that what we see seems less than worthwhile. That is, there may be a tendency for negative feedback to prevail once the goal is in sight; for the establishment of primitive pockets within a modern-neomodern society, like the legendary hippie communities on the Pacific West Coast of the US [21]. But there are, of course, also more traditional foci of identification, such as *geographical units* (a city, a county) or *organizations* — of which the latter are much more likely, since the salience of the former will continue to decrease with increasing communication capacity.

One more drastic result of this would be rejection of national policies by such subunits; in other words, open expression of the feeling that national policies, even if arrived at by a process of majority vote, are not necessarily to be obeyed. We envisage a relatively near future where one state or county or professional organization in a predominantly neomodern nation will tell the nation's capital *fate la guerra, ma senza noi.* That a value-oriented organization should do so would not be strange, for the members might be organized around precisely that value; the new factor would be that such values could predominate in subunits and even prevail over traditional national loyalties. If the subunit is geographical, the result may be a separatist movement [22]. In a sense, this is not much stranger than the idea that workers should go on strike against 'their' factory; both are based on the feeling that the demands from the rulers or owners have lost their legitimacy. But in this case the 'enemy from within' would above all be the intellectuals, and the most loyal cooperation would come from the rural and more traditionally industrial or commercial segments. This structural division will hold *a fortiori* true for foreign policies, since they more than any other type of policy will concern the nation as a whole, all citizens equally.

2. *Crossnational identification.* Much more basic to the logic of our general scheme of analysis is the idea that the neomodern societies are outgrowing their borders, so that they become dependent on corresponding or complementary segments in other nations. There is a general process of interpenetration. Invariably this will mean that individuals are brought into all kinds of crossnational contacts that are both functional, relatively symmetric, and long lasting (as opposed to the contact between the tourist and the shoeshine boy, taxi-driver or others from the lower ranks of the tertiary sector that he is likely to encounter). Contacts of this kind will not necessarily lead to a decrease in loyalty to one's own nation, but almost certainly to increase in loyalty to the other nation; and this crossnational identification may be cemented by crossnational marriage, dual position (characteristic of most professions in the neomodern segments is precisely that they do not know national borders, the skills are universally valid — i.e. valid in other neomodern segments all over the world).

Extrapolating from this well-known trend, we would predict that the amount of mobility, both of persons and of their loyalties, will lead to a reevaluation of the meaning of national citizenship, more in the direction of membership in an organization. This has two implications: that the transfer from one nation to another will become easier (the individual tears up his membership card if he dislikes the way the organization, the nation, is run — even if it is according to the expressed wishes of the majority) and that multiple membership and zero membership will become possible. Today much energy still goes into the idea that citizenship should be a classification. An individual should be member of one and only one nation: both stateless and multiple citizens are to be avoided. Well before year 2000 these problems will probably be solved as indicated, more in accordance with differential capacity for membership among people, and the fact that loyalty is, after all, distributive, even in the set of nations — and particularly under the assumption of increasing neomodern forms of social organization.

3. *Transnational identification.* For the person with crossnational identification, the unit of identification is still the nation-state — only that he takes in more than one of them (just as the person with subnational identification takes in less than one). For transnational identification the focus of identification is an organization which transcends national borders, without comprising nations; it is subnational, yet international: in other words, the INGO. Clearly, the person with subnational identification in his professional organization or value-organization will find support in his rejection of pure national loyalty if his organization is a branch of an INGO that ties him to individuals, perspectives, values rooted in other nations.

Characteristic of the INGOs (at present about 1,600 in number with about 10% growth rate) is a dynamism in the growth pattern without comparison in the system of nation-states [23]. Thus, whereas a combination of likely independence movements, fission and fusion processes will yield a maximum of around 200 nation-states (provided we do not get large-scale fission processes of the kind envisaged in connection with subnational identification above), there is no limit at all to the number of INGOs. There is nothing corresponding to a finite territory to be divided into units that somehow have to be viable, so the growth can continue in an exponential pattern for many years to come.

Since the minimum size for viability of a nation increases with increasing level of development, we predict that the number of fusion processes of existing nation-states will tend to prevail over the fission processes. Or more correctly, there will be many fission processes, but leading to (con)-federations rather than to autonomous nation-states; just as the fusion processes also will take the form of (con)federation rather than superstates. *Similarly*, we shall certainly also have fissions and fusions of INGOs, resulting in a number of super-INGOs, or organizations of INGOs [24]. But this does not restrict the number in any way, since there is almost no minimum requirement to make an INGO viable. As first steps in that direction INGOs will start exchanging *observers* to meetings of the executive council or to the general conferences; the next step will be exchange of *members* of executive and council; then there will be exchange of *missions* to each others' headquarters; and the next step is a super-INGO and possibly complete fusion. Thus, we shall probably witness a repetition of some centuries of international diplomatic history in the field of inter-INGO relations.

Most interesting from our point of view is the compatibility between INGO rules of membership and the difference in individual capacity for participation: a person can in principle become a member of almost as many INGOs as he wants, since only relatively few INGOs are mutually exclusive [25]. Three particular kinds of INGOs seem to have specific relevance for our general problem.

First, the *internationalization of political ideologies*. The socialist and communist internationals, and to some extent the universal religious movements are old examples; but the international anti-Vietnam war movement is a much better one. The characteristic feature is the more or less spontaneous, international character of demonstrations and of ideologies. In this perspective they become concretizations of what von Weiszäcker calls *Weltinnenpolitik* — world domestic policy. In other words, INGOs may be formed by people having the same or corresponding views on domestic problems — to exchange ideas and to support each other. But much more relevant are INGOs built around value-positions in international politics, where members fight not only parallel causes but a common cause. We predict that this phenomenon will show a rapid growth in the years to come, and tend to internationalize foreign policies, just as the formation of national parties gave a nationwide scope to district and regional policies.

The second factor is the possible *internationalization of age-sets*. By this we mean the following: inside each nation whose dominant social segment is neomodern there will be a rapid increase in the conflict between generations. This is not due to the traditional factors behind such conflicts (such as different position in the life cycle; different amount of available physical, intellectual, creative, and sexual energy; different degree of experience; the fact that the younger generation is in search of positions and the older generation is defending theirs), but above all due to the speed with which social change takes place in neomodern societies. If the amount of time needed before any given social phenomenon — be it population, number of cars, of scientists, of organizations — has doubled [26], becomes less than the average number of years separating generations, i.e. less than about 25 years, then parents will see their children grow up in a world quite different from that they grew up in. The rest is a question of adaptability rates for the older generation — and even if they can adapt themselves to short doubling times, they may not be able to adapt themselves to short trebling times. The net result will easily be that they are perceived as irrelevant to their own children, much like grandparents are today.

This will probably lead to increased solidarity among teenagers against parents, teachers, professors; a rejection of leadership and tutelage from persons who are so old as to represent substantially different forms of social life. They will see teenagers in other societies at the same level of development as more comparable and compatible, associate with them and form a teenager-INGO, however loosely organized, much like today's hippie--INGO. This, in turn, will lead to a corresponding effort among the older generation to organize. Thus, just as traditional societies by virtue of their stability essentially belonged to the old since they were superior in terms of experience; experience is less of an asset in a neomodern society which will belong to the young, because only they possess sufficient flexibility to adjust to the changes (or sufficiently unconditioned by irrelevant experience).

If these two bases of INGO-formation are combined, we would envisage some kind of worldwide generational conflict — the contours of which we get an idea of by observing the age of such political leaders as Fidel Castro, Che Guevara, and Stokeley Carmichael. But world-shaking events of the type presented by the war in Vietnam (and many would see that as the only positive result so far) will perhaps also be needed in the future to crystallize these types of INGO and to fuse them sufficiently.

The third factor is the *internationalization of specialists in world welfare*.

The world today faces two major problems, recognized as the two axes around which the UN system is built: the problems of *peace* and *development*. We predict the rapid emergence of *international peace specialists* [27] and *international development engineers* [28], who look at these problems from a global point of view, not from the vantage point of any smaller unit. Such professionals will be exposed to heavy pressures from the environment, particularly if they reject national loyalties. They will have to seek protection somewhere, and this is likely to be some kind of professional organization built on the model of corresponding domestic organizations. In other words: two more INGOs — probably even to be started in the beginning of the 1970's.

But we also predict denationalization for a number of old professions, not only for new professions created with denationalization as a *raison d'être*. Physicians have in a sense been denationalized since Hippocrates — whether the oath is a myth or not — and all kinds of natural and physical scientists will probably be the next to do so. Strong professional ties will control the use of innovations, much like composers' societies see to it that some revenue accrues to the composer upon public performances.

4. *Supranational identification.* We have mentioned fusion processes among nations and assume that they will continue to be very prominent features in the years to come. It is a serious analytical mistake to include only such dramatic examples as the EEC under this heading; any IGO will serve as an example of some level of fusion, with a consequent increase in supranational identification. That identification may be found among relatively few, for instance only among the secretariat members and staff in general: but people who somehow benefit from it or see the IGO as an expression of their own ideology will also easily identify.

The characteristic feature is that more and more functions will be taken care of by nations acting together; coordinating, harmonizing or even unifying their policies completely. And just as for INGOs, we predict that history will repeat itself: IGOs will become increasingly jealous of each other; they will be in conflict over functions belonging to none of them or claimed by several (just as big powers when their 'spheres of influence' do not exhaust the surface of the world or are not mutually exclusive); and they will try to regulate their conflicts by inter-IGO and supra-IGO machineries. But there is almost no limit on these processes, for if we assume than an IGO has at least three members and that there are n nations in the world, then the total number of extensionally different IGOs is $2 \div n^2/2 \div n/2 \div 1$, which could then be multiplied by the number of functions these IGOs could be concerned with. At present there are around 600 IGOs, with a very high growth rate.

Very important in this connection are the economic IGOs, the international corporations, the countless *coproduction* schemes that are rapidly becoming a normal form of neomodern economy. Another telling example of how much developed nations grow together is the tendency to form even military IGOs, called *alliances*. The intermeshing has then gone so far that the symbiotic relationship to a large extent is realized so that wars between these nations become virtually impossible. Alliances are usually formed only in the presence of a perceived common enemy, and justified in terms of this factor; but it is often forgotten that in order to share military secrets and integrate military units, a solid basis in the form of networks of cooperation in other fields may be a condition.

All these four processes (sub-, cross-, trans- and supranational) are now seen as responses to the incompatibility between development level and size of the nation. Hence, we would assume these processes take place in more developed nations much more than in less developed nations; and among the more developed nations, much more in the small nations than in the big nations — since there will be a greater fraction of neomoderns in small nations having to engage in extra-national interaction than in big nations. Big nations will be more self-sufficient even when it comes to providing a real neomodern with what he needs. Thus, we would expect small, developed nations to be particularly active and particularly well represented in IGOs and INGOs, and all relative to the size of the populations concerned. And we would expect to find the return to the subnational type of identification more frequently in the bigger nation, since only that nation will provide sufficient space and diversity. But we would also expect periods of increased nationalism in the biggest developed nations — on top of a generally downward trend — as new traditional strata grow into the nation-state, discover it, become identified with it, and fight for the national focus of identification — which maximizes their power and rank — to prevail. This is where the German NPD fits, not as neo-nazism: a revival of nationalism.

This said, our general prediction for the developed part of the world would be as follows. *We predict a steady growth in the mutual interpenetration and intermeshing of all developed, industrialized nations with neomodern segments with each other; using INGOs and IGOs as building structures and individuals with cross-, trans- and supraloyalties as building blocks.*

Small nations will be particularly important in this process. They have most to gain from the process, since their level of incompatibility is highest, so they will often deliver the best IGO/INGO personnel. They may serve as go-between for bigger nations that will still have a more purely national concept of 'national interest' and hence tend to perceive each other in competitive terms. But also for them, i.e. particularly the United States and the Soviet Union, we predict that they will be caught in this generally integrative movement. This will eventually (i.e. at the very latest by the year 2000, probably already around 1980) comprise the area from the Bering Strait to the Bering Strait; from Alaska via Canada, the United States, over the North-Atlantic Ocean into Western Europe and Eastern Europe (possibly with the exception of some Mediterranean countries), Soviet Union, Japan, and down to Australia and New Zealand: in other words, the OECD nations plus the socialist nations. The Kennedy Grand Design vision of an Atlantic Community, the de Gaulle vision of a Europe from the Atlantic to the Urals, the visions expressed in the 1957 Treaty of Rome — all are partial visions, with clearly political constraints, of this total image based more on the logic of the socio-economic forces currently in operation.

In this area there will still be nations, maybe about the same as today, but most borders will play no more role than the border between Norway and Sweden or even between two countries (where, incidentally, change of membership is usually not so difficult, although the 'one and only one' rule still obtains). As in marriage, nations will be tied; they will have less latitude; but, also as in marriage, most of them will decide that they gain more than they lose by the arrangement. There will also be regions with particularly strong supranational links: we will probably discern the EEC, the Comecon countries, etc. Some parts will call themselves socialist, others may call themselves capitalist — but that will be more like the difference between countries with socialist or with non-socialist majorities inside a nation: the logic of industrialized, highly educated societies will prevail over such ideological distinctions. The flow of persons (also as labor force: one works where one wants or is most needed,), goods, and information across borders will be considerable and this permeability of borders will contribute tremendously to the erosion of the nation-state — as indicated above. Nations will look more like Armenians and Jews before Israel. This may also sometime in the 1970's facilitate the solution of the German problem in Central Europe [30]. *Peaceful coexistence* will be the general rule.

Thus, the prediction is that East and West will rapidly disappear as meaningful contradictions, not because of any complete convergence of socioeconomic systems, but because of de-ideologization and technification of the economics and a relatively complete mutual interdependence — with the big two as the last to join (but they will be greatly stimulated to join when they see that the smaller nations on both sides and in the middle become gradually more integrated). This gigantic neomodern complex will not have a unified regional government, but rather be coordinated through a network of supranational and supraregional organizations that will have to work closely together with INGOs and super-INGOs. Thus, all

631

three conditions of peaceful relations envisaged in section 2 above will be satisfied and increasingly so, and that will serve to absorb and solve conflicts bound to arise in a process of interpenetration.

As a crowning achievement there will even be integration of military forces in this area, starting with non-aggression treaties (partly bilateral between all pairs of nations, partly between subregions such as the NATO and Warsaw Pact countries), continuing with exchanges of observation teams and mutual inspection schemes, and ending up with some kind of unified command. Thus, we do not predict disarmament so much as arms control and a pooling of military resources, that will be less and less targeted on intra-region goals. Of course, for all this to take place a common enemy would be almost, but not quite, indispensable — and this will be discussed later.

In other words, the prediction is that *in this region there will be 'no major war*, except, possibly, by technical failure or escalation in the first ten years. After that, even such factors will be under control. There may be some local conflagrations, but they will be absorbed quickly because of the high number of conflict-absorbing and conflict-solving organizations, the high entropy due to the high level of mobility, and the generally symbiotic pattern of cooperation. There is the uncertainty connected with the two big powers, not so much because of their power potential as because of their size. We may risk some kind of atavistic return to nationalistic rather that regional militarism, but this can be coped with by means of domestic opposition and the extent to which allies are able to control the superpowers and inform them that they cannot count on unconditional support. As mentioned above, it is felt that the smaller nations will increasingly feel that their interests are better served by general cooperation in the entire region than by subregional patterns of cooperation alone, and that East--West cooperation in general will have to be based on small-power interaction to a considerable extent in the beginning [31].

3.3. Trends in the less developed part of the world

Characteristic of this part of the world, now, is the manner in which the societies are *growing into* their nation-states, which are not like strait jackets, but like jackets to be filled by a very lean person. A consequence of this is a certain general building-up of the nation-state, since it is perceived as being increasingly relevant for an increasing fraction of the members of the nation. But here too there is a double process taking place. On the one hand there is the general trend in this type of nation: primitive segments becoming traditional by tying themselves to urbanized sectors and market-economies; and traditional segments becoming modernized by means of industrialization and a growing tertiary sector of professionals. These are the 'joiners'; they grow into the nation-state and are received by it. But there will also be some 'leavers': people who were formerly the leaders and who never felt at home in their own nation because the modern or neomodern segments surrounding them were too limited.

They were the Latin-American business elites and the Afro-Asian intellectual elites who felt that the environments provided for them in the more developed countries were more congenial; that only in such settings could they be sustained in the form of life they felt as theirs. The recent version of this is known as 'brain-drain', where the typical cause seems to be that the returned fellowship-holders do not feel sufficiently sustained in their old environments; there are too few people to have meaningful talks with, no professional association, no milieu, very few people trained to receive and appreciate their products, and hence little influence potential [32]. These people may still, for some time, continue to be 'leavers', and they may also feel repelled and rejected by the local stock of professionals, drawn from traditional and even primitive segments of their own less developed nation and then squeezed through a domestic educational system designed to keep them in the country and providing them with a local environment. Thus, the generation of Oxbridge and Sorbonne graduates who wanted to do in their new nations what the English and the French had done before them, but do it themselves, will be replaced by a new stock with new ideas.

Specific consequences of this should then be observable at the level of very concrete participation on behalf of the nation-state; as members of parliament or government [33], and as soldiers 'giving their lives' for their country [34]. We predict that both decisionmakers and people willing to act as soldiers will come from the center of the society; or rather that the strata and levels from which they come will look central, since an increasing fraction of the population will be located in these segments — the modern and more developed traditional segments. Our assumption is that these segments identify with the nation-state in any nation; the point is merely that in the less developed nations there is a growth into these segments, whereas in the more developed there is a growth out of them. *Just as the population as a whole will be in a process of decreasing nationalism in the more developed nations (particularly in the small ones), the populations as a whole in the less developed nations will be in a process of increasing nationalism (particularly the big ones).* Hence, the big nations of the world will increasingly understand each other's idiom.

This means that there is no question of finding alternative foci of identification, since the nation-state will provide a growing reservoir of such foci, as the internal segments become more connected to each other. On the other hand, all four alternative forms of identification will also be found, particularly the first one. However, subnational identification will not emerge as an alternative to and a rejection of national identification, but rather as an identification to be replaced with national identification when the circles of growing interdependence have grown large enough.

As to the other three, there are two reasons why there will be much slower growth in cross-, trans- and supranational identification. The first reason is simply the lack of functional necessity: for the development levels concerned, the PTM states do not *have* to be in constant interaction with other states, as the TMN states must in order to sustain their social order. They do not have a high number of businessmen and professionals who depend for highly complex cooperation and communication on colleagues and partners in other nations. An apparent exception here is trade. Less developed nations, particularly the small ones, depend for a large fraction of their GNP on trade [35]. That does not mean that many people are involved, since such trade operations are usually handled by a low number of big export-import firms, often staffed more from the TMN nation to which they export. This is due to the concentration of the commodities; the states in question often have an economy based on mono-culture. Hence, few inhabitants of the PTM states will be directly involved or exposed to a change of loyalties in the crossnational and transnational directions.

The second reason has to do with the general structure of interaction in any system, or so it seems, that is stratified: interaction tends to concentrate on the top of the system, between the center nations, to be less developed between center and periphery nations, and to be at a far lower level between two periphery nations [36]. Interaction flows in the direction of high rank; and even though this will tend to link PTM nations to TMN nations, the tendency will be less pronounced than the relations between TMN nations, and particularly low between PTM nations. Thus, the growth rate of their participation will lag behind, particularly for inter-PTM IGOs: we would expect a very low growth rate in their formation, and that such IGOs will quickly and easily split up once they have been formed [37]. The supranational identification most likely to be formed is in the direction of TMN nations, for it is in this general direction that the interpenetration takes place. More particularly, this is the direction in which military alliances are still likely to be formed, much more than TMN nations alone.

The difference between small and big PTM nations enters here. We would expect the peak of nationalism to be reached more quickly in the smaller nations, where the coincidence between society and state can be reached earlier, due to their often very small size. But at least as importantly: these nations are often far from self-sufficient, nor will they ever become self-sufficient because of their small size, which in turn also affects their growth rate negatively [38]. Thus they are less likely to ever develop substantial modern and neomodern fragments except on an IGO basis, as a spill-over from a TMN nation, often with a commercial nucleus. This makes them particularly vulnerable to all kinds of TMN manipulation. The center of gravity for decisions affecting them will still for some time be outside themselves. We only say 'less likely': there is also a chance that new forms of modern and neomodern societies requiring less in terms of size can be found, and that they can tie themselves to big PMT neighbors.

Concretely, what does all this mean for war and peace? There are three types of relations to predict: intra-PTM nations, inter-PTM nations, and the relations between less and more developed nations. We shall deal briefly with the first two here, and refer the third type to the following subsection.

Relations *within less developed nations* are likely to be increasingly characterized by all kinds of intergroup conflict, between tribes, classes, racial, and ethnic groups in general. The reason for this is generally that all three peacemaking formulas seem to be unfulfilled: there is little symbiosis because of the self-sufficiency — although at a low level of development — of the many constituent units: where there is symbiosis it tends to be asymmetric and exploitative, because of the generally low level of entropy (e. g. with tribes to a large extent occupying specific areas) even though growing urbanization tends to increase the entropy considerably [39] and because of the weakness and insufficiency of supragroup organizations. This is especially true for the bigger nations, and particularly because the 'internal development distance' will tend to make symbiotic relations particularly asymmetric.

In other words, we would predict the kind of internal antagonism that will almost call for foreign and domestic military intervention and for deposition of civilian regimes (the foreign version will be called a 'peacekeeping force'). The present trend of military coups d'etat will probably continue, and the growth will continue [40]; to some extent because the military segment is often 1. the most efficient organization in the new nation; 2. the most achievement-oriented; 3. an organization with a broad national basis; and 4. with a high level of internal entropy (both officers and soldiers recruited from different groups) — the last two points because the organization has been colored by a strong nationalist ideology [41].

But this is for the coming years, say till the end of the 1970s, when some of the imbalance between population growth and food resources has been engineered away [42]. The result will be consolidation of the regimes, concomitant with the much more rapid growth of the modern and neomodern segment we predict for that period. In the process the geo-political map will have changed, there will have been both fissions and fusions, separatist

635

and amalgamist movements, with the general consequence of increased homogeneity within nations and increased heterogeneity between nations. In other words, there will be a general loss of entropy in this part of the world, as against the predicted gain in entropy in the developed part of the world. Something called the 'rectification of articifial borderlines created by imperialism' will take place, and that, then, is one basis for the prediction of *inter*-PTM *relations*.

We predict external warfare between them, much for the same reason as we predict internal warfare within them: lack of symbiotic relationship, lack of symmetry in relations between them, very low level of entropy, and weak supranational institutions — all for reasons mentioned above. The lack of symbiosis is to a large extent due to the parallelism in the economies which directs trade in the direction of complementarity, i. e. upwards in the world ranking system. But this is also for the first decade or two; after that we would expect more possibilities of cooperative relationships. PTM nations with substantial modern sectors will expand trade relations. They will export to nations at the same level: after having exhausted the consumers' market at home they will turn to nations at the same level of development and the same demand profile. But this pattern is also likely to be asymmetric in the beginning; the smaller PTM nations will be exposed to the dominance and even exploitation stemming from the bigger ones until this to some extent can be alleviated by symmetrically designed supranational organizations [43].

In other words: the prediction for the PTM nations is a generally pessimistic one: revolutions, coups d'état and separatism internally; competition rather than cooperation, mutual irrelevance, conflict and even exploitation and war between nations; all patterns that are likely to last far into the 1970s.

3.4. *Trends in the relation between more and less developed states*

We then turn to the crucial type of relationship between more and less developed nations. If our general picture is correct, then there will be a high level of integration in the developed part of the world, and a low level of integration in the less developed part; with a low level of nationalism in the former, and a high level of nationalism in the latter — say, long into the 1970s. Thus, the stage is set in a way particularly advantageous for the developed nations, at least in a short time perspective.

To study these relations further we must introduce the value of equality. Nationalism and development are both seen as instrumental to equality, but not as identical with it. Thus, *nationalism* establishes representation in some IGOs, and *development* a move along the axis in Table 18.1 — but neither guarantees equality. The less developed nations develop, usually by emulating some of the trajectories followed by the more developed nations — but at the same time there is a change of the more developed nations: they are gradually transformed into neomodern nations. Today there is much talk about increasing gaps (very true if one chooses indicators like GNP /capita, less true if one chooses indicators like literacy and health levels), and these are clear expressions of the lack of equality. We shall now relate these gaps to the gaps in nationalism and level of integration.

We should note here that equality between nations is *not* the same as equality between individuals. There may be much inequality between nations and yet some kind of equality between individuals, viz. if they are permitted to move around freely. Thus, the world will probably always have structural or ecological pockets that are low or high on some kind of dimension, but this is intolerable under an ideology of equality only if there is no freedom to move. A poor and/or predominantly primitive/traditional nation may change character completely if linked to a rich nation, provided free flow of persons both ways is permitted.

We can now imagine the typology of possibilities as to the relation between less developed and more developed nations as shown in Table 18.3.

TABLE 18.3 *Typology of relations between more and less developed nations*

	More developed deal with less developed at the	
	Level of individuals	*Level of nations*
Low level of interunit solidarity; they are 'taken one at a time'	I	III
	a. top level approach	a. top level approach
	b. bottom level approach	b. bottom level approach
High level of interunit solidarity; they organize	II	IV
	a. bargaining approach	a. bargaining approach
	b. international revolution	b. international revolution

In the first case in Table 18.3 there is a steady drift of individuals from PTM into TMN nations, usually from (former) economic, political, and cultural colonies into the 'mother-country'. Equality is obtained at the level of individuals, i. e. for *some* individuals. The *top* of the PTM nations leave to find more congenial environments, whether in terms of political values (called 'asylum'), in terms of economic values (called 'absentee ownership'), in terms of cultural values (called 'inspiration'), or scientific values (called 'brain drain'). In general, this reduces the speed of development for the rest, but can be seen as an international expression of this very same process at the domestic level: development is seen in terms of improved chances for the individual (e.g. to go abroad), not in terms of improving the lot of society as a whole or of the underprivileged groups left behind. The perspective is individualistic.

But there is also the *bottom* level approach, whereby cheap labor is shunted into the lower echelons of the TMN society (as unskilled laborers, domestic servants, etc.) left empty by the general upward mobility in these societies [44]. Thus, the relation is highly symbiotic and generally useful for the PTM nation (in terms of accumulated cash and skills), but far from symmetric.

These processes may continue indefinitely if the diffusion rate is located well between 'too high' (which leads to resentment, because it taps the PTM nation of too much of its skilled and unskilled manpower) and 'too low' (which leads to resentment among those who are not let in, high or low). In both cases we would expect the reaction to take the form of solidification inside the PTM nation, increased loyalty, and efforts to develop local resources. In addition, automation will make cheap migrant labor less profitable, but the forces making for brain drain will increase rather than diminish. This will lead to increasingly tougher restraints on the free flow of intellectuals from less to more developed nations, in the name of the increased nationalism predicted.

This brings us to the second type in the typology in Table 18.3, where the PTM nation applies some kind of collective pressure on the TMN nation, usually a nation with which it has formerly had a symbiotic, but highly asymmetric, inegalitarian relationship. The nation may sell its cheap labor at a higher price, require many and very cheap experts in return for brain drainage [45], etc. But the resentment may also go so far as to lead to more drastic measures against representatives and symbols of the TMN nation; supposedly above all when efforts to bargain do not lead to any result.

From the second type there is a straight line leading to the third type: the nation has a high level of internal solidarity, achieved through internal development and the rising tide of nationalism, but the level of solidarity between PTM nations is still low. In this situation the stage is set for 'taking the nations one at a time' [46]. The more developed nations are greatly helped here by their high level of both internal and external cohesion. This will lead to rapid growth in the tendency to deal with the less developed nations collectively, not necessarily through the UN, but typically through the EEC, the OECD, NATO (as coordinating agency), CEMA, etc. As the integration of the industrialized part of the world proceeds, there will also be a certain unification in the approach to developing countries. Western nations will soon start helping more nations leaning to the East [47], and the East will step up their assistance to nations leading to the West. There will be joint teams of technical assistance and especially capital-absorbing projects, and mixed East-West teams of volunteers (Peace Corps) to the less developed nations [48]. In other words, there will be a general regional and industrialized approach to PTM nations; and one goal of this approach would be precisely to get one nation at a time over the wall, so as to make it 'developed'. Japan would be the typical example of a nation that engaged in type II strategies, *in extremis*, and then became the leading exponent of type III strategies. Mexico, Venezuela, Tunisia, Ghana and sometimes also India have been mentioned as examples of candidates for a joint investment, so as to get them across the line.

But there is also a bottom level approach here, applied to very poor and very small nations that are 'adopted' by a very rich and very big nation. We are thinking of the relation between the US and Puerto Rico, between France and Senegal, between Britain and some Caribbean islands — where the investment would matter little to the big nation but very much to the small. This investment would also be particularly rewarding since it might mean one supporting vote in the UN, regardless of the size of the nation adopted.

The transition to type IV in the typology is now relatively clear: the process of type III may go on indefinitely except if the diffusion rate is 'too high', or 'too low'. It can be so high that the PTM nations see that they lose an important chance to gain collectively by organized activity — particularly since the 'one at a time' approach is likely to deprive them of their best leaders in a struggle of that type. Thus, there is complete isomorphism between the transition from type I to II and the transition from type III to IV, although with the important difference that it is more difficult to build up solidarity at the international, less developed, level for the two reasons mentioned in the preceding section.

But if integration takes place, and we predict that it will take place increasingly quickly, then this will change the picture completely. Bandoeng, Beograd, Cairo conferences; caucus groups of the Afro-Asians in the UN and *its* agencies; the more or less concerted initiatives by the less developed nations in UNCTAD; the Tri-Continental movement (OSPAAAL, Habana) are all clear cases of attempts towards trade union formation among the underprivileged nations of the world — with the latter as a trade union of groups engaged in wars of liberation (second version, type II in the typology).

As mentioned under 3.3 above, such organizations work against the structural difficulty that they cannot, like the more developed nations, draw upon a rich network of already existing IGOs and INGOs to cement the relationship. We nevertheless predict that effective trade union formation will be forthcoming quite quickly, due to the resentment against type I, II, and III strategies used by the TMN nations. The situation is too analogous to

639

the corresponding situation at the domestic level when trade union formation took place not to lead to relatively similar results [49]. But since the IGO/INGO infra-structure is missing to a large extent, there must be something else to keep the members closely together, e.g. a strong ideology, a charismatic nation (not only a charismatic person), and some discontinuous event that can be seen as a signal for effective organization. We would predict this organization at least in the beginning of the 1970s — perhaps earlier.

However, it is likely that the first attempts will be in the general direction of collective bargaining. The PTM nations will approach the TMN nations collectively rather than singly, and this will also speed up the integration between the TMN nations. When this is achieved, the North-South conflict, as it is commonly called, will be well institutionalized, and since this is a class conflict in the international system the UN will probably play a role somewhat analogous to national parliament in serving as a medium, a mediator, and an arbiter of the conflict. The TMN bargaining position will be strengthened by the circumstance that there will be large groups in the PTM nations of their side — probably all three of the special INGOs mentioned under 3.2 above.

Analogous with what has taken place within many nations, it seems reasonable to predict that the bargaining will be along two important lines:

1. *Trade union policies*: the PTM nations will put higher prices on what they have to sell, above all on raw materials. More particularly, they may set the price of oil so high that the petrol derived from it will cost just below the price of petrol derived from coal or in other 'artificial' ways. Similar policies can be adopted for many products, but just as for type I strategies have to be carried out relatively quickly before the TMN nations become too clever at making synthetic substitutes.

2. *Welfare state policies*: typical of the welfare state are first, heavily progressive taxation, direct and indirect, so that the gap between the top and bottom of the societies is decreased or at least so that a brake is put on it; second, the idea that the state shall distribute goods, services, welfare in a way both *anonymous* (no specific donor is mentioned, it is from everybody to everybody, although a more authoritarian regime would like to add that it is from the state itself) and *universalistic* (according to objective criteria, not according to any particular relationship existing between donor and receiver). Translated to the international system, this would mean progressive taxation of nation-states (and possibly also of IGOs and even of INGOs) and individuals, the formation of a common pool under the leadership of the UN or some more complex international agency — and

the redistribution of the resources in forms both anonymous and universalistic [50]. This might provide resources of the magnitude needed, and also put some brakes on the further development of the TMN nations into the neomodern types of civilization — probably the only realistic way short of war of bridging the gap in this century.

The alternative to this type of development, once effective organization formation has taken place on both sides of the class wall, would be organized warfare between the two groups, for it will take more time for non-violent techniques to be sufficiently developed. Since this would be a warfare engaged in by nations that perceive themselves as exploited, oppressed, betrayed, we should not believe that balance of power policies and deterrence will work well, for these policies presuppose a certain type of rationality, symmetry, and equality absent here. Throughout the entire human history, oppressed groups have taken to arms against odds, as an expressive outlet, to get revenge or simply because it appeared as the lesser evil when all other utilities were already so negative.

Would nations or blocs be deterred from going to war by the possibly disastrous consequences? Not necessarily: they may believe they will be able to keep them limited, and they know that even though wars become more destructive, the recovery intervals become smaller. Besides, the PTM nations will know that the TMN nations by their social logic are more vulnerable, that the parts cannot function as before without the whole. They know that ten coordinated trucks with explosives in the tunnels and on the bridges leading to Manhattan will have a higher pay-off than almost anywhere else in the world in terms of destruction, and accumulated hatred may be strong enough to translate this knowledge into action. Neither should we believe too much in arms control measures, since A, B, C weapons may relatively soon be available many places in the world due to discontinuous changes in production technologies — and there are countless ways in which they can be delivered [52]. Hence, the protection against this type of war must probably be along the lines of the more associative approaches to peace, indicated in section 2 above.

The problem, then, is to what extent it will be possible to set up patterns of symbiotic and symmetric cooperation with a high level of entropy and many supranational organizations. We should note that organization-formation, types II and IV in Table 18.3, are in themselves entropy-reducing; but what is lost at one level may still be gained at the next, if one succeeds in setting up highly egalitarian and entropic supranational organizations. This in turn depends on whether such organizations are really functional, which means that we are back at the general conclusion that type IV, subtype *violence*, will be the conclusion if type IV, subtype *bargaining*, fails.

The entropy is already low, as mentioned, and particularly so since the line drawn between the PTM and the TMN nations is also to a considerable extent a geographical line (drawn along the tropics), *and* a color line.

However, these negative conditions for organized warfare are only (almost) necessary; they are not sufficient. Otherwise we would probably have the war already. Another necessary condition would usually be a leader nation, in this group a nation sufficiently identified with those less developed, yet sufficiently high on some dimensions of development to dare face the enemy — in other words, a nation with a strong *rank disequilibrium* [53]. Such a candidate is obviously present on the world scene in the form of the People's Republic of China, and predictions about its future power potential seem to indicate that it is also, in balance of power terms, a worthy candidate relative to the contenders: the USA and her allies, the Soviet Union and her allies, singly or combined [54]. But we would like to abstain from any kind of speculation as to China's inclinations in the future — and this is, of course, a crucial point.

Thus, we would expect increasingly coordinated efforts by all TMN nations to forestall such possibilities — and that these efforts will strongly color relations between less and more developed nations in the decades to come. This is a truism, but the forms these efforts will take are less trivial. More concretely, we predict the following:

1. *Strategies of types I, II and III will be increasingly given up,* partly because they create more resentment than gratitude, more enemies than friends. In some cases they may be pursued under confederate schemes, however. This means that bilateral technical assistance, as known from the 1950s and 1960s, will be on its way out (the 1966 figure was already $ 400 million below 1965).

2. *There will be a heavily ideological, rather than organic and cooperative, organization of less developed nations early in the 1970s,* pressing forwards towards type IV relations. The developed nations will realize that their only hope of forestalling an international war lies in accepting even quite heavy demands made in bargaining, of the trade union and welfare state types — and some developed nations will accept this at an early stage as a part of their foreign policy, in order to build up friendly relations.

3. *A large-scale international class war, between rich and poor nations is unlikely, but may come towards the end of the 1970s.* It was unlikely before because of the internal turmoil in the poor nations, because of their generally competitive relations and even exploitative relations, because it takes time to build up sufficient resources that can be converted into military power of any dimension, and because of the debilitation from famines, etc. Moreover, it is unlikely ever to come, because rich nations will use all

strategies, I, II, III, and IVa to prevent it, because they have a tremendous organizational advantage, and because they probably will get the time they need to understand that they must yield to type IVa in order to avoid type IVb.

4. *The rich nations will also engage in preventive military and paramilitary operations to prevent an international class war.* As mentioned, we predict large-scale foreign military intervention in the poor nations when they are engaged in internal and external warfare, and this will increasingly take the form of peacekeeping forces (PKF), not necessarily under the UN. Each domestic upheaval, each border rivalry, will be one more pretext for stationing peacekeeping forces which will essentially also be used in the interests of the more developed nations — also in this type of long-term interest. Moreover, this will serve to bring about even some measure of military unification between East and West, thus providing them with the 'common enemy' factor, Of course, all of this may be impeded by negative votes in the General Assembly, by refusals to accept PKF, by efforts to avoid the type of turmoil that will serve as a pretext for the more developed nations to intervene, etc. But again, at least in the first five — ten years to come, the rich nations will have greater resources in finding ways of getting around such hindrances. CIA-type tactics to undermine Chinese influence etc. will continue.

Thus, relations are bound to be uneasy to say the least, and there will probably be armed conflagrations somewhere along the perimeter of the modern-neomodern complex (such as the Amur and Rio Grande rivers). But whether the international class struggle is absorbed in a network of bargains of the type mentioned, or explodes in an international war depends on the relative growth rate of some of the major curves we have tried to trace — and their relative size would be a matter of pure guess, completely unguided by any theory.

4. Conclusions and policy implications

At this point we stop: we have tried to sketch some of the major structural forces shaping the landscape of the future — as we see it. It is an educated guess, intended as a baseline for discussion. The truism that non-structural factors — a technical error somewhere in a nuclear device, a particular personality type who gets power somewhere else — may completely upset this picture is no reason not to try to paint it, even if we have to use rather thick brushes. The point is to try to see some of the implications of present-day trends and values, to guess where they might lead us if we did nothing about them. As indicated in section 3.4, this leads us inevitably to predictions about second and third order phenomena, not merely predictions about trends but about how actors will react to other actors' reactions to these trends, etc. Needless to say, the speculations grow more and more tenuous, the higher the order of the trends, for actors may simply fail to do what we predict them to do.

What policy implications follow from such reflections, if we were to take the vantage point of the more globally identified decisionmaker, not the vantage point of the nationally or regionally identified politician? In very brief terms, perhaps something like this:

Do not try to pursue neocolonialist policies of tying less developed nations to more developed nations in 'regions' defined by affinity or vicinity; they will disrupt due to the social logic of the different levels of development. Rather, recognize the international class structure for what it is, and contribute to its institutionalization — at the top, at the bottom and above all at the global level. Engage in the trade union and welfare state policies on a global scale, with the less developed nations abstaining from extreme violence and the more developed nations abstaining from extreme exploitation; with large-scale redistribution of values and resources to reduce gaps, much like in a modern welfare state. On top of this, build a maximum of egalitarian INGOs and IGOs, super-INGOs and super-IGOs, improve communications in all possible directions, facilitate to the maximum the free flow of persons, goods, information. If pockets of low entropy develop, let them be small and well encapsulated, so that there will be no escalation; if there is asymmetry in one relationship, try to balance it out in the next relationship; if there is a tendency for a (con)federation to develop into a super-state, try to absorb it in a network of cooperation linking it to the rest of the world so as to soften the frontier effect.

By building on such elements, some of the trends explored may be turned in a direction more conducive to the realization of peace. If they are engaged in with sufficient vigor, they may increase the growth rates of the more peace-productive curves and thus serve as a protection against major catastrophes. And this is not merely to telescope time, to use future research to make things happen more quickly; it would also be a way of controlling trends so as to decrease the likelihood of certain predictions. For just as we feel there is quite a lot of reason to be relatively optimistic about East-West relations, one may also feel that the factors operative in that context could be put to effective work in North-South relations. And if they were, a global system (it will not be a truly international system) where really large-scale wars and large-scale exploitation would be extremely unlikely should be a possibility, even as early as sometime in the first half of the next century.

IV.19 On the Future of the World System*
Territorial and Non-territorial

From Bulletin (International House, Japan)

PRIO publication No. 25—11. (1967)

Notes on page *736.*

1. Introduction

In the preceding chapter, "On the Future of the International System," originally prepared for the First International Future Research Conference in Oslo, September 1967, an effort was made to explore one particular image of the world. Theoretically, the fundamental axis used was *socio-economic development* in a particular sense, as measured by the growth of the non-primary sectors of economic activity. In other words, development was seen in a highly horizontal sense as a decrease of the primary sector of economic activity. More precisely, human history was portrayed as a decrease of this factor from 100% to 0% in neolithic and neomodern (post-industrial) societies respectively, and one major *force motrice* of this development was, by definition, the increase in agricultural productivity and in facilities for communication/transportation. This, then, leads to a distinction between primitive, traditional, modern and neomodern societies.

Another basic factor was the division of the world into *geopolitical units* referred to as nation-states, harboring within their confines *socioeconomic systems* at highly different levels of development along the axis mentioned. By and large the highest level of *compatibility* was found between a medium sized nation-state and a socioeconomic system which could be called modern or industrial, whereas most nation-states were considered to be highly incompatible with their socioeconomic systems that were either growing *into* the nation-state (the case of primitive or traditional systems) or *out of it* (neomodern systems). As a result of this, patterns of dominance developed, and some typologies and predictions were made in that connection.

In this paper we shall not contradict this image, but try to attack the problem of developing previsions, predictions and prescriptions for the future of the world in a different way. First of all, we shall be mostly concerned with the distinction between territorial and non-territorial actors and deal with them *symmetrically*. In chapter 18 non-territorial actors (universal organization, whether they are governmental or nongovernmental, profit or non-profit) were seen as an inevitable result of the incompatibilities between the socioeconomic systems and the geopolitical systems defining the territorial actors (particularly between neomodern systems and nation-state), and we shall retain that idea. But this time we shall discuss in a more systematic manner and more symmetrically the possible changes that may happen both in the territorial and the non-territorial action systems of the world, and consequently in the relations between them.

Second, we shall be somewhat less concerned with horizontal development and more with *vertical* development. Our focus shall be on equalization of life chances rather than on moving averages; on social justice rather than on economic growth. In other words, we would like to expose all the visions that could be developed of the future world to the acid test of *social justice*, within as well as among territorial and non-territorial actors, rather than to the acid test of what it means for *economic growth*, or even for peace in the limited sense of *absence of violence*. This does not mean that we consider the other perspectives less important, only that we would like this to be the focus for the present discussion.

To start with some simple definitions:

— By a *territorial actor* we mean a political unit with effective political control over what is essentially a contiguous territory.

— By a *non-territorial actor* we mean a political unit with political control over actors that are non-contiguous.

The criterion as to whether an actor is territorial or non-territorial is whether the control center must be located in some specific area of the world, however extensive, or in principle can be located anywhere. Thus, the control center for the Common Market will have to be somewhere in the (so far) six countries concerned, whereas the location of the UN Headquarters could be in any member state and possibly also on non-claimed territory. The same applies to all universal organizations: they can have their headquarters wherever they can have members, and if this is anywhere in the world the conclusion is that they are not in any sense territorially constrained.

There is still the problem of actors that are controlling non-contiguous territory, yet unable or unwilling to move the center of control anywhere in the world. Examples would be the British Commonwealth of Nations, the OECD countries, the socialist countries. It is for this reason that we have used the term "essentially" in the definition of territorial actors: we assume that there is a contiguous center with the possibility of a more scattered periphery. Hence the control center location is a better criterion than the contiguity, but both are useful.

It should also be mentioned that an actor could be non-territorial within a region: *the regional association*. It can have its headquarters anywhere, but constrained by the confines of the region. We are less interested in this particular variety, however. Our contrast is between territorial actors, which essentially are states and superstates, and non-territorial actors, which are international organizations of the four kinds mentioned: governmental non-profit and profit, and nongovernmental non-profit and profit. It should be added that regional, non-territorial actors may lay the foundation for a regional superstate, but also for a more universal non-territorial actor.

Since we are equally interested in both types we cannot talk any longer about the future of the "international system". This term is in itself too heavily biased in favor of the territorial actors. Nor are we interested in the future of the non-territorial system alone; we are interested in exactly the sum of these two: *the world system*.

2. Six possible dimensions of change

We now enter the analysis with two types of actors, something like 135 territorial actors called nations, and something like 3,000 actors called IGOs (international governmental organizations), INGOs (international nongovernmental organizations) and BINGOs (business international nongovernmental organizations). They both form systems of interaction, and the two systems are in turn heavily interrelated. The question is what can happen to the two systems. One extremely simple typology is as follows.

For each system there are essentially three possible processes, which certainly do not exclude each other.

First, the system may *grow in number*. By this we simply mean that more nations may come into being without any changes in the nations existing today, and that more organizations may come into being with no changes in already existing organizations.

Second, there is the possibility of *integration or fusion*. Two or more nations may coalesce and become one territorial actor, one bigger nation referred to as a (con)federation or simply as a new nation, a superstate; two or more non-territorial actors may similarly integrate and become one actor in the non-territorial system.

Third, there is the possibility of *disintegration or fission*. One nation may be exposed to *secession*: a minority group may want to go its own way and establish itself as a new nation-state. And the same may happen in an organization: there may be splinter groups, for any number of reasons, that want to set up their own international organization, for instance of "new emerging forces".

In short, we get a total of six different processes that should be examined one by one. To discuss the future of the world system with little or no clear idea of these processes is not very meaningful. Particularly dangerous is the tendency to discuss the future of the world as if only one or two of these prophecies were significant. Obviously, they are not all going to have the same degree of impact on the total system, but they will all have some impact and for that reason merit a relatively extensive discussion.

We shall treat them in the order indicated in Table 19.1.

TABLE 19.1 *The six dimensions of change*

system	process growth	fusion	fission
territorial actors	1	2	3
non-territorial actors	4	5	6

3. Growth in the territorial system

The most significant thing about this dimension is its limitation. At the end of the 15th century one would not have spoken in such terms: the possibilities of growth were tremendous because the territory available was constantly expanding with new discoveries. Today one will have to go outside the earth itself to have a similar sensation, and in that case it will probably be a question of analysis at a higher level adding an interglobal system to the international system we have today, and a definition of spatial actors in addition to the territorial actors. But the Apollo moon landings have demonstrated very clearly how dependent a moon colony would be on Mother Earth even for such elementary life ingredients as oxygen and water. A Moon Colony viable enough to launch a Moon Tea Party in 1976 seems rather unlikely; their oxygen supply might simply be cut off. Of course, this does not mean that the possibilities of growth are zero. More precisely. there are three ways in which new territorial actors may come into being on this earth without affecting the existing ones.

First, there are still something like 80 territories with a total population of 50 million human beings that are not national actors because they are dependencies, even colonies, sometimes trust territories, etc. Very many of these are in the category of prospective mini-states, and it is important to have a very clear conception of them. However, it is not felt that their impact is going to be of a really major significance in the world of today, except perhaps in some regions such as Southern Africa (where independent Angola and independent Mozambique might be significant factors in changes in the balance of power), and in Oceania.

Second, there is the possibility of territory that is either unclaimed or has such a low degree of claims on it that it almost does not count developing into new territorial actors. We are thinking of certain isolated islands in the Polar areas, the Antarctic territory, Greenland and Spitsbergen, and so on. There are also some desert territories around the world, some of which are even referred to as "neutral" territory. It is well known that any such move would be met with heavy reaction from some territorial unit, but since the areas in question are (almost completely) undeveloped and unpopulated, one can nevertheless meaningfully talk in terms of the birth of new territorial actors without affecting present nation-states.

Third, there is the possibility of invading the oceans, by establishing underwater colonies and by reclaiming land. The latter possibility would probably lead to expansion of present actors (Netherlands, Japan) rather than to new ones, but the former, like space platforms, could lead to interesting constellations if they were established by non-territorial actors and not simply controlled by some rich nation-state. In the latter case this would of course add to the power potential of that nation, e.g. by controlling water, air and space transport and possibly set us back many centuries in terms of possibilities of free travel. But only the former would lead to new actors, hopefully experimenting with new forms of social life and contributing to peace through a strengthening of the non-territorial system outside the control of the territorial (so far every non-territorial organization has had to put its buildings down on territory belonging to a territorial actor).

However, it is difficult to see that it will affect the territorial system or the world system in general in any significant way in the foreseeable future. The world system has a certain absorption capacity, particularly at the periphery, and like the mini-states discussed above these new actors will certainly have to enter the system at the periphery. Hence, much more is to be expected from the next dimension, which we will have to treat at some length.

4. Fusion in the territorial system

Since fusion is tantamount to integration this possibility is very often mentioned, and usually by theorists who are rather optimistic about the prospects of this development. Since our view is just the opposite, we shall try to deal with it in some detail.

To do this some image of the world is needed so that the processes of fusion or integration or super-state formation can be discussed in a systematic manner. The image we shall use is simply as follows (Fig. 19.1).

FIGURE 19.1 *The world as nations in regions*

Top

Bottom

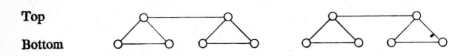

This is a world divided into 12 nations that are connected from high to low mainly, and there is also some connection at the top. The world is divided into 4 regions. and this leads us to six possible patterns of fusion.

First, the fusion may concern only one region or the whole world; it may be *regional* or *universal*. Second, the fusion may be *vertical* in the sense that it involves both levels, it may be *horizontal* involving only one level and in that case there are two possibilities, horizontal *fusion at the top* and horizontal *fusion at the bottom*.

In Fig. 19.2 some of the fusion patterns are superimposed on this world.

FIGURE 19.2 *Some fusion patterns in the world of Figure 19.1*

Top

Bottom

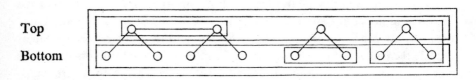

The box involving the total system stands for vertical integration at the universal level. Inside that box one may see horizontal universal integration at both levels, a case of vertical regional integration, a case of bottom-level horizontal regional integration, and a case of top-level horizontal integration which includes two regions.

These are the theoretical possibilities; some examples are spelt out in Table 19.2.

Given the low likelihood of retaining the present world structure, the question to be asked is simply: which of these types of fusion are more likely in the world today? Or rather, what will these six trends produce, as a resultant, in the relatively near future?

It seems to the present author that we are now in a typical transition phase. The simplest thing to establish, *regional vertical* integration based on a certain amount of contiguity and highly vertical relations dominated by one power, is already to some extent a thing of the past in the sense that the recent history of mankind has witnessed many life cycles leading to the ultimate dissolution of vertical empires, to their death. Examples are the processes involving the British Commonwealth and the French Com-

TABLE 19.2 *Some concrete examples*

	regional	universal
vertical	OAS,	
both levels	NATO	UN
	Warsaw Pact	UNCTAD etc.
	Common Market with associates	
horizontal,	Common Market	condominium of big
top level	North America	powers
horizontal	Latin America	Alger group of 77
bottom level	Black Africa	Non-aligned group
	Arab World	Tri-continental
	ASEAN	

munauté, and the extremely significant cracks in the systems of regional superpower domination; OEA (Organización de Estados Americanos) in the Western hemisphere and the Warsaw Pact in Eastern Europe after the interventions in the Dominican Republic in 1965 and Czechoslovakia in 1968. NATO, which is less vertical, has also shown serious cracks in Western Europe but was highly stimulated by the invasion of Czechoslovakia.

However, the important factor is that with the postwar dissolution of five colonial empires controlled from Western Europe, the British, the French, the Belgian, the Dutch and the Italian, *horizontal bottom-level and top-level* fusions start developing, partly as a cause, partly as a consequence of this dissolution. This leads to well-known integrative efforts in Black Africa, in the Arab world, and in parts of Asia. The obvious response to this is a similar pattern of horizontal fusion at the top level, known as the Common Market, where the five colonial powers are finding each other again, although Britain is still only an applicant, the German empire collapsed already after the First World War, and Luxembourg was too small to have any empire except through Brussels. But it also leads to a reverticalization through the system of associated states and neo-colonialist trade and aid patterns.

The Latin American nations find each other in horizontal, bottom-level integrative attempts as a response to highly manipulative efforts towards vertical integration inside the USA-dominated OEA system. The obvious prediction is that this will lead to a similar integration between the United States and Canada, here referred to as North America; just as more emphasis on NAFTA will lead to closer cooperation between Black Africa and Latin America, or vice versa. Of course, Latin America went through a similar process one hundred and fifty years ago against the colonial powers of those days, Spain and Portugal, but means of communication and trans-

TABLE 19.3 *The matrix of interregion relations*

	North America	Western Europe	Eastern Europe	China	Japan	Latin America	Black Africa	Arab World	South Asia	South-east Asia
1. North America										
2. Western Europe	*positive* "special relation", NAFTA, NATO									
3. Eastern Europe	*negative* WWII residues, cold war, arms race	*negative* but improving, leaving arms race to superpowers								
4. China	*negative* all kinds of reasons	*neutral* leaving conflict to superpowers	*negative* border, competition							
5. Japan	*mixed* positive: PAFTA negative: WWII, competition	*neutral!* may turn negative	*negative* WWII residues, competition	*negative* relation to US memories						
6. Latin America	*negative* exploitative relationship	*positive* but not strongly so?	*neutral*	*neutral*	*neutral* but maybe positive					
7. Black Africa	*neutral*	*negative* exploitative relationship Rhodesia, SA	*neutral* maybe positive	*neutral*	*neutral*	*neutral*				
8. Arab World	*negative* basically over Israel	*negative* exploitative and Israel	*positive* over Israel	*neutral*	*neutral*	*neutral*	*negative* Sudan, etc.			
9. South Asia	*neutral* mixed	*neutral*	*neutral*	*negative* border, subversion	*neutral*	*neutral*	*negative* Indians in Africa	*negative* Kashmir, Pakistan		
10. Southeast Asia	positive and negative, depending on country and class	*mixed* depending on country	*neutral*	*negative* subversion	*negative* memory, exploitative	*neutral*	*neutral*	*neutral*	*neutral*	

portation were not sufficiently developed at that time, before the communication revolution, to lead to any real integration, either at the bottom, or at the top level between Spain and Portugal. Because of this asynchrony Spain and Portugal lost their prestige in the European system a long time ago and are very much in the periphery of the Common Market system. And Latin America has already several premature, negative and traumatic experiences behind her in integrative attempts, often with the effect of becoming negative incentives.

When it comes to the Soviet-dominated vertical system the situation is somewhat different. There are probably tendencies towards horizontal, bottom-level integration (the horizontal top-level integration has already taken place: it is called the Soviet Union), but the level of oppression is too high for these tendencies to show. Hence, it is difficult to see that a process corresponding to what is now taking place with increasing acceleration in the Western hemisphere will take place in the Warsaw Pact area.

We then turn to the possibilities of universal fusion. At this point it should be noted that the universal integration involving all would no longer be a territorial actor: the center of power could theoretically be located anywhere. But this argument does not apply to the patterns of horizontal universal integration; they would both constitute highly interesting international, territorial actors. There are very strong factors, however, impeding their formation.

First, as to the *top-level* actors: a complete condominium looks rather unlikely in the foreseeable future. In the US-Soviet-China-Japan quadrangle relations, all pairs are somewhat negative at the time being; perhaps Soviet-China most openly so, and US-Japan least. But a "least" is not necessarily a basis for a more lasting fusion, as was so dramatically demonstrated during the Second World War. A short-time alliance might be formed, but that is not what we are discussing here.

As to the horizontal, *bottom-level* fusion we may be forced to the conclusion that the communication and transportation revolutions have not yet come far enough. It may be sufficient to lead to some integration within a region, even at the bottom level, but not to integrate universally. Within the region there is always *some* similarity and interaction around which *some* fusion can be built, but at the universal level there is so little that the motivation and the possible benefits will be highly unevenly distributed. For that reason the groupings listed in Table 19.2 are meeting on a rather ad hoc basis, but they should of course be taken into account in any future analysis.

This leaves us with *regional fusion* as a real possibility, and what we see as major events in the coming decades would be the progressive revolution against the *vertical* fusion of the past and a consequent consolidation of *horizontal,* regional integration, both at the *bottom* and at the *top* levels. However, within this fusion-oriented type of thinking we have difficulties seeing how the Soviet system could disintegrate as quickly as the US-dominated system does. There are also very many uncertainties in connection with Asia in general, by far the most complex of all regions, offering a combination of the direct East-West conflict and the structural North-South conflict, but in patterns very different from Europe on the one hand and Latin America/Black Africa/Arab World on the other.

Let us now try to project a vision of the world in line with this type of thinking, with ten regions or superstates as an outcome of the horizontal consolidation within formerly vertical regions:

1. *North America* (NA) — including USA and Canada.
2. *Western Europe* (WE) — including EEC (expanded) and the rest of non-socialist Europe.
3. *Eastern Europe* (EE) — Soviet Union and socialist Europe, i.e. the countries presently members of the Warsaw Pact.
4. *China* (C) — this is the People's Republic of China with the system she dominates.
5. *Japan* (J) — the third economic power in the world.
6. *Latin America* (LA) — including the 20 Latin American countries with the possible inclusion of the other territories in the Caribbean and South America.
7. *Black Africa* (BA) — which is Africa with the exception of Arab and white-dominated states.
8. *Arab World* (AW) — including all countries presently members of the Organization of Arab States, with the possible addition of Muslim, non-Arab states such as Turkey, Iran, Pakistan (but Indonesia and Madagascar will probably be too far away).
9. *South Asia* (SA) — this is India with the possible addition of such neighboring countries as Nepal, Burma, Ceylon. The possibility that East Pakistan might combine with Indian Bengal into a Bengali-speaking state which might eventually affiliate into this region is also a possibility.
10. *Southeast Asia* (SEA) — this is the region from Thailand via the Philippines to South Korea, comprising ten countries, the five ASEAN members and Cambodia, Laos, Taiwan, South Vietnam and South Korea.

This scheme divides the world into ten regions, and one should now look at it using the two general criteria of mutual exclusiveness and exhaustiveness. In other words, to what extent is there an overlap between the regions, and to what extent does this division of the world really exhaust the territorial actors available?

This is a somewhat pedantic question, but let us briefly touch on five of the classification problems of this division of the world.

1. *Will North America and Western Europe fuse together?* In spite of all kinds of special relationships we have put them down as separate super-states. Some kind of NAFTA (North Atlantic Free Trade Association) may come into being, but US protectionism and increasing isolationism will probably impede further fusion together with growing Western European superstate-ism.

2. *What about the OECD members outside the North Atlantic area?* Japan will be her own region, we think, and Israel will very much depend on her ties with NA and WE for future political, economic and social existence. Australia and New Zealand will retain ties with NA and WE and compensate for a lack of proximity with a high level of affinity. In addition they will orientate themselves towards both Asian and Pacific concepts.

3. *Where is the borderline between Black Africa and the Arab World?* There is the question of whether "Arab" should be taken in a religious (Muslim) or some other sense, but in either case there will be a problem of exact demarcation line. As any map of religious distribution in Africa will show, this line runs somewhere south of the Sahara from east to west in Africa, but much further down on the eastern coast. Practically speaking, nowhere does it coincide with national borders.

4. *Where is the borderline between South Asia and the Arab World?* As already mentioned this is not so clear either because of the mixed position of the Regional Corporation for Development (RCD) countries (Turkey, Iran and Pakistan). Turkey has one foot in Europe and most of its body in Asia, and Pakistan almost touches Southeast Asia — so there is also the possibility that they may crystallize into their own region, possibly including Afghanistan.

5. *Where is the borderline between South Asia and Southeast Asia?* One may have a vague racial notion in mind, "red-brown" Asia and "yellow Asia," with India to a large extent dominating the former and Japan and China (not to mention what remains of the Western powers, and to some extent Australia/New Zealand) competing in the latter, and the Soviet Union in both. There will be highly problematic border areas in the Burma-Thailand region and in the Nagaland-Assam region. But some development in this direction seems probable after the US

withdrawal from the area (when and if it ever takes place; the moral withdrawal was included in L.B. Johnson's speech of 31 March 1968).

And thus one could continue, but we want to discuss this system of ten possible superstates in more concrete terms by looking at the matrix of interrelations. More precisely, it seems fruitful to ask which relations would be *negative* (and why), which ones would be *positive* (and why) and which ones would have a *relatively neutral character* — usually for the simple reason of distance. One such vision is given in Table 19.3, and we would like to emphasize that this is neither a prediction nor a prescription, but a prevision, and more precisely of a nightmarish character.

In principle each one of these characterizations may be subject to considerable specialist argument, but we think they are generally considerably more right than wrong, and even though they will certainly be changed by the end of this century, they are not likely to change that much during the 1970's. And more fundamentally, some basic features of the structure will remain. To see them more clearly let us view the ten regions more like a map:

FIGURE 19.3 *A 10-superstates map of the world*

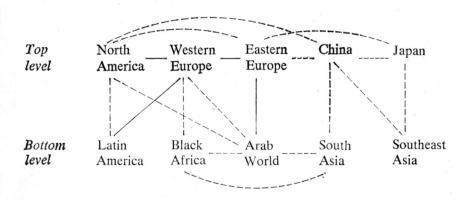

With 10 superstates there are in principle 45 pairs, and we have postulated 3 positive, 16 negative and 26 neutral or mixed relations. This gives a fairly high level of saturation of meaningful relationships, 42%, out of which 84% are negative. But the saturation level becomes even higher if we focus on the top level alone. With five superstates there are only 10 relations, with a saturation level of 70% and a proportion of negative relations as high as 86%.

Why do we have these findings? For two simple reasons:

1. Even with efforts to break down the vertical patterns of past and present, most of what happens in the world will still happen at the top level with repercussions in top-bottom and bottom-bottom relations, with positive as well as negative costs, and one has to be rich and powerful to meet the costs.
2. The non-neutral relations are predominantly negative simply because negative relations with the outside are among the most important solidifiers inside. The opposite relation also holds: fusion may lead to growth that in turn provokes fears. The superstate is formed to serve as a protective shield against outside direct or economic aggression, or sometimes as an aggressive sword — and even if the intention is the former, the perception (and even the consequence) may easily become the latter.

To all this can be added elements of contiguity, of racial and ethnic homogeneity and of shared history, and the total logic is extremely similar to the formation of the nation-state. Hence the patterns of top heaviness and negative predominance are certainly not strange; what would have been strange would have been the opposite pattern.

Another thing is what may happen to the system when it has been in existence for some time. It may be capable of developing more positive ties, so let us look more systematically at some of the relations.

Let us start with the two positive relations. The ties between North America and Western Europe are so strong that it is very difficult to envisage a near future where they would turn into negative relations. In fact, the conditions of contiguity and homogeneity are so well satisfied that strong forces are needed to prevent further coalescence, and we have mentioned North American isolationism and protectionism as one such force. This, however, may change if North America is further and consistently weakened by the disruption of the *Pax American* system, as well as by internal dissent. In that case North American self-sufficiency might disappear, and the two parties may become more equal.

The other positive ties in the system are between Eastern Europe and the Arab World, and between Western Europe and Latin America. We have put the Arab World down as the underling of Eastern Europe, but only in the sense of differential levels of development. The ties seem to be positive: Eastern Europe has no history of colonialism in the region; they have been by and large much more understanding in their relations with the developing world than the old colonialist powers with their satellites; and with Syria, Iraq, Libya and Algeria socialist and Egypt nearly so, the move in the Arab World is so definitely towards the socialist camp that it is hard to envisage a future where this will change into a negative relation.

Together with the North America-Western Europe axis this provides us with another positive axis in the system of considerable importance, since these are axes around which more comprehensive alliance systems might crystallize in the more distant future.

This does not compare to the positive tie we have postulated between Western Europe and Latin America: it is more sentimental, with Paris as the capital of the "Latin race," etc., but it exists as a contrast to the relationship with North America.

Let us look more closely at the negative relation between North America and Latin America. There is no scarcity of grievances: the whole history of hemispheric relations is by and large a rather unfortunate one with a continuous series of interventions and major conquests made by the United States, such as one half of the territory that once belonged to Mexico. Economic colonialism and neocolonialism, humiliation and imperialist commercialism have been dominant trends in these relations of dependence. But this of course is not in itself enough to start anything like a war: for a war some basic relation of *symmetry* is needed. A war is between equals, between unequals it is called *dominance*.

In order for this kind of symmetry to emerge two conditions have to be satisfied: North America has to become considerably weaker, and Latin America considerably stronger. Neither of these developments is in any sense impossible, and they may also coincide in time.

For *North America* to become weaker what would be needed would be a continuation of internal revolution with the possible secession of American Negro-dominated states as well as an accumulation to the point of internal revolt of what today is known as the New Left revolution. It is not very likely that this will happen under wise American leadership with its tremendous talent for absorption and reintegration. But one could easily imagine a scenario with the United States suffering a rather humiliating defeat in Southeast Asia, with the *Pax American* system crumbling completely, with internal rightist reaction, with increasingly conservative governments till the point of a military coup d'état, and so on.

As to *Latin America* a rather different scenario is needed to lead to conclusions of this type. Latin America is headed for modernization, for independence and autonomy and a definite farewell to dependency relations. But it is not likely that this will happen the Cuban way: Cuba was an *island*, Cuba was the *first case*, Cuba was a *small* country, and Cuba had *Fidel Castro*. This will not be repeated. A much more likely scenario is what has currently taken place in Peru and Bolivia where rather anti-US governments are installed by means of progressive military coups d'état. Instead of the classical revolutionary model of guerrillas fighting against military oligarchs one now has a model of military oligarchs themselves becoming some kind of revolutionaries, resulting in a progressive military dictatorship. They have the distinct advantage that they have the ultimate means of power under their control and they have a nationwide and even continental organization, something guerrillas all over Latin America have not been able to establish.

Of course, the Cuban model could repeat itself if the military leadership, the military oligarchs, were reactionary and completely demoralized as in the case of Batista. But it is much more likely that they will receive inspiration from the case of Peru and convert that inspiration into further action. And if that happens in a sufficient number of countries, with varying degrees of support and participation from radical civilian sectors, one might very soon arrive at a Latin America that would be integrated by means of military organizations having the tremendous advantage of *homology*. They are structurally similar and have no difficulty finding each other; they know each other and already have training in cooperation due to technical assistance and organizational elements handed to them, in the name of anti-subversive activity and counter-insurgency, by the United States and its Southern Command. For that reason it is not inconceivable that the most successful Latin American institution in the near future, within 20 years, might be *an integrated Latin American military command with a progressive tinge.*

The question is whether such a military command also would acquire nuclear arms, and although Latin America at present is a nuclear-free zone, this possibility should not be excluded. We then assume that within the next 20 years technical "progress" in this field will continue reducing the two major factors impeding such development up till now: the *costs of separating* U_{235}, from U_{238}, and the *difficulty of hiding* the activity. With the centrifuge technique both costs and difficulties of hiding are reduced considerably and there is little doubt that this reduction will continue. And if one now adds to this the possibility of inflammatory propaganda against the United States and the psychology of converting a certain creeping servility which Latin America has plenty of into arrogant disdain when or if United States is weak, anything might happen — or is at least as likely as anywhere else in the world.

The general pattern behind this is of course that it is problematic to be a topdog in difficulty, with a recent history of having subdued and humiliated underdogs. If we now turn to relations between Western Europe and Black Africa, this is less likely to be the mechanism behind a possible war. After all, Western Europe got out of Black Africa in a relatively bloodless and benign paternalistic manner, "granting" the colonies their independence. Most colonies did not *take* what rightly belonged to them, it was *given* to them from above. But they are still weak, the colonial masters are far away, and there are no grievances of the type Latin America has suffered recently with the same degree of concreteness, so we would not postulate anything like direct warlike activity.

However, what is not so unlikely is the possibility that Black Africa within 20 years might become strong enough to launch a major attack on South Africa, on the white enclave or redoubt. Western Europe would not look with complacency at the systematic extermination in warfare of some thousand or even hundred thousand whites; the rescue operation in the Congo some years ago testifies to that. In short, they might become directly involved and a general formula of topdog peacekeeping by means of the UN machinery might by that time be inapplicable simply because Western Europe will find herself in a minority position. On the other hand, we do not think that North America would become directly involved in this, although we are not so certain, considering financial interests in South Africa.

On the other hand, it looks rather likely that both North America and Western Europe might become engaged in a war with the Arab World as an ultimate guarantee of the population if not the state of Israel. Much more than the current relatively effective Al-Fatah needle-pricks would be needed for this guarantee to be invoked, but in case it is, the stage might be set for a rather inclusive war. For at this point Eastern Europe would in all probability back the Arab countries, and since the classical cold war already structures negative relations between North America and Eastern Europe on the one hand and (less so) Western Europe and Eastern Europe (particularly over Germany) on the other, we have a full-scale bipolarized system involving four of the ten superstate actors: North America-Western Europe pitted against Eastern Europe-Arab World, over Israel.

Of course, there is an incongruency here between the smallness of Israel and the bigness of that war if it should ever come about, and that incongruency will itself serve as a deterrent. Also, this system is relatively well balanced, the superpowers are involved, and all of this should guarantee a certain stability. But what is often forgotten in such calculations is that those who confront each other across the Suez Canal, in the sand dunes of Sinai or the Jordan valley or up in the Golan mountains are not so concerned with these strategic calculations. To them it is a matter of immediate passion and hatred. One party, the Palestinians, has everything to win and nothing to lose because they have already lost everything. The other party, Israel, has everything to lose and nothing to win because they have already won everything, and even more than that. In other words what might be stable in Europe, as experience has shown by and large so far, might be an extremely dangerous play in some other region of the world to which the system has been extended

As to the cold war there is little to add, nor is there much more to say about the remaining negative topdog relations. The US-Soviet-China triad is negative on all sides, and we think it is highly unlikely that some positive link will develop for any lasting period of time, as mentioned above. With more audacious and talented Western European politicians of the magnitude of de Gaulle a positive tie between Western Europe and China might develop, and might have a highly healthy and depolarizing effect at the top, but the likelihood that such statesmen will emerge again is rather low.

The newcomer in the topdog club, *Japan*, has also what we regard as negative relations with the other three, although not so strong, and with the US there are still strong (but deteriorating) positive ties. This gives Japan more leeway for maneuvers and creation of new structures, and makes Japan-watching crucial for any attempt to study world futures.

If we now go down to the underdog level again, what strikes us first is both the total absence of positive relations and the number of negative relations. There is enough material for regional level warfare between *Black Africa* and the *Arab World* over the case of Sudan alone, and if to this is added the whole sub-Saharan belt the perspectives are rather dark. One might also add that so far this has not received international attention, but the nations involved are still weak and the ethnically and racially homogeneous regions even weaker. In other words, the protection against war probably rests mainly on weakness, and that is exactly the weakness so many efforts are directed against, such as the world democratization of the right to fight one's own wars (and not have them fought by some topdog power), not to mention the arms sales.

Black Africa might get into similar relations with India over the question of Indians along the *East-African* coast, although it should be added that the distance rather than weakness is here a major peacemaking factor. At higher levels of technological development this factor disappears, but at the level likely to be maintained on both sides of the Arab Sea for some time to come it will still be of significance.

This, however, does not apply to the relationship between the *Arab World* and *South Asia*, as has already been seen in the relations between Pakistan and India and between Muslims and Hindus in general. And, to take more negative relations: *China* and *South Asia* have very long borders in common with mutual interpenetration cutting across what today is defined as nation-states, in short a multitude of possible nuclei of major conflicts. To this should then be added the quickly growing anxieties in connection with Japan's economic and also military power in the first place as a structural conflict between Japan and Southeast Asia. This concludes our review of negative relations that are easily seen today. Then there are, of course, the possible negative relations of tomorrow. But we have already more than enough speculation, so we will rather take this system as it stands and try to make some projections within this paradigm.

First of all, Fig. 19.3 is one more demonstration of how isolated *Latin America* is. Latin America is only tied to the rest of the world by some ties to Western Europe and predominantly negative feelings to North America. It is postulated that these negative feelings may be sufficient to propel further the forces of integration, but that is not the same as developing positive relations to other parts of the world. On the other hand, this relative isolation of Latin America as an appendage of North America might also become an advantage: *the region has no explicit friends, but it does not have other enemies either.* What it does not have it might get, and here is one scenario that might be promising for "el ultime rincon del mundo" — the last corner of the world.

There is actually a relevant model from the Nordic countries where there has traditionally been a certain division of labor with Finland specializing in relations with the Soviet Union; Sweden and Denmark with relations to the south; and Norway with relations with England. With really good *internal coordination* these specializations may be complementary rather than competitive; all countries may interact on behalf of the region.

One could now imagine a similar system for Latin America whereby Brazil would specialize in relations with Africa. Interesting and surprisingly positive relations already exist with the African nations in the Bay of Guinea that were the places from which the Brazilian slaves originated and to some extent returned, and relations with Portuguese-speaking Africa, Angola and Mozambique, are bound to develop in the future. Similarly, Argentina and Uruguay would continue their relations with Western Europe, but in a less egocentric fashion. And the whole Pacific Coast of Latin America, the Andean group, would engage in a really conscious and conscientious Pacific policy, developing reciprocal ties with Japan, Australia and New Zealand, with Southeast Asia and possibly even with China and South Asia. Traditionally these nations, with their strong European orientation, have been standing with their backs to the Pacific Ocean trying to get a glimpse of Europe on the other side of the Andes mountains. It is high time to turn around and face Pacific reality, and a good beginning here would be enlightened airline diplomacy.

Latin America to the north of South America would essentially have to develop its policy in all three directions, towards the Pacific side, towards the giant to the North, and towards the European and the African regions. If relations with North America should deteriorate it would be important for them to have alternatives on the other side of either ocean. And if all these policies could really be coordinated into a meaningful whole, then Latin America will have done somewhat of the same thing Norway did during the last century: convert isolation and peripheral location into a positive utility simply due to a lack of enemies. Norway could, and still can, enter in the field between belligerents elsewhere because she is not suspected. The same might apply to Latin America, and it might also apply to Japan if she does not get too entangled in conflict with SE Asia or in big power conflict and if she does not become so powerful as to raise suspicion.

The rest of the world is to some extent too burdened with conflict to engage easily in similar policies, thus leaving Latin America with more *degrees of freedom* (an entity which is roughly inversely proportionate to the *associated number* of the graphs given in parentheses next to the regions in Fig. 19.3). So, what could one predict about the rest of the world ? Our only theoretical basis would be the theory of *balanced graphs*: most of the cycles in Fig. 19.3 are unbalanced, and one would assume that they would somehow tend towards balance. In other words, there might be more alliance formation and a tendency towards bipolarization. Let us explore some of these possibilities.

One would assume that such alliances would have to be built around already existing positive axes, of which there are two. One projection would be that either axis would try to tie up with some of the other elements. The North American—West European axis would try to enlist Latin America, under the banner of "Western civilization". with its obvious racist implications. But this may be too late if the attitudes held by the present young generation in Latin America ("young" now seems to mean anybody below 45) are to be taken seriously. On the other hand, the Latin American ties with Western Europe will probably be stronger and more positive in the future, and this will have a depolarizing effect, again pointing to the possible global role of the isolated region (presupposing that Latin America develops recruitment mechanisms that put statesmen of higher average talent on top of the system).

What else can the Northwestern part of the world do ? Five hundred years of imperialism have not made them excessively popular or trusted in the rest of the world, and they are now reaping the harvest of that policy. But they will still for a long time to come harbor a tremendous amount of resources and talent, and some of this will probably be used to try to entice one or more superstates or part of a superstate over to their side. Thus, the Common Market with its famous agreements with African states is almost an immediate and direct continuation of colonialist economic principles. Indeed, this relation should be seen as the condition for the independence granted to so many nations around 1960 (the only strange thing is that Whitehall in London did not fully realize in 1957, when the treaty of Rome was signed, what great opportunities she had rejected). Chances are, however, that these policies will not be so successful in the future.

And the Northwestern corner will have no chance with the Arab World for decades to come.

More promising are the possibilities with Eastern Europe, and here one can imagine that the smaller countries might cut ties with a Soviet Union weakened by conflict and by open war with China, as well as by certain possibly secessionist tendencies in Central Asian republics (which we predict might come into being in the 1980s). All-European institutions might be created, making out of Europe a unit that would thwart the scheme in the diagram to some extent. A Europe without the Soviet Union might even develop positive relations with China, and the result would be isolation of the Soviet Union. Considering the terror over the human mind (and often also over the human body) Stalinist and neo-Stalinist regimes have spread inside their own country as well as to their neighbors, this might also be an example of the type of harvest that may even be reaped very soon after such effective seeds of violence have been sown. At any rate, an isolated Soviet Union would be of the same magnitude as North America, and might, like North America, have more than enough to do with internal problems. On the other hand, the Soviet Union seems to have a positive relation with the developing world, the Arab countries, and she may also be able to use that relation for global, not merely European politics.

Another possibility in this scheme is a positive axis between various parts of Asia. In the period of *Panch Shila* this almost looked like reality, and that reality may be reborn with the radicalization of the regime in New Delhi and a certain moderation of the regime in Peking. In that case the world would be clearly tripolar, with Asia (South and Southeast Asia, China and possibly even Japan) pitted against the "Middle World" (Eastern Europe and the Arab World), pitted against the Western World, North America and Western Europe. Latin America and Black Africa, with a possible positive tie between them, might be a fourth pole rather reduced to a spectator role with occasional skirmishes along the peripheries. But such a tripolar system, even one that spans the whole globe, is hardly completely stable in the age of modern communication and will tend to reduce to a bipolar one.

And this will not easily happen either. Thus one thing that there seems completely impossible is that the two camps should be defined according to *international stratification*, in other words with North America, Western Europe, Eastern Europe, China and Japan in the upper class, and Latin America, Black Africa, Arab World, South Asia and Southeast Asia in the lower class. The system is too complicated, there are too many positive ties between the two classes and too many negative relations within the classes for this to develop easily. A more likely configuration in the long run would be the six regions to the West against the four regions to the

East, but this presupposes that the *vertical* grievances between North America and Latin America, between Western Europe and Black Africa, between China and South Asia and between Japan and SE Asia, as well as between NATO and the Warsaw Pact, between China and Japan, and *horizontal* grievances between Black Africa and the Arab World are settled sooner and more easily than the grievances between South Asia and the Arab World, South Asia and Black Africa, or between China and the Western powers, China and the Soviet Union — and that Japan prefers to define herself as Asian. There may be some reasons for making such assumptions but the total political work needed could be overwhelming. For this reason we *conclude that it is highly unlikely that the system will be bipolarized in this century.* And this means that it will oscillate between all kinds of transient alliance formations, in all probability at ever increasing levels of military potential, and not even benefit from the meager stability a bipolar "orderly" world might enjoy.

When we have referred to this system as a nightmare it is for the simple reason that *superstates tend to differ from states mainly because they fight superwars instead of wars.* There seems to be no reason to believe that a big state has higher morality or wisdom than a small state in spite of the fact that it should have much more human manpower from whom to recruit the best men and women. What rather seems to be the case is that its definition of "best" tends to take on a rather bellicose tinge, and that makes the total system described far from reassuring. On the other hand: this is not a prediction, only a prevision with a certain degree of persuasiveness; it is not a completely unlikely turn of events. But if it is not completely unlikely, then we might not live to see the turn of the century. For this is a vision which is so ripe with possibilities of real world wars far beyond and above the two negative lines with Eastern Europe that people in the North Atlantic area have been trained to believe in as the major axis around which world politics rotates that it is very much to be hoped that there are also other tendencies in the world. And there are, but not necessarily more encouraging ones.

However, one cannot conclude this section without adding that one answer to these, in our mind catastrophic, tendencies towards *one* pattern of integration in terms of *ten superstates* lies in *other* patterns of integration. Thus, one of the dangers inherent in the pattern explored is that all ten superstates would be capable of action, including belligerent actions, and that, moreover, they would have sufficient grievances to engage in such action. In another paper *(The True Worlds,* New York 1977, Ch. 6.3) we explore other integrative patterns, both vertical and horizontal, and both regional, intermediate and universal. Thus, the vertical, regional pattern would lead to six blocks (USA with Latin America; EEC with Black Africa;

Soviet Union with the Arab World; India with the rest of South Asia; China and Japan with Southeast Asia). We regard that as an even worse arrangement because of the structural violence that is so deeply built into this way of organizing international affairs — in addition to the direct violence it would engender. At the extreme opposite end of the spectrum there would be a pattern involving horizontal, universal integration — all the rich countries in one bloc and all the poor in the other. However, this would hardly lead to a split into two parts, North vs. South, since it is likely that China would be a system of her own with associates from all over the globe. It is also hard to see that the capitalist and socialist North would really come together that closely.

And then there are all the intermediate solutions, all with their problems — but none of them quite so problematic as the one we have explored in this section. With this in mind we turn to the next possibility, fission in the territorial system.

5. Fission in the territorial system

Here we shall not discuss fission of the ten superstates that have been introduced in the preceding section, but disintegration of already existing national actors. For this we also need a general theory, and that theory is not too dissimilar to the theory already developed in connection with integration: we are thinking of Fig. 19.1. Actually, the dominance relation is usually more complete inside a nation than between nations, partly because they have had more time to establish it, and mainly because control is better because communication is easier.

One theoretical approach for studying disintegration, fission or secession from or within existing nation-states, would be as follows. There seem to be three factors involved:

1. *A relation of dominance* with groups exploiting other groups.
2. *A high correlation* between the dominator-dominated dimension and some racial and/or ethnic dimension.
3. *A high correlation* between the racial/ethnic dimension and geographical location.

Expressed in simple terms: there is an upper class and a lower class that belong to different racial or ethnic groups and live in different parts of the country. Since these conditions obtain in very many parts of the world, the possibilities of disintegration are extremely numerous.

To understand the phenomenon better let us look at the obvious counter-strategies from the point of view of the dominating group.

First of all, there is the idea of building a nation without any relations of dominance. It is quite possible that this may come into being once in the future of mankind, but so far it sounds rather difficult unless the units are very small, which would in itself point towards fission. Hence, the second possibility, that of reducing the correlation between position in the dominance system and race or ethnicity is a more likely perspective. And this is done very often all over the world: it is referred to as desegregation, and takes the form of some type of proportionate representation in government, in police forces, in top military circles, etc. This may or may not, then, be combined with an effort to eradicate any kind of residential segregation whether it is between districts or inside districts but between towns, or even inside towns.

One important strategy is to combine factors 1 and 3, spreading the dominant group in a thin layer all over the nation so that there is little or no correlation with residence, but indeed a very high correlation between dominance position and race/ethnicity. This is the solution found in such different countries as United States, most Latin American countries that are racially mixed, Ethiopia, the Soviet Union and China. However, it is very difficult to make the correlation with territory disappear completely, for which reason there will be pockets with high concentrations of the privileged and high concentrations of the underprivileged.

All these strategies are tried in various forms in many parts of the world today. Europeans have a tendency to see Africa as the region split by tribalism, quoting such figures as 6000 tribes in total, 120 of them in Tanzania alone. The tendency is to forget the time and the blood it has taken to obtain the far from perfect sorting today found on that peninsula of the Asian continent known as Europe. And these processes are going to continue, also in Europe. The idea of translating national belongingness into some kind of territorial exclusiveness known as a state is far from dead, so new states are going to be born, carved out of the territories of old ones. In all likelihood this is also going to become one of the major factors of social dynamism in the years to come, national struggle being as important as class struggle in shaping history.

6. Growth, fusion and fission in the non-territorial system

In the preceding three sections the dynamism of the territorial system was studied: growth, fusion and fission processes; in the present section some of the corresponding tendencies and trends in the non-territorial system will be analyzed.

Our basic proposition is as follows: *whereas the dynamism of the territorial system will mainly consist in fission and fusion processes, the dynamism of the non-territorial system will be in terms of growth of the system.* In a sense this is trivial: the geographical space subdivided by the territorial actors, the states or countries, is finite and relatively unchangeable (except for possibilities on the ocean floor and the ocean itself) whereas the socio-functional space over which the non-territorial actors are defined knows no limitation and has a very malleable topology, to say the least. The dynamism of the territorial system has to be squeezed into the painful exercises of disintegration and integration of the various kinds discussed above, whereas the non-territorial system is free to expand, adding to its numbers. Of course, there can also be some fission and fusion processes — and some of them will be very important politically as when the Third World establishes its own organizations, including something akin to the UN. Hence, in the total world system consisting of both, dynamism derives from the territorial system banging its head against the ceiling of its own limitation, and boiling over in the form of non-territorial growth — with the growth of the transnational corporations both in number and in assets, relative to the states, as the compelling example.

Some of the reasons behind it and the consequences of this pattern are important e.g. four of the factors directing non-territorial growth:

1. When some new elements appear in social or functional space it is often surprisingly easy to build an international organization around it. I have participated in the process a number of times, and one observation would be that it is easy because the process so often draws upon already existing non-territorial networks. One can conceive of an organization as built around people with some similarity in value and/or interests, or around some kind of task or function. In either case the task is facilitated by the principle of "neighborhood": many of the same people are already organized around some related task, or people related to them have already done something relating to the same function. To build international organizations becomes a stepping-stone game, easy for those who already know some of the structure of that space, difficult for those who have lived their entire life in a territorial cell. As there are already many stones to step on, and any number of new stones (points) that can be added, the possibilities are unlimited — except by the finiteness of the human population and the limited capacity of the transportation/communication systems.

2. The multiple function organization, often built around one ascriptive and one achieved characteristic (the association of female lawyers), or around any combination for that matter. If people feel best when they are with their own kind, they might feel even better the more characteristics they have in common, and that is precisely what the multiple function organization is about — whether it mainly serves some psychological or also

some political function. As there are many functions and characteristics, the possibilities are legion.

3. One organization may bring about an anti-organization to counteract it, even trying to negate it completely. Or at least so they may believe: in a longer term perspective it may be, for instance, that the International Peace Research Association has much more in common with the International Institute of Strategic Studies than both believed initially. Anyhow, the functions may be antithetical, the members may be opposed to the members of the other organization, or an organization may emerge to counteract some other organization — as the Group of 77 or OPEC can be regarded relative to the OECD and the European Community, not to mention trade unions relative to transnational corporations.

4. The growth process that comes out of increasingly higher levels of integration. Thus, an IGO can be seen as the outcome of a process whereby governments have come together, maybe first only bilaterally and on an *ad hoc* basis, then others have joined and on an increasingly regular basis till the institutionalization takes the form of an intergovernmental organization — which is then born. And correspondingly for the INGOs: non-governmental organizations from various countries come together after a searching process for their opposite numbers abroad, and as a result an INGO is born. But when we come to BINGOs we also see more clearly that this may also operate the other way: the non-territorial actors already exist, at least in the minds of somebody with a good national base for one "chapter" or "company" — and the rest is a question of implanting it in other countries, so that both isomorphy and homology are served at the same time. But regardless of the time order of this process: *what has happened once can happen again.* The IGOs/INGOs/BINGOs can also come together, first two at the time and on an *ad hoc* basis, exchanging information — ending up with a super-IGO/super-INGO/super-BINGO as vast integrative networks. The position as a liaison between a super-BINGO and a super-IGO certainly does not belong to the territorial system and is probably not even known as a position — yet it definitely exists and the person holding it would possess considerable power, among other reasons because of all the information that would come his way.

Compare all this to the territorial system. The period of Great Discoveries is over, one cannot simply add a new state if one runs into difficulties, or migrate to some New World. So far countries do not permit "multiple geographies", for instance interpreted as populated zones under the jurisdiction of two or more states so that everybody living there would not merely have double nationality (that exists to some extent), but some sort of mixed nationality (not British and French, but Anglo-French). But dialectics there is: countries oppose each other, even try to negate each other

— only that the way they do it is so destructive compared with the nonviolent verbal battles fought in socio-functional space, and so agonizingly slow relative to the quick, possible action in the NT system. Of course, there are also integration processes in the territorial system, but it is also a very slow and painful process, not so easily carried out as in non-territorial space.

One consequence of all this is predictable — and we are already living in the ever-growing confirmation of that "prediction": the non-territorial system will attract increasing attention, talent, dynamism. An increasing number of persons will think, act, even live in terms of international networks of which they form some part — like pilgrims have done for millenia already. For consider what these four growth factors mean, concretely, for the case of the transnational corporation. For any new product: a new corporation. For a combination of two existing products (travel agency, bank): a new corporation. Then for any product one can always imagine a number of competitive products: hence any number of competing corporations, perhaps only differentiated by trade names (Coca-Cola, Pepsi-Cola). And for corporations with some element of harmony of interests: a potential super-corporation, even concealed to the naked eye, e.g. for integration along the economic cycle (one prospecting/research/development corporation, one banking institution, one processing corporation, one for transportation/communication, one for marketing, and finally one for the consumption itself). Not strange that the field is dynamic and also attracts talent and money when it can operate under such conditions. Nor is it strange that the territorial system hits back — partly because non-territorial growth serves imperialistic interests, partly because it threatens the territorial system itself, reducing states to something stagnant, incapable of doing more than some little splitting up and joining together, lost in their zero-sum games.

7. Conclusion: territorial and non-territorial processes combined

This example also brings out the obvious: one thing is to find and analyze the possibilities of growth, quite another is to evaluate them according to such values as peace and social justice. Left to itself, given the present trends, the non-territorial system may not only attain grandiose proportions by the Year 2000 — much of this growth will also be in the wrong direction; above all strengthening the grip the North-West corner of the world has over the rest. But for good or for bad, let us imagine that the trends continue, what world would that lead to?

Building on the typology in Table 19.1 we arrive at the image of Table 19.4: To discuss the future of the world system with little or no clear idea of these six processes is not very meaningful.

670

FIGURE 19.4 *Growth, fission and fusion in the*
territorial and non-territorial systems

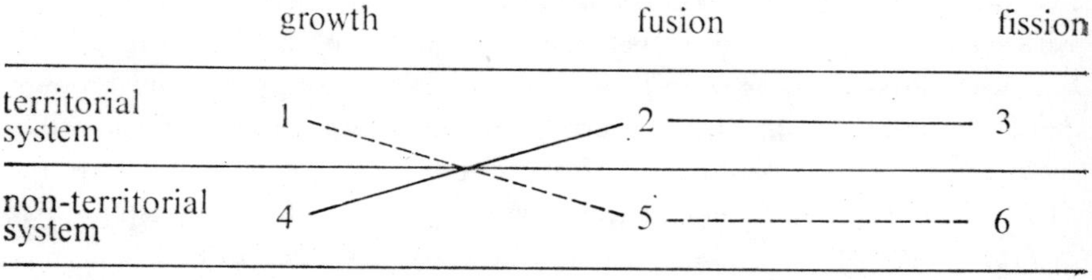

	growth	fusion	fission
territorial system	1	2	3
non-territorial system	4	5	6

Particularly dangerous is the tendency to discuss the future of the world as if only one or two of these processes were significant, e.g. the old-time favorite of territorial integration. In addition, there is also the necessity of considering some of the key interaction processes between what happens in the two systems. So, what kind of world results from the line 4—2—3— above, the line linking the most dynamic factors?

One answer to this is very easily found: that world would have many things in common with the countries with the densest number of national associations and organizations today. It would not be difficult for an historian to write the history of, say, the British Isles in the terms suggested by this paper: decreasing salience of the territorial system, of the various counties into which that piece of the territory is divided, increasing importance of nationwide factories and firms and organizations and associations of all kinds, particularly the interest organizations of employers and employees. It belongs to the picture that the system exercised considerable territorial spill-over during its age of imperialism, that some territorial part detached itself partially from the center (the Irish Republic), that others tried or are trying (Ulster, Scotland, Wales) — in other words that the *territorial* structure is more salient in some parts than others. But this will also be the case in the world as a whole. What has been said is more true for the first and second worlds than for the third. Nevertheless, we know the end result so far: it is not that territorial units disappear, *but they lose in salience* — except where there is, or has recently been, some type of external or internal colonization, and except to the extent that there may be a revival of the local community, meaning the small community which is usually smaller than the administrative units most countries are divided into.

But this, in turn, means that there are positive and negative experiences to draw upon from the domestic system that may be applicable to the global system. One of them is, in simplistic terms, that there has to be some kind of political articulation, and political institutions to steer the process. At the moment the world cannot be compared to Britain, for the countries of the world are not tied together like the counties of Britain — for world non-territorial actors are not brought openly into the process like political parties domestically, nor is there any world central authority like there is central authority in Britain. The comparison would rather be with what was on these isles before some kind of unification came about, but with criss-crossing non-territorial actors growing like mushrooms. This is counter-factual history: territorial integration came first and facilitated the growth of nationwide organizations and associations later — but then transportation/communication was developed after nationstates had emerged and before a world central authority had been established.

Thus, the nation-state analogy has its obvious limitations. Consequently, the total world system is on its own. There are some very likely processes that will dominate the near future. But the more distant future is open — for us to shape if we manage to understand and steer the processes.

Notes

IV.1. *Small Group Theory and the Theory of International Relations: A Study in Isomorphism*

* Paper prepared for the Norman Wait Harris Conference "New Approaches to International Relations", June 1—4, 1966, University of Chicago, printed here as PRIO-publication no. 1—6 from the International Peace Research Institute — Oslo. The author is indebted to the *Norwegian Council for Research on Conflict and Peace* and to the *Aquinas Fund*, New York, for financial assistance, and to the participants at the conference for valuable suggestions.

[1] P. F. Lazarsfeld and H. Menzel, "On the Relation Between Individual and Collective Properties", in A. Etzioni, ed., *Complex Organizations, A Sociological Reader* (New York: Holt, Rinehart, & Winston, 1961), pp. 422—440.

[2] For a very negative view of the possibilities of applying psychological knowledge to the problems of international relations, see Morton A. Kaplan, "Review of The Human Dimension in International Relations, by Otto Klineberg," *Amer. Polit. Sci. Review*, 1964, pp. 682—683. For another view, and particularly for a more multidisciplinary view, see J. D. Frank's answer, "Psychology and International Relations," *Amer. Polit. Sci. Review*, 1964, p. 965. Kaplan's answer is on pp. 965—966.

[3] For one review of approaches see J. W. Burton, "Recent Development in the Theory of International Relations", *The Year Book of World Affairs 1964* (London: Stevens & Sons, 1964), pp. 213—229. Typically, more intellectual energy and more pages are devoted to the development of typologies, description of variables/dimensions held to be important, and to comments on what others are doing, than to formulating and testing falsifiable hypotheses or tying them together in theoretical frameworks.

[4] Isomorphism is a relation between two sets, such as the set of points on a map and the set of points in the terrain, which holds when: 1. there is a one-to-one mapping between the elements in one set and the elements in the other; 2. there is a one-to-one mapping between relations in one set and relations in the other; and 3. these two mappings correspond to each other. If two elements in the first set are mapped on two elements in the second and there is a relation between the elements in the first set, then the image of that relation will hold between the image of the two elements (if a point is to the right of another on the map, then the image of that point is to the east of the image of the first

673

point in the terrain, because "to the right of" is mapped on "to the east of").

But this is a purely mathematical definition that may be of limited usefulness in the construction of models as a heuristic for research. Of course, one should stick to the definition, but make it more suitable by adding two more concepts, viz. *richness of isomorphism* and *degree of isomorphism*. The two are closely related since the latter is merely the relative version of the former. We shall illustrate them by means of the terrain-map example (I am indebted to Herman Kahn for this illustration).

We have the terrain, which represents "reality" (and corresponds to "international system" in the present paper) and want to use the map to obtain knowledge about the terrain. The map is then the "mode " (and corresponds to "small group" in the present paper). The usefulness of the map as a model is due to the circumstance that several relations are included in the isomorphism, for instance both distance and direction if we are dealing with maps of small bits of terrain and usually at least one of them if we are dealing with maps covering more terrain. Now, imagine the map were printed on a rubber sheet and distorted so that both distance and direction were lost. Topological relationships would, however, still be preserved (one would still know from the map what is in the neighborhood of what in the terrain), so the map would not be useless, only less useful. We shall express this by saying that the isomorphism has lost in richness, it is poorer than it was, and define the "richness of an isomorphism" simply in terms of the number of relations in the *model* that are included in the isomorphism. Similarly, "degree of isomorphism" is this number relative to the total number of relations in the model. Thus, if the degree of isomorphism of the model is very high then this means that the model has been (nearly) completely exploited for its structural content, if it is very low, then it is underutilized or simply a poor

model that in addition may be misleading. For each unutilized relation in the model is a temptation toward unwarranted conclusions and even toward poor hypotheses.

It should perhaps be pointed out that we have tied the concept of "richness" and "degree" to the model and not to that which the model is a model of. The main reason for this is that the model usually is much simpler and more explicit (even formalized), which often makes such ideas as "number of relations" and "total number of relations" meaningful. "Reality" is usually so complex that one can impute to it any number of relations. Thus the point of reference is the model itself, and — reality being the same — the task is to find a model as high on richness and degree of isomorphism as possible. However, when two models are compared in terms of richness a safer method than simply counting number of relations would be to say that "one model is richer than the other if it includes all the relations of the latter and at least one more in its isomorphism".

Where would one now put such concepts as "metaphor", "analogy", and "heuristic", which often appear in this connection? We would suggest that both "metaphors" and "analogies" are models, only that they are poor and/or low in degree of isomorphism. One reason is often that the models are in themselves so complicated, for instance because they are taken from another aspect of human reality, that the degree of isomorphism will have to be low even if the richness is quite high, and model-building as such easily falls into disrepute because of the tendency to step outside the established isomorphism. But a generalized anti-model attitude, on the basis of some poor applications, is of course equally unscientific.

The concept of "heuristic" only serves to point out that there is no *a priori* confirmation of any model of reality; the model is a reservoir of hypotheses. On the other hand, one would not do empirical work before every application of a map, one would use the map, only preserve an empirical attitude with readiness for revision if the isomorphism should fail.

Finally, it should be pointed out that there is nothing new in such heuristic devices in the study of international relations. The only new element would be the effort to make it more explicit and systematic.

[5] For an analysis of the concept of "interaction", see Johan Galtung, "Expectations and Interaction Processes", *Inquiry*, 1959, pp. 213—34.

[6] For an excellent example of this kind of analysis, see Chadwick Alger's chapter, "Interaction in a Committee of the United Nations General Assembly" in J. David Singer, ed., *Quantitative International Politics, International Yearbook of Political Behavior Research*, Vol. VI (New York; The Free Press, 1968), pp. 51—84, and other papers coming out of his UN project.

[7] The important book by Sidney Verba, *Small Groups and Political Behavior* (Princeton: Princeton University Press, 1961) is permeated with a discussion of this. For an effort to discuss a concrete case of small group interaction in terms of the representative roles of the participants, see Johan Galtung, "Summit Meetings and International Relations," *Journal of Peace Research*, 1964, pp. 36—54. The Verba book deals with small groups *in* politics, not with small groups as a *model*.

[8] See T. Parsons and R. F. Bales, *Family Socialization and Interaction Process* (Glencoe: The Free Press, 1955), pp. 47, 310—312. For a similar analysis of how a leadership structure is born in stages, see Verba (ref. [7]) p. 177.

[9] See P. E. Slater, "Role Differentiation in Small Groups", in Paul Hare et al.,

eds., *Small Groups* (New York: Knopf, 1955), pp. 498—515.

[10] See Johan Galtung, *Norm, Role and Status, A Synthetic Approach to Social Structure* (forthcoming). For precise, operational definitions of rank disequilibrium and rank incongruence, see Johan Galtung, "International Relations and International Conflicts: A Sociological Approach," *Transactions of the Sixth World Congress of Sociology*, (International Sociological Association, 1966), pp. 121—161.

[11] We are thinking of Komarovsky's finding of how American college girls play down interests and ability in order to fit into the underdog role. "At first I resented this bitterly. But now I am more or less used to it and live in hope of one day meeting a man who is my superior so that I may be my natural self." "Cultural Contradictions and Sex Roles", *American Journal of Sociology*, 1946, p. 185.

[12] For an analysis of this mechanism in case of race conflicts, see Johan Galtung, "A Model for Studying Images of Participants in a Conflict: Southville", *Journal of Social Issues*, 1959, pp. 38—43.

[13] One of the best polarization theories, and in general a model piece of theorizing in the social sciences, is found in Cartwright, Harary, "Structural Balance: A Generalization of Heider's Theory", *Psychological Review*, 1956, pp. 277—293.

[14] New York: Harcourt, Brace, 1964.

[15] Some psychological research seems to indicate that seven (or a number between 2 and 3 bits) is, for practical purposes, the maximum number of objects that most people can keep cognitively present at the same time — for ranking purposes, for instance. If the number is higher, a process of grouping and categorization takes place. Picking *a la carte* the person

will group dishes in "meat" vs. "fish", etc., and start ranking the groups, then he may do the within-group ranking and on that basis make his choice. See Duncan Luce, *Individual Choice Behavior* (New York: Wiley, 1959), Chapter I.

[16] Op. cit., p. 326.

[17] Verba emphasizes a reason why small groups are so much more homogenizing than mass media: "Through selection, mass media communications can be kept from challenging an individual's opinions. But not so with the face-to-face group. One cannot as easily tune out or ignore communications that are hostile to one's point of view" (op. cit., p. 26). It probably works the same way with nations, for if nations are in a group together, then not only do statesmen meet and there is much formal and informal diplomatic interaction; the tendency is also for all types of nongovernmental nteraction to be high so that the same

homogenizing pressure is found at many levels.

[18] Richardson's data from *Statistics of Deadly Quarrels* (Chicago: Quadrangle Books, 1960), pp. 177 and 297, are good illustrations. Of 710 "deadly quarrels" down to Richardson's magnitude $3 \pm 1/2$, 321, or 45%, were international between contiguous nations, 173, or 24%, were international between noncontiguous nations and 216, or 31%, were intranational or "civil" wars. This means that of the international wars, 65% were across frontiers — which is, of course, much higher than by chance. From this one would also expect that noncontiguous wars would be even more "deadly" since they have to be started against geography and triggered by something more serious than merely a quarrel between neighbors. This is also borne out by Richardson's data if we percentage his data in Table 1 on p. 297:

Percentage of pairs of opposed belligerents

Magnitude	International wars Contiguous belligerents, %	Noncontiguous belligerents, %	Percentage difference
6.5—7.5	12	41	—29
4.5—6.5	21	12	9
2.5—4.5	67	47	20
Sum	100	100	0

But it should also be noted that the curve of the noncontiguous pairs is U-shaped. indicating the involvement of many "small quarrels" also in the noncontiguous case. We would also expect from this general pattern that there would be a high and positive correlation between the number of a state's external wars and the number of its frontiers, and this is also borne out by Richardson's findings. The correlation is, in fact, .77 (Chapter V, section 4, pp. 176 ff.).

[19] The most crucial dyad is, of course, the marital couple. Whether it is formed

by parental choice, as in many traditional societies, or by self-selection, as in many modern societies, the tendency toward homogamy seems to be very strong as evidenced by the many high correlations found. For some data on this, see Berelson, Steiner, op. cit., p. 309.

[20] For some notes on the territorial vs. social definition of a nation especially in relation to defense, see Johan Galtung, "Different Concepts of Defense", (Oslo, PRIO-stencil, 1964).

[21] The world where geographical distance is a variable of fundamental impor-

tance is so quickly decreasing in significance due to modern transportation and COMSAT systems of communication, etc., that simultaneous coexistence of very many persons with very many others regardless of where they are located is increasing. The consequence of this is of course that social organization based on affinity will increase in importance relative to social organization based on vicinity, and that this will even permeate the loyalty ties attached to the territorial nation-state. For some comments on this see Johan Galtung, "On the Future of the International System", *Journal of Peace Research*, 1967, pp. 305—333.

[22] This is the famous cross-pressure hypothesis, tested and confirmed particularly on voting data. See Berelson, Lazarsfeld, McPhee, *Voting*, (Chicago: University of Chicago Press, 1954), p. 149.

[23] See Bruce Russett, "El problema de la identificación de regiones", paper prepared for the Centro de Sociología Comparada Conference, Buenos Aires, 1964. Actually, Argentina is the lowest of the Latin American countries on the factor "Latin America", and Portugal and Spain are almost as Latin American as Argentina. The countries with the highest loadings on "Latin Americanism" are Costa Rica, Colombia, Ecuador, Mexico, Paraguay, Panama, and Honduras. Correspondingly, the most North-Atlantic country is West Germany, the most Asiatic country Indonesia and the most East European country is Romania.

[24] For an extensive analysis see Johan Galtung, "Manuel Mora y Araujo", and Simon Schwartzman, "El Sistema Latino-Americano de Naciones: Un Analysis Estructural", *America Latina*, 1966. ("The Latin American System of Nations: A Structural Analysis", in Höglund and Ulrich, eds., *Conflict Control and Conflict Resolution*, Scand. Univ. Books, 1968.

[25] For data comparing knowledge level in the United States and Brazil see Wilbur Schramm, *Mass Media and National Development* (Stanford: Stanford University Press, 1964), p. 70. The data show that in the United States knowledge level is higher than in Brazil; much more interesting is the circumstance that whereas urban-rural differences in knowledge level are tremendous in Brazil they appear to be almost negligible in the United States. Thus, the educated urban group in Latin American nations can communicate readily with the developed nations and have become relatively similar to them, but the vast rural masses have been left behind. And interaction with, not to mention knowledge about, other developing nations appears to be negligible.

[26] For another theoretical statement on the nature of polarization see James S. Coleman, *Community Conflict*, (Glencoe: The Free Press, 1957). For a presentation in mathematical terms see Johan Galtung, *An Introduction to Mathematical Sociology* (forthcoming).

[27] See Harary, op. cit.

[28] Harary has tried it out in an article, "A Structural Analysis of the Situation in the Middle East", *Journal of Conflict Resolution*, 1961, pp. 167—178.

[29] Berelson, Steiner, op. cit., pp. 331—339.

[30] For discussion of the communication of news, see Einar Ostgaard, "Factors Influencing the Flow of News", *Journal of Peace Research*, 1965, pp. 39—63, and Johan Galtung and Mari Holmboe Ruge, "The Structure of Foreign News: The Presentation of the Congo, Cuba and Cyprus Crises in Four Norwegian Newspapers", *Journal of Peace Research*, 1965, pp. 64—91.

[31] Verba, op. cit., p. 231.

[32] *Street Corner Society*, (Chicago: University of Chicago Press, 1943), pp. 256—57.

[33] Data on trade relations between the Soviet Union and countries in the NATO alliance show in general a U-shaped pattern: high before the cold war started around 1950, a minimum in the early and mid-fifties, and then — in most cases — a rise again. This pattern is particularly pronounced for USA and Portugal on the one hand, Greece and Turkey on the other, and much less so for France, UK, and Britain. Correspondingly, there is more voting similarity between the USA and the very marginal countries in the OAS system than between USA and the topdog Latin American nations, such as Argentina, Mexico, and Brazil. For some data on East-West trade relations, see Paul Smoker, "Trade, Defence and the Richardson Theory of Arms Races: A Seven Nation Study", *Journal of Peace Research*, 1965, pp. 161—176.

[34] Berelson, Steiner, op. cit., p. 339. The leader has to conform, but whether the values have originated in the group or in the leader himself is another matter.

[35] Data from the article by Galtung, Mora, and Schwartzman illustrate this. Thus, several indicators of development were correlated with data on flights to and from the country, more precisely with the proportion of flights (of the total number of international flights) to and from the United States. The correlations were —. 62 with literacy rates, —. 52 with per capita income, —. 57 with newspapers per capita, and —. 62 with the proportion of the active population engaged in industry (ibid., Table 18). Of course, there are several ways of interpreting this, and for another interpretation, see Johan Galtung, "International Relations and International Conflicts: A Sociological Approach."

[36] For an exploration of these conditions, see Johan Galtung, "International Relations and International Conflicts: A Sociological Approach."

[37] Berelson, Steiner, op. cit., p. 341.

[38] For a more complete list of properties of nations, ascribed as well as achieved, see Johan Galtung, "A Structural Theory of Aggression", *Journal of Peace Research*, 1964, pp. 95—119, especially pp. 115—16.

[39] The degree to which this leads to correlation between centrality in the communication network and total rank is explored in Galtung, Mora y Araujo, and Schwartzman, op. cit. The article indicates how international prestige seems to be based on a mixture of achievement and ascription, and mostly on the latter.

For a study of interaction patterns in a factory, see John Cohen, Peter Cooper, Paul Thorne, "A Note on Communication in a Factory", *Occupation Psychology*, 1965, pp. 25—30. And for a very interesting demonstration of feudal interaction patterns in a biracial group, see Irwin Katz and Lawrence Benjamin, "Effects of White Authoritarianism in Biracial Work Groups", *J. Abnormal Soc. Psychology*, 1960, pp. 448—456. Sixteen task-solving groups were formed with two whites and two Negroes in each, and the conclusion was: "For the entire sample of sixteen groups it was found significantly that whites spoke more than Negroes, Negroes spoke more to whites than to one another, Negroes were more susceptible to group influence than were whites, ranked whites higher on mental ability, favored one another as future work companions, and scored lower than whites on a Group Satisfaction scale. These results indicate that even when Negroes are given objective evidence of equal mental ability in a relatively brief interracial contact they tend to feel inadequate and to orient compliantly toward whites." As is seen, this summarizes many of the general system hypotheses referred to in the text, whether at the level of individual or national actors.

[40] Thus, Lippitt writes: "This is to say, the actor's power may have initially derived from pre-eminence in some particular type of activity or characteristic, e.g., fighting, sports, campcraft, disobeying adults, strength or size, but fellow members tend to generalize this pre-eminence to the general range of group situations and activities", in "The Dynamics of Power", *Human Relations*, 1952, pp. 37—64. It is obvious that this phenomenon will greatly contribute to rank concordance; the big are made bigger and the small smaller.

[41] For a general theory, see Johan Galtung, "A Structural Theory of Aggression". Some of the findings made by R. J. Rummel in his Dimensionality of Nations Program seem to support this theory very nicely, see "Research Communication", *Journal of Peace Research*, 1967, pp. 196—206.

[42] For a general analysis of the role of rank-disequilibrium and rank-incongruence in connection with the political systems centering around the United States, the Soviet Union, and the People's Republic of China, see Johan Galtung, "East-West Interaction Patterns", *Journal of Peace Research*, 1966, pp. 146—177, especially pp. 151—155.

[43] For one description of the system, see Parsons, Bales, op. cit., pp. 38 ff. In this theory the movement from the phases of adaptation and goal-achievement via integration and latency and back again to adaptation (to new problems, or new aspects of old problems) plays a dominant role. The international system should be characterized by periods involving the first two phases, interspersed with prolonged latency periods, to permit

the system to rest. There is, in fact, some indication that there are limitations to how much the system can absorb of time- and energy-consuming conflict matter. If one analyzes the distribution of what has been defined as major international conflicts over time it is remarkable how truncated the distribution is in the sense that there are few cases of as many as four or five major conflicts coinciding in time (or, if they were, some of the conflicts would be played down simply because the machineries of data-processing and policy-making would not have sufficient time at their disposal to deal with them). Thus, the information overload factor probably forces some kind of latency phase on systems or subsystems. But the conclusion is still that the integration phase under the leadership of a unit with expressive status in the system is missing.

[44] It should be interesting to analyze relations between the United States and France during the last ten years from this point of view, through the phases of docility/subservience (relatively speaking) via high nuisance values to the phase of partial rupture. However, the transition from phase 2 to phase 3 has not really taken place: "We are all watching the French delegate. What will he say? How does he think? What is he up to now?" (quoted from a NATO delegation member, April 1966) indicates intense concern rather than rupture.

[45] Berelson, Steiner, op. cit., p. 348.

[46] See Bales, Strodtbeck, Mills, Roseborough, "Channels of Communication in Small Groups", *Amer. Sociol. Review*, 1951, pp. 461—468.

[47] For an exploration of this, see Johan Galtung, "Rank and Social Integration: A Multidimensional Approach", in Berger, Zelditsch, Anderson, *Sociological Theories*

in Progress, (Boston: Houghton Mifflin Co., 1866), pp. 145—198, especially Table 4.

[48] See T. M. Mills, "Power Relations in Three Person Groups", *Amer. Sociol. Review*, 1953, pp. 351—57.

Nils Petter Gleditsch reviews the literature in the field in an important article, "Trends in World Airline Patterns", *Journal of Peace Research*, 1967, pp. 366—408, and points out that in this example, from Mills, there is no independent criterion of rank — a point which we fully accept. However, Gleditsch points to some other and better evidence from the small group literature, viz. a study by Hurwitz, Zander, and Hymovitch where "interaction patterns in groups where the members have been assigned positions of high and low power" (Gleditsch, op. cit., p. 369) are investigated. "The data fully support the hypothesis of rank dependence." Other accounts of the literature on small group interaction patterns can be found in H. W. Riecken and G. C. Homans, "Psychological Aspects of Social Structure", in G. Lindzey, *Handbook of Social Psychology*, Ch. 22. For other comments, see Newcomb, Turner, and Converse, *Social Psychology* (New York: Holt, Rinehart and Winston, 1965).

[49] But this problem is solved if we look at the data on diplomatic relations with more refined categories. Thus, the size of the US embassy in Norway is bigger than the Norwegian embassy in the USA, indicating that there is at least a higher potential for channelling interaction from high to low than from low to high.

[50] Systematic data on size and structure of all embassies and other diplomatic stations are currently being collected and analyzed at the International Peace Research Institute in Oslo, by Reidar Kvadsheim.

[51] See Galtung, Mora, Schwartzman, op. cit., and Johan Galtung, "East-West Interaction Patterns, op. cit.

[52] Systematic data on about twenty types of interaction between all nations are currently being analyzed at the International Peace Research Institute in Oslo.

[53] Berelson, Steiner, op. cit., p. 354.

[54] The experiment is described in Berelson, Steiner, op. cit., p. 357, taken from Heise, Miller, "Problem Solving By Small Groups Using Various Communication Nets", *J. Abnormal Soc. Psychol.*, 1951, pp. 327—335.

[55] Thus, the multilateral structure of n individuals is also a setting that permits all bilateral combinations, but not vice versa.

[56] This important experiment is reported in Alex Bavelas, "Communication Patterns in Task-Oriented Groups", *J. Acoustical Soc. Amer.*, 1950, pp. 725—30; a source usually difficult to locate for social scientists, for whom the short report in Berelson, Steiner, op. cit., p. 356 may be more useful. Also see Festinger, Schachter, Back, *Social Pressures in Informal Groups* (New York: Harper, 1950), pp. 157—158.

[57] See Johan Galtung, *An Introduction to Mathematical Sociology*, Ch. 3, section 4 (forthcoming).

[58] A general theory of how rank and centrality relate to each other is given in Johan Galtung, "International Relations and International Conflicts: A Sociological Approach."

[59] This theme is developed extensively for the case of the East-West system and used as a basis for policy recommendations in Johan Galtung, "East-West Interaction Patterns", in the last section, pp. 169—

172, and in Johan Galtung, *Cooperation in Europe* (Strasbourg: Council of Europe, 1968).

[60] Berelson, Steiner, op. cit., p. 359, based on data from Bales, Borgatta, "Size of Group as a Factor in the Interaction Profile", in A. Paul Hare, and others, eds., *Small Groups*.

[61] Berelson, Steiner, op. cit., p. 360.

[62] This is also mentioned in J. David Singer, "The Political Science of Human Conflict", in Elton McNeil, ed., *The Nature of Human Conflict* (Englewood Cliffs, New Jersey: Prentice-Hall, 1965), p. 152.

[63] Efforts to develop strict criteria for comparisons of individual and national systems of interaction on these dimensions are currently being made at the International Peace Research Institute, Oslo.

[64] As an effort in this direction, see Johan Galtung, *Cooperation in Europe* (Strasbourg: Council of Europe, 1968).

IV.2. *Summit Meetings and International Relations*

* Paper presented at the First Nordic Conference on Peace Research, Oslo, 4—8 January 1963, here published as PRIO publication no. 4—1. The author wishes to express his gratitude to the *Aquinas Foundation*, New York, for financial support, to Mari Holmboe Ruge, M.A., for assistance in the data-collection, and to Dr. J. David Singer, Fulbright research fellow at the Institute for Social Research 1963/64. The article is a part of a more comprehensive study of summit meetings.

[1] For a succinct presentation of the requirements of a profession, see the article by W. J. Goode: 'The Emerging Profession', *American Sociological Review*, 1960, pp. 902—14.

[2] In a study by Svalastoga, *Prestige, Class and Mobility* (Copenhagen: Gyldendal, 1959) a population sample ranks 75 occupations with the result that 'ambassador' comes out as no. 1, and 'prime minister' as no. 2 (see insert between pages 80 and 81). Thus, public opinion in an aggregate sense does not correspond to the factual power relations in, say, Danish society. This is probably due to the circumstance that whereas both positions are among the most prestigious, the ambassador is a remote and half sacred person and the prime minister the opposite. He is controversial, and consequently suffers a certain drop in prestige.

[3] In the most important monograph on summit meetings, Elmer Plischke, *Summit Diplomacy, Personal Diplomacy of the President of the United States* (College Park, Maryland: Bureau of Governmental Research, 1958) the author says: 'Although to date the term "summit" has been applied solely to international conferences, it is equally applicable to a number of other types of diplomatic relations engaged in by the chief executive... Such diplomacy encompasses the following principal elements: 1. presidential policy formulation, enunciation and formalization; 2. personal presidential communications; 3. presidential personal representative; 4. state visits; and 5. summit conferences.' We are concerned only with no. 5 in this list, but not only with the Chief Executive — our 'summit' is broader. Also, we feel the qualifying 'ad hoc' is important; regular, institutionalized meetings are not summit meetings in our sense.

[4] For a discussion of falsifiability in survey research, see Galtung, Johan: *Theory and Method of Social Research* (Oslo: mimeo, 1964), II, 5.4.

[5] 'The struggle for the heart of Europe is much older and quite independent of

the ideological color of the Russian government; as is the struggle between Great Britain and Russia in the Middle East and that between the United States and Russia in the Far East. But for the collapse of imperial Russia during the First World War, it is a virtual certainty that Czechoslovakia, for example, would have fallen under Russian control in 1918 instead of 1948.' Geoffrey Barraclough, in a review of D. F. Fleming: *The Cold War and its Origins* (New York: Doubleday, 1961) in *The Nation*, December 2, 1961, p. 453.

[6] The methodologically oriented reader should notice that we are here dealing with the universe of summit meetings, not with any sample, so percentages are not subject to sampling variations and the percentage differences are as reliable as our method of data-collection. Hence, no tests of significance will be carried out.

[7] Thus, it is particularly important for a nation to fill the in-between status, that of the premier, with a person who is capable of engaging in both instrumental and expressive activities. The most important contemporary example is probably Nikita Khrushchev.

[8] The American president is coded as head of state when he meets other heads of state, and as head of government when he meets other heads of government. Mendès-France is coded correspondingly in the period when he functioned as both head of government and foreign minister.

[9] From *Permanent Missions to the* UN, No. 151, New York, January 1963. Some countries are without national days, and for some countries we did not get information. But generally the national day is like the flag; it is almost a part of the definition of a nation.

[10] Using the traditional definition in terms of the two tropics.

[11] Durkheim, E.: *Suicide*, American edition by J. A. Spaulding and G. Simpson (Glencoe: The Free Press, 1951), esp. p. 108.

[13] Plischke, op. cit., p. 90 calls these meetings 'pre-conference or post-conference meetings'.

[13] From Churchill, W.S.: *The Hinge of Fate* (Boston: Houghton, Mifflin, 1950), p. 664.

[14] Eden, A.: *Full Circle* (London: Cassel, 1960), p. 291.

[13] Hull, C.: *The Memoirs of Cordell Hull* (New York: Macmillan, 1948), vol. II, p. 1277.

[16] The best general discussion of polarization in the sociological literature is found in Coleman, J.: *Community Conflict* (Glencoe: The Free Press, 1957).

[17] This is the 'tight bipolar system' in the sense of Morton Kaplan in *System and Process in International Politics* (New York: Wiley, 1957), pp. 43 ff, but the discussion here is about a move towards the 'loose bipolar system".

[18] Just to quote one commentator: 'By 1945, or more conservatively 1946, it was evident that the conflict between the Soviet bloc and the West would dominate the diplomatic scene for a long time. In these historically unprecedented circumstances the so-called traditional quarrels between European nations lost all meaning'. 'Old Nations, New Europe', by Raymond Aron, in *Daedalus*, Winter 1964.

[19] Nicolson says about communiqués: (*The Old Diplomacy and the New*, London: David Davies Memorial Institute of International Studies, 1961) p. 5: 'But the politician whose journey of mission has been widely advertised does not wish to return to his own aerodrome and announce

that he has accomplished nothing. He prefers to wave triumphantly in the air a scrap of paper recording complete agreement, even though in his heart of hearts he may suspect that the paper is worthless. Thus we get that horrible document called a 'communiqué', in which the results of the meeting have to be recorded for public consumption. I recall with horror the many hours I have spent after an exhausting conference seeking to find with a foreign colleague a formula which will satisfy our chiefs.' And Thayer: *(Diplomat*, London: Michael Joseph, 1960) p. 112: 'Every newspaper reader will recognize the formulas with which varying degrees of success are announced at the end of a conference. "Full agreement" but no published agreements means doubtful: "substantial agreement" means disagreement in at least some important fields, "full exchange of views resulted" means no agreement at all. If unfriendly powers announce "full agreement", it may mean substantial success. No success is generally signalled by unilateral announcements that the con-ference adjourned *sine die*, meaning that the participants could not even agree on how to disagree'.

[20] This is a revision of the *hypothesis*, not of the *proposition* about polarization in conflict. The hypothesis gains some additional support from another, unpublished, PRIO study about conflict over the desegregation issue in a town in the southern United States. Originally there was much contact between people, then the latent issue became manifest and a period of organization-formation with a very sharp dip in contact followed. But when the organizations were formed some form for contact, not between the extremists but in the middle, was found. However, the positions were at that time relatively hardened. To the extent that this is a generally valid thesis it is a relatively tragic one: there is contact 1. when it is least necessary because of patterns of indifference or cooperation rather than conflict, and 2. when it is least efficient because of the inertia due to the conflict organizations.

IV.3. *Patterns of Diplomacy: A Study of Recruitment and Career Patterns in Norwegian Diplomacy*

* This is a part of a comprehensive study of the structure and function of modern diplomacy' published here as PRIO publication no. 13—1. The authors wish to express their gratitude to the Institute for Social Research, the Norwegian Research Council for Science and the Humanities and the Norwegian Council for Research on Conflict and Peace for financial support; to stud. mag. art. Mariken Vaa Mathiesen, stud. mag. art. Siri H. Albrechtsen, stud. mag. art. Rolf Rasmussen and Chief of Section Sigrid Garborg for assistance in the data collection; to Director General, now Ambassador Tor Brodtkorb, Chief of Section Per Pröitz and first secretary Björn Blakstad at the Ministry of Foreign Affairs for their kind permission to obtain necessary data and their general helpfulness; and to Messrs. Arne Arnesen, Knut Frydenlund, Torvald Stoltenberg and Oscar Varnö, all of the Ministry of Foreign Affairs, and also Professor Torstein Eckhoff and Dr. Knut Dahl-Jakobsen, for stimulating comments and criticism. Special gratitude is expressed to all other Norwegian diplomats with whom we have had the opportunity to discuss aspects of this report. Needless to say, opinions and conclusions of this article are the responsibility of the present authors alone.

[1] Thus, in the index for the leading sociological journal, the *American Sociological Review*, for the period 1935—60 no article was found containing an analysis of the institution from a sociological point of view. There is, however, an excellent but

so far unpublished study by Suzanne Keller, made when its author was a visiting fellow at the Center for International Studies, Princeton University. Also see article by same author, 'Diplomacy and Communication,' *Public Opinion Quarterly*, Vol. XX, No. 1, Spring 1956, pp. 176—82, and her book, *Beyond the Ruling Class*, (New York: Random House, 1963) p. 297.

[2] These themes are the themes of research which the Peace Research Institute — Oslo are interested in exploring within the framework of its program 13, Modern Diplomacy: Structure and Function.

[3] For a discussion of the problem of elite-studies see I, 6.4 in Johan Galtung, *Theory and Methods of Social Research* (forthcoming).

[4] 'A society is civilized insofar as the community is no longer small, isolated, homogenous and self-sufficient, as the division of labor is no longer simple; as impersonal relationships come to take the place of personal relationships, as familial connections come to be modified or supplanted by those of political affiliation or contract.' Robert Redfield, *The Primitive World and its Transformations*, (Ithaca, New York: Great Seal Books, Cornell University Press, 1953) p. 22.

[5] A case here is the annual conference of international organizations, another the regular trips made by an ambassador stationed in one country but accredited to another.

[6] The Finnish diplomat and scientist, Ragnar Numelin, in his presentation of diplomacy in ancient cultures and primitive societies, quotes a number of authorities to show that diplomatic practice is by no means limited to Western cultural traditions. Ragnar Numelin, *The Beginnings of Diplomacy*, (London: Oxford University Press, 1950). '...by the fifth century the Greeks had elaborated some system of constant diplomatic relations; that members of diplomatic missions were accorded certain immunities and great consideration; and that it had come to be recognized that the relations between states could not be managed or adjusted merely by ruse and violence, and that there was some implicit "law" which was above immediate national interests or momentary expediency'. Harold Nicolson, *Diplomacy*, (London: Oxford University Press, 1950, 2nd edition) p. 22.

[7] *Public Opinion Quarterly*, op. cit. p. 176.

[8] Hans J. Morgenthau, *Politics Among Nations*, (New York: Knopf, 1960, 3rd edition) p. 541.

[9] P. A. Sorokin, *Social and Cultural Dynamics*, (Boston: 1957) Ch. 26.

[10] Amitai Etzioni, *A Comparative Analysis of Complex Organizations*, (Glencoe: Free Press, 1961) p. 5.

[11] Not all acts take place beacause of anticipated consequences, however. They can also relate to some kind of general ideology, etc. For a discussion of this see Torstein Eckhoff, *Rettferdighet og sosiale avgjörelser*, (unpublished manuscript) pp. 17—18.

[12] Harold Nicolson, op. cit., pp. 127——53. The author also gives an amusing description of what to him are the two main schools of diplomatic theory, 'the military school' and 'the school of shop-keepers': 'The former believe far too much in the ability of force to produce intimidation; the latter believe far too much in the ability of the credit idea to produce confidence' (ibid, p. 54). A characterization of the third school might be the following: 'The worst kind of diplomatists are missionaries, fanatics and lawyers; the best kind are the reasonable and humane sceptics' (ibid, p. 50).

[13] Mari Holmboe Ruge, in her article 'Technical Assistance and Parliamentary Debates', *Journal of Peace Research*, No. 2, 1964, pp. 77—94, distinguishes between three styles of technical assistance diplomacy, or three patterns of motivation. Thus, Norway seems to be a nation that at least in the 50s used morality, and hence persuasion, as the motivational basis of her technical assistance activities.

[14] '...because diplomats for some centuries were the personal representatives of the head of state, and since the heads of states were royal personages, it is not surprising that the profession of diplomacy was originally entered exclusively by persons of noble rank. This meant that diplomats were usually more cultured, wealthier and better educated than the general populace in any of the nations.' Michael H. Cardozo, *Diplomats in International Cooperation*, (Ithaca, New York: Cornell University Press, 1962) p. 12.

[15] See, for instance, Burdick and Lederer, *The Ugly American* (New York, W. W. Norton & Co., 1958).

[16] The mean rank given to 'ambassador' was 1.20, 'prime minister' got 1.30. The scale from 2 to 5. Kaare Svalastoga, *Prestige, Class and Mobility*, (Copenhagen: Scandinavian University Books, 1959) p. 74.

[17] E. F. Jackson, 'Status Consistency and Symptoms of Stress', *A.S.R.*, 1962, pp. 469—80.

[18] Excessive curiosity and revelation of ignorance would be against the rules of behavior for a person with extremely high rank. It is interesting to see how compatible this simple sociological principle is with common ideas about what it means to be 'diplomatic': no emotion, not talking too much, no commitment, affable manners, but uniform facial expressions.

[19] Thayer, however, gives the other side of the picture: 'The travelling American public also expects to be entertained in the manner long associated with diplomatic tradition. Not only congressmen but businessmen, artists, writers, editors, ballet troupes, college bands and basketball teams, wrestlers, swimmers, and rope climbers, not to mention social climbers, consider it not a privilege but a right to be entertained in the grand diplomatic manner at "their" embassy. Not a few career diplomats, eyeing their precious supply of whisky, have listened tight-lipped as American visitors demanded a double Scotch from the butler explaining loudly, "What the hell, we taxpayers pay for it!"' Charles W. Thayer, *Diplomat*, (London: 1960) p. 215.

[20] 'In *The Ugly American* the authors have with considerable justification criticized the isolation in which American diplomats live in their gadget-equipped ghettos. One wonders, however, whether this is entirely the fault of the diplomat or whether it does not reflect the parochial narrowness of Washington bureaucrats and legislators.' Charles W. Thayer, op. cit., p. 237.

[21] Thus, a content analysis of the memoir literature produced by Norwegian diplomats would easily substantiate these ideas about interaction patterns if one counted systematically the social position of the persons with whom they reported interaction. But these memoirs report conditions some decades ago, or are written by people born several decades away, so it remains to know more about interaction patterns of today.

[22] Thus, the Norwegian Foreign Ministry instructs its officers not to encourage Norwegian emigration abroad, not to encourage Norwegians who want to be employed abroad, etc. *Instruction for the Norwegian Foreign Service*, § 7, § 6.

[23] 'Frequently the inexperienced diplomat, consciously or unconsciously, as-

sumes the role of advocate for his host's country *vis-à-vis* his own. Anxious to be loved, he himself falls in love with his host. The result it that his dispatches take on the color of a lawyer's brief rather than a dispassionate objective report. Occasionally the opposite temptation arises when his love is rebuffed and he takes every occasion to condemn his host unfairly.' Charles W. Thayer, op. cit., p. 233.

[24] These are frequently recurring themes in the memoir literature. Since the reports are visible and lasting documents, they are among the strings that tie the stations to the ministry. It becomes of some importance to the diplomat that his reports are well received, and we have noticed the elements of some kind of a scoring system to record how successful a report has been. The diplomat is notified as to who has received the report, and a simple mental score can be made, based on numbers weighted with the rank of the report-receiver (but much of the distribution is routine). Also there is the reward that may be due to the person who is right in specific predictions of important events — and this may discourage general, analytical reports.

[25] In so doing the diplomat is not alone. The famous study by Caplow, *The Academic Marketplace*, (New York: Basic Books, 1958) p. 105, demonstrates a general human tendency (the aggrandizement effect) to overrate one's own particular organization, to give it more importance than others are willing to give it.

[26] The current practice of the Norwegian foreign service is a maximum of about three years for lower and middle diplomatic positions and five years for heads of diplomatic missions.

[27] This might be compared with Peter Cooper's analysis of 'morality' attributed to nations by children: in early years children are willing to attribute the same

kind of morality to both parties in a conflict; later on they seem to learn that if one is 'right' then the other is 'wrong'. See Peter Cooper, 'The Development of the Concept of War', *Journal of Peace Research* ,No. 1, 1965, pp. 1—17.

[28] Each issue of *Utenrikskalenderen* contains an alphabetical list of the foreign service officers, giving their current position as well as their past career steps. In addition, the years of birth, university graduation and entrance into the service are given. For additional background information we have drawn upon a variety of sources of reference. Finally the data were checked and completed by a retired chief of section in the Foreign Ministry, who had been given access to the dossiers. The data comprise the Foreign Service officers only; they are defined in the *Instruction* (2 § 3) as having an obligation to be moved to any position of equal or higher rank within the service *(flyttepliktig)*.

[29] The growth of the foreign service during this time is almost but not quite as rapid as that of the Norwegian ministries as a whole, which show an increase from 266 civil servants in 1900 to 1,453 in 1960 (between 500 and 600 %). Vilhelm Aubert *et al.*, *The Professions in Norwegian Social Structure 1720—1955*, (Oslo: Institute for Social Research, 1961) Tables I — 6.

A study group of younger officers in the foreign service has pointed out the rapid increase of the tasks of the foreign service after the war, such as participation in the U.N. and other international organizations, the emergence of new independent nations, increase in technical assistance, 'without leading to a similar increase of the personnel in the Ministry'. *Innstilling fra Studiegruppen vedrörende utenrikstjensten*, (Oslo, 1964, 75 pp. mimeo.) p. 33.

[30] Concerning the consular service, one has to keep in mind the high number of

unpaid consuls placed all over the world. The size of this group has been remarkably constant in the last 50 years: in 1906 there were 451, in 1960, 599, with a record high of 675 just before World War II. This reflects Norway's strong shipping traditions which date back to the abolition of the Navigation Act in 1849. Hence the need for a strong consular network also before 1905. During the union between Sweden and Norway the two countries had a common consular service. Prolonged and unsuccessful Norwegian demands for a separate consular service triggered off the separation in 1905.

[31] The titles 'Ambassador I and II' do not designate ambassadors in the international sense as agreed to at the Vienna conference in 1815 (see Nicolson, op. cit., p. 32). Rather, these titles are translations of the Norwegian *sendemann* I & II, which is the official term in the Norwegian foreign service. Actually Norway had no 'real' ambassadors until after World War II.

[32] *Studiegruppen vedrörende utenrikstjenesten*, op. cit., p. 29.

[33] Ibid.

[34] The data comprise all those who have served in the foreign service of Norway as an independent nation. Thus, those Norwegian diplomats who served only in the common Norwegian-Swedish foreign service have been excluded, for lack of sufficient data.

[35] The members of the foreign service have been assigned to the different phases according to the year when they entered the service.

[36] In the period 1885—1950 the general Norwegian occupation structure changed as follows: Academic professions increased from 0.6 % to 1.5 % of the adult population, business people from 2.6% to 6%, functionaries from 7% to 19%, teachers show

a slight increase from 0.6% to 0.9%, and the group 'workers, farmers and craftsmen' has declined from 89% to 75%. Tore Lindbekk, 'Den sosiale rekruttering til de akademiske profesjoner i vår tid', *Tidsskrift for Samfunnsforskning*, Oslo 1962, p. 252. (The last figure conceals the major changes which have taken place within that group from a majority of farmers to a majority of industrial workers.)

[37] Suzanne Keller, in her unpublished study on 97 American and 120 British ambassadors summarizes findings about their fathers' positions as follows: 'The British diplomats thus come predominantly from the landed gentry (21%), from the higher ranks of the Civil Service (14%) and from the Armed Services (17%). The Americans tend to come primarily from business (31%) and professional families (21%). This corresponds, in rough form, to the general value systems of the two countries with the United States emphasizing success in the world of business and Great Britain emphasizing family tradition and public service. Each country is thus expressing some of its fundamental values through the selection of its highest national representatives' (pp. 94—95). Her data were collected in 1953—54.

[38] On the other hand, both the categories for 'father's position' and for the phases are too crude to catch the finer trends. Thus, if we look at the data for phase VI there are some differences relative to phase V: In the last phase there are 9% more professionals than in the former, 9% more workers, farmers, etc., and 14% less functionaries. We have not presented them separately, however, since the percentage for phase VI is quite high, and we have not succeeded in decreasing it.

[39] This fact is borne out in a study made of Norwegian officers as a social group. Between one-third and one-half of the officers have had a civilian occupation

in addition to their military rank in the period 1880—1930. This also accounts for the fact that the father's occupational distribution for phase I adds up to more than 100 per cent. Francesco Kjellberg, 'Offiserene som sosial gruppe', *Tidsskrift for Samfunnsforskning*, 1962, p. 130.

[40] Summarizing the trend from 1900 to 1953, Suzanne Keller states: 'The American Diplomats are not appreciably more representative of American society now than they were at the beginning of the century. In fact, the most striking overall changes occurred in the direction of greater exclusiveness in social origins... The occupational origins of these men have changed somewhat; except for lawyers' sons, there are now more sons of businessmen and professional men. A slight but noticeable increase of men from less privileged social background, appeared in the latest decade. Sons of small businessmen, on the other hand, are virtually eliminated... From this we would conclude that the alleged democratization of the United States foreign service has not occurred to any appreciable extent at the top posts of that service. Great Britain, too, seems not to have extended its democratic principles into diplomatic practice. It is true that there are now fewer sons of the landed gentry and of higher Government officials, but the difference is made up by more sons of lawyers, of judges, of bankers and of physicians, occupations usually accorded high prestige' (pp. 170—71). She then goes on to discuss various reasons for this development and suggests that the prevailing image of the diplomat's as a 'high-class profession' is partly responsible for the selection that takes place (pp. 172—73).

[41] In 1960—64, however, 13% had been working in the ministry before they were accepted for the service, but as substitutes and 'on trial' as lower rank clerks, etc.

[42] The relation between sex and position in the ministry is as follows *(Utenrikskalenderen, 1960)*:

	Men	Women	Total	% difference
Diplomats	69% (201)	1% (1)	49% (202)	+68%
Others, secretaries and consultants	9% (27)	13% (16)	10% (43)	— 4%
Others, office personnel and 'kansellister'	22% (65)	86% (107)	41% (172)	—64%
Sum	100% (293)	100% (124)	100% (417) .	0%

Thus, the correlation is overwhelming and probably serves to emphasize the highly stratified and slightly feudal character of the institution.

[43] One possibility is the idea that 1. young foreign service officers often marry female secretaries belonging to the office personnel of the service, and 2. that these female secretaries by no means represent a random sample of Norwegian girls but rather a sample located higher up socially than the attachés themselves. If there is something to this hypothesis it means a certain in-breeding in the foreign service in spite of the low rate of self-recruitment, and a flow of upper class taste into the service via the wives to compensate for 'democratization'.

[44] Suzanne Keller found that 'the pattern of their marriages conforms strikingly, both among the British and the Americans, to the pattern of their origins. The Americans, by and large, married daughters of businessmen (55% of those who married)

or of professional men (18 %), whereas the British married daughters of landed proprietors (43%) and of high Government officials (18%)' (p. 130).

[45] 'One final misconception about the diplomat's job shared by Congressmen and the public is that the chief function of an American diplomat is to be a model of the average American.' Charles W. Thayer, op. cit., p. 269.

[46] It should also be mentioned that in the first phases the lower positions in the service were either unpaid or very badly paid, this being in itself a serious obstacle to marriage. An extreme example is the secretary at the legation in Stockholm, who managed because he 'had very simple personal habits, and in addition had invitations to dinner several times a week'. Reidar Omang, *Norsk Utenrikstjeneste*, Vol. II, (Oslo: Gyldendal Norsk Forlag, 1959) p. 67. Another point worth mentioning is the low age at which persons entered the service in the first phases, see Table 18.

[47] The average age at which Norwegian men married for the first time has gone down from about 28 years in the last part of the 19th century to about 26 years in the 1960s, with a record of 29 years in the period 1930—50. For a detailed presentation see Erik Grönseth, *Early Marriage in Norway*, (Oslo, 1963, mimeo.) Appendix, Table III.

[48] The official instruction concerning recruitment and training for the foreign service demands that the candidates should be either university graduates (which presupposes high school graduation) or be high school graduates with sufficient additional occupational experience. Only in very special cases may exceptions from these rules be made. *Reglement om rekruttering og utdannelse i utenrikstjenesten* fastsatt ved Kgl. resolusjon av 5. september 1963, § 1. With minor exceptions, these rules have been used since 1948.

[49] During the last 30 years, the percentage has been very stable at 2—3%.

[50] A look at the distribution of academic graduates among the civil servants in the Norwegian ministries as a whole during the period 1900—1960 gives this result:

	No degree	Humanities	Law	Economics	Other	Total	N
1900	7%	1%	86%	0%	6%	100%	266
1920	31%	1%	60%	3%	5%	100%	477
1940	35%	1%	52%	4%	8%	100%	635
1960	40%	4%	39%	8%	9%	100%	1453

Vilhelm Aubert *et al.*, *The Professions in Norwegian Social Structure 1720 — 1955*, loc. cit.

The main way in which the Foreign Ministry differs from the other ministries seems to be the development in the number of civil servants who do not have a university degree. The proportion of lawyers is remarkably parallel.

[51] 'As yet, however, the professional diplomats are not inclined to abandon Callieres entirely in favour of the socio-anthropologists and the new scientific intelligence methods. In fact they question whether the new methods of intelligence gathering and evaluating are alone an adequate substitute for the older methods which have stood the test of generations of diplomacy.' Charles W. Thayer, op. cit., p. 178.

[52] Those who graduate as mag. art. in for instance political science get no marks,

but still have to be 'laudable' in order to pass the examination. Thus the percentage of 'lauds' is higher than the Table shows.

[53] In an article from 1954, the Norwegian Foreign Minister, Halvard Lange, comments on this fact and gives some background information about recruitment during and right after the war. He states that almost one-half of the foreign service personnel (in 1954) had been recruited to the service in an irregular way, in addition to those who had been appointed to top level positions directly. Halvard Lange, *Administrative problemer i norsk utenrikstjeneste*, Oslo, 1954, pp. 14 f. If one looks at the phases in which the course has existed (III, V and VI)

the ncreasing importance of this test is evident.

[54] The attentive reader who finds inconsistency between '10% starting in Norway' and '18% starting in the ministry' (Table 20) should remember the Norwegians who served in Stockholm before 1905.

[55] After the training course of one year, the candidates are put on a 'probation period' of usually two years, during which they serve as attachés or second secretaries in the ministry. Thus, the entire training period for the Norwegian foreign service is three years. *Reglement om rekruttering og utdannelse i utenrikstjenesten*, op. cit., p. 5.

IV.4. *The Structure of Foreign News*

* This is a much revised and extended version of a paper presented at the First Nordic Conference on Peace Research, Oslo, 4—8 January 1963 and as a guest lecture at Danmarks Journalisthöjskole, Århus, May 1964, here published as PRIO publication no. 14—2. The authors wish to express their gratitude to the Institute for Social Research, the Norwegian Research Council for Science and the Humanities, and the Norwegian Council for Research on Conflict and Peace for financial support; to stud. mag. art. Marit Halle and stud. mag. art. Elisabeth Bögh for assistance with the data-collection and to our friends and colleagues at PRIO and particularly to Einar Ostgaard for stimulating criticism and suggestions.

[1] Einar Ostgaard, 'Factors Influencing the Flow of News', *J. Peace Res.* (1965), no. 1, pp. 39 ff.

[2] For an interesting article making systematic use of these two indicators of interdependence, see Kaare Svalastoga, 'Technology and Autonomy', *Acta Sociol.*, Vol. 5, pp. 91—99.

[3] Thus, a completely realistic image of other people's image of oneself might have a harmful effect on the social adequacy of one's behavior. Thus, there is the important finding by Caplow and McGee (*The Academic Marketplace*, New York: Basic Books, 1958) that members or organizations are often subject to an Aggrandizement Effect whereby they overestimate their own organization relative to others in the field. One might argue that if they did not, the consequent drop in self-image would result in lower achievement levels. And this may have a parallel in the field of international affairs: if the news structure was symmetric, giving to each nation its due, relative to how it was estimated by other nations, an important source of self-pride and assertiveness might be too weak to spur effective action.

[4] For one way of describing this chain see Johan Galtung and Mari Holmboe Ruge, *Presentasjonen av utenriksnyheter* (Oslo: PRIO stencil no. 14—1, 1962), pp. 71—78.

[5] Östgaard, op. cit., pp. 42 f.

[6] For an impression of what sociologists can get out of the condition of sleeping see Vilhelm Aubert and Harrison White, 'Sleep: A Sociological Interpretation' *Acta Sociol.*, Vol. 4, No. 2, pp. 46—54 and Vol. 4, No. 3, pp. 1—16.

[7] This, of course, is a fundamental idea in the psychology of perception. Actually there are two separate ideas inherent here: the notion of an absolute level that must not be too low, and the notion of the increase needed to be noticed — the 'just noticeable differences' (jnd's). The jnd increases with increasing absolute level; the stronger the amplitude, the more difference is needed to be noticed (whether this is according to Weber's principle or not). This principle probably applies very explicitly to news communication: the more dramatic the news, the more is needed to add to the drama. This may lead to important distortions. The more drama there already is, the more will the news media have to exaggerate to capture new interest, which leads to the hypothesis that there is more exaggeration the more dramatic the event — i.e. the less necessary one might feel it is to exaggerate.

[8] N. R. Ashby in *An Introduction to Cybernetics* (New York: Wiley, 1957) defines noise simply as distortion that may create differences in interpretation at the sender and receiver ends of a communication channel. But one may just as well say that the signal distorts the noise as vice versa.

[9] B. Berelson and G. A. Steiner in their *Human Behavior! An Inventory of Scientific Findings* (New York: Harcourt, Brace & World, 1963) mention a number of principles under 'Perceiving', and two of them are (p. 112 and p. 100):

B7: The greater the ambiguity of the stimulus, the more room and need for interpretation.

B3.3a: There may also be decreased awareness of stimuli if it is important *not* to see (perceptual defense).

What we have been doing is to combine these theorems (but not deductively) into the idea of defense against ambiguity. There are several reasons for this. Modern newspapers are mass media of communication, at least most of them, and publishers may feel (justifiably or not) that increase in ambiguity may decrease the sales. Moreover, to the extent that news shall serve as a basis for action orientation ambiguity will increase rather than reduce the uncertainty and provide a poorer basis for action.

[10] The common factor behind both dimensions of what we have called 'meaningfulness' is probably 'identification'.

[11] Again, some findings from Berelson and Steiner are useful (op. cit., p. 101 and p. 529):

B3.2: With regard to expectations, other things equal, people are more likely to attend to aspects of the environment they anticipate than to those they do not, and they are more likely to anticipate things they are familiar with.

B3.3: With regard to motives, not only do people look for things they need or want; but the stronger the need, the greater the tendency to ignore irrelevant elements.

A1: People tend to see and hear communications that are favorable to their predispositions; they are more likely to see and hear congenial communications than neutral or hostile ones. And the more interested they are in the subject, the more likely is such selective attention.

[12] For a discussion of this see Johan Galtung, 'Summit Meetings and International Relations', *J. Peace Res.* (1964), pp. 36—54.

[13] For a discussion of this factor see Östgaard, op. cit., pp. 151.

[14] Festinger has a very interesting account of how Indians selected rumors following an earthquake, and consistent with the fear provoked by the earthquake: 'Let us speculate about the content of the cognition of these persons. When the earthquake was over they had this strong, persistent fear reaction but they could see nothing different around them, no destruction, no further threatening things. In short, a situation had been produced where dissonance existed between cognition corresponding to the fear they felt and the knowledge of what they saw around them which, one might say, amounted to the cognition that there was nothing to be afraid of. The vast majority of the rumors which were widely circulated were rumors which, if believed, provided cognition consonant with being afraid. One might even call them "fear-provoking" rumors, although, if our interpretation is correct, they would more properly be called "fear justifying" rumors'. Leon Festinger, 'The Motivating Effect of Cognitive Dissonance', in Gardner Lindzey (Ed.), *Assessment of Human Motives* (New York: Grove Press, 1958), p. 72.

[15] As an example some impressions can be given from three months' systematic reading of the Moroccan newspaper *Le Petit Marocain*. In very summarized form: the first page contained news about progress in Morocco, the second about decadence, murder, rape and violence in France — so that anybody could drawn his conclusion. Of course, such things will depend rather heavily on the value-systems of the editorial staff — but we nevertheless postulate the existence of general patterns. Ola Mårtensson, in a mimeographed report (in Swedish) of a content analysis of three major papers in the URSS, indicates both personification and elite concentration. Ola Mårtensson, *Pravda, Izvestija och Krasnaja Zvezda*

under våren och hosten 1964 (Lund: Institute for Political Science, Lund University, Sweden, 1965), 26 pp. mimeo.

[16] Östgaard, op. cit., pp. 52 ff.

[17] As an example it can be mentioned that in a survey carried out in Norway, November-December 1964, to the question 'What do you think has been the most important event in the news recently?' 53% answered in terms of elections in the US and changes of power in the Soviet Union, i.e. in terms of the top elite people in the top elite nations. The next answer category, 'events in the Congo', made 9%.

[18] Norway appears as No. 7 in a list of 125 countries, according to the UN *Statistical Yearbook 1962* (New York: United Nations, 1963). The variable used is daily newspaper circulation per 1,000 population.

[19] We omit the names of the papers, not so much out of considerateness, which would be out of order — firstly because we have nothing really inconsiderate to say about them, and secondly because they are public phenomena that might well be subject to public appraisals. The names, however, are of interest to Norwegian readers only and carry many connotations that will not be used in the analysis anyhow.

[20] Not included in our sample is the biggest Norwegian newspaper with two daily issues and an average 1964 circulation of 168,000. This paper is the one with the most complete coverage of international events. Its political attitude is moderately conservative. The reason for excluding this paper is not only the considerable extra work of coding that it would imply, etc., but also the fact that we were primarily interested in papers with a very clear political profile that would span the political spectrum better.

[21] One thing that should be explained is 'Norsk Telegrambyrå'. Only in some very few cases (nine in all) in connection with Norwegian soldiers recruited for UN service in the Congo does this mean that the Norwegian agency was actually the source of the piece of news. In all other cases NTB actually stands for AFP or Reuters and other Scandinavian agencies, since it acts as an agent for these foreign bureaux in Norway. (UPI and AP have their own offices in Oslo.)

[22] With the exception that the two less wealthy conservative papers have chosen one each of the American agencies (III does not subscribe to UPI and IV not to AP), all four papers were subscribers to these agencies in 1960 and 1964. And all four agencies (AP, UPI, Reuters, AFP) have their headquarters in the three major powers of the world's Northwest — a region where Norway is also located.

[23] It should be noted that the time-span covered in the Cyprus crisis is of a somewhat different nature than for the Congo and Cuba. The building up of the Cyprus crisis actually took a long time and only culminated during the winter months of 1963—64. For comparative reasons we still decided to analyze a short period. We chose the weeks immediately prior to and during those in which the UN was actively brought into the conflict, in order to be able to make a comparison with the Congo situation. But this excluded the period in which Greek-Turkish-Cypriot relations were most strained, probably in January-February.

[24] Bjarte Kaldhol, 'Norske soldater til Kypros', Dagbladet, 12/2 1964, p. 4.

[25] Wilbur Schramm refers in his book, Mass Media and National Development (Paris: UNESCO, 1964, p. 64), to an investigation where Indians have commented on the way India is presented in the American press. Four aspects of this particular news communication are presented, and it is claimed that they represent the greater part of the news total: India in the East-West power struggle and communism, American economic aid to India, stories about disasters and hunger, and stories about 'bizarre and outlandish things' in connection with child marriages, untouchability, etc. The first two are typical examples of increased relevance by tying what happens in remote places to one's own country, the third is a clear case of F_{12}, but also of a case where distant countries are presented as victims rather than agents of what happens. The last factor is a case of $F_{5 \cdot 1}$ — it is consonant in the sense of being predicted from 'knowledge' of Indian culture; it fits stereotypes.

[26] The Indian Express, 11 July 1962, p. 6.

[27] For some comments on the phenomenon of 'imprinting' see Berelson, Steiner, op. cit., pp. 41 and 43.

[28] Alan Coddington, in an unpublished paper, A Study of Policies Advocated in Conflict Situations by British Newspapers, studies ten national dailies over a period of two weeks (12 days) to find out how the kind of solution they recommend for conflicts in their editorials relates to whether the conflict is domestic or international. He finds quite opposite patterns for domestic and international conflicts: both are relatively low where recommendations in terms of 'external settlement' (mediation and arbitration) are concerned, but whereas domestic issues rank high on 'mutual adjustment' (compromise and reconciliation) and low on 'policies of force' (conquest and containment), the foreign issues show exactly the contrary pattern. This may be very rational and due to the more integrated nature of the domestic social system relative to the international system. But it may also be seen as a natural consequence of the structure of foreign news and as compatible with our hypotheses about the implications of that structure.

IV.5. *International Air Communication*

* The present article can be identified as publication S-3/79 from the International Peace Research Institute, Oslo (PRIO). It is based on PRIO-publication 21—11, published as "Trends in World Airline Patterns" by Nils Petter Gleditsch, *Journal of Peace Research*, vol. 4, no. 4, 1967, pp. 366—408. A first draft of that article was written as a term paper for Political Science 760 at the University of Michigan and our gratitude should be recorded to the instructor, Charles McClelland, for his inspiration and comment. Valuable comments were also received from other students in the class and from J. David Singer from University of Michigan and Harold Guetzkow and Paul Smoker, Northwestern University. The article is part of a larger project on international aviation. Most of the other publications from this project are cited in the reference section. The data collection was done at PRIO for the 1965 data and at the University of Michigan for the earlier timepoints. Per Evensen and Reidar Kvadsheim coded most of the 1965 data, and Steinar Wigtil helped with the initial data processing. The University of Michigan, the University of Oslo, and the Simulated International Processes Project, Northwestern University provided free computer time for the data analysis. Financial support during the period the article was written was provided by the Norwegian Disarmament Committee of the Norwegian Foreign Ministry, by the Department of Sociology, University of Michigan, the Simulated International Processes Project, Northwestern University, and the Norwegian Research Council for Science and the Humanities (NAVF). The present article is only a slightly revised version of the 1967 article. In addition to correcting printing errors, we have added a new introduction, simplified some of the tables slightly, and added some references to later developments and other analyses of the same data. Finally we would like to thank Wilbur and Orville Wright for making this study possible.

[1] Kenneth R. Sealy (1957, p. 127) points out that most European airlines have 'spoke patterns' with the node in the home city. The advantages are the possibility of maintaining a centralized maintenance service and the simplification of business procedures. On the other hand, a spoke pattern, particularly when the distances are short, creates certain scheduling problems.

[2] For a discussion of this and other motives behind the proliferation of national airlines in Africa, see Weeks (1965).

[3] Berelson and Steiner (1964), p. 482 ff.

[4] Galtung (1966 a), p. 18; ref. to Berelson and Steiner (1964), p. 348.

[5] Galtung (1966 b), p. 148.

[6] Galtung (1966), p. 19. The data are from Mills (1953).

[7] See e.g. Bales and Slater (1955).

[8] Hurwitz, Zander, and Hymovitch (1960), p. 806.

[9] It may be objected that there is no norm against children communicating with each other. However, in many situations involving adults as well as children (family visits, at the dinner table) children are supposed not to interact a great deal with each other, but to keep quiet, speak only when addressed (i.e. UT interaction follows TU), while the corresponding norms for adults are more relaxed.

[10] Hurwitz, Zander, and Hymovitch (op. cit) also find a tendency to exaggerate the relative participation of underdogs in

the discussion. This proposition, which fits the general picture well, could also be applied to the international system; it could be tested e.g. by having diplomats rate the amount of participation of various nations in UN debates, and then checking their estimates against an objective measure from the proceedings.

[11] Data on the degree of foreign ownership in airlines in internationally scheduled passenger traffic, can be found as an appendix to the abstract of an unpublished paper on "aviation and dominance". Cf. Nils Petter Gleditsch, ed.: Theories of Dominance and Dependency Structures. Proceedings of a seminar in Oslo, March 13—14, 1975, vol. 1, Abstracts, discussion, etc. Oslo, PRIO, 1975.

[12] Deutsch (1967), pp. 218 ff.

[13] A stronger version of the feudal hypothesis would be that the RA's (relative acceptance indices) are predicted to rank as follows: TT>TU>UU. This possibility has not been systematically investigated, but some of Deutsch's results and some preliminary tests on the airline data seem to indicate that this is generally *not* the case in international relations.

[14] A systematic model for extracting the influence of variables at the unit level (i.e. country or actor level) and thus synthesizing effects at the pair level, has been developed in Høivik and Gleditsch, 1978.

[15] Other references are given in Gleditsch 1969, 1970.

[16] For a review, see Gleditsch (1968, appendix 7; 1969).

[17] For a general formulation, see Zipf (1949). A very critical discussion of this work can be found in Simon (1957), ch. 9. Cf. also Coleman (1960) ch. 15. For an empirical test on international trade data see Linnemann (1966).

[18] For tests of the gravitation formula and related models, see Gleditsch (1969, 1970 b). For a mathematical treatment and development of alternative models, with some testing, see Høvik *et al.*, 1975.

[19] In the East—West system this did not extend as far as a general diplomatic boycott, but a partial trade boycott of the West against the East was initiated in the early days of the cold war and still exists, if in reduced scope. Cf. Adler-Karlsson, 1968.

[20] The reader might think that this is the usual state of affairs in international relations. In that case his attention is drawn to the *World Handbook of Social and Political Indicators* (Russett et al., 1964), the single most important data source for international relations research with the nation as the unit. Although the book is limited to the 133 most significant countries, there are missing data on almost every variable. Variables like the Index of Achievement, Motivation and Defense Expenditure as a Percentage of GNP have missing data percentages of 69% and 38%. In addition, the reliability of the data is frequently very low, as the authors themselves note, even for highly important variables like GNP and population. Whatever the merits of this article in other respects we see no reason for modesty with regard to the quality of the data base. The *validity* of air connections as a measure of integration is, of course, another matter (cfr. section 3.3.).

[21] Flight numbers were not used in the 1931 book, and not consistently in the 1951 book. Hence there were a few cases of the following pattern:

$$1 < {}^{2}_{3} > 4—5$$

It was decided to code all connections (except 2=3).

More importantly, overnight stays were ignored in the 1931 book. Here we felt that since nightflying was considered dangerous in many areas too much weight would be given to physical factors by interpreting an overnight stay as a change to another flight. In 1951 overnight stays were still fairly common, but no longer necessary, and have therefore been interpreted as a break. However, when (in 1930) certain air routes were interspersed with train rides or boat connections, the flight has been interpreted as broken. Thus, London—India and London—Tanganyika both appear to be broken by a rail connection between Skoplje and Saloniki; and Marseilles—Bagdad by one from Damascus to Beirut.

[22] A few asymmetric schedules were found. The connections both ways were coded. A different coding rule would probably not have affected the number of *connections*, although the number of *flights* (for the 1965 data) would have been (negligibly) smaller.

[23] In a factor analysis of the 'foreign behavior' (94 variables) of 82 nations Rudolph Rummel (1966) found the variables 'Many foreign college students in country' and 'much foreign trade' to load highly (.78 and .95), ranking no. 9 and no. 1 respectively in terms of their loadings on a factor of *participation*. This factor accounted for 19.1% of the total variance. Rummel's work seems to support the idea of a general interaction dimension.

[24] We used a modification of a clustering procedure proposed by Steve Johnson of Bell telephone labs, in a mimeographed paper 'Hierarchical clustering schemes' later published in *Psykometrika*. In the modified version the variables are added one by one to 'clusters' according to the size of the median correlation of the variable with the cluster. The procedure tends to give results very similar to a factor analysis (e.g., it reproduced McGowan's rotated factor analytic solution on the original 10 by 10 matrix in terms of the no. of independent factors and what factors the variables loaded most highly on). An approximation to factor loadings can be obtained by taking the correlation of each variable with 'the most central variable' in each cluster.

[25] A weakness of this argument, as well as of McGowan's study is that Algeria and the UAR receive very high scores on almost all of the variables. By their size alone they tend to produce exaggerated values of the product-moment correlation coefficient.

[26] See, for example, Harary et al. (1965), p. 21.

[27] For a discussion of the Gini index and other measures of inequality see Alker and Russett (1964). Useful discussions with examples are also found in Alker (1965) and Russett (1965). The Gini index measures the inequality with which a variable (e.g. votes, GNP) is distributed over a set of individuals, groups, or nations relative to some baseline (usually population). In our application here the baseline is simply the number of nations. The index varies from 0.0 (full equality) to 1.0 (full inequality). As an example, votes in the UN General Assembly are distributed with complete equality with the number of nations as a baseline (one nation, one vote) but the inequality is great with population as a baseline (one man, one vote).

[28] However, the absence of an air connection can be interpreted as uncooperative behavior where other factors would have led us to expect an air link. Thus, that Israel and the Arab states, geographically close to each other, and each with considerable air traffic, have *no* common air links, is clearly significant. Obviously, these states are locked in on mutual noncooperative behavior.

[29] An alternative approach would be through multiple regression analysis. This has been tried on the same and related data in Gleditsch 1969, 1970a, 1970b.

[30] This is a classic dilemma in both social science research and political discussin. An example is provided by the following data from Lindbekk (1968) on the percentage of workers' and academics' sons who graduate from secondary school (examen artium) in Norway:

	1930—39	About 1950
Workers	0.7%	3%
Academics	54.9%	60%
Difference	54.2%	ca. 57%
Ratio	ca. 80	ca. 20

Lindbekk concludes that 'the distance between worker's sons and the sons of academics has decreased'.

This is reasonable in terms of *ratios*, but it might equally well have been demonstrated on the basis of the percentage *difference* that the workers' sons are lagging. (I am indebted to Ottar Hellevik for calling my attention to this example.) The same problem arises in economic analysis where a country with a lower growth rate may increase its 'distance' to one with a higher growth rate, although the latter's higher growth rate can eventually reduce the "distance" to insignificance. However, the difference between a variable like economic growth on the one hand and variables normed by an absolute ceiling (like the percentage of a group that reaches a certain educational level, or airline 'density') on the other hand is that while the former may be expected to have a continued exponential growth, the latter are likely to be logistic. One might expect the bottom group to catch up more quickly whenever the growth is logistic, but this begs the issue of whether the 'ceiling effect' does not occur at a lower level for this group.

[31] Another publication (Gleditsch, 1969) which examines the relationship between distance and air communication in more detail concludes that the correlation between the two has increased over the 35 year period examined. This finding was somewhat unexpected in view of the common feeling that "distance does not matter anymore", our interpretation is that distance is no longer an absolute barrier, but continues to have an impact on the degree of interaction.

[32] The clearest everyday example is probably age (and the status differences associated with age.) Any pair of persons go through life with a constant age difference, while the ratio decreases steadily. And common sense agreement seems to be that the difference becomes less important over the years.

[33] This finding is corroborated by another more detailed study which also examines several other forms of interaction (Gleditsch, 1971a).

[34] The formidable land mass of the Soviet Union along with the physical obstacle of the Himalayas has forced air interaction between Western Europe and Asia into a narrow band in the Middle East. The Western Hemisphere is, of course, connected to Asia and Oceania over the Pacific, and there are also connections from Europe over America to Australia. The only alternative connection from Europe to the Far East has been the SAS polar route over Anchorage to Tokyo, established in 1957. In the fall of 1967, however, a 'Trans-Asia Express' was set up, running from Copenhagen over Tashkent, USSR, to Bangkok (and to be extended to Jakarta). This route, which is indicative of a softening of East-West tensions, is in return for Russian rights in Scandinavia en route to Cuba. However, the stop in Tashkent is a technical stop only, and adds no new connections.

697

[35] The same was true for international trade during the same period, cf. Adler-Karlsson, *op. cit.*

[36] Just as it was the Western European countries which maintained some contact with Eastern Europe during the coldest phase of the Cold War, Western Europeans were ahead of the us in breaking the isolation of China. This is true of international aviation as well as many other areas. The establishment of a us-China air connection was not announced until the establishment of full diplomatic relations between the two countries in late 1978.

[37] The boycott campaign against South Africa appears to have been ineffective — at least as far as air connections are concerned. We do not yet have data on a year to year basis to say whether there is a trend towards the isolation of (Southern) Rhodesia after the unilateral declaration of independence in November, 1965. In the summer of 1967 Rhodesia still had a rather low no. of connections, but through its links (with many flights per week) to the neighboring countries of Zambia and South Africa (which in turn are well connected to the rest of the world) one cannot in any sense talk of an isolation comparable to that of China.

[38] By the late 1970s Cuba is still only weakly connected to Latin America by scheduled flights and not at all to North America. However, during the entire period of "Cold war" against Cuba, it has been possible to fly to Cuba from Mexico, if one was prepared for infrequent and irregular service.

[39] For some further suggestions regarding ICAO and IATA policies, see Gleditsch (1977).

[40] The nation numbers refer to the PRIO *list of nations* (see Appendix 3).

IV.6. *The Latin American System of Nations: A Structural Analysis*

[1] This article is a product of a project on "The Structure of the World Community" now in development at the *International Peace Research Institute — Oslo*. It was partially presented by Simon Schwartzman at the Inaugural Conference of the International Peace Research Association (Groningen, Netherlands, July 1965), and first published in Spanish in *América Latina*, 1, 1966, the journal of the Latin American Center for Research in the Social Sciences, Rio de Janeiro. The present text is a revised version of the Spanish one, and can be identified as PRIO-publication no. 21—1. The authors are indebted to J. David Singer for valuable comments.

[2] A pioneer study in this perspective of international stratification is Gustave Lagos, 1963.

[3] See Galtung, 1966.

[4] This is just one technique among many others, selected because of the resulting curve of distribution. We could order the countries according to rank position or according to the values in each rank dimension (using interval scales), and the result could be dichotomized or trichotomized:

	ordinal scale	interval scale
dichotomy	I	II
trichotomy	III	IV

Our index corresponds to cell III.

[5] This division can be better seen if we divide table 5 in its two clusters:

Table 5-A. *Index of International Position: clusters.*

It is interesting to notice that Per Capita Income, the classical indicator of development lies somewhat in between the two dimensions.

The differences of the countries in the two clusters raises the question of the consequences of the *rank disequilibrium* for a given country, or the *rank incongruency* for a given pair of countires, etc. A first general theoretical study in this perspective is Johan Galtung, 1965. For

TABLE 5-A. *Index of international position. Clusters*

	average correlations with cluster 1	with cluster 2
Cluster 1: Size		
1. Area	.93	.12
2. Population	.95	.12
3. GNP	.94	.29
Cluster 2: Wealth		
4. GNP per capita	.17	.43
5. Literacy	.11	.78
6. Newspapers per inhabitants	.12	.74
7. % of population in high and middle sectors	.24	.92
8. Urbanization	.22	.75
9. % of active population in industries	.16	.58
10. % population white	.22	.60

studies on the effect of rank disequilibria at regional and international level in Latin America, cf. Peter Heintz, *Modelo de Investigación sobre Política Provincial*, FLACSO, Santiago de Chile, 1964 (mimeographed) and mainly *Análisis Contextual de los Países Latinoamericanos*, part of a book on the subject by Peter Heintz. In this work all the consequences of rank disequilibria between income, education and urbanization, and characteristics of the social structure of the countries are analysed. The conclusions of this analysis,

referring to the development of social movements, political systems and leading to a general theory of social development differ from ours in the sense that we are mainly concerned with the consequences of the stratification system for the *international* setting.

[6] These data are part of a more general multinational study on the perception of international stratification in Latin America, now in progress. For more penetrating

analyses of these data, see Manuel Mora y Araujo and Simon Schwartzman, 1966.

[7] We made use of an index constructed by Walter Soderlund (Ann Arbor, Michigan), who was kind enough to make it available to us. The index was made by the characterization of each of the last 30 years for each Latin American country according to the kind of government they had (military dictatorship, civilian dictatorship, constitutional government, provisional government) and according to the occurrence or non-occurrence of successful insurrection. The index was constructed by adding the years with dictatorships and insurrections.

[8] This means working with the universe of pairs and there is no necessity for significance tests. The situation would be different, however, if we dealt with a larger number of countries. The Dimensionality of Nations Project now in progress in Yale University under the direction of Professor R. J. Rummel works with a universe of 82 countries, which demands the selection of a sample among the more than three thousand possible pairs. Cf. R. J. Rummel, *The Dimensionality of Nations Project*, November 1964; *Dyadic Relations Random Sample*, July 1964; *Dyadic Study — First Revised Variable List*, January 1965; etc. We are indebted to Professor Rummel for making available to us a number of draft reports of the DON project (publication in progress: Rummel, 1966, and forthcoming).

[9] Fred P. Ellison (1964) notes that "the Latin American writers know each other's work less well that one might think, and there is truth in the quip that the concept of Latin America exists only in the United States, where the 'Latin American studies' are pursued".

[10] For instance, L. F. Richardson (1960) considers trade the most important factor for cooperation. In a quite different context, a factor analysis carried out by R. J. Rummel (Dimensionality of Nations Project, *Some Dimensions of International Relations in the Mid — 1950's*, August 1964, mimeographed) shows the existence of a general factor of cooperation, in which the variable trade has the higher loading, of .95.

[11] Because the *Direction of International Trade* does not always refer to one year periods, efforts were made to achieve comparability. When differences were found in the trade budget of a pair, due perhaps to differences on exchange rates (the exports of A to B differing from the imports of B from A), the average was taken. The data have, then, a fairly wide range of errors, but the differences of magnitude are so big that we may safely assume that the general tendency will not disappear or be reversed.

IV.7. *East-West Interaction Patterns*

This is a much revised and extended version of a paper originally presented at the Thirteenth Pugwash Conference on Science and World Affairs, Karlovy Vary, September 13—19, 1964, published in *Proceedings* pp. 133—139; here published as PRIO publication no. 21—4. Parts of the paper were also presented in a Lord Simon guest lecture, The University, Manchester, November 1964, and in the Quaker Seminar on European Security Problems, Gars am Kamp, Austria, April 22—30, 1966. I am very much indebted to Mr. Richard Edvardsen for imaginative assistance in the collection of data; to Pugwash friends and colleagues, particularly Professor Karol Lapter, for discussions and criticism of the ideas in the paper; and to the Norwegian Research Council for Science and the Humanities and to the Norwegian Council for Research on Conflict and Peace for financial support.

[1] The most complete theoretical formulation is found in Johan Galutng, "International Relations and International Conflicts: A Sociological Approach," International Sociological Association, Plenary Session, September 4—11, 1966. A test of the theory on the Latin-American system of nations is found in: Johan Galtung, Manuel Mora y Araujo and Simon Schwartzman: "El Sistema Latino-Americano de Naciones: Un Analysis Estructural," *America Latina*, 1966; English version: "The Latin-American System of Nations: A Structural Analysis," *Journal of Social Research*, 1966, and Simon Schwartzman "International Cooperation and International Feudalism: The Latin-American Case," First General Conference, International Peace Research Association, Groningen July 3—5, 1965.

[2] For an extensive analysis of this phenomenon for the case of interpersonal interaction see: Johan Galtung: "Small Groups Theory and the Theory of International Relations," Lecture at the 75th Anniversary of the University of Chicago, June 1—4, 1966. However, we would like to illustrate the thesis with some cases from international relations. One clear example of how interaction is concentrated on the top in the international system is found in the article by J. David Singer and Melvin Small, "Formal Alliances, 1815—1939, A Quantitive Description," *J. Peace Res.* (1966), pp. 1—32. They write: "Moreover, a large proportion of them (internation alliances) were also accounted for by the major powers, especially as regards the entente or class III alliance. That is, 30 of the 46 defence pacts in the total system, 28 of the 41 neutrality or non-aggression pacts, and all of the ententes included al least one major power." (ibid, p. 10). Thus, the major powers are overrepresented in this activity, for the major powers are only 8 of 82 nations. One could now easily calculate the probability that alliances with 2, 3, 4 etc. members would include one or more major powers if alliances were concluded by chance where membership is concerned; but this would involve us in too many unrealistic assumptions. But to illustrate: only 28 of 3321 (less than 1%) possible bilateral alliances should be between majors as against 30% in the data.

A second example is found in the pattern of bilateral conventions for the avoidance of double taxation among the 20 member countries of the OECD (The OECD Observer, December 1963, p. 35). Defining as "major powers" United States, United Kingdom, France, German Federal Republic, Canada and Italy (see Table III in the text), we get this pattern:

Bilateral conventions existing or being negotiated, OECD countries

	Major-major	Major-minor	Minor-minor
No. of pairs	15	84	91
No. of pairs with conventions	14	57	28
% with conventions	93%	68%	31%
Percentage difference		62%	

As a third example, consider the air communication network between the three Scandinavian capitals (according to SAS Worldwide Timetable, Winter 1965—66). Copenhagen is the biggest capital and also the most central one relative to the rest of Europe; Oslo and Stockholm are both smaller and further removed. Thus, we would expect least interaction between Oslo and Stockholm, and get in fact 21 weekly flights between Stockholm and Copenhagen. Exactly the same pattern is repeated inside each country for the three biggest cities.

[3] For some comments on de Gaulle's proposed three power directory for NATO, see Williams, P.M. and Harrison, M., *de Gaulle's Republic* (London: Longman's, 1960), pp. 177f.

[4] The NATO treaty was signed on April 4 1949, the Warsaw Pact on May 14 1955. EEC may be said to have been founded on March 25 1957 and Comecon on January 25 1949, but perhaps as a reaction to the Marshall plan.

[5] For an analysis of this, see Coser, Lewis, *The Functions of Social Conflict* (Glencoe: The Free Press, 1956), p. 131: "In a number of instances, for example in the garment industry, unions have forced employers to form associations so that the union might avoid bargaining with many different small employers."

[6] We are thinking particularly of the feelings of the United States and the other Western big powers when the German Federal Republic makes overtures to the Soviet Union, and the feelings of the latter when Poland encourages interaction with the big powers in the West.

[7] For a discussion of theories of incest, see Aberle, D.F., *et al.*, "The Incest Taboo and the Mating Patterns of Animals," *Amer Anthropologist*, 1963, pp. 253-265.

[8] For a generalization, see Parsons, T. and Bales, F.: *Family, Socialization and Interaction Processes*, (Glencoe: The Free Press, 1955) pp. 305-306.

[9] For a theory on the effect of congruent systems, see Eckstein, H., "A Theory of

Stable Democracy," *Research Monograph No. 10*, Centre of International Studies, Princeton University, 1961.

[10] For what is still the best discussion of polarization in sociological literature, see Coleman, J.: *Community Conflict* (Glencoe: The Free Press, 1957).

[11] One reason for this, according to the theory outlined in Galtung, Johan, "International Relations and International Conflicts" lies in the general lay in the structure of the international system of nations relative to at least many international systems of individuals or groups. Thus, in many international systems there is nothing quite corresponding to the idea of the "big power" after the abolition of nobility as a status with tremendous ramifications into economic and political life.

[12] The reason for this lies in the proposition developed in the text, *viz.*, that a rank-dependent system is also a polarized system, or a system in the process of being polarized.

[13] There are of course exceptions to this. In Latin-America, for instance, intranational conflict is far more dangerous than international conflict. But one reason for this is precisely that Latin-American societies are so rank-dependent, within as well as between. As to the latter see Galtung, Mora and Schwartzman, 1966.

[14] See Galtung, Johan, "Summit Meetings and International Relations," *J. Peace Res.* (1964), pp. 36-54, particularly pp. 38-39. For a validation of the time cuts introduced in that article and used here, see Smoker, Paul, "Trade, Defence and the Richardson Theory of Arms Races: A Seven Nation Study," *J. Peace Res.* (1966), p. 162, and also Table 8 in the text for validation in terms of note exchange.

[15] *The Military Balance 1965—1966* (London: Institute for Strategic Studies,

1965) for Population, Armed Forces, Nuclear Power Potential (table 7 parts A and B combined, p. 46) and defence expenditure (table 4, p. 43).

World Handbook of Political and Social Indicators (New Haven: Yale University Press, 1964) for area (table 40, p. 139), GNP (table 43, p. 152), GNP per capita (table 44, p. 155).

For "veto power" is used the "permanent member of the Security Council" definition (USA, UK, France, Soviet Union, "China").

For "world language" is used the UN definition (English, French, Spanish, Russian, Chinese). The "working languages" are English and French.

For "sphere of interest" is used a combination of "recognized sphere of interest" (as defined by the Monroe-Johnson doctrines, the Commonwealth and Communaute agreements, the Yalta agreement) and the refusal of the German Federal Republic to recognize borderlines in the East. It is difficult to lay down formal criteria in this field.

[16] The propositions are developed in Galtung, Johan: "International Relations and International Conflicts." The basic idea is simply that *one* unit, *in casu* a nation which is high on one rank-dimension and low on another, will tend to develop patterns of aggressive behavior if other sources of mobility are blocked, because it will try to equilibrate upwards.

[17] The propositions are developed in Galtung, Johan: "International Relations and International Conflicts." The basic idea is simply that *two* units, *in casu* two nations where one is high where the other is low and vice versa (a young nation with nuclear weapons vs. an old one without), will tend to develop patterns of either withdrawal or conflict towards each other, for many reasons (they are competitors for the top position they may arrive at if both of them are permitted to equilibrate upwards, for instance).

[18] *See World Handbook of Political and Social Indicators*, reference given in footnote 15.

[19] Op. cit., p. 77.

[20] See Frank, L. A., "Nuclear Weapons Development in China, "*Bull. Atomic Scientists*, January 1966, pp. 12—15, for much nteresting information on this issue.
i

[21] An examination of the attitudes of 115 members of the UN in 1950, 1959, 1961, 1962, 1963 and 1964 on the issue of seating the representatives of the People's Republic of China in place of those of the Republic of China shows that the nations can be divided into five groups. First, there is a group of 44 countries that have been consistently in favor when they have expressed any opinion at all (Pakistan and UK are included in this group although they were against in 1959). Then there is a group of 9 countries that have changed from being against to being in favor — six of them African, five of them again French African. Then there are two countries that changed the opposite way: Netherlands and Ireland. Fourthly, there are 55 countries that have been consistently against. And finally there are five countries (Austria, Malta, Kuwait, Portugal and Saudi Arabia) that have not expressed attitudes, for various reasons. The split is above all among African countries, East are wholly in favor, Latin America wholly against (except Cuba) and then some dissonance is brought into the picture because UK and the Nordic countries except Iceland are in favor. All of this makes the attitude to the Chinese question one of the most interesting barometers in the UN. Source: "Representation of China in the UN," prepared by Committee for World Development and World Disarmament, New York.

[22] As an expression of how far this kind of thinking has penetrated, recent pronouncements by the French Foreign Minister Couve de Murville could be quoted.

[23] It is difficult to find a better analysis of the relation between Chinese self-image and their perception of how others perceive them than the analysis given in Fitzgerald, C.P., *The Chinese View of their Place in The World* (London: Oxford University Press, 1964).

[24] Fitzgerald, op. cit., ch. 1, "Pre T'ang China," pp. 1—14.

[25] *World Handbook of Social and Political Indicators*, pp. 155—157.

[26] For operationalization of the concept of rank disequilibrium, see Galtung, Johan, "International Relations and International Conflicts." The formulae developed there are used to calculate the average rank disequilibria referred to in the text.

[27] For a general theory of this see Galtung, Johan: "A Structural Theory of Aggression," *J. Peace Res.* (1964), pp. 95—119.

[28] Data from *Europa Year Book*, 1965, checked with embassies and foreign ministries.

[29] Data from *Keesing's Contemporary Archives. Keesing's* has excellent indices so that perusal of *Keesing's* for data is greatly facilitated. Another question is to what extent *Keesing's* covers what happens in the world well enough, and we are not prepared to comment on that since we have made no thorough check of what is reported in *Keesing's* relative to an objective baseline. It is obvious that *Keesing's* would be oriented towards United Kingdom and the Commonwealth more than, say, the *New York Times* would be — and it is quite conceivable that it is big power oriented so that data from *Keesing's* will have systematic bias in favour of our hypothesis of rank dependence. To check on this we selected *Keesing's* for 1963 and counted the number

of relationships in which a nation occurred (bilateral or multilateral interaction with other nation, as listed in the index). UK appeared 54 times, then USA with 40, USSR with 32, South Africa with 28, Portugal and India with 22 each, France with 21, German Federal Republic with 17 and People's Republic of China and United Republic with 16 each — to take the top 10. There is nothing unreasonable in this list — and if we look at it from the other end (countries that are never mentioned or mentioned only once) there seems to be nothing unreasonable in that either. Later on this type research may be carried out on direct source material — where we only checked with the questionnaires. However, we doubt that this would change our conclusions.

I am indebted to Simon Schwartzman for his assistance with the data-collection.

[30] For more on this, see Galtung, Johan: "Small Group Theory and the Theory of International Relations." Lecture at the 75th Anniversary of the University of Chicago, June 1—4 1966.

[31] I am indebted to Dr. Chadwick Alger for making data available to us and to Mr. Kurt Jacobsen for assistance in the data analysis. A report on Alger's study is published in J. David Singer, ed., *International Yearbook of Political Behavior Research*, vol. VII (New York: The Free Press 1965). There is a correction for seat-mates vs. non seat-mates.

[32] The trade data are for 1962 in most cases, except 1963 for Netherlands and 1961 for USA and the German Democratic Republic. I am indebted to Dr. Simon Schwartzman and Vigdis Vollset for assistance with the data-collection.

[33] I am indebted to Reidar Kvadsheim for assistance with the data-collection. Flights are counted in one direction only.

IV.8. *Norway in the World Community*

* PRIO publication no. 21—8 from the International Peace Research Institute, Oslo. The original article was written in 1967 and the data have not been updated.

IV.9. *International Relations and International Conflicts: A Sociological Approach*

* The author expresses his gratitude to the *Aquinas Fund*, New York for a grant that made this research possible and to colleagues at PRIO, Oslo and FLACSO, Santiago, Chile for valuable discussions. The paper can be identified as PRIO-publication no. 21—7.

[1] For an extensive list of rank-dimensions at the individual and national levels see Johan Galtung, "A Structural Theory of Aggression", *J. Peace Rep.* (1964), pp. 115—16 (footnote 16).

[2] By "ordered" we refer to "complete order", not to "partial order". If the relation is not connected so that there exist pairs of elements (individuals, nations) where one cannot decide which element is higher and which is lower, then one is not dealing with a rank dimension. In such a case one may collapse some values (defining as equivalent all elements that are mutually undecidable) or split the dimensions into two or more subdimensions.

[3] This section is concerned with the operationalization of dimensions of rank analysis and is relatively technical. The reader is advised to inspect table 3 and look at some of the definitions and then turn to section 3, unless he is particularly concerned with the exact meaning of these concepts (p. 180).

[4] For one list of literature, see the references on rank disequilibrium made in Galtung, 1964, p. 118. Some other important references are: Bo Anderson and Morris Zelditch, jr., "Rank Equilibration and Political Behaviour", *Europ. J. Sociol.* (1964), pp. 112—25. G. C. Homans, "La congruence du status", *J. Psychol.* (1957), pp. 22—34; Id., "Status among Clerical Workers", *Hum. Organization* (1953), pp. 5—10.

[5] For an analysis of different dimensions of status inconsistency, see Johan Galtung, *Norm, Role and Status: A Synthetic Approach to Sociology*, ch. 6 (mimeographed, forthcoming).

[6] For other efforts to operationalize this concept, see G. E. Lenski, "Status Crystallization: A Non-vertical Dimension of Social Status", *Amer. Sociol. Rev.*, (1954), pp. 407 ff., and E. Jackson, "Status Consistency and Symptoms of Stress", *Amer. Sociol. Rev.* 1962, p. 47.

[7] For an analysis of this concept see Johan Galtung, "Balance of Power and the Problem of Perception: A Logical Analysis", *Inquiry*, 1964, pp. 277—294.

[8] For the use of the expression "relational analysis", see Lazarsfeld, P. F. and Menzel, H.: "On the Relation Between Individual and Collective Properties", in Etzioni, A., ed., *Complex Organizations, A Sociological Reader* (New York: Holt, 1 1961), pp. 442—440.

[9] For a discussion of an additive index of this kind see Johan Galtung, "Foreign Policy Opinion as a Function of Social Position", *J. Peace Res.* (1964), pp. 217 ff.

[10] See Johan Galtung, *The Measurement of Agreement* (Dept of Sociology, Columbia University, 1959, mimeo).

[11] See Johan Galtung, "Rank and Social Integration: A Multi-dimensional Approach," in Berger, Zelditch, Anderson, *Sociological Theories in Progress*, (Boston: Houghton Mifflin Co., 1966).

[12] Ibid., section 2.1 and Appendix 1.

[13] See M. Kendall, *Rank Correlation Methods*. (New York: Haffner 1955) to p. 179.

[14] See Johan Galtung: "A Structural Theory of Aggression", *J. Peace Res.* (1964), pp. 95—119.

[15] See Johan Galtung, "Rank and Social Integration: A Multi-dimensional Approach", in Berger, Zelditch, Anderson, *Sociological Theories in Progress* (Boston: Houghton Mifflin Co., 1966).

[16] Thomas Pettigrew comes very close to this concept of the generalized role as underdog in his *A Profile of the Negro American* (Princeton: van Nostrand, 1964), for instance on pp. 115 ff., where he demonstrates how playing the role of "Negro" serves as an inhibiting factor when white psychologists perform intelligence tests on Negro children (the percentage responding correctly to over half of the items increased by 17 and 10 percentage points in two tests when the interviewer was not white, but Negro). Mirra Komarowsky has similar findings in her study of how an American college girl plays down interests and ability in order to fit into the underdog role: "At first I resented this bitterly. But now I am more or less used to it and live in hope of one day meeting a man who is my superior so that I may be my natural self". From her famous "Cultural Contradictions and Sex Roles", *Amer. J. Sociol.* (1946), p. 185.

[17] For studies showing how interaction is distributed in small groups, see Bales, R. F. et al., "Channels of Communication in Small Groups", *American Sociological Review*, 1951, p. 463, and Mills, T. M., "Power Relations in Three-Person Groups". *Amer. Sociol. Rev.* (1953), p. 353.

[18] We are thinking of Bavelas' famous study "Communication Patterns in Task-Oriented Groups", *Journal of the Acoustical Society of America*, 1950, pp. 730—50, reprinted in many anthologies.

[19] For some preliminary results, see the articles by Johan Galtung, Manuel Mora y Araujo and Simon Schwartzman: "The Latin American System of Nations: A Structural Analysis", PRIO 1965, mimeo, and Galtung, Johan: "East-West Interaction Patterns", *J. Peace Res.* (1966), pp. 146—177. The general content of the research is to use, systematically, a high number of possible objective and subjective rank dimensions as independent variables, and see how all possible kinds of unilateral, bilateral and multilateral interaction variables vary as a function of the rank of the unit, pair, triple, etc.

[20] This is, of course, the major point in the meritocracy debate initiated by Michael Young in *The Rise of the Meritocracy 1870—2033* (London: Thames and Hudson, 1958).

[21] Three such possible dimensions that are less heavily correlated with intelligence are creativity, integrative capacity and different types of emotional achievement. This will be elaborated in a forthcoming article on the theory of topdog-underdog conflicts at the level of individuals.

[22] The usual Marxist scheme is, in our opinion, too narrow here because it (1) is too one-dimensional (the topdog being the owner and the underdog being the non--owner of the means of production), (2) is too tied to a particular type of rank--dimension and (3) is less open to the idea that history may offer circular or spiralling patterns of change rather than some type of rectilinear "development". But the pre-

sent scheme can, perhaps, be seen in part as a generalization of some types of marxist analysis.

[23] See Galtung, Johan, "East-West Interaction Patterns", *J. Peace Res.* (1966), pp. 146—177.

[24] See Coleman, J., *Community Conflict* (Glencoe: The Free Press, 1957).

[25] Lewis Coser discusses some aspects of this in *The Social Functions of Conflict* (Glencoe: The Free Press, 1956).

[26] See Johan Galtung, Manuel Mora y Araujo and Simon Schwartzman, "The Latin-American System of Nations: A Structural Analysis", PRIO 1965, mimeo.

[27] This is one possible explanation why the periphery so often conforms most to the center, whereas opposition and "difficulties" come from the middle. But there are also other explanations: the periphery is marginal and has to prove its right to belong, and in the middle there is more accumulation of disequilibrium that may function as a structural source of aggression.

IV.10. *Big Powers and the World Feudal Structure*

* Paper presented originally, in outline, at the *Pacem in Terris II* conference, Geneva, May 1967; and in the present version at ADIRI, Bucureşti, April 1969; at an international UN seminar, Sandefjord, Norway, June 1969; at a World Order Models Project conference in Santiago, Chile (FLASCO), August 1969, etc. The present paper is transcribed from the presentation in Norway, June 1969, and the oral form has been kept, only some footnotes have been added.

[1] For more details about this type of theory of feudal systems, see Johan Galtung, "Feudal Systems, Structural Violence and the Structural Theory of Revolutions", *Essays in Peace Research*, Vol. III (Ejlers: Copenhagen, 1978), pp. 197—267. The idea is basically taken from Marc Bloc's famous work on feudal society where the rights and duties of vassals are clearly spelt out: the lords protect, the vassals agree to be protected; the lords receive and the vassals pay homage; the vassals pay tribute including military service; the sons of the vassals may be brought up by the lord (like sending the best students for university training with the big power intellectuals?), and so on. Obviously, in comparing the domestic level at the time of the Middle Ages with the global level today we are thinking in terms of homologies

(like between the wing of a bird and the arm of a man) rather than in terms of analogies (like between the wing of a bird and the wing of an insect) — homologies are deeper, without insisting on surface similarities.

[2] *Ibid.*, pp. 215—216.

[3] For a comparison, strong on Santo Domingo, weak on Czechoslovakia, see Mercedes Acosta and Carlos Maria Vilas, "Santo Domingo y Checoslovakia en la política de bloques", *Estudios Internacionales*, 1969, pp. 565—576.

[4] The Monroe doctrine is well known. As for the Brezhnev doctrine the key expression is "the duty of all socialist countries to defend socialism not only at home but also inside a brother country if socialism is endangered" from the article "Prague: formulation d'un droit international "socialiste" ", *Le Figaro*, 10 April 1972, by Jacques Guillemé-Brulon. For a good example of how what happened in CSSR is construed as a threat to socialism, see *Neues Deutschland*, 21 August 1968: "Dies wurde notwendig nachdem, nachdem durch einen verschärften Rechtskurs einer Gruppe in der Führung der KPC und die erhöhte Aktivität der antisozialistischen Kräfte eine akute politische Krise in der CSSR

ausgelöst worden war." As it takes some time to write such things it might be surmised that the events were known beforehand (the invasion actually started on 20 August in the late evening — but *Neues Deutschland* was already that day saying that socialist internationalism includes a readiness to enlist help from the fraternal countries).

[5] For some examples of this, referring to the Latin American system and to the East-West system in Europe, see Chapters 6 and 7 of this volume.

[6] Captain Cook is reported to have said the following, taking possession of New Zealand on January 31, 1770:

"I next explained to the Old Man, and several others, that we were Come to set up a Mark upon the Island in order to show to any ship that might put into this place that we had been here before. They not only gave their free consent to set it up, but promised never to pull it down, ... we were then drank His Majesty's health in a Bottle of wine and gave the empty Bottle to the Old Man ... with which he was highly pleased".

It might have been interesting to hear the "Old Man's" version of this story, particularly after some time had passed — but leaving that aside: although the UN had laid down that outer space belongs to all mankind, the first astronauts landed with US flags in 1969.

IV.11. *A Structural Theory of Integration*

* This is a revised version of a paper originally presented as a plenary address at the Third Nordic Conference on Peace Research, Örenäs, Sweden, May 20th — 21st 1968, at the peace research seminar at PRIO on various occasions, and at the Faculty Seminar, Department of Sociology, University of Essex, 30th October 1968. I am indebted to discussants all places for valuable criticism. The paper is published here as PRIO-publication nr. 22—1 from the International Peace Research Institute, Oslo.

[1] This can be discussed as a problem of bivariate correlation. On either axis would be put the level of goal-satisfaction of the two actors, and if they are highly correlated, then there is obviously a case of coinciding interests. If they are highly correlated, but negatively, then this means that one actor's welfare is compatible with the other actor's disutility. If the correlation is low, then both tendencies are obviously present, and the question is how to locate a third variable so that the conditions for positive and negative correlation can be specified.

[2] There is then a principle of congruence between value-integration and actor-integration: the values held by the highest ranking actors become the highest ranking values. Or as Marx said: 'die herrschende Ideologie ist die Ideologie der herrschenden Klasse'.

[3] These ideas actually tie in with each other. In a situation of interdependence there is usually an element of stratification or hierarchy, as will be argued later, and integration is often based on the idea that it 'pays' to stay together. In a situation of similarity, ideas of loyalty, derived from an ideological basis which again very often stems from location in an organization, and ideas of egalitarian value-integration with bargaining leading to compromises, will be more prevalent.

[4] According to this the world state will not rest on a firm basis unless it has some contra-actor in outer space, or unless it is able to define 'nature' or 'social problems' somehow as a contra-actor.

[5] These concepts have above all been developed by the Yale school, particularly by Harold Lasswell.

[6] This is presumably different under artisanry, where the worker can 'sign' his product, much like the intellectual author does. But intellectuals rarely seem to recognize what an exceptional and in many senses enviable position they are in, even if the element of individualism is taken out of this and a book is published as a publication from an institute. There will still, usually, be recognizable elements that can be traced to individuals — as opposed to the assembly line process.

[7] For actors can occupy statuses in many systems so that their total ranks come out more or less the same; or they may be rotated so that their total rank over time comes out the same.

[8] This is the kind of problem one would imagine social scientists today should be

able to say something more precise about. How many units, in general, can be controlled from a central unit given a scope level? How many tiers can be interspersed without losing contact?

[9] This is developed at length in Johan Galtung, *Structural-Functional Analysis*, forthcoming.

[10] Thus; the factory hall is not only useful for short distance transport, but also for easy foreman supervision — somewhat like the prison.

[11] This is developed in Johan Galtung 'International Relations and International Conflicts: A Sociological Approach', *Transactions of the Sixth World Congress of Sociology* (International Sociological Association, 1966), pp. 121—161.

[12] The typical example here is the structure of the societies based on the domination by a minute racial minority over an indigenous population.

IV.12. *Non-Territorial Actors: the Invisible Continent*

* Paper prepared for "The Concept of International Organizations" within the framework of the UNESCO study on international organizations. I am indebted to Kjell Skjelsbaek for stimulating discussions and comments on this and related topics. All the data in the article, unless otherwise indicated, have been made available by him. For more data, see his *Peace and the structure of international organizations*, thesis, Oslo 1970.

[1] Of course, the two views do not exclude each other — as we hope to show. The international organizations, or non-territorial actors as they are referred to here, can be both adjuncts of the territorial system of states and a system in their own right — at the same time. Any good analysis has to reflect this doubleness

and not fall into the trap of either form of singlemindedness.

[2] Nomads should, with some hesitation, be included into this category: they constitute actors, yet do not have a definite territorial base. But our usual metaphors, such as "international", "inter-governmental", "inter-nongovernmental", "transnational" etc. do not apply. They presuppose a first phase whereby mankind, or a part of mankind, is divided into territorially based groups and then a second phase where some kind of linkage is established again — or for the first time. Nomads constitute a more primordial type of non-territorial actor, also indicating that this concept is broader than the concept of "international organization". That metaphor is probably not very good either, for if we count the monastic orders

as non-territorial actors (and we should), they are clearly "transnational" more than "international" — and have been so from the earliest orders (in the West often dated from St. Benedict, fifth century).

[3] We are, of course, thinking particularly of the transnational corporations.

[4] Theoretically territorial space is subdivisible to the extent that matter is subdivisible, but in the politics of states there is usually a limit to subdivisions defined in terms of *viability* — roughly defined as some minimal kind of self-sufficiency. Correspondingly there is a limit to subdivision in functional or social space: *meaning*. One might subdivide the area of the World Health Organization in social space, "health" into many sub-fields, but although not well-defined there is somewhere a limit, e.g. to how far the human body can be subdivided into subfields while still retaining the concept of health (which has certain holistic implications).

[5] A model here might be Roman law with its high level of formalism, expressed in the *Twelve Tables*, and the principle of *legis actio*. The idea was to express all possible forms of human action, in a system of mutually exclusive and exhaustive typologies.

[6] At least at a given point in time — the person may change later in life. Even the Chinese, who go further than most others in organizing social life so that each person is exposed to a variety of occupational tasks by more traditional standards, make a distinction between being all-round, and having a speciality. Nvertheless, Western type occupational categories, used in a census for instance, would easily break down when confronted with Chinese occupational structure.

[7] Thu-, how many people with multiple citizenship and multiple passports can the territorial system take? Countries differ as to how one gets citizenship, e.g. by the citizenship of one or both of the parents or by the place of birth, already making it possible for one child to have three different nationalities. When called upon for civic duties, such as voting or military services, interesting problems arise that can be handled when the order of magnitude of such people is low (10^3, maybe 10^4), not so easily when it is high (10^{4-6}). Given the level of international travel, interaction and intercourse (no pun intended) in the world today, this is the direction in which the world will be moving where this factor is concerned.

[8] Of course, there is also the scenario that social space may be forced into the relatively rigid regimentation of today's geographical space; not only the scenario just indicated of geographical space becoming as flexible as social space (to some extent) is today, at least in some countries. Much of this can be expressed in terms of entropy (see, for instance, Johan Galtung, "Entropy and the General Theory of Peace", *Essays in Peace Research*, Vol. I, ch. 2, pp. 47—75, Copenhagen: Ejlers, 1975). Given the close contact between the two systems it is hardly to be expected that the entropy level of the two can remain very different for a long time, however — one will have to adjust to the other.

[9] Loc. cit., p.. 51 ff.

[10] For the distinction between direct and structural violence, see Johan Galtung, "Violence, Peace and Peace Research", op. cit., pp. 109—134.

[11] For an exploration of the dialectic between the geo-political pocket in which a country is embedded and the socioeconomic system, see Johan Galtung, "On the Future of the International System", *Essays in Peace Research*, Vol. IV, ch. 18 (Copenhagen: Ejlers, 1977).

[12] For another use of this fourfold table, see Johan Galtung, "Patterns of Diplomacy", *Essays in Peace Research*, Vol. IV, ch. 3 (Copenhagen: Ejlers, 1977).

[13] The same applies to marriage: the institutional aspects constitute a signal to the outside world that the contracting parties intend to continue their relation, that it is not merely an ad hoc liaison.

[14] In fact, international relations are probably better understood by analyzing dyads than analyzing the units, the states. But there are two obvious difficulties: there are many more dyads since the number increases by the second power of the number of states; and a focus on the dyads levels out higher level relations such as triads and the m-tuples — which is another expression for an international organization (or even conference) with m participants. Thus, the dyadic approach does not solve the problem.

[15] Thus, among the Nordic countries it is fair to say that the embassies have mainly ceremonial functions, most problems being handled multilaterally. But they are not abolished: the Nordic political scene is a dense network of all four forms, of civil servants contacting their opposite numbers directly, bypassing embassies that are then used for other purposes (e.g., cultural), of countless conferences and organizations. When there are arrows in Figures 1 and 2 it is not to suggest that the lower phases are emptied, only that the process, and perhaps also the point of gravity, moves on.

[16] We shall use the commonly used terms IGO, INGO etc. For an explanation related to the type of theory developed here, see section 3. For the particular term BINGO (business internongovernmental organization) I am indebted to Tord Høivik.

[17] For a good summary of statistics in this field, see Werner Feld, *A Study of Business, Labor, and Political Groups* (New York: Praeger, 1972), especially p. 177 where the growth of IGOS and INGOS from 1860 to 1970 is given as from 1 to 242 and 5 to 2,296 respectively. These numbers differ from one study to another depending on criteria — but the substantial growth rate is always clearly demonstrated.

[18] Thus, organizations will send representatives to the UNESCO Secretariat for negotiations before UNESCO sends an observer to their meetings.

[19] A typical example would be all the resident diplomacy among the UN agencies. It is also necessary, not to streamline and "coordinate" in the sense of eliminating differences or overlaps, but in order to be informed about other approaches. For an example of totally different perspectives on the same international issue, that of transfer of technology, see the article "The Technology that can Alienate", *Development Forum*, July-August 1976, p. 8, by the present author, on WHO and UNCTAD.

[20] There are already some data available on the process. Thus, Skjelsbaek reports, on the basis of the *Yearbook of International Organizations* from 1968, 93 super-INGOS — such as the International Social Science Council with the various international social science associations as members — or 5% of the total of INGOS. But the major form of growth is, of course, new organizations and growth within the organizations. Thus, in a questionnaire study from 1967 to general secretaries of international organizations, 55% report expansion in the past, only 4% loss; and 61% predicted expansion for the future, only 2% loss (it should be added that organizations in crisis may be less inclined to answer such questionnaires). The work was carried out by Jorge Schnitman and Luis Stuhlman from Buenos Aires under the supervision of Kjell Skjelsbaek and the author (not yet published).

[21] We do not yet have the appropriate indicators here, maybe because indicators of power tend to be developed by intellectuals fascinated by the power they do not have (capital assets, military power, etc.) and less inclined to explore the distribution of the power they/we do have, such as information.

[22] I am indebted to Tony Judge for this observation.

[23] For a further discussion of the theoretical basis of this perceptive, see Johan Galtung, "A Structural Theory of Integration", *Essays in Peace Research*, Vol. IV, ch. 11 (Copenhagen: Ejlers, 1977).

[24] This may not be true inside the countries because opposing organizations are tied into an institutional framework in some kind of balance, usually in favor of the strong. Since that institutional network is largely missing at the world level, the net result may be words cancelling each other.

[25] Thus, relatively soon the Third World may organize their own secretariat, to some extent to counter the expertise possessed by such "trade unions of rich countries" as the European Community and the OECD.

[26] We are here talking about an empirically existing organization.

[27] One way of obtaining this would be to cross-classify one ascriptive dimension (women, young), one occupational dimension (particularly the professions) and one value-dimension (Socialist, Christian).

[28] This is one more example of the principle indicated in note 4 above: *meaning* is the limiting principle in sociofunctional space.

[29] From *International Associations*, 1955, no. 2. The data are old, but from the crucial period of rapid post-war expansion.

[30] There are interesting indications, particularly in New York where the INGOs surrounding the UN perhaps tend to be more Western than is the case elsewhere — thus adding to the "Westernness" of UN organizations. The question is to what extent his attitude is anti-Western, anti-imperialist, anti-NT or anti-INGO (from the UN Secretariat; the major IGO).

[31] A classic in this field is Chad Alger, "Non-resolution Consequences of the United Nations and Their Effect on International Conflict", *Conflict Resolution*, 1961, pp. 128—45. Also see Kurt Jacobsen, "Some Behavioral Characteristics of the United Nations as a Function of Rank", IPRA Proceedings (Assen: van Gorcum, 1969), where the distinction is made between the power inside and outside the organization.

IV.13. *A Structural Theory of Imperialism*

* Johan Galtung is Professor of Peace Research at the University of Oslo. This is a revised version of a paper originally prepared for the International Political Science Association World Conference in Munich, September 1970, under the title 'Political Development and the International Environment: An Essay on Imperialism'. I am grateful to Ali Mazrui for having solicited the paper, and for all other colleagues in the World Order Models Project under the direction of Saul Mendlovitz for penetrating and stimulating discussions — particularly Osvaldo Sunkel, Stephen Hymer, and Otto von Kreye. The paper has also been presented at the International Peace Academy in Vienna, in September 1970; at the University of Lund, December 1970; at the College of Europe, Bruges and University

of Groningen, January 1971 and at the PRIO Theory Weeks, January 1971. I am grateful to discussants at all places, and particularly to Lars Dencik, Egil Fossum, Tord and Susan Høivik and Knut Hongro. The article can be identified as PRIO-Publication no. 27—1 from the International Peace Research Institute, Olso.

[1] For an explanation of this concept, see Galtung, J. 1969: 'Violence, Peace and Peace Research' *J. Peace Res.* 6. pp. 167—91.

[2] This equality premise may be formulated in terms of distribution, or redistribution, of values generated by the society in liberal theory, or as absence of exploitation in marxist theory. The two approaches have in common the idea that a party may have an interest even if it does not proclaim that it has this interest, but whereas the liberal approach will keep the social structure but carry out some redistribution along the road, the marxist approach will change the social structure itself. In both cases one may actually also make a further distinction as to whether harmony is to be obtained by equalization of what the society produces of material and spiritual value, or equalization when it comes to the power to decide over what the society produces. But imperialism as a structure cuts across these distinctions and is, in our view, based on a more general concept of harmony and disharmony of interests.

[3] No attempt will be made here to explore similarities and dissimilarities between this definition of imperialism and that given by such authors as Hobson, Luxemburg, Lenin, Hilferding and very many others. This definition has grown out of a certain research tradition, partly inductively from a long set of findings about international interaction structures, and partly deductively from speculations relating to structural violence in general and the theory of inequality in particular.

[4] Particularly one aspect of Lenin's conception of imperialism has been picked up in our definition: the general idea of a labour aristocracy. Lenin quotes Engels when he says that '... quand aux ouvriers, ils jouissent en toute tranquillite avec eux du monopole colonial, de l'Angleterre et de son monopole sur le marché mondial'. *L'impérialisme: Stade supreme du Capitalisme*, (Moscow, 1969), p. 139 — The same idea is expressed by L. S. Senghor; 'les prolétaires d'Europe ont bénéfice du régime colonial; partant, ils ne s'y sont jamais reellement, je veux dire efficacement, opposes', *Nation et voie africaine du socialisme*, p. 51. And. T. Hopkins in 'Third World Modernization in Transnational Perspective' *The Annals*, (1969), pp. 126—36 picks up the 'other' angle of this; '...there are strong indications that in most Third World Countries, internal inequality is increasing. The educated are markedly more advantaged; urban workers are relatively well-off; unemployment is high and increasing; rural populations are poor'.

[5] Thus, international statistics should not be given only for national aggregates since this conceals the true nature of the relations in the world. It would be much more useful if statistics were given for the four groups defined in our definition. In general we should assume such statistics over time to show that cC and cP grow most quickly and more or less together, then follows pC and the bottom is pP that is not only located much below the other two, but also shows little growth or none at all. The more numerous is the group, the lower the growth: it is the accumulated work from these vast masses that permits the growth of the dominating minorities. One highly stimulating analysis in this direction is given by T.E. Weisskopf who tries to disaggregate the growth rates and is led to the conclusion that the growth in the developing countries has taken place in upper and middle strata of population, in the secondary

sector of economic production, and in the urban areas. The growth rates in these parts of the developing nations are not too different from growth rates in corresponding parts in developed nations, but due to the absence of mechanisms for redistribution this leaves the vast periphery of the developing nations with close to zero or even negative growth. Weisskopf, T. E., 'Underdevelopment Capitalistic, Growth and the Future of Poor Countries', World Order Models Project, 1970.

[6] This argument is carried much further for the case of inter-individual rather than international interaction in Galtung. J., 'Structural Pluralism and the Future of Human Interaction', paper presented at the Second International Future Research Conference, Kyoto, April 1970, and Galtung, J, 'Perspectives on Development: Past, Present and Future', paper presented at the International Sociological Association Conference Varna, September 1970.

[7] The basic point here is that a demand generates a chain of demands. Economists have made some estimates in this connexion. For instance, H. B. Chenery and T. Watanabe conclude, 'In the four industrial countries studied here (United States, Japan, Norway and Italy), between 40% and 50% of total domestic demands for goods and services comes from other productive sectors rather than from final users' 'International Comparisons of the Structure of Production', *Econometrica*, (1958), p. 504. The more connected the economy of a country, the more will a demand proliferate. Other social scientists should have tools corresponding to the input-output analyses of the economists in order to study the degree of connectedness of a society. Characteristic of a traditional society is precisely the low level of connectedness: the spread effect into other branches of economic activity and into other districts is much lower. Also see Stirton-Weaver, F. 'Backwash, Spread and the Chilean State', *Studies in Comparative*

International Development, vol. V. no. 12 and Hirschman, A.O., *The Strategy of Economic Development* (New Haven: Yale Univ. Press, 1958), especially his discussion of backward and forward linkages, pp. 100—119.

[8] It is this equality that we stipulate to be in the interest of both parties, both for the exploiter and the exploited. Obviously, there are two approaches: the interaction structure can be changed so that the inter- and intra-actor effects are equal, and/or redistribution can take place. But if this interaction structure has been in operation for a long time and has already generated considerable differences in living conditions then both methods may have to be used, a point to be further elaborated in section 10 below. For highly stimulating discussion of unequal exchange, see Casanova, P.G., *Sociologia de la Exploitation* (Mexico: Siglo Veintiuno, 1969), and Arghiri Emmanuel, *L'échange Inegal* (Paris: Maspero, 1969).

[9] What we have in mind here, concretely, is of course all the various forms of development assistance based on the idea that grants are given to poor countries on the condition that they use them to procure capital goods in developed countries. In an excellent article, 'Prospectives for the Third World', S. Sideri summarises much of the literature showing how well development assistance pays. However, these analyses are by no means complete since only some aspects of the economic spin-off effects are considered, not all the others that may also, incidentally, be convertible into economic effects, at least in the long run.

[10] For an analysis of social status systems using feudal interaction as the basic concept, see Galtung, J., 'Feudal Systems, Structural Violence and the Structural Theory of Revolution' *in Proceedings of*

the IPRA *Third General Conference,* — pp. 110—188. (Van Gorcum, Assen, 1970.)

[11] For a penetrating analysis of the relation between dependency and development, see Cardoso, F. H. & Faletto, E., *Dependencia y desarrollo en America Latina* (Mexico: Siglo Veintiumo, 1969). One important difference between that book and the present analysis lies in the warning the authors give against generalization beyond the concrete case. While sympathetic to this, we nevertheless feel there is considerable virtue in general theory as a baseline for understanding the concrete case.

Another basic analysis of this type of relationship is, of course, Frank, A. G., *Capitalism and Underdevelopment in Latin America* (N. Y.: Monthly Review Press, 1967). The basic key to Frank's analysis is the structure that 'extends from the macrometropolitan system center of the world capitalist system "down" to the most supposedly isolated agricultural workers, who, through this chain of interlinked metropolitan-satellite relationships, are tied to the central world metropolis and thereby incorporated into the world capitalist system as a whole' (p. 16). and he goes on (p. 17) to talk about 'the exploitation of the satellite by the metropolis or — the tendency of the metropolis to expropriate and appropriate the economic surplus of the satellite'. All this is valid as general formulae, but too litle emphasis is given to the type of exploitation referred to here as 'asymmetric distribution of spin-offs' and the special organization referred to as 'feudal interaction structure'. And economists with no marxist inclination at all are certainly not helpful when it comes to reflecting imperialistic types of relations. Thus, in Jan Tinbergen. *The Design of Development* (Baltimore: Johns Hopkins, 1966), development is discussed throughout the book as if the government in a developing country is free to make its decisions. And in T. Haavelmo. *A study in the Theory of Economic Evolution* (Amsterdam: North--Holland Publ. Co., 1954) it is difficult to see that any theory at all based on *relations* between nations is offered to explain the tremendous disparities in this world; just to mention two examples. And even Myrdal's *Asian Drama* has little to say on international relations, as pointed out by Lars Rudebeck in an excellent review article, *Cooperation and Conflict* 1969, pp. 267—81.

[12] One book that gives a fairly balanced account of Soviet dominance patterns is *The New Imperialism* by Hugh Seten-Watson (New York: Capricorn Books, 1961). Andre Amalrik's analysis *Will the Societ Union Survive Until 1984?* (New York: Harper & Row., 1970) also deserves reading, not so much for its apocalyptic scenario as for its penetrating analysis of the internal dominance system. But the elite harmonization criterion will probably hold to a large extent mediated through the cooperation between party elites. Comparative studies of imperialistic structures, in the tradition of Helio Janguaribe, comparing different types of empires in this century as well as long-time historical comparisons bringing in, for instance, the Roman Empire, would be highly useful to shed more light over this particular international structure. At present this type of exercise is hampered by the tendency to use 'imperialism' as an abusive term, as a category to describe the other camp. We have preferred to see it as a technical term, which does not mean that he who struggles for peace will not have to struggle against imperialism regardless of what shape it takes.

[13] For an analysis of international air communication, see Gleditsch, N. P., 'Trends in World Airline Patterns' (1967), pp. 366—408.

[14] For an analysis of the role of the international press agencies see Ostgaard, E., 'Factors Influencing the Flow of News', *Journal of Peace Research* 2, pp. 39—63.

[15] For an analysis of this see Galtung, J., Ruge, M. H., 'The Structure of Foreign News: The Presentation of the Congo, Cuba and Cyprus Crises in Four Norwegian Newspapers', *J. Peace Res.* 2, pp. 64—91.

[16] For an analysis of this, see Galtung, J., 'After Camelot', in Horowitz, I. L. (ed.) *The Rise and Fall of Project Camelot* (Cambridge, Mass.: M.I.T. Press, 1967).

[17] As one example, and a very explicit one, may serve the following quotation: '...can we discharge our responsibility to God and to man for so magnificent, so populous a proportion of the world — Our answer is off hand ready and simple. We are adequate. We do discharge our responsibilities. We are a conquering and imperial race. All over the world we have displayed our mettle. We have discovered and annexed and governed vast territories. We have encircled the globe with our commerce. We have penetrated the pagan races with our missionaries. We have innoculated the Universe (sic!) with our institutions. We are apt indeed to believe that our soldiers are braver, our sailors hardier, our captains, naval and military, skilfuller, our statesmen wiser than those of other nations. As for our constitution, there is no Briton at any hour of the day or night who will suffer it to be said that any approaches it'. From Lord Boseberry, 'Questors of Empire 1900', *in Miscellanies, Literary and Historical vol. II* (London: Hodder & Stoughton, 1921). I am indebted to Fiona Rudd for this remarkable reference.

[18] This is extremely clearly expressed in Report of a US Presidential Mission to the Western Hemisphere (The Rockefeller report): '... Just as the other American republics depend upon the United States for their capital equipment requirements, so the United States depends on them to provide a vast market for our manufactured goods. And as these countries look to the United States for a market for their primary products whose sale enables them to buy equipment for development at home, so the United States looks to them for raw materials for our industries, on which depend the jobs of many of our citizens ...' 'Quality of Life in the Americas', Agency for International Development, (August 1969), pp. 5—113. — The paragraph is as if taken out of a text book on imperialism, emphasizing how the Center countries provide capital equipment and manufactured goods, and the Periphery countries raw materials and markets. The only interesting thing about the quotation is that it is still possible to write like this in 1969.

[19] One example in the Brezhnev Doctrine: 'Speaking in Warsaw on November 12, 1968 to the V Congress of the Polish United workers Party Brezhnev emphasized the need for "strict respect" for sovereignty of other socialist countries, and added: "But when internal and external forces that are hostile to Socialism try to turn the development of some socialist country towards the restoration of a capitalist regime, when socialism in that country and the socialist community as a whole is threatened, it becomes not only a problem of the people of the country concerned, but a common problem and concern of all Socialist countries. Naturally an action such as military assistance to a fraternal country designed to avert the threat to the social system is an extraordinary step, dictated by necessity." Such a step, he added, "may be taken only in case of direct actions of the enemies of Socialism within a country and outside it, actions threatening the common interests of the Socialist camp." '*Keesing's Contemporary Archives*, 1968, p. 23027. Its similarity to the Monroe doctrine has often been pointed out, but there is the difference that the US sometimes seems to be acting as if they had a Monroe doctrine for the whole world.

Without implying that the following is official Soviet policy, it has nevertheless appeared in *International Affairs* (April,

1970). 'The socialist countries, united in the Warsaw Treaty Organization, are profoundly aware that the most reliable guarantee that their security will be preserved and strengthened is allround cooperation with the Soviet Union, including military cooperation. They firmly reject any type of anti-Soviet slander and resist attempts by imperialism and the remnants of domestic reaction to inject into the minds of their people any elements of anti-Sovietism, whether open or veiled. With the two worlds — socialist and capitalist — in global confrontation, any breach of international principles, any sign of nationalism, and especially any toleration, not to say use, of anti-Sovietism in policy turns those who pursue such policies into an instrument of imperialist strategy and policy, regardless of whether their revisionist slogan is given a Right or ultra-Left twist, regardless of the subjective intentions of the advocates and initiators of the course. And whether it is very big or very small, it remains nothing but an instrument in the hands of imperialism and in either case retains its ignominious essence, which is compatible with truly revolutionary socialist consciousness.' (V. Razmerov: Loyalty to Proletarian Internationalism — Fundamental Condition for Success of All Revolutionary Forces). — What this quotation says is in fact that not only hostile deeds, but also all hostile words are to be ruled out. It is also interesting to note that the types of attitudes that are not to be expressed are referred to as 'anti-Soviet'. In other words, the reference is to the Center country in the system, not even to the masses of that country, nor to anti-socialism.

[20] In general, international contacts between ministries seem to become increasingly transnational. Where the minister of defence in country A some time ago would have to use a channel of communication involving at least one embassy and one ministry of foreign affairs to reach his opposite number in country B, direct telecommunication would now be the ade-

quate channel. What this means in terms of cutting out filtering effects and red tape is obvious. It also means that transnational ties may be strengthened and some times be posted against the nation state. Obviously, this system will be expanding, for instance with a system of telesatellites available for elite communication between Center and Periphery countries within a bloc. For the Francophone countries the projected satellite Symphonie may, perhaps, be seen as a step in this direction, although it is targeted on audiences rather than on concrete, specific persons. The NATO satellite communication system is another example.

[21] Very important in this connection is, of course, the quick development of the telephone concept from essentially bilateral (one person talks with one other person, possibly with some others listening in at either end, or in the middle!) towards the telephone as a multilateral means of communication. Bell Telephone Company can now organize conferences over the telephone by connecting a number of subscribers. Obviously, if combined with a videoscreen the conversation may be more orderly because participants may also react on non-verbal, visual cues such as facial expressions, etc. More particularly they may raise a finger and ask for the 'floor'.

[22] The battle between the two types of imperialism is perhaps more important in the imagination of those who try to uphold one of the types than in social reality. Thus, what happened in the Dominican Republic in 1965 was interpreted by those who are upholding a pattern of economic imperialism as an attempt by 'the other bloc' to establish political imperialism; just as the events in Czechoslovakia in 1968 were interpreted by the servants of political military imperialism as an effort by 'the other bloc' to introduce economic imperialism. Whatever history's judgement may be in terms of these two hypotheses it is obvious that two types of imperialism,

directed from antagonistic blocs, cannot at the same time be in the same phase. One pattern would be that the dominant types are in phase 3 and the competitive type is in phase 1 — and that is what was claimed by the Center countries in the two cases.

[23] The best analysis we have read of division of labor in multinational corporations is by Stephen Hymer 'The Multinational Corporation and the Law of Uneven Development' to appear in Bhagwati, J.N. (ed.): *Economics and World Order* (New York: World Law Fund, 1970).

[24] This is not a random event: international organizations are in that phase because they reflect the relationships between national actors, that in the present stage of development are the major carriers in these relations.

[25] Thus, when Stalin died in 1953 there must have been great expectation in China that Mao Tsetung would be the next head of the International Communist Movement. His revolution was more recent, the country in which the revolution had taken place was by far the biggest, and he was also older as a revolutionary fighter in a leading position than possible competitors. Nevertheless, it was quite clear that the Soviet conception was that the leader of the International Communist Movement would have to be the leader of what they interpreted as the leading Communist nation: the Soviet Union herself.

[26] This is a major difference between liberal and structural peace theory. It is hardly unfair to interpret liberal peace theory as somehow stating that 'peace' is roughly proportionate to the volume of trade, possibly interpreted as an indicator of the level of interdependence, whereas structural peace theory would bring in the factor of equality and ask for the composition as well as the volume of trade. If structural theory is more correct and if the present trade structure is such that only the

Center nations can enjoy both high level of interdependence and high level in equality in exchange, then 'peace' is one extra benefit that will accrue to the Center layer of the world.

[27] Another concept would be the frequently quoted saying that 'technical assistance is taken from the poor man in the rich country and given to the rich man in the poor country.' The model of the world implied by the dominance theory would certainly not contradict this quite elegant statement: technical assistance is to a large extent paid for by tax-payers' money, not to mention by the surplus produced by the masses working in the rich countries, and given via public channels, often for the benefit of the layers in the poor countries that have a consumption structure compatible with a production structure that the rich countries can offer.

[28] Galtung, J., 'International Relations and International Conflicts: A Sociological Approach', *Transactions of the Sixth World Congress of Sociology* (International Sociological Association, 1966), pp. 121—61.

[29] E.g. Magdoff, H., *The Age of Imperialism*, (N.Y.: Monthly Review, 1969).

[30] Research on this is currently in progress at the International Peace Research Institute, Oslo.

[31] But it is still an open question whether this should really be referred to as imperialism, since so many of the criteria do not seem to be fulfilled. Once more this seems to bring up the importance of seeing imperialism as a special case of a wider set of social relationships, conveniently lumped together under the heading 'domination'.

[32] Relations between Soviet Union and the Arab World and Japan and Southeast Asia are being explored at the International Peace Research Institute, Oslo by Tormod Nyberg and Johan Galtung respectively.

[33] This type of structural reasoning seems particularly important in the Soviet case. It can hardly be claimed that the Soviet periphery participates more in the decision-making made by the Soviet center than the Czech periphery participated in the months prior to the invasion in August 1968. On the contrary the opposite hypothesis seems more tenable. And if this is the case the Soviet center could no longer necessarily count on the allegiance of its own periphery, particularly not on the Ukrainian periphery, bordering Czechoslovakia not only geographically, but also linguistically and culturally (and apparently listening attentively to broadcasts). This means that what happened in Czechoslovakia became a threat to the Soviet center, perhaps more than to the Soviet Union as a Center nation.

[34] See Appendix for data for 60 nations on these seven variables (but missing for most of the nations for Gini i, and for many of the nations for Gini 1).

[35] The trade composition index was developed by Knut Hongro after some suggestions by the present author. It may, however, well be that the index $\frac{(a + d) - (b + c)}{(a + d) + (b + c)}$ would be better since values of trade are usually added, not multiplied, and since this would attain the value I not when b *or* a equals 0, but when b *and* c equal 0. (Galtung, J., 'Vertical and Horizontal Trade Relation. A Note on Operationalization', WOMP 1970).

[36] Reference are given in the Appendix.

[37] In this connection it should be pointed out that the theory of imperialism would not be disconfirmed if these correlation coefficients had been much lower. It is only the theory as a model for the concrete empirical world here and now that would have been disconfirmed, not imperialism as one factor in systems of collectivities, and particularly as a factor that together with other factors may rise to the constellation known in the present world. What Table VIII seems to indicate is that the theory of imperialism as presented there is not a bad map for orientation in the contemporary world.

[38] For one exposition of the center-periphery theory for individuals see Galtung, J. 1964: 'Foreign Policy Opinion as a Function of Social Position' *J. Peace Res.* I, pp. 206—31.

[39] This, of course, would also be true inter-individually: division of labor may be organized in such a way that it is personality expanding for some actors and personality contracting for others so that they 'sort' themselves away from each other by participating in this type of vertical interaction.

[40] See the article by Stephen Hymer referred to in footnote 23 above.

[41] We are thinking particularly of the Pakistan consortium and the India consortium.

[42] Thus, center-periphery theory in connection with non-territorial actors should perhaps not be stated so much in terms of size or age of organizations, as in terms of whether they are able to establish bridgeheads in other non-territorial actors, and whether they are able to organize systematically some vertical type of division of labour. Thus, the system of 'consultative status' clearly indicates who is to decide and who to be consulted.

[43] It should be pointed out that no strategy seems to exist for reducing the gap. There is not even any strategy for reducing the increase of the gap, the only strategy that perhaps may be said to exist is a strategy for improving the level of poor nations. A strategy for reducing the gap does not necessarily imply a basic change of the structure of the relations

719

between rich and poor nations, however. It might also come about by reducing significantly the growth in the rich nations.

[44] Few statesmen seem to have put this point more strongly than Julius Nyerere in the famous Arusha Declaration: 'If every individual is self-reliant the ten-house cell will be self-reliant; if all the cells are self-reliant the whole ward will be self-reliant; and if the wards are self-reliant, the District will be self-reliant. If the Districts are self-reliant, then the Region is self-reliant, and if the Regions are self-reliant, then the whole Nation is self-reliant and this is our aim.' — In this there is of course also an implicit theory: self-reliance has

to be built from the very bottom, it can only be basically a property of the individual, not of the nation. — And Kenneth Kaunda has this to add in *Humanism in Zambia*, (Lusaka, 1968), 'We all know that a man who has developed a genuine sense of self-reliance will not in any way wish to exploit his fellow men', p. 50.

[45] In the present phase of imperialism, cP would use their good contacts with cC through international organizations to get resettled in the Center. This seems to work for businessmen in the capitalist world as well as for high-ranking party officials in the communist world. For the latter, 'reasons of health' are often invoked.

IV.14. *Cultural Contact, Technical Assistance, Peaceful Relations*

[1] More explicitly, the principle could be formulated as follows. Man divides objects into good, bad, and neutral; and he sees objects as facilitating or implying each other and as impeding or denying each other. There are simplistic and sophisticated versions of this. In the simplistic version, there are no longer any neutral objects: all positive objects support each other and all negative objects support each other, whereas they impede each other mutually. In other words, the world is divided into internally consistent hell and heaven. Another version of the same pattern is the polarization found in conflict. The world is divided into those who are for us and those who are against us (there are no neutrals), with positive interaction within the two camps and negative interaction between. Thus, the world appears more manageable, less ambiguous, and hence less threatening. In the more sophisticated versions, all kinds of complications are introduced: two objects may *both* facilitate *and* imply each other; there are neutral objects: *some* negative objects facilitate positive objects and *some* positive objects impede positive objects, nor do negative objects necessarily support each other — and time-lag, stochasticity, and

feedback are introduced into the patterns. Obviously, the action-directives that can be derived are less clear.

[2] By "depolarization", then, we mean the process leading away from the pattern described in the note above. Links of positive interaction and cooperation are established between the two camps.

[3] The strongest peacebuilding factor is probably cultural cooperation particularly via supranational organizations (arguments 3 and 10). But this is true only if it can compete successfully with other agents of cultural transfer, such as the organizations of nation-states — otherwise there will hardly be a loyalty transfer. Badly organized supranational activity at a lower level of efficiency than bilateral cooperation may decrease rather than increase supernational identification, since the output probably is compared to other outputs, not to the output of zero. For some evidence in connection with the three principles mentioned, see Berelson, Steiner: *Human Behavior: An Inventory of Scientific Findings* (New York: Harcourt, Brace & World, 1965), p. 513.

[4] Thus, much research shows that people have a remarkable capacity for behaving differently under different circumstances: in other words *not* to generalize experiences. Norms of action are seen as or are made *situation specific*.

[5] As formulated in the preamble to the United Nations Charter. With the prominence given to these values one would expect many people to regard it as axiomatic that they support each other, almost automatically, and this is probably a very widespread belief.

[6] By "rank disequilibrium" we mean the condition that obtains when a person or a nation is strong in some characteristic considered desirable and weak on another. "Rank equilibrium" obtains when the person or nation is weak in both (for instance,

both poor and illiterate) or strong in both (for instance both rich and powerful).

[7] By "supranational" we mean any kind of international organization, governmental or nongovernmental, which is an "actor" in its own right, and has its own existence. In a special class among the supranational organizations are the (very few) international organizations that can adopt resolutions with binding power over member states. We do not have them particularly in mind.

[8] For more details about this argument, see Johan Galtung and Tord Høivik: "On the Definition and Theory of Development with a View to the Application of Rank Order Indicators in the Elaboration of a Composite Index of Human Resources", (Mimeo. 1967), 52 p.

IV.15. *Peace Corps: Structure and Function*

* I wish to express my gratitude to members of the staff of the US Peace Corps, particularly to Mr. J.L. St. Lawrence, Regional Director for Far Eastern Programs and to fellow members of the "Komiteen for utredning av spørsmålet om opprettelse av et norsk fredskorps" and the Council of the War Resisters' International for stimulating debates and information provided; and to Norges Almenvitenskapelige Forskningsråd and Institute for Social Research for economic support.

[1] In *Memories and Studies*, (Longmans, Green and Co., New York, 1911).

[2] *ibid.*, p. 264.

[3] *ibid.*, p. 269.

[4] *ibid.*, pp. 293 f.

[5] *ibid.*, p. 274.

[6] *ibid.*, p. 275.

[7] *ibid.*, p. 276.

[8] *ibid.*, p. 283.

[9] *ibid.*, p. 287.

[10] *ibid.*, p. 290.

[11] *ibid.*, p. 291 f.

[12] *ibid.*, p. 291.

[13] *Op. cit.*

[14] For an elaboration of this, see Galtung, J.: *Notes on Technical Assistance*.

[15] So far, it seems as if the pedagogical aspect has been largely neglected both by the Norwegian and Danish Peace Corps committees and to some extent even by the US Peace Corps. Sooner or later this problem will have to be faced.

[16] International Edition, January 8, 1962, p. 8.

[17] Dodd's article "A Social Distance Test in the Near East" (*Amer. J. Sociol.*, vol. 41, pp. 194—204) is interesting for many reasons. It shows (which is primarily a kind of validation of the instrument) that "the two outstandingly large distances or hostilities are of the Armenians for the Turks ($_A$d$_T$ = 82) and of the Palestinian Arabs for the Jews ($_{PA}$d$_J$ = 75) (p. 198) and "at the other end of the scale the outstanding friendships which a historian would expect are those of Armenians for Americans, largely as a result of the aid given by Americans through the Near East Relief and other channels ($_{Ar}$d$_{Am}$ = 20). Another outstanding friendship at present is that of Iraqis for the British, as the result of the peaceful relinquishing of British control in Iraq and the granting of independence to it ($_I$d$_B$ = 12) (p. 199). That there would be friendly feelings toward Americans in general when the test is given by an American to "170 freshmen at the American University of Beirut" (p. 196) is certainly not strange, but it is interesting that the Armenians range particularly high here. It certainly supports the author's conclusion (p. 199) that "the general finding from this table of nationalities is that social distances are not determined by geographic proximity nor by abundance of contacts, as much as by definite acts of a benevolent or malevolent sort between groups. Processes of cooperation or conflict seem to have determined these distances more than the mere amount of interaction. Of course, it is probably true that much of the positive feeling Armenians had for the Americans can be attributed to their negative feelings for the Turks — the Americans rank high because the Turks committed the massacres they did. But the effect has been a lasting one, transmitted from one generation to the next — and the American aid must have been given in such a way as not to provoke the many counter-feelings technical assistance in the 'fifties has encountered.

[18] For a discussion of the role of indigenous vs. migrant status in a country with ethnic conflict, see Liebersohn, Stanley: "Theory of Race and Ethnic Relations", *Amer. Sociol. Rev.* (1961), 26, pp. 902—909.

IV.16. *Notes on Technical Assistance: The Indo-Norwegian Project in Kerala*

* This is an abbreviated version of a mimeographed publication prepared in 1961, at the Section for Conflict and Peace Research, Institute for Social Research, Oslo. The reader is referred to "Development from Above and the Blue Revolution: The Indo-Norwegian Project in Kerala", *Essays*, Vol. V, chapter 12, for an account of what happened to the project later.

[1] The Oslo School of Economics, University of Oslo, has done some work on the economics of developing countries. See Ragnar Frisch: *Economic Planning and the Growth Problem in Developing Countries*, 1961 (reprint series) and Trygve Haavelmo (edited by Per Schreiner): *Ökonomiske problemstillinger i underut-* viklede områder, Memorandum 30 August 1960.

[2] Or, to be more precise: at least not what both parties recognize as complete, economic compensation.

[3] For valuable information on TA from an administrative point of view, see UN publications and Sharp, W. R.: *International Technical Assistance Programs and Organization*, Public Administration Service. Chicago 1952, Glick, P.M.: *The Administration of Technical Assistance*, Growth in the Americas, University of Chicago Press, 1957. Engen-utvalget, Oslo 1961 chs. I—III has a good survey of TA organizations and their monetary resources, with particular relevance to Nor-

way. Somewhat dated but excellent is Erling Nypan: *FN og de underutviklede land*, Bergen 1952.

[4] By collectivity we mean a super-national collectivity with a special organizational structure. The distinction can be made between *regional* and *universal* collectivities of nations, the former comprising such international organizations as the Nordic Council, the Organization of American States, the EEC, etc. and the latter being United Nations and its specialized agencies. This distinction is of tremendous importance but for our purpose here "regional" and "universal" is combined. The term "multilateral" is often used so as to cover both of these, and the case of more yielders to the same receivers.

[5] Two figures giving an impression of the size of bilateral aid are: USA for 1958/59: close to 2 billion dollars, Soviet Union for 1954 till May 1960: 1.8 billion dollars. See Olav Dörum: "Multilaterale og bilaterale tiltak", *Internasjonal Politikk*, nr 1, 1961, p. 39.

[6] Says Glick *(op. cit.,* p. 359 f) "there is little doubt that the United Nations program enjoys inherent advantages in meeting the problems of sensitivity and sovereignty, in emphasizing the role of the host countries as donors, and in making clear that international technical cooperation is a two-way street. There is a reverse side, however, to this coin. In the United Nations agencies to say "No" or to insist on the meeting of preconditions before aid is given.

[7] *Arbeiderbladet*, 12/6—1961, p. 8

[8] See Gerhardsen, G.M.: *Fredens våpen*, Bergen 1960, p. 90.

[9] Annex I to Resolution 222 (IX) adopted by ECOSOC August 1949 in connection with the Expanded Program of Technical Assistance (EPTA) says in its *Guiding Princi-*

ples: (The assistance) "...shall not be a means of foreign economic and political interference in the international affairs of the country concerned and not be accompanied by any considerations of a political nature".

[10] The ECOSOC resolution on the EPTA program *(op. cit.)* calls upon requesting governments "normally to assume responsibility for a substantial part of the costs of technical services with which they are provided, at least the part which can be paid in their own currencies". This pattern is extremely important in this connection. In the receiving country assistance via collectivity makes the donor anonymous, and their own contributions will easily dominate psychologically.

[11] The structure of TA may in many cases permit both parties to claim responsibility for success (receivers: we have actually done the job, donors: and our purpose was to train you) and to blame the other party for failure (receivers: you thought the job was easy, just to copy your own institution and procedures, donors: there was no real support and interest in the receiving country).

[12] For the receivers welfare boards as well as international TA organizations have the function of making what *others* receive much more visible, and this may lead to claims for universalism, thus multiplying the request for TA. "Country A has received TA in the fields X, Y, Z, ... we need it even more than they do."

[13] "Erfaringer fra det norske hjelpeprosjekt i India", *Internasjonal Politikk*, 1961, nr. 1, p. 84.

[14] Technical assistance is a part of the foreign policy of most countries, see *Engen-utvalget*, pp. 2 and 27. A contemporary theory of balance of power would have to take TA into account, if power is defined as "capacity to influence".

[15] As an example of explicit but non-tangible counter-value consider the following from *Programme for Cooperation with Developing Countries*, State of Israel, Ministry for Foreign Affairs, Jerusalem June 1961, (p. 3): "Israel is a small country and there is no fear that with her assistance there can be inroads for colonial purposes. The developing countries realize that Israel needs friends to secure her place in the international community among other small states, and that in an atmosphere of friendship Israel is prepared to enter into programmes of cooperation. These technological and scientific programmes, therefore, are to the benefit of all concerned."

[16] Even the system with counterparts has led to difficulties, as good counterparts are scarce, and often too busy to enter into a fruitful cooperation with a temporary expert. The expert has often found that he has to work in isolation, communicating to future counterparts and experts via a "report", instead of directly to a counterpart.

[17] In stressing what the experts offer it should certainly not be forgotten what he receives: a high salary, interesting, work, prestige (at least as long as it lasts), and important experience. Countries that participate disproportionately much also get much back in terms of experienced experts.

[18] The internationalization of TA will never prevent countries that participate disproportionately much, for instance small countries that are often preferred for political reasons, from stealing some of the success fron the collectivity, and getting an additional quota of honor.

[19] This may be facilitated by the export as well as the counterpart factually belonging to the same culture by both of them having received a Western education.

[20] In many cases it is probably also true that mutual acceptance is furthered by a vertical dividing line. Says Williams (*Reduction of Intergroup Tension*, Social Science Research Council, Bulletin 57, 1947, p. 72); "In any integration of minority members into a work situation *on the initiative of higher control-groups in any organization*, acceptance is facilitated by arranging for representation of the minority in the upper as well as the lower levels of the organization".

[21] Quoted from a speech given at the University of Kerala January 1961 by former Union Minister of Finance, C. D. Deshmukh.

[22] *Monthly Public Opinion Surveys* of the Indian Institute of Public Opinion, no. 32, May 1958, pp. 16—22.

[23] *Ibid*, p. 21.

[24] See article by Ithiel de Sola Pool and Kali Prasad in *Public Opinion Quart.*, Vol. XXII, pp. 292—304. The volume is a special issue on "Attitude Research in Modernizing Areas", and contains much valuable material.

[25] *ibid.*, pp. 302 f.

[26] *ibid.*, p. 304.

[27] For an interesting account of an experiment with education for cooperatives, see Albert Mayer and assoc.: *Pilot Project, India*, University of California Press, 1949, pp. 303—310.

[28] *J. Educ. Sociol.*, pp. 184—190.

[29] *Ibid.* p. 184.

[30] The best treatment of the problem of multiple loyalties we have encountered is: Guetzkow, Harold: *Multiple Loyalties*, Theoretical Approach to a Problem in International Organization, Publication no.

4 of the Center for Research on World Political Institutions, Princeton University, Princeton 1955.

[31] Cultural relativism, when it becomes an ideology more than a theoretical perspective, is hardly conducive to anthropological research in this field, unless the motivation is to reveal the evil effects of TA. See the famous "Statement on Human Rights" by the Executive Board, American Anthropological Association, in *American Anthropologist*, XLIX, pp. 539—543. For a comment, see Bay, Chr.: *The Structure of Freedom* (Stanford University Press, 1958), p. 376.

[32] This also applies to "concrete persons". A TA project always creates conflict and antagonism, and the researcher will have to use all his skills and methods to avoid the trap of taking criticism at its face value. Criticism is important as a symptom of something, but must be understood in its social context. The TA administration may, often rightly, fear that this understanding will not be the right one, and try to discourage certain contacts, and steer the understanding.

[33] In Albert Mayer: *Pilot Project, India*, University of California Press, p. 319, "And it is still the habit of mind of our project leaders in India not to deviate appreciably from set patterns, nor to exercise initiative and originality — not to have, in short, an empirical urge and outlook. The inevitably competitive race toward fixed goals also militates against questioning the set pattern, against developing any new "angles" or methods, for fear of falling behind". This lack of empiricism, except in certain limited fields closely connected with the immediate goal of the project, is interesting and understandable, but also detrimental in the long run.

[34] For an interesting account of how the main impact of a sociologist partici-

pating in a TA community development program was "a much greater acceptance by the administration of the methods of scientific analysis and evaluation as tools of administration", see J. W. Green: "Success and Failure in Technical Assistance: A Case Study", *Human Organization*, vol. 20, no. 1, p. 9. An empirical, analytical and questioning attitude is less widely distributed than ordinarily believed, and a main function of the social scientist for which he will hardly be applauded, may well be to force empirical attitudes and evaluation studies on TA projects.

[35] For a brief survey of research in this field sponsored by the UNESCO see *The Social Sciences*, UNESCO and its Programme XI, UNESCO 1955, chapter III, "The International Aspects of Social Evolution". Also see the special issue of *Public Opinion Quarterly*, vol. XXII, no. 3 and the reader by Shannon: *Underdeveloped Areas*, New York 1957. See also: *Social, Economic and Technological Change*, A Theoretical Approach, UNESCO, Paris 1958 and Mead, Margaret, ed.: *Cultural Patterns and Technical Change*, UNESCO, Paris 1953.

[36] For instance, at a theatre evening January 1961 arranged in Puthentura, very few people from Catholic Sakthikulangara were present. In this case, however, one reason and a rather important reason may be that the theatre evening had a pronounced communist flavor, as the Kerala People's Art Society that had arranged the evening was recognized by everybody as an organization with a communist tinge.

[37] *A Census of the Fisherfolk and the Fishing Implements of the Project Area*, INP item. no. 12, 13th Meeting, standing committee, November 1960. Hereafter called "Census".

[38] Miller points out an important characteristic of the Kerala village: "Instead of

living huddled in a street as so many other Indians do, the Malayali prefers the privacy of his own fenced compound, at a distance from his neighbors. The density of palm trees, plantains, and other vegetation often renders one house invisible from the next." And he continues: "...settlement is usually haphazard, with no special tendency for houses of a particular caste to cluster together." Miller, E. J.: "Village Structure in North Kerala", in Srinivas, M. N., ed.: *India's Villages*, Asia Publishing House, 2nd ed. 1960, p. 43.

[39] Actually, although the palms seem to be scattered everywhere 37% of 380 households in Sakthikulangara and 57% of 372 households in Neendakara owned no palm trees at all. P. Bog.: *A Statistical Survey of Economic Conditions in the Project Area*, Oslo 1954, p. 35.

[40] In 1961, however, a massive concrete wall with broken glass on top of it was constructed between the camp and the village.

[41] H. J. Ustvedt: "Sakthikulangara og Puthentura — arbeidsfeltene for den norske hjelpen til India", *Norwegian Broadcasting Corporation*, April 14, 1953, 19.40 hours.

[42] A Kerala exhibiton not too far from the project area, late 1960, had a pavilion for the Indo-Norwegian project. A poster with some statistical information made use of these figures:

	Norway	India	Kerala
Area, sq. miles	124,000	1,259,983	14,992
Population	3,541,000	397,500,000	15,230,000
Density, pop. sq. mile	28	315	1,016
Per capita income (rupees)	5,910	314	218
Urban population	52.2%	17.3%	13.2%

[43] The first director of the project (1952—1957), Diderich H. Lund, a remarkable personality, engineer, Quaker and pacifist.

[44] According to Per Vokso: *Framtid for India*, Folkeaksjonen, Bergen 1953, p. 37, Kerala communists and independents were against U S assistance but welcomed the Norwegians officially.

[45] According to P. Bog; *(Report no. 2*, p. 13) the sand contains ilemite and monazite that are exported, and the fraction of thorium is retained. (The Indian Government does not permit any export.)

[46] If an expert wants to maintain a favorable self-image he must not necessarily claim that he has *nothing* to *learn*, but he must claim that he has *something* to *teach*. His skill must be scarce, otherwise he could just as well be replaced by a native. See Gerhardsen: *Det norske eksperiment i India*, Gyldendal, 1959, p. 101.

[47] Norwegian salaries are considerably above corresponding salaries in Norway, but also considerably below corresponding UN salaries. The project director, however, is paid according to the salary he obtained in the position from which he is given leave. For an ambassador this means about N. kr. 120,000 a year. For the other positions there is a 25% addition for stay in India (tax exempt), a 5% annual increase (but maximum stay is 4 years) and free stay and transportation.

[48] It should also be noted that although a tremendous difference in economic stand-

ing may make contacts at home awkward, because of the extreme visibility of the difference in clothing, manners, etc. the work-situation induces a certain equivalence that may facilitate contact. *Health Survey*, no. 5, p. 8.

[49] This important factor is also mentioned by Evang, K.: "Våre oppgaver idag", *Internasjonal Politikk*, nr. 1, 1961, p. 102 in an interesting analysis.

[50] Stycos discusses the problem of using natives for proper translation of questionnaires and says (Stycos, J. M. "Studies of Fertility in Underdeveloped Areas, in Shannon, L. W.: *Underdeveloped Areas*, New York 1957 p. 396): "Such individuals tend to have as little or even less understanding of their lower classes than we do of ours. Moreover, they have as often as not been trained in Britain or the United States, further removing them from an understanding of their cultures." We do not necessarily imply that this applies to the project area, but the point is important.

[51] The highest castes with 10% of the population are said to command 90% of administrative positions in India.

[52] And certainly, nor do we say that exactly the same thing does not happen in a Norwegian fishing village.

[53] It has been pointed out that even Norwegians who express themselves quite fluently in English may not have the command of the language that makes it possible to express feelings in a polite and smooth way.

[54] Recently, efforts have been made to do something about this. Literature on India was almost not available to project personnel in the project library, however. It should be pointed out in this connection that project libraries are not usually supposed to contain literature on local customs and conditions when the project is

an ordinary engineering enterprise in Norway, by Norwegians, for instance. But our requirements are higher when it comes to cross-cultural contacts, it seems.

[55] For some accounts of conflict situations and issues see Gleditsch, K.: "Erfaringer fra det norske hjelpeprosjektet i India", *Internasjonal Politikk* nr. 1, 1961, p. 77 and p. 99. Also see Gerhardsen, G.M.: *Det norske eksperiment i India*, Gyldendal 1959, chapter called "Sol og skygger" pp. 102—126. It is interesting to compare these reflections with the testimony of good relations given in *Report no. 1.* Oslo 1954 p. 8.

[56] Nor must this particular argument or the whole section be conceived of as a criticism of high level contact. The latter is indispensable; our task is only to try and explain why this kind of contact seems to have increased and the more local contact seems to have decreased — not to state which one is more important.

[57] See Gleditsch, *op. cit.*, pp. 83 f, for arguments re choice of a diplomat as director. Another possibie function of appointing a top level diplomat has been pointed out to us: this may prove to the Indians that "Norwegians consider this an important undertaking". On the other hand it may also prove to the Indians that there is a hidden purpose, or at least that Norway must be a strange little country when an ambassador is used for a small fisheries project.

[58] See Sorokin, P.: *Social and Cultural Dynamics*, Boston 1957, Introduction.

[59] See *Health Survey*, 1960, p. 5.

[60] Sivertsen mentions the importance of a situation "which provides the Parias with an active participant role in the common struggle of the less privileged sections of all castes for better conditions" — it is not enough to reduce "the problem of

caste differences... to a moral question". See Sivertsen, D.; *Political Development and Organizational Change in a South Indian Village*, Oslo 1959, p. 170. What role the INP has played in this connection in the project area we do not know.

[61] *Op. cit.*, p. 26.

[62] Information by courtesy of the Project office in Oslo.

[63] For an interesting comment about this point of lack of communication downwards, of *success*, not only of failure, see J. Vedel-Petersen: "Lad os ikke snuble i starten", *Aktuelt*, 19/1—1961 p. 8; "Det er helt klart, at vi kan rejse flere hospitaler a la Korea-hospitalet, men befolkningen vil i så fald forblive uengageret. Det er den fejl. nordmændene har gjort. Jeg har besögt deres store projekt i Kerala det er i mange henseender fortræffeligt — men det har ingen kontakt med hjemlandet, og ingen i Norge er opptaget av denne gode — indsats. *Hjemme i Norge*

er den en fiasko. — Vi må ikke begå de samme fejl." There is hardly any doubt that a visit to India is more gratifying in terms of understanding and appreciation of the purposes and achievements of the project than exposure to Norwegian criticism at home.

[64] During the first four years the Norwegian personnel were paid according to the regular salary of the person hired + something more. From September 1 1957 salaries for the positions in the project area have been fixed. This does not mean that the personnel has not been carefully selected — only that the basis for fixing the salary is more according to the position the person shall fill in the project than the position in Norway he has to leave.

[65] And, indeed that insight in such factors may facilitate transitions that are only partly seen by the administrators. On the other hand, although "freedom is insight in necessity" (Spinoza, Lenin) — "necessity" will always have local facets the sociologists will hardly catch.

IV.17. *European Security: An Era of Negotiations?*

* This is a slightly revised version of a paper presented at the Twelfth Annual Conference, Institute for Strategic Studies, Evian, 11—13 September 1970.

[1] For further exploration of these two types of violence' see Johan Galtung, 'Violence, Peace and Peace Research', *J. Peace Res.* (1969), pp. 167—91.

[2] The peace thinking in this paper in connection with Europe is clearly in the liberal tradition on this criterion, but should also be compatible with the socialist concept of 'active peaceful coexistence'. See Johan Galtung, 'Analyses and Recommendations', in Johan Galtung, ed., *Cooperation in Europe* (Oslo: Universitetsforlaget, 1970), pp. 3—103.

[3] It is difficult to understand how the theory of peaceful coexistence can be compatible with this, except under the assumption that the coexistence will prove the superiority of socialism so convincingly that the other regimes will crumble not only because of their internal contradictions, but also because of the demonstration effect from the other party in the coexistence.

[4] The word *détente* should preferably be used about something that took place at the end of the 1950s and lasted for some years — not as a state of affairs that is still lasting; it is like capital spent, or eroded, not like unlimited reserves.

[5] This is spelt out in detail in the reference in footnote 2. Particularly important

is the degree of dependence, of whether one party's latitude depends on what the other party does. Political, not to mention military, domination are clear cases; and so is the tendency to become dependent on consumer goods development in other countries as has been mentioned above.

[6] See footnote [5].

[7] *Images of the World in the Year 2000: A Synthesis of the Marginals,* available from the Vienna Center, Franz Josefs Kai 3—5, Vienna.

IV.18. *On the Future of the International System*

* This is a revised version of a paper originally presented as a public lecture, Makerere University College, Kampala, 16 August 1967; at the International Future Research Inaugural Congress, Oslo, 12 September 1967; as a George A. Miller Centennial Lecture, University of Illinois, 10 October 1967; and for the Seminar on Peace Research and International Relations, University of Essex, 7 November 1967. I am indebted to discussants all places for important comments and criticism, but the standard phrase that 'the responsibility rests entirely with the author' has rarely been felt as more appropriate — since there are no data available so far that can serve as arbiters in any dispute. This article can be identified as PRIO-publication no. 25—6, from the International Peace Research Institute, Oslo.

[1] A claim of this kind cannot be based on lack of data from the future, since that also applies to the natural scientist whose predictions have usually been regarded as legitimate. Rather, the claim must be based on the idea that a prediction becomes an element in the predicted system, and that this may create the wellknown self-fulfilling and self-denying mechanisms. Although this often is a highly exaggerated picture of what the publication of future oriented studies of social affairs may entail, it is difficult to see it as an objection against such studies. Rather, it should predispose one for the term *prevision* rather than

prediction, as most authors in the field of futurology seem to agree. That such prevision may highlight attractive and objectionable points in the map of the future is obvious, just as obvious as it is that the researcher who wants to predict rather than to preview should lock up his findings rather than publish them.

[2] For some statements on this, see articles in the excellent *Daedalus* issue 'Toward the Year 2000: Work in Progress' (summer 1967) by Herman Kahn and Anthony J. Wiener (particularly pp. 705f), and by Ithiel de Sola Pool (particularly pp. 930f). Another article with some valuable ideas is Bruce Russett: 'The Ecology of Future International Politics', *Int. Studies Quart.* (1967), pp. 12—31.

[3] Thus, one would and should expect social scientists to be able to map out viable worlds nobody else has thought of, discussed from the point of view of current values, but also to introduce new values that these constructs may realize.

[4] In general, the social sciences are remarkably inept in dealing with discontinuities, probably because they are engaged in by predominantly gradualistically oriented people who are sufficiently in opposition to want change, yet not so alienated from their society that they want absolute change, i.e. discontinuity. Marxist and neo-Marxist thinking have discontinuities built

into their schemes, but are on the other hand usually not empirical enough in their approaches. A synthesis here should bring interesting insights, and is bound to come about with the current growth in cooperation between the Marxist and positivist camps.

[5] Because pure ideologists are more likely to be located so far from the decision-making nucleus that they do not feel the urge or the challenge to work out more continuous trajectories and feel that scientists who try to do so only try to reduce the degree of freedom in order to protect the *status quo*. For some efforts to analyze this relation, see Johan Galtung, 'Foreign Policy Opinion as a Function of Social Position', *J. Peace Res.* (1964), particularly pp. 207—216.

[6] Thus, an issue leaves Ideology and becomes Technology as soon as these conditions are fulfilled, much as a problem leaves Philosophy and becomes Science as soon as consensual criteria of validation (formal or empirical) are found — *and* there is consensus that the problem is still worth pursuing.

[7] This theme is developed further in Johan Galtung, *Theories of Peace* (forthcoming), section 1.3.

[8] Ibid., sections 4.3 and 4.4.

[9] A crucial example is balance of power politics, one of the classical, dissociative formulas for peace-making. It presupposes a certain polarization and distance in general, and should, hence, work better for low levels of communication than for high levels. But it also presupposes communication of intentions and a certain measure of tacit agreement; which means that it should work relatively well when the international system has a well integrated elite. But when popular and populist forces press for other values as well and constrain the delicate maneuvers of the

diplomats in maintaining balance of power, at the same time as the communication potential doubles and trebles, this mechanism will be of decreasing utility.

[10] For more details about this, see Johan Galtung, 'Cooperation in Europe, A Report to the Political Commission, Council of Europe'.

[11] For more details about this, see Johan Galtung, 'Entropy and the General Theory of Peace', *Proceedings*, Second IPRA General Conference; and Ch. 5. in *Theories of Peace*.

[12] Thus, in this paper we locate the basic source of change inside nations. This does not mean that there is no feedback from the international system to the domestic systems, or no dynamism in the international system *sui generis*. We only use this as a way of organizing the theory.

[13] This Table is taken from 'Socio-economic Development: A bird's-eye view', section 1.2 in Johan Galtung, *Members of Two Worlds* (forthcoming).

[14] This is done in the Fisher-Clark-Fourastié tradition. However, we very much agree with Kahn (op. cit., p. 720) when he, as do other authors in this field, starts splitting the tertiary sector into some of its components, such as 'quaternary occupations /that/ render services mostly to tertiary occupations or to one another'. The crucial factor, as we see it, is the general tendency towards occupations where the work consists mainly in the manipulations of symbols — direct contact with matter for extraction or processing has been automated.

[15] Thus, in neomodern society, or post-industrial society as some authors refer to it, close to 100% would be in the tertiary sector, manipulating symbols (science, arts, education, computers, etc.); traditional occupations would be automated. The

urban 'form of life would be shared by most Education would be a form of life, shared by almost all throughout their lifespan; not a preparation for an occupation. To make such a society run, many people are needed; the high level of symbolic activity and communication facilities will make the society global because inhabitants will often have to travel far to find partners for meaningful symbolic interaction (so far above all in arts and sciences, later on probably also in styles of life, in tastes and manners, etc.). The society would also be highly vulnerable because of the high level of automation and the proliferation of complex machinery — and the removal of one part will affect many people, since they cannot fall back on 'simple life on the farm' or anything like that.

[16] Kahn's distinctions (op. cit., pp. 716f) are in our mind too much based on GNP/capita, which is an aggregate measure and hence one that obscures the qualitative differences between the segments inside a nation-state. But his post-industrial is our neomodern, his 'mass consumption or advanced industrial' is a mixture of modern and neomodern; his industrial is our modern; and his partially industrial and preindustrial are modern with increasing ingredients of traditional or perhaps even primitive segments. When his typology is based on GNP/capita and ours to some extent on % *not* in primary sector, comparisons can only be made under the assumption that there is a high correlation between these two measures; and that is a rather well established fact: it is 0.84, based on 76 nations (Russett et al., *World Handbook of Political and Social Indicators*, p. 279). Kahn's projections as to which nations will be in which stage in Year 2000 are, hence, very useful for our purposes, although some of the dynamics is lost when GNR/capita measures are used.

[17] There are two kinds of these cross-national, social orders, viz., the egalitarian ones, where the segments are at the same level of development; and the inegalitarian ones. The latter easily become exploitative and oppressive. Cross-national links at the N-N level may take the form of international conferences organized around some value or profession; at the M-N level it may take the form of exchange of manufactured goods and expertise; at the T-T level, the exchange of manufactured goods form of traditional trade; at the P-P level, the form of cross-national tribalism. But then there are the M-T forms (manufactured goods against raw materials), the T-P forms (primary products against slaves) and the N-M form yet to flower: highest level expertise against manufactured goods. 'Imperialism' is a term often used for the T-P and M-T relations.

[18] One logical pattern here seems to be as follows: the organizers of industries want to make a profit, whether they are private or public, whether they want the profit for own consumption or for investment, whether they want to invest in more industries or in some other goods. The less they can pay their workers, the more profit can they make. One solution is to keep low wages by keeping workers' expenses low. One such expense would be transportation to the place of work: this is cut down by urbanization. Another expense is food: this is cut down by paying farmers badly for their products. The major reason why this works is that farmers are badly organized; unlike workers their form of production is still very often neolithic, i.e. one family, one farm — whereas work organization brings workers together and facilitates union-formation. The theory may be that this is justified because the country gets industrialized so that it can later on pay the farmers back — but in the meantime these may have escaped from the countryside and settled in slums outside the cities — as found all over the Third World today.

[19] We are thinking here of the relatively low number of high-ranking intellectuals participating in national assemblies and governments in most developed nations — to some extent isolating the universities.

[20] We are thinking here of the concentration of resistance to the Vietnam war on the campus, in terms of opinion-formation as well as in terms of such active forms of resistance as draftcard burning, etc. Interviews and stories from the US soldiers actively fighting in the war give an impression of a very strong rural, even peripheral element. For an example of this, see the story of 'The Anderson Company' in *Le Figaro*, January 1967.

[21] For one description, see *Time* Magazine, 7 July 1967, pp. 12—20.

[22] The recent example of the poll in San Francisco over a proposal calling for an immediate cease-fire and withdrawal of American troops from Vietnam without prior negotiation is very interesting as a case here. The proposal was rejected by a majority of nearly two to one (132,402 against, 76,632 in favor) — but a pattern has been indicated that will definitely be followed in other local communities around the world, not only in the US, but predominantly in the most neo-modern parts of TMN nations (we would have predicted California or somewhere in the Boston—Washington range in the US), and in low entropy segments of PTM nations. (More details in *The Guardian*, 9 November 1967).

[23] INGOS are presently being studied in a joint project by the International Peace Research Institute, Oslo and the Peace Research Centre, London. For some preliminary results, see Paul Smoker, 'A Preliminary Empirical Study of an International Integration Sub-system', *Proceedings of the IPRA Inaugural Conference*, (Assen: van Gorcum, 1966), pp. 38—51. Richard Meier has brought to our attention a report indicating an even higher growth rate among international business corporations (INGOS are by definition non-profit) of as much as 15% — according to a study reported in *Chemical Abstracts*.

[24] An example of the International Social Science Council, coordinating activities of international social science associations, with headquarters in Paris and supported by the UNESCO.

[25] INGOS can generally be divided according to focus in three groups: ideology-oriented, status-oriented, and profession-oriented. In a world where a person is seen as having only one profession, most professional INGOS would be mutually exclusive; but typical of neomodern societies seems to be persons with more than one profession, at least, during their life-time. And who knows whether ideologies will not once be conceived of that way too — not only that a basic chance during one's life-time will be seen as quite normal, but also simultaneous belief in contrary or even contradictory ideologies?

[26] I am indebted to Herman Kahn for drawing my attention to this factor.

[27] This is currently being studied under the auspices of the International Peace Research Association.

[28] This was suggested at the International Future Research Inaugural Congress by Richard Meier.

[29] This corresponds exactly to Kahn's list of 'visibly postindustrial' and 'early postindustrial' nations by Year 2000 — but Kahn is more interested in their relative power positions whereas our position is that that question will have lost much of its meaning in the web of affiliations spun by neomodern societies growing into each other.

[30] In other words, that unification takes place not so much by a change in the legal and political order within and between

the two Germanies, as by increasingly rapid diffusion across the border leaving the border issue uninteresting. Parallel with this development, towards higher entropy except in the early 1970's there will probably also be a growth in the supra-German institutional network with increasingly symbiotic and symmetric patterns of cooperation, and, hence, good prospects for very peaceful relations.

[31] One particular reason for this is the degree to which small nations even today depend on their environment much more than big nations. Thus, on the basis of *World Handbook of Political and Social Indicators* data we calculated the correlation (Yule's Q) between size (population) and foreign trade as a percentage of GNP, and found a correlation —.79. In other words, the bigger the nation, the less does it depend on trade for its GNP. Most spectacular in this connection is the position of the three biggest powers in the world USSR, USA, and China — at the bottom of the list, with their allies usually quite high, and higher the smaller they are.

Of both economic and political significance are the famous 'Club of 9' initiatives, to try to find platforms for all-European cooperation. For an empirical and theoretical analysis of bilateral patterns of interaction in Europe, see Johan Galtung, 'East-West Interaction Patterns', *J. Peace Res.* (1966), pp. 146—177.

[32] See studies by Ingrid Eide Galtung, 'Student Scholars as Culture Carriers: A Study of Eastern Students Who Have Received Western University Training', 'Brain Drain: An Attempt at Diagnosis and Therapy', both forthcoming.

[33] We are thinking here of the legendary participation by teachers — the current intellectual elite — in many African parliaments and governments, of the participation of the 'abogado' in Latin America, etc.

[34] Characteristic of the many movements currently known under the initials of NLF or FLN in various countries (Algeria, Vietnam, Venezuela, Aden, etc.) is that students always seem to play a dominant and positive role — compare this with the draftcard burners in the US.

[35] This does not mean that many of them have, in fact, high trade loadings in their GNP, because they may not have anything to trade with. See footnote 38 for further comments.

[36] For a general exposition of this theory, the feudality thesis, see Johan Galtung, 'International Relations and International Conflicts: A Sociological Approach' *Transactions of the Sixth World Congress for Sociology*, pp. 121—161, particularly pp. 146—148. For a good test of this theory, see Smoker, op. cit., pp. 46—49

[37] For data on how slowly the poorer nations develop air communication between themselves, see Nils Petter Gleditsch: 'Trends in International Air Communication', *J. Peace Res.* (1967), pp. 366—408.

[38] We have already mentioned (footnote 31), that small nations depend much more on their environment for trade. But big nations also have a much higher growth-rate, on the average, as seen from Table A. To be big means to have internal markets, under central control at least to some extent, and hence possibilities of expansion

TABLE A. *Relation between size, development level and growth rate*

	Average growth rate		
	Big	Small	Difference
Rich	3.9	3.0	0.9
Poor	2.1	0.8	1.3

and transformation of less developed segments into more developed ones. Industries can grow big without having to engage in complicated international transactions. But size is most important for the poor nations, leaving the small and poor very much behind. To the extent they do develop, however, they will outgrow themselves.

[39] Thus, one typical formula for national integration is the coexistence, in every ecological unit, of many different tribes and races, but not so many of any single group that they can run a viable society alone. Also to be avoided is the low entropy formula whereby tribes and races specialize in occupations or groups of occupations, so that tribes and races become stratified in accordance with the stratification of occupations.

[40] This coincides with the prediction made by Ithiel de Sola Pool, op. cit., p. 932.

[41] For an important analysis of the conditions that favor military coups d'etat, see Egil Fossum, 'Factors Influencing the Occurrence of Military Coups d'etat in Latin America', *J. Peace Res.* (1967), pp. 228—251.

[42] To many this will sound too optimistic. They may point to pollution, growth curves for populations, and to dwindling food resources, e.g. caused by the circumstance that agricultural output of industrialized nations may decrease because migration to the cities offsets the effects of automation. That this will lead to some large-scale famines early in the 1970's is perhaps correct — and is in case a most telling indictment against professionals and politicians for not having engaged in sufficient future research when there was still time to remedy the evil. But after that, we would predict that we shall start reaping the benefits of what has been invested in propaganda for family planning and invention of contraceptive devices (probably more innovations in this field during the last 7

than in the preceding 7000 years); and that completely new methods of increasing food supply (ocean farming, three-dimensional agriculture, synthetic products) will start to pay off. Thus we are more in line with Colin Clark in his 'Agricultural Productivity in Relation to Population' (Wolstenholme, ed., *Man and His Future*, London: Churchill, 1963) and Richard Meier in *Science and Economic Development: New Patterns of Living* (Cambridge: MIT Press, 1966).

[43] The stage is already set for large-scale exploitation of small PTM nations by the larger ones by very feudal interaction patterns between nations in, say, Latin America. This theme is investigated in Johan Galtung, Manuel Mora and Simon Schwartzman, 'El sistema latino-americana de naciones: Un analisis estructural', *America Latina*, 1966, pp. 59—94 and developed further, in a context of analysis of integration, in Per Olav Reinton, 'International Structure and International Integration: The Case of Latin America', *J. Peace Res.* (1967), pp. 334—365. In this context it is not strange if the smaller nations look to their trade partners among the more developed nations for protection and recognition.

[44] In societies in the Northern hemisphere there is a general drift of this kind from South to North, within nations (Italy) and between nations (Puerto Rico to the US; Italians, Spaniards, and Yugoslavs to Central and Northern European nations). In the Southern hemisphere this is reversed: there is migration into South Africa, into the southern part of Brazil, and so on. Inside nations this is probably one of the most important mechanisms in coping with accumulated frustration that may be converted into revolutions, but also a risky method since it is irreversible.

[45] Herman Kahn on what this means to the neo-modern nations: 'This does not mean, as the Europeans think, that the

United States is depending on this importation, but it does mean that we are benefitting; we are getting a subsidy from the rest of the world' (*Daedalus*, p. 962). This seems to be a fair assessment.

[46] I am indebted to Immanuel Wallerstein for this idea and expression.

[47] Thus, we predict that in the beginning of the 1970's, perhaps before, Western assistance in many forms will be forthcoming to Cuba, with the US reluctantly joining this effort, in the end.

[48] This has been a recurrent theme in all Pugwash conferences from the 12th conference January 1964 in Udaipur, India.

[49] This argument is developed in Johan Galtung, 'A Structural Theory of Integration', *J. Peace Res.* (1968).

[50] This is brilliantly argued by Dudley Seers in 'International Aid: the Next Steps', *J. Modern African Studies*, pp. 471—489. In practice this means that the amount of 'aid' given will be decided by the rich nations alone only for some more years; we would be surprised if the point of gravity in the decision-making here would not be in the hands of the less developed nations as late as in 1975. Aid is already deeply resented as alimony and neo-colonialism, as a means in foreign policy strategies, much like domestic alimonies to 'the poor' some generations ago. Thus, a taxation system is bound to emerge, and is actually less novel and utopian than many may think: it can be seen as an extrapolation of what nations may to IGOS, particularly to UN specialized agencies and to the UN itself — e.g., to participate in UNDP programs.

[51] This is an important line of argument in explaining why the Kaiser went to war in 1914 according to Robert North and his associates; and in explaining the Japanese attack on Pearl Harbor as done by Bruce Russett in 'Pearl Harbor: Deterence Theory and Decision Theory', *J. Peace Res.* (1967), pp. 89—106.

[52] To believe that nuclear explosive devices will have to be delivered by rockets (and that the adequate defense, hence, is of the ABM variety) is to believe in the Maginot line once more. Much more likely is delivery in a suitcase, eg. by using a dwarf submarine, and a strategically well chosen site for the suitcase with an electronic long distance ignition mechanism combined with a trip-wire to avoid detection and dismantling. A 100% failsafe protection against this is not easily devised.

[53] The theory of this is outlined in Johan Galtung, 'A Structural Theory of Aggression', *J. Peace Res.* (1964), pp. 95—119.

[54] One such prediction study is carried out in Wilhelm Fucks, 'On the Future Development of Potentials of the Major and the Big Powers', Paper delivered to the International Political Science Association, Brussels, September 1967. On the basis of production capacities (that can be converted into military power) Fucks concludes: ' — the Soviet Union will never reach or exceed the power of the USA in the next decades — China should reach and exceed the virtual military-political power of the Soviet Union in the course of the seventies — the virtual military-political power of China will reach and exceed that of the USA in the eighties — in the nineties this virtual power should exceed that of the USA and her allies and in the next century even that of the Soviet Union added to these countries' (ibid., p. 9). We have doubts about these predictions since they are not also based on assessments of the structure of the international system that will put a multiplier on any development figure for the strongly industrialized and integrated parts of the world. But they are interesting, particularly because many decision-makers are probably reflecting along such lines.

IV.19. *On the Future of the World System: Territorial and Non-Territorial*

* Paper presented at the Third International Future Research Conference in Bucuresti, Sept. 1972. A first version of the paper was delivered as a lecture at the 102nd Foreign Relations Dinner Address Meeting, held on February 20, 1970 at the International House of Japan under the chairmanship of Mr. Michio Royama. Parts of the paper can also be found in chapters 6 and 7 of my book *The True Worlds, A Transnational Perspective*, (New York, MacMillan-Free Press, 1980), and in the *bulletin*, April 1970, no. 25, pp. 46—73 of the International House of Japan. It is a follow-up of the article "On the Future of the International System" printed in the *Journal of Peace Research*, 1967, pp. 305—333, and in the proceedings from the First International Future Research conference, *Mankind 2000*, pp. 12—41 — edited by Robert Jungk and myself (Oslo, Universitetsforlaget, 1971); also published as Chapter in this volume (*Essays in Peace Research*, IV, Ejlers, Copenhagen, 1980), pp. 615—644.